For Jack & Kathryn,

a little light reading with the author's compliments!

all best,   Peter

THE ROMAN AUDIENCE

THE
ROMAN AUDIENCE

CLASSICAL LITERATURE
AS SOCIAL HISTORY

T. P. WISEMAN

Great Clarendon Street, Oxford, OX2 6DP,
United Kingdom

Oxford University Press is a department of the University of Oxford.
It furthers the University's objective of excellence in research, scholarship,
and education by publishing worldwide. Oxford is a registered trade mark of
Oxford University Press in the UK and in certain other countries

© T.P. Wiseman 2015

The moral rights of the author have been asserted

First Edition published in 2015

Impression: 1

All rights reserved. No part of this publication may be reproduced, stored in
a retrieval system, or transmitted, in any form or by any means, without the
prior permission in writing of Oxford University Press, or as expressly permitted
by law, by licence or under terms agreed with the appropriate reprographics
rights organization. Enquiries concerning reproduction outside the scope of the
above should be sent to the Rights Department, Oxford University Press, at the
address above

You must not circulate this work in any other form
and you must impose this same condition on any acquirer

Published in the United States of America by Oxford University Press
198 Madison Avenue, New York, NY 10016, United States of America

British Library Cataloguing in Publication Data

Data available

Library of Congress Control Number: 2015936005

ISBN 978–0–19–871835–2

Printed and bound by
CPI Group (UK) Ltd, Croydon, CR0 4YY

Links to third party websites are provided by Oxford in good faith and
for information only. Oxford disclaims any responsibility for the materials
contained in any third party website referenced in this work.

IN MEMORY OF
Winifred Agnes Rigby and Stephen Wiseman,
Nancy Ernestine Rigby and Henry Cecil Geipel,
and all that generation.

Preface

> The modern reader, who is accustomed to taking in literature through the eye rather than through the ear, cannot be too frequently reminded that nearly all the books discussed in this history were written to be listened to.

So wrote E. J. Kenney in 1982, in the opening paragraph of the Roman volume of the *Cambridge History of Classical Literature*. But he did not follow his own excellent advice. The brilliant introductory chapter that follows is all about books and readers, about 'a highly developed and intensive literary and scholarly culture' in which literature 'was from first to last the preserve of the relatively small elite in which high culture flourished'. The audience implied in his opening paragraph somehow fades out of mind.

This book is an attempt to rethink the whole history of Roman literature from the point of view of those who *heard* it, and thus both endorse Ted Kenney's original advice and question his subsequent assumption that literature was mainly a matter for the cultured few.

It is, inevitably, a historian's book. I try to insist on primary sources and contemporary evidence wherever they are available, in the hope of helping readers of classical texts towards a better understanding of the changing social and cultural conditions in which the texts were composed. In particular, I want to counter the idea that Jacques Derrida's dictum, 'il n'y a pas de hors-texte', excuses us from the effort of finding out what can be known, or reasonably inferred, about the world for which the classic authors wrote.

In a sense, this is a companion volume to *The Myths of Rome* (Exeter, 2004), which also attempted a chronological rethink on a large scale. Because I hope it may be of interest to non-specialist readers, as in the previous book I have left the text free of numbered notes and segregated the technical apparatus at the end, where reference to the primary evidence and modern discussions is keyed by the page-number and a brief identifying phrase. Except where otherwise stated, all translations are mine.

Contents

List of Illustrations   xii

1. **Times, Books, and Preconceptions**   1
   1.1 The *longue durée*   1
   1.2 Paper   3
   1.3 Books   4
   1.4 Literature as a Public Performance   6

2. **Rome Before Literature: Indirect Evidence**   10
   2.1 Evidence from Homer   10
   2.2 Evidence from Terracotta   14
   2.3 Rome and Athens   19
   2.4 Honouring Gods   21
   2.5 Fragments and 'History'   24
   2.6 Marking the Days   25

3. **Rome Before Literature: Dionysus and Drama**   29
   3.1 Pots Painted, Bronze Engraved   29
   3.2 Republican Rome   36
   3.3 The Roman Games   42
   3.4 Rome and Alexandria   45
   3.5 The Turning-point   47

4. **An Enclosure with Benches**   50
   4.1 *Theatrum* and *Scaena*   50
   4.2 Plautus and the *Cauea*   51
   4.3 In the Forum, in the Circus   55
   4.4 Terence and the *Cauea*   59
   4.5 Curtains and Steps   61

5. Makers, Singers, Speakers, Writers — 63
- 5.1 Ennius and the *Vates* — 63
- 5.2 Ennius as Impersonator — 68
- 5.3 Cato and Polybius — 70
- 5.4 Lucilius and Varro — 73

6. A Turbulent People — 79
- 6.1 The Political Stage — 79
- 6.2 Pompey and the Theatre — 81
- 6.3 When Cicero Wasn't in Rome — 82
- 6.4 Pompey's Games — 85
- 6.5 Poets and Dancers — 88
- 6.6 Before the Disaster — 93

7. Rethinking the Classics: 59–42 BC — 94
- 7.1 Lucretius and Philodemus — 95
- 7.2 Demetrius, Historians, Caesar — 98
- 7.3 Caesar and Catullus — 102
- 7.4 Catullus 61–64 — 105
- 7.5 The Greek Stage in Rome — 110
- 7.6 The Ides of March, and After — 113

8. Rethinking the Classics: 42–28 BC — 114
- 8.1 Virgil's *Eclogues* — 114
- 8.2 Sallust — 115
- 8.3 Horace's *Satires* — 118
- 8.4 Virgil's *Georgics* — 121
- 8.5 Virgil's 'Epyllion' — 125
- 8.6 Livy and Horace — 129
- 8.7 The Republic Restored — 134

9. Rethinking the Classics: 28 BC–AD 8 — 138
- 9.1 The Citizens, the Audience — 139
- 9.2 Horace's *Epistles* — 141
- 9.3 Tibullus and Propertius — 146
- 9.4 Ovid and Virgil — 150
- 9.5 Augustus and the 'Secular Games' — 152
- 9.6 Horace and Ovid — 156
- 9.7 Ovid's *Fasti* — 159

10. Under the Emperors   163
    10.1 First-Century Poets   164
    10.2 First-Century Playwrights   166
    10.3 Prose Fiction and History   169
    10.4 Lucian in the Theatre   172
    10.5 Integrating Evidence   175
    10.6 Christians   180

Notes   183
Bibliography   293
Index of Passages   315
General Index   318

List of Illustrations

Figures marked with an asterisk are also in the colour plates section

Fig. 1.	Time-line, 1300 BC to the present	2–3
Fig. 2.	Map of Italy and the Mediterranean	12–13
Fig. 3.	Terracotta statue-group from a temple of c.530 BC	16
Fig. 4.	Terracotta revetment plaques, 'Veii–Rome–Velletri' group, c.530 BC	18
Fig. 5.	Satyr-mask terracotta antefixes from Rome, c.500 BC*	21
Fig. 6.	Attic *chous*, c.420 BC	29
Fig. 7.	Attic volute-krater, c.400 BC (the 'Pronomos Vase')	30–31
Fig. 8.	Apulian *phiale*, c.350 BC*	32
Fig. 9.	Areas of production of red-figure pottery in Italy, fourth century BC	34
Fig. 10.	Paestan kalyx-krater, c.350 BC*	35
Fig. 11.	Faliscan cup, fourth century BC	36
Fig. 12.	Praenestine(?) mirror, late fourth century BC	37
Fig. 13.	'Unrolled' engraving on cylindrical *cista*, late fourth century BC	38–9
Fig. 14.	'Unrolled' engraving on cylindrical *cista*, late fourth century BC	38–9
Fig. 15.	Elevation and cross-section of the temple of Magna Mater	56
Fig. 16.	Theatre of Pompey, conjectural reconstruction	87
Fig. 17.	Theatre of Pompey, plan of archaeological remains	90
Fig. 18.	Reconstruction of part of the Severan Marble Plan of the city of Rome	127
Fig. 19.	*Aureus* of 28 BC*	136
Fig. 20.	The theatre and *odeion* at the Pausilypon villa	144–5
Fig. 21.	Roman sarcophagus, late second century AD*	177
Fig. 22.	Roman sarcophagus, c. AD 130*	178
Fig. 23.	Roman sarcophagus, c. AD 190–200*	179

Poetry is for the people, and can fill theatres.
                              Strabo of Amaseia

One uses what one has, and there is work to be done.
                              Sir Ronald Syme

Ask yourself, What does this presuppose?
                              William Arthur Heidel

I

Times, Books, and Preconceptions

How can we know what people did thousands of years ago? The short answer is that we can't: those people are all long dead, and beyond the possibility of interview. All we can do is make fragile inferences from what texts or artefacts happen to survive from the distant past.

There is also a longer answer, one as long as the history of scholarship. An astonishing number of texts and artefacts *have* survived, and thanks to several centuries of intense study some of the inferences that can be made from them are not so fragile after all. Of course it is still true, and inevitable, that every statement about the past is a hypothesis that may one day be refuted if better evidence turns up; nevertheless, some of those hypotheses are so secure that without misuse of language they can be called facts.

For instance, if you are interested in Roman drama, it is a fact that comedies by Plautus and Terence were performed in Rome in the second century BC; it is a fact that three permanent stone theatres were constructed in Rome in the first century BC; and it is a fact that Nero's adviser Seneca, before committing suicide in AD 65, wrote tragedies that had a profound effect on English and French drama in the sixteenth and seventeenth centuries. But how do those facts relate to each other?

This book is an attempt to understand literature, including drama, as a constituent part of Roman society as it developed over a very long period of time.

1.1. The *longue durée*

Our first task is to understand the chronology. Figure 1 is a time-line of the history of Rome, from the first archaeological evidence of continuous habitation, dated roughly 1300 BC, to the present day. Each of the subdivisions is a hundred years—three or four generations, a period longer than living memory.

As we read it from left to right, at first there is no history to report. For our purposes the first significant stage is the seventh century BC, when the community

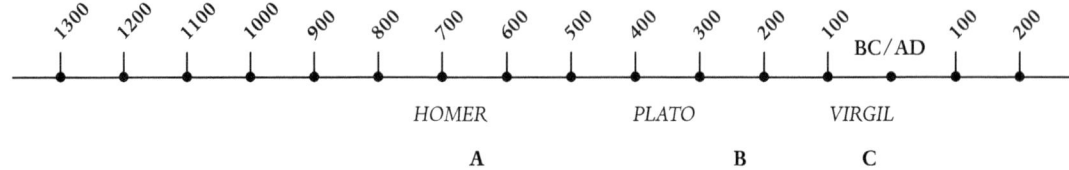

FIG. 1. Time-line, 1300 BC to the present. **A**: Approximate date of the first public open space on the site of the Roman Forum. **B**: Approximate date of the first written works of Latin literature. **C**: End of the Roman republic, principate of Augustus; 'classic' period of Roman literature; first permanent theatres built in Rome. **D**: Abolition of pagan festivals in Rome. Chronology of the book's argument: **A–B**, chapters 2–3; **B–C**, chapters 4–6; **C**, chapters 7–9; **C–D**, chapter 10

(or communities) on the high ground by the crossing-point of the Tiber developed the stream valley between the Palatine and Capitol hills and laid out the gravelled public area which became the Roman Forum. This first evidence for Rome as a recognizable city-state is marked as point A on the time-line.

The use of writing was known, but still a novelty. In the Greek-speaking world, the epics of Homer may have been written down not long after this, and western literature thus initiated. But the Latins and other peoples of Italy did not yet use their alphabets to record the bard's chant or the storyteller's tale or the stage-performers' cross-talk. It was not until four centuries later, when their republic was already in control of Italy and challenging Carthage for supremacy in the western Mediterranean, that the Romans had their own Latin literature created for them, in epic poetry and drama. That is marked as point B on the time-line.

Those four centuries from A to B, for which the only contemporary evidence is archaeological and iconographical, present us with a very particular methodological problem, addressed in Chapters 2–3. Thereafter, literary evidence becomes available—though not equally for all periods—and the argument becomes a little more straightforward.

Point C on the time-line is placed in the second half of the first century BC. That was the 'classic' period of Roman literature, from Cicero to Ovid, and the period of political crisis and civil war that saw the end of the Roman republic and the first stages, under Augustus, of the rule of the Roman emperors. Point C also marks a major development in the public culture of Rome, the creation of purpose-built stone theatres. Those great buildings remained central to the life of the city throughout the principate.

Point D on the time-line marks the end, not of Rome, but of the Roman culture this book is about. Since my argument is much concerned with games and festivals, the prohibition of sacrifice in AD 391 and the consequent obsolescence of the traditional—that is, 'pagan'—public holidays, in order to make the life of Rome irreversibly Christian, is as appropriate a finishing-point as any. In 410 Alaric and his Goths would sack the city, a disaster that clearly symbolized the end of an era.

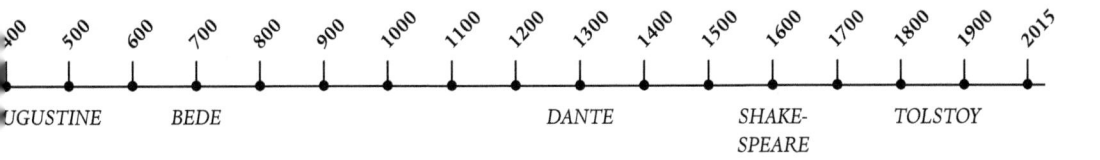

1.2. Paper

When texts are created (point B), history becomes possible. Texts can give meaning to artefacts that are otherwise enigmatic. Through texts the people of the past can speak to us.

It's not just the craft of writing that matters, but what gets written and what it gets written on. The Romans had long been used to inscribing public documents on stone, bronze, wood, leather, or even linen. For letters, legal documents, and other everyday business they used wooden tablets (*tabulae*), often covered with a wax writing surface; tied together, such tablets formed a *codex*, literally 'wood-block'. (The diminutive form *codicillus* was often used, or *pugillar*, meaning a 'fistful'.) For literature, however, you need books, and for books you need paper; and paper, in the ancient world, was made from the pith of the papyrus plant, which grew in Egypt.

Greeks had been trading with Egypt since at least the seventh century BC, and the pharaoh Amasis (570–526 BC) eventually granted them a permanent commercial centre at Naucratis, on the western branch of the Nile delta. It is probably no accident that the first clear evidence for Greek literary texts (of Homer) refers to the 530s BC, the time of Pisistratus' rule in Athens. The modern misconception that 'the Greeks came before the Romans'—an absurdity in historical or archaeological terms—may be largely due to the accident that the Greeks had the means to create a written literature about three centuries before the Romans did.

As we shall see in Chapter 3, the Roman republic first established diplomatic relations with the Ptolemaic kingdom of Egypt in about 273 BC. The ruler at that time was Ptolemy II Philadelphus, second of the dynasty and founder of the great library at Alexandria. Whether or not this contact was the catalyst, the Romans' first use of papyrus volumes to record sung and spoken speech can be dated to the mid-third century BC.

We may begin to get an idea of the impact of the innovation if we listen to what learned Romans of later ages said about papyrus. First, Gaius Plinius Secundus, soldier, historian, and encyclopaedic polymath, in the first century AD:

> Civilized life, and certainly memory, depends above all on the use of paper.... [It is] the product on which the immortality of human beings depends.

Pliny, *Natural History* 13.68 and 70

Second, and nearly half a millennium later, Magnus Aurelius Cassiodorus Senator, senior administrator in the regime of Theodoric the Ostrogoth:

> What crop grows in any field to equal this, on which the thoughts of the wise are preserved?... Preserving a faithful witness of human deeds, it speaks of the past, and is the enemy of oblivion.

Cassiodorus *Variae* 37.3 and 5

Without record on paper, what was done and said would be forgotten. The creation, preservation, discovery, and copying of texts is what makes historical enquiry possible. Although paper is vulnerable to fire, water, and vermin, a surprising number of texts in ancient Greek and Latin survived long enough to be reproduced in print and become 'classical literature' for the modern world. What those texts say is most of what we think we know about ancient Greece and Rome.

In this book I shall constantly be citing passages from ancient texts and trying to understand what they imply. The result will not be a confident narrative offering easy answers, but I hope it will reflect the necessarily provisional nature of any reconstruction of the distant past. And because my argument will contradict what most classical scholars take for granted about Roman literary culture, it is important to remind ourselves right at the start what Roman books were like.

1.3. Books

The scroll on which a text could be written had to be manufactured in Egypt, before the papyrus pith from which it was made became too dry. As the standard account describes it:

> the pith having been cut with a sharp knife into strips, these strips were laid down in two layers, in one of which the fibres were placed horizontally, in the other vertically. The two layers were then fastened together by moisture, glue and pressure until they formed one fabric.

Kenyon 1951.48

The sheets of paper so produced were usually about 30cm x 20cm. They were then glued together in sequence to form a continuous scroll, which might be anything up to 10 metres in length. In Egypt, the cost of such a scroll was the equivalent of two to five days' pay for an agricultural worker; anywhere else, transport costs would make it substantially more expensive. An anecdote about the impoverished philosopher Cleanthes confirms that in Athens in the third century BC paper was more than a poor man could afford.

Then the text had to be written on the scroll. The wealthy might have skilled slaves to do such things; failing that, in the market-place a copyist's charge for a mere 200 lines was the equivalent of a day's pay for a skilled artisan, or two days' pay for a farm labourer. Add the wooden rollers that had to be attached at each end of the papyrus to make it usable for reading, and it becomes clear that the final result was an expensive artefact.

The best evidence for what finished books cost to buy is provided by Martial: he gives 6 or 10 *sestertii* (24 or 40 bronze *asses*) as typical prices, with 5 silver *denarii* (80 *asses*) for a de luxe product. As a comparison, before Domitian raised their pay, Roman legionaries received 10 *asses* per day, from which food and equipment had to be found. In effect, if an ordinary Roman wanted to buy a book, he would need to find the equivalent of several days' living expenses; for about the same outlay he could buy a whole amphora of wine (say 26 litres).

Only the rich could collect books. The first libraries were funded by kings— Ptolemy in Alexandria, Eumenes in Pergamum, Antiochus III in Antioch—and when substantial book collections first came to Rome, they came as war booty. In the late republic, libraries were part of the luxury goods in the country houses of the seriously wealthy. Bringing books to the Roman People in a public library was one of the projects Caesar would have carried out if the aristocrats had not murdered him. As it was, it fell to his friend Pollio in 39 BC, who used the profits of a military campaign in Illyria to set up a library in the Hall of Liberty; as a later Roman recorded with admiration, Pollio was the first to make works of genius public property. Thereafter, emperors provided libraries, as they provided baths and porticos and gymnasia.

There was nothing like a publishing industry in the ancient world. An author would create his text on wax tablets, either writing it himself or dictating it to a slave. Having it written on to a scroll, or more than one, was a sign of completion, though advice from friends or exposure at an invited reading might cause some revisions to be made. At this stage there would still be just one copy, safe in the author's control. 'It's a big thing', said Pliny, 'to put something into other people's hands.' 'Sit on it for nine years', advised Horace, though few did.

The act of 'making it public' (*publicare*) was the investment in further handwritten copies to be 'given out' (*edere*) or 'sent out' (*emittere*) to whomever the author considered appropriate. The nearest modern parallel is not a published edition but an author's complimentary copies; how many there were depended on what he could afford, and how many people he could rely on to appreciate the text and not just recycle the papyrus. Probably each separate scroll would have a personalized dedication.

The best chance of finding readers beyond one's own acquaintance (*diuulgare*) was the *librarius*, whose business was as much a copy-shop as a bookshop. You sent him your book, and he put it on display with all the others. Perhaps someone might be prepared to pay that steep price to buy it or have it copied. Failing that, since people who liked books gathered in the shop to read and gossip and argue, at least it was available for the browsers to unroll.

1.4. Literature as a Public Performance

If books were luxury items, it seems to follow that literature was the concern only of the privileged. But in that case, what about drama? Plautus and Terence were poets who wrote for public performance, and it would be an odd definition of literature that excluded dramatic poetry. Or consider epic poets: when Virgil began the *Aeneid* with 'Arms and the man I sing', was the verb just an empty metaphor? Was he writing just for those who could read his words on papyrus?

If we were talking about the Greek world, these questions would be absurd. Homer and the Athenian dramatists composed their works for oral delivery or performance at public festivals; copying them into books for readers was a secondary phenomenon. It is usually supposed that at some time between Homer and Virgil, perhaps in the fourth and third centuries BC, the secondary stage became primary, and poets began to write for readers rather than audiences. It is taken for granted that Romans writing in Greek genres—as they nearly all did—were book poets imitating oral poets across a great cultural divide.

For instance, Peter Bing's exploration of Hellenistic poetry in his influential book *The Well-Read Muse* (1988, reissued 2008) takes it as a given that by the third century BC 'the primary experience of literature was through books'. The poet did not 'sway large audiences in a public forum any more through the skillful use of words: performance...had given way to the private act of reading'. Why should this have come about? No evidence is offered, but we are told it was

> because the coherent fabric of the polis-community had disintegrated, supplanted by the remote, dislocated mass of the Oikoumene. Poetry, in concert with this change, became a private act of communication, no longer a public one.

Bing 1988.17

One should be cautious in drawing conclusions from historical developments described with quite so broad a brush. It is true that the Hellenistic monarchies had destroyed the political independence of the few city-states—like Athens—that had enjoyed such a thing. But does the rest follow?

1.4. Literature as a Public Performance

No, it does not. It was pointed out with devastating erudition by Alan Cameron in *Callimachus and his Critics* (1995) that though 'modern scholars have often posited a radical discontinuity between Hellenistic and earlier Greek culture',

> this unargued dogma rests in the last analysis on nothing more than a feeling that sophisticated and allusive poetry *cannot* have been publicly performed, that it was 'by its very nature, poetry to be read'.
>
> Cameron 1995.30

The fact is, as Cameron demonstrates at length, that 'Greek poetry and ceremonial literature of every sort from the Dark Ages down to the Crusades was written for performance'.

To prove Cameron's point, you have only to read the two main surviving works of Hellenistic literary criticism, Demetrius *On Style* and 'Longinus' *On the Sublime*. Where a modern critic would say 'the author' and 'the reader', Demetrius and 'Longinus' consistently refer to 'the speaker' and 'the audience'. Exactly the same usage appears in the Greek *scholia*, the commentaries that feature in the medieval manuscripts of classic authors, and derive from a long tradition of critical scholarship that lasted from the fourth century BC down into the Roman empire. The commentators take it for granted that you would *hear* Homer, just as you would *see* Attic tragedy; indeed, one of the ways poetry affected the audience was the voice the speaker used in delivering it.

And yet, even the best scholars can still write as if Cameron's decisive refutation had never happened. It is a sign of the power of preconception that René Nünlist, in his excellent analysis of the critical assumptions of the *scholia*, systematically translates their term *akroatēs* ('listener') as 'reader'. His justification for that is an equally excellent article by Dirk Schenkeveld, who demonstrated the existence of a Greek idiom, 'I have heard X saying Y', meaning 'I have read in X that Y'. It is a metaphor like the one I used above ('where a modern critic would *say*...'), and as Schenkeveld rightly points out, it probably reflects the ancient habits of reading aloud and of having books read *to* you.

The latter custom is particularly important: in a world without reading-glasses, many people were physically unable to read for themselves. But that is no reason to mistranslate *akroatēs*. The Greek critics referred not only to 'the listener' in the singular—who might just be what we would call a reader, having her book read to her—but equally often to 'the listeners' in the plural, and that can only imply an audience in the true sense, literature as a public performance.

This reluctance to let ancient texts mean what they say is particularly prevalent in the study of Latin literature, where Cameron's argument is simply ignored. Rather than try to do justice to the huge bibliography, I shall simply cite one authoritative contribution (from Michèle Lowrie's discussion of

Horatian lyric), which offers an admirably clear statement of what most scholars don't even feel required to spell out:

> Ideas about ancient song need to take account of the break in historical times from real or imagined tradition. Despite great activity in popular entertainment, there was no continuous formal performance tradition for high literature in Augustan Rome. Any performance medium that may have transmitted Horatian lyric or other genres was, if not an outright invention, some sort of reconstruction, whether Greek or Roman. Once there has been a break in the tradition, restarting it is an act of will that constitutes the literary.

Lowrie 2009.49

It is worth noticing that no evidence is offered either for the break in tradition or for the distinction between popular entertainment and high literature. The two notions are so widely accepted that no justification is thought to be necessary.

Antitheses like 'Greek/Roman' and 'popular/elite' are too crude to be historically useful, and the first of them has been fatally undermined by advances in archaeology. We now know, for instance, as we did not know thirty years ago, that there were Greek-speakers in the land of the Latins as early as about 800 BC. Scholarly specialisms have been unhelpful here. Archaeologists and historians are familiar with the cultic and artistic influence of the Greek world on Latium from at least the sixth century BC; specialists in Latin literature, on the other hand, rarely query Horace's misconceived idea that the Latins were unaware of Greek culture until after the Punic Wars (say, 200 BC); and one still finds authorities on ancient theatre writing as if the Romans had to conquer the cities of south Italy and Sicily before they could have any idea of what Greek drama was like.

As for the distinction between popular and 'elite' culture, that depends on a quasi-sociological abstraction which is not well suited to historical enquiry. Who were the 'elite' when Roman literature began? As it happens, the third century BC seems to have been a time when plebeian magistrates hostile to social and financial privilege were particularly influential in the Roman republic; and though it is true that distinctions of rank subsequently multiplied, two centuries later Marcus Varro still insisted that from the beginning Rome had been a community of equals.

Or are we to think of an elite defined by education rather than social status? The extent of literacy in the ancient world is a controversial question; but even if it was very limited, as seems likely, that does not mean that education, in a broad sense, was limited to the same degree.

To avoid anachronism on this point, it is important to remember that our ancient sources had no need to record what people in their world simply took for granted. Sometimes only a comment in passing alerts us to circumstances which would otherwise not have occurred to us. For instance, Plato in the fourth

1.4. Literature as a Public Performance

century BC refers to people's knowledge of the gods from 'stories heard in prayers at sacrifices'; Cicero in the first century BC refers to the stage as one of the sources of people's opinions, and to ordinary working people's enthusiasm for 'listening to history'; Pausanias in the second century AD refers to people believing 'whatever they have heard from childhood in choruses and tragedies'. These casual remarks reveal what was obvious to their authors but alien to us: the cultural heritage of the Greco-Roman world was transmitted through speech, song, and stage performance. You didn't have to be able to read.

There is a revealing anecdote in one of Pliny's letters, written about AD 104. It concerned his rival and fellow-senator Aquillius Regulus, whose young son had just died. Not content with commissioning images and statues of the boy 'from every workshop, in paint, wax, bronze, silver, gold, ivory, and marble', Regulus

> recently collected a huge audience and read them, in person, a book about his life—yes, a child's life, but still, he read it. He had a thousand copies made, and distributed the book throughout Italy and the provinces. He wrote to the local authorities requesting that someone with the best voice from among the town councillors should be selected to read it to the people—and it was done.
>
> Pliny *Letters* 4.7.2

Perhaps it wasn't literally a thousand copies: since the point of the story was Regulus' astonishing energy, we may allow Pliny a little exaggeration. What matters for our purpose is the light it throws on how texts reached their public. The oral delivery to an audience came before the distribution of written copies, and the written copies themselves were to make possible further oral delivery to audiences.

Regulus wanted 'the people' to know about his son's life. Was that exceptional, part of his over-the-top behaviour, or was it the norm? If we want to believe in a 'two cultures' model, with literature restricted to a small world of book-readers, we must assume that it was exceptional. I think it was the norm, and this book is an attempt to collect the evidence for that view.

2

Rome Before Literature

Indirect Evidence

Fig. 1   The story begins (point A on our time-line) with the creation of an *agora*, a common public space for what had probably been independent communities. The work that was involved required substantial resources as well as a common commitment, and I think it is likely that the newly unified 'city-state' now for the first time called itself *Roma*, Latinizing the Greek *rhōmē*, which meant 'strength'.

That is not the story the Romans themselves told. Their version of their own origins, as narrated for us by Cicero, Livy, and Dionysius in the first century BC (point C on our time-line), is no more than a legend; even the earliest authorities those writers could have used—the first Roman historians, Fabius Pictor and Cincius Alimentus about 200 BC—were centuries too late to record any accurate oral tradition. What we need is *contemporary* evidence for the seventh century BC. It does exist—not from Rome itself, but from a world with which those proto-Romans were not unfamiliar, the world of Homer.

2.1. Evidence from Homer

As it happens, the earliest independent evidence for both the Homeric epics comes from the west coast of Italy: 'Nestor's cup', from the *Iliad*, is referred to on a cup from a grave at Ischia of about 720 BC; and the blinding of Polyphemus, from the *Odyssey*, is illustrated on a mixing-bowl at Etruscan Caere about 650 BC. If we want to imagine what the *agora* of a seventh-century BC community was like, Homer can give us a contemporary view.

Let's look at the first and last of the scenes of everyday life, of peace and war and agriculture and celebration, fashioned by the craftsman-god Hephaestus on the shield of Achilles in the great set-piece description in book 18 of the *Iliad*. In the city at peace, 'the people were crowded in the *agora*', where a

2.1. Evidence from Homer

dispute about a killing was being heard, with compensation refused and arbitration demanded:

> The people around shouted in support of each side, while heralds were keeping the crowd back. The elders sat on polished stone seats in a sacred circle, and took the sceptres in their hands from the loud-voiced heralds, and leapt to their feet and gave their verdict.
>
> Homer *Iliad* 18.502–6

No doubt the judges' circle was sacred because the *agora* and the place of judgement were also where the altars of the gods were set up. The last scene created by the god (apart from the river of Ocean round the edge of the shield) was a *choros*, a dancing-place where young men and marriageable girls danced in circle and in line:

> A large crowd stood round, enjoying the lovely dance; and among them two tumblers whirled around, leading the dance in the centre.
>
> Homer *Iliad* 18.603–6

Was the dancing-place also the *agora*? On the shield that is not made explicit, but the *Odyssey* suggests that it probably was.

Here we have to do not with a generic scene, but with part of the narrative. Odysseus has been washed ashore on the island of Phaeacia. The king's daughter Nausicaa tells him how to get to the city. He will see high walls and towers, and harbours on each side of the entrance, with ships drawn up on shore: 'that is where the *agora* is, around the splendid precinct of Poseidon, fitted with dragged stones set deep.' (That probably means walled with stone rather than paved.) As Odysseus makes his way past the harbours, he is duly impressed by 'an *agora* of heroes'.

The ruler, Alcinous, receives Odysseus in his house, and the following morning leads the way to 'the *agora* of the Phaeacians, by the ships'. The leading citizens are summoned, 'and swiftly the *agora* and the seats were filled with people as they assembled'. He issues an invitation to a banquet, and all return to the king's house. After the banquet Alcinous announces athletic competitions, and again leads the way to the *agora*: 'and a great crowd followed with him, in their thousands.'

The games take place—running, jumping, wrestling, boxing, discus-throwing—and then Alcinous announces dancing, and sends to his house for the lyre of Demodocus the bard:

> Nine magistrates of the people all stood up, chosen to organize everything properly concerning competitions, and they cleared a dancing-place [*choros*] and opened up a fine space for the contest. From close by came the herald, bringing the clear-sounding lyre for Demodocus. He came to the centre, and around him stood young boys skilled in dancing, and they struck the sacred dancing-place with their feet.
>
> Homer *Odyssey* 8.258–64

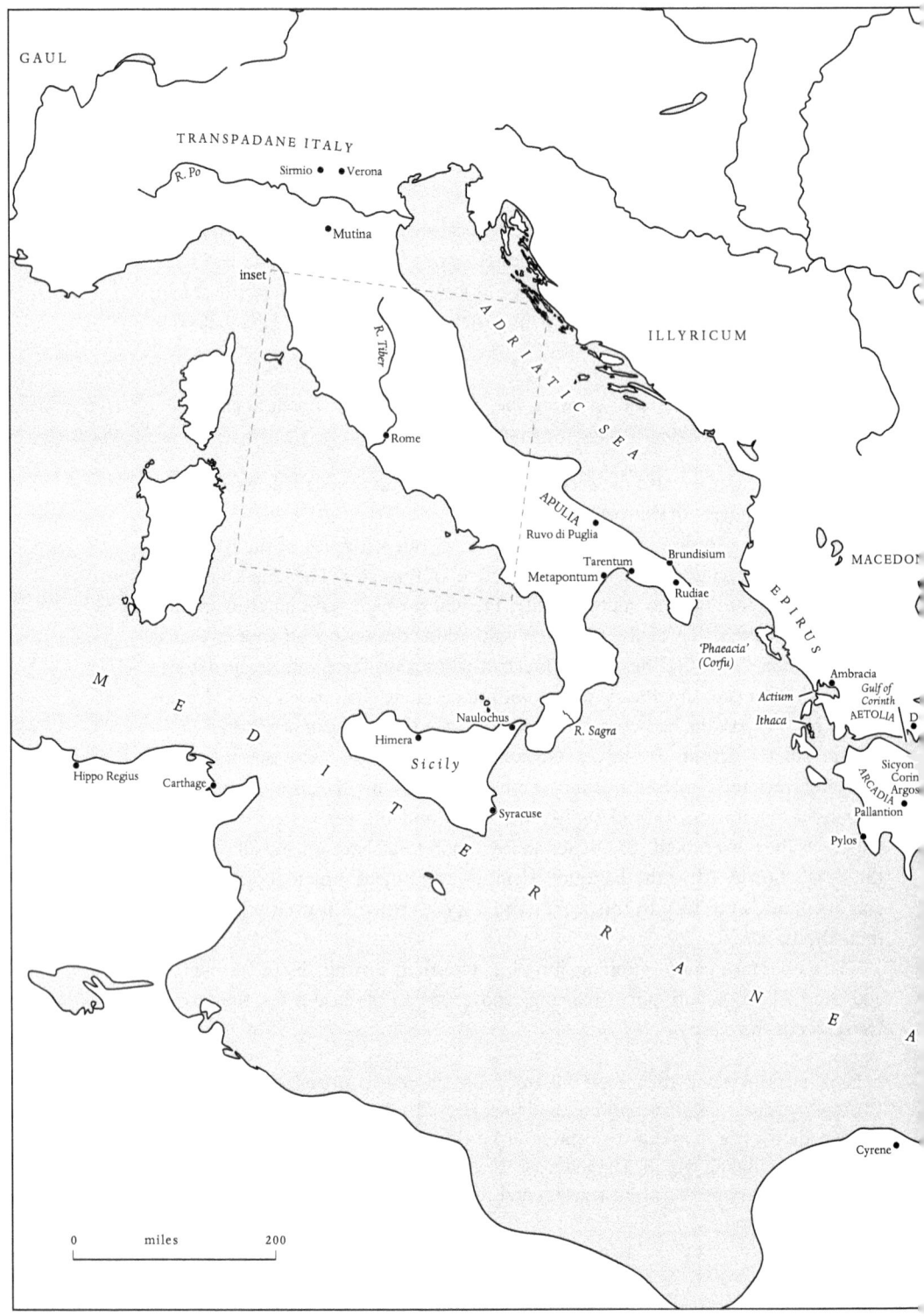

FIG. 2. Map of the Mediterranean; inset, central Italy. © Andras Bereznay: <www.historyonmaps.com.>

Demodocus then sings of the adulterous love of Ares and Aphrodite, and when he has finished Alcinous brings on two virtuoso dancers to give a display. Are we to suppose that the boys were dancing throughout Demodocus' song? If so, was it mimetic, a ballet representing the events? Homer's first audiences didn't need to be told, and we can only guess.

Demodocus sings at least four times in the king's hall (like Phemius in the house of Odysseus), and only once, on this occasion, in the *agora*. For an epic tale of kings and heroes, that was no doubt the proper balance—and we may note that his lyre was kept in the ruler's house. But since his name means 'honoured by the people', and he is twice given a formulaic epithet to the same effect, we need not suppose that it was unusual for a bard to perform at a festival in the *agora*, before that 'great crowd, in their thousands'.

Of course this is all idealized, and in any case reflects the experience of a poet—or more than one—composing for Greek audiences. We cannot simply impose such scenes on the newly created *agora* of embryonic Rome. But Homer's world and the land of the Latins were not wholly alien to each other. We may still make a reasonable inference: at Rome too, the *agora*—the Forum—was the place of judgement and the place of festival. Law and dance were equally sacred in the eyes of the community and its gods.

What we have to remember is that 'the people were crowded in the *agora*', 'heralds were keeping the crowd back', 'a large crowd stood around, enjoying the lovely dance', and the bard was 'honoured by the people'. In the mind's eye we need to summon up the first *populus Romanus* in its public space.

2.2. Evidence from Terracotta

No doubt they had a ruler, as the Phaeacians did. Recent archaeological research has even uncovered the remains of what may have been his house. But here again, we must not be led astray by the Romans' own pseudo-history. Although the *Cambridge Ancient History* confidently registers '672–640 [BC], Reign of Tullus Hostilius' and '640–616, Reign of Ancus Marcius', there is in fact no good evidence for the existence of those monarchs (I think they were probably invented to flatter the later families whose names they bear), and the chronological framework that made it possible to assign dates to them was itself only a creation of the third century BC.

As always, we need contemporary evidence, and to find it we now have to come forward a century or more, to the time when the Romans and their Latin and Etruscan neighbours were building stone temples for their gods, and decorating them with terracotta statues and terracotta revetment plaques that masked the roof-timbers.

The remains of one particularly fine statue-group were found in 1938 near the church of S. Omobono in Rome, just south-west of the Capitol, close to the river harbour of the ancient city and the open area known as Forum Bovarium ('cattle market'). A temple was built there about 530 BC, and the statue-group stood either on its roof or at ground level as a dedication to the deity. Enough survives of it to reveal the iconography: the helmeted Minerva (Pallas Athene), slightly behind Hercules (Hēraklēs), who has the lion-skin knotted round his neck, is evidently escorting the newly deified hero to Olympus.

Fig. 3

What makes this discovery particularly precious is its relevance to a story we know from Virgil, Livy, and Ovid 500 years later. A generation or so before the Trojan War, while Hercules was working his way through his Labours, Evander, a Greek exile from the Arcadian town of Pallantion, came to the banks of the Tiber and founded a settlement there. He named it after his native town, and in later times *Pallantion* became Latinized to *Palatium*, the Palatine hill. Hercules came there, driving the cattle of Geryoneus back to Argos (capturing them had been his tenth Labour); he killed a monstrous brigand who had been plaguing the place, and Evander's mother, who was a prophetess, revealed that the hero was destined to become a god. So a sacred precinct with an altar, the Ara Maxima, was made for him just south of the Forum Bovarium, which itself was named after the cattle.

We now know that this story—at least in its essentials—was already important in the sixth century BC. And we can make a good guess about how it came to be so.

About fifty years before the S. Omobono temple was built, the classic narrative of Hercules' tenth Labour had been created by one of the great masters of archaic Greek poetry, Stesichorus of Himera, whose home on the north coast of Sicily was just across the water from the land of the Latins. In his poem *Geryoneis* he broke with previous tradition, which saw Hercules as a conventional warrior, by giving him the lion-skin costume, just as on the Rome statue-group.

Stesichorus' name, evidently assumed for professional purposes, meant 'he who sets up the dance (or the dancing-place)', and it is likely that his lyric narratives, of which only fragments survive, were designed for choral performance at festivals not unlike those of Homer's Phaeacians. We know he worked for the cities of south Italy, and addressed himself to their citizens; whether or not he also set up the dance as far afield as Rome (that Latin city with the Greek name), at least the S. Omobono group suggests that his work was known there. And since it happens to be recorded that Arcadian Pallantion was mentioned in the *Geryoneis*, it is possible that the whole Evander story goes back to Stesichorus, or was elaborated from his famous poem.

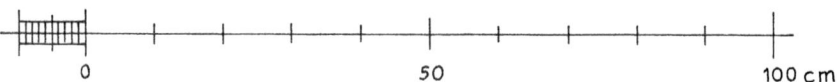

FIG. 3. Terracotta statue-group from a temple of c.530 BC, from the Forum Bovarium (S. Omobono), Rome; reconstruction drawing by Renate Sponer-Za, reproduced by permission of Dr Nancy A. Winter. Winter 2009.378, item 5.E.1.a. The original height of the group was about 150 cm (5 feet).

2.2. Evidence from Terracotta

Here we should remember again that in antiquity most of what ordinary people knew about the world beyond their own experience—the doings of gods and heroes and the men of the past—was what they learned from priests and poets at festivals and sacrifices (Ch. 1.4 above). We may be sure that when that temple by the Forum Bovarium was dedicated, the citizens were told in song and speech what the deity had done to deserve it, and that every year the lesson was repeated when the day of the festival came round.

The form such festive solemnities took will have differed from one community to another, as resources allowed and traditions developed. Thanks to Herodotus, and a digression in his history of Athenian politics, we happen to know what they were like about this time in the city of Sicyon, on the southern coast of the gulf of Corinth. The Athenian Cleisthenes was a grandson of the Cleisthenes who had been ruler of Sicyon in the early sixth century BC:

> That Cleisthenes, at war with the Argives, put an end to the rhapsodes' competitions at Sicyon, because the Homeric epics constantly celebrate the Argives and Argos. Also, there was, and still is, a hero-shrine of Adrastus the son of Talaus, actually in the *agora* of the Sicyonians, and Cleisthenes wanted to banish him from the country because he was an Argive.... Part of the Sicyonians' cult of Adrastus was the custom of commemorating his sufferings in tragic dances [*choroi*], in honour not of Dionysus but of Adrastus.

Herodotus 5.67.1 and 5

The end of the story was that Cleisthenes transferred the *choroi* to Dionysus and the rest of the cult to a rival hero from Thebes.

At about the same time (we have this too from Herodotus), Cleisthenes' neighbour Periander, ruler of Corinth, imported a poet-musician from Lesbos to organize the Corinthians' traditional festivals. His name was Arion:

> He was the leading cithara-player of his time, and the first person we know of to have made a dithyramb and given it that name, and he produced it in Corinth. Though Arion spent most of his time with Periander, they say he was very keen to sail to Italy and Sicily, and only having done so, and made a great deal of money, did he decide to return to Corinth.

Herodotus 1.23–24.1

The dithyramb was a danced choral hymn to Dionysus; according to Aristotle it was the origin of tragic drama.

Arion too was a setter-up of dances, no doubt in competition with Stesichorus. The fact that it was worth his while to sail to the west implies significant cultural innovation in sixth-century Italy, and there is no reason to suppose that it was confined to the Greek cities of the south. What Latins and Etruscans took from the Greek world was more than just imported pottery and artistic techniques.

Let's return to Rome, and the c.530 BC archaeological horizon of the S. Omobono temple. The terracotta plaques used on that building, and on several others in Rome and its vicinity, from Etruscan Veii (10 miles north) to

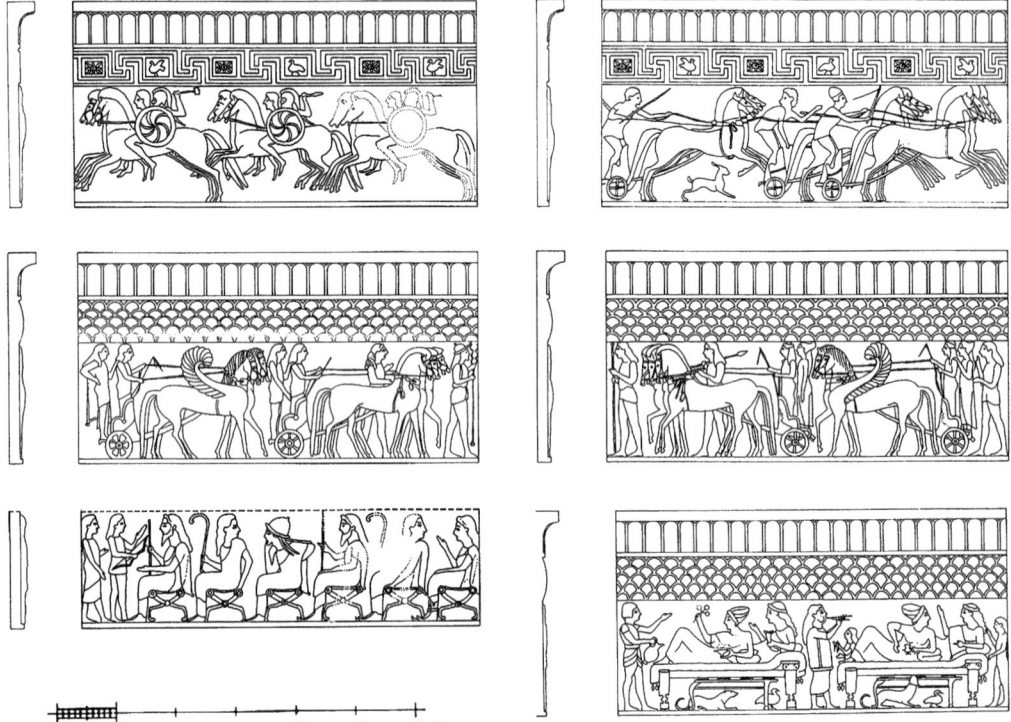

FIG. 4. Terracotta revetment plaques, 'Veii–Rome–Velletri' group, c.530 BC; reconstruction drawings by Renate Sponer-Za, reproduced by courtesy of Dr Nancy A. Winter. Winter 2009. 354–74: items 5.D.1.a (chariot race), 5.D.1.c (armed riders), 5.D.2.a (procession to right), 5.D.2.c (procession to left), 5.D.2.e (banquet), 5.D.5.a (seated assembly).

Fig. 4

Latin Velitrae (20 miles south), came from one particular workshop. Some of its designs may give us a sense of how the Romans and their neighbours idealized their world—armed horsemen parading at the gallop; a chariot race; two processions of ceremonial chariots, one led by Mercury (Hermes), the herald-god, with his *caduceus*, the other by a presumably mortal herald with a staff (in each case the winged horses suggest divine participation); a banquet, with couples reclining together in the Etruscan fashion; a session of elders or magistrates with rods of office—or is it a session of immortals, receiving Hercules to Olympus?

For some of these scenes we may imagine the citizens of the community as an audience, enjoying the spectacle or witnessing what is being done in their name. In the case of the chariot race, the bizarre idea that the 'Circus games' were named after Circe, the witch-goddess of *Odyssey*, book 10, would make perfectly good sense in the sixth century BC, when many elaborations of the *Odyssey* story were being composed, including one that made 'Latinus, ruler of the famed Etruscans', a son of Circe and Odysseus. Even more revealing is the story that

Romulus set up the games in honour of Poseidon Hippios, the presiding deity of the Isthmian Games at Corinth. The Romulus narrative is probably no older than the fourth century BC, but Poseidon Hippios looks like an earlier tradition.

2.3. Rome and Athens

That Corinthian connection is unlikely to be a coincidence. The last king of Rome, 'Tarquin the Arrogant'—the only one whose historical existence can be confidently asserted—claimed descent from a Corinthian aristocrat who had escaped to Italy after a *coup d'état*. For this reason, and because after his expulsion he made an alliance with 'Aristodemus the Effeminate', ruler of the Greek city of Cumae, Tarquin was of interest to Greek writers, and as a result the Romans' tradition about him may contain some accurate information. In particular, the Greeks' date for his expulsion—'twenty-eight years before Xerxes crossed into Greece'—is more likely than not to be right.

That was three years after the expulsion of Hippias son of Pisistratus, ruler of Athens. The Tarquins evidently held power at Rome in much the same way as the Pisistratids did in Athens, and the removal of one dynasty may have provided an inspiring example for that of the other. The extensive import of Athenian pottery, archaeologically attested, makes it likely that Romans of the late sixth century BC were familiar with the affairs of Athens. Two centuries later, when they were creating the narrative of their own history, the Romans used 'after the expulsion of the kings' as a dating-era modelled on the Athenians' 'after the expulsion of the tyrants'.

As Aristotle later remarked, despotic regimes liked to keep their subjects poor and busy, by taxing them heavily and employing them on huge, labour-intensive building projects. Among his examples of the latter are the pyramids of Egypt and 'the Olympieion of the Pisistratids'—that is, the great temple of Olympian Zeus just south-east of the Athenian acropolis, twice the size of any other temple west of the Aegean. (It had to be abandoned when the Pisistratids were expelled, and was only completed by Hadrian in AD 132.) Tarquin too built a great temple to Zeus (Jupiter Optimus Maximus) on the Capitol, 61m long by 55m wide, 'one of the largest temples in the Mediterranean world'.

In the Romans' own account of their history, wicked King Tarquin was thrown out before the temple was quite complete, and its dedication to the ruler of gods and men was carried out by one of the consuls in the first year of the republic. That is a little too good to be true, no doubt just one of the many exemplary stories that were told about the origin of Roman freedom. Dating 'from the expulsion of the kings' probably superseded an original dating-era 'from the dedication of the Capitoline temple' (used in the late fourth century BC), once the two events had been merged in the tradition.

The contemporary evidence is purely material: parts of the huge stone platform of the temple survive, and may be seen in the Museo dei Conservatori, but we have no idea how its dedication was marked and made significant to the Roman community—perhaps still the king's subjects—at the time. We can guess that the miraculous discovery of a human head, divine indication that the site was the destined capital (*caput rerum*), was celebrated in song or story or even performance, but a guess is all it can be.

Another guess is that the new cult of Ceres, Liber, and Libera, introduced soon after the expulsion of Tarquin, was influenced by the Athenian cult of Dionysus Eleuthereus: Liber is what the Latins called Dionysus, and *liber* and *eleutheros* are respectively Latin and Greek for 'free'. What is certain is that Dionysus' followers, the satyrs or *silēnoi*, were very widely portrayed as temple-antefixes, in Rome and the towns of Latium and south Etruria, about the turn of the sixth and fifth centuries BC.

Fig. 5 and colour plate 1

Satyrs are creatures who perform, whether impersonated by worshippers in Dionysiac rites or played by actors in Dionysiac drama (if indeed it makes sense to distinguish the two categories). 'Drama' is now a word we can use, for it was precisely at this time that the performance traditions of tragedy, comedy, and satyr-play were being formalized at the Athenian festival in honour of Dionysus Eleuthereus. At the same time, closer to Rome but detectable even in our Athenocentric sources, an independent tradition of comic drama was already established at Syracuse. It is inconceivable that the Romans were unaware of these developments, but we have no way of telling how far they imitated them.

The greatest Syracusan dramatist of the time was Epicharmus, later believed (perhaps rightly) to have been a follower of Pythagoras. He is quoted as saying—in a prose work, not a play—that the Romans honoured Pythagoras with the grant of their citizenship; even if, as is often supposed, the philosophical interests of Epicharmus are an invention of fourth-century BC Pythagoreans, that is still early enough for this alleged citation to add to our evidence for Roman engagement in the cultural developments of the Greek cities of south Italy and Sicily, and through them, of the Greek world as a whole.

Did they have 'drama' yet? Was their Liberalia festival on 17 March an occasion for stage performance like the Athenian Dionysia? The later Romans thought not: their historical tradition (Ch. 2.5 below) put the introduction of 'stage games', *ludi scaenici*, in 364 BC, and it may well be that for historians working in the first century BC (point C on our time-line), that was as far back as their documentation went. For us, however, new evidence may change the picture.

Fig. 1

Very recent archaeological research at the Etruscan city of Caere, less than 30 miles from Rome, has detected a fifth-century BC cult site of the same triad of gods—local versions of Dionysus, Demeter, and Persephone—associated with a performance area described by the excavators as a 'proto-theatre'. It is not

FIG. 5. Satyr-mask terracotta antefixes from Rome, c.500 BC. (*a*) and (*c*) reproduced by permission of the Ministero per i Beni e le Attività Culturali—Soprintendenza Speciale per i Beni Archeologici di Roma; (*b*), (*d*), and (*e*) reproduced by permission of the Sovrintendente e Direttore dei Musei Capitolini, Rome.

(*a*) From the site of the Basilica Iulia, perhaps from the temple of Castor: Antiquarium forense 1916, Cristofani 1990.63 (3.4.1).
(*b*) From near SS. Luca e Martina, probably from a temple on the north-eastern summit of the Capitol: Antiquarium comunale 16230, Cristofani 1990.69 (3.6.1).
(*c*) From near the 'House of Livia' at the west corner of the Palatine: Antiquarium palatino 12008, Cristofani 1990.91 (4.1.4).
(*d*) From the Via dei Serpenti, near the ancient Subura: Antiquarium comunale 3348, Andrén 1940. pl. 107 no. 384.
(*e*) From the Esquiline, near S. Antonio: Antiquarium comunale 3374, Cristofani 1990.254 (10.1.4).

unlikely that the Romans of that time were also seeing stories performed at the festivals of their gods.

2.4. Honouring Gods

When we tried to imagine the *agora* of a seventh-century BC community, the *Iliad* and *Odyssey* offered a vivid picture. We have no Homer for the world of

500 BC, only the fragments of lost works; but even they can be useful. Here are a couple of stray sentences from the philosopher Heraclitus (quoted by another philosopher nearly a thousand years later):

<small>Heraclitus fr. 104 Diels = 59 Kahn (trans. adapted from Kahn 1979.57)</small>

> What wit or understanding do they have? They believe the bards of the peoples and take the crowd as their teacher, not knowing that 'the many are worthless', good men are few.

Many years ago, Eric Havelock spotted the significance of this passage:

> This is an unmistakable vignette, sharply etched, of the epic recital being given in a city square as a regular civic performance attended by the populace, who in the intervals of the recitation discuss the performance, compare notes on the story, and thus renew for themselves that instruction in their own traditions which Plato was later to characterize in his descriptions of poetic performance in the *Republic*. The audience is pluralized as *dēmoi* ['peoples']; that is, the minstrel is presumed to be moving from city to city.

<small>Havelock 1966.56 = 1982.243–4</small>

That too has a Homeric precedent: as examples of those who are welcome guests to the community as masters of a craft, Eumaeus in the *Odyssey* mentions a prophet, a healer, a carpenter, and also 'an inspired bard who gives delight with song'.

Since Heraclitus was an Ionian aristocrat from Ephesus, the peoples he had in mind were no doubt those of the cities of Ionia, on the coast of Asia Minor and the islands of the Aegean. But people like him had been trading along the west coast of Italy for generations (we know them from the names they wrote on dedications at the Etruscan harbour-sanctuary of Gravisca), and when in due course the free Romans wanted to draw up a written law-code, they brought in an Ionian aristocrat from Ephesus, Hermodorus, to help them do it.

Certainly the post-Tarquin regime was still prosperous enough to attract such people. One good index of prosperity was the creation of new public cults, and in all the later Romans' elaborate (and often very implausible) 'historical' tradition on the early republic, temple dedications are among the few items that have a good chance of being authentic, and more or less accurately dated. Four new temples are said to have been built in the first dozen or so years of the free city. One of them, that of Ceres, Liber, and Libera, we have mentioned already; the others were dedicated to Saturn, to Castor and Pollux, and to Mercury.

Saturn is the god who carries a sickle. As the Greek Cronos, he used it to castrate his tyrannical father and depose him as king of the gods; when he threw it down from heaven, it landed in Sicily. Deposed in his turn, he lay low in the land of the Latins, and gave it its name. Castor and Pollux are the twin *Dioscuri*,

Spartan heroes who twice miraculously appeared in battles in Italy—at the river Sagra in 540 BC for Locri against Croton, and at the lake Regillus in 499 BC for Rome against the exiled Tarquin and his Latin allies. In Rome these stories were surely told or sung each year, on 15 July for Castor and Pollux and on 17 December for Saturn.

What song was sung on 15 May for Mercury? The month was named after his mother, and the day of his birth was the day he invented the lyre. Mercury is the Greek Hermes, son of Zeus and Maia, 'many-talented, charmingly clever, a thief and a bringer of dreams'. A hymn that survives from the sixth century BC gives an idea of how he might be celebrated, with the invention of the lyre offering the singer an opportunity for self-reference:

> He took the plectrum and tried each string in turn. Under his hand it made a wondrous sound, and as he tried it the god sang a lovely song, improvising like the young men who mock with double meaning at festivals. He sang of Zeus the son of Cronos and Maia of the fair sandals, how they used to converse in the intimacy of love, and he made famous his own renowned begetting.

Homeric Hymn to Hermes 53–9

The last phrase means literally 'he named his own begetting as a famous name'. The god's Latin name was derived from *merces*, 'price', and he looked after commerce as well as theft.

For a generation or two after the expulsion of the Tarquins, Rome was still a prosperous commercial centre. From about the middle of the fifth century BC, however, an economic downturn can be inferred from the archaeological evidence, or its absence. Among the reasons were military pressure, from highland peoples attacking Latium, and plague and famine; the only new cult recorded at Rome between 466 and 392 BC is that of Apollo the Healer. The conquest and absorption of the Etruscan city of Veii should have marked a great recovery, but it was followed by a great catastrophe—the sack of Rome by the Gallic Senones in 387 BC.

This is the period for which it is most difficult to imagine the Roman audience. How many people in Rome were aware of the glorious maturity of Athenian drama, whether tragic (Aeschylus, Sophocles, Euripides) or comic (Cratinus, Eupolis, Aristophanes)? Some, certainly. Aeschylus worked in Sicily, and died there in 456 BC; Euripides was all the rage in Syracuse in 415 BC; Plato was well aware of theatre competitions in Sicily and Italy. And Romans also found their way to 'old Greece', as in 393 BC, when they took their thank-offering for the Veii victory to Delphi and dedicated it in the treasury of the Massilians. However, knowing about Athenian drama was not the same as being able to afford it. When the great tragedians left imperial Athens, they went to the courts of wealthy autocrats like Hiero of Syracuse and Archelaus of Macedon.

2.5. Fragments and 'History'

At this point, we have for the first time usable evidence from the Romans' own later literature. It offers only a couple of glimpses of a lost world, but it is precious for all that.

First, a passage in Pliny's *Natural History*, written in the seventies AD. The author is discussing crowns and coronets, whether made of flowers or leafy twigs or precious metal. They were used as prizes at the games:

> There was always distinction in the winning of them, even in sporting competitions. For [Romans in the past] used to go down to the *circus* themselves to compete at the games, as well as entering their slaves and horses. Whence that law in the Twelve Tables: 'Whoever wins a crown, either himself or his property, or it be given him for his bravery...' Nobody has ever doubted that by 'won by his property' the law means the crown that his slaves or horses had earned. So what was the honour? That at his death and that of his parents it might legally be placed on the body while it lay in the house or was carried out for burial.

Pliny Natural History 21.7

Pliny is quoting from the ancient law-code of the Roman republic, the original text of which probably dated back to the fifth century BC. He infers from this ancient document that in those days Roman citizens might compete in person as charioteers at the games, or else take the credit if their slaves were victorious. That is certainly consistent with the contemporary visual evidence for aristocratic chariot-racing.

Fig. 4

Humbler entertainments are attested in our other possible fragment of archaic information. It comes in the entry on *cernuus*, 'head-first', in Nonius Marcellus' dictionary of Latin word meanings:

> See Varro *On the Life of the Roman People*, book I: 'They also used to run along ox-hides soaked in oil and go head-first there, which is the origin of the old verse in the *Songs*: "There the shepherds hold their games with hides, the festival of Consus."'

Nonius 31L

We have three levels of evidence here. Nonius' dictionary was probably compiled in the fourth century AD, near to point D on our time-line. The Varro passage it cites was written in the forties BC (point C), and Varro himself cited an earlier source, a collection of anonymous 'old songs' which were believed to pre-date the beginning of written literature in Latin (point B).

Fig. 1

Consus had two festivals, on 21 August and 15 December. There were probably 'games' on each occasion, in the valley between the Palatine and the Aventine where the god had his underground altar. The August games were the setting for Romulus' capture of the Sabine women; that story, probably created in the late fourth or early third century BC, evidently presupposed the shepherds' festival referred to in the old song.

These tenuous indications provide evidence that is more likely to be authentic than the 'historical' tradition about the origin of Roman drama. Our fullest version of that tradition is in Livy's seventh book, narrating the supposed events of the year we would call 364 BC. Rome was recovering from her humiliation by the Gauls; internal strife between the rich and the poor, the privileged and the exploited, had just been alleviated by a new power-sharing agreement (two consuls per year, one patrician, one plebeian); the territory of newly conquered Veii provided land for the needy and stone-quarries for a huge new defensive wall.

But there was no defence against natural disaster, and for three years plague afflicted Rome. Here is Livy's account:

> People's minds were overcome by superstitious terror. Among other attempts to placate the wrath of heaven, it is said that stage games were also instituted—something new to a warlike people, since hitherto there had been only the spectacle of the *circus*. They were also something small, as beginnings usually are, and the thing itself was foreign. No singing, no acting in imitation of song: the players summoned from Etruria danced to the accompaniment of a pipe-player's measures and made quite graceful movements in the Etruscan manner. Then the young men began to imitate them, at the same time exchanging repartee in improvised verses, with movements appropriate to the words. So it was taken up and established by frequent repetition. The name given to these native performers was *histriones*, since *ister* was the Etruscan word for a player. They didn't throw out rough improvised exchanges like Fescennine verse, as had been done previously, but began to perform satires filled with musical measures in what was now a written song accompanied by a pipe-player and with appropriate movement.

Livy 7.2.7–8

Livy was writing in the twenties BC (point C on the time-line), and exploiting the recent research of Marcus Varro, the most learned Roman of his time. But even Varro only knew what he could infer from written sources, like that collection of old songs. So far as 364 BC is concerned, Livy's scenario must be largely guesswork.

Fig. 1

2.6. Marking the Days

The Romans of the fourth century BC were familiar with Greek culture, or at least some parts of it. Archaeology reveals the work of Greek architects and engineers; it was they who created the great new defensive wall of Rome, 7 miles long and 40 feet high, and designed the fortified 'maritime colonies' manned by Roman citizens at Ostia, Tarracina, and other coastal sites. By a very fortunate chance, we even have some contemporary evidence from the Roman colonists at Circeii: on what had once been Circe's island, proud of their little town's Homeric past, they showed visitors the ancient tomb of Elpenor, the young comrade of Odysseus who fell off the witch-goddess's roof when he was drunk, and broke his neck.

According to one story current at the time, the Romans were descended from Achaeans who were blown off course as they returned from the Trojan War and settled in the land of the Latins with the captive Trojan women they had brought with them. We don't know the origin of that tradition, but it was accepted by Aristotle, who was interested in the Romans' institutions. He was right to be interested. By the time he was collecting his data on political systems in the 320s BC, Rome had established herself as a major power in central Italy. Her settlers now occupied the north Campanian plain, only 20 miles from the Greek cities of Cumae and Neapolis. Soon they would be overlooking the Adriatic.

One of Rome's leaders in this great period of military and political success was a man called Gaius Maenius. He is important for our purposes because as consul in 338 BC he created a new speakers' platform (called *rostra* from the rams of captured ships that decorated it), and as censor in 318 he put up balconies (called *maeniana* after their originator) above the shops and porticos in the Forum, 'in order to give more room for spectators'. Now for the first time we can begin to imagine the Roman audience, whether as citizens or as spectators, in a relatively intelligible architectural environment.

At about the same period (the archaeological remains are not precisely datable, but could easily have been part of Maenius' programme), a new assembly-place for the citizen body was built at the north corner of the Roman Forum. It probably imitated the theatre-like circular form used by the Greek cities of southern Italy: the Latin term was *comitium*, where the People 'come together'; the Greek was *ekklēsiastērion*, the place for the 'summoned-out' citizens. For Romans as for Greeks, it was a venue that could be used both for political decision-making and for the festivals of the gods.

At this point we must take account of a very particular kind of contemporary evidence, the Roman calendar. Various examples of Roman calendars survive, painted on plaster, carved in stone, or copied in manuscript. None of them is earlier than point C on our time-line, but what they all have in common is an identifiable nucleus of named days which evidently goes back at least as far as the fourth century BC.

Fig. 1

Most of the days in the calendar are marked as F (*fastus*) or N (*nefastus*), 'speaking' or 'non-speaking' days, when the judicial business of magistrates—and thus the 'speaking' of their legal formulae—respectively could or could not be carried out. On the F days the Forum crowd would be noisily jostling round the praetor's tribunal; on the N days they might be jostling round the very same platform to hear a prophet or a storyteller, or watching a funeral procession and listening to the dead man's praises being spoken and sung from the same *rostra* from which a consul or tribune had addressed them the previous day.

The named days in the calendar—or at least thirty-five out of the total forty-five—are not marked with F or N, but with a monogram of N and P. So are the Ides of every month (the 15th of March, May, July and October, the 13th of the others), which were sacred to Jupiter. We don't know what the monogram letters stood for, but it seems clear that the days they marked were in some sense public holidays in honour of the gods. Twenty of the named days are indeed named after gods, and the list itself is an insight into the unfamiliar world of pre-literary Rome:

11 and 15 January: *Carmentalia*, for the goddess Carmentis; *carmen* could mean 'song', 'prophecy' or 'incantation'.

17 February: *Quirinalia*, for Quirinus, whose priest (*flamen*) ranked equal with those of Jupiter and Mars.

23 February: *Terminalia*, for Terminus, god of boundaries.

17 March: *Liberalia*, for Liber, identified as the Greek Dionysus (Ch. 2.3 above), and Libera.

19 April: *Cerialia*, for Ceres, identified as the Greek Demeter, with whom Liber and Libera shared their temple.

21 April: *Palilia*, or more usually *Parilia*, for Pales, goddess of shepherds.

25 April: *Robigalia*, for Robigus or Robigo, god or goddess of rust and mildew.

9, 11, and 13 May: *Lemuria*, for the Lemures, ghosts of the dead.

9 June: *Vestalia*, for Vesta, goddess of the hearth.

11 June: *Matralia*, for Mater Matuta, whose name seems to mean 'morning mother'.

23 July: *Neptunalia*, for Neptunus, identified as the Greek Poseidon.

25 July: *Furrinalia*, for Furrina; this otherwise unknown goddess had her own priest, the *flamen Furrinalis*.

17 August: *Portunalia*, for Portunus, god of gates and harbours.

21 August and 15 December: *Consualia*, for Consus; *condere* means 'to store'.

23 August: *Volcanalia*, for Volcanus, identified as the Greek Hephaestus, god of fire and metalworking.

27 August: *Volturnalia*, for Volturnus, who also had his own priest, the *flamen Volturnalis*.

13 October: *Fontinalia*, for Fons, god of springs and water sources.

17 December: *Saturnalia*, for Saturnus, identified as the Greek Cronos.

19 December: *Opalia*, for the goddess Ops; *opes* meant 'resources', 'wealth'.

23 December: *Larentalia* for Larentia, or Lara or Larunda; she may be the mother of the Lares, guardian gods of the city and its streets and houses.

Several of the other named days were no longer understood at the time our literary sources were writing, three centuries later; the names *Agonalia*, for instance (9 January, 21 May, 11 December), and *Feralia* (21 February) gave rise to many implausible explanations, while the name *Lupercalia* (15 February: *lupus* means 'wolf') seems inappropriate to that festival's consistent association with goats.

The best guess for *Agonalia* is that it referred to *agones*, the Greek word for contests and competitions. We have good evidence from later times that the young men who ran naked at the *Lupercalia* were thought of as performers (*ludii*) before an audience. As we shall see in the next chapter, it is likely that the *Liberalia*, like the Athenian Dionysia (Ch. 2.3 above), honoured the god with dance and drama. Whatever the truth of that, the balconies Maenius set up 'to give more room for spectators' clearly imply that Rome in the fourth century BC was already familiar with public spectacles of one kind or another.

Necessarily, this chapter has had to deal with indirect evidence for early Rome, using analogies from the better-attested archaic Greek world, especially Homer, to provide a context for what little contemporary evidence survives in the archaeological record. We have reached the second half of the fourth century BC, still two or three generations before Roman literature begins. But at this point archaeology provides some new categories of contemporary evidence, and what they reveal deserves a chapter to itself.

Fig. 1, point B

3

Rome Before Literature

Dionysus and Drama

What sort of spectacles did the Roman audience watch from Maenius' balconies? To find a likely answer to that, we need to go back a little in time, to the Athens of Euripides and Aristophanes.

3.1. Pots Painted, Bronze Engraved

A modest late fifth-century red-figure jug from Attica shows an actor dancing on stage in the role of Perseus; he carries that hero's characteristic sickle-

Fig. 6

FIG. 6. Attic *chous*, c.420 BC (Athens, National Museum BΣ 518); Beazley 1963.1215.1, Taplin 1993. fig. 8.25; drawing by Elizabeth Malyon, reproduced by permission of Eric Csapo (Csapo 2010.25, fig. 1.10).

FIG. 7. Attic volute-krater, c.400 BC (Naples, National Museum 81673); Beazley 1963.1336.1, Taplin and Wyles 2010. fi
Reproduced by permission of the Beazley Archive, Oxford.

Fig. 7

shaped weapon and the bag that will contain the Gorgon's severed head. Two people on chairs represent the audience, or competition judges, and what looks like a curtain or screen marks off the performance area. This is evidently a comic parody of a tragedy plot.

Athenian tragedies of the fifth century BC were performed as tetralogies, three successive tragic plays followed by a satyr-play. A much more famous Attic vase, datable to about 400 BC, depicts the winning chorus after the final play. One of the chorus-men (20), with his mask still on, is dancing right out of the picture; the rest are relaxing with their masks off, accompanied by two of the tragic actors, still dressed for their roles as an oriental king (4) and Herakles (9). In the foreground are the playwright Demetrios (19), the pipe-player Pronomos (21), and the impresario Charinos (22); in the background are the gods—Dionysus and Ariadne (5 and 6), Himeros ('Desire', 7), and Tragoidia, the divine personification of tragedy (8), holding a mask as if she were one of the actors. Most of the chorus wear the usual Athenian satyr-play costume of furry pants with a tail at the back and an erect phallus at the front. One of them, however (10), has an old man's mask and wears a hairy body-suit; his character is conventionally named as Papposilenus, the father of the satyrs.

On the other side of the vase we are out of the theatre and into the wild; watch out for the panther (29). Here, Dionysus and Ariadne (14 and 15) are in their own element, with maenads and 'real' satyrs ecstatically dancing. We can't hear the music, but Himeros (13) is about to clash cymbals, and one of the satyrs (16) is playing the pipes. His colleague (12) symbolically links the two scenes by pouring the wine of Dionysus to fall on one of the unwitting chorus-members.

The reason this vase matters to us is that it was found in non-Greek Italy. It was owned by, buried with, and quite possibly made to order for a wealthy Apulian of the people who called themselves Rubustini. Their cemeteries, excavated in the nineteenth century at the town of Ruvo di Puglia, revealed a huge trove of elaborate red-figure vases, either Athenian or from the neighbouring Greek city of Tarentum. They are the most spectacular evidence for a phenomenon which is only now receiving the attention it deserves—the export of Athenian comedy and tragedy, not only beyond Athens but beyond the Greek-speaking world.

Which side of the vase mattered more to its Apulian owner, the theatrical scene or the Dionysiac ecstasy? Or were they inseparable, dramatic performance considered as a part of Dionysiac ritual, with its promise of bliss in this world and the next? A juxtaposition similar to that on the Ruvo vase can be seen on a Tarentine dish about fifty years later: on one side, a scene from Euripides' *Bacchae*, with the disguised Pentheus being attacked by the Bacchants; on the other, a scene of Bacchic revelry, with a young satyr, a piper on a panther-skin, and a naked dancing-girl.

Fig. 8 and colour plate 2

Painted pottery, the medium that gives us these images, was not a craft skill that could be taken for granted. For a long time it was an Athenian speciality; but late in

FIG. 8. Apulian *phiale*, c.350 BC (British Museum F 133). For the *Bacchae* scene on the left, see Taplin 2004 and 2007.156–8; for the satyr and dancing girl on the right, see Wiseman 2008.107–8. © The Trustees of the British Museum, all rights reserved.

Fig. 9

the fifth century BC it began to be practised also in the Greek cities of Sicily and south Italy, and by the middle of the fourth century—the date of the Tarentine dish—there were schools of craftsmen also producing it in various areas of Italy where Greek was not the local language. There seem to have been no vase-painters in Latium, but there certainly were among the Latins' neighbours, both to the north (Etruria) and to the south (Campania).

Paestum, just south of the bay of Naples, had once been Greek Poseidonia, but in the late fifth century BC it was taken over—'barbarized', a Tarentine philosopher said—by Oscan-speaking Lucanians. Two or three generations later,

3.1. Pots Painted, Bronze Engraved

the vase-painters who worked there were fond of comic-theatre scenes. In one example, the dancing-girl is on stage performing for Dionysus himself; two masked comic actors look on, and two more, in female roles, appear in the windows of the stage-set.

Fig. 10 and colour plate 2

From much closer to Rome, about 30 miles north, comes a Faliscan cup showing another dancing-girl, not on stage this time but performing with a man in a hairy 'Papposilenos' suit. He has a Bacchic *thyrsus*, and his hand is in the 'tilted' position characteristic of dancing satyrs.

Fig. 11

The absence of vase-painting in fourth-century Latium is more than made up for by the bronze-engravers who worked there at that time. The scenes with which they decorated mirrors and large cylindrical boxes (*cistae*) are directly comparable with the repertoire of the red-figure painters. One particularly elaborate mirror (no provenance, but perhaps from Praeneste) shows a drinking-party scene surrounded by a long, grape-laden vine. In the centre is another hairy-suited performer with a *thyrsus*, turning to a half-naked girl piper.

Fig. 12

Compare that with the scene round a *cista* from Latium, in which the hairy-suited *thyrsus*-bearer advances with two dancing girl musicians and a dancing satyr towards a dramatic scene—the decapitation of the Gorgon Medusa by Perseus. (The winged horse Pegasus springs out of the wound.) As on the Tarentine dish, Dionysiac revelry and mythological narrative merge into each other; and as the Athenian cup reminds us, Perseus was a drama character as well as a mythic hero.

Fig. 13

Fig. 8
Fig. 6

The last item in our sequence is a *cista* scene of a Euripidean tragedy plot, Iphigeneia at Aulis. Reading from right to left, we have a naked girl, as in Figures 10, 11, and 12, not dancing this time but holding a mirror; a satyr piping, as in Figure 7; a satyr dancing, with 'tilted hand' as in Figure 12; a young man with a staff, unidentified; an older man with a staff, recognizable as Agamemnon; a female character at a window, as in Figure 10 (she may be Artemis/Diana); two armed figures apparently in eastern costume, one carrying an axe; the stag which the goddess will substitute for Iphigeneia at the last minute; Iphigeneia herself, dramatically disrobing; grieving Achilles, who had hoped to marry her; and an unidentified warrior with his horse.

Fig. 14

By the fourth century BC the plots of Athenian drama, like those of Homeric epic, had become international, a cultural common ground familiar to speakers of Latin, Oscan, and Etruscan as well as those who spoke the various dialects of Greek. That is something we would never have guessed from the later Roman literary sources, but the contemporary visual evidence puts it beyond doubt. The iconography also implies that Rome and Latium were familiar with types of performance which could be described equally as drama or as Dionysiac ritual.

Yet again, we look for a context in contemporary Greek sources, and this time our informants are Aristotle and Plato. In the very first paragraph of his *Poetics*,

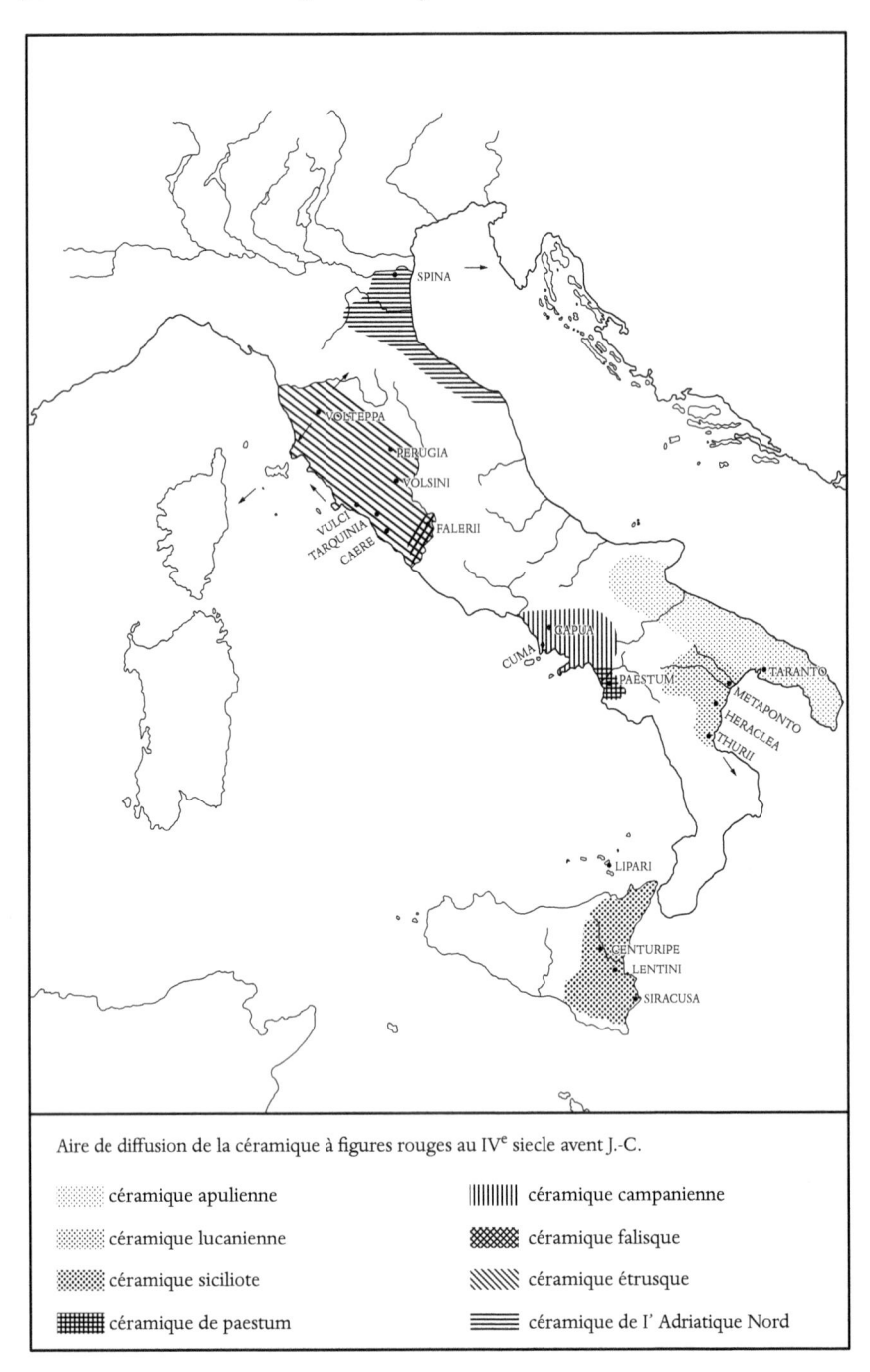

Aire de diffusion de la céramique à figures rouges au IVe siecle avent J.-C.

- céramique apulienne
- céramique lucanienne
- céramique siciliote
- céramique de paestum
- céramique campanienne
- céramique falisque
- céramique étrusque
- céramique de l' Adriatique Nord

FIG. 9. Areas of production of red-figure pottery in Italy, fourth century BC (Cristofani 1980.174). Reproduced by permission of the Musées Royaux d'Art et d'Histoire, Bruxelles.

FIG. 10. Paestan kalyx-krater, c.350 BC (Lipari, inv. no. 927). Reproduced by permission of Regione Sicilia, Dipartimento per i Beni Culturali, Museo Archeologico Regionale Luigi Bernabò Brea, Lipari (ME), Italy.

the foundation-text of literary criticism, Aristotle declares that all poetry—epic, dramatic (tragedy and comedy), dithyrambic (hymns to Dionysus)—as well as most music for the pipe and the lyre, consists of imitation, *mimēsis*. A few years earlier, Plato in the *Laws* had used the same concept when discussing ecstatic dance, such as that used in Dionysiac mystery-cult:

> Any [dancing] that is Bacchic in nature, or that resembles those in which, while celebrating certain ceremonies of purification and initiation, the dancers 'imitate',

FIG. 11. Faliscan cup, fourth century BC (Rome, Villa Giulia, inv. no. 43608). Reproduced by permission of the Soprintendenza per i Beni Archeologici dell'Etruria Meridionale.

Plato *Laws* 7.815c

as the saying is, drunken persons, calling them nymphs, Pans, Sileni and satyrs—this kind of dancing is, as a whole, neither peaceful nor warlike, and it is hard to determine what its purpose is.

He clearly disapproved of it, but even his law-code had to allow for its existence.

'Imitating satyrs' is what Athenian satyr-play did; 'imitating Sileni' may refer to the hairy-suit impersonation illustrated in Figures 7, 11, 12, and 13; the figure on the right in Figure 12 may be 'imitating Pan', to judge by the horns in his hair; and the girls in Figures 8, 10, 11, and 14 could easily be thought of as imitating the naked nymphs.

If we find it hard to imagine Romans enjoying performances like this from Maenius' new balconies, that is only because we give too much weight to literary evidence, necessarily anachronistic, from centuries later. It is better to take seriously what the contemporary pots and bronzes show us.

3.2. Republican Rome

So far as we can tell, the various Italian schools of bronze-engravers and red-figure vase-painters lasted only two or three generations. Then their world was disrupted by war.

FIG. 12. Praenestine(?) mirror, late fourth century BC (Baltimore, Walters Art Museum). Gerhard et al. 1897.52–3; Wiseman 2008.66–9.

Already dominant in central Italy, from 282 to 241 BC the Romans were involved in a succession of major conflicts in the south: with Tarentum, the greatest of the Greek cities of Italy; with King Pyrrhus of Epirus, who was hoping to conquer an empire in the west as his relative and role-model

FIG. 13. 'Unrolled' engraving on cylindrical Praenestine(?) *cista*, late fourth century BC (Battaglia and Emiliozzi 1979.41-3: Baltimore, Walters Art Museum 54.136). Drawing by John Spurbeck, reproduced by permission of the Museum.

FIG. 14. 'Unrolled' engraving on cylindrical Praenestine(?) *cista*, late fourth century BC (Battaglia and Emiliozzi 1990.273-7: Rome, Villa Giulia). Drawing by M. Tibuzzi, reproduced by permission of the Istituto di Studi sul Mediterraneo Antico (CNR, Rome).

3.2. Republican Rome

39

Alexander the Great had done in the east; and with the Carthaginians for the control of Sicily and the western seas, in a twenty-four-year struggle which a well-informed Greek historian a century later described as 'the longest-lasting, most continuous, and most extensive war I have ever heard of'.

'Latin colonies' were being established all over Italy, with conquered lands parcelled out in equal lots for Roman and loyal allied settlers. The first 'Roman roads' were being built, newly engineered with cuttings, embankments, and bridges. The first aqueducts also date to this period, supplying the needs of an expanding city population. The first coined money was now being minted, to pay for these public projects and for the soldiers and ships that fought the great wars. Rome was becoming powerful.

Her citizen body was no longer defined by the city itself; the absorption of most of the Latin communities in 338 BC and of the highland Sabines (who had their own language) in 290 made it necessary to develop a concept of citizenship that was more than just *Romani*, 'the men of Rome', or even *Latini*, 'the men of Latium'. This extraordinary period of achievement and expansion may have been when the term *Quirites* was coined, embracing all citizens in a common identity without reminding the new ones that Rome had conquered their ancestral homes.

It was a warlike title, derived from the Sabine word *curis* (or *quris*), meaning a spear; and it was war, the common dangers and the common profits of war, that held the *Quirites* together. The Romans' foundation legend of Romulus, son of Mars, was developed to incorporate first a war with the Sabines that resulted in a merging of the two peoples, and then a posthumous appearance by the deified founder instructing his citizens to practise the arts of war and worship him under the name Quirinus. The temple of Quirinus, on the Quirinal hill where the epiphany had taken place, was dedicated in 293 BC.

Many other new temples were built in Rome in the years of strife that followed. War provided both the motivation, to win the favour of the gods, and the means, by using the spoils of victory. Even with our very limited information, more than twenty new temple foundations are known from the period 295–240 BC—and at every dedication there would be a public holiday to give thanks to the deity for what he or she had done for the community of the *Quirites*. Similarly, no fewer than fifty-six triumphs are known to have been celebrated at Rome during the same period; and at each triumph there would be a public holiday, as the successful commander processed through the city to pay his vows to Jupiter Optimus Maximus on the Capitol.

That brings us back to the Roman audience. We have now reached the stage where the later Roman historiographical tradition had reliable information, at least on major events like wars fought, colonies founded, roads built. But we still have no contemporary evidence that would give us a sense of what it felt like to be in Rome in the mid-third century BC.

3.2. Republican Rome

For what it's worth, here is a story told by Aulus Gellius in the second half of the second century AD. He had it from Ateius Capito, a legal expert of the Augustan period, who dated the event to 246 BC:

> The daughter of the famous Appius Claudius [consul 307 and 296 BC] was coming away from the games she had been watching when she was jostled by the crowd as the People surged together from all sides. She got out of the situation, but complained of being badly treated. 'What would have happened to me,' she said, 'how much worse would I have been buffeted and knocked about, if my brother Publius Claudius hadn't lost a fleet of ships and a huge number of citizens in a sea-battle? I'd surely have been crushed to death if the People had been any more numerous. If only my brother would come back to life and lead another fleet to Sicily, and destroy that crowd that has just ganged up to attack a poor woman like me!'

Aulus Gellius 10.6.2

The plebeian aediles put her on trial and fined her 25,000 pounds of bronze, thus creating the legal precedent that interested Capito. What *we* would like to know is what she and the boisterous Roman People had been watching at the games.

Bearing in mind the common culture revealed by the fourth-century BC Greek, Etruscan, and Latin visual evidence, and on the assumption that it was still alive two or three generations later, let us make one final appeal to contemporary Greek literature as a way through to what may have been happening in Rome. This time the analogy is with a Greek literary genre of which practically nothing survives. It was called 'Italian comedy', and its most famous exponent, a Sicilian called Rhinthon, worked in Tarentum in the early third century BC.

Rhinthon's plays did not fit into the traditional Athenian categories. They were called *phlyakes*, 'fooleries', and later authors defined them as 'cheerful tragedy', or 'transforming tragedy into the laughable'. This is what it said on his tombstone:

> Laugh aloud as you go by, and give me a friendly word. I am Rhinthon of Syracuse—only a minor songbird of the Muses, but from my tragic fooleries I gathered ivy that was all my own.

Nossis *Anthologia Palatina* 7.414

Ivy, of course, was sacred to Dionysus, a god whom the Tarentines of the early third century BC worshipped with enthusiasm.

Besides Rhinthon, three other writers of *phlyakes* are known: Skiras of Tarentum, Sopatros of Paphos in Cyprus, and Blaisos of Capri. The reported titles of their plays reveal a remarkably Euripidean repertoire: *Herakles* (Rhinthon), *Hippolytus* (Sopatros), *Iphigeneia at Aulis* (Rhinthon), *Iphigeneia in Tauris* (Rhinthon), *Medea* (Rhinthon), *Meleagros* (Rhinthon, Skiras), *Orestes* (Rhinthon, Sopatros), *Telephus* (Rhinthon). Was the Dionysiac 'Iphigeneia at Aulis' scenario on the Latin *cista* a *phlyax* 'foolery'? That was probably a bit earlier than Rhinthon, but it confirms the impression that Latins and Tarentines shared a common culture.

Fig. 14

Blaisos of Capri lived not far from the Latin colonists of Paestum, Cales, and the Pontiae islands; one of his plays even had a Latin title, *Saturnus*, presumably about the god who hid from Jupiter in the land of the Latins, and thus gave it its name. Much later authors, listing all the types of comedy known in Rome, included *Rhinthonica*, plays in Rhinthon's style. These little scraps of information cannot give us any sort of reliable picture of what the Roman audience enjoyed in the mid-third century BC, but it is a reasonable guess that it included performances that parodied the mythological themes of classic tragedy, and did so in a Dionysiac context of revelry and eroticism.

3.3. The Roman Games

In Latin, Dionysus was *Liber pater*, 'Father Liber', an appropriate god for the Roman People, long liberated from their kings. The temple of Ceres, Liber, and Libera was the headquarters of the plebeian aediles, the officials whose job it was to protect the People's liberty. It was they who fined the patrician lady who thought the populace might usefully be thinned out by another naval disaster.

A few years later they imposed another hefty fine, this time on wealthy landowners occupying publicly owned land. They put the money towards a new temple for *Flora mater*, 'Mother Flora', adjacent to that of Ceres, Liber, and Libera. As the goddess of fertile vegetation, Flora had much in common with Ceres (in Oscan-speaking Italy they called her *Fluusa Kerríia*), and it was a crop-failure that caused the Romans to honour her.

But the juxtaposition of the temples also marked Flora's association with Liber. The Romans may have thought of her as Liber's mother; certainly the games that accompanied the new temple's dedication were famously erotic, an indication of the goddess' interest in human as well as vegetable fertility. We cannot be sure whether Liber's games, the Roman *Dionysia*, were erotic as well, because they were later discontinued, probably in 186 BC when the Roman Bacchic cult was emasculated in a violent police action by the Senate and consuls. All we know is what we can guess from a precious one-line quotation that happens to survive from the third century BC: 'At the *Liberalia* games we speak with free tongues.'

That was written by Gnaeus Naevius, evidently a Campanian (and therefore a neighbour of Blaisos of Capri), who was well known for using his own free tongue to criticize the Roman aristocracy. It looks as if increasing prosperity and military success were putting the egalitarian ethos of the *Quirites* under increasing pressure. The Senate seems to have disapproved of Flora's games too, but in her case traditional licentiousness eventually won the day.

The festivals of Liber and Ceres (*Liberalia* and *Cerialia*) were on 17 March and 19 April; that of Flora (*Floralia*) was on 27 April. We may think of them as 'rites

3.3. The Roman Games

of spring'. In the autumn, on the Ides (13th) of September and November, two great festivals of Jupiter Optimus Maximus were also celebrated with games—the *ludi Romani* and *ludi plebeii* respectively. The former, sometimes called 'the great games' (*ludi magni* or *maximi*), were organized not by the plebeian aediles but by their patrician counterparts, the 'curule' aediles.

By great good fortune, we happen to have an eyewitness description of the *ludi Romani* from the third century BC. It comes from Quintus Fabius Pictor, a patrician senator who wrote the first-ever history of Rome, in Greek and for a Greek audience who needed to have such things explained to them. Fabius' history is lost, but this passage is quoted at length by Dionysius of Halicarnassus, writing two centuries later but also with a Greek audience in mind.

The following translation is of the Fabian material only, omitting Dionysius' running commentary on it, and I have numbered the paragraphs for reference.

> (1) Before they began the games, those who held the highest authority conducted a procession for the gods, from the Capitol [i.e. Jupiter's temple] through the Forum to the Circus Maximus.
>
> (2) The leaders of the procession were those citizens' sons who were adolescent and old enough to take part, on horseback if their fathers were of the equestrian property class, on foot if they were going to serve as infantry, drawn up respectively in cavalry and infantry units as if on their way to training. This was in order to show visitors the size and excellence of the city's rising generation of manhood.
>
> (3) They were followed by charioteers in four-horse and two-horse chariots, and riders on unyoked horses. After them came the contestants in the lightweight and heavyweight competitions, naked except for loincloths. Following the contestants were many groups (*choroi*) of dancers arranged in three categories—the men, the youths, and the boys. They were accompanied by pipers playing old-fashioned short pipes and string-players plucking seven-string ivory lyres and the instruments called *barbita*.
>
> (4) The dancers were dressed in scarlet tunics with tight bronze belts, armed with swords and comparatively short spears. The men also had bronze helmets decorated with conspicuous crests and plumes. Each *choros* was led by a single man who gave the others the steps of the dance, leading their presentation of sudden warlike movements, mostly in a staccato four-beat rhythm.
>
> (5) After the armed choruses, the procession featured *choroi* of satyr-performers, presenting the Greek dance called *sikinnis*. The costumes were as follows: for those imitating *silēnoi*, the shaggy tunics some call *chortaioi*, girded round with flowers of all kinds; for those imitating satyrs, loincloths, goatskins, headdresses with hair sticking up, and other things like that. These [choruses] mocked and mimicked the serious movements, turning them into something laughable.

The *chortaios* was evidently the hairy suit attested in the visual evidence; the flowers can hardly be irrelevant to the cult of Flora; and 'turning the serious into the laughable' is what Rhinthon and his followers did.

Figs. 7, 11, 12, and 13

> (6) After these *choroi* paraded throngs of lyre-players and numerous pipers, and after them the men who carried the vessels in which perfumes and frankincense were burned all along the route, and the men who carried the display-items made of silver and gold, both sacred and secular.
>
> (7) Last of all in the procession came the images of the gods, carried on men's shoulders; their appearance was the same as those made by Greeks, as were their dress and their symbolic attributes and the gifts which each of them is said to have invented and bestowed on mankind.
>
> (8) There were images not only of Zeus [Jupiter], Hera [Juno], Athena [Minerva], Poseidon [Neptune], and the others whom the Greeks number among 'the twelve gods', but also those of the earlier generation, from whom the legends say the twelve were born—Kronos [Saturn], Rhea, Themis, Leto [Latona], the Fates, Mnemosyne [Moneta], and all the others who have temples and precincts among the Greeks—and those who the legends say were born later, after Zeus succeeded to power—Persephone [Proserpina], Eileithyia [Lucina], the Nymphs, the Muses, the Seasons, the Graces—and the demigods whose souls are said to have left their mortal bodies and ascended to heaven, who enjoy equal honours with the gods—Herakles [Hercules], Asklepios [Aesculapius], the Dioskouroi [Castor and Pollux], Helen, Pan [Faunus], and countless others.

It is not clear whether this all-encompassing claim that the Roman pantheon was identical with the Greek goes back in its entirety to Fabius, or whether Dionysius has filled it out. But the fact that not all the divinities have separate Latin names does not in itself make it any less likely that they were worshipped in Rome in Fabius' time (neither did Apollo).

> (9) When the procession was finished, the consuls and the priests whose duty it was immediately carried out a sacrifice of oxen. Having washed their hands and purified the sacrificial animals with pure water and sprinkled the fruits of Demeter [Ceres] on their heads, they then made the prayer and gave the order to the attendants to sacrifice them. One group struck the standing victim on the temples with a club, another applied the knives to it as it fell. They then flayed it and cut it in pieces. They took first-offerings from each of the internal organs and each of the other members, scattered grains of spelt over them, and took them in baskets to those in charge of the sacrifice, who set them on the altars, lit a fire beneath them, and made a libation of wine as the purification took place.
>
> (10) It remains for me to give a brief account of the competitions they held after the procession. The first was four-horse chariot races, two-horse chariot races, and races of unyoked horses. After the horse races were over, it was the turn of those competing with their own physical strength—runners, boxers, and wrestlers. In the intervals between the competitions, they presented honorific crowns and made proclamations of the honours granted to their benefactors (as was done in Athens at the festivals of Dionysus), and they exhibited the spoils they had taken in war to those who had assembled for the spectacle.

That final phrase provides us with our earliest explicit reference to the Roman audience.

Fabius was describing the *ludi circenses*, 'games in the Circus'; the charioteers, riders, and athletes who processed in paragraph 3 were performing in paragraph 10. But there were also *ludi scaenici*, 'stage games'; and although the satyr-impersonators and musicians who processed in paragraphs 5–6 do not have their performances described, it is clear that even in the games for Jupiter, the Dionysiac element was still an important part of Roman festivity.

We don't know what form it took. Perhaps it was just informal jesting, 'like the young men who mock with double meaning at festivals', 'exchanging repartee in improvised verses, with movements appropriate to the words' (Ch. 2.4, 2.5 above). Or perhaps it included dramatic plots, comic or erotic parodies of tragedy in Rhinthon's manner, as suggested by the *cista* scene at Figure 14 (Ch. 3.1 above). By Fabius Pictor's time, however, something more serious was also on the programme.

3.4. Rome and Alexandria

On 4 October 241 BC Gaius Lutatius Catulus held his triumph for the decisive naval battle of the Carthaginian war. Now dominant in the western Mediterranean, the Romans were quick to announce their new status as an international power. They sent an embassy to King Ptolemy at Alexandria (whose predecessor had already congratulated them on their defeat of Pyrrhus), offering their support in his war against King Antiochus of Syria. Ptolemy was grateful, but declined the offer: he had already won his war while the ambassadors were on their way.

The first *ludi Romani* of the glorious peace would be on 13 September 240 BC. Naturally, they would want to present themselves impressively to visitors, and the new Alexandrian connection enabled them to make a remarkable cultural statement. To understand it, however, we must make a short digression.

King Ptolemy will certainly have taken the Roman ambassadors to see the famous library of Alexandria. The Librarian at the time was the great polymath and historian Eratosthenes of Cyrene, who seems to have been well informed about the Romans: he admired their system of government, he knew that Evander had introduced the cult of Pan at the Lupercal, and he believed that Romulus, the founder of the city, was a son of Aeneas' son Ascanius.

One of Eratosthenes' many learned works was a multi-volume investigation of Athenian 'Old Comedy'; his fellow-countryman the poet Callimachus (who also regarded the Romans favourably) had recently compiled a bio-bibliographical catalogue of 'all the tragic and comic poets in chronological order, from the beginning'. The history of literature was being created, and those who composed the scripts for stage performances were a major part of it.

By using the phrase 'tragic and comic poets', I have over-translated the title of Callimachus' work. He called them just *didaskaloi*, 'teachers'—and that usage is what will lead us to understand how the Romans of 240 BC exploited the work of the great scholars of Alexandria.

The first Greek dramatists were both scriptwriters and directors, or in their own terms, both 'makers' of the plot (*poiētai*) and 'teachers' of the chorus (*didaskaloi*), just as Stesichorus and Arion had 'set up the chorus' for their dithyrambs in the previous generation (Ch. 2.2 above). The drama competitions at the Dionysiac festivals in Athens were an important part of public life, and were therefore recorded on stone like everything else in the public life of the Athenian democracy. The lists of who won what and where were called 'teachings', *didaskaliai*, because what mattered most was the performance of the citizens who had been taught to master the intricate song and dance of the choral parts.

Although in due course amateur choral performance gave way to the employment of professionals, the terminology of teaching survived. The *didaskaliai* lists became archival evidence for people like Aristotle who were interested in the history of drama, and thus also for Callimachus when he compiled his great historical catalogue. The 'teachers' he listed were the poets who had written tragedy, comedy, and satyr-play in the Athenian tradition, from the late sixth century BC down to his own time two and a half centuries later. Alexandria, the new cultural centre of the Greek world, was where their precious scripts were now collected.

Our surviving texts of the plays of Aeschylus, Sophocles, Euripides, and Aristophanes are transmitted with an apparatus of scholarly annotation which goes back ultimately to Callimachus, and preserves much of his terminology. For instance, most of them have a note (*hypothesis* is the technical term) specifying in which year and at which festival the play was 'taught'; similarly, the biographies of dramatists in the Byzantine encyclopaedia known as *Suda*, which also exploited the Callimachean scholarly tradition, normally say 'He taught [not 'he wrote'] the following plays...'.

This traditional phraseology was an anachronism even in Callimachus' own time. By the third century BC, comic and tragic drama in the Athenian manner was performed at festivals all over the Greek world, and beyond, by international guilds of professional actors who needed no instruction from the men who made their plots. That is why it is significant that our sources for those epoch-making *ludi Romani* in 240 BC use a Latin version of Callimachus' archaizing terminology.

The phrase 'to teach a play' (*fabulam docere*) occurs only rarely in our surviving Latin texts. A few examples refer to the great dramatists of fifth-century Athens (one of them quoting Eratosthenes), but nearly all the other usages of the phrase come in the context of early Roman drama, and in particular the moment in 240 BC when 'the poet Lucius Livius was the first of all to teach plays at Rome, more than 160 years after the deaths of Sophocles and Euripides and about fifty-two years after that of Menander'.

The playwright's full name was Lucius Livius Andronicus, and he was a Greek by birth, perhaps from Tarentum. What we know about him comes (indirectly) from the researches of two learned authors of the first century BC, Varro and Atticus, writing at point C on our time-line about an event at point B. They used documentary evidence (*commentarii*), perhaps from an archive of the curule aediles, who were responsible for the *ludi Romani*, or conceivably from the actors' guilds, which are likely to have kept records of who won what in which play in which year.

Fig. 1

Wherever the information came from, it was evidently expressed in the idiom of Alexandrian literary history. The plays 'taught' by Livius and his successors were tragedy and comedy in the great tradition, but in Rome and in Latin. Their texts could now be preserved, like those of the Greek classics in Alexandria, because now papyrus was available across the open seas from Egypt. In due course these texts too would be studied by scholars, one of whom—a poet and dramatist himself—even called his study of literary history 'The Teachings', *Didascalica*, thus making explicit the continuity from ancient Athens, via the scholarship of Callimachus and Eratosthenes, to a Rome that was now giving itself a literature.

3.5. The Turning-point

As Fabius Pictor reported (Ch. 3.3 above), the procession from Jupiter's temple to the Circus Maximus at the *ludi Romani* was led by 'those who held the highest authority'—which must mean the consuls, if they were in Rome in mid-September. While the great war was being fought, the consuls were normally commanding legions and battle-fleets far away, but in 240 BC we may be sure that Gaius Claudius Cento and Marcus Sempronius Tuditanus were conspicuously in Rome to celebrate peace and victory.

The consul Gaius Claudius was the youngest brother of the man who had lost one disastrous sea-battle and of the lady who hoped for another, to thin out the crowds. His *cognomen*, Cento, meant 'patchwork', and a coin-issue by one of his distant descendants may give us an idea of how he came by it. The coins, of gold and silver, were struck in or about 41 BC, and carried on their obverse the head of the goddess Flora, whose games had been instituted 200 years before (Ch. 3.3 above). Since it was the custom to wear multicoloured clothes at the games of Flora, perhaps Gaius Claudius the consul of 240 BC had made a point of forgetting his dignity and joining in the fun. Some such popular gesture, to counter his sister's patrician arrogance, could have earned him a nickname that stuck.

That can only be guesswork; but even in this most ill-attested period (Livy's history for 292–220 BC is lost), it is clear that the introduction of Flora's games was an event of some importance. One historian dated it by years from the foundation of Rome; another used it as a chronological marker in its own right;

a young aristocrat boasted of his connection with it as many as seven generations later. The celebration of peace and victory took many forms, and for most Romans the licensed raunchiness of Flora's games, by torchlight in the warm spring evenings, probably made more impression than the masked and booted interpreters of Greek tragedy at the *ludi Romani*. For us, however, the opposite is true.

With the advantage of historical perspective, we can see in the events of 240 BC the juxtaposition of traditional Dionysiac eroticism (compare Fig. 14, Ch. 2.2 above) with the new phenomenon of written texts preserved on Egyptian papyrus. For the ordinary Romans in the piazza, the texts made no difference: they were just seeing performances in different styles at different times, and it didn't matter to them that some of what they saw was scripted. But it mattered for posterity, because now the words need not be lost.

Livius and his near-contemporary Gnaeus Naevius did not restrict themselves to plays. They also wrote narrative poetry—a Latin version of the *Odyssey* (Livius) and a heroic epic on the Roman past, from Aeneas and Romulus down to the great war with Carthage (Naevius). For the latter, at least, we know how the poet's work was turned into literature.

The evidence comes from a learned author of the time of the emperor Hadrian. Suetonius put the origin of Roman literary scholarship in the first half of the second century BC. At that time, he says,

> they took the trouble to reconsider poems that had not yet been properly made public, those of deceased friends or any others they approved of, and by reading them and commenting on them make them known to everyone else. That is what Gaius Octavius Lampadio did in the case of Naevius' *Punic War*: it was set out in a single roll as a continuous text, and he divided it into seven books.

Suetonius *De grammaticis* 2.2

The implication is that each poet had just a master text, through which his work could only live on after his death if there were well-wishers to give it publicity. In Naevius' case, the single long script was presumably his own prompt-copy; in performance, he could pick out which episodes to 'sing', but now it had to be divided up into separate volumes of a size convenient for consultation—just as the librarians of Alexandria had divided up the *Iliad* and *Odyssey* into twenty-four books each.

A similar inference can be made about a late work of Livius Andronicus. Livy reports on how the Romans reacted to alarming portents in 207 BC:

> The pontiffs also decreed that three bands of maidens, each consisting of nine, should go through the city singing a hymn. This hymn was composed by the poet Livius, and while they were practising it in the temple of Jupiter Stator, the shrine of Queen Juno on the Aventine was struck by lightning.... Then twenty-seven maidens, vested in long robes, walked in procession singing a hymn in honour of Queen Juno, which was perhaps admired in those rude days but would be considered very uncouth and unpleasing if it were recited now.

Livy 27.37.7 and 13 (trans. W. M. Roberts, Everyman Library, 1912, slightly adapted)

3.5. The Turning-point

The word for 'composed' (*conditum*) means literally 'stored away', and we must assume that that is what the pontiffs did with the text of Livius' hymn, either in the temple of Juno or in an archive of their own. Two centuries later Livy the historian could pass his damning judgement on it because the text was still there to be read.

From 218 to 202 BC, Rome was engaged in a second, and no less desperate, war with Carthage. One wonders whether the lady Claudia lived long enough to see her wish come true, as Hannibal's forces, in two successive battles in 217 and 216, reduced the Roman citizen body by about 40,000 men. One indirect result of Hannibal's presence in Italy was the introduction of two new sets of games, in honour of deities who the Romans hoped would help them to drive him out. These were the games of Apollo (*ludi Apollinares*) and the games of the Great Mother (*ludi Megalenses*).

The annual programme of publicly funded games—*ludi circenses* in the Circus, *ludi scaenici* on stages in the Forum and elsewhere—eventually settled at something like this:

ludi Megalenses (curule aediles in charge), 4–10 April;
ludi Ceriales (plebeian aediles in charge), 12–19 April;
ludi Florales (plebeian aediles), 27 April–3 May;
ludi Apollinares (urban praetor in charge), 6–13 July;
ludi Romani (curule aediles), 5–19 September;
ludi plebeii (plebeian aediles), 4–17 November.

Of course the old festival dates (Ch. 2.6 above) were still observed as well, but what made this new sequence different was the expenditure on professional actors and all the equipment they required.

At the *ludi plebeii* of 200 BC, just a year after Publius Scipio 'Africanus' had celebrated his triumph for the final defeat of Hannibal, the audience gathered to watch a Roman adaptation of Menander's comedy *The Brothers*. The scriptwriter was Titus Maccius Plautus; the lead actor was Titus Publilius Pellio; the musician was Marcipor, slave of Oppius, playing Tyrian pipes throughout; and the plebeian aediles who hired the troupe and produced the games were Gnaeus Baebius and Gaius Terentius.

How do we know these details? Because they were recorded at the time, and the records were there to be consulted when Plautus' play-texts were being collected, copied, and annotated as classics of Latin comedy, just as those of Greek drama had been collected, copied, and annotated at the Library of Alexandria. And it is not just the play's performance details that survive; we have the text as well, and twenty others written by Plautus, and seven written by Publius Terentius Afer ('Terence') a generation later.

At this point, the nature of our historical enquiry changes fundamentally. Now, for the first time, we have direct contemporary written evidence. From now on, we shall be able to listen to what Romans themselves had to say at the time.

4

An Enclosure with Benches

Figs. 6, 10, 14

Fig. 1

We have the texts of Plautus and Terence; what we don't have is a clear picture of the physical context of their performance. The newly ambitious 'stage-games' (*ludi scaenici*) of the late third and second centuries BC must have required something more elaborate than the simple stages we have imagined for earlier periods. Now that the Romans had taken over the Greek notion of 'literature', and were adapting Greek tragedy and Greek comedy for their own dramatic festivals, one might have expected them to take over the corresponding Greek architectural form—a purpose-built, horseshoe-shaped stone theatre. But that didn't happen until much later (point C on the time-line).

4.1. *Theatrum* and *Scaena*

The careers of Plautus and Terence roughly correspond to the fifty-three years, described by a contemporary Greek historian as unparalleled in human history, in which Rome brought under her rule 'almost the whole inhabited world'. Terence's last play was performed at the funeral games for Lucius Aemilius Paullus, the Roman commander who had conquered Greece and Macedon and led in his triumphal procession the last successor of Alexander the Great.

Perhaps because of the wars in Greece and Asia Minor, the first part of the second century BC provides our earliest evidence for influential Romans who were actively hostile to Greek culture, as if it were a threat to traditional Roman values. Their attitude evidently affected public policy, resulting from time to time in book-burnings and expulsions of Greek intellectuals from the city.

The earliest and most extraordinary example of their influence came in 186 BC with a fierce crackdown on the 'Bacchanalia', practices supposedly introduced by a 'lower-class Greek' and denounced by Spurius Postumius, one of the consuls of the year, as a dangerous foreign cult. As it happens, thanks to archaeology we know more than Postumius knew: far from being an alien innovation, Dionysiac worship had been part of Rome's experience for well over 300 years (Chs. 2.3, 3.3 above). But in 186 BC the Senate felt the need to control it, and controlled it was. This was probably the moment when the stage-games of Liber were amalgamated with those of Ceres, and the god of liberty was given a newly subordinate place in the Roman republic.

What matters for our argument at this point is that building a permanent theatre, as in a Greek city, was evidently regarded as unacceptable. The attempt was made, first in 154 BC and then again in 107 BC, but in each case conservative opinion prevailed and the building was demolished as an incitement to 'Greek luxury'. However, two archival items in Livy's history suggest a more complicated picture.

Among the public works for which Marcus Lepidus contracted as censor in 179 BC were a *theatrum* and a *proscaenium* at the temple of Apollo, evidently for the *ludi Apollinares*. Five years later, the censors' contracts were for roads, bridges, and various items in the Circus Maximus including 'a *scaena* for the aediles and praetors'. But what exactly did these terms describe?

All three are Latinized Greek nouns. *Theatrum*, Greek *theatron*, means literally just 'a place for watching'; in Rome in 179 BC it may not yet have specified a particular structural form. *Scaena* represents the Greek *skēnē*, of which the primary meaning is a booth or hut. In a theatrical context, strictly speaking it denotes the building behind the stage; hence the later phrase *scaenae frons*, 'front of the *scaena*', for the elaborate architectural façade in front of which the actors in a permanent theatre performed. *Proscaenium*, Greek *proskēnion*, means the stage itself, the platform in front of the *scaena*. But *scaena* and *skēnē* were also used for the stage, no doubt because the building and the platform were thought of as a single unit. In Latin as in Greek, an actor on stage could be described either as *in scaena* or as *in proscaenio*.

However, the praetors and aediles, for whom a *scaena* was provided in 174, were not actors. On the contrary, they were the magistrates responsible for organizing the games (Ch. 3.3 above). Their *scaena* in the Circus Maximus was evidently some kind of pavilion appropriate to their dignity, no doubt on a raised platform or tribunal.

4.2. Plautus and the *Cauea*

It is time to see what the texts of Plautus and Terence can tell us. First, a negative item: in all the twenty-seven surviving play scripts, the word *theatrum* occurs only once. When Ballio, the pimp in Plautus' *Pseudolus*, is asked what somebody has called him, he replies:

> Oh, theatre rubbish, what normally gets said to a pimp in comedies, the stuff boys know. Told me I was wicked, a villain, a perjurer.

Plautus *Pseudolus* 1081–3

Since this may come from Plautus' Greek original (Aristophanes has a similar crack about boys in the audience), it offers no reason to suppose that the idea of a 'theatre' was current in Plautus' own time.

The term Plautus uses is *cauea*, which means literally a cage or coop. Here, for instance, is the actor playing Mercury in *Amphitruo*, urging the audience not to tolerate actors' fans trying to influence the prize-judges:

> Now, I have orders from Jupiter to make this request of you: that inspectors go through the whole *cauea* to each of the spectators' benches, and if they see supporters assigned to any individual, that their togas be taken as security while they're in the *cauea*.

Plautus *Amphitruo* 64–8

The metaphor clearly implies an enclosure of some kind, as confirmed by the slave Palaestrio in the delayed prologue of *Miles Gloriosus*:

> I'm obliging enough to tell you the plot of this play, if you'll be kind enough to listen. Anyone who doesn't want to listen can get up and go outside [*foras*], so there's space to sit for someone who does.

Plautus *Miles Gloriosus* 79–82

Inside the enclosure are the benches (*subsellia*) on which the spectators sit. The fact that they are sitting is often referred to—'Get up and stretch your legs', but only before or after the play—and comments are even made on it during the action. 'Not too loud, do you want to wake the spectators?' 'Make it quick, the sitters are getting thirsty.'

There may have been standing spectators as well, but the evidence suggests they were not welcome. At the start of *Captiui*, the eponymous prisoners of war are already on stage as the actor-manager delivers his prologue:

> See these two prisoners standing here? They're both standing, not sitting, because those people there are standing. It's true what I say, and you're my witnesses for it. [He explains the plot situation.] Got that now? Excellent. Oh God, that chap right at the back says no. Come forward, please. If there's no room for you to sit, there's room for you to walk, since you force an actor to shout like a beggar. Don't kid yourself, I'm not going to rupture my lungs for you.

Plautus *Captiui* 1–3, 10–14

Presumably he wants his victim to 'walk' out of the *cauea*. He then goes on to flatter those who do have seats as 'you who have property to declare at the census', and the same assumption of privilege may be implied in *Aulularia*, where old Euclio comes on bewailing his lost money and pleading for help to find the thief:

> You sir, what do you say? I know I can trust you, I can see from your face you're a good man. What's the matter, what are you lot laughing at? I know all of you,

> I know there are plenty of thieves here, hiding in clothes and chalk and sitting as if they were honest men. What, none of them has it? You've destroyed me!
>
> Plautus *Aulularia* 717–20

'Clothes and chalk' means laundered white togas, as worn by posh people.

The most elaborate of all the Plautine prologues is that of *Poenulus*, where the actor-manager kicks off in tragic style:

> I am minded to rehearse Aristarchus' *Achilles*; that is the tragedy from which I shall commence. Be silent, hold your peace, and pay attention. The commander—of the actors—bids you listen, that they may sit on benches in good heart, both those unbreakfasted and those well fed. You who've eaten first have been much more sensible; you who haven't, make yourself full on plays! For someone who's had a meal prepared for him, coming in to sit here unfed on our account is the height of foolishness!
>
> Plautus *Poenulus* 1–10

There are the benches again, and 'coming *in*' (*incedere*) implies an enclosure. Pseudo-Achilles continues:

> Herald, arise, and make the People listen. Long have I been waiting to see if you know your duty. Employ the voice through which you live and dwell. If you speak not, hunger will take you silent and unaware. All right, now sit down again and you'll get double pay!
>
> *Poenulus* 11–15

The joke on heralds demanding payment comes in the *Asinaria* prologue too. The fact that a herald was used at all—and later sources refer to a trumpeter as well—is a reminder that these were public games, for the whole of the Roman People. Appropriately, the speaker now impersonates a magistrate addressing the citizens, and begins by quoting the praetor's traditional edict formula:

> Good is done, that you observe my edicts! Let no worn-out tart sit on the *proscaenium*. Let no lictor, or his rods, mutter a word. Let no seat-assignment agent [*dissignator*] walk around in front of people's faces or lead anyone to a seat while an actor's on the *scaena*. Those who've been lazy and slept long at home, it's right that now they should be content to stand—or else cut down on sleeping.
>
> *Poenulus* 16–22

The usual job of lictors was to act as escorts and bodyguards for the senior magistrates, but there were also 'People's lictors' (*lictores populares*) who were responsible for keeping order at the games. Their presence, and their title, reminds us again that the potential audience was the entire Roman People. But the seating space was limited. The *dissignator* decided who could sit where, and if you came late you shouldn't expect to be shown to your seat.

> Let slaves not occupy seats, but leave room for free men—or else give cash to buy their freedom. If they can't do that, let them go home and avoid a double disaster, being striped with rods here and with whips at home if they haven't done their work when their masters get back.

Poenulus 23–7

If the seating was privileged, how could there ever be any question of slaves sitting there? Perhaps they were saving seats until their late-rising masters arrived.

> Let nurses look after their tiny infants at home. Let no one bring them here to watch the show, lest the nurses dry up and the kids starve to death, or else get hungry and wail here like little goats. Let ladies watch in silence and laugh in silence, control while they're here their bird-voiced twittering, take their gossipy conversations home and not irritate their husbands here as well as there.

Poenulus 28–35

The train of thought suggests that the nurses too are slaves, no doubt accompanying their mistresses. What is clear is that the audience includes women and children.

> Now here's something for the organizers of the games. Don't let the prize be given to any artist unfairly; don't let any be driven outside [*foras*] for the sake of favouritism so that worse ones are put above good ones. Oh, and there's this too, that I almost forgot. Manservants, while the games are on, make your attack on the cookshop! Now, while you have the chance and the pies are hot—charge!
> These are the commands from the high command—of the actors—and by God, good is done if everyone remembers them for himself.

Poenulus 36–45

Again, as we saw in *Miles Gloriosus*, 'outside' must refer to the enclosure.

In all this busy scene, there is no hint that some seats were more privileged than others. For that, we must insert into the Plautine evidence what Livy reports about the games put on by the curule aediles of 194 BC:

> It was at the *ludi Romani* of these aediles that the Senate for the first time watched separately from the People. This gave rise to comments, as innovations usually do. Some considered it a tribute which had long been owed to the highest rank. Others argued that whatever enhanced the senators' status meant a loss of dignity to the People, and that all such distinctions separating the different orders of society were designed to diminish concord and equal liberty.
> 'For 557 years [since the foundation of the city] the games have been watched by all together. What has suddenly happened to make senators not want to have plebeians among them in the *cauea*? Why should a rich man object to a poor man sitting next to him? It's a new and arrogant fancy, something no other nation's senate has ever wanted or put into practice.'
> They say that even [Scipio] Africanus himself eventually regretted that as consul he had been responsible for the change.

Livy 34.54.4–8

This infringement of the traditional equality of Roman citizens was still controversial in Cicero's time, over a century later. What matters for our purposes, however, is the use of the term *cauea*: the newly reserved senatorial seats were on the benches in the enclosure.

4.3. In the Forum, in the Circus

The annual public games were all in honour of particular deities—the Great Mother, Ceres, Flora, Apollo, Jupiter. Naturally the god or goddess had to be able to watch them, and the easiest way to ensure that was to hold them in front of the temple.

The Ceres and Flora temples evidently faced out on to the Circus Maximus, still a largely open area in the second century BC; the only permanent viewing arrangements were the 'public decks' (*fori publici*), wooden platforms about 12 feet high supporting covered booths (*skēnai*) for privileged spectators at the chariot races. Although we don't know where they were or how far they extended, there is no reason to doubt that Ceres—like Liber before her—and her neighbour Flora had ample space available in front of their temples.

The temple of Apollo was similarly well placed at the Circus Flaminius piazza, where there was room for markets to be held, magistrates to address public meetings, and returning commanders to prepare their triumphal parades; since we know that games for the dedication of temples were held in the Circus Flaminius in 179 BC, we can be sure it was also the venue for the *ludi Apollinares*. For Jupiter's games, the *ludi Romani* and *ludi plebeii*, there was the wide *area Capitolina* in front of the great temple of Jupiter Optimus Maximus on the Capitol; this too was a regular venue for magistrates holding public meetings.

The temple of the Great Mother, on the other hand, was situated at the top of the slope at the western corner of the Palatine, with only a limited terraced space in front of it. It was built on a high podium, with a long, wide flight of steps at the front which would have accommodated about 1,300 spectators to share the goddess' view of whatever was performed there. It is usually assumed nowadays that what was performed there was drama like Plautus' comedies, but that is not necessarily the case. After all, there must have been similar steps at the temple of Apollo, but the censors of 179 BC still contracted for a *theatrum* and *proscaenium* to be erected there. There would be no room to do that for the Great Mother, but the need there must have been much the same.

Fig. 15

It is important to remember that a wide variety of entertainments took place at the Roman *ludi*, and that more than one stage could be used at the same time. The relevant god or goddess could still be thought of as being present even at a venue away from the temple, represented by his or her particular symbol—the

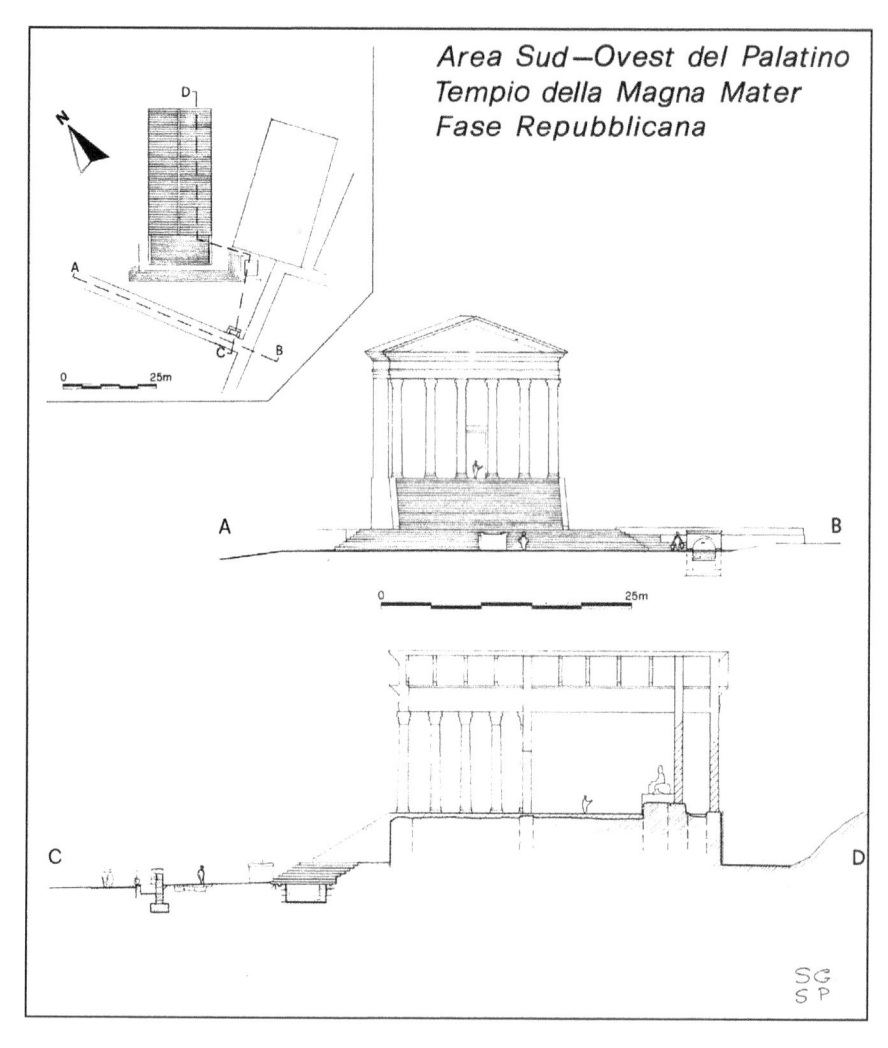

FIG. 15. Elevation and cross-section of the temple of Magna Mater, first phase (second century BC), drawing by Sheila Gibson and Simon Pratt. Reproduced by permission from Pensabene 1988.58, fig. 5.

Great Mother's turreted crown is the best attested example—placed on the seat of honour in the middle at the front. The obvious places to exploit, where there was room for a big crowd, were the Roman Forum and the Circus Maximus. The Forum was notionally under the eye of Jupiter, and the Great Mother looked out over the Circus from her temple 250 metres away and 30 metres above. As it happens, we have good contemporary evidence for both these sites being used for stage-games in the second century BC.

4.3. In the Forum, in the Circus

In Plautus' *Curculio*, while the slave, the pimp, and the banker have gone off to fetch the girl, the property-manager comes on stage worrying about the costumes he's hired out:

> I entrusted them to Phaedromus in person, but I'm going to keep a sharp lookout all the same. Anyway, until he comes out I'll just give you an easy guide to which places you can find which people in, so if you want to set up a meeting with anyone, good or no good, honest or crooked, you won't trouble yourself with too much trouble.
>
> You want to meet a perjurer? Go to the Comitium. A boastful liar? Shrine of Cloacina. For rich, spendthrift husbands, look near the Basilica—and there'll be worn-out tarts there too, and people who like to do deals, and dining-club subscribers at the Fishmarket. Respectable wealthy gents walk about in the lower Forum; in the middle by the channel, they're nothing but show-offs. Above the Pool are confident malicious talkers who boldly slander other people for no reason, though there's plenty that could truly be said about themselves. By the Old Shops, that's where they give and take at interest. Behind the temple of Castor, that's where you don't want to trust them too easily. In Tuscan Street, that's where there are people who sell themselves, in Velabrum either a baker or a butcher or a soothsayer or people who turn themselves round and offer themselves to others to be turned round.
>
> But there's a sound at the door—I must control my tongue.

Plautus *Curculio* 465–86

Though the in-jokes and topical allusions have long been lost, what is clear is that this was written for a play performed in the Forum, and in particular for an audience facing south-east, sitting below the Capitol to watch what Jupiter was imagined to be watching, from his temple above and behind.

About thirty years later, on 23 February of 166 BC, Lucius Anicius Gallus held a triumph for his victory over the Illyrians. It was followed by celebratory games in the Circus Maximus, which were witnessed—fortunately for us—by Polybius of Megalopolis, a Greek hostage newly arrived in Rome after the defeat of Macedon. They evidently made a big impression on him, since he gave a detailed description of them in his great history of the Roman conquest of Greece.

That part of Polybius' work has been lost, but this particular passage was reproduced—how accurately we cannot know—by Athenaeus of Naucratis in the second century AD:

> As Polybius records in book 30, what [Anicius] produced was totally laughable. He sent for the most famous performers from Greece, and having set up a huge *skēnē* in the Circus, he first brought on all the pipe-players together. They were Theodorus of Boeotia, Theopompus, Hermippus, and Lysimachus, very distinguished musicians. So he stationed them on the *proskēnion* and told them all to play their pipes at the same time to accompany the *choros*.

As they were going through their pieces, along with the appropriate movement [by the *choros*-dancers?], he sent them a message saying they weren't playing well, and told them to be more competitive. They didn't know what to do, but one of the lictors indicated that they should turn and advance on each other, as if in battle. The pipe-players quickly understood and took a suitable initiative, creating great confusion with their own outrageous behaviour.

Wheeling the *choroi* in the centre round to face those on the wings, the pipe-players blew unintelligible and discordant notes and led them against each other in turn; at the same time the *choroi*, stamping their feet and shaking their costumes in unison [?], advanced on their opponents and then reversed their position and retreated again. And when one of the *choros*-dancers girt himself up, spun round at just the right moment, and raised his fists as if to punch the advancing pipe-player, at that point there was a sudden roar of applause from the audience.

While these performers were still competing in battle-lines, two dancers came into the *orchēstra* with accompanying musicians, and four boxers got up on the *skēnē* with trumpeters and horn-players, and what happened as all these people were competing together was indescribable.

As for the tragedy-actors, says Polybius, what I could say about them would just make people think I'm joking.

Polybius 30.22.1–12 = Athenaeus 14.615a–e

Leaving aside the Greek authors' patronizing amusement, this passage has some interesting things to tell us.

It may be that Anicius held his games in the Circus in order to exploit the temporary stands that had been put up there three months before, to enable people to watch Aemilius Paullus' triumphal procession. But the huge *skēnē* he erected—evidently big enough to accommodate dancing *choroi* engaged in quasi-military manoeuvres—would have had to be dismantled before the first chariot races of the season, at the *ludi Megalenses* in April.

The most interesting feature of Anicius' games is the prominence of group dancers. I have left *choros* (plural *choroi*) untranslated, in order to bring out a remarkable long-term continuity, going back through the *choroi* of Fabius Pictor's description of the *ludi Romani* procession, still Dionysiac in those days (Ch. 3.3 above), to the *choroi* taught by the Athenian *didaskaloi* (Ch. 3.4), and those 'set up' by Stesichorus and his sixth-century competitors (Ch. 2.2), and even those who performed at Alcinous' Phaeacian games in the *Odyssey* (Ch. 2.1). Indeed, Anicius did exactly what Alcinous had done, following the group *choroi* with two individual virtuoso dancers.

They and their accompanists were not on stage but 'in the *orchēstra*'. That was obvious for a Greek author, since the word meant 'dancing-place'—but when the Romans eventually came to build permanent theatres, the *orchestra* was reserved for the senators' seats. It seems that did not yet apply in 166 BC, if there was still space for performers at ground level in front of the stage. Perhaps we should remember Caere in the fifth century BC, with a performance area in front of the temple of Demeter, Dionysus, and Persephone (Ch. 2.3 above); the exact equivalent at Rome, in front of the temple of Ceres, Liber, and Libera, would have been just here, in the Circus Maximus.

4.4. Terence and the *Cauea*

What seems to have surprised Polybius most about Anicius' games was the rapid sequence of different types of entertainment—pipe-players with *choros* groups, individual dancers with their own accompanists, boxers, brass players, actors of tragedies. The last category, about which he is disappointingly reticent, brings us back to the performance of formal drama with written texts.

The comedies of Terence belong to the years 166–160 BC, twenty years or so after the death of Plautus. His politer style avoided audience participation, and though all the plays have prologues, they are concerned with professional rivalries and self-defence, offering—with one exception—little insight into the physical conditions of their performance.

The exception is *Hecyra*, 'The Mother-in-Law', which according to the production-notice that accompanies the text was staged three times: first at the *ludi Megalenses* of 165 BC, then at the games for the funeral of Aemilius Paullus in 160, and a third time, evidently in the same year, at either the *Megalenses* or the *ludi Romani*. The two prologues in the transmitted text were clearly written for the second and third productions respectively, and this is how the actor-manager introduced it on the occasion of the funeral games:

> The name of this play is *Hecyra*. When *Hecyra* was given as a new play it suffered a strange disaster, with the result that it couldn't be seen or appreciated—so stupidly had the People in their enthusiasm devoted their attention to a tightrope-walker! Here it is, clearly as good as a new play now.
>
> Terence *Hecyra* 1–5

That looks like a dangerous gambit, criticizing the Roman People—and sure enough, the production-notice reveals that the play was not well received (*non est placita*).

At the third production the prologue-speaker was much more conciliatory. Lucius Ambivius was a veteran who was able to play on his old age and distinguished record. Only when he had made his pitch did he talk about the play's chequered past:

> For my sake, listen sympathetically to what I ask. I bring you *Hecyra*, which I have never been allowed to act in silence, because disaster has overwhelmed it. That disaster your good sense will mollify, if it will act as an ally to our hard work.
>
> When I started its first production, the boasting of boxers, the gathering of fans, the din, the screaming of women, caused me to make an untimely exit. For a new play, I begin by using my old method, just to keep trying: I produce [*Hecyra*] again. The first bit goes well, but then, when the cry comes that there are going to be sword-fighters, the People come rushing together, they make an uproar, they shout, they fight for places. Meanwhile, I couldn't keep my own place safe.
>
> But now there's no crowd, there's leisure and silence. I have been given time to produce the play, and you are given the power to make the stage-games honourable.

Hecyra 28–45

It worked. This time the play was a success (*placuit*).

As at Anicius' victory games, we see a swift succession of different types of entertainment. It's not clear where the tightrope-walker was performing when he distracted the audience at *Hecyra*'s first production, but the boxers on that occasion and the sword-fighters at the second one were evidently booked to perform on the same stage as Ambivius' troupe. That is the point of his last appeal to the audience: high-class Greek comedy in Latin honours the *scaena*, boxers and sword-fighters do the opposite.

The *scaena* was not just a platform (which was all the boxers and fighters needed); it was the stage plus the stage-building, purpose-built for Greek drama. Here are the prologue-speakers in Plautus' *Truculentus* and *Menaechmi*:

> Let's get on with what you've come here for. This *proscaenium*, just as you see it here, I shall change to Athens for as long as it takes us to play this comedy. Here lives a woman whose name is Phronesium...

Plautus *Truculentus* 9–12

> This city is Epidamnus while this play's being performed. When another play's performed it'll be another town. It's just like the way families move house too—one moment a pimp lives here, then a young gent, then an old one, a poor man, a beggar, a king, a parasite, a soothsayer...

Plautus *Menaechmi* 72–6

The beggar and the king are proof, if it were needed, that the same three-door building was used for tragedy too. We can well imagine that actors felt it as an affront when 'their' stage was used for mere displays of fighting.

But what does Ambivius mean when he says that the boxers and their fans caused his untimely exit? The literal meaning of the Latin is 'caused me to go outside before the time' (*fecere ut ante tempus exirem foras*). Obviously he went off the stage, but 'outside'—a term we have already met twice in Plautus—must mean something more.

We are back with the idea of a 'cage' (*cauea*), the enclosure for those who watch the play on benches and those who act it on the stage, imitating the permanent theatres of the Greek world but without their architectural form. Only by building a permanent theatre in Rome, a wish frustrated by conservative opinion in 154 and 107 BC, could the enclosure have been made secure. As it was, a handful of lictors and ushers were clearly unable to police it when enthusiastic crowds of fans wanted to get seats in advance for more downmarket entertainment while the play was still on.

4.5. Curtains and Steps

The development of the second-century BC 'theatre' included two important later innovations, for which we do not have contemporary evidence.

The first is said to date from 132 BC. Attalus, the king of Pergamum, had died, leaving his kingdom to the Roman People, and now the royal property was being auctioned off. His cloth-of-gold tapestries, which came to be known as 'Attalic', were particularly sought after, and among the buyers were the actors' companies. They called them 'court furniture' (*aulaea*), and used them as screens while the stage was being prepared. In the Roman theatre the curtain was lowered to start the play, and raised again at the end of it.

We also hear of an ordinary screen curtain called *siparium*, and since it seems that *siparia* and *aulaea* were used together, we may guess that the sumptuous *aulaeum* was for the benefit of the audience in the *cauea* facing the stage—to make them feel like guests of a king—while the plain *siparia* masked the sides of the stage from everybody else.

The second innovation is less easy to date and less easy to define. The evidence is late, and needs to be looked at carefully.

When Tacitus (early second century AD) had to narrate the institution of Nero's quinquennial games in AD 60, he imagined some objections by old-fashioned moralists:

> There were those who said that even Gnaeus Pompeius had been criticized by older men because he had established a permanent theatre site [in 55 BC]; before that, they said, the games were regularly produced with improvised *gradus* and a *scaena* constructed for the occasion.

Tacitus *Annals* 14.20.1

Literally, *gradus* means 'steps'. Three centuries later still, a Virgilian commentator explained a passage in the *Georgics* about stage-games:

> In our ancestors' time, 'theatres' were just *gradus*; the *scaena* was built of wood for each occasion, whence even today the custom has survived of scaffolds being constructed by those responsible for producing theatre games.

Servius on Virgil *Georgics* 3.24

Servius cites 'Varro and Suetonius' for this information, which probably means that his source was Suetonius (early second century AD), and that Suetonius quoted Varro (first century BC). Varro was probably well informed, but whether 'even today' refers to his time or Suetonius' or Servius', it is impossible to tell.

'Steps' (*gradus*) are not mentioned in Plautus or Terence, but they are regularly referred to in later authors as meaning the ascending rows of seats in a permanent theatre. We must assume that at some point in the second century BC it became customary to erect raised tiers of wooden seats—bleachers, in American English—which, like the *scaena* itself, would then be taken down after the *ludi* were over. The *cauea* was still an enclosure with benches, but it was becoming more defined and more secure. For each set of public games, ad hoc wooden theatres were now constructed and then dismantled again, regardless of expense.

5

Makers, Singers, Speakers, Writers

The word 'poet' (Greek *poiētēs*, Latin *poeta*) means literally 'maker'—and as Aristotle insists in the *Poetics*, the meaning was not so much 'maker of verses' as 'maker of plots' (*muthoi*, stories), whether in verse or prose.

That sense of the word is well illustrated by Plautus' Pseudolus, no mean plotter himself, when he has to find big money fast. So far he hasn't the least idea how he's going to do it,

> but just like a *poeta*, when he's taken up his tablets, searches for what's nowhere on earth and finds it, and makes what's a lie look like truth—now I'm going to be a *poeta*! Those twenty *minae*, that are now nowhere on earth, I'll find them all the same.

Plautus *Pseudolus* 401–5

The ancient world did not have a word for fiction: a lie (*mendacium*) was how Latin-speakers thought of a made-up story.

The maker of a play-text wrote words for others to deliver, and stayed out of sight himself. 'I bring you Plautus,' said the actor-manager from the stage, 'but not in person.' But there was also a quite different type of poet, one who not only delivered his own lines but did so in character, as an inspired interpreter of divine knowledge.

5.1. Ennius and the *Vates*

Narrative poets in the epic tradition were thought of not as creative artists but as transmitters of knowledge by inspiration. Right from the beginning ('Sing, goddess, the wrath...'), the narrative poet had relied on the Muse—or the Muses—to provide his material. They were the daughters of Memory (*Mnēmosynē*), and without them not even the most skilled singer could carry in his own head all the deeds of gods and men from the beginning of time. For that sort of poet the proper Latin term was *uates*, which also meant 'prophet'.

Here too we have an idea dating back to Homeric times: Apollo's gift to Calchas the prophet in the *Iliad* was the same as the Muses' gift to Hesiod the poet, knowledge of 'what is, what will be, and what was', a divinely inspired range of mastery that covered the present and future as well as the heroic past. The verb for what poet and prophet did was *canere*, to sing or chant, and the noun for what they produced was *carmen*, a song or incantation, and thus by extension a poem or prophecy.

It is one of the most regrettable gaps in our understanding of the ancient world that we have no first-hand description of a *uates* in action. The *uates* as prophet was a familiar figure at Rome, a consultant seer whose revelations might be taken seriously even by the Senate and magistrates; thanks to Cicero's dialogue on divination we know that he was characterized by *furor*, meaning perhaps 'frenzy' or 'delirium'. Did the same apply to the *uates* as poet?

In the absence of Roman evidence we must look back to Athens. Here is Plato's Socrates, in conversation with the Homeric rhapsode Ion:

> S.: When you give a good recitation and specially thrill your audience, either with the lay of Odysseus leaping forth on the threshold, revealing himself to the suitors and pouring out the arrows before his feet, or of Achilles dashing at Hector, or some part of the sad story of Andromache or of Hecuba, or of Priam, are you then in your senses, or are you carried out of yourself, and does your soul in an ecstasy suppose herself to be among the scenes you are describing, whether they be in Ithaca, or in Troy, or as the poems may chance to place them?
>
> I.: How vivid to me, Socrates, is this part of your proof! For I will tell you without reserve: when I relate a tale of woe, my eyes are filled with tears; and when it is of fear or awe, my hair stands on end with terror, and my heart leaps....
>
> S.: And are you aware that you rhapsodes produce these same effects on most of your spectators also?
>
> I.: Yes, very fully aware: for I look down upon them from the platform and see them at such moments crying and turning awestruck eyes upon me and yielding to the amazement of my tale.

Plato *Ion* 535b2–c8, d8–e3 (trans. W. R. M. Lamb, Loeb edn.)

We are so used to highly sophisticated narrative media that we may find it difficult to take such descriptions literally. So let me add another, from just a century ago. It is the performance of an itinerant storyteller in Sicily, as observed by a young Irish fiddler in 1919:

> The lanky Michele then started to tell his story, a traditional one, ... but it was not the story-telling to which I was accustomed. Rather was it a species of monodrama in which Michele spoke and made all the gestures of a whole company of actors. He told the complicated story of the Paladins' enterprises, their battles against the Saracens, and as he became launched into the throes of the drama he intoned his voice like a priest. He moved his body up and down. He stepped forward and backwards as if he was dancing in honour of some ritual. He stamped upon the

ground and at times raised his voice into a hoarse shriek. When the battle scenes reached their height he overwhelmed his audience with a torrent of adjectives, describing the flashing of the swords and the resounding blows on the armour, the horses rolling on the plain, the heap of bleeding corpses and the cries of triumph of the Christians.

The behaviour of the rustic audience was at times as surprising as that of the rhapsodist. At moments they hung upon his words, at other moments they gave shouts of approval when the favourite Christian Paladin destroyed his enemy. Occasionally they would burst into harsh roars of laughter when the story-teller gave some humorous twist to the events. Occasionally, also, they would curse under their breath and roar their disapproval when a traitor escaped punishment for his misdeeds.

Starkie 1938.278–9

Add in the poet's metre, and the presumption of divine inspiration, and we may just begin to imagine the impact of a *uates*-poet on his Roman audience.

The pioneering poets of Latin literature—Livius Andronicus and Gnaeus Naevius in the third century and Quintus Ennius in the early second—were not only *poetae* but *uates* as well, makers of play-texts for actors to perform and also singers of epic narrative in their own persons.

Livius opened his Latin version of the *Odyssey* by translating Homer's 'Tell me, Muse...' into 'Tell me, Camena...'. The Camenae were goddesses whose cult centre, a grove with a spring of pure water, was just outside the Porta Capena; the Romans identified them as Muses because they derived their name from *carmen*, 'song'. Naevius, for his 'song of the Punic War' (*carmen belli Punici*), invoked 'the nine daughters of Jupiter, sisters in harmony', describing the Muses without naming them. Ennius, on the other hand, using Homer's hexameters, gave them their Greek name and placed them in their Greek context: 'You Muses, who tread great Olympus in your dance...' At some point (we don't know where), Ennius seems to have brought the Muses into his narrative, to explain to mortals that 'we Muses are those they call Camenae'.

Of course the *uates*-poet wrote his material down (see Ch. 3.5 above for Naevius' master-copy); even the *uates*-prophet kept his oracles in books. But we should probably not imagine him reading from his text. The Muses were daughters of Memory—in Latin *Moneta*, 'the prompter'—and it was from memory that the song of the *uates*-poet reached his audience.

I think it is important to try to imagine the epic poet in public performance, if only because recent scholarship, focusing on book-texts and 'elites', is so unhelpful on the subject. These days, even the best-informed authorities can affirm without hesitation that early Latin literature was 'an agent of aristocratic acculturation', and that epic in particular 'was written for and eventually written by the Roman elite whose education best equipped them to reap literature's reward'. That seems to me a seriously misleading idea.

Unlike Plautus and Terence, the early Latin epic poets survive only in fragments. Bereft of their context, these short quotations are not easy to interpret, and inevitably one brings to the interpretation what one thinks the context ought to be. An example may give an idea of the problem.

A late grammatical treatise cites the first book of Ennius' *Annales* to illustrate the point that neuter plural nominatives end in a short syllable even in Greek loan-words. The transmitted text runs as follows:

'Probus' *De ultimis syllabis* in *Grammatici Latini* 4.231 Keil

Ennius in primo nam latos populos res atque poemata nostra cluebant.

The word the grammarian needed for his example is *poemata*, and the last five words can be translated 'the matter [or subject] and my poetry became famous'. Either *res atque poemata nostra* or *poemata nostra cluebant* would offer a good hexameter ending, but the combination of them is unmetrical. More important, the accusative phrase *latos populos* ('wide peoples') has no syntactical context: it ought to be the object of a verb (but *cluebant* is intransitive) or else dependent on a preposition.

This reference in the first book to the poet's own work suggests that the citation comes from a prologue passage, but in that case the past tense of the verb is unexpected. Help is provided by a passage in Lucretius, from his own first book:

Lucretius 1.117–19

...as our own Ennius sang, who first brought down from pleasant Helicon a crown of unfading leaves which would become bright and famous throughout the peoples of Italy.

Here is the same verb (*cluere*) and the same concept, widespread fame. For Lucretius, Ennius' fame had already been won; for Ennius himself, it would have been a confident prediction in the future tense.

So how should the corrupt text be read? Let's look at three suggested versions, the first by Hugo Ilberg in his 1852 dissertation on the first book of Ennius' *Annales*:

Ennius in primo ann.: latos per populos terrasque poemata nostra | ...clara cluebunt.

Ennius in the first book of *Annales*: 'throughout wide peoples and lands my poetry will be bright and famous.'

Ilberg emends *nam* to *ann.* (for *annali*), *res atque* to *terrasque*, and *cluebant* to *cluebunt* (future), adding *clara* from the Lucretius allusion to make it a two-line quotation. Lucretius also gives him the preposition for *latos populos*: the abbreviated form of *per* (*p.*) could easily have been overlooked by a copyist.

5.1. Ennius and the Vates

Next, Emil Baehrens in his collection of the fragments of Roman poets, published in 1886:

> Ennius in primo ann.: latos | per populos os atque poemata nostra cluebunt | clara.
>
> Ennius in the first book of *Annales*: 'throughout wide peoples my voice and poetry will be bright and famous.'

Baehrens takes over most of Ilberg's contributions, but extends the quotation over three lines and offers a different emendation of *res*. Finally, there is the version of Otto Skutsch in his great text and commentary of 1985:

> Ennius in primo annali: latos per populos res atque poemata nostra | ... clara cluebunt.
>
> Ennius in the first book of *Annales*: 'throughout wide peoples the subject and my poetry will be bright and famous.'

Skutsch keeps the manuscript reading *res* ('the phrase is odd but the sense satisfactory'), and returns to Ilberg's more convincing two-line structure.

It is a fine example of what traditional classical scholarship can achieve: though we still cannot be sure of Ennius' exact wording, the sense of what he said is as secure as such things ever can be. But what does it tell us about his poetic practice?

For Skutsch, the key word is *poemata*, transliterated from the Greek (*poiēmata*) and an indicator of Ennius' intention 'to subject Roman poetry more closely to the discipline of Greek poetic form':

> As the *Camenae*, who may owe their connection with poetry to an etymology linking their name with *carmen*, are replaced by the Muses, so *carmen* is replaced by *poema* (12), *uates* by *poeta* (3), and the Saturnian line by the hexameter (206–7).

Skutsch 1985.144

Skutsch's line 12 is the passage we have just examined; line 3 refers to Homer, of whom Ennius believed himself to be the reincarnation, as a *poeta*, not a *uates*; and at lines 206–7 the poet distances himself from Naevius' version of the first Punic War, written 'in verses which once the Fauns and prophets sang'.

But the Camenae and their *carmina* were not in fact 'replaced', and we may just as easily choose to focus on the phrase 'widespread peoples' (*latos populos*). A man who thought of himself as Homer reincarnate necessarily thought of himself as a bard travelling from city to city to sing at festivals:

> Farewell to you all, and in times to come remember me whenever any one of mortal men, some stranger who has suffered much, comes here and asks you, 'Who in your opinion is the sweetest singer who travels this way, and whom do you most enjoy?' Then all of you together give this answer: 'He is a blind man, and dwells in rocky Chios. All of his songs will be the best hereafter.'

Homeric Hymn to Apollo 166–73

The plural peoples (*populi*) among whom Ennius' poetry will achieve bright fame may remind us of the plural peoples (*dēmoi*) visited by the bards in Heraclitus' time, 300 years before (Ch. 2.4 above). Trilingual in Greek, Oscan, and Latin, Ennius may well have been familiar with every *agora* and marketplace in Italy south of the Tiber.

Even without the plural, if we were to think just of the *populus Romanus*, the grammarian's citation would still be enough to refute the notion that Ennius wrote just for the 'elite'. The likely venue for his heroic story of the Roman past—from Venus and Anchises, great-grandparents of Romulus, right down to the wars of his own time—was surely the *ludi Romani* each September, where the audience included everyone, rich and poor, plebeian and patrician, educated and illiterate.

5.2. Ennius as Impersonator

A poet with Ennius' scope and experience was well equipped to instruct and entertain that varied audience in many different ways.

He could tell them fables from Aesop, or stories from Euhemerus, the Sicilian romancer who claimed to have found, on an island in the Indian Ocean, an inscription on a golden pillar recording all the deeds of Zeus when he was king of the world before he became a god:

Ennius = Euhemerus FGrH 63 F 20 (Lactantius *Institutio diuina* 1.11.35)	In those days Jupiter used to spend most of his life on Mount Olympus, and people used to come before his judgement seat to decide disputed matters. And if anyone had discovered some innovation which would be useful to the life of mankind, they used to come and show it to Jupiter.

Or he could impersonate another Sicilian, old Epicharmus the playwright-philosopher (Ch. 2.3 above), who dreamed that he had died and learned how the universe is ordained. 'The gods are wind, water, land, sun, fire, stars':

Ennius fr. 39 Courtney = Epicharmus PCG F 287 (Varro *De lingua Latina* 5.65)	*That* is the Jupiter I speak of, whom the Greeks call Air—who is wind and clouds and then rain, and from rain cold, and after that wind and air again. This is the reason why those things I tell you of are Jupiter, because he helps all mortals, fields, cities, and animals.

The verb to help is *iuuare*, whence 'Jove'; Ennius' elaboration of his Greek original was a reassuring message of divine providence.

5.2. Ennius as Impersonator

Two other Ennian avatars, at opposite ends of the scale of respectability, were the unknown author of a Greek *Protrepticus* (moral precepts), from which his good advice on keeping your fields well weeded happens to survive, and at the other extreme the poet Sotades, from Maronea on the north coast of the Aegean, who specialized in 'low-life literature' (*kinaidologia*). Sotades was notorious for vulgar personal comments, and came to a bad end when one of the recipients, King Ptolemy Philadelphus, took offence. No doubt the Roman audience enjoyed hearing foreign bigwigs being insulted.

A more upmarket poet Latinized by Ennius was Archestratus of Gela in Sicily, whose hexameter mock epic on luxury cuisine he called *Heduphagetica*, 'Pleasure of Eating'. The only surviving passage is about fish:

> The *sargus* is good at Brundisium; get it, if it's big.
> Be aware that little boar-fish is first-rate at Tarentum.
> At Surrentum make sure you buy *elops*, and *glaucus* at Cumae.
> Why have I missed out *scarus*, almost the brain of almighty Jove?
> In Nestor's homeland this is caught big and good.

Ennius fr. 28.4–8
(Apuleius *Apologia* 39.2)

Nestor's homeland was Pylos in south-west Greece, 300 miles across the Ionian Sea from Ennius' native Rudiae in the heel of Italy. The other fish-markets mentioned were Ennius' neighbours (Brundisium, Tarentum) or Campanian harbours well known to his Roman audience (Surrentum, Cumae).

We know these works only from scattered quotations, and since the authors who cite them vary between 'as Ennius says' and 'as Epicharmus says' or 'as Euhemerus says', it is clear that Ennius not only translated his Greek originals but impersonated them too, delivering their first-person discourse through his own mouth. More often, however, he spoke in his own voice, and after 184 BC (when he was 55) he did so as a Roman citizen to Roman citizens.

The type of poetry he used was called by the Romans *satura*. Later generations argued over what the term meant: was it to do with satyrs (Ch. 3.1, 3.3 above), or was it part of the adjective *satur*, meaning 'full, replete, well-stocked'? The former sense might have appealed to Livius Andronicus, who had evidently used the style back in the third century, but would hardly be still applicable after the ruthless censoring of Dionysiac cult in 186. The latter meaning took the term as short for *satura lanx*, 'well-filled dish', which well describes the miscellaneous fare that *satura* poetry offered.

The few surviving fragments include some pointed comments about extravagant banqueters, greedy parasites, and malicious slanderers, but it looks as if personal attacks were something he avoided: 'Behaving as though a dog had bitten me, that's not my style.' His style was celebration, both of himself—'Hail, poet Ennius, you who raise your glass to mortals in verses that flame from the heart'—and of the great men of his time: 'From the rising of the sun above the marshes of Maeotis, there is no one who could equal him in deeds.' This nonpareil was Scipio Africanus, conqueror of Hannibal, on whom Ennius' praise-poems were collected in a whole volume to themselves. He even impersonated the hero himself:

> If it is permitted to anyone to ascend into the regions of the heaven-dwellers, to me alone the great gate of heaven is open.

Quoted in Lactantius Institutio diuina *1.18.10*

No doubt that dates to 183 BC, the year of Scipio's death.

Six years earlier, Ennius had accompanied the consul Marcus Fulvius Nobilior on his victorious campaign in Aetolia (north-west Greece). The main action was the siege of the city of Ambracia, about which Ennius wrote a historical drama (*fabula praetexta*) for performance at Nobilior's triumph in 187. Naevius had already added that dramatic form to the tragedy and comedy inherited from Athens: his two known *praetextae* were on Romulus and on Marcus Marcellus' victory at Clastidium in 222 BC. Ennius' chronological range was equally wide, with a play on the Sabine women as well as the *Ambracia*.

It was not just with his great ongoing epic saga that Ennius taught the Romans their own history. Every part of his poetic output justified the inscription he wrote for his own honorific statue:

> Citizens, behold the shape of old Ennius' image.
> It was he who composed your fathers' mighty deeds.

Ennius fr. 45 Courtney (Cicero Tusculan Disputations *1.34)*

5.3. Cato and Polybius

The seamless continuity of the Roman past into the Roman present was expressed also in prose. The great men of Rome could speak for themselves, and expect the citizens to listen. Politics was the art of persuasion; 'sweet-speaking' oratory was praised and valued.

Here too there was a great Athenian tradition to follow: 'the Roman Demosthenes' was Marcus Cato, who had been consul in 195 BC and censor in 184. His manner as a speaker was 'both graceful and forceful, pleasant and striking, witty and severe, aphoristic and belligerent'. He made sure the texts of his speeches were preserved; a century later, Cicero was able to collect over 150 of them.

Cato spent the whole of his long career campaigning against luxury and self-indulgence, vices he attributed in particular to the Roman aristocracy. He took the view that men in public life should make rational use of their leisure time, and he used his own to write a history. Entitled *Origins*, it began with the foundation stories of Rome and the other cities and peoples of Italy, but soon turned to the Punic Wars and the events of his own lifetime. With no false modesty about his personal contribution to Roman history, he found it natural to include some of his own political speeches verbatim in the narrative.

But it was another type of oratory, speeches at funerals, that most directly connected the Roman People with their own past, and we happen to have precious contemporary evidence of its impact. In book 6 of his history, Polybius tried to explain to his fellow-Greeks how the Romans were able to survive the dreadful losses inflicted on them by Hannibal. He offered this striking scene as an indication of their moral strength:

> Whenever one of their celebrated men dies, in the course of the funeral procession his body is carried with every kind of honour into the Forum to the so-called Rostra, sometimes in an upright position so as to be conspicuous, or else, more rarely, recumbent. The whole mass of the People stand round to watch, and his son, if he has left one of adult age who can be present, or if not some other relative, then mounts the Rostra and delivers an address which recounts the virtues and the successes achieved by the dead man during his lifetime. By these means the whole populace—not only those who played some part in these exploits, but those who did not—are involved in the ceremony, so that when the facts of the dead man's career are recalled to their minds and brought before their eyes, their sympathies are so deeply engaged that the loss seems not to be confined to the mourners but to be a public one which affects the whole People.

Polybius 6.53.1–3 (trans. Ian Scott-Kilvert, Penguin Classics)

That sense of community was reflected equally in Marcus Cato's history: it reported 'the deeds of the Roman People' (*populi Romani gesta*) and regularly left out commanders' names in order to emphasize the common achievement.

But how did Cato's history reach the Roman People? Here too, for historical prose as for epic poetry, we have to go back to the beginning.

Herodotus, the father of history, presented his work as an *apodexis*, a 'display' or oral performance, and we know he delivered at least part of it on one famous occasion at the Olympic festival. Thucydides too took a festival audience for granted, though they were not his main target:

> For an audience, perhaps the unmythical nature of my material will appear rather unpleasing; but if those who wish to look at the clarity of the past ... should judge it useful, that will be enough. It is set down as a permanent possession rather than as a competitive display for immediate hearing.

Thucydides 1.22.4

Rather than the audience at a one-off oral performance, Thucydides wrote for the future readers of that permanent possession, the written text.

Polybius, a Greek in Rome in the mid-second century BC, saw himself as another Thucydides. He was certainly writing for readers, and took care to point out how much easier and more convenient it was to have just his forty volumes of 'universal history' rather than trying to read or obtain all the various authors who dealt with the different regional events. And when he insisted on the necessity of proper analysis, he did so in Thucydidean terms:

> If one takes away from history the questions why, how and for what purpose something was done, and whether it had the expected outcome, what is left of it becomes just a competitive display, not something one can learn from, and though it pleases for the moment it is of no use at all for the future.

Polybius
3.31.12–13

But even he didn't think that history was only for readers of books.

Immediately after this very passage, Polybius went on to claim that his particular type of history was 'as much superior to the partial ones as acquiring knowledge is to simply *listening*'. And he returned to the subject in his programmatic introduction to book 9:

> I am aware of the fact that my work has a certain austerity, and is suited to and approved by only one type of *audience*, because the composition is of a single type.

Polybius 9.1.2

Other historians used various different modes, thus 'attracting many to make the acquaintance of their work', including people who just liked to *listen*. He knew very well that his 'pragmatic' history of politics and war would be 'unattractive to most types of *listener*'.

So even this most reader-centred of historians also assumed an audience for history, even if the 'lovers of knowledge' who appreciated his works would be in a minority. Polybius took for granted a Hellenistic world in which historians, like poets, were welcome visitors to the cities of Greece and Asia Minor, and their public performances (*akroaseis*) were evidently major events. It is a world we know only from scattered evidence, fragmentary inscriptions recording the civic honours their efforts earned them.

There is no reason to suppose that such events were unique to Greek-speaking communities. Cato and his successors were now writing history for Romans, and what was obvious to Polybius was no doubt equally obvious to them. The Romans were perfectly familiar with Greek historiography as a literary genre—and had indeed contributed to it, with senators writing Roman history in Greek in order to bring their city into the cultural mainstream. The Greek *historia*, literally 'enquiry', was transliterated as a Latin noun, and the Greek word for a historian, *syngrapheus* ('writer'), was Latinized as *rerum scriptor* ('writer of events'), normally shortened to just *scriptor*, as if 'writer' and 'historian' were practically the same thing.

The *ludi scaenici* were the equivalent of a Greek festival, and we may imagine that the magistrates in charge of them would be glad to have inspiring patriotic narratives read to the Roman People for their instruction. The chance survival of a couple of sentences from a lost work of the late second century BC enables us to see how one historian, at least, thought his work should be used:

> Mere chronicles cannot make men more eager to defend the republic, or more reluctant to do wrong. Just to write in whose consulship a war began or ended, and who held a triumph as a result of it, and not to make clear in the book what was done during the war, what the Senate decided at that time, what laws or plebiscites were passed, or recount what policies led to these events—that's telling stories to children, not writing history.

Sempronius Asellio *FRHist* 20 F2 (Aulus Gellius 5.18.9)

Writing real history was telling stories to adults that would make them good citizens.

There is much we don't know. Some of the Roman historians were senior senators, men of dignity whom it is hard to imagine reading their works at the games; but they had educated slaves and freedmen who could do it for them. On the other hand, historians like Vennonius, Cassius Hemina, and Claudius Quadrigarius, whose names do not sound aristocratic, may have been happy to appear in person. What matters is that working people of humble station were interested in history and eager to listen to it. That is what Cicero tells us, in a throwaway remark that shows it was nothing unusual, and we have no reason to suppose it was any less true two generations before his time.

5.4. Lucilius and Varro

Compelled by the necessities of war and politics to spend much of his adult life in Rome, Polybius greatly admired his adopted country's political system. He thought it combined elements of monarchy (the consuls), aristocracy (the Senate), and democracy (the People), in a 'mixed constitution' where the powers of each of the constituent parts checked and balanced each other, preventing any one element from lording it over the other two. But quite apart from that theoretical analysis, he admired the way the Romans behaved: the citizens acted in concord for the public good; bribery was regarded as disgraceful; magistrates kept their oaths and were scrupulous with public money; individuals sacrificed their own interests, even their own lives, for the welfare of the community.

Alas, Polybius lived long enough to see that admirable republic fatally corrupted by the avarice and arrogance of the Roman aristocracy. He was probably in his seventies when the plebeian tribune Tiberius Gracchus was murdered, while presiding over an assembly of the Roman People, by a group of senators and their dependants armed with clubs. Two or three hundred other citizens were killed too, and many more later executed without trial. It was sacrilege as well as murder, but no one was ever punished for it. Indeed, the men who carried it out claimed that they were defending the republic.

It was a disastrous precedent, repeated in 121 and 100 BC, when armed force and summary execution were again used to settle political crises. Once lethal violence was accepted as a possible political option, it was only a matter of time before armies were used in civil war. That happened in 88 BC, when the patrician Lucius Sulla marched on Rome to eliminate his political opponents. He did the same thing again in 82, executing his prisoners *en masse* and then getting rid of over 4,000 Roman citizens by the simple expedient of listing their names and announcing that anyone who brought in the head of a listed person would be rewarded. The heads were set up in public, to make sure everyone understood.

Sulla's aim was to reverse the historic compromise between the interests of rich and poor, patrician and plebeian, that had been worked out with difficulty, but without bloodshed, in the fifth and fourth centuries BC. The plebeian tribunes were now stripped of their political powers. The aristocracy, 'the best men', were to be in control. The Roman People, said Sulla, were just irritants to be disposed of like lice in a tunic.

Sulla died in 78 BC. Although more civil war followed, his aristocratic friends kept their control. But their greed and abuse of power were so blatant, and popular resentment of it so fierce, that in 70 BC the traditional checks and balances were brought back: the tribunes regained their political role and the censorship was restored, to try to police the behaviour of the rich and powerful. An uneasy equilibrium was established.

Our understanding of this pivotal period—two generations, sixty-three years, from the murder of Gracchus to the restoration of tribunician authority—is made difficult by the almost total absence of contemporary literature. In particular, we have lost two great satirical voices, those of Gaius Lucilius and Marcus Varro.

Lucilius was writing in the last three decades of the second century BC (he died in 103/2). He was well placed to write satire, being both an outsider, born in the Latin colony of Suessa Aurunca, and a man of wealth and standing, quite possibly a senator. He was well-read, funny, and aggressively opinionated on every subject, from sex through politics to philosophy. He was happy to attack anyone, high or low, just like the poets of 'Old Comedy' in Periclean Athens. One of the more substantial fragments to survive gives a vivid idea of his view of Rome:

> Now indeed from dawn to dusk, on holidays and workdays, all the People and all the senators alike busy themselves in the Forum, never leaving it. All have given themselves over to one and the same study and art—to be able to swindle without getting caught, to fight by cunning, to compete by smooth talking, pretend to be a fine fellow, to lay traps as if all are enemies of all.

Lucilius 1145–51W (Lactantius *Diuinae institutiones* 5.9.20), trans. Frances Muecke

'The People and the senators alike'—but lower-class vices are an easy target. What made Lucilius famous was attacking the great.

Three names in particular were remembered—Lupus, Metellus, and Mucius. They were Lucius Lentulus Lupus, consul in 156 BC, censor in 147; Quintus Metellus Macedonicus, consul in 143, censor in 131; and Quintus Mucius Scaevola, consul in 117 and a famous jurist. The details of Lucilius' treatment of them are lost; but we happen to know that he summoned up a council of the gods to deliberate on the posthumous fate of Lentulus Lupus, in a famous scene imitated by Virgil a hundred years later in *Aeneid* book 10. Some other high-born names turn up in the surviving fragments (the bribe-taker Lucius Cotta, the thief Gaius Cassius, the perjurers Tubulus and Carbo), as does a stray couplet that seems to sum up Lucilius' general attitude:

> To the verses he's put together, such as he can, Lucilius imparts a matter of importance, the People's security, and all this with honest care and commitment.

Lucilius 791–2W (Nonius 54L, 481L)

Doing that meant exposing a corrupt aristocracy.

But it wasn't all politics. Lucilius wrote about anything he thought his listeners would be interested in, including himself. His whole life was his subject, and he evidently had no inhibitions:

> When Cretaea came to my place for it, I got her to throw off her dress and everything else of her own accord.

Lucilius 897W (Varro *De lingua Latina* 6.69)

We only know that quotation because it was used sixty years later in a learned work on linguistics, to illustrate the phrase *sua sponte*.

Lucilius called his poems 'play' and 'conversations'. He started off with the metres of drama, and then turned to hexameters, the epic rhythm that Ennius had used so variously. Like Ennius and the dramatists, he was addressing an audience of the Roman People. Here he is in a scene imagined by Horace, who knew his work much better than we ever can:

> He arraigned the People's leaders and the People tribe by tribe, well-disposed to Virtue alone, of course, and her friends. In fact when the brave scion of Scipio and gentle, wise Laelius had withdrawn from the crowd, leaving the public stage for a private place, they used to fool around with him and play in casual clothes while waiting until the vegetables cooked.

Horace *Satires* 2.1.69–74 (trans. Frances Muecke)

Modern scholarship likes to take this as metaphorical. Lucilius is seen as a poet 'from the very ranks of the aristocracy', who 'had no need to cultivate access to an audience [and] needed only to circulate his poems among his friends'. But why should we think that?

Of course he collected his poems into volumes for reading (or we wouldn't even have the fragments that survive); and he famously announced in the preface to one of them that he didn't want readers who were either too learned or too ignorant. But that was normal, as the secondary means of getting a message across. Equally normal, as Horace knew, was the primary means—literally addressing the crowd, and literally from a stage.

Marcus Varro was about 14 when Lucilius died. He too was an outsider, from the Sabine prefecture of Reate; he too was from a landowning senatorial family; he too was well-read, funny, and opinionated, though less personally aggressive than Lucilius had been. When Varro was getting *his* message across to the Roman People in the seventies BC, the Forum had not long been cleansed of the rotting heads of Sulla's opponents. Perhaps that was why he assumed the role of a Cynic philosopher, and named his satires after a famous Cynic of the past, Menippus of Gadara. But he too, like Lucilius, spoke in his own name.

Among Varro's targets were venal judges, extortionate praetors, 'the dregs of the Senate-house', men who cheated the Roman People 'in broad daylight in the middle of the Forum', and he wanted to shame them before as wide an audience as he could find. No doubt he was more learned and literary than Lucilius, but it is clear that he too used a stage to address the crowd:

> And you in the theatre, who have rushed together here from your homes to hunt for pleasure for your ears, stay here and learn from me what I have for you, so you can take literature home from the theatre.

Varro *Satires* 218 (Nonius 510L)

Not a permanent theatre, of course: we must imagine something like Plautus' 'enclosure with benches', though by now the ad hoc structures were handsomer and more substantial.

Varro's satires referred quite often to the great comic poets of the previous century, and it may be that he thought of himself as part of their tradition. In *Double Marcus*, evidently a programmatic piece about his inspiration to write satire, he matched himself against a poor contemporary comedian:

> When Quintipor Clodius has made so many comedies with no help from the Muse, shall I not 'hack out' (as Ennius puts it) just one little book?
>
> Varro *Satires* 59 (Nonius 719L)

As with Lucilius, we need not suppose it was a book only to be read. The fragments of the satires are full of stage allusions, and like Lucilius in his early years, Varro used the metres of drama. So when he refers to his own 'stage style' (*modus scaenatilis*), there is no reason to doubt that he meant it literally.

Was he on stage himself, or impersonated by somebody speaking for him? The latter is more likely, for both external and internal reasons: Varro was a soldier as well as a satirist, often away on campaign at the time of the *ludi*; and in the fragments themselves the frequent use of vocatives and second-person-singular verbs strongly suggests dialogue, and therefore performers to deliver it. Dialogue is directly attested in a quotation from *Marcus' Boy*:

> —What about the people standing round watching? Aren't they laughing?
> —I *think* they are. I can't hear them laughing, but I see their mouths are open.
>
> Varro *Satires* 277 (Nonius 499L)

Who were the speakers? What were they doing? We have no idea. But this was evidently a script for performance.

The best-attested of Varro's satires, with forty-nine fragments surviving, is *Eumenides*, 'Kindly Ones', the euphemistic name for the Furies. Much of it was first-person narrative, with the speaker describing his efforts to find sanity in a mad world by sampling various philosophical and religious cults. The narrator used conversational prose, but also iambic *senarii* and iambic and trochaic *septenarii* and *octonarii*, appropriate to dramatic monologue and recitative; and when reporting his vision of the Furies themselves, he broke into the short anapaestic lines of a sung aria. There was clearly a variety of different episodes: someone gave an exposition in hexameters on the madness of ambition, avarice, and luxurious living, and there was a dialogue in iambic *septenarii* and *octonarii* in which the narrator's slave Strobilus told him some home truths and was threatened with a beating for his impudence.

The most spectacular scene was evidently set into the narrator's account of his visit to the temple of the Great Mother. He described in *senarii* the glamour and gorgeous costumes of the Galli, her eunuch priests, whose moral excellence someone commended to him in trochaic *septenarii*. And then they performed their frenetic cult-dance for the goddess, in the headlong Galliambic metre that only they used. Were there dancers on stage, with real horns and drums driving them on, or was their hymn just part of the narrative, a virtuoso performance by a single reciter? We certainly need not rule out the first alternative; but whichever it was, we may be sure that this multi-metric extravaganza was not written just to be read on papyrus.

A striking feature of the *Eumenides* fragments is the instability of the *mise-en-scène*. At one moment it's Rome, as we join the aedile responsible for the Great Mother's games, but then we're in Athens for the Dionysia, visiting Zeno's portico and Diogenes' barrel; and perhaps at the end the two became one, if it was 'Truth, the foster-child of Attic philosophy' who persuaded the people in the Forum to declare the narrator sane.

What that means, I think, is that Varronian satire was an art form that needed a stage and an audience, but did not need a *scaenae frons*. The three-door backdrop of traditional tragedy and comedy required the audience to think itself into a specific place and time until released by the closure of the plot. *Satura* was not like that. It was a 'well-filled dish' (Ch. 5.2 above), a miscellany where words, music, and dance could take the audience to any place at any time.

Among many other things, Marcus Varro was a man of the theatre—an expert on Plautus, a writer of 'pseudo-tragedies', an authority on the history and practice of drama. Although it cannot be more than a conjecture, I think Cicero was talking about Varro in this passage from a speech he gave in a court case in 64 BC:

Cicero *Pro Gallio* fr. 2 Crawford (Jerome *Epistles* 52.c. 8)

> At this year's games (for I speak from recent experience) there is one particular dominant poet—a very cultured man, the author of those *Poets' and Philosophers' Dinner-Table Discussions* in which he has Euripides arguing with Menander and another time Socrates with Epicurus, though we know that their lifetimes were not years but centuries apart. And what thunderous applause he gets for them! There are plenty of his fellow-pupils in the theatre audience, who never learned their lessons at the same time.

As it happens, Menander, Socrates, and Epicurus all appear in the surviving fragments of Varro's Menippean satires, as do Euripides' most famous heroines, Medea and Andromeda. And *Eumenides* itself, with its title from Attic tragedy, evidently featured a philosophers' banquet hosted by the narrator.

6

A Turbulent People

Gaius Lucilius' great-nephew was a good friend of Marcus Varro. He was also a precociously brilliant military commander, a charismatic young man whose good looks endeared him to the Roman People, and the consul of 70 BC whose legislation restored the traditional powers of the plebeian tribunes. He was Gnaeus Pompeius Magnus, 'Pompey the Great'.

During that epochal year Pompey was on bad terms with his consular colleague Marcus Crassus, and both of them had armies still in being after their recent campaigns. Would they turn them on each other, as had happened twice in recent years? The Roman People did not want their restored constitution to be threatened again by armed force. What happened provides us with a picture of the Roman audience on a working day.

6.1. The Political Stage

In December of 70 BC the Roman People were assembled in the Forum. What they were voting on is not recorded. The two consuls were seated separately on their curule chairs, probably at opposite ends of the Rostra. The citizens were anxious and unhappy, and seers were prophesying disaster if the consuls were not reconciled. A man called Gaius Aurelius, equestrian in rank but a farmer with no interest in politics, went up on the Rostra and made a declaration. Jupiter himself, he said, had ordered him in a dream to tell the Roman People not to allow the consuls to lay down their office until they became friends.

The citizens pleaded with Pompey and Crassus to heed the divine warning and not plunge Rome back into civil war. Crassus, the presiding magistrate, took the initiative and descended from his chair. He walked across to Pompey and offered his hand. Pompey stood up to meet him, and the handshake took place. 'Citizens,' said Crassus, 'I see no humiliation in making the first move towards friendship and goodwill with a man whom you called "the Great" before he had grown a beard, and to whom you gave a triumph before he was even a senator.'

Scribes were summoned. The orders for the disbandment of the two armies were formally announced, and the inscribed tablets were sealed and taken to the treasury in the temple of Saturn for safe keeping. The grateful People shouted their approval. The three men—Crassus, Pompey, and farmer Aurelius—had played out a real-life drama before the same audience, and on the same stage, as the actors who performed at grand funerals or in plays at the *ludi scaenici*.

A little over two years later, the Forum's political theatre staged a drama with a more contentious outcome. Two issues were at stake. The first was straightforward: Rome's authority was being contemptuously defied by pirate fleets; Ostia had been attacked, and even praetors in their robes of office had been abducted for ransom. It was intolerable; they must be eliminated. But how? That was the second issue, and it polarized the politics of Rome.

The People knew what they wanted. Pompey had given them their authority back, and now their tribune Aulus Gabinius was proposing that one of the ex-consuls (who but Pompey himself?) be granted full powers to do whatever was needed. To the aristocracy, however, 'full powers' meant monarchy (unless wielded by one of their own, like the late dictator Sulla); their oligarchic point of view had even given rise to a revisionist account of Romulus, in which the founder-king became 'tyrannical' and was killed by his own senators.

When Gabinius brought up his proposal for discussion in the Senate, the hostility against him was so threatening that the crowd outside invaded the Senate-house to protect their tribune. The presiding consul, Gaius Piso, was arrested and only freed at Gabinius' insistence. The People were then summoned for the voting assembly, filling the whole Forum, crowding the steps of every temple that gave a view of the Rostra.

Gabinius commended his bill to the People, and called on the consul to speak. Piso turned to Pompey. 'Remember what happened to Romulus', he said, and there was a furious surge of anger from the assembled People. Eventually calm was restored and speeches given, including one from Quintus Catulus, a leading opponent but recognized by the People as a man of integrity. It was not good, he told them, to trust everything to one man. Suppose some accident happened to Pompey—who would they give the command to then? 'You!' roared the crowd.

It would be easy to describe a dozen or more such scenes taking place during the next forty years, as polarized politics—the many against the few, incompatible visions of what the republic was and whose interests it should serve—destroyed that precarious equilibrium. (The fatal symptoms soon returned: execution without trial, political murder, civil war deliberately provoked.) For our purposes what matters is the crowd, the Roman People as the Roman audience.

The last generation of the Roman republic was a time of political disaster and literary brilliance. The audience had the chance to hear the poetry of Catullus, Lucretius, Virgil, and Horace, and the prose of Cicero, Caesar, and Sallust; and we have the chance of imagining their experience, because so many of those authors' texts survive.

Here, for instance, is Cicero in action, just a year after the debate on Gabinius' bill. Pompey has sorted out the pirates, and the tribune Gaius Manilius is proposing another special command for him, against King Mithridates in the east. Marcus Cicero, elected to the praetorship at the top of the poll, is called for his opinion:

> To face the crowded ranks of your Assembly has always given me a very special satisfaction. No place, it has seemed to me, lends greater dignity to the proposal of a motion, no environment is more impressive for a speech. You provide here, citizens, a road to fame which has always been wide open to every man of merit....
>
> I could see very clearly [from my election], citizens, that you intended to pass a generous verdict upon myself, and that you commended a similar course of behaviour to others. And now the influence which you indicated—by entrusting me with this office—that you desired to place in my hands, is mine. Whatever capacity for public speaking I may have been able to derive from almost daily experience and close attention in the courts is mine also.
>
> As to the influence, I am happy to exercise it in front of the men who bestowed it upon me. And if I have any ability as a speaker, this too I shall be especially glad to display before those very people who decided that oratory was one of the qualifications that deserved to be rewarded by public office.

Cicero *De imperio Cn. Pompei* 1–2 (trans. Michael Grant)

Three years later the Roman People would give this master-orator the consulship, and five years after that they would banish him for the unlawful killing of Roman citizens.

No fewer than nine of Cicero's extant speeches were addresses from the Rostra to the Roman People: *De imperio Cn. Pompei* (66 BC), *De lege agraria* 2 and 3, *Pro Rabirio perduellionis reo*, *In Catilinam* 2 and 3 (all 63 BC), *Post reditum ad Quirites* (57 BC), *Philippics* 4 and 6 (44–43 BC). And the great majority of his forensic speeches were delivered in the Forum, where his audience was not just the magistrate on his tribunal and the judges on their benches, but also the *corona*, the people crowding around to listen and make comments. For good reason, orators thought of themselves as actors on a stage.

6.2. Pompey and the Theatre

Pompey completed his second great popular command, hugely extending Rome's eastern empire and more than doubling the tributary income of the Roman People. Like his great predecessor Alexander, he took his historian with him to record his conquests at first hand. This was Theophanes of Mitylene, to whose home city Pompey made a complimentary visit on his way back to Rome in 62 BC.

Plutarch has an interesting report of the occasion, which may very well derive from Theophanes himself:

> When [Pompey] came to Mitylene he gave the city its freedom for the sake of Theophanes, and he was a spectator of the traditional competitions held there for poets, who this time had only one theme, which was the exploits of Pompey. He was very pleased with the theatre itself, and had sketches and plans made of it for him, with the intention of building one like it in Rome, only larger and more magnificent.

Plutarch Pompey 42.4 (trans. Rex Warner)

We may be sure that extracts from Theophanes' own history were also conspicuous on the programme of the theatre festival. What Pompey intended to build in Rome would not be just for plays.

Among other things, it would be for the display of Pompey himself. Already, before the conquering hero had returned, the Roman People had voted him the unheard-of privilege of wearing full triumphal regalia at the Circus games and a purple-bordered toga at the stage-games, with a gold crown as part of the costume in each case. One can see why the aristocrats complained about monarchy.

Back in Rome, Pompey tried to reassure them, but without much success. As Cicero complained to his friend Atticus in 60 BC:

> There isn't a statesman to be found, or even a dream of one. The man who could be, my friend Pompey (for so he is, I want you to know that), looks after that fancy embroidered toga of his by saying nothing.

Cicero Ad Atticum 1.18.6

He had been happier about him a year earlier:

> The crowd at public meetings—the miserable starving *plebs*, that leech of the treasury—thinks the Great Man is devoted to me alone! And yes indeed, we've been brought together by a lot of pleasant familiarity—so much so that those conspiratorial drunkards, the boys with the little beards, call him Gnaeus Cicero in their discussions. And so I get away with wonderful applause, both at the games and at the gladiators, without any shepherd-style whistling.

Cicero Ad Atticum 1.16.11

The games were the *ludi Apollinares* in July; and the implication is that before he had the benefit of Pompey's friendship, the crowd at the games used to whistle at him in disapproval.

6.3. When Cicero Wasn't in Rome

Suddenly, we get vivid insights like that. This is another point where the nature of our evidence changes, in both quantity and quality. The extraordinary survival of so much of Cicero's correspondence, over 900 letters dating from 68 to 43 BC, makes a huge difference to our understanding of Roman society—or at least of one section of it, since Cicero, as the last quotation illustrates, was not a man of the People. What gives the extra dimension is not only the direct evidence, as when we 'overhear', as it were, what Cicero confides to Atticus about Pompey; no less important is the information he doesn't know he is giving us, in the inferences we can make from the letters about things he and his correspondents never needed to spell out, because they took them for granted.

For instance, since many of the letters are dated, it is possible to work out when Cicero was in the habit of leaving Rome to stay at one or other of his country houses, or make a tour of several of them.

Naturally, spring was a favourite time. A departure date about 8 April was evidently normal, with the expectation of returning either mid-May or as late as 1 June. Other senators did the same thing (the social life between neighbouring villas could be like Rome in miniature), and in fact senatorial business was normally postponed at this time, though whether that was the cause or effect of the exodus is not known.

More surprising is the evidence for Cicero leaving town in November, when the weather was much less suitable for a holiday. We may get a hint of the reason for it from a passing comment in a letter to Atticus in November 56 BC: since the games have been extended for an extra day, Cicero will be glad to have one more day in the country, talking literature with Atticus' learned freedman Dionysius. He evidently went to his country house to avoid the games.

That is confirmed by the settings Cicero liked to use for his philosophical dialogues. For example, *De oratore* is set in 91 BC at the Tusculan villa of Lucius Crassus, where the presence of several other senators is explained by the fact that it was September, and the *ludi Romani* were on in Rome. So too *De finibus*, which is given a contemporary setting:

> I was at my place in Tusculum and wanted to consult some books in young Lucullus' library, so I went to his villa to help myself to them, as I normally did. When I got there, I found Marcus Cato sitting in the library surrounded by books on Stoicism...
>
> 'What brings you here?' he asked. 'I imagine you've come from your villa? If I'd known you were here I'd have called on you myself.'
>
> 'I left town yesterday,' I said, 'when the games began, and only got here in the evening.'

Cicero *De finibus* 3.7–8

But it seems that Cicero regarded some games as more to be avoided than others.

There is very little evidence in the correspondence for his being away from Rome during the *ludi Apollinares* in July or the *ludi Romani* in September. On the contrary, he reported several times on what was happening at Apollo's games, and on at least one grand occasion (as we shall see) he deliberately chose to be in Rome at the time of the *ludi Romani*. Not only that, but his regular April departure date was three or four days after the start of the *ludi Megalenses*.

It is clear that the games Cicero regularly chose to avoid were the *ludi Ceriales* from 12 to 19 April, the *ludi Florales* from 28 April to 3 May, and the *ludi plebeii* from 4 to 17 November. It can hardly be an accident that those were the three sets of games presided over by the plebeian aediles (Ch. 3.5 above). Cicero himself had once been plebeian aedile, proud of his responsibility for these very games; but that was when he was a newcomer in politics, making his way as a critic of aristocratic corruption. Since then, and in particular since December 63 BC, when as consul he had had five men executed as public enemies with no more legal authority than a resolution of the Senate, many citizens on what we would call the left of the spectrum had come to see him as an enemy of the People. It is likely that the games, and especially the 'plebeian' ones, offered them an opportunity to make their feelings known.

On 15 May 61 BC, Cicero was challenged in the Senate by one of the quaestors: why hadn't he been in Rome for the games of Ceres and Flora? Since the heckler, a young patrician called Publius Clodius, had a reputation as an extravagant playboy, Cicero replied with heavy irony:

Cicero
In P. Clodium et Curionem fr. 19 Crawford (Bobbio scholiast 88 St)

> This tough, old-fashioned type has complained about those who were taking the waters at Baiae in the month of April. What can we do with someone so gloomy and strict? Here's a magistrate too austere and outspoken for our modern lifestyle! He won't allow older gentlemen even to be at their own properties with impunity to look after their health at a time when there's nothing going on at Rome.

But things soon went beyond sarcastic jokes. Clodius got himself adopted into a plebeian family and elected as a plebeian tribune. It was his bill to the People in 58 BC that sent Cicero into exile.

The following year Cicero's friends, including Pompey, mustered enough support to get him recalled. The vote was passed early in August, and Cicero timed his return very carefully to arrive in Rome on 4 September, the opening day of the *ludi Romani*. He duly enjoyed the holiday crowd's applause, but Clodius and the *populares* kept hounding him, demonstrating in the Forum a few days later about the high price of grain, and shouting at the audience in the temporary theatre that Cicero was to blame for it.

Conspicuously visible from the Forum was a splendid new portico, dedicated to the goddess of Liberty; it stood on the site of Cicero's town house, destroyed at the time of his exile and consecrated under the terms of Clodius' bill. A bitter dispute now arose, with Cicero maintaining that the procedure had been illegal and he was therefore entitled to have his house restored to him, and Clodius determined to protect 'the People's Liberty'. Cicero won his case, and the portico was demolished in its turn; but supervising the rebuilding of his house kept him in Rome for the *ludi plebeii* in November.

Reporting events to Atticus, Cicero didn't even mention the games themselves. What mattered to him was Clodius' reckless violence:

> On 11 November he pursued me with his men as I was going down the Sacra Via. Shouts, stones, clubs, swords, and all without any warning. I withdrew into Tettius Damio's forecourt. The people with me easily prevented the hired men from getting in. He himself could have been killed—but I'm starting to use diet treatment, I'm tired of surgery.

Cicero *Ad Atticum* 4.3.3

Both men evidently had armed guards, described pejoratively in Clodius' case as 'hired men', and it is clear from the outcome that Cicero's escort was the stronger of the two; even killing Clodius while they had the chance was a possible option. Of course this was particularly shocking, as Cicero makes clear in his letter; but even so, it is interesting to see what sort of popular demonstration Clodius knew he could get away with at the time of the Plebeian Games, and what precautions Cicero knew he had to take.

Five months later, at the *ludi Ceriales* of 56 BC, Cicero wrote from Arpinum asking Atticus (now back in Rome) to make sure there were guards posted at Cicero's house. He knew what to expect; and sure enough, Clodius, now in office as aedile and directing some street theatre of his own, led a crowd of citizens to the house as if to demolish it again and claim it back for Liberty. The following year Atticus was again requested to keep an eye on the house during the games of Ceres and Flora, though so far as we know nothing happened that time.

It was at those *ludi Florales*, in 55 BC, that Marcus Cato chose to get up and leave the audience. We have no contemporary evidence for that event, and the later moralizing tradition tells the story as a tribute to Cato himself: so great was his moral authority that the Roman People were unwilling to watch erotic shows in his presence. But we may equally suspect that they just made it clear he wasn't welcome.

6.4. Pompey's Games

Meanwhile, in the Campus Martius the great bulk of Pompey's theatre was taking shape. The traditional opposition to permanent theatres had been partly ideological, an aristocratic prejudice against the Greek habit of using theatres for popular assemblies, a seated citizen body deliberating on policy. That did not happen in Rome; but in so far as the theatre was the People's place, it was appropriate that Pompey, the People's favourite, should break the old taboo.

Now, in 55 BC, Pompey was consul for the second time (again with his rival Crassus), much to the anger of the aristocrats. Since the theatre was close enough to completion to be used, this was the moment for Pompey to show off his magnificent gift to the city. Lavish votive games were staged in September for Victoria, in thanks for Pompey's triumphs over the pirates and Mithridates. Her temple towered more than a hundred feet above the Campus Martius, with the theatre as its supporting platform: the rising tiers of seats in the semicircular auditorium were in effect a huge extension of the steps giving access to the temple.

Two Ciceronian texts may help us to think ourselves into the world of 55 BC. The first comes from a speech he made in the Senate just before Pompey's games. The occasion was the return to Rome of Lucius Piso, lately proconsul of Macedonia and a man with whom Cicero had unfinished business. As consul in 58, Piso had not only refused to support Cicero against Clodius but had even supervised the demolition of his house after his departure into exile. Now it was payback time.

In the course of his pitilessly prejudicial character-assassination, Cicero taunted Piso about his Epicurean beliefs:

Cicero *In Pisonem* 65

> The games are approaching—the most elaborate and magnificent in living memory, such as have never been seen before and I can't believe will ever be seen again. Offer yourself to the People, be present at the games. Afraid of whistles? Where are your learned discussions now? Afraid you'll be shouted at? A philosopher shouldn't care about that either. Afraid someone will hit you? Well, pain is an evil, as you contend—even if reputation, disgrace, infamy, and baseness are just words and nonsense. No, I'm sure of it: he won't dare to go near the games.

Cicero himself *would* be there, of course—if only to gratify Pompey, who had helped bring him back from exile.

The disrespectful treatment to which he hoped Piso would be subjected—and from which he himself would be shielded by Pompey's friendship—was in fact minimized by the design of the great building. The auditorium, still called the 'cage' (*cauea*), is reported to have had a capacity of nearly 18,000. It was divided horizontally by two semicircular corridors (*praecinctiones*), and the resulting three sections, the lower, middle, and upper *cauea*, were kept separate from each other by the *praecinctio* walls, which were as high as the corridors were wide. Though the physical evidence is lost, it is clear from the design of subsequent stone theatres that the access stairs to the respective sections were strictly segregated. Whether or not crowd control was the motive, it was certainly the effect.

Fig. 16

The other Ciceronian evidence for Pompey's games is very different. Marcus Marius was a friend of Cicero's living in Pompeii, a man of means and evidently

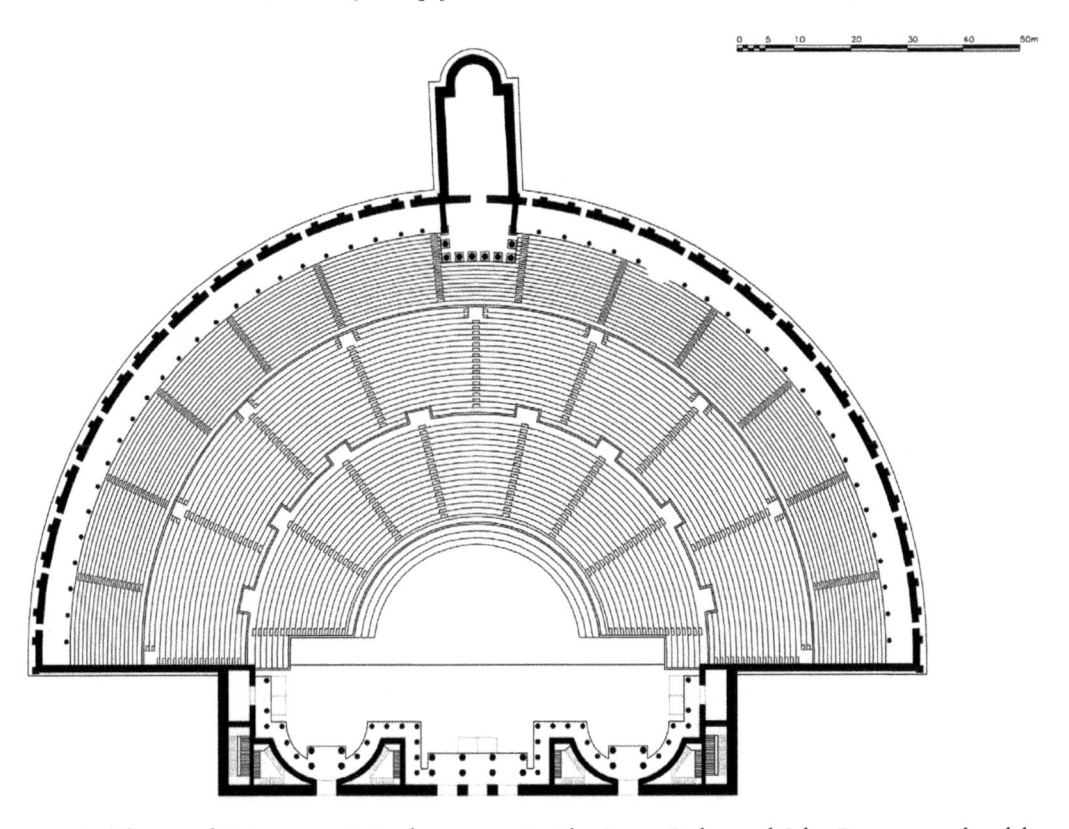

FIG. 16. Theatre of Pompey: conjectural reconstruction by James Packer and John Burge, reproduced by permission of James E. Packer.

a man of taste and learning as well. In October 55 Cicero sent him a letter reporting on the games and elaborately congratulating him on not having come to Rome to see them:

> Just so long as you've made good use of your leisure! You certainly had a wonderful opportunity to enjoy it, left almost to yourself in that beautiful place. I've no doubt at all that throughout those days you spent the mornings on little readings in that private room of yours with the window you had made to open up the view over the bay of Stabiae, while those who left you there were half asleep watching mimes for the public taste; and that the rest of your day was taken up with pleasures you arranged at your own choice, while we had to endure whatever Spurius Maecius had approved for us.

Cicero *Ad familiares* 7.1.1

Yes, everything at Pompey's games was very magnificent, 'but not to your taste, if I may judge by my own'. There were 600 mules in Accius' *Clytemnestra*, 3,000 wine-bowls in Naevius' *Trojan Horse*, not to mention all the battle scenes with infantry and cavalry exotically armed.

Though that won popular admiration, it would have given you no pleasure. But if through those days you were giving your attention to your man Protogenes (so long as he read you anything but my speeches!), then surely you had much more enjoyment than any of us.

<small>Cicero *Ad familiares* 7.1.2–3</small>

Protogenes was the slave *lector*, an important figure in any cultured man's household.

In a sense, the whole argument of this book turns on those 'little readings' (*lectiunculae*) that Marius enjoyed in his morning-room with the view across the bay. What I see as the modern misconception is elegantly stated in two very authoritative translations of Cicero's letter:

<small>Wilkinson 1949.58</small>

I can see you all those days spending the morning dipping into a book in your bedroom there...

<small>Shackleton Bailey 1978.79</small>

Throughout the period of the show you have spent the mornings browsing over your books in that bedroom of yours...

L. P. Wilkinson and Shackleton Bailey were two of the finest Latinists of modern times, but I think they each grossly misinterpreted the scene Cicero imagined at Marius' villa. They knew, of course, that a *cubiculum* was not necessarily a bedroom: it was a private chamber that might or might not be used for sleeping. Even more obviously, they knew about Protogenes the *lector*, mentioned just a few lines later. But because they assumed that *lectio* means 'reading' in the modern sense, they seem to have forgotten all that and imagined Marius alone in his room, reading books. In fact, he was enjoying his view (why mention it otherwise?), while listening to Protogenes reading books to him.

The point of Cicero's contrast is that Marius and the thousands in the theatre were doing the same thing—but he was an audience of one, who could choose his own programme. There is no need to suppose that what Spurius Maecius approved for the theatre audience was restricted to plays. He was known as a critical judge of poetry in general, and poetry in general was written for performance. If Cicero chose to report on the tragedians, that was no doubt because of the scope they offered for grandiose display. We can be sure there was much more variety on offer, but of course it had to be acceptable to the taste of the majority. There was plenty of variety on offer for Marius too—the whole content of his library—but he could enjoy whatever suited *his* taste.

6.5. Poets and Dancers

That literature was something spoken and heard is nicely illustrated in one of Cicero's letters to his brother. Quintus had been reluctant to come to Cicero's country house for fear of disturbing him. No need to be, says Cicero:

> I assure you, no Muse-struck poet is more eager to read his own recent work than I am to hear you talking about anything, public or private, country or town.

Cicero *Ad Q. fratrem* 2.9.1

Where, and to whom, would such a poet read his work? Two more *obiter dicta* give us an idea of what was involved.

Defending the Greek poet Archias in a court case, and making the most of his client's aristocratic connections, Cicero remarks that Archias 'was listened to by Marcus Aemilius', a prominent ex-consul of the previous generation. No doubt that means that he read his work at Aemilius' house, in what Varro the satirist described as 'an audience of fine gentlemen'. That is good evidence for those who think literature was just a matter for the 'elite', but an equally casual comment in one of Cicero's philosophical works opens up a quite different perspective.

Discussing the correction of faults, Cicero draws an analogy with what was evidently a familiar phenomenon:

> For as painters and those who make statues, and even poets too, wish their works to be put before the public [*uulgus*], so that if anything is criticized by the majority it may be improved, and try to find out on their own account and from others what is wrong with their work, so we should use the judgement of others about many things that should be done and not done, altered and corrected.

Cicero *De officiis* 1.147

Since one could hardly attract a public audience on a working day, these poets were evidently performing at festivals, and in particular at the games.

We have no direct evidence for how the new 'stone theatre' was used for the regular annual *ludi scaenici*. The traditional wooden structures were still erected and taken down each year in front of the relevant temples—on the Palatine for the Great Mother, in the Circus for Ceres and Flora, in the Circus Flaminius piazza for Apollo, on the Capitol for Jupiter's *ludi Romani* and *ludi plebeii*—and we may assume that for events in Pompey's theatre the magistrate in charge led a procession (Ch. 3.3 above), with the divinity's symbolic attribute, just as he would have done to a temporary theatre in the Forum or the Circus. It may be that one effect of the new building was to free up the Forum for performances attracting relatively smaller crowds: it is not long before we get our first direct evidence for poets reading their work in the middle of the Forum.

Because the ground-plan of Pompey's theatre survives, embedded in the cityscape of modern Rome, we know that its stage was about 70 metres wide. It's not surprising that the companies putting on classic tragedies did so with hugely elaborate spectacle and armies of extras. More puzzling—but perhaps more interesting, if we can get the inferences right—is the case of those 'mimes for the public taste' that were on the morning programme at Pompey's games (Ch. 6.4 above).

Fig. 17

'Mime' could mean many things in the Roman entertainment tradition. The term had no necessary connotation of silent performance, as it has nowadays; it simply meant 'imitation'. For Cicero, it evidently implied physical clowning,

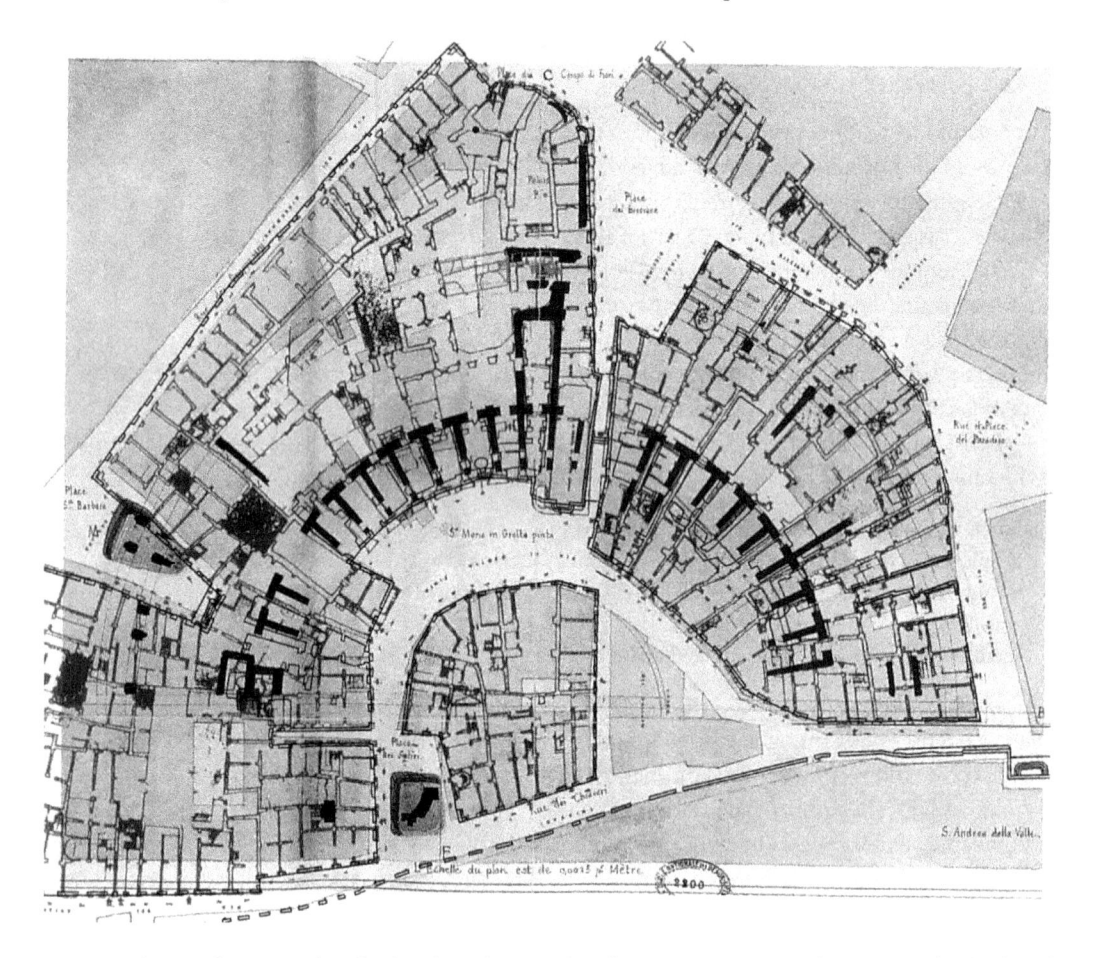

FIG. 17. Theatre of Pompey: plan of archaeological remains by John Burge, superimposed on Victor Baltard's plan of the site in 1837. Reproduced by permission from Packer 2007.275, fig. 14.

obscene language, improvised plots, and topical comment; but it was now also a dramatic genre scripted by serious poets of his own social background. He barely alludes to the most conspicuous feature of mime, the participation of female performers (*mimae*); and that may not be accidental, since the *ludi Florales*, where they were most notorious, were one of the games he regularly avoided. The *mimae* were variety artistes, simultaneously actresses, singers, and dancers, and it was surely their dancing, and the musicians who played for it, that filled the vast performance area of Pompey's theatre.

We happen to have precious eyewitness testimony from exactly this time (the fifties BC) on how sitting in the audience watching the *ludi scaenici* affected people's dreams. What stayed in the mind was not actors but dancers:

6.5. Poets and Dancers

> For many days the same things pass before their eyes, with the effect that even when they are awake they seem to see dancers with their soft limbs moving, to hear in their ears the liquid song of the lyre and its speaking strings, and to see the same audience and the various shining splendours of the stage.
>
> Lucretius 4.978–83

A stray quotation from one of Varro's satires refers to Actaeon as a subject for 'dancers in the theatre'. They were plural and masculine, therefore probably playing the dogs that tore Actaeon to pieces; but the play must have had fine roles for the *mimae* too, as vengeful Diana and her naked nymphs. (In the poets, the nymphs of Diana and Venus dance by night, and it was at night that the *mimae* featured in Flora's licentious games.)

In the fourth century BC we saw women performers in erotic mythological scenarios (Ch. 3.1 above); in the second century BC we heard of a huge stage filled with dancers, musicians, and battle scenes (Ch. 4.3 above); closer to Pompey's own time we identified the 'full dish' of *satura* as a type of topical quasi-drama that may well have involved music and dance (Ch. 5.4 above).

Fig. 14

Such scattered pieces of a lost jigsaw are all we have for the history of show-business in the Roman republic. Even now, in the uniquely well-attested 'age of Cicero', things Cicero was not interested in go practically unrecorded. We are still dependent on just a few random scraps for even a hint of what happened now that the huge stage was not just a one-off expedient but a permanent feature of Rome's cultural landscape. Let's look at what evidence there is.

The first item comes from a grammarian of late antiquity, whose chapter on types of poetry (*de poematibus*) includes under 'comedy' a quotation from a lost work of Suetonius, written about AD 100:

> Originally, everything that [now] happens on stage was performed in comedy. For the *pantomimus*, the *pythaules* and the *choraules* used to sing in comedy. But because not everything could be equally excellent in the performance of everyone, those among the comedy performers who had greater ability and skill each claimed the artistic primacy for himself. So it came about that the *mimi* were unwilling to yield to the others in their own speciality, and so there was a split from the rest. For since, being more skilled, they were not prepared to serve the less skilled in the work they shared, they separated themselves from comedy; and so it happened that once the precedent had been established, the practice of each speciality began to follow suit, and not appear in comedy.
>
> Diomedes in *Grammatici Latini* 1.491–2 Keil

By 'originally' (*primis temporibus*), Suetonius evidently meant the origins not of comedy itself but of something that evolved from comedy. It counted as 'mime'—including 'all-mime', *pantomimus*, a new type of dance drama that came to its definitive form during the first thirty years of the existence of Pompey's theatre.

One of the great pioneers of 'all-mime' was a dancer from Alexandria, a fact which may help to explain an enigmatic comment of Cicero's in 54 BC. He was trying to discredit Alexandrian witnesses in a court case:

<small>Cicero *Pro Rabirio Postumo* 35</small>
> We used to hear about Alexandria, but now we know about it. It's where all trickery comes from, and yes, all deceit as well—and from trickery and deceit it's the source of all the mime plots.

The implication, however disdainful, is that something new was happening in the entertainment world. That may be borne out by the fact that only now—but precisely now, in the fifties BC—do we have evidence of serious poets writing 'mime'. We know three names: Publilius 'the Syrian', a freedman; Decimus Laberius, a Roman knight; and Valerius Catullus, evidently the famous poet Catullus of Verona, whom we shall meet in the next chapter. What matters at this point is that a century or so later a well-informed author called Publilius 'the founder of the mimic stage'. Of course Publilius didn't invent mime, which dates back at least to the fifth century BC; but in some sense he must have been an innovator.

By a very fortunate chance we happen to know that Catullus wrote a prose work about mime. An ancient commentator on Lucan, annotating a reference to the sun's refusal to look on the 'banquet of Thyestes', explains it with a rationalization:

<small>Scholiast on Lucan 1.543–4 (35–6 Usener)</small>
> That is, the sun was eclipsed, and there was night at Mycenae. But I have found in a book of Catullus entitled *On Mime-Performances* that this is a legend. He says that Atreus was the first to explain to his fellow-citizens the true and hitherto unfamiliar courses of the sun, and convince them that it rises opposite the signs [of the Zodiac], and what the other planets are said to do, and that becoming famous through this expertise he supplanted his brother and became king.

The astrological angle is particularly interesting, because five out of the forty-four known titles of Decimus Laberius' mime-plays are *Aries*, *Cancer*, *Gemelli* (i.e. *Gemini*?), *Taurus*, and *Virgo*.

If 'mime-performances' could involve the quasi-historical reinterpretation of plots from Greek tragedy, that is a sobering index of how little we know. But at least we can say that this practitioner's theoretical work on the subject may confirm our sense of a period of rapid change and experiment.

It is obviously impossible, from such fragmentary and haphazard evidence, to offer any kind of confident reconstruction of what went on at the *ludi scaenici*, every year from 55 BC onwards, on that enormous stage in Pompey's theatre. But I think it is reasonable to make two suggestions. First: what was needed to fill the space was not words alone but music and dance as well. And second: any poet who hoped to reach those tens of thousands in the theatre audience would have to write with the new conditions in mind.

6.6. Before the Disaster

The purpose of this chapter has been to convey, however inadequately, something of the energy and vitality of late republican Rome; and in so doing to avoid separating out 'political history' as if it were a thing apart. Much of the energy and vitality stemmed from the determination of the Roman People to support 'their' politicians against the arrogant aristocracy: first it was Pompey 'the Great', then Pompey's ally and father-in-law Julius Caesar, consul in 59 BC. The result was great military commands authorized by the People in the teeth of senatorial opposition—Pompey against the pirates and Mithridates, and now Caesar in Gaul—and in consequence a great influx of the spoil of conquest, to be spent on grand projects for the benefit of the People themselves.

As Cicero once remarked to a jury, 'the People hate private luxury, but love public magnificence'. The aristocracy took the opposite view: in 133 BC they had protected private wealth illegally acquired by killing the People's tribune who tried to correct the abuse. Now they saw Pompey and Caesar as quasi-kings, and they knew enough Greek political theory to justify a convenient killing as 'tyrannicide'. Pompey did not often appear in public, and when he did it was with a large escort. Both he and Caesar knew very well that there were plenty of distinguished Romans who quite seriously wished them dead. It was a dangerously unstable situation, and within a very few years the reckless intransigence of the aristocracy, and the jealous rivalry of the People's champions, would destroy the precarious balance and bring civil war back to Rome.

But let's pause the chronology while the news was still good, in July 54 BC. Caesar has conquered Gaul and taken Roman arms beyond the known world, across the Rhine into Germany and across the Channel into Britain. His daughter Julia, beloved wife of Pompey, having survived one miscarriage, is pregnant again. Cicero, chastened perhaps by the experience of exile (and to the disgust of his aristocratic friends), has lent his eloquence to the popular cause. Now it's the time of the *ludi Apollinares*, and he wants to oblige the praetor in charge. As he tells Atticus:

> I came back to Rome for Fonteius' sake on 9 July. I went to the show, and the first thing is that I got loud and steady applause—but never mind that, it's stupid of me to write it down.

Cicero *Ad Atticum* 4.15.6

He was pleased about it, all the same.

7

Rethinking the Classics

59–42 BC

Fig. 1 We are now at point C on our chronological diagram. Just a point without extension on a 3,400-year time-line, it was in reality a full human lifetime, during which the Roman republic collapsed into civil war, peace and the rule of law were restored by Caesar Augustus, and his indirect rule developed into a dynastic monarchy. The same lifetime witnessed an extraordinary profusion of literary talent, as Lucretius, Catullus, Caesar, Sallust, Virgil, Horace, Propertius, Livy, and Ovid created the masterpieces of 'classic' Latin literature.

This chapter and the next two are attempts to read those classic texts in the light of what we have learned so far about authors and their audiences. If our premise is valid, that the creation of expensive written books was the secondary, not the primary, form of 'publication', there may be indications in the texts of how their authors intended them to be first presented.

'Authorial intention' has been a bone of tedious literary-critical contention for a long time, but a historical enquiry like this one can afford to be relaxed about it. 'What did the author intend?' is a factual question like any other, to be empirically—and therefore provisionally—answered by evidence and argument. To insist that we can never *know* is true but trivial: strictly speaking, we can never *know* anything about the past, but we can still make statements about it that are more or less confident according to the strength or weakness of the evidence they are based on.

I define the 'point C' period, not quite arbitrarily, as the sixty-seven years from Caesar's first consulship to the banishment of Ovid, and divide it into three chapters at 42 BC, the deification of Caesar, and 28 BC, the restoration of constitutional government.

Triumphantly elected as the People's champion, in 59 BC Caesar as consul forced through legislation dividing up public land into small plots for ordinary citizens. (Marcus Varro, now 56, served on the commission appointed to administer it.) The aristocrats regarded that as tyranny. 'The republic is finished,' Cicero wrote to Atticus. 'We're slaves, and we do nothing about it.' The republic was not finished yet—but it couldn't survive their diehard intransigence much longer. Fifteen years later they did do something about it, on the Ides of March.

Caesar's son, born Gaius Octavius and adopted in his will, avenged his father's murder and liberated the republic, as he put it, 'from the domination of a faction'. Fourteen years later, when his army entered Alexandria, he not only ended the civil wars but took over the last and richest of the Hellenistic kingdoms, thus giving himself the means to fund what everyone longed for— peace, prosperity, and the rule of law. And during those dangerous and sometimes desperate decades, the long-suffering Roman populace had the chance to hear some of the greatest poets who ever lived.

7.1. Lucretius and Philodemus

Titus Lucretius was a man with a mission: to bring peace of mind to suffering mortals by freeing them from the fear of the gods. He could do it, because he understood the reasoning (*ratio*) of Epicurus, that 'the nature of things' is not divinely ordained. But people had to be persuaded:

> It is essential that this dread and darkness of the mind be dispersed—not by the sun's rays and the shining shafts of day, but by the appearance and reasoning of nature. We shall take its first principle as our starting-point, that nothing is ever created out of nothing by divine will. Why are all mortals so beset by fear? It's because they observe many things happening on earth and in the sky, they have no reasoning to enable them to see what makes them happen, and they assume that they come about by divine power.

Lucretius 1.146–54

And because they think gods control the world, they think gods will also punish them after death:

> As for Cerberus and the Furies and the loss of light, the jaws of Tartarus belching horrible fumes, it is certain that they do not, and cannot, exist anywhere. What does exist is fear of punishment for misdeeds in life (the worse the deeds, the worse the fear), and expiation for wrongdoing—the prison, the dreadful hurling from the rock, beatings, executioners, the cage, the pitch, the hot iron, the firebrands. Even if they aren't there, the guilty conscience is terrified in advance and applies the goads to itself and burns with whips.

Lucretius 3.1011–19

Not knowing that there is nothing after death, they make their own hell here on earth—unless Lucretius' passionate argument can save them from it.

What sort of people was he trying to reach? Notionally, Lucretius' poem was addressed to Memmius, a prominent senator whose public responsibilities he referred to with proper respect. The phrase he used of the two of them, 'the hoped-for pleasure of sweet friendship', reveals a poet looking for patronage, help from a wealthy man to support the time-consuming hard work of understanding science and making it intelligible. And he probably got what he wanted: the many vivid vignettes in his argument suggest a familiarity *both* with the world of work *and* with the life of luxury. But the fact that he had grand friends doesn't mean he was writing only for a literary elite. On the contrary: people like Memmius were unlikely to be terrified by the Roman state's instruments of torture and coercion.

The classic statement of Lucretius' mission and his way of carrying it out comes in a famous passage in book 1, later reused as the introduction to book 4:

> I am well aware how obscure it is. But a great hope has struck my heart with the Bacchic wand of fame, and beaten into my breast the sweet love of the Muses. Inspired by that, I now with vigorous mind traverse the pathless places of the Pierides, trodden by no one's foot before. My pleasure is to approach untouched springs and drink from them, to pluck new flowers and gather for my head a glorious garland from where the Muses have wreathed the brow of nobody before. Firstly because I teach about great things, and aim to free the mind from the tight knots of religion that bind it, and then because on a dark subject I put together songs so full of light, coating them all with the Muses' charm.
>
> For that too is seen to be not without reasoning. What I do is what healers do when they try to give children foul-tasting wormwood. They first coat the rim round the cup with the sweet, yellow moisture of honey, so that the children's unsuspecting age may be tricked as far as the lips, and meanwhile swallow down the bitter wormwood draught; deceived, they are not harmed but rather cured by this method, and get well. In just the same way, since this reasoning usually seems too unpleasant to those who haven't tried it, and the crowd shrinks back from it, I have wished now to set out our reasoning for you in sweet-speaking Pierian song, and coat it, so to speak, with the sweet honey of the Muses.

Lucretius
1.922–47

'For you' (singular)—meaning Memmius, in whose country villa we may perhaps imagine Lucretius addressing an audience of fine gentlemen. But they were not the suffering mortals he most wanted to save from fear.

How does he know the crowd (*uulgus*) shrinks from the hard work of reasoning? No doubt because he has already tried it out on them.

If we look sideways for a moment (still in the fifties BC) to the palatial villa of another wealthy and cultured senator, we find another poet and Epicurean, a learned Syrian called Philodemus of Gadara. His patron was Lucius Piso, Cicero's enemy (Ch. 6.4 above), and in Piso's villa at Herculaneum there was a library full of his philosophical works. Unlike Lucretius, Philodemus kept his poetry for elegant entertainment (evidence for his patron's depravity, Cicero said), and did his philosophy in prose treatises from which the Muses' charm was conspicuously absent.

We know that, because the books were still there when Vesuvius' 'pyroclastic surge' of superheated ash and gases engulfed the villa in August AD 79, and the carbonized scrolls were brought to light in 1752 by the Bourbons' tunnelling treasure-hunters. The immensely difficult work of retrieving their texts has now revealed, among other things, precious remains of Philodemus' *On Poems*, a critical review of theories on the nature and effect of poetry.

This literary-critical commentary is important for our purposes because of what it takes for granted. Some thought the power of poetry was only in the sound; others insisted on its intellectual content as well; but nobody ever doubted that the poets' words and rhythms were received through the ear. These learned authors would have found modern critics' obsession with books and reading very odd indeed.

At one point in *On Poems*, Philodemus was discussing the views of a certain Andromenides. This author defined the poet as unlike the 'sophist', who delivers his public address in prose, in that the sophist aims at truth and the poet only at what pleases the multitude. Philodemus glosses that as 'the most beautiful diction is what enthrals the crowds', as opposed to what is admired by the educated few. What the arguments of the professors presuppose is a 'literary' world where authors in both prose and verse made their work known by oral delivery to a public audience, often a very large one.

Who or what was the Roman equivalent of Andromenides' sophist? Cicero gives us a possible answer, in a passage which takes as its premise the Lucretian observation that the Roman public 'shrinks from the science and learning of the Greeks'. The speaker is Marcus Varro, imagined as talking to Atticus and Cicero himself:

> Of course you understand that *we* can't be like Amafinius and Rabirius, who use no art and discuss matters obvious to everyone in the language of the crowd.
>
> Cicero *Academica* 1.5

Elsewhere Cicero refers to the multitude being drawn to the Epicurean way of life by the 'giving out' of Amafinius' books. That seems to refer to copies being used by his disciples to reach multiple audiences, though Cicero also claims, disdainfully and inconsistently, that they preached only to the converted.

What matters is that moral lectures from philosophers of one persuasion or another were a familiar phenomenon in Rome. Cicero remarks that the stricter schools found it hard to keep their audiences, but evidence from just a few years later suggests that the Stoics, at least, were still in business. As with all public performers, we may imagine them in action on the N days of the Roman calendar (Ch. 2.6 above), when the city's piazzas were free from public business and available to whoever could attract an audience.

What made Lucretius different was his ambition to be *both* the sophist who seeks the truth *and* the poet who pleases the multitude. Hence the honey on the cup, the technical argument coated with the Muses' charm. The crown of fame he sought was the one Ennius had brought down from the Muses' mountain; his poem was like a six-lap chariot race, with Calliope, Muse of epic, guiding him to the victor's prize.

The great opening hymn to Venus is a magnificent example of how his audience, like the children taking their wormwood medicine, were tricked into hearing his message. Later, that message would tell them that the gods live far away in a totally different dimension, with no concern at all for mortal affairs. That was a doctrine that upset the conventionally pious; the prophets, competitors of the poet for the public's attention, no doubt denounced it as a blasphemy to be punished as Jupiter punished the impious Giants. So here the honey of the Muses conceals it, and Venus, creator of all life in the world, is asked to bestow on the Romans the blessings of peace: 'for in our country's time of trouble I cannot perform my task with ease in my heart, nor in such circumstances can noble Memmius forsake the common safety.'

The goddess is hymned as mother of the Romans, *Aeneadum genetrix*. That makes particular sense if the poet was addressing the Roman People; and he may have been reminding them that noble Memmius, who claimed descent from Troy, would soon be asking for their votes as a candidate for the consulship. A prayer for peace was certainly appropriate at a time (55 BC) when electoral contests led repeatedly to bloodshed.

7.2. Demetrius, Historians, Caesar

It may have been about this time—or perhaps a generation or two earlier—that the otherwise unknown Greek author Demetrius wrote his treatise *On Style*. We used it in the introductory chapter (Ch. 1.4 above) as proof that Greek literature continued to be written primarily for audiences, and not just for lone readers with their own texts. And that applied to prose as well as poetry: *On Style* pays almost as much attention to Xenophon, Plato, and Demosthenes as it does to Homer. Two particular passages, referring to two different prose genres, may be helpful at this point.

The first concerns the fourth-century BC historian Ctesias of Cnidos, cited as an example of *enargeia* (vividness):

Demetrius *On Style* 215	And in general this poet—for one may reasonably call him a poet—is in all his writing a creative artist of *enargeia*.

7.2. Demetrius, Historians, Caesar

A poet (*poiētēs*) is a 'maker', and as Aristotle insisted, what he makes is not just verses but plots (*mythoi*). Ctesias was famous for his tall stories, and that may be what Demetrius had in mind. But Ctesias was not necessarily a special case. Some authorities regarded all writers of narrative or persuasive prose as *poiētai* too. Here is Heracleodorus, as cited by Philodemus:

> The works of Demosthenes and Xenophon are poems (*poiēmata*), and even more so those of Herodotus, though each of these is a prose-writer according to the convention.

Quoted in Philodemus On Poems 1.199

If such authors counted as poets, it should follow that they drew audiences in the same way poets did.

That was what we inferred from Polybius in an earlier chapter (Ch. 5.3 above). Confirmation of it for the mid-first century BC comes from Cicero and his younger contemporary Sallust, both of whom repeatedly use the phrase 'hearing or reading' with reference to history. Those who couldn't read, or couldn't afford books, evidently got their knowledge of the past by *hearing* it narrated.

The historians of the first century BC are lost, except for fragments, but we know that one of them, at least, was in the Ctesias tradition of mixing real history with mythological narrative. This was Valerius Antias, who not only dealt with the events of his own time but also told how King Numa kidnapped Faunus and Picus on the Aventine and bargained with Jupiter about the expiation of thunderbolts. The fragments of Antias reveal a consistent interest in the history of the games; it also seems likely that he wrote the patrician Valerii back into every stage of the 'history' of early Rome. Putting all that together, one might guess at a historian with aristocratic backing who found his audience at the *ludi scaenici*—and who no doubt helped to encourage the Roman People to vote for the two noble Valerii Messallae who became respectively consul in 61 BC and censor in 55, and consul in 53.

In 55 BC, Cicero too wanted political publicity. Having made his peace with Pompey and Caesar, he was hoping to attain the honours appropriate to a senior statesman—the censorship, or one of the great priesthoods—or perhaps a consulship for his brother Quintus. He wrote a long, elaborate letter to his friend the historian Lucius Lucceius, who had just finished writing the history of 'the Italian and civil wars' (91–83 BC), asking him to jump forward twenty years and deal with the period from 63 to 57 BC as a thematic narrative of Cicero's own consulship, exile, and return:

> My experiences will supply your writing with plenty of variety, full of a certain enjoyment which (since you are the author) will really be able to grip people's minds in the reading. For there is nothing more suited to a reader's pleasure than

> Cicero
> *Ad familiares*
> 5.12.4–5

> changes of circumstance and the vicissitudes of fortune. Although they were unwelcome to me as I experienced them, they will be enjoyable in the reading... and if they end with a remarkable outcome, the mind of the reader is filled with the most pleasurable enjoyment.

Only readers are referred to, because Cicero is pretending that all he wants is the approval of posterity; besides, it would have been tactless to refer to Lucceius, himself a senior senator, offering his work to a popular audience. But if such a narrative had been available, we can be sure Cicero would have arranged for it to be publicized as widely as possible.

In fact, the idea of history as public performance is already implicit in Cicero's argument. Narrating the events of those years as the ups and downs of one man's experience would, he says, make it like a play with various acts. And the artistic advantage to which he draws Lucceius' attention is precisely the vividness (*enargeia*) that made Demetrius say that historians like Ctesias 'may reasonably be called poets'.

Appropriately, our other significant Demetrius passage is concerned with letter-writing, which he treats as appropriate to the 'plain style'. Since a letter is not spoken, but written and sent 'as a sort of gift', the question of oral delivery is less relevant than in other modes; on the other hand, he says, a letter on a serious subject may resemble a speech given in public (*epideixis*).

That ambivalent definition is well illustrated by Cicero's correspondence. Although most of the letters are informal, often confidential, for the eyes of the recipient only, others are much more elaborately composed, in a style that would certainly be appropriate to rhetorical delivery. It is clear that some were even designed to be read to other people, and not just informally. (Cicero at one point refers to a letter from his son in Athens 'so affectionately and elegantly written that I'd even venture to read it before an audience'.) The letter to Lucceius is one such; the letter about Pompey's games, sent to Marcus Marius a few months later (Ch. 6.4 above), is another.

One example particularly useful for the present argument is a long letter written to Atticus, who was away in Greece, in the summer of 61 BC, bringing him up to date on three very eventful months in Cicero's political life. Since both men were very familiar with Greek literature and Greek literary scholarship, it was natural to begin his narrative in professorial style ('I'll tell you Homerically, in reverse order'), and proceed with casual allusions to Greek history and even a Homeric invocation of the Muses. But it was surely not just for one man to read. In Greece just as much as in Rome, Atticus was constantly active in furthering Cicero's interests and publicizing his works. He must have known perfectly well that this brilliantly vivid and lively narrative was to be read to a suitably influential audience just as soon as it could be arranged.

7.2. Demetrius, Historians, Caesar

There was one type of narrative letter with which all Romans were familiar: the proconsul's dispatch from his province. Addressed to the Senate and magistrates, such letters were read aloud to the senators in their meeting, and then, if they authorized it, read aloud again to the Roman People assembled outside. However, that order of procedure was not quite appropriate to the great commands of Pompey and Caesar in the sixties and fifties BC, all of which were conferred directly by order of the People against the Senate's wishes.

The constitutional position was made very clear by Pompey himself in a letter to the Senate in 50 BC: his province and his army, he said, had been granted to him for the public good, and he would resign them only when those who granted them (the Roman People) wished to take them back. A change in protocol may even be detected in the addresses of later proconsuls' dispatches, 'to the magistrates, Senate, People, and *plebs* of Rome'.

Given all that background information, we are now better placed to understand the significance of one of the most famous prose texts in Roman literature, Caesar's *Commentaries* on the conquest of Gaul. When the People first gave him the Gallic command, Caesar had taunted his opponents in the Senate: 'now I'll trample on your heads!' His conquests were at the People's order and for the People's benefit, as he emphasized over and over in the first of his reports. Naturally, the *Commentaries* were reporting to them, not just to the Senate.

Readers of 'Caesar's *Gallic War*' in a modern translation read a single continuous narrative in seven chapters, one for each year from 58 to 52 BC (followed by Hirtius' later addition on 51–50); but that is not how the *Commentaries* were composed. The People's commander needed to report after each year's campaign, and in any case it is certain from internal evidence that book 2 was already 'published' before book 5 was written. Caesar spent the first four winters of his command, from 58–57 to 55–54 BC, holding assizes in Transpadane Italy, which was also part of his province. That must have been where each year's report was written and dispatched; in Rome, no doubt his agents Gaius Oppius and Lucius Balbus would arrange for its copying, distribution, and public reading.

The format was like a historical narrative rather than an ordinary proconsul's dispatch. Caesar wrote in the third person, not only to give the illusion of objectivity but also, perhaps, to avoid placing the burden of impersonating him on whoever had the task of reading his narrative to the People. As it was, they would be 'listening to history' only a few weeks or months after the events themselves had taken place, with 'Caesar' as much the hero of the drama as Scipio Africanus and Aemilius Paullus and Gaius Marius were of the great wars of the past.

In the spring of 53 BC, for the first time in five years, there was no report on the previous year's campaign: Caesar was too busy trying to recover from the disastrous attacks on his legions' winter camps. Probably 'books 5 and 6' were composed together when he was in north Italy during the winter of 53–52. For that more problematic narrative (the People were not used to hearing of major losses), and even more for the great story of the rebellion and defeat of Vercingetorix, perhaps composed at Bibracte in the winter of 52–51, Caesar now allowed himself some of the conventions of real history-writing, such as ethnographic excursuses and set-piece speeches which he could not possibly have heard.

The combined text of books 5 and 6 takes up fifty-three pages of the Oxford text; that of book 7 alone takes up fifty. The four earlier books are thirty-three, seventeen, thirteen, and nineteen pages respectively. Texts of that length were probably intended to be heard not by the People's assembly, standing in the Forum, but by an audience of citizens seated in a theatre. Although it can only be guesswork, we may reasonably suppose that Balbus and Oppius aimed to exploit the games of the Great Mother. Beginning on 4 April, they were the first of the annual sequence of *ludi scaenici*, the earliest opportunity of the year to get the Roman People all together. Besides, the Mother herself, traditionally a bringer of victory, was the goddess of Mount Ida, where Caesar's ancestors came from.

If that guess is correct, then the first three of the Gallic war commentaries were probably heard in an ad hoc theatre in the Forum. For the fourth, however, in April 54, the fifth and sixth in April 52, and the seventh in April 51, Caesar's agents must surely have used the great new permanent theatre built by the People's other champion, Caesar's ally and son-in-law Pompey the Great.

7.3. Caesar and Catullus

As we saw in the last chapter (Ch. 6.4 above), the great games for Victoria at the opening of Pompey's theatre took place in September 55 BC. Pompey was consul in that year; at his triumph six years earlier he had paraded a trophy representing the entire known world (*oikoumenē* in Greek, *orbis terrarum* in Latin), and now the temple that dominated the theatre carried an inscription recording Pompey's extension of the empire of the Roman People to the very limits of the world.

Caesar, meanwhile, his ally and father-in-law, was leading his legions beyond those limits, across the waters of Oceanus that formed the world's boundary. Of course it was all for the People's benefit: Britain was believed to be a source of gold and silver, and Caesar's officers and men expected to come home rich.

The third member of the popular alliance was Marcus Crassus, who had equally ambitious imperialist plans: his command in Syria would be a base to attack Parthia and annex all its territory as far as the Caspian and the Indian Ocean. Crassus himself was nearly 60, but his son Publius was a dashing commander with ambitions to emulate Cyrus, conqueror of Babylon, and Alexander the Great, whose conquests had reached as far as India.

Of course there was opposition. Such open acquisitiveness enabled the traditionally dominant aristocrats, no mean acquisitors themselves, to claim the moral high ground. Lucius Domitius Ahenobarbus, who had only been kept out of the consulship by strong-arm tactics, was now standing again, on the promise that he would get Caesar recalled from his command; and with Pompey and Crassus already at the tail-end of their year of office, he was getting plenty of support.

When Caesar brought his two legions back across the Channel about the middle of October in 55 BC, the report of his spectacular campaign in Britain was no doubt already on its way to Rome. Who carried it? Probably Mamurra, Caesar's chief of staff (*praefectus fabrum*), who had served earlier with Caesar in Spain, and before that with Pompey in the east. Certainly Mamurra was in Rome about that time, squandering Gallic gold and arrogantly exploiting the glamour of military success. And if he got there, as he surely intended to, before the *ludi plebeii* ended on 12 November, he had a fine tale to tell to the Roman People in the theatre: Caesar, not content with conquering the existing world, had found a new world and conquered that!

Not everyone was impressed. One young man who resented Mamurra as unwelcome competition was the brilliantly versatile poet and playwright whose treatise on mime-writing was quoted in the previous chapter (Ch. 6.5 above). Gaius Valerius Catullus was a dangerous enemy, a writer not only of satirical stage-plays but also of invective poems short enough to be easily learned and chanted in the Forum. With over four months to wait before the next theatre games, the latter mode was called for now, and Catullus used it with no inhibition at all.

Here he is, attacking first Pompey and then Caesar as the sources of Mamurra's disappearing fortune, and ending with the conservatives' charge that the People's champions had destroyed the republic:

> Who can watch this? Who but a pervert, a glutton, and a gambler can endure Mamurra getting all the fat that used to belong to long-haired Gaul and Britain? Pansy Romulus, you'll watch this and do nothing? He's going to saunter through everyone's bedrooms, overbearing and overflowing like a white dove [of Venus], or Adonis? Pansy Romulus, you'll watch this and do nothing? You're a pervert, a glutton, and a gambler!
>
> And you, Commander One-and-Only, is it for this that you've been in the furthest island of the west—so that that shagged-out prick of yours could eat his way through twenty or thirty million? That's real left-handed generosity! Hasn't he done enough screwing and stuffing? First of all he shredded his inheritance, then the booty from Pontus and then from Spain, as the gold-bearing river Tagus

knows—and now there are fears for his Gallic and British loot. For heaven's sake, why do you keep him? What's he good for, except swallowing fat fortunes? Father- and son-in-law, you [*text corrupt*] of the city, is it for this that you've ruined everything?

Catullus 29

He followed that up with a series of squibs on 'The Prick' (*Mentula*), mocking Mamurra's expensive mistress (ten thousand? she should look in the mirror), Mamurra's country estates (pity they can't support his expenses), Mamurra's literary ambitions (the Muses chuck him off their sacred mountain), in fact everything about him (just one big menacing Prick!). The news got back to Caesar, who wasn't pleased. Catullus didn't care: 'Once again, Commander One-and-Only, you're going to be cross with my innocent iambics.'

Like his good friend Licinius Calvus, Catullus was quite prepared to go for Caesar himself on a personal level:

The shameless pansies get on fine, pathic Mamurra and Caesar too. No wonder—equal brand-marks on them both, one from the city, one from Formiae, are stamped in deep and won't be washed away. Diseased alike, each other's twins, two little intellectuals on one little bed, you can't tell which is more greedily adulterous. Companionable rivals of the girls, the shameless pansies get on fine!

Catullus 57

What happened next is reported by Caesar's biographer, as an example of his political pragmatism:

Caesar made no secret of the fact that Valerius Catullus had inflicted on him a permanent mark of infamy with his lines about Mamurra; but when Catullus apologized he invited him to dinner the same day, and continued as before to accept the hospitality of Catullus' father.

Suetonius
Diuus Iulius 73

Where did that dinner take place? Certainly not in Rome.

Catullus came from Verona. To be exact, his home was the island or peninsula of Sirmio in lake Garda, at the western extreme of Verona's extensive territory. Evidently Caesar was in the habit of staying as a guest at that beautiful site when he went through the Transpadane part of his province each winter to hold the assizes. We know Catullus cared deeply about family ties, and we can be sure he was back at Sirmio every year for the family-reunion festival (*Caristia*) on 22 February. We can be equally sure that his father was furious at this public humiliation of their famous guest.

Caesar meanwhile had his own problems. His enemy Ahenobarbus was now consul, and news had come in of attacks on the very furthest part of his province, Illyricum on the eastern Adriatic coast. So in January, while the ships were being built for the proper invasion of Britain that summer, he made the necessary journey across Europe (in modern terms, from Boulogne to Dubrovnik), taking in the Transpadane assizes en route and no doubt dictating his fourth set of commentaries as he went. Having sorted out the Illyricum problem, he was back in Transpadane territory by late May, writing flattering letters to prominent people in Rome and authorizing a huge public building programme to be paid for with the profits of conquest.

What matters for the argument of this chapter is that in the middle of all these preoccupations Caesar thought it worthwhile to receive a penitent poet, accept his apology, and treat him with conspicuous generosity. He did the same for Calvus, but that was to be expected: Calvus was an orator as well as a poet. If he needed Catullus too on his side, it was because Catullus too was a significant public figure.

7.4. Catullus 61–64

When Catullus died young a few years later (we last hear of him in 53 BC), there was 'public mourning' at his funeral. So at least we are told in the biographical sketch that introduces the first and second printed editions of his poems (Venice 1472, Rome 1475), and it is likely that the information derives ultimately from Suetonius' *De poetis*, possibly still extant as late as the 1450s.

Modern scholarship neglects this evidence, preferring to believe in a Catullus who shunned the crowd and wrote only for *readers*. Here is a thoughtful recent statement, by a very distinguished Latinist:

> Catullus...keeps reminding us that our only access to a poet is via his text, a medium which he is at pains to depict as at once compellingly vivid and evocative and yet profoundly opaque in its mimetic dimension. Even for his immediate and contemporary audience, let alone for a wider public or posterity, his stance on the question of textual access is consistently the same, as he invariably presents poems as being read by readers, rather than being recited by a poet to his audience.

Feeney 2012.43

It is not that Denis Feeney is wrong about Catullus' interest in 'the materiality of the book', but rather that he deals with one part of the poet's 'representation' as if it necessarily ruled out every other. If the Roman public mourned Catullus, the Roman public must have known him well.

One single copy of a collection of poems entitled 'The Book of Catullus of Verona' survived from the ancient world. When, how, and by whom it was put together are questions to which there is no certain answer. It is structured in three parts, of which the first and third (in modern editions poems 1–60 and 69–116) consist of short pieces in lyric, iambic, or elegiac metre on a very wide range of subjects. There are poems of love and hate and jealousy, celebrations of friends, denigrations of foes, jokes, anecdotes, letters, even a hymn. The longest is only thirty-four lines, and most are much shorter than that; references to writing-tablets (Ch. 1.2 above) suggest that that was where they were normally written down.

Many of these poems were evidently meant to be read aloud at parties ('in the fun and the wine' is a recurring phrase); on the other hand, the hymn to Diana was self-evidently for public performance, and the satirical pieces too seem to presuppose a wide audience. See, for instance, Catullus' warning to a hapless rival (poem 40):

> Poor little Ravidus, what insanity is driving you into range of my iambics? What god improperly invoked is setting you up to pick a crazy quarrel? Do you really want to end up on the lips of the crowd? What are you after? Just to be famous, no matter how? You will be, since you've chosen to love my love—and it'll last a long time, as punishment.

Catullus 40

This was a poet who knew he could reach the general public.

The second part of the transmitted collection (poems 61–8) is much the most interesting in the evidence it implies for the Roman audience. Omitting poem 65, a twenty-five-line covering letter for the translation that follows, and dividing 'poem 68' into two, as the different addressees require, we have eight long poems in four different metres, their lengths varying from forty lines (68a) to 404 (64). Of these at least the first three, and perhaps the first four, are best understood as scripts for performance.

The first is the easiest (poem 61). It happens to be the only work named in the 1472 biographical sketch of Catullus:

> He was particularly elegant in jests, but a man of great gravity on serious matters;
> he wrote erotic poems, and a marriage-song to Manlius.

'Manlius' was a patrician bridegroom, a Manlius Torquatus whose ancient family is mentioned by the poet with due honour, and the text maps precisely on to what we know about the ceremony of aristocratic weddings in Rome. It is composed in lyric stanzas, presumably to be sung and danced.

In Latin, to marry a wife is to 'lead' her (*ducere*), or 'lead her away' (*deducere*), from her family home to your own; the wedding is, in essence, the evening procession that brings her from one garlanded house to the other. Torches are lit from the hearth in the bride's house; some are set up along the route, where there may also be wooden stands for the spectators; others are distributed to the choruses of girls and boys in the street outside.

The pipe-player strikes up the *hymenaeus*; a solo singer begins the hymn that summons the marriage-god ('Come, Hymen Hymenaeus') and then brings in the girls' chorus to celebrate the deity and the institution of marriage. When they have sung, the solo singer resumes, calling for the doors to be opened and encouraging the bride to come out. All that takes twenty-four stanzas of Catullus' text.

The remaining twenty-three stanzas take place at the bridegroom's house. At first we are in the street outside, as the solo singer sees the procession coming and calls on the boys' choir to sing; when they have delivered the traditional 'Fescennine' mockery and advice to the bride and groom, the solo singer directs the bride's reception into the house. The final part is the *epithalamium* proper, sung at the nuptial chamber itself as the bride is taken within, the groom follows, and the girls who have escorted her all the way close the doors on them.

The choral songs in the street, and the procession between the two houses, were of course a public occasion for all the neighbourhood to enjoy. Catullus' 'poem 61' was evidently a script for public performance—but in saying so we must reject a very authoritative scholarly consensus. Here, for instance, is C. J. Fordyce in 1961:

> Catullus' poem is clearly not a hymn to be sung on the actual occasion of the marriage which provides its theme. There is no ground for distributing the lines between two choruses, one of girls and one of boys, or for assigning the successive parts of the poem to successive stances, and attempts to synchronize the lines with the stages of the ceremony are quite unconvincing.

Fordyce 1961.236

I find that a quite baffling judgement, but here is Oliver Lyne, another excellent Latinist, who explicitly endorses Fordyce's dogma:

> Poem 61, in stanzas of glyconics and a pherecratean, seems to have been written with a real Roman wedding in mind; yet it too is a complex imaginative enactment rather than an actual hymenaeal or epithalamium.... It is essentially dramatic— things *happen* in the course of the poem—so that in its effect, or for part of its effect, it is a *narrative*—much of it Grecizing fancy.

Lyne 1978.175, 183

That view seems to me both improbable a priori (why should Manlius be invited to imagine his own wedding?) and illogical as an argument; since the lyric form implies a text to be sung, the onus of proof is on those who say it can't have been.

The next long poem (62) is also for choral song at a wedding, but it is very different. It consists of antiphonal texts for two choruses, of young men and of young women, competitively praising marriage and virginity respectively after a banquet at the bridegroom's house, as they await the arrival of the bride. The occasion is not specific (references to Olympus and Oeta suggest a Greek context), the bride and groom are not named, and the tone is rather brutally insistent on the bride's duty of submission. What is the poem *for*? Eduard Fraenkel's judgement in his classic commentary, that 'it moves in the free sphere of poetry', is not particularly helpful.

Again, remember the onus of proof. Other things being equal, a poem in dramatic form should be written for performance; and the fact that the choruses were competing for a prize may suggest performance at a festival. What sort of festival, what sort of competition, the limits of our evidence prevent us from knowing. Another possibility, equally untestable, is that this wedding was part of a play on a Greek subject. We know that Catullus was interested in Greek myth as a subject for mime as well as tragedy (Ch. 6.5 above), and three of the four drama titles attributable to him are Greek in form. It could even be the choral part of a performance otherwise danced.

'Poem 63' is in Galliambics, the staccato rhythm of the Galli, eunuch acolytes of the Great Mother, in their frenetic dance to the sound of drums and cymbals and the deep-toned Phrygian pipe. It is in the form of a hymn, a story illustrating the divinity's power concluded by a prayer. The narrative is structured around speeches:

1–11. Attis disembarks on the forested coast of Phrygia. Driven by madness, he castrates himself. Now an initiate of the Great Mother, he takes up the drum to sing to his companions (only now mentioned).
12–26. *Attis' song: come on, Gallae (feminine), up to the wild forest of the goddess, to dance in her mysteries!*
27–38. They rush headlong to Ida, the goddess's sacred mountain, and fall asleep in exhaustion.
39–49. Attis wakes at dawn. Now sane, he understands what he has done. In despair, he returns to the shore and stares out to sea.
50–73. *Attis' speech of repentance, addressing his lost home across the seas.*
74–7. Cybele hears, and looses one of the lions from her chariot.
78–82. *Cybele's instruction to the lion: drive him back into the forest!*
83–90. The lion attacks. Attis flees from the shore to the forest, and lifelong slavery.
91–3. *Prayer to the great goddess: drive other men mad, not me!*

To understand this extraordinary text, we must respect what the metre implies: it is a script for dancers. Attis, of course, is the protagonist throughout; the companions disappear without explanation at the mid-point, where the choreography moves from the team dance of the *chorus* to Attis' solo and then to the *pas de deux* of Attis and the lion. It must surely have been for performance at the games of the Great Mother (*ludi Megalenses*).

When we try to imagine the demands made on the lead dancer, who also had to sing two contrasting arias, we should bear in mind the evidence for the development of dance-drama in the following generation. A fragment from Suetonius' history of the *ludi* happens to survive in St Jerome's *Chronica*, under 22/1 BC:

> Earlier performers used to dance and sing themselves. Pylades, the Cilician 'all-mime' [*pantomimus*] was the first at Rome to have a chorus and piper accompany him.
>
> Jerome *Chronica* Ol. 189.3

That first sentence is repeated in Lucian's essay *On Dance*, where the innovation is then explained more clearly:

> Because the heavy breathing caused by their movement disturbed their singing, it seemed better that others should sing as accompaniment for them.
>
> Lucian *Saltatio* 30

It looks as if Catullus' 'poem 63' was written for a virtuoso of the pre-Pylades era.

'Poem 64' is normally regarded nowadays as the defining example of a literary genre which ancient authors never refer to, 'the mannered miniature *epos* which we conveniently call epyllion'. Rather than just assigning it to an unattested modern category, it might be worth asking whether it too could be a performance script.

We need to remember, first, that filling the huge stage of Pompey's theatre demanded music and dance, and not just words; second, that the star singer-dancers of that age were female as well as male, *mimae* as well as *mimi*; and third, that eroticizing Greek myth had been a feature of the Latin stage for at least 300 years (Ch. 3.1 above, Fig. 14). Literary scholarship sees 'epyllion' as just a form of hexameter epic—'that brief, highly-wrought *epos* which more or less ostentatiously dissociated itself from traditional *epos*'. But perhaps its episodic and discontinuous style could also be evidence for the real world, where there were dancers in the theatre and glamorous showgirls who had even senators in thrall.

So let's imagine Catullus' poem 64, 'The wedding of Peleus and Thetis', as it might have been performed. There is a narrator, maybe the poet, maybe an actor, maybe singing, maybe reciting; there is a large *corps de ballet*, male and female; there are solo and small-group singers, male and female; and there is a *prima donna assoluta* whose role explodes into the narrative as a spectacular *tour de force*.

Lines 1–30, the meeting of Peleus and Thetis. Dancers on stage: Peleus and the Argonauts, Thetis and the bare-breasted Nereids, gradually receding to leave the two principals alone together.

Lines 31–51, preparation for the wedding. The dancers return, now as Thessalian rustics, miming awe and wonder at the wealth of the king's palace. By the time the narrator describes the marriage-bed, and the scene embroidered on its coverlet, they have left the stage and the music has totally changed.

Lines 52–75, Ariadne abandoned. Enter the star actress, miming grief and despair, her clothes dropping off her as she stares numbly out to sea.

Lines 76–115, flashback to Ariadne and Theseus in love. A *pas de deux*, the young girl besotted, the killing of the Minotaur, the labyrinth dance.

Lines 116–23, a narrative catch-up, allowing a costume change.

Lines 124–206, Ariadne on the shore again, not static now but hyperactive, delivering her great aria, all seventy lines of it, to the heedless winds. Gods, give me justice for Theseus' betrayal! As she leaves the stage, the thunder rolls for Jupiter's assent.

Lines 207–37, flashback to Theseus' instructions from his father. Another aria, this time for a male singer, expressing old Aegeus' doomed love for his son.

Lines 238–50, Theseus' forgetfulness and Aegeus' suicide. At the end, Theseus in grief-stricken Athens and Ariadne on the shore of her desert island share the narrative for a moment, and no doubt also share the stage.

Lines 251–64, Iacchus and his *thiasus*. Wild Dionysiac music, wild Dionysiac dancing by satyrs, Sileni, and bacchants. They are looking for Ariadne, but she has already gone; the deafening drums and horns mark the end of the inserted narrative.

Lines 265–302, Peleus' palace again, where the mortal guests depart and the gods arrive bearing gifts. Two of the dancers play Chiron the centaur, another impersonates a river-god carrying trees.

Lines 303–83, the Fates (*Parcae*) spin their threads and sing the wedding song. Sinister music marks a deliberately ominous narrative; in the usual version of the story the wedding song was provided by Apollo and the Muses. As the three crones sing in unison, a solo dancer mimes first the murderous Achilles and then the innocent victim Polyxena. So on with the wedding! But the story is over.

Lines 384–408, narrator's epilogue. Yes, once the gods used to visit mortals, but not anymore. Offended at the violence and immorality that now infect the earth, they refuse even to come into contact with the light of day.

'A man of great gravity on serious matters', Catullus knew that the *ludi scaenici* were not only to entertain the Roman People—and he certainly did that—but also to instruct them. With a bit of imagination, the long poems in the surviving collection can offer us a glimpse of how he may have reached his Roman audience.

7.5. The Greek Stage in Rome

The gods might well be offended at what happened in January 52 BC. A prominent popular politician was murdered in cold blood on the public highway; and honourable men like Cato, Brutus, and Cicero praised the killer as a patriot and a benefactor. The Roman People disagreed, and at the funeral they made their point by burning down the Senate-house.

7.5. The Greek Stage in Rome

Pompey restored order, consul for the third time, and without a colleague, but the Fates had already spun their threads. Caesar's daughter, Pompey's wife, was dead, and so were Marcus Crassus and his glamorous son and much of the army that had set out to conquer as far as India. The conservative oligarchy sensed things moving their way, and it was clear what Caesar could expect when he came back from Gaul.

The People tried to protect Caesar by giving him special permission to go straight from his province to a second consulship (to which they would elect him *in absentia*), but the aristocrats frustrated that. They persuaded Pompey to 'protect the republic' by force of arms, and defied the People's tribunes with a declaration of martial law. Two of the tribunes fled to Caesar, who marched south across the Rubicon to protect their authority and 'free the Roman People from the factious domination of the oligarchs'. The die was cast.

That was in January 49 BC. Three and a half years later, the Roman People believed (wrongly, the Fates were still spinning) that the civil war was over and their champion had prevailed. One of their champions, that is: Pompey was dead, having chosen the wrong side. After Caesar's triumph, the most spectacular ever, in September 46 BC there were games for the dedication of the temple of his divine ancestress, Venus Genetrix. They took place in two theatres, one for Latin and one for Greek. Caesar himself presided over the first, and put his great-nephew Gaius Octavius, just 17 years old, in charge of the second.

There is good, but neglected, evidence for 'Greek games' (*ludi Graeci*) at Rome in the second and first centuries BC, and we even have a posthumous message from one of the performers, a young freedwoman called Licinia Eucharis. Her epitaph is in iambic *senarii*, the metre of stage dialogue:

You there, whose wandering eye looks on the houses of death! Halt your step and read my inscription to the end. My father's love gave it to his daughter where the remains of my body were to be laid down. Here, when my fresh youth was flowering in the arts and attaining glory as my age increased, the gloomy day of my fate came too quickly, and denied breath to my life from then on.

Skilled and taught almost by the Muses' hand, I who recently graced with my dancing the games of the nobles and played the lead before the People on the Greek stage—see how the cruel Fates with their song have laid down the ashes of my body in the tomb.

The help of my patroness, care, love, applause, and honour are mute at the body's cremation, are silent in death. A daughter, I left grief to my father; born later, I went to the day of death before him. Twice seven birthdays the eternal house of Dis holds fast in the darkness here with me. As you leave, please pray that the earth may be light on me.

CIL 6.10096

Already a rising star at 14—but what did she appear in before the People on the Greek stage?

Casual allusions in Cicero and Varro may help us to guess. They had the classics of Syracusan drama in their heads—not only Epicharmus and Rhinthon (Chs. 2.3, 3.2 above) but also Sophron, the supposed inventor of 'mime'—and the easiest explanation is that they were familiar with them from the stage. The last of the great Syracusans was Theocritus, who made his name in Alexandria in the 270s BC; like Sophron, he wrote 'mimes', and unlike Sophron his works (or some of them) survive to be used as evidence.

Modern Theocritus scholarship is cautious, perhaps even evasive, about performance. But most of the poems are dramatic in form, sometimes with a narrative frame that makes the narrator a character too, and even the short epic-narrative poems feature long speeches not necessarily spoken by the narrator himself. 'Poem 27', a rustic dialogue of two young lovers, would have provided a good role for Eucharis.

Two texts in particular presuppose dramatic action. 'Poem 15', the dialogue of the two Syracusan ladies going to the Adonis festival at Ptolemy's palace, has a couple of extra speaking parts in the crowd scene, and forty-five of its 148 lines are devoted to the lament for Adonis sung at the festival itself. Catullus evidently knew the song, and may well have seen the whole little drama performed. 'Poem 2', on the other hand, is a dramatic monologue, as Simaetha casts her moonlight spells to bring back the lover who has spurned her. On this we have some precious external evidence, in the passage on prayers and incantations in Pliny's encyclopedia:

> There is no one who isn't afraid of being bound by magic spells.... That's what lies behind the erotic incantations imitated by Theocritus among the Greeks and by Catullus and most recently Virgil among the Romans.

Pliny *Natural History* 28.19

Only two words survive of the spells of Catullus' sorceress, referring to her magic wheel; the spells of Virgil's sorceress are sung by Alphesiboeus in the eighth *Eclogue*, a performance within a performance.

Publius Vergilius Maro ('Virgil') was a Transpadane like Catullus, but from a humbler background; the proconsul was never a guest at *his* father's house. Although we don't know when he first came to Rome, the games in September 46 after Caesar's triumph were not something an aspiring poet of 23 would be likely to miss. He described his own poetic beginnings as Thalea, the Muse of comic drama, playing with Syracusan verse. It is quite possible that he first made the acquaintance of his great model Theocritus at the *ludi Graeci* presided over by young Octavius.

7.6. The Ides of March, and After

In late 45 or early 44 BC the Roman People granted Caesar the same sacrosanct inviolability that protected their tribunes: any violence towards him would count as sacrilege against the gods. In addition, all senators and *equites* swore a solemn oath to guard his safety. He dismissed his bodyguard, and in March 44 he was killed, stabbed to death in a Senate meeting by men who thought of themselves not as assassins or oath-breakers but as liberators of the republic. The Roman People demanded vengeance.

Cicero, once Caesar's friend and collaborator, was delighted by his murder. In the hope that the republic was back to 'normal', he threw himself into active politics again, attacking Caesar's right-hand man, the consul Antony, in the interests of the assassins and their sympathizers. His last attested speech to the Roman People was on 1 January 43 BC, when Antony was besieging Decimus Brutus, one of the leaders of the conspiracy, at Mutina. Called to the Rostra by one of the tribunes, Cicero invited the People to remember that Decimus was 'a Brutus, born for your freedom', and to resist the threat of slavery by declaring war on Antony. What their reaction was is not reliably recorded.

Meanwhile, young Octavius, adopted in Caesar's will, had set about claiming his inheritance and his filial duty of revenge. As he himself put it many years later:

> when I was 19 years old I raised an army on my own initiative and at my own expense, and with it I freed the republic from the domination of a faction.

Augustus *Res gestae* 1.1

The Roman People voted him the consulship, and then, when he was barely 20, elected him to supreme power with Antony and Lepidus, as 'triumvirs for the establishment of the republic', to bring the conspirators to justice or destroy them.

On 7 December 43 BC Cicero was killed on the triumvirs' orders. On 1 January 42 Caesar was officially consecrated as a god. On 23 October 42 Antony and the young Caesar (né Octavius) completed the defeat of the conspirators' armies at Philippi. At one end of the Roman Forum, work was starting on the site of the new temple of Divus Julius; at the other, the head and hands of Cicero were nailed up on the Rostra.

8

Rethinking the Classics

42–28 BC

Later blamed conveniently on Antony alone, the atrocity of Cicero's death was never forgotten. For us, it marks another change in the nature of our evidence. The huge corpus of Cicero's works—so many of his speeches, so much of his correspondence—provides the modern historian with a privileged insight into the day-to-day business of social and political life that is unique in the history of the ancient world. With that gone, normal conditions resume: the social and political history of the 'triumviral period' is desperately difficult to piece together.

Nevertheless, many texts survive. In Latin prose, we have Sallust's two historical monographs and extracts from his *Histories*, three dialogues on farming by the octogenarian Marcus Varro, and a selection of short biographies from Cornelius Nepos' *De uiris illustribus*; in Greek prose, fifteen of the forty books of Diodorus Siculus' universal history, and thirty-six short mythological narratives written by Parthenius of Nicaea for the poet Cornelius Gallus to turn into hexameters or elegiacs. As for poetry, the works of Gallus are almost wholly lost, but great works do survive—the *Eclogues* and *Georgics* of Virgil, and Horace's *Epodes* and *Satires*. Can they tell us anything about the Roman audience?

8.1. Virgil's *Eclogues*

The *Eclogues* provide the clearest evidence. Seven of the ten poems are dramatic in form like their Theocritean models (two of them with a narrative frame), and the later Virgilian commentators knew that they were sung on stage. Virgil's singing herdsmen might also dance, or provide a scene for dancers; once again, the wide stage of Pompey's theatre comes to mind.

Eclogue 6 is in narrative form, with Silenus' song reported in indirect speech, but the poet as narrator identifies himself as Tityrus, one of the characters from the bucolic dialogues. On at least one occasion we know the poem was sung by

Rome's leading mime-actress; with Apollo opening and closing the action, it may well have been composed for the *ludi Apollinares*.

Apollo featured also in *Eclogue* 4, which was neither drama nor narrative but prophecy: notionally addressing the incoming consul (Pollio, 40 BC), the poet as *uates* promised the Romans an escape from their 'sinful' present into an age of peace divinely guaranteed. Once again the Fates were spinning, but this time, in a conscious reversal of the Catullan scenario, they would bring about Apollo's golden age.

That would be a long time coming. The republic was terminally divided, along a deadly fault-line opened up years before by the murder of Tiberius Gracchus and the brutal regime of Sulla (Ch. 5.4 above). Caesar had done his best to heal the rift: victorious in the civil war that was forced on him, he had treated his aristocratic opponents with conspicuous clemency. He had also announced his rejection of Sulla's two disastrous precedents, the proscription and summary execution of his personal enemies and the dispossession of entire communities to reward his soldiers. But as soon as they had the chance, the aristocrats broke their oath and killed him anyway. Drawing their own conclusions, the triumvirs declared an end to clemency. Both proscription and mass dispossession were duly applied in the war of vengeance.

The Roman People had granted Caesar the same sacrosanctity that should have protected Gracchus. For them, the murder of Caesar was never just a crime; it was an offence against the gods, a pollution that rendered those responsible accursed. No doubt they took the view that the proscription victims were just the arrogant rich, tainted by sympathy with the assassins (if not conspirators themselves), and that their great estates were rightly forfeit to citizens who had served in the legions to carry out the People's sentence. But now the assassins were dead; the young Caesar was back in Italy supervising the redistribution of land, and suddenly the issues were less clear-cut.

Rome was full of desperate refugees. The mass-expropriation policy meant that the dispossessed were not just the great landowners but thousands of small farmers as well, who now came to Rome to complain of brutality and injustice. Equally unnerving were the victorious veterans themselves, in Rome to insist on delivery of what they had been promised, often insolent and undisciplined, throwing their weight around at the theatre games. That was what lay behind the bitter-sweet conversations of Tityrus and Meliboeus in Virgil's first *Eclogue*, and Lycidas and Moeris in his ninth.

8.2. Sallust

The old aristocracy were hoping to turn the clock back to a pre-Caesarian republic where they would again be dominant. With Lucius Antonius in 41 BC they did what Caesar had never done and turned Italy itself into a war zone. When that failed, they supported Pompey's son Sextus in his naval blockade, to cause famine at Rome. They must have been pleased when the starving citizens rioted at the Plebeian Games in 40 BC, stoning the young Caesar in the Forum until forcibly dispersed by Antony's soldiers.

At some time close to this low point in the People's fortunes Sallustius Crispus, a senator with a questionable past, presented them with a way of making sense of recent history. We know it as 'Sallust's *Catiline*'.

The narrative, when we get to it, is of events that took place in 64–62 BC. But since it begins as the study of a political conspiracy, and ends as the description of a civil-war battlefield in Italy, with repeated references along the way to the greed of Sulla's veterans and the despair of those they had dispossessed, the world of 44–41 BC must have been constantly evoked for Sallust's audience.

That he was indeed writing for an audience, not just for readers of books, is clear from his own words. He opens with a discursive comparison between the life of action and the life of the mind, in which the case that interests him is engaging in politics versus writing about politics:

> It is splendid to do good things for the republic, and to *say* good things is not inappropriate either. Distinction in peace and distinction in war are equally permissible, and many are praised both of those who have done things and those who have written of others' doings. Although it is by no means equal glory that follows the writer and the doer of deeds, nevertheless, to me at least, writing about deeds seems particularly difficult, first of all because what is done must be matched by what is *said*.

Sallust *Catiline* 3.1–2

He later comes back to the subject, in contrasting the Romans with the Athenians, whose deeds were magnified by their historians even beyond their great deserts:

> But the Roman People never had that advantage, because all the cleverest among them were also the busiest; no one used just his mind and not his body; all the best men preferred to do things rather than *say* them, to have their good deeds praised by others rather than themselves narrate the deeds of others.

Sallust *Catiline* 8.5

The recurring words are *dicere* and *dicta*; historical narration was a matter of 'saying'. And the speaker might also be a listener:

> It so happens that when reading, or hearing, of the many glorious deeds done by the Roman People, at home and on campaign by sea and land, I liked to focus on what above all had made such great enterprises possible.

Sallust *Catiline* 53.2

The history of Rome was a subject expounded, and understood, by the spoken word no less than the written. But where, and for whom, is not obvious.

Sallust's introductory disquisition was all about fame and reputation and how they were acquired. It was also an apologia for his own inglorious public career. Ten years earlier he had been one of the People's tribunes, speaking out against political murder and the protection of those who committed it. Expelled from the Senate by aristocratic censors in 50 BC, he had regained his position after Caesar's victory, but lost his reputation by notorious profiteering as governor of Africa in 45. Whereupon he retired from politics:

> It was not my intention to waste good leisure in sloth and idleness, nor indeed to spend my time devoted to agriculture or hunting, activities appropriate to slaves. Instead, I returned to the original enthusiasm from which evil ambition had kept me away, and resolved to write down the deeds of the Roman People—selectively, as each seemed worthy of being remembered—for the particular reason that my mind was free from political hope, fear, and partisanship.

Sallust *Catiline* 4.1–2

Sallust's repeated emphasis on the Roman People can hardly be accidental. It was their good opinion he had to regain.

Of course we should not imagine an audience as big as for the *Eclogues*. What Sallust offered was not Arcadian escapism but a serious historical analysis of how things had come to this state. Even so, we know that ordinary people were interested in history, and no doubt the desperate Romans of the late 40s BC wanted explanations more than ever.

Sallust's explanation began with a general maxim: when the mental and physical vigour required to create an empire in war is not also deployed to maintain it in peace, then everything starts to go wrong. In particular:

> when idleness has come in instead of hard work, and lust and arrogance instead of self-control and fairness, fortune changes along with behaviour.

Sallust *Catiline* 2.5

That had happened in Rome a century earlier, after the destruction of Carthage in 146 BC:

> There grew a lust first for money and then for power; those were the building materials, so to speak, of every kind of evil. For avarice destroyed honesty, integrity, and all the other virtues; instead of them, it taught arrogance, cruelty, neglect of the gods, the belief that everything can be bought.

Sallust *Catiline* 10.3–4

So power passed to the acquisitive, the 'powerful few' who effectively monopolized positions of authority and privilege. The republic had been corrupted by an oligarchy devoted to its own enrichment.

For his next historical work, the *Jugurthine War*, Sallust went back to an earlier stage in the process, where responsibility could be more clearly assigned:

> I am going to write the war which the Roman People waged with Jugurtha, king of the Numidians [111–105 BC]—first because it was a great and fierce war with varied

success, and then because it was at that time that the first challenge was offered to the arrogance of the aristocracy, a conflict that convulsed everything, human and divine, and reached such a level of insanity that only warfare and the devastation of Italy could bring an end to civil strife.

<small>Sallust *Jugurthine War* 5.1–2</small>

If indeed it *had* brought an end to it. That was probably written about the same time as the fourth *Eclogue*; people needed to believe there was a better world to come.

The arrogance of the aristocracy was the recurring theme of Sallust's Jugurthine War narrative. It was the arrogance of those who believed that their own wishes were identical with the public good, the arrogance that had made Caesar's assassins think of themselves as liberators. In 40 BC, the men who shared that view were hoping that Sextus Pompeius in Sicily would bring them back to the power they thought was their right, and the lands they had lost to the veterans. The young Caesar would soon have another civil war on his hands.

During the four difficult years of the Sicilian war (39–36 BC), Sallust brought before the Roman audience an ongoing narrative of the post-Sullan period, the time when aristocratic abuse of power was at its most blatant. Taken together, the *Jugurthine War* and the new *Histories* enabled the Roman People to hear again their champions of the previous two generations—Gaius Memmius in 111 BC, Gaius Marius in 108, Marcus Lepidus in 78, Licinius Macer in 73—urging them to be worthy of their ancestors and resist the oligarchs' usurpation of the republic. It was a reminder of what Caesar had stood for, and why the civil wars were still going on.

Sallust died in 36 or 35 BC. He probably lived just long enough to see the young Caesar, now 28, return victorious after the long war and receive from the grateful People the same sacrosanct immunity they had granted his father. It seemed things were back to where they had been before the Ides of March.

8.3. Horace's *Satires*

Political morality and personal morality are different things, and Sallust's playboy lifestyle was always a poor match for the gravity of his message. In the city that loved to criticize (Cicero's description of Rome) there were plenty of satirical observers who were happy to point a finger. One of them was Quintus Horatius Flaccus ('Horace').

Unlike his great satirical predecessors Lucilius and Varro (Ch. 5.4 above), Horace was not socially or financially secure—or at least not at first. Many years later he portrayed his young self as distinctly unprivileged: after a good education in Rome, he had gone to Athens to study philosophy

> but the difficult times [42 BC] took me out of that pleasant place, and the tumult of civil war brought me untrained to arms that would be no match for the strength of Caesar Augustus. As soon as Philippi got me out of that, humbled, wings clipped, paternal farm and homestead lost, reckless poverty drove me to writing verses.
>
> Horace *Epistles* 2.2.46–52

He was a freedman's son, as nobody let him forget, and he used his talent to make his way in the world. Eventually, probably in 37, he was taken into the patronage of the young Caesar's luxurious friend Gaius Maecenas, and from then on his troubles were over. Before that, however, it is hard to see how he could have made a living from poetry except by selling his work to the aediles for the annual *ludi*.

What Horace wrote in the thirties BC is known to us from three published collections, two of hexameter satires and one of (mostly shorter) 'iambic' epodes. There are thirty-five poems in all, of which eight are in dramatic form; another is a *uates*-poet's address to the People, like the fourth *Eclogue*; and yet another is a moral homily addressed to an explicitly plural audience. So when the poet refers to the ears of the listener, we need not assume, as modern commentators do, that he is merely offering book-readers the illusion of an oral performance. An oral performance is what it was in the first instance—but not on a big scale.

Horace referred to his satires as 'like conversation', a poetic genre that didn't soar but walked, or even crept along the ground. We are not dealing here with music or dance, or the great stage of Pompey's theatre.

In the old days, young aristocrats had lavished huge sums on the games they gave as aediles, so that the People would later vote them into praetorships and consulships. Now many of the young aristocrats were dead or in exile, and most of the great families had lost their wealth in the proscriptions. That economic revolution would have been reversed if Brutus and Cassius had won at Philippi in 42, or Sextus Pompeius in Sicily in 36. Horace, who took part with his patron in a late stage of the Sicilian war, knew that if it went the other way he would be in exile himself. But the young Caesar's luck held; there was no comeback for the old nobility, and lavish spending on the games would have to come from somewhere else.

In the thirties and twenties BC, the expense of the aedileship made people reluctant to hold the office at all—and those who did may have been glad to hire low-maintenance poets instead of expensive dancers and musicians. With that complicated context in mind, we may try to puzzle out what Horace himself says about his audience and his readers.

Satires 1.4 begins with a resounding tribute to the great Athenian comic dramatists, who exposed without inhibition the vices and crimes of their fellow-citizens. 'Lucilius derives wholly from them', and at Rome too people with a bad conscience have reason to fear the satirist:

> 'Keep well away, he's got hay on his horns [like a dangerous bull]. As long as he gets a laugh, he won't spare either himself or any of his friends. Whatever he's once smeared on to his pages, he'll be dying for all the people coming back from the bakehouse and the water-fountain to know about it, even the boys and the old ladies.'

Horace *Satires* 1.4.34–8

Like Eupolis, Cratinus, and Aristophanes, Roman satirists too were addressing the entire citizen body.

Horace claims to be not like that. He distances himself from Lucilius, not only in writing better but also in not making personal attacks:

> Fierce Sulcius and Caprius are on the prowl, horribly hoarse, with their books in their hands. Muggers are afraid of them both, but no one who lives properly and keeps his hands clean need pay any attention to either. Suppose you were like the muggers Caelius and Birrius—well, I'm no Caprius or Sulcius, so why be afraid of me?

Horace *Satires* 1.4.65–70

Of course it would be a help if we knew what Horace's audience knew about Sulcius and Caprius (or even if they were real names). The context seems to require that they were satirists, hoarse from recitation and with written copies of their work always available. Horace goes on:

> No shop or column would have *my* books for the hands of the crowd or Tigellius Hermogenes to stain with sweat. And I don't recite to anyone except friends, and then only when forced to—not just anywhere or to just anybody. There are many who recite their writings in the middle of the Forum, or at the baths; the enclosed space gives the voice a lovely resonance! This pleases the inane, but not those who wonder whether what they do lacks sense or could be better-timed.

Horace *Satires* 1.4.71–8

As for Horace, what *he* did (or so he tells us) was observe people's behaviour, draw moral lessons from it, and keep his mouth shut. 'And if I have time to spare, I waste a bit of paper.'

He came back to the subject in a later poem, insisting again on the difference between Lucilius and himself:

Horace *Satires* 1.10.37–9

> These things I play about with aren't meant to resound in the temple, in a competition with Tarpa judging, or to come back again and again as theatre shows.

His advice is not to waste effort trying to please the crowd, but be content with just a few readers.

Oblique, evasive, ironical, Horace is never going to provide modern historians with straightforward evidence for the Rome of his time. Part of what he was doing in these poems was boasting of his newly privileged status. Those who enjoyed Maecenas' Esquiline estate regarded themselves as 'far, far removed from the crowd', and Horace could afford to take a detached view of human folly while at ease on Maecenas' dining-couch or strolling in his colonnade. But that didn't last for long.

It is only in the first collection of satires that Horace refuses the Lucilian role of public critic: 'I'm afraid to recite to the crowd, because satirists aren't popular with those who deserve blame.' The second collection, however, begins with a quite different manifesto:

> Let no one harm me, I'm eager for peace. But if anyone gets me angry he'll regret it (better not touch me, I cry), and he'll be notorious, chanted throughout the city. . . . To put it briefly—whether a peaceful old age awaits me or death is circling round on black wings, whether rich or poor, in Rome or in exile (if luck so orders it), whatever my life's complexion, I will write.

Horace *Satires* 2.1.44–6, 57–60

The example he now cites is fearless Lucilius himself. So why is he no longer afraid of the people he'll offend? Because Caesar approves of him, and it is Caesar's judgement that matters.

Commander Caesar, son of the deified Julius (*Imperator Caesar Diui filius*), had ended the civil wars—or so he thought—with the defeat of Sextus Pompeius in Sicily, at the great naval battle of Naulochus. The People's cause had prevailed. Now that the seas were free for trade, and the import of grain in particular, the famine in Rome was over. Now that the allies of Caesar's assassins were defeated, the veterans could be confident that their farms would not be claimed back. Now the People must have the benefits of peace.

The commander himself had a war to fight in the Balkans (protecting the vulnerable north-east frontier), so his friend Maecenas, in an informal capacity, was looking after Rome and Italy. Naturally, anyone living at Maecenas' expense would be required to do his bit. It can hardly be a coincidence that the six Horatian satires in dramatic form are all in the second collection, and that in the last and most farcical of them the poet refers to watching the games. As always, the theatre games were for the entertainment and instruction of the Roman People. If impoverished aediles found it difficult to deliver that, no doubt wealthy Maecenas and his poet friends would be able to help out.

8.4. Virgil's *Georgics*

It was Marcus Agrippa, the young Caesar's oldest friend and closest ally, who trained and commanded the fleet that won at Naulochus. Now he turned his organizational skills to a great peacetime project, the repair and extension of

Rome's aqueduct system. No new aqueduct had been built for ninety years, and even the old ones were illegally tapped by the rich for their country estates before they reached the city. Agrippa's programme was a practical demonstration that the People's needs were now at last being taken seriously.

Just to make the point explicit, the new aqueduct Agrippa constructed was called Aqua Iulia. To mark the completion of the project in 33 BC, even though he had been consul four years earlier he took on the aedileship, a lesser magistracy but one directly responsible for the fabric of the city and the welfare of the citizens. Agrippa's own account of his year in office is quoted by the elder Pliny:

> Agrippa in his aedileship, having added the Aqua Virgo [Pliny's error for the Aqua Iulia] and re-channelled and repaired the other aqueducts, created 700 basins, 500 free-running pipes, and 130 distribution tanks, many of them magnificently decorated; and on these constructions he erected 300 bronze or marble statues and 400 marble columns. All this was done in the space of a year. He himself, in the record of his aedileship, adds that games were held on fifty-nine days, and 170 bath-houses were provided free of charge.

Pliny *Natural History* 36.121

Those 59 days probably represent the regular annual games for which all six aediles were normally responsible, the *ludi Megalenses* (7 days), *Ceriales* (8), *Florales* (6), *Romani* (16), *Victoriae* (7), and *plebeii* (14), with an extra day added, perhaps in honour of victorious Caesar's return from Illyricum.

They were not just ordinary games. Agrippa had tokens thrown out over the heads of the audience, redeemable for cash or clothes or other goods, and hired barbers so that anyone could have a shave or haircut free. Going unshaven and letting your hair grow was a sign of mourning, all too familiar during the civil wars; now Agrippa's games were saying goodbye to all that, as the water ran free and the fountains played.

Meanwhile, another great peacetime project was slowly coming to fruition. After the great success of the *Eclogues*, Virgil seems to have tried to avoid publicity. Where he liked to be was in Naples, studying philosophy with the Epicureans Siro and Philodemus. But he too was now one of Maecenas' poetic friends, and naturally he would be receptive to his patron's suggestions. What was needed now was something more substantial than the *Eclogues* and their Theocritean Arcadia.

Why not turn to Hesiod's *Works and Days*, updating it in a more optimistic vein, to celebrate the labour of small farmers and the revival of agriculture in Italy now that peace had returned? Though he didn't enjoy doing it, Virgil was evidently a very attractive public performer (one of his contemporaries commented that it was no use stealing Virgil's lines unless you also had his face, his voice, and his delivery), and so we can hardly doubt that he too was on stage at

8.4. Virgil's *Georgics*

Agrippa's games, enthralling the Roman audience with what he had so far written of the *Georgics*.

Virgil was a learned poet, and Latinists who focus on his learning do not normally think of the *Georgics* as performance poetry. Even the most admirably historical of recent critics still takes it for granted that the poet had only readers in mind:

> The leisured men who had received the profound education in Greek literature necessary for understanding the poem would be quite likely to own large rural estates, and almost certain not to do much of the kind of physical work which the poem enjoins.... This argument was not addressed to the farmers themselves, any more than the poem was meant as a handbook for peasants who had somehow acquired the education needed to appreciate Virgil's play on literary genres. The argument, the poem, was addressed to the literate class.

Powell 2008.228, 263

Agreed, it was certainly not a handbook. But Seneca's often-quoted remark that Virgil wanted to please readers, not teach farmers, was only half correct. Virgil does, in fact, address the farmers themselves, in the second-person plural, and he calls them not *agricolae* but *fortes coloni*, brave settlers. He was talking directly to the veterans.

Once we relegate the writing and distribution of papyrus scrolls to their proper position as secondary publication, we may begin to understand how Virgil's poetic message could have been delivered. Traditionally, the games were the time when country people might come in to the city; and the games were about education as well as entertainment. Apply that to the years 36–33 BC, and it's not too difficult to guess what Virgil may have been doing.

The *Georgics* begin with an invocation, first to Liber and Ceres for the grape and the grain, to the gods of the countryside and the inventors and protectors of pasture and agriculture. And then:

> Yes, and you too, Caesar, whose place one day in the councils of the gods is still unknown, whether you may choose to watch over cities and take care of the lands, and the great world, binding your brow with a mother's myrtle, accept you as an authority with power over crops and seasons... grant me an easy course, approve my bold endeavours, and take pity with me on countrymen who do not know the way. Step forward, and accustom yourself already now to be invoked with prayer.

Virgil *Georgics* 1.24–8, 40–2

(Myrtle was sacred to Venus, mother of Caesar's ancestor Aeneas.) The poet then gets down to Hesiodic business about the farmer's tasks, and goes on to explain the weather-signs given by the moon and sun:

> Who would dare to call the Sun a liar? He even gives warning when hidden revolts are under way, and crime and secret wars are swelling up. In pity for Rome at the

death of Caesar, he even hid his shining head in iron-grey darkness, and the impious generations were afraid of eternal night... [The following twenty lines list other portentous events on that occasion.] That was the reason why Philippi twice saw Roman battle-lines clash with matching arms. It seemed right to the gods that Emathia and the broad plains of Haemus should twice be made fertile with our blood. You can be sure the time will come when a farmer in those fields, working the earth with his curved plough, will find javelin-heads eaten away by scabby rust, or strike empty helmets with his heavy hoe, and marvel at the great bones dug out from their graves.

Virgil Georgics 1.463–8, 489–97

The veterans had fought for the Caesars, father and son, for twenty years or more. Many of them had been in Rome on the Ides of March, and many more had fought the armies of the assassins at the two battles of Philippi. From the vantage-point of Agrippa's games, that was less than eight years ago.

The second book of *Georgics* is famous for two great purple passages—in praise of Italy (lines 136–76) and in praise of the rustic life (lines 458–540). A detail from each of them may help to set our scene. First, in celebrating Italy's lakes, the poet moves on swiftly from the great lakes of his Transpadane homeland to something much less predictable:

Or should I speak of harbours, and the barriers added to the Lucrine lake, and the loud roaring of the indignant sea where the Julian waves sound afar as the deep flows back, and the Tyrrhenian tide is let in to Avernus' channel?

Virgil Georgics 2.161–4

This is the complicated description of a great feat of engineering, consul Agrippa's creation in 37 BC of Portus Iulius, a safe haven in which to train his crews to face Sextus Pompeius' fleet in the last great showdown. For the veterans that was an even more recent memory.

Virgil contrasts country life with the hectic ambition and avarice of the city, which is symbolized, with emphatic repetition, by murderous strife between brothers. For many people in the thirties BC, that would be a reminder of Romulus' killing of his brother Remus, cited by Horace in a famous poem as the primal curse that doomed Rome to civil war. So it is surprising to see how Virgil concluded his eulogy of virtuous families on frugal farms:

This was the life once led by the Sabines of old, this the life led by Remus and his brother; this was how brave Etruria grew—yes, and how Rome was made the fairest of all things and surrounded her seven hills with a wall as a single city.

Virgil Georgics 2.532–5

The Sabines, of course: they were proverbial for old-fashioned frugality. But why refer to the fratricidal twins? The answer must be that for Virgil they were not fratricidal at all.

There were, in fact, various legendary traditions about Romulus and Remus. According to one of them, the twins founded the city together on equal terms, and ruled it together as well; that version, stressing consensus and cooperation, may well have been attractive in the war-weary thirties BC. Certainly Agrippa cared about fraternal concord, as Seneca reports:

> The magnanimous Marcus Agrippa, the only one of those whom the civil wars raised to fame and power who was fortunate for the public welfare, used to say that he owed much to this maxim: 'Through concord small things grow, through discord great things fall apart.' It helped him, he said, to become both an excellent brother and an excellent friend.

Seneca
Letters 94.46

We happen to know where the maxim came from—one of the speeches in Sallust's *Jugurthine War*, which Agrippa must have heard or read in 41 or 40 BC.

As all Virgil's audience knew, from the very beginning of his meteoric career the young Caesar had associated himself with Romulus (who fought a war of vengeance at the age of 18). Many of the veterans had witnessed the twelve vultures appear over the Campus Martius on 19 August 43 BC, as the young Caesar inaugurated his first consulship, or escorted him in 36 BC to the house on the Palatine that looked out on Romulus' hut. Agrippa, his exact contemporary, had been with him from the beginning, a brother in arms if not by blood. Of course he was thought of as Remus to Caesar's Romulus, and Virgil's line can only have been an honorific allusion to him.

8.5. Virgil's 'Epyllion'

The four books of *Georgics* deal in turn with agriculture, arboriculture, livestock, and bees. Half-way through the last book, the text moves unexpectedly from didactic instruction to a mythological narrative of recognizably the same type—'epyllion' is the unhelpful modern term—as Catullus' poem 64. There is no good reason to doubt Servius' report that it was a late insertion into the text, replacing a eulogy of the poet Cornelius Gallus after Gallus' disgrace and suicide in 27 or 26 BC. Since Virgil was a famously slow composer, and so could hardly have produced this masterly narrative at short notice, we must assume that it already existed as an independent composition before its insertion into the *Georgics*' apicultural context.

At lines 315–32 Aristaeus, son of Apollo and master of all the rustic crafts, has lost his bees, and complains to his mother Cyrene. He is presented as a surprisingly helpless character, not at all like the inventive hero of the traditional Aristaeus legend. He has come to the head-waters of the river Peneus in Thessaly, but his mother is not there in person. She is an immortal, a nymph who dwells 'in the depths of this water'. That too is unexpected: Cyrene was a mortal shepherdess and huntress, daughter of the king of the Lapiths and loved by Apollo; the god did indeed make her a nymph, but not a water-nymph—and her home was in Libya, where a famous city was named after her. It looks as if both mother and son have been stitched in to a scenario not originally designed for them.

But what a scenario it is! Cyrene in her underwater chamber is surrounded by her sister nymphs, spinning wool and listening to one of their number sing of the loves of the gods from the beginning of time. Eventually (Arethusa has gone to the surface to investigate) she realizes that her son has need of her:

> 'Bring, oh bring him to me! No harm for him to approach
> The gods' threshold.' At once she bade the stream roll back
> And leave a wide path, an entrance for him. But the water
> Stood up on end in a mountainous curve, stood all around him,
> Laid him in its huge lap and bore him beneath the surface.
> Marvelling now at his mother's home and aqueous kingdom—
> The pools enclosed in caverns, the sighing woods of weed—
> He went along: the enormous passage of waters dazed him,
> For he viewed all the rivers that glide below great earth
> Far and wide—Phasis, Lycus,
> The spring from which the deep Enipeus first leaps forth,
> The source of father Tiber and the flowing Anio,
> Of Hypanis roaring down through rocks, Mysian Caicus,
> Of Eridanus, depicted with golden horns on his bull-head—
> Eridanus, than which through fertile fields no river
> Rushes with more momentum to the pansy-purple sea.

Virgil *Georgics* 4.358–73 (trans. Cecil Day Lewis)

One wonders why it mattered so much to the poet to have 'water, water everywhere'.

Let's break off for a moment and take a walk in the streets of Rome. Out of the Forum by Caesar's new Senate-house, along the Argiletum, through the Subura, up the steep street (*cliuus Suburanus*) as if you were going to the Esquiline Gate—in modern terms, it's roughly up Via Cavour and Via Giovanni Lanza as far as Piazza S. Martino ai Monti. Facing you at the top of the slope was the richly decorated façade of one of Agrippa's main distribution tanks (*castella*), and from it the waters of the culverted river Anio gushed out among the statues. A century and more later, Martial would describe the scene:

> Keep going: once you're through the Subura it's a brief effort to climb the uphill way. There straight away you'll see slippery Orpheus at the top of his watery theatre, and the beasts amazed, and the king of birds that brought the kidnapped Phrygian to thundering Jupiter.

Martial 10.20.4–9

Fig. 18

From a century later again, we even have a plan of it, three great basins evidently fed by three cascades. Ganymede and the eagle must have decorated one of the

8.5. Virgil's 'Epyllion'

FIG. 18. Reconstruction of one of the slabs of the Severan Marble Plan of the city of Rome: north is to the bottom left. The three circular features in the piazza at the top left are the *lacus Orphei*; the wide street coming up diagonally from the right is the *cliuus Suburanus*, leading from the Forum to the Esquiline Gate. Rodriguez Almeida 1981, Tav. IX, reproduced by permission of Edizioni Quasar, Rome.

side basins; the main one was certainly for Orpheus taming the beasts with his singing, because we know that this fountain complex was called 'the Orpheus pool', and that the people who lived near it were called *Orphienses*.

Thanks to the survival of the city-plan fragment, we also know that the Orpheus pool faced an irregular-shaped piazza about 25 m wide, extensive enough to accommodate a temporary stage and seating. And that in turn means that Martial's reference to the 'watery theatre' may not have been wholly metaphorical. The main aqueduct terminals (the Trevi fountain, still fed by Agrippa's own Aqua Virgo, is a fine eighteenth-century version) were like theatre stage-sets, obvious sites for the stage-games of Agrippa's aedileship. Water meant nymphs, and nymphs meant dancing-girls. For the 'Aristaeus epyllion', as for Catullus 64 (Ch. 7.4 above), it is worth testing the hypothesis that it was written as a dance-performance script.

Back in the text (lines 387–414), the nymph Cyrene in her chamber among the waters instructs her son to consult Proteus, the Old Man of the Sea, who happens to be in the neighbourhood. He knows everything, but he is a shape-shifter, and must be subdued by force before he will speak. She escorts her son to a great sea-cave, where Proteus likes to bring his herd of seals out of the hot summer sun:

Virgil *Georgics*
4.429–32
(trans. Cecil
Day Lewis)

> Now Proteus came to his customed
> Den from the water: around him the dripping tribes of the deep
> Frolicked, flinging the bitter spray far and wide about them.
> All over the beach the seals were sprawled for their siesta.

We have already met 'dancers in the theatre' who played Actaeon's dogs, and shared the stage with nymphs (Ch. 6.5 above); these frolicking seals were surely dancers too.

As for Proteus, he was the dancer par excellence, his shape-shifting an allegory of mimetic ballet:

Lucian
Saltatio 19

> That is exactly what characterizes present-day dancers, and you can see them swiftly changing as the moment demands, and imitating Proteus himself.

Lucian had in mind the later 'all-mime' style, where the dancer never opened his mouth. In Virgil's time the virtuoso dancer still sang as well, and singing, or chanting, was exactly what prophets like Proteus did. So now, having gone through his transformational repertoire, he sings the great story of Orpheus and Eurydice.

Commentators are puzzled: 'Why Orpheus and Eurydice should have been chosen as the mortals whom Aristaeus has wronged, and so incurred divine displeasure, we cannot tell.' I suspect that may be putting it the wrong way round, if Orpheus was the original *raison d'être* of the piece and Aristaeus the bee-keeper spliced in for its new purpose. Certainly his offence—an otherwise unattested pursuit of Eurydice that caused her to step on a snake—is dealt with quite perfunctorily, and soon gives way to a chorus of Dryads mourning her death. Dryads as Eurydice's companions are another mythological innovation, but easily intelligible if we imagine the return of a female *corps de ballet*, the girls who played the water-nymphs in the first scene.

Of course we cannot *know*; it's like trying to solve a thousand-piece jigsaw puzzle with only a few dozen pieces available. But it is a possibility surely worth considering that Virgil's revised version of his book about bees exploited a previously composed libretto for Agrippa's aedileship, and that the Roman audience first enjoyed it at that watery theatre by the Orpheus pool.

8.6. Livy and Horace

No holiday lasts for ever, and grim reality soon returned. The last day of Agrippa's aedileship was also the last day of the triumvirate. Of the three men to whom the People had given absolute power ten years before, Lepidus was long out of the picture, living in ignominious retirement on his country estate, and Antony was in Alexandria with his ally and mistress the queen of Egypt, ruling Rome's eastern empire as if he too were a Hellenistic monarch.

In 32 BC Antony concentrated his military forces in north-western Greece, with the intention of invading Italy; he also divorced Octavia, Caesar's sister, to whom he had been married for seven years. In the face of this crisis, Caesar had to renew his popular mandate by other means. As he put it many years later, 'the whole of Italy swore allegiance to me and demanded me as its commander for the war in which I conquered at Actium'.

Caesar did indeed conquer, in the naval battle in 31 BC and at Alexandria itself the following year, when Cleopatra and Antony committed suicide. But this was not like previous civil wars against arrogant aristocrats and enemies of the People; Antony too had been a popular hero. It was still a very uneasy time, and as Caesar's deputies in Rome Maecenas and Agrippa had to deal with riots and an assassination plot.

It was probably during those anxious years that Titus Livius ('Livy') began the great historical work that would occupy his whole life. The first question he asked himself was, is it *worth* writing the history of the Roman People from the beginning? He decided it was, but only for a very particular reason:

> Most readers... hurry to reach these recent events by which the forces of the all-powerful People are destroying themselves. I on the other hand shall seek this reward for my labours, that I may avert my eyes—at least as long as I devote my whole attention to that early period—from the evils that our age has witnessed for so many years.
>
> Livy pref. 4–5

Livy saw Roman history as a moral parabola. The excellence of the Romans in both peace and war won them an empire, but then discipline began to slip and morality declined, gradually at first and then in a headlong rush 'down to the present time, when we can endure neither our vices nor the remedies for them'.

In the context, the vices must be public ones—civil strife, citizen killing citizen—and since the Romans were very familiar with the metaphor of the 'body politic', the remedies Livy refers to were no doubt political too. What he probably had in mind was a dictatorship like Julius Caesar's, an outcome that might well be expected when the young Caesar returned.

Inevitably, we read Livy in book form; but even in the continuous text it is not difficult to identify dramatic episodes, often with direct speech or even dialogue, written with an audience rather than a readership primarily in mind. (Even the more prosaic factual narrative sections would have appealed to the smaller audience of history enthusiasts that we know from Polybius and Cicero, interested in information for its own sake.) Livy was famous for his eloquent speeches, and that alone should be enough to prove that he didn't write only for readers. On the contrary: as a later historian expressly remarked of him, he wrote for the Roman People.

What he gave them in his opening narrative—the story of the Roman kings—was interestingly different in tone from Virgil's Caesarian commitment. For instance, Livy referred at the start to the claim of the Iulii that their ancestor Iulus was a son of Aeneas, but deliberately did not endorse it—'for who could affirm as a fact so ancient a matter?' His version of the foundation story had no room for concord and cooperation: he attributed the quarrel between the twins to 'the ancestral evil, lust for power', and having reported Remus' death in a faction-fight between their supporters, he then went on to give 'the more common story' that Romulus killed him in person.

Romulus himself was 'more popular with the multitude than with the Senate, and appealed most of all to the minds of the soldiers'. Livy gave the traditional account of his uncanny disappearance and presumed deification, but then added this unsettling comment:

> I believe that even at the time there were some who would secretly assert that the king had been torn to pieces at the hands of the senators; for this story too has come down to us, deeply obscure though it is. But the other story [the deification] has been ennobled by admiration for the man and the fear felt at the time.

Livy 1.16.4

No one could have failed to think of Julius Caesar—now Divus Iulius, with a temple under construction in the Forum. And when Livy came to tell of the expulsion of Tarquin, he presented the liberator Lucius Brutus addressing the Forum crowd in a scene deliberately reminiscent of Marcus Brutus and the Ides of March.

The Divus Iulius temple was only one of many building projects being carried out in the name of 'Commander Caesar'. At the other end of the Forum the new Senate-house was also nearing completion; it was called Curia Iulia, replacing one that had borne the hated name of Sulla. In the Campus Martius, celebrating popular sovereignty, the voting area was being surrounded by a long, high portico adorned with elaborate reliefs and wall-paintings; the new enclosure was called Saepta Iulia, so both Senate and People would soon be performing their functions in a conspicuously Caesarian setting. No less symbolic was the new temple of Apollo on the Palatine, being built on the site of a large and luxurious private residence that had been bought by the young Caesar and demolished; when complete, the temple would look out over the forecourt of his own house, which everyone knew was much more modest.

The purpose of all this building was to make available to the Roman People the lavish architecture and fine art that had hitherto been the privilege of the rich. The Apollo temple would feature sumptuous colonnades full of Greek sculpture, and a library too, while the great new burial-mound of the Julian family in the Campus Martius, pointedly outdoing the Alexandrian monument that held the bodies of Cleopatra and Antony, would be surrounded by shady trees and walks for the benefit of the public. When all was done it would convey a powerful message, that nowadays Rome's resources were for the benefit of all citizens alike, and not just the powerful few. In the meantime, however, the experience of living amid the dust and din of multiple building-sites probably did little to lift the sense of unease that Livy's early history seems to have reflected.

That sense is also manifest in two of Horace's early odes, unusual in their explicit address to the Roman People. Normally, as the poet says, the lyre was 'a friend to temples and the tables of the rich', and many of the odes are songs for a banquet or party, or hymns to be sung in a respectfully formal context. It can't have been easy to sing for a mass audience, but in the tense and anxious months of Caesar's absence in the east, Maecenas' protégés were no doubt expected to do what they could.

One of the signs of Rome's malaise was temples in disrepair or ruinous because responsibility for their maintenance had been neglected. In *Odes* 3.6 Horace took on the role of prophet:

> Though innocent, Roman, you will pay for the sins
> of your fathers, until you restore the crumbling temples
>   and shrines of the gods
>   and their filthy smoke-blackened images.
> You rule because you hold yourself inferior to the gods.
> Make this the beginning and this the end of all things.
>   Neglect of the gods has brought many ills
>   to the sorrowing land of Hesperia.
> Already, Monaeses and the army of Pacorus
> have twice crushed our attacks made without auspices
>   and they grin as they add plunder taken from us
>   to their worthless neckbands.
> Our city, seized by internal strife, has been almost
> destroyed by the Dacian and the Ethiopian,
>   Ethiopian formidable for his fleet,
>   Dacian prevailing with flights of arrows.

Horace *Odes* 3.6.1–16 (trans. David West)

The allusions were to Antony's disastrous invasion of Parthia in 36, and to the young Caesar's supposedly defensive wars in Illyricum ('Dacians') and at Actium (the 'Ethiopian' fleet) in 33 and 31. The prophet-bard then blamed Rome's troubles on sexual permissiveness, a modern and aristocratic vice:

> Not from such parents sprang the men
> who stained the sea with Punic blood
>   and cut down Pyrrhus, mighty Antiochus,
>   and the deadly Hannibal.
> That was the manly stock of farmer-soldiers
> taught to turn the sod
>   with Samnite mattocks and cut and carry logs
>   under the authority
> of their strict mother when the sun was moving
> the shadows of the mountains
>   and loosing the yoke from weary oxen
>   as its departing chariot brought the longed-for hour.

Horace *Odes* 3.6.33–44 (trans. David West)

The echo of the *Georgics* is not accidental; precisely in 30 BC, thousands more veteran legionaries were demobilized and settled in farms in Italy. Would they reverse the cycle of decline?

In the poem we know as *Odes* 1.2, Horace was no longer a sermonizing prophet, but sang to 'Quirinus' people' as one of themselves:

> Already Father Jupiter has sent enough fierce hail
> and snow and his red right arm has struck
> his holy citadel and brought
>   fear to the city...
> We have seen yellow Tiber wrench his waves back
> from the Tuscan shore and rush
> to hurl down king Numa's memorials
>   and Vesta's temple,
> to show himself the avenger of Ilia's loud grievances.
> Leaving his course, without the blessing
> of Jupiter, the doting husband flooded
>   the left bank.

Horace *Odes* 1.2.1–4, 13–20 (trans. David West)

Ilia was 'the Trojan woman', descendant of Aeneas and mother of the twins; thrown in the Tiber by her wicked uncle Amulius, she became the bride of the river-god, who now takes revenge by adding to Jupiter's storms with a flood of his own. Not too serious a story—but 'avenger' (*ultor*) was an ominous word, and one that easily evoked the memory of the Ides of March (Caesar too was descended from Aeneas). So now the poet showed what had caused these portents:

> Young men will hear that fellow citizens sharpened swords
> that should rather have slain Persians. They will hear—
> what few there are, thanks to the sins of our fathers—
>   of the battles that were fought.
> What god can the people call upon to shore up
>   their crumbling empire?

Horace *Odes* 1.2.21–6 (trans. David West)

Vesta, perhaps, or Jupiter or Apollo or Venus or Mars? His final choice was Mercury:

> ... or if you, winged son of bountiful Maia,
> have changed shape and are imitating
> a young man on the earth, accepting the name
>   of Caesar's avenger,
> do not return too soon to the sky. For long years
> be pleased to stay with the people of Romulus,
> and may no breeze come and snatch you up too soon,
>   angered by our sins.
> Here rather celebrate your triumphs.
> Here delight to be hailed as Father and Princeps
> and do not allow the Medes to ride unavenged
>   while you, Caesar, are our leader.

Horace *Odes* 1.2.41–52 (trans. David West)

The news was getting better. It must have been late 30 or early 29 BC when the citizens who had listened to Horace lined up to pass their votes on a law defining the authority of the Prefect of Egypt. Now that the Ptolemies' kingdom had passed into the power of the Roman People, it would be governed by *their* representative, and not by a senatorial proconsul like the other provinces.

At last Caesar was coming home. At some time in the early summer of 29 BC he stopped for a few days at Atella, just inland of Naples, to recover from a throat infection. There he heard the full text of the *Georgics*, read by Virgil and Maecenas in turn. It must have been the poet himself who delivered the signing-off passage:

> Thus of agriculture and the care of flocks I sang
> And forestry, while great Caesar fired his lightnings and conquered
> By deep Euphrates, and gave justice to docile peoples,
> Winning his way to the immortals.
> This was the time when I, Virgil, nurtured in sweetest
> Parthenope, did follow unknown to fame the pursuits
> Of peace, who dallied with pastoral verse, and by youth emboldened,
> Tityrus, sang of you in the shade of a spreading beech.

Virgil *Georgics* 4.559–66 (trans. Cecil Day Lewis)

8.7. The Republic Restored

The Senate had decreed that the day of Caesar's return to Rome would be a public holiday. We don't know exactly what day that was, but it is not hard to guess. He would of course avoid 18 July, the most ill-omened day in the Roman calendar, but immediately after that (20–30 July) came the games established by his father in honour of Venus as ancestress of the Iulii, known as 'the games of Caesar's victory'. And immediately after *that*, on 1 August, came the anniversary of the conquest of Egypt, which the Senate had declared a public holiday 'because on that day the republic was freed from a most dreadful danger'.

Perhaps the arrival ceremony was on 19 July. 'After that', Dio Cassius' history reports (and it was surely on 1 August itself), Caesar presided over a great public meeting in which he not only praised and decorated his senior officers (Agrippa, who already had the 'naval crown' for the battle of Naulochus, now received a symbolic blue flag for the battle of Actium), but also distributed cash grants to the veterans and to the citizens of Rome 'out of the spoils of war'. Cleopatra's palace had been stripped and her treasury confiscated, but there had been no sacrilege: no temples had been plundered. Each veteran farmer got 1,000 sesterces, each member of the Roman *plebs* got 400; for comparison, a legionary soldier was paid 225 sesterces per year. Egypt was now the Roman People's property, and the Roman People were getting the benefit directly.

There followed a lavish programme of spectacle and celebration. Caesar's three successive triumphal processions, for the Illyrian, Actian, and Alexandrian campaigns, took place on 13–15 August. On 18 August the temple of Divus Iulius in the Roman Forum was dedicated, with elaborate games and wild-beast shows. On 28 August the completion of the Curia Iulia was celebrated with the dedication of a grand altar to the goddess of Victory. On 2 and 3 September there were two further anniversary holidays, respectively for the battle of Actium in 31 BC and the victory in Sicily in 36. They led straight in to the annual *ludi Romani* (4–19 September), and then, on 23 September, came the public holiday for Caesar's birthday. He was 34 years old.

Meanwhile, there was serious business to be done. Caesar and Agrippa, elected as consuls for the following year, were granted the authority to hold a census. Now that the civil wars were definitively over, and emergency powers no longer necessary, the normal working of the republic would resume; and that meant that every Roman citizen must be morally and financially assessed and properly registered in his appropriate voting unit. Traditionally, that had been done by two senior senators elected every five years as censors, but the system had broken down in the corrupt aristocratic republic of the last forty years.

8.7. The Republic Restored

The last act of the census, the *lustrum*, was a purification sacrifice symbolizing the cleansing of the citizen body. The last time it had been carried out was in 70–69 BC, and even then nothing like a full numeration of citizens had been achieved. Since then, censors had been elected in 65, 64, 61, 55, 50, and 42 BC, but political machinations had always prevented the completion of a *lustrum*. Now it was going to be done properly.

Caesar himself took on the drastic revision of the Senate's membership, and the creation, specifically authorized by the People, of new patrician families. Agrippa seems to have concentrated on private luxury, to judge by an admiring passage in the elder Pliny a century later. Describing Agrippa as a man 'closer to country manners than to sophistication', Pliny observed:

> At any rate, there survives a magnificent speech of his, worthy of the greatest of citizens, that all paintings and statues should be public property, something that would have been preferable to having them banished into exile in country houses [by the rich].

Pliny *Natural History* 35.26

Certainly Agrippa acted on this ideal, using the suburban estates in the Campus Martius that had once been Antony's (and Pompey's before that) for public building on a very large scale, with generous provision of works of art.

In January 28 BC, Caesar's sixth consulship (and Agrippa's second) was marked with all possible publicity as the return of constitutional government and the rule of law. Cataloguing his achievements forty years later, he drew attention to it on three separate occasions:

Fig. 19 and colour plate 3

> In my sixth consulship I carried out a census of the People with Marcus Agrippa as my colleague. I performed the *lustrum* after forty-two years, and at that *lustrum* 4,063,000 individual Roman citizens were registered.

Augustus *Res gestae* 8.2

The figure on the previous occasion had been 910,000.

> As consul for the sixth time, I restored eighty-two temples of the gods in the city, without omitting any that needed restoration at that time.

Augustus *Res gestae* 20.4

So the anxiety expressed by Horace about crumbling temples and smoke-blackened images was laid to rest.

> In my sixth and seventh consulships, after I had extinguished the civil wars, being with universal consent in complete control of affairs, I transferred the republic from my power to the dominion of the Senate and the Roman People.

Augustus *Res gestae* 34.1

(The seventh consulship, 27 BC, opens our next chapter.)

After the celebration of the *lustrum* (date unknown), the great spectacle of the sixth consulship came in the autumn, with the first of the quadrennial games in

FIG. 19. *Aureus* (= 100 sesterces). Obverse: head of Caesar with laurel wreath; legend *Imp. Caesar Diui f. cos. VI*. Reverse: Caesar wearing toga, seated on curule chair, holding scroll and with box of scrolls at his feet; legend *leges et iura p.R. restituit*. 'Commander Caesar, son of Divus [Iulius], consul for the sixth time, has restored laws and justice to the Roman People.' © The Trustees of the British Museum, all rights reserved.

honour of the victory at Actium, and the dedication on 9 October of the great marble temple of Apollo, the god who had brought that victory about. Virgil later re-created the scene, as pictured on Aeneas' shield:

> But Caesar, who had entered the walls of Rome in a triple triumph, was consecrating an everlasting vow to the gods of Italy—three hundred great shrines throughout the whole city. The streets were loud with gladness and games and applause; at all the temples there were matrons dancing, and altars, and before the altars slain bullocks strewed the ground. He himself, seated in the snow-white threshold of gleaming Phoebus, is reviewing the gifts of nations and fixing them to the proud doors. The conquered peoples process in a long line...

Virgil *Aeneid* 8.714–22

In the real world, the main venue of the games was probably the *area Palatina*, an open area or piazza on the summit of the Palatine, no longer recognizable among the ruins of the imperial palaces but clearly attested by earlier references. As always, we must imagine a wooden stage and auditorium put up for the occasion. It is likely—though the question is very controversial—that the Apollo temple looked out over this piazza, and also over the forecourt of Caesar's house.

Of all the many items that must have been on the performance programme, we know of only one, a tragedy *Thyestes* for which the poet Lucius Varius—a friend of Virgil, Horace, and Maecenas—received an honorarium of 1 million sesterces. But we can make a guess about some surviving works that must date to about this time—Horace's Cleopatra ode, for example, or perhaps Livy's narrative of the beginning of the republic:

> The free Roman People's history in peace and war, annual magistracies and the laws' commands more powerful than those of men—that shall be my theme from now on.
>
> Livy 2.1.1

It was certainly a topical one.

9

Rethinking the Classics

28 BC–AD 8

Not many people give their names to an entire age. The young Caesar was one of them—but first he had to receive the name.

On 13 January 27 BC, as consul for the seventh time, he formally handed back his power of military command to the Senate and People of the restored republic, and accepted their mandate to hold proconsular authority over Spain, Gaul, and Syria for a ten-year period. 'For this benefit,' he wrote forty years later,

> I was called 'Augustus' by decree of the Senate, the doorposts of my house were publicly decorated with laurels, the oak wreath which is given for saving fellow-citizens was fastened above my door, and a golden shield was placed in the Curia Iulia, which, as attested by the inscription on the shield, the Senate and the Roman People were giving to me for the sake of my valour, clemency, justice, and piety.

Augustus *Res gestae* 34.2

The name referred to a line in Ennius' epic history: 'After famous Rome had been founded by august augury.' The site of that original augury, when Romulus sought and received divine approval for his rule, was the piazza immediately outside Caesar's house, over which the towering marble temple of 'augur Apollo' now presided.

Within three or four generations, the men who bore the names Caesar and Augustus would be absolute rulers in a dynastic autocracy, and *Palatium*, the Palatine, would have come to mean 'palace'. But that was still in the womb of time. Rome in the 'Augustan' age was a working republic, in which one citizen, by the will of the great majority, enjoyed unequalled honour and influence. He had earned it by defeating the arrogant aristocrats, by conquering Egypt, and by bringing back peace and prosperity.

The Roman citizens who crowded the Palatine piazza when the laurels and the oak-leaf crown were put in place, or the Roman Forum when the golden shield was dedicated, did not think of Caesar 'Augustus' as an emperor. There was no such word in their vocabulary.

9.1. The Citizens, the Audience

It is clear that the Romans took huge pride and pleasure in their restored republic, and in the grand new marble buildings, adorned with the spoils of Egypt. That pride and pleasure extended to literature as well. They knew they now had poets and historians who could stand comparison with the old Greek masters.

Virgil's fame—to take the greatest of them first—was remembered a century later by one of the speakers in Tacitus' *Dialogue on Oratory*:

> Witness the People themselves, who on hearing Virgil's poetry in the theatre, rose as one man and honoured Virgil, who happened to be present in the audience, just as if he were Augustus.

Tacitus *Dialogus* 13.2

For Horace, as always, the evidence is less direct. In *Odes* 2.13 he sang of his narrow escape from a fatal accident:

> How nearly did we see the kingdom
> of dark Proserpina, and Aeacus in judgement,
>   and the seats of the holy set apart,
>   and Sappho complaining
> of her young countrywomen to her Aeolian lyre,
> and you, Alcaeus, sounding in fuller tones
>   with your golden plectrum the rigours of shipboard,
>   the cruel rigours of exile, the rigours of war.
> The shades listen in wonderment and sacred silence
> to the words of both, but with more willing ear
>   the crowd packed shoulder to shoulder drinks in
>   battles and expulsions of tyrants.

Horace *Odes* 2.13.21–32 (trans. David West)

In the world above, we must infer, Horace too had sung the themes of Sappho and Alcaeus, in the metres of Sappho and Alcaeus, before equally crowded audiences.

As for history, Livy was giving his audience battles (lake Regillus) and the expulsion of tyrants (the Tarquins) at just this time. He too enjoyed widespread fame, with a reputation far beyond Rome itself.

His main rival was a senior senator, Asinius Pollio, who had been consul in 40 BC and held a triumph the following year. A distinguished orator, Pollio was also known as a poet and dramatist (tragedies), and now he was taking on a great Sallustian narrative, the dangerous history of the civil wars. He had spent the booty of his triumph to create Rome's first public library, and he invited people into his own house to hear him read his works, not as a grandee but as a citizen. Perhaps he held his readings at home because the history of the civil wars, now so mercifully over, was not the sort of thing the aediles would want to include in the programme of the public games.

Attention now was directed to more traditional types of warfare. Caesar Augustus had had the province of his military command defined so that he could deal with the Roman People's unfinished business, in Britain and against the Parthians. In 27 BC he left for the north—but the intended invasion of Britain did not take place. Instead, Caesar concentrated on Spain, which he declared finally conquered in 25 BC. The 'Gate of War' (Ianus Quirinus) was closed, to signify that 'peace had been won with victories by land and sea throughout the whole empire of the Roman People'.

So far, we have looked for the Roman audience in the twenties BC in various ways. Tacitus has given us a direct view of the theatre audience applauding Virgil; Horace's vision of the underworld has allowed us to guess at his own experience; and Pollio's home readings have suggested another way of reaching the people for whom his history was written. Now we must consider an extraordinarily tenuous testimony, which may just tell us how Caesar Augustus himself communicated with his people.

It comes in a voluminous commentary on the Song of Songs, written in the fifth century AD by an otherwise unknown author called Apponius. Like all Christian exegetes, Apponius interpreted the erotic imagery allegorically, and the passage that concerns us is his treatment of chapter 8, verse 10, which the New English Bible renders as 'I am a wall and my breasts are like towers; so in his eyes I am as one who brings contentment'. In the Latin translation used by Apponius, however, the word was not 'contentment' but 'peace' (*pax*).

That naturally suggested the familiar Christian belief that the peace supposedly established by Augustus throughout the world was divinely ordained in preparation for the birth of Christ. As Apponius put it,

> on the day of His manifestation, which is called Epiphany, Caesar Augustus (so Livy narrates), on his return from the island of Britain, reported to the Roman People at the spectacles that the whole world had been subdued to the Roman empire in the abundance of peace, either by war or by treaties.

Apponius
In Canticum canticorum 12.53

The narrative he refers to would have been in Livy's book 135, out of the total 142. It is unlikely that Apponius consulted it directly ('a complete Livy must have been a rare and precious item'), and it is easy to see some of the ways he has garbled what Livy may have said.

We can be sure that Livy didn't use the phrase 'abundance of peace', which is a quotation from the Psalms, and that he didn't say Augustus had returned 'from the island of Britain', since he must have known he never went there. It is also very unlikely that Augustus would have addressed the People on 6 January, the day of Epiphany, because in the Roman calendar that was one of the unlucky days (*dies atri*) when no public business took place if it could possibly be avoided. Probably what influenced Apponius was the Christian belief (erroneous) that Epiphany was also the day when Augustus received his honorific name—but that was in 27 BC, not 24.

On the other hand, the reference to Britain must come from somewhere, and the careful qualification 'by war or by treaties' certainly sounds authentic. Three years earlier, Horace had prayed to the goddess Fortuna to preserve Caesar, 'soon to set out against the Britons at the end of the world'. Now Caesar was back, announcing peace throughout the world, and the Britons had not been conquered. They were, however, once more tributary to Rome, 'subdued to the Roman empire' by diplomacy (threats and sweeteners), not by war. Augustus would soon do the same with the Parthians.

So it seems that Apponius does indeed preserve, no doubt at second or third hand, the gist of what Livy wrote about an event he himself must have witnessed, Caesar Augustus' report to the Roman People in 24 BC. And that means we must take seriously the little phrase 'at the spectacles' (*in spectaculis*), which is hardly something an author in late antiquity would have added on his own account. Were they special games for the occasion, perhaps at an ad hoc theatre in the piazza on the Palatine? Or did Augustus time his return to coincide with the *ludi Megalenses* in April, the first of the regular theatre games of the Roman year? Either way, Apponius' confused quotation provides good evidence for what the Roman audience might find itself listening to.

Like his father Julius Caesar, Augustus wrote commentaries on his military campaigns, up to and including the war in Spain in 26–25 BC. It could only be a guess (Ch. 7.2 above) that those of the elder Caesar were meant to be read to the Roman People seated in a theatre rather than standing in the Forum; but now the unlikely witness of an Old Testament commentary confirms that that was indeed where the People's commander told the story of what he had done in the People's name.

9.2. Horace's *Epistles*

The return of free elections, with ambitious candidates canvassing voters in the streets, provided Horace with perfect material for his moral reflections:

> Of the candidates coming down to compete in the Campus, A is more aristocratic, B has a better character and reputation, C's crowd of clients is more numerous.
>
> Horace *Odes* 3.1.10–14

> If appearance and influence make a man fortunate, then let's buy a slave as a name-prompter—his dig in the ribs will get us crossing the cobbles with hand outstretched. 'This chap's big in the Fabia tribe, that one in the Velina. This one will give the *fasces* and curule chair to whoever he likes, and deny them to whoever he likes if he wants to be awkward.'
>
> — Horace *Epistles* 1.6.49–54

'The crowd of fickle citizens' could raise a man to honour and authority, or bring him down in shameful defeat. Horace's privileged position as a friend of Maecenas meant that he was now on easy terms with men whose whole life consisted of such triumphs and disasters.

It is interesting that he describes literary life in the same terms, with ambitious poets soliciting the People's favour. Modern literary scholars see it merely as a metaphor, but I don't think that's quite right: the Roman People *were* the poets' audience. As Horace put it to one of his privileged friends:

> Some time, if you're not busy, come along and listen at a distance, to hear what each poet is offering and how he's weaving a victor's crown for himself.
>
> — Horace *Epistles* 2.2.95–6

(No need to wait for a written scroll to read in private.) It matters that Horace says 'at a distance'. He was evidently not thinking of a private recitation, and there is no need to accept the current orthodoxy that 'the Augustan audience for poetry was coextensive with the social and cultural elite of Rome'. Of course poets *did* write for that elite, but not for them alone. Fame and honour were in the People's gift.

That basic fact is presupposed in a fascinating but difficult passage in one of Horace's *Epistles*, discussing with Maecenas the tepid reception of the *Odes*:

> If you want to know why the ungrateful reader praises and loves my little pieces at home, but unjustly disparages them as soon as he's outside the door, it's because I don't go hunting after the votes of the fickle *plebs* at the cost of dinners and giving away used clothes.
>
> — Horace *Epistles* 1.19.35–8

The *Odes* were evidently made available as written texts in 23 BC, arranged in the form we know as books 1–3. Horace was proud that his scrolls were 'read and handled by the respectable', but he expected more enthusiasm for such wonderfully innovative songs. That much is clear, but the explanation is baffling.

If poets had to hunt for votes and offer favours like ambitious politicians, what sort of election was involved? We must read on:

> As one who listens to noble authors and avenges attacks on them, I don't see fit to canvass literary constituencies and stages.
>
> — Horace *Epistles* 1.19.39–40

Horace is still talking about voters. 'To canvass constituencies' is my inexact translation of *ambire tribus*, literally 'to go round the tribes'—not of course tribes in the ethnographical sense, but the thirty-five voting units of the Roman republic, like the Fabia and Velina tribes mentioned by the imagined slave prompter in the passage quoted above. But what could *literary* tribes be (*grammaticae tribus*), and what had they to do with stages?

Horace himself has already given us the answer. About ten years earlier (Ch. 8.3 above) he had boasted that his poems would not be subject to the judgement of Maecius Tarpa or regularly performed for theatre audiences. 'Theatres' in the earlier poem matches 'stages' here: what is at issue is evidently the competitive selection of items for the *ludi scaenici*. We know of two other 'judges of poetry' at about this time, Vibius Viscus and Valerius Cato, of whom the latter at least was a well-known teacher of literature (*grammaticus*). A contemporary poet, with some exaggeration, called Cato 'the one selector and maker of poets'. Naturally, the magistrates in charge of the various games would turn to experts to pick their literary programmes for them.

So Horace's 'literary constituencies' seem to be the consultant *grammatici* with whom the ambitious poet had to plead to get his work accepted for a big public occasion. To unpack the nuances of that phrase *grammaticae tribus*, we should remember Cicero's recollection of his own experience of canvassing for office: 'I appealed to the People tribe by tribe; I humbled myself and pleaded.' When every vote counts, and all citizens are equal, social eminence counts for nothing; election to office depended on 'demeaning supplications' to people the candidate might normally despise. So too the privileged poet—and Horace makes sure we know what exalted circles he moves in now—might find it demeaning to humble himself to mere teachers who had to work for a living.

'*I* listen to *noble* authors'—and the implication is, they listen to me. In the earlier poem Horace named them as Messalla Corvinus and his brother Publicola (orators), Calpurnius Bibulus (historian), and Servius Sulpicius (poet); he could now have added another orator, Manlius Torquatus, and perhaps another poet, the young Iullus Antonius. Out of context, the names don't mean much, but archaeology allows us an insight into the world of luxury Horace now frequented.

At Pausilypon (Posillipo), a promontory just west of Naples, was the sumptuous seaside estate of a wealthy equestrian called Vedius Pollio, who died in 15 BC. This villa, explored in the nineteenth century, may give us an idea of the sort of place Maecenas would have owned, where Horace, like his noble friends, could count on a generous welcome. Conspicuous among its architectural features were a private theatre big enough to accommodate about 1,700 spectators, and facing it a smaller *odeion* or recital hall with a capacity of over 300.

Fig. 20

As we saw in an earlier chapter (Ch. 6.3), it was precisely when the games were on in Rome that rich villa-owners were likely to be in residence, enjoying

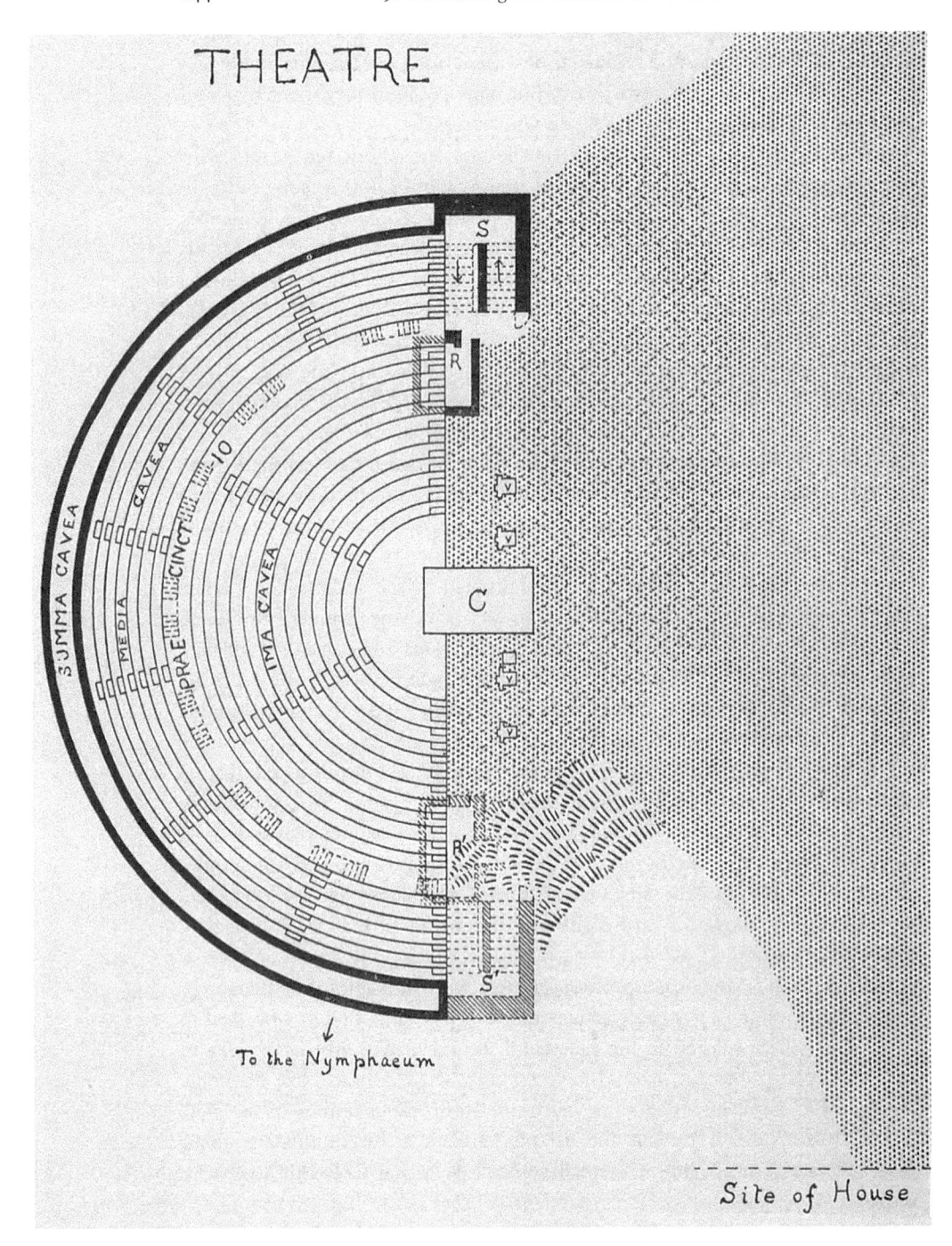

FIG. 20. The theatre and *odeion* at the Pausilypon villa (Günther 1913.32–3, fig. 11). No scale provided, but 'the theatre measures about 51 yards in diameter' (Günther 1913.34), about one-third the size of Pompey's theatre in Rome (Fig. 16). Unlike the *odeion*, the theatre had no permanent stage; presumably a wooden platform was erected in the garden (*uiridarium*).

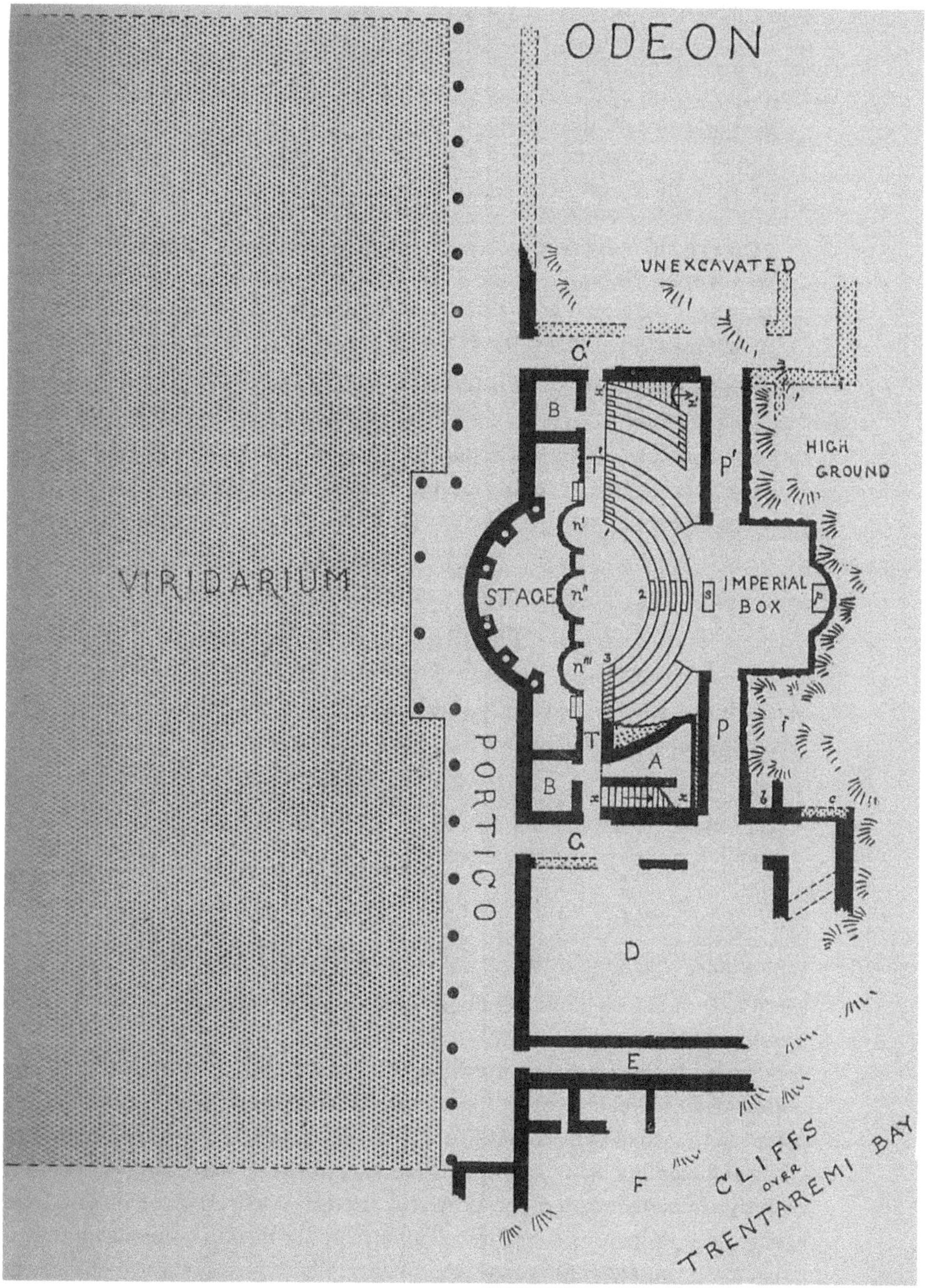
ODEON
UNEXCAVATED
HIGH GROUND
VIRIDARIUM
STAGE
IMPERIAL BOX
PORTICO
D
E
F
CLIFFS OVER TRENTAREMI BAY

an idyllic retreat from the city and the People's boisterous pleasures. If Horace often went with them as a favoured guest, it's easy to see why he was unpopular. As he goes on to explain:

> *That*'s what causes the trouble. If I say 'I'm ashamed to recite my unworthy writings in crowded theatres and add weight to trifles', then someone replies: 'You're laughing—you keep your stuff for the ears of Jove, so confident that you alone distil poetic honey. You really fancy yourself!'
>
> I'm afraid to treat that sort of criticism with contempt, and in case he fights and I get cut by his sharp nails, I shout 'I don't like that venue', and ask for a break. For the games have given rise to alarming competitiveness and anger, and anger has given rise to grim feuds and deadly war.

Horace *Epistles* 1.19.41–9

That last sentence may not have been much of an exaggeration. The outrageous rivalries of the star dancers (and their fans) had already led to one of them being banished for sedition. In 22 BC the games were transferred from the aediles' jurisdiction to that of the praetors, more senior magistrates with the power to suppress violence.

9.3. Tibullus and Propertius

Meanwhile, a whole new literary genre had been created: the Roman love elegy. A century later Quintilian put it like this:

> In elegy too [as well as epic] we challenge the Greeks. Of this genre I think the most polished and elegant author is Tibullus. Some may prefer Propertius. Ovid is more playful than either, and Gallus more severe.

Quintilian 10.1.93

Of Gallus, the originator, practically everything is lost—though the few scraps that do survive reveal that he too needed to please those 'judges of poetry', Vibius Viscus and Valerius Cato. Ovid was the youngest of the four, and we shall come to him before long. For the twenties BC, the two that matter are Albius Tibullus and Sextus Propertius.

Some of their poems were evidently delivered on grand public occasions; others may have been written for dramatic performance, like Virgil's eclogues; many, addressed to individuals or to 'my friends' in general, clearly belong in the privileged world of private parties. These categories are not, of course, mutually exclusive. Poems written for powerful friends—Messalla in Tibullus' case, Maecenas in Propertius'—might well involve public themes, especially if Caesar himself was present at the party. And Vedius Pollio's private theatre reminds us that a rich man's hospitality might easily extend to dance, music, and dramatic performance, amateur as well as professional.

Cicero described the life of the self-indulgent rich as 'shows, and what follows shows'. The erotic nature of such performances, discreetly hinted at in a philosophical dialogue, could be alluded to more openly in the slanderous mode of political oratory. Here is Cicero on his enemies the consuls of 58 BC:

> While the house of [Gabinius] was resounding with song and cymbals and he himself was dancing naked at the banquet, even whirling round in the circle of the dance he wasn't afraid of the turn of Fortune's wheel. [Piso] on the other hand, not so elegant or artistic in his extravagance, was sprawled among his Greeks in the stink and the wine; his banquet was said to be a sort of Lapiths and Centaurs affair...

Cicero *In Pisonem* 22

The Centaurs, of course, had got drunk at a feast and tried to rape the Lapith women.

The young Caesar himself had once played Apollo at a banquet masquerade of the twelve Olympians. Lucius Plancus, consul in 42 BC, the man who proposed the name 'Augustus' in the Senate in January 27 and held the proverbially austere post of censor in 23, had notoriously acted the sea-god Glaucus at a banquet, 'naked, painted blue, his head wreathed in reeds, on his knees, dragging a fish-tail'. He may well have been performing the narrative poem on Glaucus by his fellow-senator Quintus Cornificius.

But we should not be misled by pejorative rhetoric: not all wealthy Romans were playboys and exhibitionists. Messalla and Maecenas were cultured men with serious literary talents of their own. There's no reason to doubt the artistic quality of any entertainments they provided.

With all that in mind, let's look at one of Propertius' early poems, the twentieth in his first collection. It's addressed to Gallus (who may be Cornelius Gallus the poet), as a friendly warning. Gallus' boyfriend Hylas is being pursued by the girls:

> Whether you sail the Umbrian forest's sacred stream or the wave of Anio bathes your feet or you walk on the shore of the Giants' coast, or wherever the wandering river receives you, always protect him from kidnap by predatory nymphs. The Dryads are no less amorous in Italy.

Propertius 1.20.7–12

At one level, the poet is listing the sites of grand country estates: by the river Clitumnus and its sacred grove, by the river Anio at Tibur (Tivoli), on the bay of Puteoli where the Giants had once fought the gods, or wherever you called in overnight as you cruised down the Tiber in your pleasure-boat.

It was in those surroundings, among the leisured class enjoying itself, that seductive ladies or good-time girls might have an eye on your young friend. For the poet's purposes, however, these rivers, woods, and seas are the haunts of nymphs, to whom Gallus' Hylas may fall victim just like his mythical namesake. So Propertius goes on to tell that particular story.

The Argonauts have landed on the Mysian coast. Hercules' young friend Hylas goes to look for a spring to get water. The next six lines are difficult, and there may be some textual corruption, so I rely on a leading Propertian scholar's translation:

> Two brothers followed him, sons of the North Wind, both Zetes above him and Calais above him; their hands in mid-air, they pressed upon him to snatch kisses, and one after the other rushed to seize kisses from his uplifted face. He, swinging beneath a wing-tip, is shielded and with a branch wards off the winged ambush.

Propertius 1.20.25–30 (trans. Francis Cairns)

They try it on, they get nowhere, they give up. 'No other extant account of the expedition includes such an incident... Artistic representations do not exist.' So what is the point of the episode? And why is it so hard to visualize what is happening?

Perhaps it was meant to be seen, not described. Were Zetes and Calais played by dancers? The poet now brings us to the pool of Pegae, 'the beloved watery home of Bithynian nymphs'. Hylas is entranced, and leans forward to gaze in its reflecting waters:

> Fired by his beauty, in amazement the Dryad girls abandoned their accustomed dances, and as he fell lightly forward they dragged him through the yielding water.

Propertius 1.20.45–7

Their *accustomed* dances? Perhaps the audience has been watching them already. Of course there is a limit to what one can infer from just the bare text—but it is worth remembering a very conspicuous feature of Vedius Pollio's private theatre at Pausilypon:

> In the middle of the arena is a shallow rectangular pit, shown in fig. 13 [our Fig. 20] and marked C on the plan, measuring 20 feet long by 13 feet wide and sunk out to a depth of 2 feet. Its sides are faced with tufa (*opus reticulatum*), but originally it undoubtedly had an inner lining of marble veneer.... On either side of the tank are two deep holes (v, v, v, v), the purpose of which seems to have puzzled the original excavators. We believe them to have been part of the contrivances for supporting stage scenery, curtains or awnings, carried on wooden masts or uprights stepped in the holes.

Günther 1913.34

A similar marble-lined cistern was recently excavated in Rome, at the cult site of Anna Perenna and the 'consecrated nymphs', where inscriptions record competitive performances, evidently dramatic. As always, we can only guess. But if Vedius Pollio had ever wanted to put on a danced performance of 'Hylas and the

Nymphs', his private theatre was well equipped to present the pool of Pegae. And Propertius could have written the libretto.

What made the elegists famous was their love poetry, the quasi-autobiographical records of their respective relationships with 'Delia' (in Tibullus' first collection), 'Nemesis' (in his second), and the tempestuous 'Cynthia' (in Propertius' first three). Since they were clearly party girls, and 'Cynthia' also a dancer, we might suppose that these poems as well were written for the privileged few and their lavish entertainments. But it may not be that simple.

Both Tibullus and Propertius were of equestrian rank; their mistresses were socially inferior, but made up for that with beauty and talent. This is how Propertius put it:

> It's not just respectable beauty I admire, or a woman who boasts of noble ancestors. I like to have read my writings in the lap of a girl who knows the arts, and have had them approved by her pure ears. When *that* happens, then goodbye to the confused talk of the People: with my mistress as the judge, I shall be safe.

Propertius 2.13.9–14

Like Horace, Propertius linked the judgement of poetry with the People—and he may have shared some of Horace's resentment. In a later poem, imagining his own funeral, he looked forward to a posthumous reputation: 'what the envious crowd detracts from me in my lifetime, honour will pay back double after my death.' No doubt, as with Horace, what the crowd envied was the poet's life of privilege as a friend of Maecenas.

Unlike Horace, however, who wouldn't even try to get his poems selected for the *ludi*, Propertius evidently did try, but could not be sure of acceptance. If the People's voice was 'confused', that may mean that he wasn't always turned down; and if he and his mistress were indeed notorious 'throughout the city', as he boasts, that surely implies something more public than just the circulation of written texts. It is not hard to imagine his brilliantly varied reports from the front line of a demanding love affair being looked forward to by audiences at the games like the episodes of a modern sitcom or soap-opera.

Propertius was not only a house-guest of the rich. He was also a man about town, and the public theatre and games were an integral part of his and 'Cynthia's' world. All the poems of his fourth collection, in or after 16 BC, were evidently written for public performance, including an appearance by 'Cynthia's' ghost that any actress would have loved to play. And there is now something more: newly published evidence from the poet's home town of Asisium reveals that the Umbrian city, like many others in Italy and elsewhere, built a permanent theatre in the Augustan period—and the wealthy citizen responsible for its construction was none other than Sextus Propertius.

9.4. Ovid and Virgil

We have had to work quite hard to get the texts of Horace and Propertius to reveal anything about the practicalities of the poet's trade, and still we can offer no more than educated guesswork. So it is a relief to turn to a text that was actually *meant* to convey information. It is the autobiography of Publius Ovidius Naso ('Ovid'), the youngest of the love-elegists and the most prodigiously talented. When he wrote it he was in his early fifties, in exile far from Rome, reviewing a ruined life:

> I, whom you read, used to play the tender Loves. Who was I? Listen, posterity, if you want to know!

Ovid *Tristia* 4.10.1–2

Place of birth, Paelignian Sulmo, 90 miles east of Rome among the cold streams of the central Apennines. Date of birth, 43 BC, 'when both consuls fell by the same fate' (at Mutina, the young Caesar's first command). Rank of family, equestrian, and by inherited status, not recent gift.

Publius and his brother were sent to Rome for their education. The brother, who died at 20, was a promising orator, but everything Publius wrote came out as verse. To please his father ('there's no money in poetry'), Ovid persevered with his oratorical training, and even served as *triumuir capitalis*, one of the junior posts held by young men who were on track for entry to the Senate. But in his early twenties he turned his back on a public career and chose the Muses instead.

At that point, looking back, the exiled poet provides us with a precious first-hand account of the world of poetry in the early years of Caesar Augustus:

> The poets of that time I cultivated and cherished; however many bards were present, I thought it was that many gods. Often Macer in his old age read his birds to me, and his poisonous snakes and healing plants. Often Propertius used to recite his flames of love, by right of the comradeship that joined him to me. Ponticus famous for epic, and Bassus also for iambics, were delightful members of my company, and Horace, the master of metre, captured our ears while striking his cultivated songs on the Ausonian lyre. Virgil I only saw, and the greedy fates gave Tibullus no time to be my friend. He was your successor, Gallus, and Propertius was his. The fourth after them in order of time was myself.
>
> As I cultivated the older men, so the younger ones cultivated me. My [Muse] Thalea was not slow in becoming known. My beard had been cut only once or twice when I first read my youthful songs to the People. The woman who had got my talent going was sung throughout the city—Corinna, I called her, but it wasn't a real name.

Ovid *Tristia* 4.10.41–60

There is no mention of reading books. Even the greatest and most godlike of the Augustan poets gets only half a line, because Ovid never *heard* him read. Of course the passage is about friendship, not literary practice as such, but even so, it assumes that poetry is to be heard. The question is, where, and in what audience? Ovid gives us the answer: he read his poems to the People, and his fictive mistress was on everybody's lips.

Thalea was the Muse of comedy and mime, presenting human behaviour good and bad. The 'naughtiness' (*nequitia*) of the elegiac lover-poet was exactly in her territory, and when Ovid introduced his second collection with the warning that ladies of strict morals were 'not the right *theatre*' for his erotic themes, we needn't suppose he was being merely metaphorical. This was poetry performed in public, for an audience that knew what to expect.

Virgil and Tibullus both died in 19 BC. It had been known for years that Virgil was writing a great epic poem on Augustus' legendary ancestor Aeneas. His rare readings of extracts from the master-copy were enough to show that, as Propertius put it, 'something greater than the *Iliad* is being born'. A slow and anxious composer, Virgil was not going to make any part of his text public until he was sure it was perfect, but already in 25 BC Augustus had been impatient. 'Please,' he wrote from Spain, 'send me anything of your *Aeneid*, even just the first sketch of the poem, or whatever part of it you choose.'

Now Augustus was away again. Of the three provinces the People had entrusted to him, Gaul and Spain had been dealt with and it was now the turn of Syria, facing the dangerous Parthians across the Euphrates. His winter headquarters were on the Aegean island of Samos. Perhaps Virgil wanted to see the birthplace of Pythagoras: at any rate, in 19 BC he left for 'Greece and Asia', hoping to spend three years perfecting the poem. In Athens, however, he met Augustus and his entourage on their way back to Rome, and it's not hard to guess how the plan changed. Virgil and his text came back with them—but only as far as Brundisium. He had caught a fever in the dangerous autumn heat.

Dying, he called for the boxes that held the twelve scrolls. They were still imperfect, and he wanted them burnt. No one acted on his wish, not even his executors, Lucius Varius and Plotius Tucca. The veto came from Augustus himself, as celebrated by a poet of the time:

> Virgil had ordered these songs, that sang of the Phrygian leader, to be destroyed by swift flames. Tucca and Varius say no—and you too, great Caesar, forbid it, taking thought for the history of the Latins.

Donatus *Vita Vergili* 38

The unknown poet had it exactly right. This was the story of the origins of Rome, and great Caesar was making sure the Roman People would get to hear it.

9.5. Augustus and the 'Secular Games'

Caesar Augustus himself was lucky to be alive. Never robust, subject to constantly recurring illnesses, he had nevertheless spent the whole of his adult life in the most physically demanding of activities, warfare and political conflict. Only four years earlier his life had been despaired of, his affairs set in order, and his signet ring given to Agrippa. Without Caesar, what would happen to the People's victory over the arrogant aristocrats? They were still there, waiting for their moment—and when, against all expectation, Caesar recovered, two of them had conspired to do to him what Brutus and Cassius had done to his father.

Their plot failed, but the trial and execution of two senators only added to the tensions of a disastrous year of floods, plague, and food shortages. Augustus had already had his ideological position as the People's protector formalized by a law granting him all the powers of the tribunes of the *plebs*, and not limited, as theirs were, to just the city and a mile beyond. But the People wanted more than that. They demanded that he be made dictator, or consul for life. He refused, accepting only the responsibility for food supply, and in 21 BC went off to arrange the affairs of Syria and the eastern provinces.

Now he was back, and the manner of his reception showed how much it mattered to Rome that Caesar (this time) should stay alive:

> In thanks for my return, the Senate consecrated an altar of Fortune the Bringer-Home in front of the temple of Honour and Virtue at the Porta Capena; it ordered the priests and Vestal Virgins to make an annual sacrifice there on the day on which I had returned to the city from Syria in the consulship of Quintus Lucretius and Marcus Vinicius [19 BC]; and it named the day *Augustalia* after my *cognomen*.
>
> On the Senate's authority, some of the praetors and tribunes of the *plebs*, together with the consul Quintus Lucretius and other leading citizens, were sent to meet me in Campania, an honour that has been decreed for no one other than myself up to this time.

Augustus *Res gestae* 11–12.1

(It was in Campania that Virgil was laid to rest, close to his beloved Naples.)

To get some sense of what the introduction of the *Augustalia* meant, look back to Ch. 2.6, where the 'named days' in the Roman festival calendar were used as evidence for the thought-world of the early republic. Cautiously, we said there that the calendar list of days named in capital letters 'evidently goes back at least as far as the fourth century BC'. Most scholars put it at least two centuries earlier: as the standard modern account of Roman religion points out, 'in no case can it be proved that a capital-letter festival was introduced later than the regal period'. Until 19 BC, that is. So great was the relief at Augustus' safe return that only a quite unprecedented honour was adequate to express it.

9.5. Augustus and the 'Secular Games'

Caesar Augustus was 44 years old. While he was alive and well and looking after the public interest, the old aristocracy was not going to gets its arrogant supremacy back. For the Roman People, what mattered above all was the favour of the gods. The juxtaposition of flood, plague, and famine with an assassination attempt spoke for itself. The elder Caesar, killed by men, was now a god, as the People knew his son would also be one day; meanwhile, it was right and proper that there should be *Augustalia* among the festivals of the religious year.

As it turned out, Caesar lived on earth for another thirty-one years, habituating a whole generation of Romans to the new 'state of the republic' that he had brought about, and securing the favour of the gods was a large part of his achievement. About one such initiative, the *ludi saeculares* of 17 BC, we happen to be helpfully well informed. The normal English translation 'Secular Games' is quite misleading, because they were anything but secular in the modern sense. 'Epochal' might be a more accurate rendering, since they were intended to mark the start of a new age, or *saeculum*.

Portentous events announced the end of one *saeculum* and the beginning of the next. The Sibyl's books of prophecy, now housed in Apollo's new temple on the Palatine, were duly consulted by the priestly college responsible (the *quindecimuiri sacris faciundis*), with Augustus presiding. They reported her response:

> Whenever the longest time of life for humans passes,
> making its journey as a cycle of a hundred and ten years,
> remember, Roman, even if you are unaware of it,
> remember all these things: to sacrifice to the immortal gods
> in the plain by the boundless waters of Thybris,
> at the narrowest point, when night comes upon earth
> while the sun hides his light.

Phlegon *FGrH* 257 F 37.5.4, lines 1–7

In particular, sacrifice must be made to the Fates (*Moírai*), to the goddesses of childbirth (*Eileithyiai*), to Earth (*Gaia*), to Jupiter and Juno, and to 'Apollo who is also called Helios [the sun]'. Choirs of boys and girls must dance and sing, matrons must pray, all must be ritually purified and bring appropriate offerings to the 'gentle powers' and the gods of heaven. When that has been done,

> in the days and nights that follow, let there be
> a thronged festival on seats fit for gods,
> and let gravity mix with laughter.

lines 33–5

For the Roman People, that meant three days of solemnity followed by seven days of fun.

On the night of 31 May 17 BC, by the Tiber in the Campus Martius, Caesar Augustus carried out the sacrifice to the Fates 'by the Achaean ritual', praying for the prosperity and safety of the *populus Romanus*, the Quirites. 'Games' were performed 'on a stage with no theatre attached and no seats provided'—no doubt in the belief that that was what the ancient Achaeans did. The following day, 1 June, Augustus and Agrippa sacrificed two bulls to Jupiter on the Capitol, with the same prayer, and 'Latin games' were performed 'in a wooden theatre which has been set up in the Campus next to the Tiber'. That night, still by the Tiber and still with the same prayer, Augustus carried out the sacrifice to Eleithyia.

The following day, 2 June, Augustus and Agrippa sacrificed two cows to Queen Juno on the Capitol, and games were held as on the day before. Next day, 3 June, Augustus and Agrippa made a bloodless sacrifice to Apollo and Diana on the Palatine, and two choirs, of twenty-seven boys and twenty-seven girls, sang the hymn 'composed by Quintus Horatius Flaccus'. Then they sang it again on the Capitol. There were stage-games (*ludi scaenici*), site not stated, followed by chariot races on an ad hoc race-track, 'next to the place where the sacrifice had been made on the previous nights and the theatre and stage set up'. That concluded the serious business of the ritual.

On 4 June the college of *quindecimuiri* issued an edict to the populace announcing seven days of 'complimentary' games:

> We shall begin them on the Nones of June [the following day]: Latin games in the wooden theatre by the Tiber at the second hour, Greek *thymelici* games in the theatre of Pompey at the third hour, and Greek *astici* games in the theatre which is in the Circus Flaminius at the fourth hour.

CIL 6.32323.156–8

Explanation of the technical terms may provide interesting evidence for what the Roman audience liked to watch.

The Greek word *thumelē*, meaning a sacrificial hearth or altar, was used in particular for the altar in the *orchēstra* of the theatre of Dionysus in Athens. It then came to refer to the *orchēstra* itself as opposed to the stage, and the dancing chorus as opposed to the actors. There is good evidence, contemporary with the *ludi saeculares*, that that distinction was still recognized in Augustan Rome. It is provided by the architect Vitruvius in the twenties BC, discussing Greek theatres:

> The Greeks have a wider *orchestra*, the stage-building further back, and the stage-platform, which they call *logeion*, of lesser width. This is because in the Greek theatre tragic and comic performers present their activities in the *orchestra*, and for that reason in Greek they are named separately as *scaenici* and *thymelici*.

Vitruvius 5.7.2

As for the other descriptive term, the Greek word *astikos*, meaning 'of the city', was applied in particular to the 'City Dionysia' theatre festival at Athens, where the drama competitions were, precisely, for tragedy and comedy. So it looks as if the separate Greek *ludi* at the games of 17 BC were respectively danced performances at Pompey's theatre and plays on the stage at the theatre in the Circus Flaminius.

The theatre in the Circus Flaminius had been a project of Julius Caesar's. It was taken up again by Augustus in 23 BC in honour of his deceased nephew Marcellus, and eventually dedicated—with spectacular games, of course—in 11 BC. It was on the same huge scale as the theatre of Pompey, though it is not known how much of the auditorium was complete at the time of the *ludi saeculares*. Nor is it known what sort of Greek stage-plays—if that is indeed what *ludi astici* were—the Roman audience watched on that famous occasion. As we have seen in previous chapters (Chs. 2.3, 3.1–2 above), 'Greek drama' in the wider world was vastly more diverse than just tragedy and comedy in the old Athenian style.

When the Sibyl (or her interpreters) referred to 'seats fit for gods', what she (or they) must have had in mind was the theatre of Pompey. But what exactly would that huge audience be watching? What *were* the 'Greek *thymelici* games'? In part, at least, the question is easily answered.

This was the heyday of Pylades and Bathyllus, two virtuoso performers whose new 'all-mime' dance style (*pantomimus*) excited enormous enthusiasm in audiences, and such violent rivalry among their supporters that Pylades had even been banished from Rome as a threat to public order. ('It's in your interests, Caesar,' he told Augustus on his return, 'that the People should spend their spare time on us.') They were both Greeks, Bathyllus from Alexandria, Pylades from Cilicia in what is now southern Turkey. Their art was Greek; their roles were from Greek mythology; and Pylades' repartee with Augustus was in Greek, as were his notorious exchanges with his rivals and with hecklers in the audience ('I'm dancing a madman, you idiots!').

'All-mime' was a very extravagant spectacle. Besides the musicians—some of whom might be flying across the stage on a crane—the star dancers each had a chorus of singers, and speaking actors too in supporting roles. When Livy narrated the supposed origins of the Roman stage-games in book 7 of his history (Ch. 2.5 above), he noted how their modest beginnings contrasted with 'this present madness, which wealthy kingdoms would hardly tolerate'. Later, reporting the games of 17 BC, he merely noted their 'lavish provision', and kept any disapproval to himself.

Even with no expense spared, it is obvious that such extravagant shows could not have filled the whole ten days' programme of the priestly college's complimentary games. We should think of Roman *ludi*, even special ones like these, as a variety show, with many different types of entertainment presented in succession, including what we call 'literature'. Another contemporary witness, the historian and geographer Strabo of Amaseia, reminds us of what the ancient world took for granted:

Strabo 1.2.8 C20

While philosophy is for the few, poetry is more useful to the people and can fill whole theatres, that of Homer above all.

The Romans now had a Homer of their own. They had lost the man himself, but Caesar Augustus had rescued the great poem. Tidied up by Varius and Tucca, the text Virgil wanted to burn was now ready for the Roman People. What better opportunity to present it than the games of the new age?

It is the Sibyl who guides Aeneas through the Underworld in the sixth book of the *Aeneid*. She brings him to Elysium, where his father Anchises shows him his descendants awaiting their time on earth:

Virgil *Aeneid* 6.788–84

'Now turn your eyes this way. Look on this race, your Romans. Here is Caesar, and all the progeny of Iulus that is to come beneath the great vault of heaven. Here is the man, here he is whom you have so often heard promised to you—Caesar Augustus, son of a god, who will establish again the golden *saecula* in Latium, through the lands once ruled by Saturn.'

Here he is. I think it is more likely than not that that passage was first delivered in the presence of Caesar Augustus, to thunderous applause, at the 'Latin games in the wooden theatre by the Tiber', on or soon after the Nones of June 17 BC.

9.6. Horace and Ovid

As it turned out, it really was a new age. Augustus had strengthened his position as the People's choice and the guarantor of stability, and the aristocracy learned to live with it. Twenty years of calm and prosperity followed.

One small index of easier times was that Horace, still proud of his aristocratic friendships, was now less unpopular for it:

Horace *Odes* 4.3.13–16

Rome's offspring (chief of cities) sees fit to place me among the pleasing choirs of bards, and now I am less chewed by envy's tooth.

He was evidently performing more often in public, on themes that appealed to the People's pride. In the very last of his *Odes*, addressing Augustus on some public occasion, he was once again their spokesman. He began, with characteristic obliquity, by excusing himself for not being Virgil:

> Phoebus, when I wanted to tell of battles and conquered cities, struck a disapproving note on his lyre to stop me spreading little sails across the Tyrrhenian sea.

Horace *Odes* 4.15.1–4

The honorific opening name suggests that this was a Palatine occasion, in the piazza by the temple of Apollo and the house of Augustus. It was to Augustus that the poet immediately turned:

> Your age, Caesar, has brought back rich crops to the fields, and restored to our own Jupiter the standards torn down from the Parthians' proud doors.

Odes 4.15.4–8

That invited the audience to look at Augustus' own doors, decorated with Apollo's laurel and the oak crown for the saving of citizens. Direct quotation of Virgil's great post-Actium scene (Ch. 8.7 above) made the parallel inescapable.

The new age, he went on, has brought peace, improved moral standards, restored sound government, and extended 'the fame and majesty of empire' from the rising to the setting sun—just as Jupiter had decreed in the first book of the *Aeneid*.

> While affairs are in Caesar's charge, neither fury nor violence between citizens shall drive peace away, nor anger that forges swords and sets unfortunate cities at enmity.

Odes 4.15.17–20

No one in the wide world, not even as far as China, will disobey 'the Julian edicts'. As for the citizens of Rome,

> we, both on working days and at festivals amid the gifts of playful Liber, with our wives and children will first pray duly to the gods, and then, in song mingled with Lydian pipes, sing of the leaders who lived virtuously in the ancestral way, and of Troy and Anchises and the offspring of kindly Venus.

Odes 4.15.25–32

The standard commentary refers dismissively to 'propaganda and cliché', but that is too easy a judgement. Why should we doubt the reality of Rome's gratitude, to Caesar Augustus for securing peace and plenty, and to Virgil for creating a history that made sense of it?

Ovid is more congenial to modern taste. Twenty years younger than Virgil and Horace, with no adult memory of civil war, he could take the peace and plenty for granted and feel no obligation to be virtuous in the ancestral way. What he enjoyed was present-day life in 'golden Rome':

> Others may like the old ways. As for me, I'm glad I was born now. This era suits my style.

Ovid *Ars amatoria* 3.121–2

Contemporaries saw Augustus' *saeculum* as a golden age—and Ovid filled it with 'the arts and eloquence of love'.

He too had aristocratic friends, but his poetry was for everyone. Only three of the fifty poems in the *Amores* collection are addressed to individuals. The great majority were, as he says, 'read to the People'; and in one case he even specifies the occasion, the games of Ceres on 19 April. Several of them required performance, with actors or actresses taking speaking roles, and in two poems the mention of nymphs may suggest a supporting cast of dancers. 'My poems', he later remarked, 'have often been danced for the People.'

The *Heroides* are particularly tantalizing. At first sight, they are wholly dependent on the written word, presented as letters to be read, with frequent internal references to the letter-writer in the act of writing. But reason rebels at the notion that these intensely rhetorical monologues were composed just to be read on papyrus, and seizes with pleasure on textual evidence that suggests otherwise. It comes in the seventh poem, which begins as follows:

> Ovid *Heroides* 7.1–4
>
> So the white swan sings when the Fates call, throwing itself down in the wet grass by the Maeander. I speak to you, but not because I hope you may be moved by my prayer; it is against the god's will that I have begun this.

As the swan sings (*concinit*), so the speaker speaks (*alloquor*). She reveals herself as Dido, at a moment precisely identified in the fourth book of Virgil's epic: Aeneas is resolved to leave Carthage, but has not yet set sail. Only at the end do we realize that this soliloquy is meant to be a letter. Dido has taken the sword Aeneas left and is going to use it on herself:

> *Heroides* 7.183–4
>
> If only you could look at an image of the writer! I am writing, and the Trojan sword is on my lap.

The *reader* of the poem is invited, like Aeneas, to imagine the scene. But elsewhere, describing the poem as 'what pitiful Dido *says* with the drawn sword in her hand', Ovid seems to have in mind an actress before an audience.

With the 'Art of Love' and 'Cures for Love', the question of presentation is much more straightforward. Since Ovid consistently used the second-person plural, and sometimes even addressed his audience collectively, it is clear that these works, like the *Amores*, were 'read to the People'. Notionally, the first two books of *Ars amatoria* were for men only, and the third for women; but of course much of the humour of his 'school of love' depended on each class hearing the other's lessons, and in *Remedia amoris* he addressed both together. They were simply the Roman People, men and women, rich and poor, together at the games.

Not everyone approved of such openly erotic public entertainment, but Ovid didn't care:

Some people lately have criticized my little books. According to their view, my Muse is shameless. Well, while I'm this popular, and sung throughout the world, any odd critic who wants to is welcome to damn my work.... So burst, you envious backbiters! I've got a great name already, and it's going to be greater.

Ovid *Remedia amoris* 361–4, 389–90

That was written probably in AD 1, just a couple of years after Augustus had banished his own daughter for precisely the sort of behaviour that Ovid's poetry took for granted. Eighteen years had passed since the games of the *saeculum*. Horace was dead, Maecenas was dead, Agrippa was dead. Caesar Augustus was 63 years old, and about to face the unusual experience of popular demonstrations *against* him. The People wanted him to bring Julia back; but he was adamant.

9.7. Ovid's *Fasti*

Rome's citizens now enjoyed the luxury of three permanent theatres. Augustus rebuilt the theatre of Pompey at great expense; Balbus' theatre was constructed between 19 and 13 BC, and the theatre of Marcellus was finally completed in 11 BC. The 'regionary catalogues' of the fourth century AD, which evidently preserve some Augustan data, give a capacity of 11,510 for Balbus' theatre, 17,580 for Pompey's, and 20,500 for Marcellus'.

What were those huge audiences watching? Primarily, no doubt, the exciting new 'all-mime' ballets of Pylades, Bathyllus, and their rivals. But we must also remember that the triumphantly popular Ovid was now turning to epic, of a kind no one had ever seen before. *Metamorphoses* was a whole world of stories, introduced as 'a continuous song from the beginning of the world to my own time'. Recent scholarship has noted analogies with 'all-mime' dance, and with tragedy; less serious spectacle is suggested by the many episodes that involve nymphs or Nereids *en masse*, and heroines or goddesses without their clothes. Was *Metamorphoses* a repertoire of performance libretti? Or were the poet's words alone enough to create the illusion? Perhaps Ovid, like Homer, could fill whole theatres.

Of course, those alternatives are too crudely distinguished. We can imagine a solo recitation, the poet at a lectern reading from his scroll. We can imagine, with a bit of help from modern analogies, the lavish spectacle of 'all-mime', with its singing choruses and flying musicians. But it's not as if that was all there was. A praetor booking the entertainments for his *ludi scaenici* might well want more than a poetry reading but less than the whole expensive apparatus of the Pylades company; a college of priests (and Augustus was a member of all of them) might well want more than just a hymn to the relevant deity on the 'NP' days of the festival year (Ch. 2.6 above). *Fasti*, Ovid's calendar poem, gives us an idea of what might be on offer.

It is a conspicuously didactic work, conveying information to an anonymous pupil (the reader) who is addressed throughout in the second-person singular. What makes it a great poem, however, is the series of extended narratives and dialogues that explain the name of a month or the significance of a ritual. In four of these—aetiologies of the hymn of the Salii on 1 March (NP), of the name of the month of May, of the *ludi Florales*, and of the *Matralia* in honour of Matuta on 11 June (NP)—use of the second-person *plural* confirms that Ovid meant them for delivery to an audience. That is exactly what we should expect, since religious occasions were for instruction as well as enjoyment. When the best poets were available, why not employ them?

The games too were religious occasions, and Ovid was there. At the *ludi scaenici* for the Great Mother on the Palatine:

> Ovid *Fasti* 4.187–90
>
> The stage resounds, the games are calling. Come to watch, Quirites, and leave the litigious forums empty of strife! I feel like asking many questions, but I'm terrified by the noise of the high-pitched bronze and the curved pipe whose sound makes your hair stand on end.

Or at the *ludi circenses* for Flora in the Circus Maximus:

> Ovid *Fasti* 5.183, 190
>
> Be present, mother of flowers, to be honoured with fun-filled games! ... Let this song too go with the Circus' show.

Flora's cult site at the Circus was next to that of Ceres and Libera. That in turn prompted Ovid's aetiology of the *ludi Ceriales*, the ancient story of the goddess's search for her lost daughter: 'The place itself demands that I tell of the virgin's abduction.'

At the Great Mother's games, the Muse Erato answered the poet's questions. At Flora's, the goddess herself did the honours—and three other Muses had just given the poet competing explanations of the month of May. Similarly on 1 June, when sacrifice was offered to Juno on the Capitol, the goddess herself and her daughter Iuuentas disputed the meaning of the month at the poet's enquiry. Who spoke those goddesses' lines? The poet himself in a solo recitation, or actresses sharing the performance? Either guess is possible; there is no reason to privilege the first.

The close relationship of *Fasti* with stage performance is attested in one passage—on the reception of the Great Mother in 204 BC—and easily detectable in many others. A particularly interesting example is Ovid's aetiology in book 3 of the constellation called 'Ariadne's crown'. A sequel to the Ariadne and Theseus story in Catullus 64 (Ch. 7.4 above), it featured the heroine once more soliloquizing on a deserted beach, this time about the supposed infidelity of Liber (Bacchus) himself:

> 'Again! Waves, listen to the same complaints. Again! Sand, receive my tears. I used to say, I remember, "Forsworn and faithless Theseus!".'
>
> Ovid *Fasti* 3.471–3

Why 'used to say'? Since she was quoting herself on a particular occasion in the Catullus story, we should expect 'I *said*' in the perfect tense, as in other Ovidian quotations. But here, and again later in her speech, Ariadne used the imperfect appropriate to repeated actions. If she was not just Ariadne but also an actress, the line may mean 'I used to say it every time I played the Catullus piece'.

For a high-profile poet, association with the stage was now perhaps a dwindling asset. In AD 4, Fortune finally deserted Caesar Augustus. His two heirs—Julia's sons, adopted as his own—were dead, one at 18, the other at 23. He adopted his stepson, the patrician Tiberius Claudius Nero, 45 years old and disliked by the Roman People. Tiberius did not share Augustus' indulgent view of popular pleasures, and at just this time the behaviour of the 'all-mime' dancers and their fans was becoming particularly outrageous.

What would happen when Augustus died? Could anyone inherit such personal authority, and if so, who should it be? The question of 'succession' was now toxic, and political anxieties were made worse by a dangerous military crisis and flood, fire, and famine in Rome. It was not a good time to do something stupid.

What exactly Ovid did in AD 8, nobody knows. But it evidently involved prominent people, it was too sensitive to talk about, and it made Augustus very angry. After *Ars amatoria*, the poet would not be given the benefit of any doubt; in fact the poem was added to the charge against him. There was no trial by jury, no debate in the Senate, just Caesar's edict announcing the sentence. Ovid was banished, and the place of his banishment was specified: not Athens or Ephesus or any other cultivated city that would appreciate his gifts, but Tomis at the very edge of empire, just south of the Danube delta.

Fasti had to be left half-finished, but Ovid kept on writing. With no restrictions on his correspondence, he sent a constant stream of poems and verse epistles to Rome, where his well-wishers kept them safe. The five books of *Tristia* and the four books of *Epistulae ex Ponto* constitute a substantial part of his surviving oeuvre. At the time, however, written copies were a poor consolation.

Ovid knew perfectly well what his sentence meant. He excused himself to a friend and fellow-poet for not having sent him a poem before:

> It's partly because I get so little benefit from writing—so much so that that's the main part of my misfortune—and partly because writing a poem you don't read to anyone is the same as doing dance movements in the dark. An audience stimulates

> Ovid *Ex Ponto* 4.2.31–8
>
> creativity, praise for talent increases it, and glory carries a huge spur. Who is there here I can recite my work to, except blond-haired Corallians and all the other tribes of the barbarous Danube?

That was what Augustus wanted, and his edict was a proof of our main argument. To neutralize an author, you didn't have to stop him *writing*. You had to take away his audience.

10

Under the Emperors

Now at last we can turn back to the time-line, and readjust our focus to the *longue durée*. In Chapter 1 we posed a dilemma about the nature of Roman literature. Should we assume that it was a matter only of books and readers, the preserve of a cultured elite? Or should we take the norm to be the 'Regulus model' (Ch. 1.4 above), with oral delivery to a large audience as the primary mode of 'publication', and the making of written copies only a secondary stage?

Fig. 1

Chapters 2 and 3 (A to B on the time-line) were an attempt to understand the cultural conditions of early Rome, from the creation of the Roman Forum in the seventh century BC to the availability of papyrus in the third. In Chapters 4–6 (B to C on the time-line) the story was taken forward into the second and first centuries BC—from the evidence of Plautus and Terence, Ennius and Lucilius, Varro and Cicero—with particular attention to the stage-games (*ludi scaenici*) and the wooden enclosures (*caueae*) that were constructed to accommodate their audiences. Then followed three chapters (7–9) dealing with a single point on the time-line, less than one person's lifetime. (Caesar Augustus lived from 63 BC to AD 14.)

Those three chapters were necessarily dense and demanding. Interpretation of the 'classic' authors' texts, from Cicero to Ovid, had to be interwoven with two complex narratives—the political story of an arrogant oligarchy tamed by the Caesars, father and son, on behalf of the Roman People, and a story of 'show business', with the development of new forms of mass entertainment and new permanent theatres to house them. We have now reached the point where Caesar Augustus has banished the People's favourite, and 'the three theatres' are policed by the Praetorian Guard.

On his way into exile, the first thing Ovid wanted to know was what the People thought, and he knew that, as was proper, they would take their cue from Caesar. The republic that the People's champion had restored thirty-four years earlier was becoming a hereditary monarchy. A century later, Tacitus would begin his history of Rome under the emperors from the moment when Caesar Augustus' unique authority was transferred, awkwardly but decisively, to the man he had had to adopt as his successor.

From this point onwards, from C to D on the time-line, there is no need to pin the argument to an exact chronology. But we shall still be looking for contemporary evidence, to test the hypothesis that Roman literature, and Greek literature in the Roman empire, was primarily written for delivery to a popular audience.

10.1. First-Century Poets

Our first witness is the astronomical poet Manilius, whose second book, written some time between AD 9 and 14, begins with the great sequence of poets from Homer to the present. Every subject has now been dealt with, all the paths to Helicon have been trodden, the springs of the Muses are drunk dry by 'the crowd that rushes to familiar themes'. Manilius, however, will sing of a subject all his own, nothing less than the workings of the universe:

Manilius 2.136–8 (trans. Katharina Volk)
> Since I desire to carry these things to the stars with inspired breath, I shall compose my songs neither in the crowd nor for the crowd, but alone—carried, as it were, in an empty orbit.

Like Lucretius, his great predecessor as a poet of hard science, Manilius glories in being different, separate from the common run of authors.

He doesn't write for the crowd (*turba*), as everyone knew that other poets did. *His* audience, he says, is the smallest crowd in the world, just those few who understand astronomy. The majority, on the other hand, as he goes on to explain, are interested only in money, power, easy living, and undemanding entertainment, 'the sweet pleasure of *listening*'.

The same Lucretian image of following untrodden paths is found in another poet of science, anonymous but evidently writing in the first century AD. His subject was Mount Etna, and the causes of volcanic eruptions. We must not be taken in, he says, by the 'deception' of the bards, with their 'base and impious' stories of Vulcan and the Cyclopes or buried Enceladus:

Aetna 74–9, 91–2
> Such is the common licence of faulty rumour. Bards have creative power: from that, their song is called noble. The greater part of the subjects of the stage is deception. Bards have seen in song the black *manes* beneath the earth and the pale realm of Dis among the ashes; bards have lied about the waves of Styx and the hounds of hell.... That is the licence granted to poetry, but all *my* concern is with the truth.

What is interesting here is the reference to the stage. The train of thought requires that the bards (*uates*) with their songs or poems (*carmina*) were heard in theatres.

The same combination of terms occurs in Tacitus' report of an event in AD 47: the emperor Claudius,

> exercising his censorial responsibilities, in stern edicts berated the People's recklessness at the theatre, because they had hurled abuse at the consular Publius Pomponius (he produced songs for the stage) and at illustrious ladies.

Tacitus *Annals* 11.13.1 (trans. A. J. Woodman)

Pomponius was a senior senator, and soon an active army commander in Germany, but he was equally well known as a poet and playwright. He was evidently performing in person when the audience treated him so discourteously.

A few years later, a young equestrian called Aulus Persius Flaccus took a satirical view of contemporary literature:

> Behind closed doors we write—one in verse, another in prose—something grand for a huge lungful of air to puff out. This is for the People, of course, and eventually you'll read it from your lofty position, well combed, all white in a fresh toga, wearing the sardonyx you got for your birthday.

Persius 1.13–17

But then he imagines an objector:

> 'You laugh,' he says, 'and you're overdoing the curled nostrils. Who's going to say no to the desire to earn the People's voice?'

Persius 1.40–2

When the poet persists, so does the objector: 'What do the People say about it?' It was clearly a question that mattered.

To read 'from a lofty position' must mean on a stage or platform. But where were the audience? One answer is provided by Juvenal, in his own satirical account of the meanness of literary patrons:

> He knows how to provide freedmen to sit at the end of the row, and distribute the loud voices of his friends—but none of the top people will give you what benches cost, or seats on hired stands, or an *orchestra* consisting of portable chairs.

Juvenal 7.43–7

That was clearly an occasion organized by the poet himself, perhaps the sort of reading that caused the famous rant that begins Juvenal's first satire ('Shall I always be just in the audience?'), with long-winded reciters delivering tedious mythological poems among Fronto's plane trees, marble statues, and columns—evidently the peristyle garden of the patron's grand house.

But that cannot be the whole story. Persius was, after all, talking about poems 'for the People'. Another passage in Juvenal opens a different perspective:

> Everyone runs to hear the pleasing voice and the song of the beloved *Thebaid* when Statius has made the city happy by promising a day. Such is the pleasure with which he captures their minds, and such the desire with which the crowd [*uulgus*] listens to him. But when he's broken the benches with his poetry, he still starves unless he can sell Paris his virgin *Agave*.

Juvenal 7.82–7

(Paris was an 'all-mime' dancer, and writing libretti for him was what paid the bills.)

That was Statius in the 80s, an ambitious poet still making his way. Ten years later he had made it, and for one who enjoyed the emperor's favour it was no longer a question of benches. Now the venue might be one of the three great theatres, with the audience in the wedge-shaped divisions of the semicircular auditorium. Here he is in AD 95, addressing a young friend about to leave on a military commission:

Fig. 16

> Alas for me! But if I should happen to summon my usual gatherings, and the Romulean fathers come to hear my poems, I shan't have you there, Crispinus, and my Achilles will look round through all the wedges for the absentee.

Statius
Siluae 5.2.160–3

There we have a glimpse of a real poet, not a pretentious amateur, performing to a real audience worthy of his talent.

10.2. First-Century Playwrights

Pomponius the playwright, barracked in the theatre despite his status as a senior senator, was well known for discussing his work with his peers. Pliny, for instance, reports that Pomponius would say 'I'll appeal to the People' whenever one of his friends suggested something should be cut from the text; and according to Quintilian, Pomponius and Seneca argued 'even in their prefaces' about whether a particular Latin phrase was acceptable in a tragedy. The two anecdotes evidently refer to successive stages of a play's existence: performance before the People, where applause or silence would show whether or not the critical friend was right, followed by distribution in a written text with a preface for the benefit of the learned.

Seneca too was a senior senator (consul in AD 56) and a writer of tragedies. However, modern scholarship is divided on whether his surviving texts were meant for performance at all. One widely held view is that they were written for recitation to a private audience:

> Tragedy neither could nor should compete with the public spectacles, and the best way to avoid that competition was to change it from a public to a private activity. By becoming private and rhetorical, aristocratic poetasters could separate themselves from the world of bluster and vulgarity that had ridiculed the elegance of Pomponius Secundus.

Goldberg
2000.225

Here I think we can detect the preconception noted in the introduction (Ch. 1.4 above), that sophisticated literature must be intended only for a cultured elite.

10.2. First-Century Playwrights

There is no evidence—and I think no reason to suppose—that Seneca's practice was any different from Pomponius'. But so powerful is the idea of 'recitation drama' that it seems to neutralize all evidence to the contrary:

> The setting and resources implied by the text of Seneca's dramas are those of a full-scale theatre. Medea needs to appear on the roof of a stage-building, and to be lifted from it in a dragon-chariot. Phaedra appears on a balcony in the upper storey of the *scaenae frons*. And use of the *exostra* to reveal an interior scene is implied in the *Thyestes* and *Hercules*. But these indications are scarcely conclusive, since it could have been simply conventional practice to write tragedy as if for a full-scale theatre.
>
> Fitch 2000.7

It could have been—but where does the burden of proof lie? Other things being equal, texts written in dramatic form, implying the use of a theatre's resources, should be for public performance. What evidence is there to defeat that expectation?

The setting of Tacitus' *Dialogue on Oratory* (dramatic date AD 75–6) is the town house of Curiatius Maternus, senator and playwright, the day after he had given a private reading of his historical drama *Cato*. That was the usual procedure, to collect comments and possible criticisms before finalizing the text. On this occasion, the political content of the play had 'caused offence to the powerful'. Maternus is now looking over his text when visitors are announced—Julius Secundus, Marcus Aper, and the young Tacitus.

> Secundus said: 'Maternus, don't the spiteful stories that are going around frighten you into loving this unpopular Cato of yours a little less? Or perhaps you've taken the book in hand to give it a thorough revision and cut out the parts that have given a handle to misrepresentation: so that *Cato* on publication [*emittere*, Ch. 1.3 above] may turn out, if not better, at least safer?'
>
> 'You will find in the book,' he replied, 'what Maternus owed it to himself to put there—and you will recognize what you heard at the recitation. If Cato has left anything out, Thyestes will repair the omission at the next recital. I've already got that tragedy organized in my mind—and I'm hurrying on the publication [*edere*, Ch. 1.3 above] of *Cato* so that I can put that care aside and concentrate wholeheartedly on the new one.'
>
> 'You're never tired of these tragedies of yours,' said Aper. 'You still neglect oratory and the law-courts, and spend all your time on Medea and now Thyestes, though you're constantly being summoned to the Forum by your friends' cases and countless obligations to colonies and municipalities. You'd hardly have time for them even if you hadn't brought this new business on yourself of lumping in Domitius and Cato—Roman names and Roman episodes—with Greek mythology.'
>
> Tacitus *Dialogus* 3.2–4 (trans. M. Winterbottom

At first sight, this seems to be exactly the evidence that's needed—plays recited before small groups and then distributed in written form.

However, we can hardly generalize from Maternus' case. The whole point of the discussion is that his plays were politically sensitive, and therefore unlikely to be chosen by the praetors for the *ludi scaenici*. It doesn't follow that they were not intended for performance at all. No doubt Maternus hoped that one day they would indeed be staged, when 'the powerful' were less censorious. At any rate, when Tacitus made Aper summon Maternus 'away from auditoria *and theatres* to the Forum and lawsuits and real battles', he evidently took it for granted that Maternus wrote for public performance.

So I think we can forget the phantom genre of 'recitation drama'. Plays were plays, to be performed. As the younger Pliny put it (and he was a connoisseur of recitations), if you wrote tragedy, you needed not a private auditorium but actors and a stage.

Maternus' *Cato* is actually evidence for something much more interesting, the continued political relevance of the Roman theatre. A century and a half earlier, Cicero usually left Rome when the stage-games were on (Ch. 6.3 above), and when he did go to the theatre, he was relieved to get a friendly reception (Ch. 6.6 above). The Roman People *en masse* were no respecters of persons, and they knew who was on their side and who was not. When Pomponius Secundus was treated so rudely in AD 47, it was only six years since his brother's consulship at the time of the assassination of the emperor Gaius ('Caligula'), when the Senate had rejoiced prematurely at the end of the 'tyranny' of the Caesars and proposed to destroy the temples of Divus Iulius and Divus Augustus. When Claudius came to power there had been an amnesty; but the People did not forget.

A historian writing in the nineties AD, whose source for the death of Gaius may well have been there at the time, makes it clear that the ideological tension between the People and the Senate, the many and the few, was as strong as ever:

> The aim of the senators was to regain their former dignity; they owed it to their pride to free themselves, now that it was possible at last, from the slavery imposed on them by the tyrants' insolence. The People, on the other hand, resented the Senate; they saw the emperors as a curb on its rapacity and a protection for themselves. They were delighted at the seizure of Claudius [by the Praetorian Guard], believing that if he became emperor he would save them from the sort of civil strife there had been in the days of Pompey.

Josephus *Jewish Antiquities* 19.227–8

Maternus' hero Cato had been deeply involved in that civil strife, as Caesar's opponent in his lifetime and as a symbol of principled resistance after his death. Since the Roman People, and therefore the theatre audience, were naturally loyal to the Caesars, a historical drama with Cato as its protagonist might have failed the selection process even without the disapproval of those powerful courtiers.

By great good fortune, the text of a first-century historical drama happens to survive; it was wrongly attributed to Seneca, and thus included in a collection of his tragedies. The dramatic date is AD 62. Octavia, the eponymous heroine, is the daughter of the late emperor Claudius, now unhappily married to Nero—Claudius' stepson, adopted son and successor in power—who banishes her and marries the 'haughty harlot' Poppaea Sabina. When the Roman People violently protest, Nero crushes them and plans the burning of Rome as their punishment. There are two choruses, one of Roman citizens supporting Octavia, one of courtiers in attendance on Poppaea. The most likely date for the production is soon after the fall of Nero in June 68, in a Rome still devastated by the great fire of 64.

It is the citizens' chorus that matters most for our argument. They remember the great tradition of Roman popular power from the expulsion of the Tarquins onwards, and they honour the Gracchi as the People's friends (Ch. 5.4 above), though Lucan in his recent epic had put them in Tartarus. Nero was the Caesar who failed the People, using the fire to create his own luxurious urban estate. Augustus' great-great-grandson, dead without an heir, he was, in the words of the Sibyl herself, 'the last of the line of Aeneas'. The play that tried to make tragic sense of his failure still caught an echo of the ideological conflict that had freed the People from the oligarchs four generations before.

10.3. Prose Fiction and History

It was prose as well as poetry that Persius imagined being puffed out for the People in a huge lungful of air. What sort of prose he had in mind is not easy to guess, but one possibility is narrative fiction.

The ancient 'novels', Greek and Roman, have been studied intensively in recent years, but not much attention has been paid to the question of their delivery. Petronius' *Satyrica*, almost certainly contemporary with Persius' satires, is supposed by its latest commentator to have been written in episodes 'intended as recitations for a literary coterie associated with Nero'. We can certainly agree about episodes for recitation, but why should we assume a restricted audience?

Notoriously, there is no ancient critical discussion of the novel. The nearest approximation to it comes in Macrobius' discussion of different types of fiction in the fifth century AD. His purpose was to justify the philosophical validity of Platonic 'myths', as exemplified by the dream of Scipio in Cicero's *De republica*.

He carefully distinguished such narratives from stories that merely gave enjoyment to the listener:

> Stories (their very name is an admission of falsehood) are invented *either* just to give pleasure to the ears *or* as an encouragement to good works as well. The ones that charm the sense of hearing are comedies, such as those Menander or his imitators have presented for performance; or else the plots full of invented vicissitudes of lovers that [Petronius] Arbiter spent much effort on or that Apuleius, to our astonishment, sometimes played with. A philosophical treatise expels from its sanctuary this entire category of stories, which offers delights only for the ears, and relegates it to the cradles of the nursery.

Macrobius In Somnium Scipionis *1.2.7–8*

The astonishment about Apuleius was because the author of *Metamorphoses* (also known as *The Golden Ass*) was thought of in Macrobius' time as a Platonic philosopher.

In fact he was a sophist, in north Africa in the second century AD—a professional in the art of words who could perform in any genre, prose or verse. And he did so in theatres:

> Such a great multitude of you has come to listen to me that I ought to praise Carthage for having so many friends of learning rather than apologize for not, like a philosopher, refusing to speak! For the assembled audience is appropriate to the greatness of the city, and the chosen venue is appropriate to the magnitude of the audience. Besides, in an auditorium of this sort what should draw your attention is not the marble of the floor, the many storeys of the proscenium, or the columns of the stage; nor the height of the roof, the brilliance of the coffering, or the circumference of the seating; nor the fact that here on other occasions the mime actor makes a fool of himself, the comic actor makes conversation, the tragic actor makes loud speeches, the tightrope-walker takes risks, the conjuror makes things disappear, and all the other performers at the games [*ludiones*] demonstrate their particular arts to the people. Leaving all these aside, there is nothing that should draw your attention more splendid than the mind of the audience and the words of the speaker.

Apuleius Florida *18.1–5*

That elaborate exordium introduced a display speech which itself served as an introduction to another performance, a hymn to Aesculapius in both Greek and Latin. That in turn was to be followed by a three-part dialogue, also in Greek and Latin and also in honour of the god, in which the two other performers were Sabidius Severus and Julius Persius, learned local worthies who may well have been sophists themselves.

Reference to other types of theatre performance, particularly mime and comedy, is a notable feature of both the *Satyrica* and *The Golden Ass*. As for the Greek novels, or 'romances', as they are sometimes called, one of the earliest of them, Chariton's *Chaereas and Callirhoe* (first century AD?), ends with the young hero

10.3. Prose Fiction and History

telling the whole story to the people of Syracuse assembled in their *theatre*. The only extant discussion of the Greek novels, by Photius in the sixth century AD, calls them 'dramas', and refers to the author of one of them as 'the poet of a comedy'.

A prose author described as a poet may remind us of what Demetrius, seven centuries before Photius, said about the historian Ctesias (Ch. 7.2 above). History, too, is a possible candidate for the prose that Persius imagined puffed out for the People.

Cicero, the master-orator, declared that history was 'the orator's job above all', and by that he meant not the contentious oratory of the law-courts and the political arena, but the 'easy-listening' style of the sophist. As it turned out, for two or three generations after his time Roman historians *were* contentious and political, and some of them paid for it with their lives. Perhaps for that reason, much of our evidence for the recital of history in Rome presupposes the 'audience of fine gentlemen' mode, with the historian addressing a polite gathering of his peers. But that was not typical.

The evidence for mass-audience history in Rome is inconspicuous and easy to ignore, but it does exist; and once we look beyond the capital to the cities of the empire, we can see that mass audiences were the norm. Our best witnesses are the sophists Aristides and Lucian, contemporaries of Apuleius who were doing in the cities of the Greek East what he was doing in Latin-speaking Carthage.

When Aristides wanted to talk about historians, he referred to them as 'those between the poets and the orators', and of course he meant the sophistic style of oratory, as used by people like himself in competitive display at city festivals. The theatre audience was a cross-section of the whole population, not just the educated but 'those whom we call "the many"', even if the latter sometimes preferred dancers, mimes, and jugglers to the liberal education the sophist provided.

Exactly the same general audience is assumed in Lucian's dissertation on how to write history. There are two things, he says, that the true historian must avoid, and they are eulogy (*enkōmion*) and poetic myth (*muthos*):

> Mythical fiction isn't even enjoyable, and panegyric of one side or another is particularly repugnant to listeners—if you're thinking not of the mob and the common people but of those who listen critically, and yes, even forensically as well.

Lucian *Historia* 10

You must be absolutely objective, honouring truth alone and ignoring everything else:

> In short, the one yardstick and exact measure is to look not to those who are listening to you now, but to those who hereafter will make the acquaintance of your writings.

Lucian *Historia* 39

The true historian wrote for posterity as well as for the present day. But he had to satisfy his present-day audience, by using a style 'which the many can understand and the educated can applaud'. And the nature of his material enabled him also to be entertaining:

Lucian *Historia* 58

If ever you need to bring on someone making a speech, then that's your opportunity to be rhetorical and display the brilliance of the words.

Why were there so many speeches in ancient historiography? Partly, perhaps, because popular audiences enjoyed having characters 'brought on stage' to speak their parts.

Lucian's own works, a wonderful collection that fills eight volumes of the Loeb edition, provide an unparalleled insight into this world of cultural entertainment. In an autobiographical piece, he described Education (*Paideia*) appearing in a dream when he was a boy and promising him fame and fortune:

Lucian *Somnium* 12

All eyes will be on you, and whenever you happen to speak the multitude will listen to you open-mouthed in amazement, and congratulate you on the power of your words.

So he got an education and became a *rhētōr*, a sophist, one of 'those who come before the masses and announce their recitals', paid to perform at civic festivals (the equivalent of the Roman *ludi*) and charging top fees for their 'rhetoric in public'.

The sophist too, like the historian, addressed both an immediate audience in person and a subsequent readership via the written text. That double purpose was precisely invoked when Lucian imagined his friend Sabinus' reaction to reading the text of one of his performances:

Lucian *Apologia* 3

'My friend, for a long time, and rightly, this composition of yours has been admired, both when it was presented before a great crowd, as those who were then in the audience used to tell me, and in private among those of the educated who have thought it worth visiting and handling.'

'Before a great crowd' was no exaggeration. Throughout his works Lucian took it for granted that his audience might consist of 'the general public' or 'the mass of the people'.

10.4. Lucian in the Theatre

Not all of Lucian's works were written for his own voice. No fewer than forty-four of the eighty-two surviving texts were composed in dialogue form, and though in some cases the dialogue is merely a frame for an extended speech,

10.4. Lucian in the Theatre

most of them keep up the conversation among the characters throughout. Since Lucian presented his work in theatres, and referred to his own dialogues as acted dramas, it is reasonable to conclude that they reached their public by being performed on stage.

That is not the commonly accepted view. On the contrary, according to one distinguished Lucian scholar, 'it has been demonstrated that the dialogues are carefully written in order to be read aloud by a single performer'. The reference is to Alfred R. Bellinger's essay 'Lucian's Dramatic Technique', published in 1928. It is a beautiful piece of work, full of acute observations and written with an elegance to which modern scholarship no longer aspires; but it is not in any sense a demonstration. In fact it is a *petitio principii*, a circular argument that claims to prove what has been taken for granted from the start.

This is what Bellinger says in his first paragraph, comparing Lucian's work with that of real dramatists:

> In the drama, the highest flights of genius would be lost if the playwright had not first informed his audience as to the place, the situation, and the *dramatis personae*. These same problems confront the writer of dramatic dialogues intended to be read aloud by the author, instead of acted. Moreover, these problems are much more difficult to solve, for here the audience can see the scene only in imagination, the actors do not appear at all, and the same voice delivers the speeches of them all.
>
> Bellinger 1928.3

All those presuppositions recur in his text: 'Lucian had neither costume nor action to assist him'; 'innumerable subtleties of tone, with perhaps some help from pose or gesture...would assist the understanding of the piece'; 'the intangible power of his voice and presence supplied the deficiencies of the written words'; 'much of this burden was borne by the reader's tone and by the use of appropriate pauses'. And so to the final paragraph:

> We must conclude that Lucian wrote his dialogues to be read aloud, and to be self-sufficient, relying on the imagination of the audience and on the ingenuity of his work to make them enjoyable and understandable without the necessity of any inartistic interjection of his own personality into the scene.
>
> Bellinger 1928.40

One may wonder why he would choose to make things so difficult for himself.

Bellinger was too good a scholar to ignore evidence that counted against his own assumptions. He noted several dialogues where the text alone—and therefore the putative single reader—gives no indication of how many characters are involved in the conversation, a failing he could only put down to the author's carelessness or poor technique. And there is one case where he simply throws up his hands, a dialogue that opens with six or seven characters all shouting in rapid succession. As Bellinger admits, the stage is crowded, and it is hard to see how any ingenuity on the part of the reader could make it clear who speaks each time. But this exception, puzzling as it is, cannot be allowed to controvert the testimony of the rest, because experiment will show that it cannot be read aloud without confusion, even naming the characters as they speak, unless the reader continually interjects stage directions to the utter ruin of all continuity.

<small>Bellinger 1928.35</small>

The proper inference is surely that it was not read aloud at all. 'The stage is crowded', literally, and the audience can *see* who speaks each time.

Why write in dramatic form at all, if not for performance? The idea of a single voice taking all the parts was always counter-intuitive, and once we are free of it we can try to imagine what Lucian's audience may have seen. In two dialogues, for instance, we have gods on Olympus commenting on conversations or debates on earth. That presumably means actors both on stage and on the roof of the proscenium building. Another begins with Charon coming up from the underworld, no doubt via the 'Charon's ladder' trapdoor in the stage, and Hermes giving him a good view of the upper world by piling Oeta on Ossa and Parnassus on both; since the mountains are 'rolled' (the verb is used twice), and described as 'stage-machinery' (*mēchanē*), we must imagine three cylindrical platforms set upright on top of each other, and the actors climbing up to continue their conversation on the 'twin peaks' of Parnassus.

The 'Judgement of the Goddesses' dialogue starts 'in heaven', from where Hermes points out to Hera the herdsman Paris far below on Mount Ida.

'Since we're close now, if you don't mind let's land on earth and walk. We don't want to alarm him by suddenly flying down from above.' 'Very well, let's do that. Now we've come down, it's time for you to lead the way for us, Aphrodite. I suppose you're familiar with the district, since they say you often came down to visit Anchises.'

<small>Lucian *Dearum iudicium* 5</small>

Between the first and second sentences of Hera's speech, the four deities have descended the stairs of the proscenium building and emerged onto the stage. Of course we *could* simply imagine all that, just as we could imagine the goddesses undressing for the judgement of Paris, but what would be the point? The theatre was the place for looking (*theatron*), not just for seeing with the mind's eye.

Hermes comes down again in the 'Twice Accused' dialogue, this time with Justice (*Dikē*); together with Pan, a local resident, they watch an Athenian law-court hearing the case of Dialogue versus 'the Syrian orator' (Lucian himself, of course). The plaintiff complains of outrageous treatment: he has been used to the high-flying style of Plato's *Phaedrus*, but now the Syrian has broken his wings and put him on the level of 'the many', making him wear a 'comic and satyric' mask, and confining him with Mockery and Invective and old comedians like Eupolis and Aristophanes:

> 'So of course it's outrageous! I'm no longer in my proper state, but playing comedy and farce and acting absurd plots for him!'

Lucian Bis accusatus *33*

He should be grateful, retorts the defendant: joining him with comedy has made him popular with the audience.

There's no need to doubt the literal meaning of 'acting'—or of the mask, for that matter. The interpretation of Lucian's dialogues is analogous to that of Varro's satires (Ch. 5.4 above), and no doubt it is not accidental that both authors saw themselves as modern avatars of Menippus, a Cynic philosopher of the third century BC. This was how Menippus got his message across:

> He had reached such a level of wonder-working that he went around in the guise of an avenging Fury [*Erinys*], saying that he had come from Hades as an inspector of sins, and was going to go back down and report to the powers below. This was the costume he used: a grey ankle-length tunic with a crimson belt round it; an Arcadian hat on his head with the twelve signs [of the Zodiac] embroidered on it; tragic boots, a very long beard, and a staff of ash-wood in his hand.

Suda s.v. *Phaios* (Φ 180 Adler)

He certainly didn't rely on 'innumerable subtleties of tone, with perhaps some help from pose or gesture' to 'assist the understanding' of what he had to say.

It seems clear that when the city authorities hired Lucian for their festival, the theatre audience might see just the man himself, giving a lecture or telling a story; or he might have a little help from his friends—like Apuleius in Carthage with Sabidius Severus and Julius Persius—to provide some conversation as a frame for his speech; or his performance could be part of an extended dramatic scene, with actors and spectacle and all the resources of the theatre. He was a star, and would deliver whatever his hosts could afford.

10.5. Integrating Evidence

Repeatedly in the course of the argument, we have found authors reciting their work in the theatre (Chs. 5.4, 9.2, 10.1 above). Now for the first time, in the second century AD, we have clear evidence that the old classics were recited there too. It comes from the learned Aulus Gellius, recalling the time, probably in the 140s, when he was studying rhetoric with Antonius Julianus in Campania. During a summer festival at Puteoli,

> it was reported to Julianus that a reader [*anagnōstēs*] of some learning, with a really skilled and musical voice, was reading Ennius' *Annales* to the populace in the theatre. 'Let's go,' he said, 'and hear this "Ennianist"' (that was what the performer wished to be called), 'whoever he may be.' When we arrived he was already reading, to huge applause. He was doing book 7 of the *Annales*, and the first thing

Aulus Gellius 18.5.2–4 — we heard was his wrong pronunciation... He finished a few lines later, and left amid the applause and praise of all.

Julianus and his pupils were less impressed.

Another second-century theatre scene, this time in Corinth, is presented by Apuleius in the tenth book of *The Golden Ass*. He describes in detail an elaborately staged ballet of the judgement of Paris, performed by a troupe of young dancers of whom at least two—the boy playing Hermes and the girl playing Aphrodite—were practically naked. It was all music, dance, and spectacle: unlike the Pylades–Bathyllus 'all-mime' mode, there was no chorus singing a libretto. Nevertheless, Apuleius presents it as a dramatization of Homer, presumably from the epic *Cypria*, the original narrative of the judgement of Paris story, which in his time was believed to be by Homer himself.

As always, what we happen to be told is largely random. But it does seem reasonable to take these passages as exemplifying in two very different ways the symbiosis of literature and the stage. At Puteoli there was a single reciter, and his whole performance consisted of reading the words; at Corinth, there were no words, but what was performed was still classic literature. Between those two extremes, we may imagine all kinds of permutations in the way poetry and prose were presented to an audience.

Lucian's treatment of the judgement of Paris is a case in point. Words are his business, but when the goddesses undress for inspection by the judge we are entitled to infer a less intellectual style of entertainment coming into play. That applies even more to Lucian's 'marine dialogues', where the characters are sea-gods, Tritons, and Nereids, and their conversations are brief enough to suggest that they served as interludes between dance routines. Here too there must have been a strong erotic element, provided not only by the sea-nymphs themselves but also by the heroines of the story-lines (Andromeda, for instance) that the dialogues presuppose.

The last of the 'marine dialogues' features two wind-gods, with Zephyrus telling Notus about the 'delightful spectacle' he missed when Zeus, in bull-form, swam off from Tyre with Europa on his back:

> We [winds] all kept calm and just followed along as spectators. There were Cupids flying alongside just above the sea, so that every now and then their toes touched the water. They were carrying lighted torches and singing the wedding song, and the Nereids came up, mostly half-naked, and rode along on dolphins, clapping their hands, while the Tritons and the other sea-creatures that aren't terrifying to look at all danced round the girl. Poseidon, riding in a chariot with Amphitrite as his consort beside him, led the way rejoicing for his swimming brother, and finally there was Aphrodite, carried by two Tritons as she lay in a shell and scattered all kinds of flowers over the bride.

Lucian *Dialogi marini* 15.3

10.5. Integrating Evidence

FIG. 21. Roman sarcophagus showing the *Seethiasos* of Nereids, Tritons, and Cupids, late second century AD, built into the *cortile* of the Palazzo Giustiniani in Rome. Archivio fotografico, Senato della Repubblica © 2014.

Art historians will recognize the scene: it is a *Seethiasos*, 'marine revelry', the aquatic equivalent of Dionysus' riotous retinue of satyrs and maenads. And it takes us to an unexpected source of information about theatrical performance in this period.

Fig. 21 and colour plate 3

In the early part of the second century a far-reaching change took place in Roman funerary practice. Cremation had previously been the norm, but now, and for the next two centuries and more, Romans who could afford it normally placed their dead in stone sarcophagi that were housed (literally) inside tombs designed to look like private dwellings, or even temples. Despite not being on public show, the sarcophagi were lavishly decorated with mythological scenes in high relief, originally painted or gilded; when viewed by torchlight in the darkness of the tomb, they must have presented a dramatic illusion of actually seeing the world of gods and heroes, goddesses and heroines.

Dramatic, literally. Theatrical masks are a very common feature of the decoration of sarcophagi, particularly on the lid, where they often mark the corners and frame the shallow sculpted frieze along the front. There is a fine Hadrianic example in the Louvre: the masks have closed mouths, evidently representing 'all-mime' rather than traditional tragedy or comedy, and the frieze on the lid shows the *Seethiasos* of Nereids, Tritons, and sea-monsters. At this comparatively early stage of sarcophagus design, the main decoration often consisted of lavish fruit-and-flower garlands held up by Cupids, with either masks or narrative scenes in the lunettes above them. Here, however, the garlands are held by nymphs, no doubt the companions of Diana, who is seen bathing in the right-hand lunette; two Cupids attend her, and at the top right we see the hunter Actaeon, spying on her from a tree; the left-hand lunette shows the voyeur punished, torn to pieces by his own dogs.

Fig. 22 and colour plate 4

FIG. 22. Roman sarcophagus showing Diana and Actaeon, c. AD 130. Paris, Louvre inv. MA 459.

We know the Actaeon story was performed by 'dancers in the theatre' as far back as the early first century BC (Ch. 6.5 above), and an author writing about the time this sarcophagus was made tells us there was a special mask for actors playing Actaeon, featuring antlers to indicate his metamorphosis. It may be that the sarcophagus scene alluded not just to a myth but to the performance of a myth. Note the figure of Priapus in the left-hand lunette, leaning back to achieve a vertical erection; he was a familiar character in the erotic stage-world of Roman mime. To get an idea of what this scene was about, we should perhaps remember Rhinthon and his 'tragic fooleries' four centuries before (Ch. 3.2 above).

The sculptors soon abandoned the 'garland and lunettes' design, and began to fill the whole front face of the sarcophagus with multiple scenes in very high relief, creating an extraordinary profusion of overlapping images to illustrate their stories. Again, one fine example must suffice—a sarcophagus in the Basel Museum of Ancient Art, probably from the last decade of the second century. The lid shows the story of Jason and the Golden Fleece, and on the sarcophagus itself we see a later episode in Jason's life, the death of his bride Creusa in the poisoned wedding-dress sent her by Medea.

Fig. 23 and colour plate 4

Here the masks are not boundary markers on the lid but integral to the main scene, on the footstool beneath Creusa's knee. What is being illustrated is not a woman dying in agony but the stage performance of a woman dying in agony, complete with audience. ('The introduction of a large number of grief-stricken

PLATE 1. Satyr-mask terracotta antefixes from Rome, c.500 BC. (*a*) and (*c*) reproduced by permission of the Ministero per i Beni e le Attività Culturali—Soprintendenza Speciale per i Beni Archeologici di Roma; (*b*), (*d*), and (*e*) reproduced by permission of the Sovritendente e Direttore dei Musei Capitolini, Rome.

(*a*) From the site of the Basilica Iulia, perhaps from the temple of Castor: Antiquarium forense 1916, Cristofani 1990.63 (3.4.1).
(*b*) From near SS. Luca e Martina, probably from a temple on the north-eastern summit of the Capitol: Antiquarium comunale 16230, Cristofani 1990.69 (3.6.1).
(*c*) From near the 'House of Livia' at the west corner of the Palatine: Antiquarium palatino 12008, Cristofani 1990.91 (4.1.4).
(*d*) From the Via dei Serpenti, near the ancient Subura: Antiquarium comunale 3348, Andrén 1940. pl. 107 no. 384.
(*e*) From the Esquiline, near S. Antonio: Antiquarium comunale 3374, Cristofani 1990.254 (10.1.4).

PLATE 2. (top) Apulian *phiale*, *c*.350 BC (British Museum F 133). For the *Bacchae* scene on the left, see Taplin 2004 and 2007.156–8; for the satyr and dancing girl on the right, see Wiseman 2008.107–8. © The Trustees of the British Museum, all rights reserved.

(bottom) Paestan kalyx-krater, *c*.350 BC (Lipari, inv. no. 927). Reproduced by permission of Regione Sicilia, Dipartimento per i Beni Culturali, Museo Archeologico Regionale Luigi Bernabò Brea, Lipari (ME), Italy.

PLATE 3. (top) *Aureus* (= 100 sesterces). Obverse: head of Caesar with laurel wreath; legend *Imp. Caesar Diui f. cos. VI*. Reverse: Caesar wearing toga, seated on curule chair, holding scroll and with box of scrolls at his feet; legend *leges et iura p. restituit*. 'Commander Caesar, son of Divus [Iulius], consul for the sixth time [28 BC], has restored laws and justice to the Roman People.' © The Trustees of the British Museum, all rights reserved.

(bottom) Roman sarcophagus showing the *Seethiasos* of Nereids, Tritons, and Cupids, late second century AD, built into the stile of the Palazzo Giustiniani in Rome. Archivio fotografico, Senato della Repubblica © 2014.

PLATE 4. (top) Roman sarcophagus showing Diana and Actaeon, c. AD 130. Paris, Louvre inv. MA 459.

(bottom) Roman sarcophagus showing Medea and the death of Creusa, c. AD. 190–200. Antikenmuseum Basel und Sammlung Ludwig/Andreas F. Voegelin.

FIG. 23. Roman sarcophagus showing Medea and the death of Creusa, c. AD. 190–200. Antikenmuseum Basel und Sammlung Ludwig/Andreas F. Voegelin.

spectators . . . appears to be aimed at mobilizing sympathy and emotions'—just as in the theatre.) The masks decorating the footstool have open mouths, signifying traditional tragedy, and the conspicuous bearded figure just behind Creusa—not a named character in the myth—is evidently another iconographic allusion, indicating the messenger's speech that reports her dreadful death in Euripides' *Medea*. It couldn't be shown on stage in Athens in the fifth century BC, but in Rome in the second century AD it was probably danced.

It is only by trying to integrate these disparate bits of evidence that we can hope to get some idea of how the Roman theatre audience engaged with literature, whether classic or contemporary. The uncertainties involved are nicely illustrated by a literary text, precisely contemporary with the Basel sarcophagus, which might illuminate the question for us if only we could be sure what it means.

It comes in the passage of Tertullian's *De spectaculis* where good Christians are warned to shun the indecency of the theatre games, lest they be defiled by what they see and hear. This is what the author seems to say:

> If we despise the teaching of secular literature, defined in God's eyes as the teaching of foolishness, then we are also sufficiently instructed about those types of spectacle which mark off [?] from secular literature the stage of the games [?] or of athletic contests.

Tertullian *De spectaculis* 17.6

'Mark off' is *dispungere*, a favourite word of Tertullian's. Its literal sense was 'to check', as in ticking items on a list, and from there it came to mean 'to distinguish'. 'The stage of the games or of athletic contests' is my over-literal translation of *lusoriam uel agonisticam scaenam*, where the second term is straightforward, since Tertullian uses *agones* to refer to athletics in the Greek style, but the first is ambiguous, since *ludi*, the noun implied by his adjective, could be either *ludi circenses* or *ludi scaenici*, games in the Circus or games in the theatre, with 'stage' (*scaenam*) apparently favouring the latter.

The only way I can make sense of the passage is by assuming that *scaenam* is used very loosely of any kind of performance, including 'athletics', and that Tertullian was distinguishing both drama and dance (*lusoriam*) and boxing and wrestling (*agonisticam*) from secular literature, which itself was a type of spectacle, referred to later in the work as 'stage teachings' (*scaenicae doctrinae*). His argument here seems to be *a fortiori*: if even this (apparently innocuous) type of theatre occasion is prohibited, how much more so must all the others be!

I am not confident of this interpretation; but if it has any merit, then perhaps we can claim Tertullian too as evidence for what this book has tried to show—that poets and prose authors wrote for a popular audience, and that the *ludi scaenici* provided them with the means to find it.

10.6. Christians

'Indecency' was an easy target for Christian preachers. Erotic entertainment had been a part of Roman culture as far back as our evidence allows us to see (Ch. 3.1 above), most conspicuously at the games of Flora, in the 'ancient custom of fun' from which the austere Cato famously absented himself. They were still notorious in the third and fourth centuries AD.

Again and again over that long period (the final stage of our chronological journey) the games of Flora were brought up as evidence of pagan depravity. A good polemicist concentrates on the opponent's weakest point, and Tertullian, Arnobius, Lactantius, and Augustine were nothing if not good polemicists. Their point was not just that shows with explicit sexual content were disgraceful, but that since they were put on in honour of the gods, they revealed what sort of deities Flora, and all the other gods honoured at the *ludi scaenici*, really were.

The beauty of that argument was that it came from the pagans themselves. The great Marcus Varro, unrivalled as an authority on traditional religion, had complained centuries earlier that the 'mythic theology' of the poets, as shown in the theatre, produced stories unworthy of the true nature of the gods. On the contrary, said the Christian apologists, the true nature of the gods was exactly what it *did* show. They were demons, and the theatre was their citadel.

Varro tried to distinguish the gods of the poets from the gods worshipped in public cult, but that was never a convincing argument. The theatre was a part of public cult, as Arnobius pointed out in a bravura passage that provides a satirist's view of the Roman audience about AD 300:

10.6. Christians

> There they are at the public shows! The members of all the priesthoods and magistracies, and the chief *pontifices* and *curiones*, are sitting there. The *quindecimuiri* in their laurel wreaths, and Jupiter's *flamines* in their pointed caps, are sitting there. The augurs, interpreters of the divine mind and will, are sitting there, as are the chaste Virgins who nurse and guard the undying fire. The entire People and Senate are sitting there, including ex-consuls, supremely august and regal, the next thing to gods.
>
> What's on show would be sinful even to hear—the mother of the race of Mars, ancestress of the sovereign People, Venus herself, is being danced as a woman in love, portrayed by indecent imitation as revelling in all the emotions of a vile harlot.
>
> The Great Mother is danced too, with the sacred ribbons in her hair. Regardless of the dignity of her age, the goddess of Pessinus and Dindyma is represented as writhing with outrageous desire in the embrace of a herdsman.
>
> Then there's the famous son of Jupiter, Hercules in Sophocles' *Trachiniae*, caught in the trap of his death-dealing shirt. He's brought on stage screaming piteously, destroyed by the violence of his agony, consumed to the last putrefaction by the dissolution of his disintegrating entrails.

Arnobius 4.35

And so on, and so on. Like the virtuoso carving of the sarcophagi, this gleeful description gives us just a hint of what the dancers of the late-Roman stage were capable of.

A recurring feature of Christian attacks on the traditional *ludi scaenici* was the notion of their impact on the 'eyes and ears' of their audience. 'Eyes' are sufficiently accounted for by the kind of danced spectacle Arnobius described; but what about 'ears'? All Christians were aware of the insidious attraction of pagan literature, and for generation after generation they were warned to deal with it as Odysseus' men dealt with the song of the Sirens—by blocking their ears and not hearing it at all. That preacher's cliché wasn't just a metaphor, meaning 'don't read the pagan poets'. It meant 'don't *listen* to them', literally.

Everyone knew that poetry was received through the ears, and since Tertullian, Arnobius, and Augustine, in their polemics against the theatre games, referred explicitly to the poet's song as well as the actors' performance, it is clear that they regarded literature as an integral part of the *ludi scaenici*. Blocking your ears to it meant not going to the theatre.

Our final witness was the bishop of Hippo Regius in north Africa from 395 to 430. In his twelfth Easter sermon, on the resurrection of the body, Augustine attacked the teaching of 'the philosophers' that blessed souls in heaven, having had all traces of earthly corruption purged away, are then born again in bodily form and live another life on earth. Not only Christians resisted this idea:

> Virgil doesn't like the doctrine of souls returning to bodies. On that view, he thinks, the souls cannot be blessed. Even he, the philosophers' spokesman, was horrified

by it—he, to whom it was shown, or who at least presented a father in the underworld showing it to his son. Of course nearly all of you know this, and I wish only a few of you did. But a few of you in books, and many of you in theatres, know that Aeneas descended to the underworld, and his father showed him the souls of great Romans before they took bodily form. Aeneas himself was afraid, and said

> 'O father, are we to think there are souls that go
> from here to the world above, and return once more
> into encumbering bodies?'

Can we believe, he says, that they go to heaven, and come back again?

> 'Poor wretches—why this dreadful longing for daylight?'

The son's understanding was better than the father's explanation.

Augustine Sermones 241.5

Secondary education in late imperial Rome was largely based on the study of four classic authors, Terence, Cicero, Sallust, and Virgil, and of those it was Virgil in particular who was 'branded on the memory' of every educated person. Those in Augustine's congregation who knew the *Aeneid* from books were the educated few; everyone else knew it from the theatre. It was a fact that he deplored, but it was a fact.

In the preface and the first chapter (Ch. 1.4 above), we noted the prevailing consensus that Roman literature was only for the educated few, 'the preserve of the relatively small elite in which high culture flourished'. We proposed a different idea, that all non-technical poetry and prose was composed in the first instance for oral delivery to a large general audience, and that the distribution of written texts was a secondary stage of 'publication'. The purpose of this book has been to justify that idea, where possible from contemporary evidence, over the whole long history of Rome. Now we have passed point D on the timeline, I think we can say the demonstration is complete.

Fig. 1

Notes

ABBREVIATIONS

CIL   *Corpus inscriptionum Latinarum* (ed. T. Mommsen et al., Berlin, 1863–)
FGrH   *Fragmente der griechischen Historiker* (ed. F. Jacoby, Berlin, 1923–)
FRHist *The Fragments of the Roman Historians* (ed. T. J. Cornell et al., Oxford, 2013)
IGUR   *Inscriptiones Graecae urbis Romae* (ed. L. Moretti, Rome, 1968–73)
ILLRP   *Inscriptiones Latinae liberae rei publicae* (ed. A. Degrassi, Florence, 1957–63)
ILS   *Inscriptiones Latinae selectae* (ed. H. Dessau, Berlin,1892–1916)
PCG   *Poetae comici Graeci* (ed. R. Kassel and C. Austin, Berlin, 1983–)

PREFACE

Epigraph: Kenney 1982.3, cf. 4 and 10 for the following quotations. For the 'relatively small elite' see also Quinn 1982.101 ('We have to remember that we are talking about a cultural élite, not the whole population'), 164 ('The problem which dogs Roman literature throughout its history is the lack of an audience large and representative enough to make the writer feel he is fulfilling a valid social function').   vii

'Nothing outside the text': Derrida 1976.158; for critical discussion, see e.g. Patai and Corral 2005.173 (John R. Searle, 1994), 227–8 (Frederick Crews, 1986), 250–1 (Brian Vickers, 1993).

EPIGRAPHS

Strabo 1.2.8 (C20); Syme 1979.711; Heidel (*c*.1935) quoted in Pearson 1987.vii.   xiii

1. TIMES, BOOKS, AND PRECONCEPTIONS

1.1. The *longue durée*
Literature created for them: by 'half-Greeks', *semigraeci* (Suetonius *De grammaticis* 1.2), like Livius Andronicus and Quintus Ennius; see Feeney 2005.   2

1.2. Paper

Public documents, stone: e.g. CIL 6.36840 (Volcanal regulations), misunderstood by the sources of Dionysius of Halicarnassus *Roman Antiquities* 2.54.2 and 3.1.2 (Wiseman 2008.10). Bronze: Polybius 3.26.1 (Carthage treaties), Dionysius of Halicarnassus 4.26.5 (Latin League list at Diana temple), Livy 3.57.10 ('Twelve Tables' law code). Wood: Cicero *De oratore* 2.52, Servius *auctus* on *Aeneid* 1.373 (pontifical records on *album* or *tabula dealbata*); Livy 9.46.5 (legal calendar on *album*). Leather: Dionysius of Halicarnassus *Roman Antiquities* 4.58.4 (Gabii treaty). Linen: Livy 4.20.7 (captured spoil in Jupiter Feretrius temple); Livy 4.7.12, 4.20.8 (magistrate list in Juno Moneta temple).

Tabulae, codicilli, pugillaria: e.g. Catullus 42.4–12, Laberius fr. 49 (Panayotakis 2010.331–4), Aulus Gellius 17.9.17. Meyer 2004.22: '*Tabulae* were smallish rectangles, often of wood, itself usually (but not always) hollowed out and coated with wax into which letters were incised with a stylus. They could be hung on walls, or two, three, or more of these could be folded together or stacked to form diptychs, triptychs, or polyptychs, and in these multiples could be called a *codex* or *codices*.' Detailed evidence and discussion in Meyer 2004.21–43.

Papyrus: Pliny *Natural History* 13.68–89 (Varro fr. 297 Funaioli); commentary at Lewis 1974.34–69.

Greek trade with Egypt: Herodotus 4.152.1, Diodorus Siculus 1.66.8 and 67.9; Lloyd 1975.1–60, esp. 24–7. Naucratis: Herodotus 2.178–9. Pisistratus and the texts of Homer: *Anthologia Palatina* 11.442 (Page 1981.338–9), Cicero *De oratore* 3.34, Pausanias 7.26.13.

Diplomatic relations: Livy *Epitome* 14 (*societas*), Dionysius of Halicarnassus *Roman Antiquities* 20.14, Dio Cassius fr. 41 (ὁμολογία). Philadelphus and the library: Fraser 1972.1.320–35, 2.473–94.

Pliny *Natural History* 13.68 and 70:

> *chartae usu maxime humanitas uitae constet, certe memoria... rei qua constat immortalitas hominum.*

Cassiodorus *Variae* 37.3 and 5:

> *quid tale in qualibet cultura nascitur quam illud, ubi prudentium sensa seruantur... humanorum actuum seruans fidele testimonium, praeteritorum loquax, obliuionis inimica.*

1.3. Books

Standard account: Kenyon 1951.48–55 (quotation from p. 48); see also Winsbury 2009.15–20.

Cost of papyrus roll: Lewis 1974.129–34. Cleanthes: Diogenes Laertius 7.174.

Slave copyists: e.g. Nepos *Atticus* 13.3–4, Cicero *Ad Atticum* 12.40.1. Cost of professional *scriptores*, with comparisons (baker, blacksmith, etc): *Edictum Diocletiani* 7.1–12 (Giacchero 1974.150–1). Rollers (*umbilici*): e.g. Catullus 22.7, Seneca *Suasoriae* 6.27, Horace *Epodes* 14.8, Martial 1.66.11, Statius *Siluae* 4.9.8.

Cost of books: Martial 1.66.4, 1.117.15–17 (5 *denarii* = 20 *sestertii*); cf. 13.3.1–2 (just 4 *sestertii* for a little book of gift-tag couplets). Legionary pay: Tacitus *Annals* 1.17.4; cf. Suetonius *Domitian* 7.3, Zonaras 11.19 (pay rise AD 83). Wine: Martial 12.76.1 (20 *asses* per amphora).

Kings' libraries: Strabo 13.1.54 C608, Pliny *Natural History* 13.70, 35.10 (Ptolemy, Eumenes); *Suda* E3801, 2.478 Adler (Antiochus). War booty: Plutarch *Aemilius Paullus* 38.11 (Macedon, 168 BC), Strabo 13.1.54 C609 (Athens, 86 BC).

Country houses: Cicero *De finibus* 3.7–8 (Lucullus at Tusculum), 3.10 (Cicero at Tusculum); *Ad Atticum* 4.4a.1 and 8.2 (Cicero at Antium), 4.10.1 (Faustus Sulla at Cumae). Lucullus did at least make the books available to scholars (Plutarch *Lucullus* 42.1–2).

Caesar: Suetonius *Diuus Iulius* 44.2 (M. Varro in charge of the project). Pollio: Pliny *Natural History* 7.115 (*ex manubiis*, contained portrait of Varro), 35.10 (*qui primus bibliothecam dicando ingenia hominum rem publicam fecit*). *Atrium Libertatis*: Suetonius *Diuus Augustus* 29.5, Ovid *Tristia* 3.1.71–2; cf. Livy 43.16.13, Festus 277L, Granius Licinianus 28.35 (record office).

Emperors: e.g. Ovid *Tristia* 3.1.63–70, Suetonius *De grammaticis* 20.2, 21.3 (Augustus' libraries on the Palatine and in the Porticus Octaviae); Aulus Gellius 13.20.1, Suetonius *Tiberius* 74, Martial 12.2(3).7–8 (Tiberius' libraries on the Palatine and at the 'new temple' of Divus Augustus).

No publishing industry: see Winsbury 2009 for an excellent up-to-date discussion; also Hutchinson 2008.31–33, though his phrase 'general circulation' remains undefined.

Waxed tablets: e.g. Callimachus *Aetia* 1.21–2 (δέλτος); Catullus 50.2, Ovid *Fasti* 1.93 (*tabellae*); Quintilian 10.3.31–2 (*cerae, codices*); Pliny *Letters* 1.6.1 (*pugillares*). Dictation: e.g. Horace *Satires* 1.4.9–10, Quintilian 10.3.18–22.

'*A big thing*': Pliny *Letters* 7.17.15 (*quam sit magnum dare aliquid in manus hominum*). 'Sit on it': Horace *Ars poetica* 388–90, cf. Pliny *Natural History*, pref. 20.

Publicare: e.g. Pliny *Letters* 1.1.1, Statius *Siluae* 4 pref. *Edere* (very frequent): e.g. Cicero *Ad Atticum* 13.21a.1, *De legibus* 1.7. *Emittere*: e.g. Pliny *Letters* 9.1.1, Suetonius *Diuus Claudius* 33.2. Personalized dedication: implied by Pliny *Natural History*, pref. 6 (*neque enim similis est condicio publicantium et nominatim tibi dicantium*); dedications that feature in our surviving texts may be evidence for no more than one original copy. See Goldberg 2005.40: 'A Roman author not only knew who his readers were but could, at least for a time, choose them. They were, literally, his friends.'

Diuulgare: e.g. Cicero *Orator* 112, *Ad Atticum* 12.40.1, 13.21a.1. Bookshops: White 2009; cf. Winsbury 2009.58 for the copy-shop analogy.

On display: Horace *Epistles* 1.20.1–13, Martial 1.117.11–17. Bookshop gossip: Aulus Gellius 5.4.1, 13.31.1, 18.4.1, Galen 19.8–9 Kühn; that is probably what Catullus meant by looking for Camerius *in omnibus libellis* (55.4).

1.4. Literature as a Public Performance

The Well-Read Muse: Bing 1988.23, 82, 17 (quotations); cf. also 61 ('poetic works... were now communicated not by one human being to another, but by an object—the scroll'). *Callimachus and his Critics*: Cameron 1995.24–70 (32–8 on Bing); quotations from 27, 30 (quoting Gelzer 1993.144), 64. Cameron's chapter-title, 'The Ivory Tower', describes the fallacy he attacks.

Demetrius and 'Longinus': see Halliwell, Russell, and Innes 1995.143–523. Speaker and audience: most explicitly at Demetrius *On Style* 75, 201, 'Longinus' *On the Sublime* 41.2. Cf. also Demetrius 1, 27, 95, 135, 255, 271, 288, 303 (ὁ λέγων); 15, 17, 39, 45, 202, 216, 279 (ὁ ἀκούων, οἱ ἀκούοντες); 222, 247 (ὁ ἀκροατής); 'Longinus' 8.1 (τὸ λέγειν), 18.2 (ὁ λέγων); 1.4 (οἱ ἀκροώμενοι), 7.3 (ἀκοή); 16.2–3, 22.3, 30.1, 38.2 (οἱ ἀκούοντες); 3.5, 12.5, 16.3–4, 22.4, 26.2, 32.4, 34.4 (ὁ ἀκροατής, οἱ ἀκροαταί).

Greek scholia: Nünlist 2009 *passim*, esp. 135–56 for 'effects on the reader [sic]'; 243, 342 for οἱ θεαταί and τὸ θέατρον in *scholia* on drama; 350 for the speaker's voice.

Refutation ignored: in the preface to the 2008 reprint of Bing 1988, Cameron is not mentioned, and 'the shift from public staging of poetry to its reception in the solitary act of reading' is still presented as a given. Preconception: Nünlist 2009.12 n. 41, referring to Schenkeveld 1992.

Ancient habits: Schenkeveld 1992.130, 131; details in Starr 1991, Horsfall 1995. None of the alleged examples of ἀκρόασις = 'reading' and ἀκούειν = 'to read' (Schenkeveld 1992.135 n. 38, 141) seems to me at all compelling.

Plural listeners (οἱ ἀκροαταί, οἱ ἀκούοντες): see the *scholia* quoted in Nünlist 2009.58, 61, 137, 146, 149, 150, 154, 165.

Roman literary culture: bibliography listed in Werner 2009; see also the bibliographies of Hutchinson 2008, Lowrie 2009 and Winsbury 2009. Clear statement: Lowrie 2009.49. See also Parker 2009.194: 'Though literature at Rome could be (but need not be) *presented* orally on occasion, literature at Rome did not *circulate* orally. Rather, Roman authors explicitly directed their books to a group of men and women who could read them.'

Greek-speakers in Latium: Osteria dell'Osa tomb 482 (*cultura laziale* IIB2), Bietti Sestieri and De Santis 2000.53; for rival readings (*eulin, euoin, nikē* in retrograde), see Ridgway 1996, Peruzzi 1998.19–22, Canali De Rossi 2005.165–8. Greek influence on archaic Latium: brief summary in Wiseman 2008.231–3.

Horace on early Latium: *Epistles* 2.1.156–63. Authorities on ancient theatre: e.g. Dearden 2004.129–30.

Plebeian magistrates: e.g. C. Fabricius, Manius Curius and M. Regulus (Wiseman 2004.153–8, 2009b.41–4). Community of equals: Dionysius of Halicarnassus *Roman Antiquities* 2.15.4, 2.28.3 (Wiseman 2009b.81–98 for Varro as the source); cf. Ovid *Metamorphoses* 14.805–6 on Romulus' *aequata iura*.

Literacy: Harris 1989 is still the standard work; see also Beard *et al.* 1991.

Oral heritage: Wiseman 2008.237–9.

Plato *Laws* 10.887d, on those who doubt the existence of gods:

> ...οὐ πειθόμενοι τοῖς μύθοις οὓς ἐκ νέων παίδων ἔτι ἐν γάλαξι τρεφόμενοι τροφῶν τε ἤκουον καὶ μητέρων, οἷον ἐν ἐπῳδαῖς μετά τε παιδιᾶς καὶ μετὰ σπουδῆς λεγομένων καὶ μετὰ θυσιῶν ἐν εὐχαῖς αὐτοὺς ἀκούοντές τε, καὶ ὄψεις ἑπομένας αὐτοῖς ἃς ἥδιστα ὅ γε νέος ὁρᾷ τε καὶ ἀκούει πραττομένας θυόντων.

Cicero *De legibus* 1.47, on the superiority of the senses over *opiniones*:

> nam sensus nostros non parens, non nutrix, non magister, non poeta, non scaena deprauat.

Cicero *De finibus* 5.52, on why history gives pleasure:

> quid quod homines infima fortuna, nulla spe rerum gerundarum, opifices denique delectantur historia? maximeque eos uidere possumus res gestas audire et legere uelle qui a spe gerendi absunt.

Pausanias 1.3.3, on Athenian democracy 'introduced by Theseus':

> λέγεται μὲν δὴ καὶ ἄλλα οὐκ ἀληθῆ παρὰ τοῖς πολλοῖς οἷα ἱστορίας ἀνηκόοις οὖσι καὶ ὁπόσα ἤκουον εὐθὺς ἐκ παίδων ἔν τε χοροῖς καὶ τραγῳδίαις πιστὰ ἡγουμένοις.

Pliny *Letters* 4.7.2, on Regulus:

> ipse uero nuper adhibito ingenti auditorio librum de uita eius recitauit, de uita pueri: recitauit tamen; eundem in exemplaria mille transcriptum per totam Italiam prouinciasque dimisit. scripsit publice, ut a decurionibus eligeretur uocalissimus aliquis ex ipsis qui legeret eum populo: factum est.

2. ROME BEFORE LITERATURE: INDIRECT EVIDENCE

Independent communities: perhaps including the Querquetulani and Velienses mentioned on a list of the participants in the common cult of the Latins (Pliny *Natural History* 3.69, with Wiseman 2010a.435–6); according to Tacitus (*Annals* 4.65), Querquetulanus was the ancient name of Mons Caelius, and Festus (182L) mentions a *curia Veliensis*.

Work involved: Ammerman 1990.

Rome as rhōmē: Plutarch *Romulus* 1.1 ('founded by Pelasgians'); also Hyperochus of Cumae *FGrH* 576 F3 (Festus 328L), Ateius Praetextatus fr. 14 Funaioli (Servius on *Aeneid* 1.273), Solinus 1.1 ('originally Valentia, translated into Greek by Evander').

Roman legend: Cicero *De republica* 2.4–63, Livy 1, Dionysius of Halicarnassus 2–4; Wiseman 1995.

2.1. Evidence from Homer

Nestor's cup (*Iliad* 11.623–7): Ridgway 1992.55–7. Polyphemus (*Odyssey* 9.371–97): Schweitzer 1955.

City at peace: Homer *Iliad* 18.497 (λαοὶ δ' εἰν ἀγορῇ ἔσαν ἀθρόοι).

11 Homer *Iliad* 18.502–6:

> λαοὶ δ' ἀμφοτέροισιν ἐπήπυον, ἀμφὶς ἀρωγοί·
> κήρυκες δ' ἄρα λαὸν ἐρήτυον· οἱ δὲ γέροντες
> ἥατ' ἐπὶ ξεστοῖσι λίθοις ἱερῷ ἐνὶ κύκλῳ,
> σκῆπτρα δὲ κηρύκων ἐν χέρσ' ἔχον ἠεροφώνων·
> τοῖσιν ἔπειτ' ἤισσον, ἀμοιβηδὶς δὲ δίκαζον.

Altars to the gods: *Iliad* 11.807–8, on the Greek camp at Troy (ἵνα σφ' ἀγορή τε θέμις τε | ἤην, τῇ δὴ καί σφι θεῶν ἐτετεύχατο βωμοί).

Homer *Iliad* 18.603–6:

> πολλὸς δ' ἱμερόεντα χορὸν περιίσταθ' ὅμιλος
> τερπόμενοι· δοιὼ δὲ κυβιστητῆρε κατ' αὐτοὺς
> μολπῆς ἐξάρχοντες ἐδίνευον κατὰ μέσσους.

Nausicaa's directions: Homer *Odyssey* 6.266–7 (ἔνθα δέ τέ σφ' ἀγορή, καλὸν Ποσιδήιον ἀμφίς, | ῥυτοῖσιν λάεσσι κατωρυχέεσσ' ἀραρυῖα); 7.43–4 (θαύμαζεν δ' Ὀδυσεὺς λιμένας καὶ νῆας ἐίσας | αὐτῶν θ' ἡρώων ἀγοράς).

Alcinous: *Odyssey* 8.5 (Φαιήκων ἀγορήνδ', ἥ σφιν παρὰ νηυσὶ τέτυκτο); 8.15–16 (καρπαλίμως δ' ἔμπληντο βροτῶν ἀγοραί τε καὶ ἕδραι | ἀγρομένων); 8.109–10 (βὰν δ' ἴμεν εἰς ἀγορήν, ἅμα δ' ἕσπετο πουλὺς ὅμιλος | μυρίοι).

Homer *Odyssey* 8.258–64:

> αἰσυμνῆται δὲ κριτοὶ ἐννέα πάντες ἀνέσταν
> δήμιοι, οἳ κατ' ἀγῶνας ἐῢ πρήσσεσκον ἕκαστα,
> λείηναν δὲ χορόν, καλὸν δ' εὔρυναν ἀγῶνα.
> κῆρυξ δ' ἐγγύθεν ἦλθε φέρων φόρμιγγα λίγειαν
> Δημοδόκῳ· ὁ δ' ἔπειτα κί' ἐς μέσον· ἀμφὶ δὲ κοῦροι
> πρωθῆβαι ἵσταντο, δαήμονες ὀρχηθμοῖο,
> πέπληγον δὲ χορὸν θεῖον ποσίν.

14 Demodocus in the king's hall: *Odyssey* 8.41–99, 469–541; 9.1–11; 13.23–30. Phemius: *Odyssey* 1.144–55, 324–59; 17.260–71; 22.330–53 23.129–51. Demodocus' lyre: *Odyssey* 8.105–7, 254–7. Demodocus as λαοῖσι τετιμένος: *Odyssey* 8.472, 13.28.

2.2. Evidence from Terracotta

House of the ruler: Filippi 2004, elaborated by Carandini 2007.60–70 (development stages dated 770–600 BC).

Tullus Hostilius and Ancus Marcius: Walbank *et al.* 1989.647–8; *contra* Wiseman 2008.314–15. Chronological framework: Dionysius of Halicarnassus 1.74–5 (Timaeus his earliest authority), with Feeney 2007.86–100.

15 Statue-group: Sommella Mura 1990, with Arata 1990.119–20; Winter 2009.377–81.

Hercules and Evander: Virgil *Aeneid* 8.102–369; Livy 1.5.1–2, 1.7.3–15; Ovid *Fasti* 1.469–584, 5.643–50; Dionysius of Halicarnassus *Roman Antiquities* 1.31–42. The Ara Maxima was probably close to the church of S. Maria in Cosmedin.

Deification of Hercules as an early Italian story: Pindar *Nemean Odes* 1.67–72, with Wiseman 2010b.78–81.

Stesichorus (Davies 1991.133–234, Curtis 2011): *Suda* Σ 1095, 4.433 Adler (name and origin); 'Longinus' *On the Sublime* 13.3 ('most Homeric'), Quintilian 10.1.62 ('his lyre is equal to the weight of epic poetry'); Megaclides of Athens, quoted in Athenaeus 12.512f–513a (Hercules' lion-skin).

Address to citizens (Locri): Aristotle *Rhetoric* 2.1394b–95a, Philodemus *De musica* 1.30 (Davies 1991.136–7); cf. Stesichorus fr. 212 = Scholiast on Aristophanes *Peace* 797 (Stesichorus' δαμώματα, songs for the people). Pallantion: fr. 85 = Pausanias 8.3.2 (Davies 1991.175), inexplicably omitted by Curtis 2011; one version of the poet's life (*Suda*) has him born in Pallantion and exiled, just like Evander.

Herodotus 5.67.1 and 5:

Κλεισθένης γὰρ Ἀργείοισι πολεμήσας τοῦτο μὲν ῥαψῳδοὺς ἔπαυσε ἐν Σικυῶνι ἀγωνίζεσθαι τῶν Ὁμηρείων ἐπέων εἵνεκα, ὅτι Ἀργεῖοί τε καὶ Ἄργος τὰ πολλὰ πάντα ὑμνέαται· τοῦτο δέ, ἡρώιον γὰρ ἦν καὶ ἔστι ἐν αὐτῇ τῇ ἀρορῇ τῶν Σικυωνίων Ἀδρήστου τοῦ Ταλαοῦ, τοῦτον ἐπεθύμησε ὁ Κλεισθένης ἐόντα Ἀργεῖον ἐκβαλεῖν ἐκ τῆς χώρης. [...] τά τε δὴ ἄλλα οἱ Σικυώνιοι ἐτίμων τὸν Ἄδρηστον καὶ δὴ πρὸς τὰ πάθεα αὐτοῦ τραγικοῖσι χοροῖσι ἐγέραιρον, τὸν μὲν Διόνυσον οὐ τιμῶντες, τὸν δὲ Ἄδρηστον.

Herodotus 1.23–24.1:

...ἐόντα κιθαρῳδὸν τῶν τότε ἐόντων οὐδενὸς δεύτερον, καὶ διθύραμβον πρῶτον ἀνθρώπων τῶν ἡμεῖς ἴδμεν ποιήσαντά τε καὶ ὀνομάσαντα καὶ διδάξαντα ἐν Κορίνθῳ. τοῦτον τὸν Ἀρίονα λέγουσι, τὸν πολλὸν τοῦ χρόνου διατρίβοντα παρὰ Περιάνδρῳ, ἐπιθυμῆσαι πλῶσαι ἐς Ἰταλίην τε καὶ Σικελίην, ἐργασάμενον δὲ χρήματα μεγάλα θελῆσαι ὀπίσω ἐς Κόρινθον ἀπικέσθαι.

Cf. Aristotle *Poetics* 1449a10–11, on the origin of tragedy 'from those who led out the dithyramb'.

Arion as a *stēsichoros*: *Suda* A3336, 1.351 Adler ('Arion...is said to have been the inventor of the tragic mode and the first to set up a *choros* (χορὸν στῆσαι) and sing a dithyramb and name what was sung by the *choros*, and bring in satyrs speaking verse'); Scholiast on Pindar *Olympian Odes* 13.26b ('The serious element of the dithyrambs of Dionysus first appeared at Corinth; that is where the dancing *choros* was first seen, and he who first set it up (ἔστησε) was Arion of Methymna').

Terracotta plaques: Andrén 1940.lxxi–ccxlii, Fortunati 1993, Winter 2009.350–76. Specialists' rival interpretations of the S. Omobono plaques: Torelli 2011.5–8, Mura Sommella 2011.182–5. For the 'Veii-Rome-Velletri decorative system' in general, see Winter 2009.311–93, esp. 392–3: 'The Ionicizing style...suggest[s] that the artisans responsible for making these moulds were East Greek immigrants.'

Circe: Tertullian *De spectaculis* 8.2, Lydus *De mensibus* 1.12 (founds *ludi circenses*); Hesiod *Theogony* 1011–16 (mother of Latinus), with Wiseman 1995.45–50. Circus

Maximus and *ludi Romani*: ps.Asconius 217 Stangl (*Romani ludi sub regibus instituti*); Cicero *De republica* 2.36, Livy 1.35.8–9 (attributed to Tarquinius Priscus).

19 Poseidon Hippios: Dionysius of Halicarnassus *Roman Antiquities* 1.33.2, Plutarch *Romulus* 14.3, *Moralia* 276C (*Quaestiones Romanae* 48), Lydus *De magistratibus* 1.30; cf. Livy 1.9.6 (*Neptunus equester*), Servius on *Aeneid* 8.636 (*eques Neptunus*); Wiseman 2008.149–51.

2.3. Rome and Athens

Tarquin as descendant of Demaratus: Polybius 6.2.10, Cicero *De republica* 2.34, *Tusculan Disputations* 5.109, Livy 1.34.2, Dionysius of Halicarnassus *Roman Antiquities* 3.46.3–5, Strabo 5.2.2 C219–20, Zonaras 7.8. Aristodemus his heir and ally: Livy 2.21.5, 2.34.4, Dionysius of Halicarnassus 6.21.3, 7.2.3, 7.12.1; Zevi 1995, esp. 296–8 (doubted for no good reason by Gallia 2007).

Date of expulsion: Polybius 3.22.1–2; cf. Eratosthenes *FGrH* 241 F1(a) for Xerxes' invasion as a chronological fixed point.

Date of Hippias' expulsion (511/510 BC): Thucydides 8.68.4, [Aristotle] *Athenaion politeia* 19.6, 21.1; Rhodes 1981.191–9. Attic pottery in Rome: Meyer 1980.

Dating *post reges exactos*: Cicero *Brutus* 62, Varro *De re rustica* 1.2.9, Livy 7.3.8, 10.9.3, Dionysius of Halicarnassus *Roman Antiquities* 7.1.5, Asconius 76C, Tacitus *Annals* 11.22.4 (cf. *Histories* 3.72.2, *pulsis regibus*), Pomponius in *Digest* 1.2.2.3, 16, 20. Probable fourth-century BC creation of the Roman historical tradition: Gabba 2000.16–19, Wiseman 2004.70–3.

Dating μετὰ τὴν τῶν τυράννων ἐκβολήν: Aristotle *Politics* 3.1.10 (1275b36), [Aristotle] *Athenaion politeia* 32.2. The alternative phrase μετὰ τὴν τῶν τυράννων κατάλυσιν (Thucydides 8.68.4, [Aristotle] *Athenaion politeia* 20.1, 21.1, Aristotle *Politics* 5.8.21 (1312b31), Diodorus Siculus 11.55.1) was also adapted to apply to the Tarquins: Polybius 3.22.1 (μετὰ τὴν τῶν βασιλέων κατάλυσιν).

Aristotle on tyrannies: *Politics* 5.9.4 (1313b18–26); cf. Herodotus 2.124–5 on the pyramids (misdated). Olympian Zeus temple: Vitruvius 7.pref.15 (attributed to Pisistratus himself), Philostratus *Lives of the Sophists* 1.25.6 (Hadrian). Jupiter Optimus Maximus temple: Livy 1.55.1–6 (1.56.1 for plebeian labour), Dionysius of Halicarnassus *Roman Antiquities* 4.59–61; Tagliamonte 1996; quotation from Cornell 1995.96.

'Dedicated by consul M. Horatius': Cicero *De domo* 139, Livy 1.8.6–8, 7.3.8, Dionysius of Halicarnassus *Roman Antiquities* 5.35.3, Plutarch *Publicola* 14; cf. Polybius 3.22.1 for M. Horatius' consulship. Dating *post [aedem] Capitolinam dedicatam*: Pliny *Natural History* 33.19, citing an inscription of 304 BC; Werner 1963.6–37, Purcell 2003.26–33.

20 Evidence purely material: see Hall 2014.145–65 for the difficulties of interpretation.

Caput rerum story: Varro *De lingua Latina* 5.41, Livy 1.55.5, 5.54.7, Dionysius of Halicarnassus *Roman Antiquities* 4.59.2; cf. Arnobius 6.7, Servius *auctus* on *Aeneid* 8.345 for 'the head of Olus' (*caput Oli*), whence *Capitolium*.

Ceres, Liber, and Libera temple, evidently archaic: Pliny *Natural History* 35.154 (inscription naming Greek artists), Vitruvius 3.3.5 (Etruscan style with terracotta sculpture). Traditional foundation date (493 BC): Dionysius of Halicarnassus *Roman Antiquities* 6.10.1, 6.17.2–4, 6.49.3; Wiseman 2004.73, 2008.136–9.

Liber as Dionysus Eleuthereus: Aleander Polyhistor *FGrH* 273 F 109 (Plutarch *Moralia* 289a = *Roman Questions* 104). Satyr/*silēnos* antefixes: Carlucci 2006, giving a chronological range of 510–470 BC.

Impersonating satyrs: e.g. Plato *Laws* 7.815c. Modern literature on the origins of drama is very extensive: see now the studies (and bibliography) in Csapo and Miller (2007).

Syracusan drama: Aristotle *Poetics* 1448a33–4 on Dorian comedy ('the Sicilian Epicharmus was much earlier than Chionides and Magnes'); Chionides won the prize for comedy at the Athenian Dionysia in 486 BC, Magnes in 472.

Epicharmus: Theocritus *Epigrams* 18 (Syracusan); Diogenes Laertius 8.78 (Pythagorean); Plutarch *Numa* 8.9 (Pythagoras and the Roman citizenship). For Romans among Pythagoras' followers, see Diogenes Laertius 8.14, Iamblichus *De uita Pythagorica* 34.241. Later pseudo-Epicharmus: *PCG* (Kassel and Austin 2001) F 240–97; the Plutarch citation is F 296.

Liberalia as Dionysia: Festus (Paulus) 103L, quoting Naevius. Origin of *ludi scaenici*: Livy 7.2; Oakley 1998.40–71. Caere evidence: Bellelli 2011.

2.4. Honouring Gods

Heraclitus fr. 104 Diels = 59 Kahn, cited by Proclus *On Plato's Alcibiades* 1.117 Westerink:

τίς γὰρ αὐτῶν νόος ἢ φρήν; δήμων ἀοιδοῖσι πείθονται καὶ διδασκάλῳ χρείωνται ὁμίλῳ οὐκ εἰδότες ὅτι οἱ πολλοὶ κακοί, ὀλίγοι δὲ ἀγαθοί.

Commentary: Havelock 1966.56 = 1982.243–4, cf. 1982.124–5 on Plato *Republic* 2.377b–d, 10.598d–600e.

Homer: *Odyssey* 17.383–5 (οἳ δημιοεργοὶ ἔασι, | μάντιν ἢ ἰητῆρα κακῶν ἢ τέκτονα δούρων, | ἢ καὶ θέσπιν ἀοιδόν, ὅ κεν τέρπῃσιν ἀείδων).

Ionians at Gravisca: *Supplementum Epigraphicum Graecum* 27.671, 32.940–1017; Solin 1981. Hermodorus and the Twelve Tables: Pliny *Natural History* 34.21, Pomponius in *Digest* 1.2.2.4.

Saturn temple, attributed to various dates between 501 and 495 BC: Macrobius *Saturnalia* 1.8.1 (citing Cn. Gellius fr. 24P and Varro *Antiquitates diuinae* fr. 73 Cardauns), Livy 2.21.2, Dionysius of Halicarnassus *Roman Antiquities* 6.1.4. Castor temple, attributed to 499 or 484: Livy 2.20.12, 2.42.5; cf. Dionysius of Halicarnassus 6.13.4. Mercury temple, attributed to 495: Livy 2.21.7, 2.27.5–6.

Saturn and his sickle: Varro *Antiquitates diuinae* fr. 243 Cardauns (Augustine *City of God* 7.19); Virgil *Georgics* 2.406; Ovid *Fasti* 1.234, 5.627, *Ibis* 214; Martial 5.16.5, 11.6.1; Juvenal 13.39–40; Plutarch *Moralia* 275a (*Quaestiones Romanae* 42); Festus 202L, 432L; Arnobius 3.29, 6.12; Macrobius *Saturnalia* 1.7.24. Cronos and the castration of Ouranos: Hesiod *Theogony* 173–82. Sicily (Zancle or Drepanon): Hecataeus *FGrH* 1 F2, Callimachus *Aetia* fr. 43.69–70, Servius on *Aeneid* 3.707, Macrobius *Saturnalia* 1.8.12. Latium from *latere*: Virgil *Aeneid* 8.319–23, Ovid *Fasti* 1.233–8.

23 Epiphanies of *Dioscuri*: Cicero *De natura deorum* 2.6, 3.11, 3.13; Strabo 6.1.10 C261, Justin 2.3.8 (Sagra); Dionysius of Halicarnassus *Roman Antiquities* 6.13.1, Valerius Maximus 1.8.1a, Frontinus *Stratagems* 1.11.8, Plutarch *Coriolanus* 3.4, *De uiris illustribus* 16.3 (lake Regillus).

Festal days: Livy 2.21.7 (Mercury), 2.42.5 (Castor), Macrobius *Saturnalia* 1.10.2 (Saturn).

Many-talented: *Homeric Hymn to Hermes* 13–14 (πολύτροπον, αἱμυλομήτην, | ληιστῆρ', ἐλατῆρα βοῶν, ἡγήτορ' ὀνείρων).

Homeric Hymn to Hermes 53–9:

πλήκτρῳ δ' ἐπειρήτιζε κατὰ μέρος· ἢ δ' ὑπὸ χειρὸς
σμερδαλέον κονάβησε· θεὸς δ' ὑπὸ καλὸν ἄειδεν
ἐξ αὐτοσχεδίης πειρώμενος, ἠύτε κοῦροι
ἡβηταὶ θαλίῃσι παραιβόλα κερτομέουσιν,
ἀμφὶ Δία Κρονίδην καὶ Μαιάδα καλλιπέδιλον,
ὡς πάρος ὠρίζεσκεν ἑταιραίῃ φιλότητι,
ἥν τ' αὐτοῦ γενεὴν ὀνομακλυτὸν ἐξονομάζων.

Derivation from *merces*: Festus (Paulus) 111L, Servius on *Aeneid* 4.638. God of commerce and gain: Horace *Satires* 2.3.25 and 68, Ovid *Fasti* 5.671–92, Persius 5.112, Petronius *Satyrica* 77.4, Arnobius 3.32.

Economic downturn: Cornell 1995.225–6, 265–6. Plague and famine in the tradition: Livy 3.6–7 (463 BC), 3.32.2 (453), 4.20.9 (437), 4.21.2 (436), 4.21.6 (435), 4.25.3–4 (433), 4.26.5 (431), 4.30.7–9 (428), 4.52.2–5 (412–11), 5.13.4–5 (399), 5.31.5 (392). Apollo Medicus temple: Livy 4.25.3, 4.29.7, 40.51.6.

Aeschylus in Sicily: *Vita Aeschyli* 8–11, 18; cf. Macrobius *Saturnalia* 5.19.17 on Aeschylus as 'a genuine Sicilian'. Euripides and Syracuse: Satyrus *Life of Euripides* 39.19, Plutarch *Nicias* 29.2–3. Competitions: Plato *Laws* 659c.

Embassy to Delphi: Appian *Italian Wars* 8.1; cf. Diodorus Siculus 14.93.3–5, Livy 5.28.2–4, Plutarch *Camillus* 8.4–5 (aid given by Timasitheus of Lipara en route).

Autocrats: *Vita Aeschyli* 8–9 (Aeschylus and Hiero); Aulus Gellius 15.20.9–10, *Suda* E 3695 Adler 2.468–9 (Euripides and Archelaus); Aelian *Varia historia* 2.21, 13.4 (Agathon and Archelaus). For the expense of the Athenian dramatic festivals, see Wilson 2008.

2.5. Fragments and 'History'

24 Pliny *Natural History* 21.7 (Crawford 1996.708–10):

semper tamen auctoritas uel ludicro quaesitarum fuit. namque ad certamina in circum per ludos et ipsi descendebant et seruos suos equosue mittebant. inde illa xii tabularum lex: 'qui coronam parit ipse pecuniaue eius uirtutisque suae ergo duitur ei.' quam serui equiue meruissent pecunia partam lege dici nemo dubitauit. quis ergo honos? ut ipsi mortuo parentibusque eius, dum intus positus esset forisue ferretur, sine fraude esset imposita. See Rawson 1981.1–4 = 1991.389–93.

Nonius 31L (Varro *De uita populi Romani* fr. 23 Riposati):

Varro de uita populi Romani lib. I: etiam pellis bubulas oleo perfusas percurrebant ibique cernuabant. a quo ille uersus uetus est in carminibus: ibi pastores ludos faciunt coriis Consualia.

Collection: Macrobius *Saturnalia* 5.20.18 (*in libro . . . uetustissimorum carminum, qui ante omnia quae a Latinis scripta sunt compositus ferebatur*); cited also by Nigidius Figulus *Commentarii grammatici* fr. 4 Swoboda (Aulus Gellius 4.9.1), Festus (Paulus) 82L, Festus 214L; see Horsfall 2003.36–47, Wiseman 2008.45.

Consualia dates: Degrassi 1963.499–500, 538. Underground altar in the Circus Maximus valley: Dionysius of Halicarnassus *Roman Antiquities* 2.31.2–3, Plutarch *Romulus* 14.3–4, Tertullian *De spectaculis* 5.7, 8.6 (at the turning-point, *apud metas*).

Rape of the Sabines 'in the fourth month after the foundation': Fabius Pictor *FGrH* 809 F5 (Plutarch *Romulus* 14.1). Probable date of rape story: Wiseman 2004.143–4. Romulus' proto-Romans as shepherds: Cassius Hemina *FRHist* 6 F14 (Diomedes *Grammatici Latini* 1.384 Keil); Varro *Res rusticae* 2.pref.4, 2.1.9; Propertius 4.4.73; Ovid *Fasti* 2.365, 4.810; *Origo gentis Romanae* 22.3, *De uiris illustribus* 1.4.

Power-sharing probably reflected in the myth of the twin founders: Wiseman 1995.103–7. New defensive wall: Andreussi 1996. Plague, 365–363 BC: Livy 7.1.7–8, 7.2.1–3, 7.3.1–3.

Livy 7.2.3–8:

. . . uictis superstitione animis ludi quoque scaenici—noua res bellicoso populo, nam circi modo spectaculum fuerat—inter alia caelestis irae placamina instituti dicuntur; ceterum parua quoque, ut ferme principia omnia, et ea ipsa peregrina res fuit. sine carmine ullo, sine imitandorum carminum actu ludiones ex Etruria acciti, ad tibicinis modos saltantes, haud indecoros motus more Tusco dabant. imitari deinde eos iuuentus, simul inconditis inter se iocularia fundentes uersibus, coepere; nec absoni a uoce motus errant. accepta itaque res saepiusque usurpando excitata. uernaculis artificibus, quia ister Tusco uerbo ludio uocabatur, nomen histrionibus inditum; qui non, sicut ante, Fescennino uersu similem incompositum temere ac rudem alternis iaciebant sed impletas modis saturas descripto iam ad tibicinum cantu motuque congruenti peragebant.

See also Valerius Maximus 2.4.4; detailed discussion at Oakley 1998.40–58 and 776–8. For 'Fescennine verse' (abusive ribaldry, often sung at weddings), see Catullus 61.120, Horace *Epistles* 2.1.145–6, Festus (Paulus) 76L.

2.6. Marking the Days

City wall: Säflund 1932 (esp. 109–11 on the Greek-letter masons' marks), Holloway 1994.91–101 (whose third-century dating I find unconvincing), Andreussi 1996, Sewell 2010.172. Livy 6.32.1 (*murum a censoribus locatum saxo quadrato faciundum*, 378 BC).

26

Maritime colonies: Sewell 2010.48–50 (design identical with that of the Massiliot settlement at Olbia); Justin 43.5.8–10, cf. 43.3.4 and 5.3 (long-standing alliance between Massilia and Rome). Circeii: Theophrastus *Historia plantarum* 5.8.3 (Wiseman 2004.71); cf. Homer *Odyssey* 10.551–60 (Elpenor), Diodorus Siculus 14.102.4 (colony 393 BC).

Romans descended from Achaeans: Aristotle fr. 609 Rose (Dionysius of Halicarnassus *Roman Antiquities* 1.72.3–4); cf. fr. 604 Rose (Varro *De lingua Latina* 7.70) for Roman funeral customs discussed in Aristotle's *Nomima barbarica*.

Rome as major power: see Oakley 1998.538–59 on the political settlement following the Latin war in 338 BC. Campania: Livy 8.16.4, Velleius Paterculus 1.14.3 (Latin colony at Cales, 334 BC). Adriatic: Livy 9.26.5, Diodorus Siculus 19.72.8 (colony at Luceria, 314 BC).

Maenius and the *rostra*: Pliny *Natural History* 34.20, Varro *De lingua Latina* 5.155, Livy 8.14.12, Asconius 42C. Maenius and the *maeniana*: Festus 120L (*primus in foro ultra columnas tigna proiecit quo ampliarentur superiora spectacula*), Cicero *Academica* 2.70, Valerius Maximus 9.12.7, Pliny *Natural History* 35.113.

Comitium and *ekklēsiastērion* (Dionysius of Halicarnassus *Roman Antiquities* 4.38.5 for the equivalence): Coarelli 1993, Carafa 1998.132–55, Sewell 2010.36–47. Date: Humm 1999.647–75, cf. Wiseman 2004.320. *Comitium* used for *ludi Romani*: Livy 27.36.8 (207 BC); Marshall 2006.44–5 for its possible use as a theatre.

Calendar: Degrassi 1963, Michels 1967, North 1989.574–6, Beard, North, and Price 1998.1.5–8, 2.60–9. *Dies fasti* and *nefasti*: Varro *De lingua Latina* 6.29–30, Ovid *Fasti* 1.45–56, Macrobius *Saturnalia* 1.16.14.

Praetor's tribunal: Kondratieff 2010, esp. 92–5 on multiple uses of the Forum. Noise: Seneca *Controuersiae* 9.pr.5 (*fremitus consonantis turbae*), cf. Cicero *Ad Atticum* 1.16.3, *Ad Quintum fratrem* 2.3.2 etc for shouting at trials.

27

Prophets in the Forum: Livy 25.1.8–10, Appian *Civil Wars* 1.121.563; cf. Lucretius 1.102–11, Dio Cassius 41.14.4. Storytellers in the Forum: Pliny *Letters* 4.7.6; cf. 2.20.1, Quintilian *Institutio* 10.1.8 (voluble *circulatores*). Funeral: Polybius 6.53–4 (53.1 and 9 for the *rostra*), Dionysius of Halicarnassus *Roman Antiquities* 7.72.12 (procession).

NP monogram: Festus 162L, where the MS is too damaged to be intelligible. Ides and Jupiter: Ovid *Fasti* 1.56.

List of named days: Gaius *Institutiones* 1.112 (*flamines maiores* of Jupiter, Mars and Quirinus); Varro *De lingua Latina* 6.15 (*Palilia* named after Pales), *Res rusticae* 2.1.9 (shepherds); Varro *Res rusticae* 1.1.6 (Robigus), Ovid *Fasti* 4.905–32 (Robigo); Varro *De lingua Latina* 7.45 (*flamines* of Furrina and Volturnus); Festus (Paulus) 106L (Larentia), Ovid *Fasti* 2.583–616 (Lara), Lactantius *Diuina institutio* 1.20.35 (Larunda). It is not known why the *Lemuria*, *Vestalia*, and *Matralia* were marked *N* rather than *NP*.

Literary sources' rival explanations: e.g. Varro *De lingua Latina* 6.12–13, with Ovid *Fasti* 1.317–36 (*Agonalia*), Festus (Paulus) 75L (*Feralia*).

Lupercalia: Cicero *Pro Caelio* 26, Ovid *Fasti* 2.381–422, Plutarch *Moralia* 280c = *Roman Questions* 68 (wolves); Ovid *Fasti* 2.361, Valerius Maximus 2.2.9, Plutarch *Romulus* 21.4, Quintilian *Institutio* 1.5.66, Servius on *Aeneid* 8.343 (goat sacrificed); Justin 43.1.7 (goatskin cape); Dionysius of Halicarnassus *Roman Antiquities* 1.80.1, Nicolaus of Damascus *FGrH* 90 F 130.71, Ovid *Fasti* 2.445–6, Plutarch *Romulus* 21.5, Festus (Paulus) 75–6L (goatskin loincloth and whip); see in general Wiseman 2008.52–83.

Contests and performers: Ovid *Fasti* 1.329–30 (*Agonalia* from *agones*); Varro *Antiquitates diuinae* fr. 80 Cardauns = Tertullian *De spectaculis* 5.3 (Luperci as *ludii*), Valerius Maximus 2.2.9 (Luperci as a *spectaculum*); cf. Velleius Paterculus 1.15.3 (plan for theatre at the Lupercal).

3. ROME BEFORE LITERATURE: DIONYSUS AND DRAMA

3.1. Pots Painted, Bronze Engraved

Attic jug with Perseus dancer (Fig. 6): detailed discussion in Hughes 2006; see also Csapo 2010.25–7.

'Pronomos vase' from Ruvo (Fig. 7): detailed discussion in Taplin and Wyles 2010; see also Robinson 2004.197–201 (for the significance of the Ruvo vases) and Csapo 2010.18–22. Rubustini: Pliny *Natural History* 3.105, *Corpus agrimensorum* 202.25 Campbell.

Non-Greek reception of Attic drama: Green 1996, Robinson 2004, Taplin 2012. For Dionysiac ritual see Burkert 1987, esp. 22 ('Dionysiac mysteries are seen to develop especially in Italy as a kind of analogue to the Eleusinian rites. An elaborate funerary symbolism of Bacchic character is seen to flourish on southern Italian vases of the fourth century, and it also spread to the Etruscan and the Italiote world'). For the Eleusinian rites see Aristophanes *Frogs* 316–459, with Dover 1993.57–62.

Red-figure pottery in Italy: Trendall 1989 (esp. 270–1 for the chronology), Torelli 1992.186–201, with figs. 136–47.

Paestum 'barbarized': Aristoxenus fr. 124 Wehrli = Athenaeus 14.632b (οἷς συνέβη τὰ μὲν ἐξ ἀρχῆς Ἕλλησιν οὖσιν ἐκβαρβαρῶσθαι Τυρρηνοῖς ἢ Ῥωμαίοις γεγονόσι). Writing about a century after the event, Aristoxenus alleges that the Greeks of Poseidonia became 'Etruscans or Romans', though in fact the Romans sent a colony to Paestum only after his time, in 273 BC (Velleius Paterculus 1.14.7, Livy *Epitome* 14).

Paestan comedy scene: Trendall 1987.46 no. 99; for other examples showing stage windows, see Green 1995.109–10, fig. 10 a–d.

'Tilted hand' dance move (χεὶρ σιμή, Athenaeus 14.630a): Wiseman 2008.104–8, cf. 59 (fig. 10), 94 (fig. 22).

Bronze *cistae*: Battaglia and Emiliozzi 1979 and 1990; detailed discussion in Wiseman 2004.87–118 (Roman historical context) and 2008.84–124 (Dionysiac imagery). One of the best-known *cistae* was certainly made in Rome (*ILLRP* 1197, Wiseman 2004.89–97).

Perseus, Medusa, and Pegasus: Hesiod *Theogony* 270–94, a story set in the far West, connected with that of Herakles and Geryoneus.

Iphigeneia *cista*: Wiseman 2008.113–17. The figure identified as Agamemnon has the same pose as 'Acmemeno', named on a *cista* in New York (Battaglia and Emiliozzi 1979.146–50, Wiseman 2008.94); the dog beneath the window may indicate the divine huntress Artemis.

Like Euripides' play, the scene presupposes the plot of the post-Homeric epic *Cypria* (summarized in Proclus *Chrestomathia* 1, Davies 1988.32): 'When the force was gathered at Aulis for the second time, Agamemnon shot a stag while hunting and boasted that he excelled even Artemis. The goddess was angry, and sent storms to prevent them from sailing. When Calchas tells them about the goddess's anger, and orders them to sacrifice Iphigeneia to Artemis, they send for her as if to be married to Achilles, and prepare to carry out the sacrifice. But Artemis snatches her away, takes her to the Taurians, and makes her immortal; and she puts a stag on the altar in place of the girl.'

Oscan speakers: Taplin 1993.40–1, pl. 16.16 (Campanian jug showing a comic character named in Oscan). Etruscan: Wiseman 2008.111–13 ('Clusium group' cups showing naked showgirls, a dancing satyr, and a scene from Euripides' *Helen*).

35 Aristotle: *Poetics* 1447a.13–16 (ἐποποιία δὴ καὶ ἡ τῆς τραγῳδίας ποίησις ἔτι δὲ κωμῳδία καὶ ἡ διθυραμβοποιητικὴ καὶ τῆς αὐλητικῆς ἡ πλείστη καὶ κιθαριστικῆς πᾶσαι τυγχάνουσιν οὖσαι μιμήσεις τὸ σύνολον).

Plato *Laws* 7.815c:

ὅση μὲν βακχεία τ' ἐστὶν καὶ τῶν ταύταις ἑπομένων, ἃς Νύμφας τε καὶ Πᾶνας καὶ Σειληνοὺς καὶ Σατύρους ἐπονομάζοντες, ὥς φασιν, μιμοῦνται κατῳνωμένους, περὶ καθαρμούς τε καὶ τελετάς τινας ἀποτελούντων, σύμπαν τοῦτο τῆς ὀρχήσεως τὸ γένος οὔθ' ὡς εἰρηνικὸν οὔθ' ὡς πολεμικὸν οὔθ' ὅτι ποτὲ βούλεται ῥᾴδιον ἀφορίσασθαι.

36 Imitating satyrs, etc: the standard work is Seaford 1984.1–44. Imitating Pan: e.g. the figure playing the *syrinx* on a mirror in the Villa Giulia museum in Rome (Gerhard *et al.* 1897.51–2, Wiseman 2008.68, fig. 15).

Anachronistic evidence: practically all our literary sources long postdate the Roman Senate's crackdown on Dionysiac mystery-cult in 186 BC (Livy 39.8–19). The *sacrificuli ac uates* who attracted the Senate's disapproval (Livy 39.8.3–4, cf. 25.1.8–12) no doubt offered the sort of 'purification and initiation' to which Plato objected (*Laws* 7.815c); before 186, however, they had presumably practised their cult undisturbed.

3.2. Republican Rome

First Punic War: Polybius 1.63.4 (πόλεμος ὧν ἡμεῖς ἴσμεν, ἀκοῇ μαθόντες, πολυχρονώτατος καὶ συνεχέστατος καὶ μέγιστος).

Latin colonies: Cales (334 BC), Fregellae (328), Luceria (314), Saticula (313), Suessa Aurunca (313), Pontiae islands (313), Interamna Lirenas (312), Sora (303), Alba Fucens (303), Narnia (299), Carseoli (298), Venusia (291), Hadria (289), Paestum (273), Cosa (273), Ariminum (268), Beneventum (268), Firmum (264), Aesernia (263), Brundisium (244), Spoletium (241).

Roads: Diodorus Siculus 20.36.2, Cicero *Pro Caelio* 34, Livy 9.29.6, Frontinus *De aquis* 1.5 (Via Appia, 312 BC); Livy 9.43.25 (Via Valeria, 307); the Via Clodia through Etruria, the Via Caecilia through the Sabine highlands, and the Via Aurelia up the coast to Cosa all probably belong to this period, though the exact dates are not known.

Aqueducts: Frontinus *De aquis* 1.5 (Aqua Appia, 312 BC), 1.6 (*Anio nouus*, 272); the latter was paid for with booty from the war with Pyrrhus.

Coinage: Crawford 1985.28–42 (first silver issue c.310–300 BC; continuous production of silver and bronze from the war with Pyrrhus); see now Coarelli 2013.17–29 on Pliny *Natural History* 33.42–44, who dates the introduction of regular silver coinage to 269 BC.

Sabines given Roman citizenship: Velleius Paterculus 1.14.6 (*ciuitas sine suffragio*, 290 BC), 1.14.7 (full citizenship, 268); cf. Servius on *Aeneid* 7.709 for Romulus giving the Sabines *ciuitas sine suffragio*.

Populus Romanus (et) Quirites formula: Varro *De lingua Latina* 6.86 (from the *tabulae censoriae*), CIL 6.32323.92–141 (17 BC *ludi saeculares*), Degrassi 1963.11, 67 (*Fasti Antiates* and *Caeretani* on 25 May); Livy 1.24.5, 1.32.11–13, 8.6.14, 8.9.7–8, 9.10.9, 10.28.14, 22.10.3, 41.16.1; Festus (Paulus) 59L (*dici mos erat in omnibus sacrificiis precibusque*). For the interlocking etymologies of *Quirites*, Quirinus, and the *tribus Quirina* (created for the new citizens of the Sabine country in 241 BC), see Wiseman 2009b.42–4.

Foundation legend: Wiseman 1995.127–8; Mommsen 1886 = 1906.22–35 for the historical context. Romulus' merging of peoples: Varro *De uita populi Romani* fr. 285 Salvadore = Nonius 787L (*mixtura*); Cicero *De republica* 2.13; Livy 1.13.4; Dionysius of Halicarnassus *Roman Antiquities* 2.46.2–3; Plutarch *Romulus* 14.2, 14.6, *Comparison of Theseus and Romulus* 6.2–3.

Epiphany of deified Romulus: Cicero *De republica* 2.20, *De legibus* 1.3; Livy 1.16.7 ('*proinde rem militarem colant*'), Plutarch *Romulus* 28.2. Quirinus temple: Livy 10.46.7, Pliny *Natural History* 7.213.

Temples: evidence and argument in Ziolkowski 1992.17–189. Triumphs: evidence and argument in Degrassi 1947.543–9.

Aulus Gellius 10.6.2 (from Ateius Capito *De iudiciis publicis*):

Appi namque illius Caeci filia, a ludis quos spectauerat exiens, turba undique confluentis fluctuantisque populi iactata est. atque inde egressa, 'Quid me nunc factum esset' inquit 'quantoque artius pressiusque conflictata essem, si P. Claudius frater meus nauali proelio classem nauium cum ingenti ciuium numero non perdidisset? certe quidem maiore nunc copia populi oppressa intercidissem. sed utinam' inquit 'reuiuiscat frater aliamque classem in Siciliam ducat atque istam multitudinem perditum eat quae me nunc male miseram conuexauit!'

Her brother's naval disaster was at Drepanum in 249 BC.

Italian comedy: Athenaeus 9.402b. Rhinthon 'in the reign of Ptolemy I' (305–283 BC): Suda P 171 = 4.295 Adler.

Rhinthon PCG T 1–2: Suda P 171 = 4.295 Adler ($Ταραντῖνος$ $κωμικός$, $ἀρχηγὸς$ $τῆς$ $καλουμένης$ $ἱλαροτραγῳδίας$, $ὅ$ $ἐστὶ$ $φλυακογραφία$); Stephanus Byzantinus 603.1 ($Ταραντῖνος$ $φλύαξ$, $τὰ$ $τραγικὰ$ $μεταρρυθμίζων$ $ἐς$ $τὸ$ $γελοῖον$).

Epitaph, Nossis *Anthologia Palatina* 7.414 = Gow and Page 1965.2827–30:

$$καὶ\ καπυρὸν\ γελάσας\ παραμείβεο,\ καὶ\ φίλον\ εἰπὼν$$
$$ῥῆμ'\ ἐπ'\ ἐμοί.\ 'Ρίνθων\ εἴμ'\ ὁ\ Συρακόσιος,$$
$$Μουσάων\ ὀλίγη\ τις\ ἀηδονίς·\ ἀλλὰ\ φλυάκων$$
$$ἐκ\ τραγικῶν\ ἴδιον\ κισσὸν\ ἐδρεψάμεθα.$$

Ivy: e.g. *Homeric Hymns* 7.40, 26.1. Tarentum and Dionysus: Dio Cassius 9.39.5 and 10.

Euripidean titles: see Kannicht 2004.554–68 for Euripides' lost tragedy *Meleagros*, which dealt with the hero's love for Atalanta. That story was evidently exploited for erotic parody: Suetonius *Tiberius* 44.2, Ovid *Amores* 3.2.29–30, *Ars amatoria* 3.775). A naked 'Ateleta' appears on a Latin *cista* (Battaglia and Emiliozzi 1979.64–5, Wiseman 2004.108–9); see *CIL* 6.37965.21 (with Horsfall 1985 and 2003.126–8) for Atalanta on the later Roman comic stage.

Skiras: Athenaeus 9.402b, Lydus *De magistratibus* 1.41. Sopatros: Athenaeus 2.71a–b (lived into the reign of Ptolemy II, 285–246 BC); 3.85f, 6.56f, 14.644a, 14.649a, 15.702b ($φλυακογράφος$); 4.158d, 4.175a, 4.183b, 6.230e, 8.341e, 11.784b ($παρῳδός$). Blaisos: Stephanus Byzantinus 357.1 ($σπουδογελοίων$ $ποιητὴς$ $Καπριάτης$), Lydus *De magistratibus* 1.41. Titles: Kassel and Austin 2001.262–6 (Rhinthon), 271–85 (the others).

Latium from Saturnus *latens*: Virgil *Aeneid* 8.322–3, Ovid *Fasti* 1.238, Servius on *Aeneid* 1.6.

Rhinthonica: Rhinthon PCG T 5 = Caesius Bassus in *Grammatici Latini* 6.312 Keil, Evanthius *De fabula* 4.1, Donatis *De comoedia* 6.1, Donatus on Terence *Adelphoe* 7, Lydus *De magistratibus* 1.40.

3.3. The Roman games

Plebeian aediles' headquarters: Livy 3.55.13, Pomponius in *Digest* 1.2.2.21 (archive of *plebiscita* and *senatus consulta*); Livy 3.55.7, Dionysius of Halicarnassus *Roman Antiquities* 6.89.4, 10.42.4 (confiscations for infringements of plebeian rights payable to the cult).

Flora mater: Cicero *In Verrem* 2.5.36, Lucretius 5.739, Ovid 5.183. Temple of Flora: *Fasti Praenestini* 28 April = Degrassi 1963.132–3 (*propter sterilitatem frugum*); Tacitus *Annals* 2.49.1 (*eodem in loco*). Oscan name: Crawford 2011.1204 (Terventum 34, line 24).

Games of Flora: Varro *Res rusticae* 1.1.6 (vegetation), Ovid *Fasti* 5.277–94 (plebeian aediles), Velleius Paterculus 1.14.8, Pliny *Natural History* 18.286. Association with Liber: Ovid *Fasti* 5.261–74; Ampelius 9.11 ('Liber son of Flora'). Erotic: Ovid *Fasti* 5.331–54, Valerius Maximus 2.10.8 (*priscus mos*), Seneca *Letters* 97.8, Martial 1. pref; Wiseman 2008.175–86. Human fertility: Ovid *Fasti* 5.273–4.

Games of Liber: Paulus (Festus) 103L for the equivalence with Διονύσια and the Naevius quotation (fr. 113 Ribbeck: *libera lingua loquimur ludis Liberalibus*); ps. Cyprian *De spectaculis* 4.1 (*ludi scaenici et Cereri et Libero dicati*); Ovid *Fasti* 3.785–6 (merged with those of Ceres); Wiseman 1998.35–43 for the context of their suppression (Livy 39.8–19).

Naevius and the Roman aristocracy: Aulus Gellius 3.3.15, cf. 7.8.5–6; ps.Asconius 215 Stangl (his feud with the Metelli). Campanian: Aulus Gellius 1.24.2.

Senatorial objection to Flora's games: Ovid *Fasti* 5.295–330 (312, 328 for the *patres*); they were established as a regular annual festival in 173 BC, after another crop failure.

Ludi Romani: Cicero *De republica* 2.36 (*maximi*); Livy 1.35.9, ps. Asconius 217 Stangl (*magni*). Not the plebeian aediles: Livy 6.42.12–14 (367 BC). Dates of introduction of *ludi*: Wiseman 2008.167–74.

Fabius Pictor *FGrH* 809 F 13(b) = *FRHist* I F 15 = Dionysius of Halicarnassus *Roman Antiquities* 7.72.1–2, 5–6, 10, 13, 15; 7.73.1, 3–4. The context is Dionysius' narrative of '490 BC' (7.68–9), when an elderly farmer called Titus Latinius reported to the Senate, on the order of Jupiter himself, that the god was dissatisfied with the conduct of the festival and demanded that it be repeated.

According to Dionysius (6.10.1, 6.17.2, 7.71.2), these 'sacrifices and games' had been set up at the same time as the temple of Ceres, Liber and Libera in '496 BC'. Whether the long digression describing the festival (7.70.1–73.5) came from the same context in Fabius is not known; what matters is that Fabius was reporting what he knew himself (7.71.1, ἐξ ὧν αὐτὸς ἔγνω).

Shaggy tunics (μαλλωτοὶ χιτῶνες): see Aelian *Varia historia* 3.40 on Silenoi wearing tunics 'shaggy on both sides' (ἀμφίμαλλοι). Turning the serious into the laughable: cf. Stephanus Byzantinus 357.1 and 603.1 (quoted above) on Blaisos and Rhinthon.

3.4. Rome and Alexandria

End of the First Punic War: Polybius 1.61–2 (battle of Drepanum); Degrassi 1947.76–7 (*fasti triumphales* on Catulus' triumph). Diplomatic contact with Alexandria: Dio Cassius 10.41 (c.273 BC), Dionysius of Halicarnassus *Roman Antiquities* 20.14 (269 BC), Eutropius 3.1.1 (241 BC).

Eratosthenes as Librarian: *Oxyrhynchus Papyri* 10.1241 (*FGrH* 241 T7), Tzetzes *Prooemia in Aristophanem* 1.21 (Kaibel 1899.19); Fraser 1972.330–2.

Eratosthenes on Romans: Strabo 1.4.9, C66 ('marvellously governed'); scholiast on Plato *Phaedrus* 244b, Wiseman 2008.55 (Evander); Servius *auctus* on *Aeneid* 1.273 = *FGrH* 241 F45 (Romulus).

Eratosthenes on Old Comedy (Pfeiffer 1968.159–62, Fraser 1972.457–8): fragments collected in Strecker 1884.

Callimachus on Rome as part of 'Pan-Hellas': *Aetia* fr. 106 Pfeiffer (with the *diegesis*). Callimachus' catalogue (πίναξ καὶ ἀναγραφὴ τῶν κατὰ χρόνους καὶ ἀπ' ἀρχῆς γενομένων διδασκάλων): *Suda* K 227, 3.19 Adler (Pfeiffer 1968.132, Fraser 1972.452–3); quoted by the scholiasts to Aristophanes *Clouds* 553 and *Birds* 1242.

History of literature: *Suda* K 227 also reports Callimachus' 'Catalogue of those who were conspicuous in every kind of literature, and of their writings, in 120 books' (πίνακες τῶν ἐν πάσῃ παιδείᾳ διαλαμψάντων καὶ ὧν συνέγραψαν ἐν βιβλίοις κ' καὶ ρ'); fragments collected in Pfeiffer 1949.344–9; discussion in Pfeiffer 1968.126–31, Fraser 1972.452–3).

46 Dramatic poets as *didaskaloi*: Simonides 147.5 Bergk = 28.5 Page; Cratinus fr. 276 Kassel–Austin; Aristophanes *Acharnians* 628, *Peace* 738, *Birds* 912; Antiphon 6.13. As *chorodidaskaloi*: Aristophanes *Ecclesiazusae* 809; Plato *Alcibiades* 1 125d–e, *Laws* 655a.

Makers (ποιηταί) of the plot: Aristotle *Poetics* 1451b27–8.

Production of play as *didaskein*: e.g. *Supplementum Epigraphicum Graecum* 23.102 (trans. Csapo and Slater 1994.360–1); documents collected in Snell 1971.22–5 and 38–40; Parian Chronicle *FGrH* 239 F43 (on Thespis, ὃς ἐδίδαξε δρᾶμα ἐν ἄστει).

Lists as *didaskaliai*: e.g. scholiast on Aristophanes *Frogs* 67, *hypothesis* II to *Peace* (φέρεται ἐν ταῖς διδασκαλίαις); Csapo and Slater 1994.39–44. Aristotle's book of *didaskaliai*: Diogenes Laertius 5.26.

Plays 'taught': see the texts collected in Snell 1971.45–51 (*hypotheses*, etc), and 61, 66, 84, 89, 92, 94, 95, 115, 132, 208, 210, 227 (*Suda* biographies). For the *hypotheses*, see Pfeiffer 1968.192–6 on Aristophanes of Byzantium, Eratosthenes' successor as Librarian at Alexandria.

International drama and actors' guilds: good summaries in Griffith 2007.24–6, Rehm 2007.190–2, Csapo 2010.95–107.

Fabulam docere, of fifth-century BC authors: Cicero *Ad Atticum* 6.1.18 (quoting Eratosthenes on Eupolis), *Tusculan Disputations* 4.6.3 (Euripides); Vitruvius 7. pref.11 (Aeschylus), Valerius Maximus 8.7.ext.13 (Simonides).

Fabulam docere, of 240 BC: Cicero *Brutus* 72–3, *De senectute* 50; Aulus Gellius 17.21.42 (*primus omnium L. Liuius poeta fabulas docere Romae coepit post Sophoclis et Euripidis annis fere centum et sexaginta, post Menandri annis circiter quinquaginta duobus*). Of early Roman drama in general: Cicero *Brutus* 73, 78 (Ennius), 229 (Accius and Pacuvius); Horace *Ars poetica* 288. The only other attested use of the phrase is

Suetonius *Diuus Claudius* 11.2, where Claudius 'taught' a Greek comedy by his late brother Germanicus at a festival in Naples.

Livius the playwright: Cicero *Brutus* 72–3, *Tusculan Disputations* 1.3, *De senectute* 50; Horace *Epistles* 2.1.69; Livy 7.2.8, 27.37.7, 31.12.10; Suetonius *De grammaticis* 1.2. Named as Livius Andronicus: Festus 446L, Aulus Gellius 18.9.5, *Historia Augusta Carinus* 13.5, Priscian *Grammatici Latini* 2.308 and 321 Keil; cf. Terentianus Maurus *Grammatici Latini* 6.383 Keil (*Graio cognomine*). Praenomen: Aulus Gellius 6.7.11, 17.21.42, Cassiodorus *Chronica* 316 Mommsen = *MGH Chronica minora* 2.128 (Lucius); Jerome *Chronica* 188–6 BC ('Titus', presumably by confusion with T. Livius the historian).

Livius from Tarentum: Accius fr. 18 Funaioli (Cicero *Brutus* 72), wrongly asserting that he was captured when the Romans took the city in 209 BC; see Welsh 2011.32–8 on Accius' mistaken chronology.

Varro on Livius: *De poetis* fr. 55 Funaioli (Aulus Gellius 17.21.42), with Welsh 2011.40–5. Atticus on Livius: *Liber annalis* fr. 5P (Cicero *Brutus* 72–4).

Documentary evidence: Cicero *Brutus* 60 (*in ueteribus commentariis*) on Naevius, challenged by Varro; *Brutus* 72 (*in antiquis commentariis*) on Livius, followed by Atticus. Possible aediles' archive: cf. Polybius 3.26.1 on Rome's treaties with Carthage, 'preserved even now on bronze tablets beside the temple of Jupiter Capitolinus in the treasury of the aediles'. Curule aediles and *ludi Romani*: Livy 6.42.12–14 (with Wiseman 2008.169–70), Dio Cassius 37.8.1 (Caesar as curule aedile).

Tragedy and comedy: Cassiodorus *Chronica* 316 Mommsen = *MGH Chronica minora* 2.128 (*his consulibus* ['239 BC'] *ludis Romanis primum tragoedia et comoedia a Lucio Liuio ad scaenam data*). Known tragedies by Livius: *Achilles, Aegisthus, Aiax mastigophorus, Andromeda, Danae, Equus Troianus, Hermiona, Ino, Tereus*. Known comedies: *Gladiolus, Ludius, Virgo* (or *Virga*).

Didascalica (in at least 9 books): Accius frr. 1–10 Funaioli, on Homer and Hesiod (Aulus Gellius 3.11.4), Euripides (Nonius 262L), etc.

Continuity: see Moretti 1968.184–98 (*IGUR* 215–34, cf. Csapo and Slater 1994.12–13, 119–20) for fragments of lists, in Greek, of Greek playwrights' and actors' victories from fifth-century Athens onwards, mostly found in the Via Arenula area of Rome, close to the theatres of Pompey, Balbus, and Marcellus, and dated by the editor to the time of Augustus or Tiberius.

3.5. The Turning-point

Consuls at the *ludi Romani*: Dionysius of Halicarnassus *Roman Antiquities* 7.72.1 (οἱ τὴν μεγίστην ἔχοντες ἐξουσίαν); Ennius *Annales* 79–81 Skutsch (Cicero *De diuinatione* 1.107); Livy 45.1.6, cf. 8.40.3 (*imperium* required).

C. Claudius Cento, brother of Ap. Claudius Russus (consul 268 BC) and P. Claudius Pulcher (consul 249 BC): all three are identified as 'Ap.f. C.n.' in the consular *fasti* (Degrassi 1947.40–3), and were therefore sons of the great Ap. Claudius C.f.

Caecus, censor in 312 BC and consul in 307 and 296; the dates suggest that Caecus' other son Ti. Claudius Nero (Suetonius *Tiberius* 3.1), who evidently did not live to reach the consulship, was probably older than Cento.

Coins of C. Clodius C.f. Vestalis: Crawford 1974.521 (no. 512), where the connection with C. Claudius Cento is wrongly dismissed (Wiseman 1979.94 n. 124). Vestalis was patron of the *Claudienses* from the *praefectura Claudia* of Forum Clodi (*CIL* 11.3310, Pliny *Natural History* 3.52) on the Via Clodia (or Claudia: Degrassi 1963.130–1, Frontinus *De aquis* 11.3); the builder of the Via Clodia and founder of Forum Clodi is not recorded, but Cento is one of three or four possibilities (Rawson 1991.229–30).

Dating of Flora's games: Pliny *Natural History* 18.286, *urbis anno DXVI* (238 BC on Varro's chronology); Velleius Paterculus 1.14.8 on the foundation of Spoletium, *quo anno Floralium ludorum factum est initium* (241 BC on Varro's chronology); see Wiseman 2009b.93–6 (on Dionysius of Halicarnassus *Roman Antiquities* 2.25.7 and Aulus Gellius 4.3.2 and 17.21.44) for similar rival datings of another third-century event, due to the use of non-Varronian chronological systems.

48 Young aristocrat: C. Servilius C.f. in 57 BC (Crawford 1974.447, no. 423), whose coin-legend *FLORAL. PRIMVS* evidently refers to an ancestor who was either (a) first to celebrate the *ludi Florales* or (b) the first *flamen Floralis* (Ennius *Annales* 117 Skutsch = Varro *De lingua Latina* 7.45).

Raunchiness: Ovid *Fasti* 5.331–54, Valerius Maximus 2.10.8, Seneca *Letters* 97.8, Martial 1.pref., 1.35.8–9; *Historia Augusta Elegabalus* 6.5, scholiast on Juvenal 6.250; Tertullian *De spectaculis* 17.3, Arnobius 7.33, Lactantius *Diuina insitutio* 1.20.10, Ausonius 14.16.25–6. Torchlight: Ovid *Fasti* 5.361–8, Dio Cassius 58.19.1–2. Tragic boots not appropriate to Flora: Ovid *Fasti* 5.347–8.

Livius' and Naevius' epics: excellent discussion of the fragments in Goldberg 1995.58–83, though I cannot agree with his assumption that epic was 'a genre for private circulation rather than public performance' (1995.43).

Suetonius *De grammaticis* 2.2:

> hactenus...ut carmina parum adhuc diuulgata uel defunctorum amicorum uel si quorum aliorum probassent diligentius retractarent ac legendo commentandoque etiam ceteris nota facerent: ut C. Octauius Lampadio Naeui Punicum bellum, quod uno uolumine et continenti scriptura expositum diuisit in septem libros.

Livy 27.37.7 and 13:

> decreuere item pontifices ut uirgines ter nouenae per urbem euntes carmen canerent. id cum in Iouis Statoris aede discerent conditum ab Liuio poeta carmen, tacta de caelo aedis in Auentino Iunonis Reginae... tum septem et uiginti uirgines, longam indutae uestem, carmen in Iunonem Reginam canentes ibant, illa tempestate forsitan laudabile rudibus ingeniis, nunc abhorrens et inconditum si referatur.

49 Trasimene and Cannae casualties: Livy 22.7.2–4 (Fabius Pictor *FGrH* 809 F22), 22.49.15, 25.6.13; Polybius 3.84.7, 3.117.4 (giving a higher figure for Cannae).

New games: Livy 25.12.1–15 (*Apollinares*, 212 BC), 27.23.5–7 (*Apollinares*, 208); 29.10.4–11.8 and 14.5–14 (*Megalenses*, 204), 34.54.3 (*Megalenses*, 194), 36.36.4 (*Megalenses*, 191); see Wiseman 2008.168–9. Motive for their introduction: Livy 25.12.9–10 (Apollo), 29.10.5 (Magna Mater).

Games programme: calendar evidence summarized in Degrassi 1963.435, 439, 449, 477, 506, 528. Curule aediles: Livy 34.54.3 (*Megalenses*), Dio Cassius 37.8.1 (*Megalenses* and *Romani*). Plebeian aediles: Cicero *In Verrem* 2.5.36 (*Cerialia, Florales, plebeii*), with Wiseman 2008.169–70; Ovid *Fasti* 5.287–92 (*Florales*), Dio Cassius 47.40.6 (*Ceriales*). Urban praetor: Livy 27.23.5 (*Apollinares*).

I have omitted the games of Liber, about 17 March, which were merged with the *Ceriales* (Ovid *Fasti* 3.785–6), probably at the time of the Senate's crackdown on the 'Bacchanalia' in 186 BC (Livy 39.8–19, *ILLRP* 511). *Ludi Victoriae* were later instituted by Sulla (81 BC: Velleius Paterculus 2.27.6, Appian *Civil Wars* 1.99.464), from 26 October to 1 November (Cicero *In Verrem* 1.31, Degrassi 1963.525), with a praetor in charge (Crawford 1974.445, no. 421); and by Caesar (46 BC: Suetonius *Diuus Augustus* 10.1, *CIL* 6.37836), from 20 to 30 July (Degrassi 1963.485).

Theatre equipment (the technical term was *apparatus*): Cicero *Pro Sestio* 116, *In Pisonem* 65, *Ad Atticum* 15.2.3, 15.12.1, *Ad familiares* 7.1.2, *De officiis* 2.55, *Tusculan Disputations* 5.9; Livy 1.9.7, 27.6.19, 27.31.1, 31.49.4, 31.50.2, 32.7.14, 40.45.6, 45.32.8; Valerius Maximus 2.4.2, Ulpian in *Digest* 7.1.15.5, Tertullian *De spectaculis* 4.4, 10.2.

200 BC *ludi plebeii*: Plautus *Stichus*, preliminary annotation in *A*, the Milan palimpsest (for which see Tarrant 1983b). See Jocelyn 1980.387–93 for discussion of such annotations (with bibliography); Marshall 2006.89–90 (on Pellio), 234–7 (on Marcipor and musicians).

4. AN ENCLOSURE WITH BENCHES

Simple stages: Bacilieri 2001 collects the visual evidence (from vase-paintings) for early south-Italian performance settings. Architectural form: Sear 2006.48–9 on fourth- and early third-century stone theatres in south Italy and Sicily; the late fourth-century theatre at Metapontum (Todisco 2002.149–56, Sear 2006.147–8) is contemporary with the 'Lycurgan' Theatre of Dionysus at Athens (Csapo and Slater 1994.79–81, Sear 2006.388–9).

4.1. *Theatrum* and *Scaena*

Fifty-three years (220–167 BC) according to Polybius 1.1.5: σχεδὸν ἅπαντα τὰ κατὰ τὴν οἰκουμένην ἐν οὐχ ὅλοις πεντήκοντα καὶ τρισὶν ἔτεσιν, ὑπὸ μίαν ἀρχὴν ἔπεσε τὴν Ῥωμαίων, ὃ πρότερον οὐχ εὑρίσκεται γεγονός.

Terence *Adelphoe*, prefatory note: *acta ludis funerib. L. Aemilio Paulo quos fecere Q. Fabius Maxumus P. Cornelius Africanus* (160 BC). Paullus' triumph (167): Diodorus Siculus 31.8.10–12, Plutarch *Aemilius Paullus* 33–4, Florus 1.28.12–13.

Hostility to Greek culture: e.g. Marcus Cato, censor in 184 BC, in his book of advice to his son (Pliny *Natural History* 29.13–14, Plutarch *Cato maior* 23.2–3); see Astin 1978.170–8.

Book-burnings: e.g. Pythagorean writings in 181 BC (Cassius Hemina FRHist 6 F35, Piso FRHist 9 F14, Valerius Antias FRHist 25 F9—quoted in Pliny *Natural History* 13.84–7 and Livy 40.29.3–14); books of prophecy, before 186 BC (Livy 39.16.8).

Expulsions: e.g. philosophers and rhetoricians in 161 BC (Suetonius *De rhetoribus* 25.2); Epicurean philosophers probably in 154 BC (Athenaeus 12.547a, Aelian *Varia historia* 9.12); Chaldaean astrologers and Jews in 139 BC (Valerius Maximus 1.3.3, with Lane 1979).

Bacchanalia: ILLRP 511; Livy 39.8–19, 39.41.6, 40.19.9, esp. 39.8.3 (*Graecus ignobilis*), 39.15.2–3 (danger from *externae religiones*), 39.16.8–9 (danger from *sacra externa* and *externus ritus*). Games of Liber: Ovid *Fasti* 3.785–6, with Wiseman 1998a.35–43, 2008.127–9 and 192–3.

51 Abortive theatre project, 154 BC: Livy *Epitome* 48, Velleius Paterculus 1.15.3, Valerius Maximus 2.4.2, Augustine *City of God* 1.31 (*Graeca luxuria*), Orosius 4.21.4. 107 BC: Appian *Civil Wars* 1.28.125 (Ἑλληνικαῖς ἡδυπαθείαις), with North 1992.

Censors of 179 and 174 BC: Livy 40.51.3 (*theatrum et proscaenium ad Apollinis*), 41.27.5 (*scaenam aedilibus praetoribusque*); for the latter, cf. Wiseman 2009b.163–4.

Scaenae frons: Vitruvius 5.6.1, 5.7.1, 7.5.2.

Actor on stage: Plautus *Amphitruo* 91 (*in proscaenio*), *Poenulus* 20 (*in scaena*), *Pseudolus* 568 (*qui in scaenam prouenit*). As in Greek: when Polybius metaphorically describes the goddess Tyche bringing historical events 'on stage', he uses both ἐπὶ σκηνήν (29.19.2) and ἐπὶ προσκήνιον (fr. 212 B–W).

Dignity of magistrates in charge of games: Dionysius of Halicarnassus *Roman Antiquities* 6.95.4 (like kings).

4.2. Plautus and the *Cauea*
Plautus *Pseudolus* 1081–3:

> nugas theatri, uerba quae in comoediis
> solent lenoni dici, quae pueri sciunt:
> malum et scelestum et peiurum aibat esse me.

52 Boys: Aristophanes *Clouds* 539 (τοῖς παιδίοις ἵν' ᾖ γέλως).

Plautus *Amphitruo* 64–8:

> nunc hoc me orare a uobis iussit Iuppiter
> ut conquistores singula in subsellia
> eant per totam caueam spectatoribus,
> si quoi fauitores delegatos uiderint
> ut is in cauea pignus capiantur togae.

Cauea also at *Truculentus* 931 (evidently including the stage); and in its literal sense at *Captiui* 124, *Cistellaria* 732, *Curculio* 449.

Plautus *Miles Gloriosus* 79–82:

> mihi ad enarrandum hoc argumentum est comitas,
> si ad auscultandum uostra erit benignitas;
> qui autem auscultare nolet exsurgat foras,
> ut sit ubi sedeat ille qui auscultare uolt.

Stretch legs: Plautus *Epidicus* 733, *Pseudolus* 2. During the action: *Mercator* 160 (*dormientis spectatores metuis ne ex somno excites?*), *Poenulus* 1224 (*in pauca confer: sitiunt qui sedent*).

Plautus *Captiui* 1–3, 10–14:

> hos quos uidetis stare hic captiuos duos,
> illi quia astant, hi stant ambo, non sedent;
> hoc uos mihi testes estis me uerum loqui. [. . .]
>   iam hoc tenetis? optume est.
> negat hercle illic ultumus. accedito.
> si non ubi sedeas locus est, est ubi ambules,
> quando histrionem cogis mendicarier.
> ego me tua causa, ne erres, non rupturus sum.

For standing at the back, cf. Valerius Maximus 4.5.1 (184 BC); for *ultumus* at line 11, cf. Aristophanes *Knights* 704 (ἔσχατος). Flattery: *Captiui* 15 (*uos qui potestis ope uestra censerier*).

Plautus *Aulularia* 717–20:

> quid ais tu? tibi credere certum est, nam esse bonum ex uoltu cognosco.
> quid est quid ridetis? noui omnis, scio fures esse hic compluris,
> qui uestitu et creta occultant sese atque sedent quasi sint frugi.
> hem, nemo habet horum? occidisti.

Chalk (*creta*): Plautus *Poenulus* 969–70, Titinius *Fullones* 29R (Nonius 369L).

Plautus *Poenulus* 1–10:

> Achillem Aristarchi mihi commentari lubet:
> inde mihi principium capiam, ex ea tragoedia.
> sileteque et tacete atque animum aduortite,
> audire iubet uos imperator—histricus,
> bonoque ut animo sedeant in subselliis,
> et qui esurientes et qui saturi uenerint:
> qui edistis, multo fecistis sapientius,
> qui non edistis, saturi fite fabulis;
> nam cui paratumst quod edit, nostra gratia
> nimia est stultitia sessum impransum incedere.

Poenulus 11–15:

> exsurge, praeco, fac populo audientiam.
> iam dudum exspecto, si tuom officium scias;
> exerce uocem, quam per uiuisque et colis.
> nam nisi clamabis, tacitum te obrepet fames.
> age nunc reside, duplicem ut mercedem feras.

Herald and *populus*: Plautus *Asinaria* 4–5. Trumpeter: Livy 33.32.4; Juvenal 6.249 (at the *ludi Florales*); cf. Virgil *Aeneid* 5.113.

Poenulus 16–22:

> *bonum factumst, edicta ut seruetis mea.*
> *scortum exoletum ne quis in proscaenio*
> *sedeat, neu lictor uerbum aut uirgae muttiant,*
> *neu dissignator praeter os obambulet*
> *neu sessum ducat, dum histrio in scaena siet.*
> *diu qui domi otiosi dormierunt, decet*
> *animo aequo nunc stent, uel dormire temperent.*

Formula *bonum factum (sit)*: ILLRP 485.4; Suetonius *Diuus Iulius* 80.2, *Vitellius* 14.4; *De uiris illustribus* 49.17; Tertullian *De pudicitia* 1.

Lictores populares (also called *denuntiatores*, 'announcers'): CIL 6.1869, 6.32299, 10.515, 10.5917 (= ILS 1908, 1917, 1909, 340); cf. CIL 6.975, 6.10095 (= ILS 6073, 5270); Kübler 1927.515–17. Lictors at *ludi*: Cicero *De legibus* 2.61 (funeral games), Polybius 30.22.6 (votive games for victory).

Dissignator: Porphyrio on Horace *Epistles* 1.7.6; CIL 6.32332.12 (at the Severan *ludi saeculares*); Ulpian in *Digest* 3.2.4.1 (a lucrative position in the emperor's gift).

Poenulus 23–7:

> *serui ne obsideant, liberis ut sit locus,*
> *uel aes pro capite dent; si id facere non queunt,*
> *domum abeant, uitent ancipiti infortunio,*
> *ne et hic uarientur uirgis et loris domi,*
> *si minus curassint, quom eri reueniant domum.*

Saving seats: as suggested by Michael Fontaine in an unpublished paper.

Poenulus 28–35:

> *nutrices pueros infantis minutulos*
> *domi ut procurent neu quae spectatum adferat,*
> *ne et ipsae sitiant et pueri pereant fame*   30
> *neue esurientes hic quasi haedi obuagiant.*
> *matronae tacitae spectent, tacitae rideant,*
> *canora hic uoce sua tinnire temperent,*
> *domum sermones fabulandi conferant,*
> *ne et hic uiris sint et domi molestiae.*

Nurses (*nutrices*) as slaves: e.g. Aulus Gellius 12.1.17.

Poenulus 36–45:

> *quodque ad ludorum curatores attinet,*
> *ne palma detur quoiquam artifici iniuria*
> *neue ambitionis causa extrudantur foras,*
> *quo deteriores anteponantur bonis.*
> *et hoc quoque etiam, quod paene oblitus fui:*   40

> *dum ludi fiunt, in popinam, pedisequi,*
> *inruptionem facite; nunc dum occasio est,*
> *nunc dum scriblitae aestuant, occurrite.*
> *haec quae imperata sunt pro imperio histrico,*
> *bonum hercle factum pro se quisque ut meminerit.*

The organizers (*curatores*) are elsewhere referred to as *conductores*, 'those who've hired us' (*Asinaria* 3). 'Outside': *Miles Gloriosus* 81.

Livy 34.54.4–8 (194 BC):

> *horum aedilium ludos Romanos primum senatus a populo secretus spectauit praebuitque sermones, sicut omnis nouitas solet, aliis tandem quod multo ante debuerit tributum existimantibus amplissimo ordini, (5) aliis demptum ex dignitate populi quidquid maiestati partum adiectum esset interpretantibus et omnia discrimina talia quibus ordines discernerentur et concordiae et libertatis aequae minuendae esse: (6) ad quingentesimum <quinquagesimum> octauum annum in promiscuo spectatum esse; quid repente factum cur immisceri sibi in cauea patres plebem nollent? (7) cur diues pauperem consessorem fastidiret? nouam, superbam libidinem, ab nullius ante gentis senatu neque desideratam neque institutam. (8) postremo ipsum quoque Africanum quod consul auctor eius rei fuisset paenituisse ferunt.*

Traditional equality: e.g. Dionysius of Halicarnassus *Roman Antiquities* 2.7.4, 15.4, 28.3 (Romulus); Valerius Maximus 4.3.5b, Frontinus *Stratagems* 4.3.12, *De uiris illustribus* 33.6 (Manius Curius, 290 BC); Cicero *De republica* 1.53, *De legibus* 3.24 (resisted by *optimates*).

Still controversial: Asconius 70C, contrasting Cicero *Pro Cornelio* fr. 27 Crawford (*popularis causa*) with *De haruspicum responso* 24 (addressed to the Senate); according to Valerius Antias *FRHist* 25 F41 (Asconius 69C, Livy 34.44.4), the innovation was by order of the censors.

Benches: confirmed by Cicero *Pro Cornelio* fr. 27 Crawford (Asconius 69C, *tum primum a populari consessu senatoria subsellia separari*).

4.3. In the Forum, in the Circus

Ludi in front of temple: Cicero *De haruspicum responso* 24 (*ante templum*), Augustine *City of God* 2.26 (*ante ipsum delubrum*), of Magna Mater and Flora respectively.

Deity watching in person: Cicero *De haruspicum responso* 24 (*in ipso Matris magnae conspectu*); Arnobius 7.33 (*conspexerit*, of Flora and Magna Mater); Augustine *City of God* 2.4 (*coram deum matre*), 2.26 (*ante illam [Flora] turpia celebrari*). For the juxtaposition of theatre and temple, see in general Hanson 1959, Goldberg 1998.

Temple of Ceres, Liber, and Libera *ad circum maximum*: Vitruvius 3.3.5, Pliny *Natural History* 35.154; Dionysius of Halicarnassus *Roman Antiquities* 6.94.3 (above the starting-gates), Livy 40.2.2 (on the Aventine side). Temple of Flora at the same place: Tacitus *Annals* 2.49.1 (*eodem in loco*).

Fori publici: Livy 1.35.8–9 (*spectauere furcis duodenos ab terra spectacula alta sustinentibus pedes*), Dionysius of Halicarnassus *Roman Antiquities* 3.68.1 (ὑποστέγους ποιήσας περὶ αὐτὸν καθέδρας...ἐπ' ἰκρίοις, δοκῶν ξυλίναις σκηναῖς ὑποκειμένων); Livy 1.56.2, 29.37.2 (204 BC), 45.1.7–8 (168 BC); Festus (Paulus) 74L.

Temple of Apollo in circo Flaminio: Livy 3.63.7 (cf. 3.54.15), Asconius 90C; Augustus *Res gestae* 21.1 (site of Marcellus' theatre). Market: Cicero *Ad Atticum* 1.14.1. Public meetings: Plutarch *Marcellus* 27.3, Livy 27.21.1 (*ingenti concursu*), Cicero *Pro Sestio* 33, *Post reditum in senatu* 13. Triumphs: Livy 39.5.17, Plutarch *Lucullus* 37.2. Temple dedication games: Livy 40.52.3.

Public meetings in area Capitolina: Livy 25.3.14 (*multitudo*), Velleius Paterculus 2.3.2. Usually just in Capitolio: Livy 33.25.7, 34.1.4, 43.16.9, 45.36.6; Plutarch *Aemilius Paullus* 30.8, *Tiberius Gracchus* 17.2, *Gaius Gracchus* 13.3; Appian *Civil Wars* 1.15.64, 1.24.106.

Temple of Magna Mater: Goldberg 1998.4–8, cf. 14 for the estimated numbers.

179 BC: Livy 40.51.3; there is no need to accept the arbitrary assumption (e.g. Goldberg 1998.2, 10) that the contract was never carried out.

Wide variety: Terence *Hecyra* 5 (rope-walker), 33 (boxers), 40 (gladiators); Horace *Satires* 2.1.86 (boxers, bears); Phaedrus 5.5 (animal imitators). Simultaneous stages: Cicero *De haruspicum responso* 25, Plutarch *Cato minor* 46.4, with Wiseman 2009b.166–8.

56 Deity's symbol on seat: Varro *Menippean Satires* 150 Astbury, with Goldberg 1998.11. Turreted crown: Vermaseren 1977.42–3 and pl. 33.

Jupiter looking out on the Forum: Cicero *In Catilinam* 3.20, 22; cf. Livy 27.36.8 (Comitium used at the *ludi Romani* of 208 BC), Cicero *Ad Atticum* 4.1.6 (*theatrum*, probably in the Forum, at the *ludi Romani* of 57 BC).

57 Plautus *Curculio* 465–86:

>   ipsi Phaedromo
> credidi. tamen asseruabo. sed dum hic egreditur foras,
> commonstrabo, quo in quemque hominem facile inueniatis loco,
> ne nimio opere sumat operam si quem conuentum uelit,
> uel uitiosum uel sine uitio, uel probum uel improbum.
> qui periurum conuenire uolt hominem ito in comitium;   470
> qui mendacem et gloriosum, apud Cloacinae sacrum,
> ditis damnosos maritos sub basilica quaerito,
> ibidem erunt scorta exoleta quique stipulari solent,
> symbolarum collatores apud forum piscarium.
> in foro infimo boni homines atque dites ambulant,
> in medio propter canalem, ibi ostentatores meri;
> confidentes garrulique et maleuoli supra lacum,
> qui alteri de nihilo audacter dicunt contumeliam
> et qui ipsi sat habent quod in se possit uere dicier.
> sub ueteribus, ibi sunt qui dant quique accipiunt faenore.   480
> pone aedem Castoris, ibi sunt subito quibus credas male.
> in Tusco uico, ibi sunt homines qui ipsi sese uenditant,

> in Velabro uel pistorem uel lanium uel haruspicem,
> uel qui ipsi uorsant uel qui aliis ubi uorsentur praebeant.
> sed interim fores crepuere; linguae moderandum est mihi.

Basilica (line 472), unidentified: Plautus *Captiui* 815, cf. Livy 26.27.3 (no basilicas yet in 210 BC); the Basilica Porcia (184 BC), the Basilica Sempronia (170), and the Basilica Aemilia (?164 BC, cf. Wiseman 1998.106–9) are probably not relevant, since Plautus died in 184 (Cicero *Brutus* 60).

Fishmarket (line 474), on the north-east side of the Forum: Livy 26.27.3 (burned in 210 BC), 27.11.16 (rebuilt the following year), 40.51.5 (redeveloped in 179).

Pool (line 477), i.e. *lacus Curtius* in the middle of the Forum: Pliny *Natural History* 15.78, cf. Livy 7.6.1.

Old Shops (*tabernae ueteres*, line 480), on the south-west side of the Forum: Cicero *Academica* 2.70 (shady side), Livy 44.16.10.

Tuscan Street (*uicus Tuscus*, line 482), leading from the Forum to the Circus Maximus: Dionysius of Halicarnassus *Roman Antiquities* 5.36.4; cf. Porphyrio on Horace *Satires* 2.3.228 (*quo itur in Velabrum*).

Velabrum (line 483), 'a place on the street from the Forum to the Circus' (Plutarch *Romulus* 5.5): Plautus *Captiui* 489 (oil-sellers), Horace *Satires* 2.3.229 (food shops), Macrobius *Saturnalia* 1.10.15 (busiest place in the city); cf. Livy 27.37.15 (*inde uico Tusco Velabroque*).

Sitting below the Capitol: as argued in Marshall 2006.40–3 (the site of the later Rostra Iulia, Dio Cassius 56.34.4).

Anicius' triumph: dated by the Capitoline *fasti* (Degrassi 1947.80–1) as *ab urbe condita* 586, the equivalent of 167/6 BC, at the *Quirinalia* (Ch. 2.6 above). Year *ab urbe condita* began on 21 April: Cicero *De diuinatione* 2.98, Varro *De lingua Latina* 6.15; Degrassi 1963.9 (*fasti Antiates*).

Anicius' games: Polybius 30.22.1–12 = Athenaeus 14.615a–e.

At 30.22.9, 'shaking their costumes in unison' translates the emendation proposed by Gottfried Hermann in 1843 (συνεπισείοντες τὴν σκευήν), which is accepted by the Teubner editor of Athenaeus (Georg Kaibel, 1890) and the successive Loeb editors of Athenaeus (Charles B. Gulick and S. Douglas Olsen, respectively 1937 and 2011); the Teubner editor of Polybius (Theodor Büttner-Wobst, 1914) keeps the manuscript reading συνεπεισίοντες τὴν σκηνήν, which would mean 'making a joint attack on the *skēnē*'.

For the ῥαβδοῦχοι at 30.22.6 as lictors, see Diodorus Siculus 5.40.1, Dionysius of Halicarnassus *Roman Antiquities* 3.30.5, Plutarch *Romulus* 26.3.

Temporary stands for Paullus' triumph: Plutarch *Aemilius Paullus* 32.2 (ἰκρία πηξάμενοι).

Roman theatre's *orchestra* reserved for senators: Vitruvius 5.6.2, Suetonius *Nero* 12.3, Juvenal 3.178.

4.4. Terence and the *Cauea*

Hecyra production notice: *tertio relata est Q. Fuluio L. Marcio aedilib. curulib.* (identifiable as the consuls of 153 and 149 respectively); according to Suetonius (*Terence* 5), the playwright died in Greece in 159.

Terence *Hecyra* 1–5:

> *Hecyraest huic nomen fabulae. Hecyra quom datast,*
> *nouae nouom interuenit uitium et calamitas,*
> *ut neque spectari neque cognosci potuerit:*
> *ita populus studio stupidus in funambulo*
> *animum occuparat. nunc haec planest pro noua.*

Hecyra 28–45:

> *nunc quid petam mea causa aequo animo attendite.*
> *Hecyram ad uos fero, quam mihi per silentium*
> *numquam agere licitumst, ita eam oppressit calamitas.*   30
> *eam calamitatem uostra intellegentia*
> *sedabit, si erit adiutrix nostrae industriae.*
> *quom primum eam agere coepi, pugilum gloria,*
> *[funambuli eodem accessit exspectatio]*
> *comitum conuentus, strepitus, clamor mulierum*
> *fecere ut ante tempus exirem foras.*
> *uetere in noua coepi uti consuetudine,*
> *in experiundo ut essem: refero denuo.*
> *primo actus placeo. quom interea rumor uenit*
> *datum iri gladiatores, populus conuolat,*   40
> *tumultuantur clamant pugnant de loco;*
> *ego interea meum non potui tutari locum.*
> *nunc turba non est, otium et silentiumst;*
> *agendi tempus mihi datumst, uobis datur*
> *potestas condecorandi ludos scaenicos.*

Line 34 is probably an interpolation, to make this prologue consistent with the first.

Plautus *Truculentus* 9–12:

> *sed hoc agamus qua huc uentumst gratia.*
> *Athenis mutabo ita ut hoc est proscaenium*
> *tantisper dum transigimus hanc comoediam.*
> *hic habitat mulier nomen cui est Phronesium . . .*

Plautus *Menaechmi* 72–6:

> *haec urbs Epidamnus est, dum haec agitur fabula;*
> *quando alia agetur, aliud fiet oppidum.*
> *sicut familiae quoque solent mutarier:*
> *modo hic habitat leno, modo adulescens, modo senex,*
> *pauper, mendicus, rex, parasitus, hariolus . . .*

Three-door set: Vitruvius 5.6.3 and 8; Duckworth 1952.82–3 for a summary of the Plautine evidence.

'Outside' (*foras*): Terence *Hecyra* 36; Plautus *Miles Gloriosus* 81, *Poenulus* 38.

4.5. Curtains and Steps

Auction of 132 BC: Pliny *Natural History* 33.148–9. 'Attalic' textiles: Propertius 2.13.22, 2.32.12, 3.18.19, 4.5.24; *CIL* 6.1375.9 = *ILS* 917; Valerius Maximus 9.1.5, Pliny *Natural History* 8.196. Used in theatres: Pliny *Natural History* 36.115, Donatus *De comoedia* 8.8 (Kaibel 1899.71), Servius *auctus* on Virgil *Aeneid* 1.697.

Aulaea: Cicero *Pro Caelio* 65, Virgil *Georgics* 3.24–5, Horace *Epistles* 2.1.189, *Ars poetica* 154–5, Ovid *Metamorphoses* 3.111–14; 'when the *aulaea* are stored away' meant the actors' close season between the *ludi plebeii* in November and the *ludi Megalenses* in April (Juvenal 6.67–9).

Siparium (often mentioned in the context of mime): Cicero *De prouinciis consularibus* 14, Seneca *De tranquillitate animi* 11.8, Juvenal 8.185, Festus (Paulus) 459L, Donatus *De comoedia* 8.8 (Kaibel 1899.71). Used with *aulaeum*: Apuleius *Metamorphoses* 10.29.5; cf. 1.8.5 (metaphorical).

Tacitus *Annals* 14.20.2:

> quippe erant qui Cn. quoque Pompeium incusatum a senioribus ferrent quod mansuram theatri sedem posuisset, nam antea subitariis gradibus et scaena in tempus structa ludos edi solitos.

Servius on Virgil *Georgics* 3.24:

> apud maiores theatri gradus tantum fuerunt, nam scaena de lignis ad tempus fiebat, unde hodieque consuetudo permansit ut componantur pegmata a ludorum theatralium editoribus.

'Even today' (*hodieque*): for the continued use of temporary theatres, see Vitruvius 5.5.7; *CIL* 6.32323.108, 156–7, 161 (*ludi saeculares*, 17 BC); Josephus *Jewish Antiquities* 19.75, 90 (*ludi Palatini*, AD 41).

Gradus: Vitruvius 5.3.4, 5.6.3–5, Horace *Satires* 1.6.40, Ovid *Ars amatoria* 1.107, Livy *Epitome* 99, Martial 5.14.1. *Ordines* ('rows') in the same sense: Cicero *Philippics* 2.44, Pollio in Cicero *Ad familiares* 10.32.2, Asconius 79C, Tacitus *Annals* 15.32, Juvenal 14.324.

Still benches (*subsellia*): Vitruvius 5.6.3 (*gradus spectaculorum ubi subsellia componantur*), Martial 5.8.2–3, 5.27.3, Suetonius *Diuus Augustus* 43.4.

Expense: Tacitus *Annals* 14.21.2.

5. MAKERS, SINGERS, SPEAKERS, WRITERS

Aristotle *Poetics* 1451b27–8: τὸν ποιητὴν μᾶλλον τῶν μύθων εἶναι δεῖ ποιητὴν ἢ τῶν μέτρων. Verse or prose: Aristotle *Poetics* 1447a28–b24 (e.g. Socratic dialogues); cf. Dio of Prusa 36.26 (Plato as ποιητής), Aelius Aristides 28.72–3 (Thucydides as ποιητής).

Plautus *Pseudolus* 401–5:

> sed quasi poeta, tabulas quom cepit sibi,
> quaerit quod nusquam gentiumst, reperit tamen,
> facit illud ueri simile quod mendacium est,
> nunc ego poeta fiam: uiginti minas,
> quae nunc nusquam sunt gentium, inueniam tamen.

For the deviser of clever schemes as a *poeta*, see also Plautus *Asinaria* 748, *Casina* 860–1.

Lies and fiction: see Gill and Wiseman 1993.

Not in person: Plautus *Menaechmi* 3 (*apporto uobis Plautum, lingua non manu*).

In character: e.g. Donatus *Vita Vergilii* 29 (Virgil's face, voice and *hypocrisis*); cf. Plutarch *Moralia* 711C, Dionysius Thrax 6.5–11 Uhlig, Longinus *Ars rhetorica* 310.21 Spengel (ὑπόκρισις as expressive delivery).

5.1. Ennius and the *Vates*

From the beginning: Homer *Iliad* 1.1 (μῆνιν ἄειδε, θεά); cf. 2.761, *Odyssey* 1.1 (ἔννεπε, Μοῦσα); *Iliad* 2.484, 11.218, 14.508, 16.112 (ἔσπετε νῦν μοι, Μοῦσαι).

Bard taught by Muses: Homer *Odyssey* 8.63–4, 8.481, 8.488. Taught by Apollo (god of prophecy): *Odyssey* 8.488; cf. 8.44, 22.347–8 ('the god').

Daughters of Memory: Hesiod *Theogony* 54; implied already in Homer *Iliad* 2.492 (μνησαίαθ').

'Prophet': Varro *De lingua Latina* 7.36 (*antiqui poetas uates appellabant*); Homer *Iliad* 1.70, Hesiod *Theogony* 38 (τά τ' ἐόντα τά τ' ἐσσόμενα πρό τ' ἐόντα). Plato's Socrates includes prophets and seers in his account of the divine inspiration of poets: *Ion* 534b7 (ποιεῖν καὶ χρησμῳδεῖν), 534c (τοῖς χρησμῳδοῖς καὶ τοῖς μάντεσι).

Canere: *Thesaurus linguae Latinae* 3.269.12–271.11 (poets), 271.12–272.62 (prophets).

Carmen: *Thesaurus linguae Latinae* 3.464.9–49 (prophets), 466.4–75 (poets).

Vates as prophet: Cicero *De diuinatione* 1.4, 18, 34, 66, 67; 2.101, 110, 111–12; cf. 1.34 (*instinctu diuino afflatuque*), 1.89 (*mentis incitatione et permotione diuina*), 2.100 (*furore diuino incitatus animus*).

Familiar figure: e.g. Livy 25.1.8–10 (213 BC), Appian *Civil Wars* 1.121.563 (71 BC), Dio Cassius 41.14.4 (49 BC). Senate: Sallust *Histories* 1.77.3M (*uatum carmina*). Magistrate: Cicero *De diuinatione* 1.4 (*uatum furibundae praedictiones*), with Plutarch *Marius* 42.4. See in general Wiseman 1994.49–67, but I was wrong to suppose (1994.57) that the '*uates* as poet' usage went back no further than Varro; in fact, Varro ascribes it to 'the ancients' (*De lingua Latina* 7.36, above).

Socrates' conversation: Plato *Ion* 535b2–c8, d8–e3 (trans. W. R. M. Lamb, Loeb edn.).

Michele's story: Starkie 1938.278–9.

Livius *Odussia* fr. 1 Warmington (Homer *Odyssey* 1.1). Camenae: Livy 1.21.3, Plutarch *Numa* 13.2, Juvenal 3.10–16, Frontinus *De aquaeductibus* 4. Derivation of name: Varro *De lingua Latina* 7.26–7, Festus (Paulus) 38L, Servius on *Eclogues* 3.59; cf. Augustine *City of God* 4.11 (*quae canere doceat*).

Naevius *Bellum Punicum* fr. 1 Warmington. Title of *carmen belli Punici*: Festus 306L, Nonius 290L, Priscian in *Grammatici Latini* 2.198, 242, 351 Keil; cf. Aulus Gellius 17.21.45 (*in eo carmine quod de eodem bello scripsit*).

Ennius *Annales* 1 Sk (*Musae quae pedibus magnum pulsatis Olympum*), 487 Sk (*Musas quas memorant nosce nos esse Camenas*).

Books of *uates*-prophets: Livy 25.1.12, 25.12.3, Macrobius *Saturnalia* 1.17.28; Horace *Epistles* 2.1.26, Suetonius *Diuus Augustus* 31.1.

Moneta as the Muses' mother: Livius *Odussia* fr. 30 Warmington (Homer *Odyssey* 8.481), Hyginus *Fabulae* pref. 27.

Agent of aristocratic acculturation: Habinek 1998.54; cf. 3 (Latin literature emerged from 'the elite sector of a traditional aristocratic empire'), 37 (late third- and early second-century culture 'was intimately connected with the preservation, importation, and circulation of texts'), 44 ('the invention of literary Latin and the production of a sizable number of texts in it gave them [members of the elite] just the vehicle needed for communication among themselves').

Epic for the elite: Goldberg 2005.43; cf. 27 ('epic might by its very nature appeal to the people of education and privilege most reachable by scholarly efforts'), 153 ('epic's literary conceits played to an audience that was smaller, more coherent, and more bookish, a group that would have comprised only a small part of the public that was drawn to the *ludi scaenici*').

'Probus' *De ultimis syllabis* in *Grammatici Latini* 4.231 Keil (Ennius *Annales* 12–13 Sk); Ilberg 1852.13–14, Baehrens 1886.61, Skutsch 1985.71 (text), 167–9 (commentary).

Lucretius 1.117–19:

> *Ennius ut noster cecinit qui primus amoeno*
> *detulit ex Helicone perenni fronde coronam*
> *per gentis Italas hominum quae clara clueret.*

Poemata and Ennius' intention: Skutsch 1985.144. Ennius as Homer reincarnate: Persius 6.10–11 and scholiast; full references in Skutsch 1985.150–3. 'Fauns and prophets': Wiseman 2008.39–51.

Homeric Hymn to Apollo 166–73:

> χαίρετε δ' ὑμεῖς πᾶσαι· ἐμεῖο δὲ καὶ μετόπισθεν
> μνήσασθ', ὁππότε κέν τις ἐπιχθονίων ἀνθρώπων
> ἐνθάδ' ἀνείρηται ξεῖνος ταλαπείριος ἐλθών·
> ὦ κοῦραι, τίς δ' ὔμμιν ἀνὴρ ἥδιστος ἀοιδῶν
> ἐνθάδε πωλεῖται, καὶ τέῳ τέρπεσθε μάλιστα;
> ὑμεῖς δ' εὖ μάλα πᾶσαι ὑποκρίνασθαι ἀφήμως·
> τυφλὸς ἀνήρ, οἰκεῖ δὲ Χίῳ ἔνι παιπαλοέσσῃ
> τοῦ πᾶσαι μετόπισθεν ἀριστεύσουσιν ἀοιδαί.

68 Trilingual: Aulus Gellius 17.17.1. Ennius came from Rudiae in Messapia (*Annales* 525 Sk, Silius Italicus 12.393–8), and claimed to be descended from the eponymous Messapus himself (Servius on *Aeneid* 7.691).

Venus and Anchises: Ennius *Annales* 15 Sk; Servius on *Aeneid* 1.273, 6.777 (Aeneas' daughter the mother of Romulus). Contemporary wars: Pliny *Natural History* 7.101; Macrobius *Saturnalia* 6.2.32 (Istrian War, 178 BC).

5.2. Ennius as Impersonator

Aesop: Ennius fr. 17 Courtney (Aulus Gellius 2.29.20).

Euhemerus of Messene and his *Sacred History* (*FGrH* 63): Diodorus Siculus 6.1.1–11; cf. 5.41.4 (island of Panchaea), 5.46.7 (golden pillar). Ennius' version (Warmington 1935.414–31): Cicero *De natura deorum* 1.119; Lactantius *Institutio diuina* 1.11.33–49, 1.11.63–5, 1.13.2, 1.13.14, 1.14.1–12, 1.17.10, 1.22.21–7, evidently using a prose paraphrase.

Ennius = Euhemerus *FGrH* 63 F 20 (Lactantius *Institutio diuina* 1.11.35):

> *ea tempestate Iuppiter in monte Olympo maximam partem uitae colebat et eo ad eum in ius ueniebant, si quae res in controuersia errant. item si quis quid noui inuenerat quod ad uitam humanam utile esset, eo ueniebant atque Ioui ostendebant.*

Epicharmus: Kassel and Austin 2001.8–138. Ennius' version (Courtney 1993.30–8): Cicero *Academica* 2.51 (dream); Varro *De lingua Latina* 5.59–60, 5.64–5; Priscian in *Grammatici Latini* 2.341 Keil.

Epicharmus fr. 239 Kaibel = Menander *PCG* F 838.1–2:

> ὁ μὲν Ἐπίχαρμος τοὺς θεοὺς εἶναι λέγει
> ἀνέμους ὕδωρ γῆν ἥλιον πῦρ ἀστέρας.

Ennius fr. 39 Courtney = Epicharmus *PCG* F 287 (Varro *De lingua Latina* 5.65):

> *istic est is Iuppiter quam dico, quem Graeci uocant*
> *aerem, qui uentus est et nubes, imber postea,*
> *atque ex imbre frigus, uentus post fit, aer denuo.*
> *haece propter Iuppiter sunt ista quae dico tibi,*
> *qui mortales <arua> atque urbes beluasque iuuat.*

69 Good advice (Ennius fr. 42 Courtney): Priscian in *Grammatici Latini* 2.532 Keil (*Ennius in praeceptis*); cf. Charisius 68 Barwick = 1.54 Keil (*Ennius in Protreptico*).

Sotades (Hendriks, Parsons, and Worp 1981.76–8): Strabo 1.41 C648 (originator of κιναιδολογεῖν), Martial 2.86.2 (*Sotaden cinaedum*), Athenaeus 14.620f (κιναιδολόγος), Suda Σ871 4.409 Adler (ἔγραψε φλύακας ἤτοι κιναίδους); cf. Quintilian 1.8.6 (unsuitable for children). Ptolemy's revenge: Athenaeus 14.620f–621a, Plutarch *Moralia* 11a; Cameron 1995.18–20.

Ennius' version (Courtney 1993.4–7): Paulus (Festus) 51L (*Sotadico uersu*); Varro *De lingua Latina* 5.62, Festus 488–90L, Fronto 1.78 Haines (*Sota Ennianus*).

Archestratus (Olson and Sens 2000): Athenaeus 1.4d–e, 3.104b, 7.278a–b, 8.335d–f; Justin *Apologia* 2.25.3 (as immoral as Sotades).

Ennius fr. 28.4–8 (Apuleius *Apologia* 39.2):

> *Brundisi sargus bonus est; hunc, magnus si erit, sume.*
> *apriculum piscem scito primum esse Tarenti.*
> *Surrenti elopem fac emas, glaucumque aput Cumas.*
> *quid scarum praeterii cerebrum Iouis paene supremi*
> *(Nestoris ad patriam hic capitur magnusque bonusque)* ...

For the fish named, see Olson and Sens 2000.61–2 (*elops*), 68–9 (*scarus*), 79 (boar-fish), 94 (*glaucus*), 156 (*sargus*).

Ennius' impersonations: Varro *De lingua Latina* 5.59 (*Epicharmus dicit*), cf. 5.64 (*ut ait Ennius*); Lactantius *Institutio diuina* 1.11.63 (*dicit Euhemerus*), cf. 1.13.14 (*Ennius in Euhemero dicit*).

The best introduction to this part of Ennius' oeuvre is Gratwick 1982.156–60 (esp. 160: 'A judicious modern account of fourth- and third-century Greek literature as it relates in style, intent and variety to *all* of Ennius' minor works remains a *desideratum*').

Ennius as a Roman citizen: Cicero *Brutus* 79 (Livy 39.44.10 for the date), *Pro Archia* 22. He was born in 239 BC: Cicero *Brutus* 72, Varro *De poetis* fr. 61 Funaioli (Aulus Gellius 17.21.43).

Meaning of *satura*: Diomedes in *Grammatici Latini* 1.485–6 Keil; full discussion in Oakley 1998.55–8 (on Livy 7.2.7). Livius Andronicus: Livy 7.2.8 (supposedly pre-dating his plays).

Ennius' *saturae* (Courtney 1993.7–21): frr. 7 (banqueter), 11 (*Enni poeta salue qui mortalibus | uersus propinas flammeos medullitus*), 12 (slanderer), 15 (parasite), 19 (*meum non est ac si me canis memorderit*).

Ennius on Scipio: Cicero *Tusculan Disputations* 5.49 (*a sole exoriente supra Maeotis paludes | nemo est qui factis aequiperare queat*). Volume: Aulus Gellius 4.7.3 (*ex libro qui Scipio inscribitur*); Suda E 1348, 2.285 Adler ('only Homer could do him justice'); Courtney 1993.26–30. Scipio impersonated: Lactantius *Institutio diuina* 1.18.10 (*si fas endo plagas caelestum ascendere cuiquam est, | mi soli caeli maxima porta patet*).

Aetolia campaign: Cicero *Pro Archia* 27, *Brutus* 79, *Tusculan Disputations* 1.3. Siege of Ambracia: Livy 38.3–9; cf. *De uiris illustribus* 52.3 for Ennius' celebration of it.

Fabulae praetextae: Manuwald 2001.134–41 (Naevius' *Clastidium*), 141–61 (Naevius' *Romulus* or *Lupus*), 162–72 (Ennius' *Ambracia*), 172–9 (Ennius' *Sabinae*).

Ennius fr. 45 Courtney (Cicero *Tusculan Disputations* 1.34):

> *aspicite, o ciues, senis Enni imaginis formam.*
> *hic uestrum panxit maxima facta patrum.*

5.3. Cato and Polybius

Sweet-speaking oratory: Ennius *Annales* 304–8 Sk (*orator... suauiloquenti ore*), on M. Cornelius Cethegus *cos.* 204 BC, 'the chosen flower of the People, the very marrow of Persuasion'.

M. Cato as orator (Astin 1978.131–56): Cicero *Brutus* 61–9; cf. Livy 39.40.7 (*eloquentissimus*), Pliny *Natural History* 7.100 (*optimus orator*), Quintilian 12.3.9 (*in dicendo praestantissimus*). Called 'Demosthenes': Diodorus Siculus 34/35.33.3, Plutarch *Cato maior* 4.1, Appian *Iberica* 39.160.

Plutarch *Cato maior* 7.1 (trans. Astin 1978.141): εὔχαρις γὰρ ἅμα καὶ δεινὸς ἦν, ἡδὺς καὶ καταπληκτικός, φιλοσκώμμων καὶ αὐστηρός, ἀποφθεγματικὸς καὶ ἀγωνιστικός.

Cato and the aristocracy: Livy 39.40.9–10; Plutarch *Cato maior* 3.5–7 (Scipio), 16.3–4; see Astin 1978.91–8 for his attack on luxury. Cato on leisure: *Origines* fr. 1.2 Chassignet (Cicero *Pro Plancio* 66, *clarorum hominum atque magnorum non minus otii quam negotii rationem exstare oportere*); cf. Plutarch *Cato maior* 24.8.

Cato's *Origines* (Astin 1978.211–39, Chassignet 1986): Nepos *Cato* 3.3–4 (structure); Livy 34.15.9, cf. Plutarch *Cato maior* 14.2, 19.7 (self-praise). Speeches included: Aulus Gellius 6.3.6–7 (in the Senate for the Rhodians, 167 BC); Cicero *Brutus* 80, 89, Livy *Epitome* 49 (before the People against Ser. Galba, 149 BC).

Funeral orations (Kierdorf 1979): e.g. Pliny *Natural History* 7.139 (L. Metellus, 221 BC), Livy 27.27.13 (M. Marcellus, 208); Cicero *De senectute* 12, Plutarch *Fabius Maximus* 1.5, 24.4 (Q. Fabius *filius*, *c.*207–203).

Polybius 6.53.1–3 (trans. Ian Scott-Kilvert, Penguin Classics):

ὅταν γὰρ μεταλλάξῃ τις παρ' αὐτοῖς τῶν ἐπιφανῶν ἀνδρῶν, συντελουμένης τῆς ἐκφορᾶς κομίζεται μετὰ τοῦ λοιποῦ κόσμου πρὸς τοὺς καλουμένους ἐμβόλους εἰς τὴν ἀγορὰν ποτὲ μὲν ἑστὼς ἐναργής, σπανίως δὲ κατακλιμένος. πέριξ δὲ παντὸς τοῦ δήμου στάντος, ἀναβὰς ἐπὶ τοὺς ἐμβόλους, ἂν μὲν υἱὸς ἐν ἡλικίᾳ καταλείπεται καὶ τύχῃ παρών, οὗτος, εἰ δὲ μή, τῶν ἄλλων εἴ τις ἀπὸ γένους ὑπάρχει, λέγει περὶ τοῦ τετελευτηκότος τὰς ἀρετὰς καὶ τὰς ἐπιτετευγμένας ἐν τῷ ζῆν πράξεις. δι' ὧν συμβαίνει τοὺς πολλοὺς ἀναμιμνησκομένους καὶ λαμβάνοντας ὑπὸ τὴν ὄψιν τὰ γεγονότα, μὴ μόνον τοὺς κεκοινωνηκότας τῶν ἔργων, ἀλλὰ καὶ τοὺς ἐκτός, ἐπὶ τοσοῦτον γίνεσθαι συμπαθεῖς ὥστε μὴ τῶν κηδευόντων ἴδιον, ἀλλὰ κοινὸν τοῦ δήμου φαίνεσθαι τὸ σύμπτωμα.

Populi Romani gesta: Cato *FRHist* 5 F1b (Pompeius in *Grammatici Latini* 5.208 Keil), cf. T7 (Festus 216L). Commanders' names omitted: Nepos *Cato* 3.4, Pliny *Natural History* 8.11; e.g. F76, F79 (Aulus Gellius 2.19.9, 3.7.3–19).

Herodotus 1.pref (ἱστορίης ἀπόδεξις); Cicero *De legibus* 1.5 (*pater historiae*), cf. *De oratore* 2.55 (*princeps*); Lucian *Herodotus* 1 (ᾄδων τὰς ἱστορίας, Olympia).

Thucydides 1.22.4:

καὶ ἐς μὲν ἀκρόασιν ἴσως τὸ μὴ μυθῶδες αὐτῶν ἀτερπέστερον φανεῖται· ὅσοι δὲ βουλήσονται τῶν τε γενομένων τὸ σαφὲς σκοπεῖν...ὠφέλιμα κρίνειν αὐτὰ ἀρκούντως ἕξει. κτῆμά τε ἐς αἰεὶ μᾶλλον ἢ ἀγώνισμα ἐς τὸ παραχρῆμα ἀκούειν ξύγκειται.

Writing for readers: e.g. Polybius 3.31.11 (τοῖς ἀναγινώσκουσι τὰς ἱστορίας), 3.32.2–3 (his 40 volumes).

Polybius 3.31.12–13:

> ἱστορίας γὰρ ἐὰν ἀφέλῃ τις τὸ διὰ τί καὶ πῶς καὶ τίνος χάριν ἐπράχθη, καὶ τὸ πραχθὲν πότερα εὔλογον ἔσχε τὸ τέλος, τὸ καταλειπόμενον αὐτῆς ἀγώνισμα μὲν, μάθημα δὲ οὐ γίγνεται· καὶ παραυτίκα μὲν τέρπει, πρὸς δὲ τὸ μέλλον οὐδὲν ὠφελεῖ τὸ παράπαν.

Polybius 3.32.10:

> ὅσῳ διαφέρει τὸ μαθεῖν τοῦ μόνον ἀκοῦσαι, τοσούτῳ καὶ τὴν ἡμετέραν ἱστορίαν ὑπολαμβάνω διαφέρειν τῶν ἐπὶ μέρους συντάξεων.

Polybius 9.1.2:

> οὐκ ἀγνοῶ δὲ διότι συμβαίνει τὴν πραγματείαν ἡμῶν ἔχειν αὐστηρόν τι, καὶ πρὸς ἓν γένος ἀκροατῶν οἰκειοῦσθαι καὶ κρίνεσθαι, διὰ τὸ μονοειδὲς τῆς συντάξεως.

Different modes: Polybius 9.1.3 (πολλοὺς ἐφέλκονται πρὸς ἔντευξιν τῶν ὑπομνημάτων), 9.1.4 (τὸν φιλήκοον), 9.1.5 (τῷ πλείονι μέρει ἀκροατῶν ἀψυχαγώγητον); cf. 1.13.6, 9.1.6 for the audience (ἀκούοντες) of his own work. Lovers of knowledge (φιλομαθοῦντες): Polybius 2.56.11–12, 9.2.5.

Hellenistic historians' *acroaseis*: e.g. Aristheos of Troezen at Delphi in 158/7 BC (FGrH 835), and an anonymous example at Amphipolis, evidently in the third century BC (Robert 1979.454–5); for the general background see Robert 1959.233–4, Clarke 2008.337–69.

Senators writing Greek history: Q. Fabius Pictor (FGrH 809) and L. Cincius Alimentus (FGrH 810) in the late third century, A. Postumius Albinus (FGrH 812) and C. Acilius (FGrH 813) in the second.

Rerum scriptor: e.g. Sallust *Catiline* 3.2; Livy 21.1.1, 38.56.5, 39.50.10. *Scriptores* as historians: Livy pref. 2–3, 1.44.2, 3.23.7, 4.23.2, 8.30.7, 9.18.5, 23.6.8, 26.11.10, 29.14.9, 33.36.15, 36.38.7, 38.55.8, 45.44.19.

Sempronius Asellio *FRHist* 20 F2 (Aulus Gellius 5.18.9):

> nam neque alacriores, inquit, ad rem publicam defendundam neque segniores ad rem perperam faciundam annales libri commouere quicquam possunt. scribere autem bellum initum quo consule et quo confectum sit et quis triumphans introierit ex eo, et eo libro quae in bello gesta sint non praedicare aut interea quid senatus decreuerit aut quae lex rogatioue lata sit, neque quibus consiliis ea gesta sint iterare: id fabulas pueris est narrare, non historias scribere.

Senior senators: e.g. Q. Fabius Servilianus (cos. 142 BC), L. Calpurnius Piso (cos. 133, censor 120), C. Sempronius Tuditanus (cos. 129), C. Fannius (cos. 122), P. Rutilius Rufus (cos. 105); fragments in *FRHist*, nos. 8, 9, 10, 12. Lower-status historians: *FRHist* nos. 6 (Cassius Hemina), 24 (Claudius Quadrigarius).

Working people of humble station: Cicero *De finibus* 5.52 (*homines infimae fortunae...opifices denique delectantur historia*), where the next sentence refers casually to history being listened to as well as read (*res gestas audire et legere*).

5.4. Lucilius and Varro

'Mixed constitution': Polybius 6.11–18, esp. 6.18.5–7 on the prevention of hubristic arrogance. Civic virtues: Polybius 6.18.2–3 (citizens in concord), 6.54.3–6 (self-sacrifice for public good), 6.56.2 (bribery disgraceful), 6.56.14–15 (oaths and public money); the same judgement in 1 Maccabees 18: 4–6.

For the nature of the Roman republic before 146 BC, see also Sallust *Catiline* 9.1 (*boni mores, concordia maxuma*), *Jugurthine War* 41.2 (*bonae artes*), *Histories* 1.11M (*maxuma concordia*), Diodorus Siculus 37.3.1 (good customs), Dionysius of Halicarnassus *Roman Antiquities* 2.11.2 (concord and compromise).

74 Avarice and arrogance: Sallust *Catiline* 10.3–4, *Jugurthine War* 31.12, 84.5 (cf. 5.1, 64.1 on *superbia nobilitatis*). Avarice in particular: Sallust *Catiline* 12.1–2, *Jugurthine War* 15.4, 41.9, *Histories* 1.11M, 1.16M, 4.69.5M; Lucretius 2.11–13, 3.59–63; Varro *Res rusticae* 2.pref.4, Diodorus Siculus 31.26.2, Justin 38.6.8.

Murder of Ti. Gracchus: Plutarch *Ti. Gracchus* 18–19, Appian *Civil Wars* 1.16.67–70; the earliest description is in *Rhetorica ad Herennium* 4.55.68 (80s BC). Other citizens: Livy *Epitome* 58, Plutarch *Ti. Gracchus* 19.6 ('more than 300'), Appian *Civil Wars* 1.16.70, Orosius 5.9.3 ('200'). Summary executions: Sallust *Jugurthine War* 31.7, Plutarch *Ti. Gracchus* 20.3.

Sacrilege: Appian *Civil Wars* 1.2.5, 1.17.71 (μύσος); the tribunes of the *plebs* were sacrosanct (Livy 2.33.1, 3.55.10, Dionysius of Halicarnassus *Roman Antiquities* 6.89.3–4, Festus 422L).

'Defending the republic': Valerius Maximus 3.2.17, Plutarch *Ti. Gracchus* 19.3, Appian *Civil Wars* 1.16.68; Wiseman 2009b.179–87.

Precedent leading to civil war: Velleius Paterculus 2.3.3–4, Plutarch *Ti. Gracchus* 20.1; Appian *Civil Wars* 1.2.4–8, 1.17.71, 1.60.268.

121 BC: Cicero *Philippics* 8.14, Livy *Epitome* 61, Plutarch *C. Gracchus* 16.3–4, Orosius 5.12.6–8 (armed force); Sallust *Jugurthine War* 31.7, Velleius Paterculus 2.7.3, Plutarch *C. Gracchus* 17.5, Orosius 5.12.10 (3000 executed without trial); Sallust *Jugurthine War* 16.2 ('the victory of the aristocracy over the common people').

100 BC: Cicero *Pro Rabirio perduellionis* 20, Livy *Epitome* 69, Appian *Civil Wars* 1.32.144–5, Orosius 5.17.6–9 (armed force equivalent to war).

88 BC: Velleius Paterculus 2.19.1, Plutarch *Sulla* 9.5–7, *Marius* 35.4, Appian *Civil Wars* 1.58.257–63 (storming of Rome). For the sequel, the 'war of Octavius' in 87 BC, see Cicero *De natura deorum* 2.14, *De diuinatione* 1.4, *Philippics* 14.23; Appian *Civil Wars* 1.65–70, Plutarch *Marius* 42–3.

82 BC: Plutarch *Sulla* 29.2–7, Appian *Civil Wars* 1.93.428–32, Orosius 5.20.5 (battle of the Colline Gate); Livy *Epitome* 88, Valerius Maximus 9.2.1, Seneca *De clementia*

1.12.2, Plutarch *Sulla* 30.1–2, *De uiris illustribus* 75.10, Augustine *City of God* 3.28.2 (mass executions, estimates vary from 3,000 to 9,000).

Proscription lists: Valerius Maximus 9.2.1 (total 4,700), Plutarch *Sulla* 31.3, Appian *Civil Wars* 1.95.442 (40 senators, 1,600 *equites*), Orosius 5.21.3. Severed heads in the Forum: Cicero *Pro Roscio Amerino* 87, Seneca *De prouidentia* 3.7–8, Plutarch *Sulla* 32.2, Dio Cassius 30–35.109.21.

Early republican compromise without bloodshed: Dionysius of Halicarnassus *Roman Antiquities* 7.66.4–5, Plutarch *Ti. Gracchus* 20.1, Appian *Civil Wars* 1.1.1, 1.2.4.

Tribunes' powers cancelled: Cicero *De legibus* 3.22, Caesar *Civil War* 1.7.3, Sallust *Histories* 3.48.3M, Livy *Epitome* 89, Dionysius of Halicarnassus *Roman Antiquities* 5.77.5, Velleius Paterculus 2.30.4, Appian *Civil Wars* 1.100.467.

Aristocracy: Cicero *Pro Roscio Amerino* 135–42 (*causa nobilitatis*), 149; cf. *De republica* 1.50–5 (*optimates* as the equivalent of Greek *aristoi*), *Ad Atticum* 1.14.2 (μαλ' ἀριστοκρατικῶς meaning 'like an optimate'). Lice in a tunic: Appian *Civil Wars* 1.101.471–2.

More civil war (77 BC): Livy *Epitome* 90, Valerius Maximus 6.9.5, Plutarch *Pompey* 16.1, Appian *Civil Wars* 1.107.501–4, Florus 3.23.5–7, Orosius 5.22.16. The victor was Q. Catulus *cos.* 78, *Sullanus dux* (Orosius 5.22.16), 'standard-bearer of Sullan domination' (Florus 3.23.6), 'more brutal than Sulla' (Sallust *Histories* 3.48.9M), the archetypal optimate (Cicero *Ad Atticum* 1.20.3).

Aristocratic *dominatio*: Cicero *In Verrem* 1.35, 2.5.175; Sallust *Histories* 3.48.3 (*nobilitas*), 6 (*pauci*), 11, 23, 28 (*pauci*). Aristocratic arrogance: Cicero *In Verrem* 1.15, 2.5.180–2; Sallust *Catiline* 23.6.

Avarice and corruption: Cicero *Diuinatio in Caecilium* and *In Verrem*, *passim*. Popular resentment: Cicero *Diuinatio in Caecilium* 8–9, *In Verrem* 1.35–6, 1.42–50; *Pro Cluentio* 77, 79, 110, 130, 136.

Almost total absence: speeches by the young Cicero give us contemporary views for 80 BC (*Pro Roscio Amerino*) and the late 70s (*In Verrem*); but Cicero was away for two years in Athens and Rhodes (Cicero *Brutus* 314–16), thus missing the civil war of 77.

Lucilius: good summaries in Coffey 1976.24–32, Gratwick 1982.162–71, Gowers 2012.8–11. Date of death: Jerome *Chronica* Ol.68.2 ('in Naples, aged 46'), where the age must be wrongly reported since Lucilius presented himself as an old man, *senex* (Horace *Satires* 2.1.32–4). Place of birth: Juvenal 1.20, Ausonius 27.11.9 OCT.

Wealth: Horace *Satires* 2.1.75; cf. Asconius 13C on his town house, built for a Seleucid prince. Status: Velleius Paterculus 2.29.2 (*stirps senatoria*); cf. Cicero *De oratore* 2.284 on a senatorial landowner c.114 BC whose name is transmitted in the MSS as either Lucilius or Lucullus.

Well-read: Cicero *De oratore* 1.72, 2.25 (*doctus et perurbanus*). Funny: Cicero *Ad familiares* 9.15.2, *De oratore* 3,171, *De finibus* 1.7; Horace *Satires* 1.4.7–8, 1.10.3–4. Aggressive: Trebonius in Cicero *Ad familiares* 12.16.3; Horace *Satires* 2.1.62–70, Persius 1.114–15, Juvenal 1.165–6.

75 Old Comedy analogy: Horace *Satires* 1.4.1–8, Diomedes in *Grammatici Latini* 1.485K (Kaibel 1899.55), John Lydus *De magistratibus* 1.41 (via Rhinthon).

Lucilius 1145–51W = Lactantius *Diuinae institutiones* 5.9.20 (trans. Muecke 2005.46):

> nunc uero a mani ad noctem festo atque profesto
> totus item pariterque die populusque patresque
> iactare indu foro se omnes, decedere nusquam;
> uni se atque eidem studio omnes dedere et arti,
> uerba dare ut caute possint, pugnare dolose,
> blanditia certare, bonum simulare uirum se,
> insidias facere ut si hostes sint omnibus omnes.

Three names: Cicero *De oratore* 1.72 (Mucius), Horace *Satires* 2.167–8 (Metellus and Lupus), Persius 1.114–15 (Mucius and Lupus), Juvenal 1.154 (Mucius). Council of gods: Servius on *Aeneid* 10.104; part of their agenda may have been 'to save the Roman People' (Lucilius 6–7W = Veronese scholiast on *Aeneid* 12.680).

L. Aurelius Cotta *cos.* 144 BC: Lucilius 440–2W (Nonius 33L, 533L); cf. Cicero *Brutus* 81–2, Appian *Civil Wars* 1.22.92. C. Cassius (probably Cassius Sabaco, expelled from the Senate in 115 BC): Lucilius 445–7W (Nonius 424L); cf. Plutarch *Marius* 5.3. L. Hostilius Tubulus *pr.* 142 BC: Lucilius 1138W (Cicero *De natura deorum* 1.63); cf. Cicero *Pro Scauro* (quoted in Asconius 23C), *De finibus* 2.54. M. Papirius Carbo *pr. c.*114 BC: Lucilius 1139W (Cicero *De natura deorum* 1.63); cf. Cicero *Ad familiares* 9.21.3.

Lucilius 791–2W (Nonius 54L, 481L): *rem, populi salutem fictis uersibus Lucilius | quibus potest impertit, totumque hoc studiose et sedulo.*

Lucilius on himself: Horace *Satires* 2.1.30–4 (entrusting secrets, whole life on view).

Varro *De lingua Latina* 6.69 (Lucilius 897W): *itaque Lucilius scribit de Cretaea, cum ad se cubitum ueniret, sponte ipsam suapte adductam ut tunicam et cetera reiceret.*

Play and conversations: Lucilius 1039W (Nonius 502L, 581L), *ludo ac sermonibus nostris.*

76 Horace *Satires* 2.1.69–74 (trans. Muecke 1993.21):

> primores populi arripuit populumque tributim,
> scilicet uni aequus Virtuti atque eius amicis.
> quin ubi se a uulgo et scaena in secreta remorant
> uirtus Scipiadae et mitis sapientia Laeli,
> nugari cum illo et discincti ludere, donec
> decoqueretur holus, soliti.

The virtuous friends were P. Scipio Africanus (*cos.* 147 and 134) and C. Laelius (*cos.* 140). For the 'tribe by tribe' criticism, cf. Lucilius 1132–3W (Bobbian scholiast 153St on Cicero *Pro Plancio* 19; Festus 212L).

Metaphorical: e.g. Muecke 1993.112; the quotations are from Goldberg 2005.166 and 170. Lucilius on his readers: Cicero *de oratore* 2.25, cf. *De finibus* 1.7; Pliny *Natural History* pref.7 (Lucilius 632–5W).

As Horace knew: e.g. *Satires* 1.4.74–5 (*in medio foro*); *Satires* 1.10.39, *Epistles* 1.19.41–2 (*theatris*); cf. *Satires* 1.10.72–4 for the contrast between pleasing the *turba* (like Lucilius) and writing 'for a few readers' (like Horace himself?).

Varro's Menippean satires (fragments numbered as in Astbury 1985): see in general Coffey 1976.149–64, Wiseman 2009b.131–51.

Reate (Coarelli 2009, De Santis 2009): Symmachus *Letters* 1.2; cf. Varro *Res rusticae* 2. pref.6, 2.8.3, 3.2.3–5. Senatorial: the earliest known Terentius Varro was the ill-fated consul of 216 BC (Livy 22.25.18–26.4); for Varro's own senatorial career (he was praetor in 70 or 69) see Wiseman 2009b.113–15. Funny: Cicero *Academica* 1.8 (*quadam hilaritate conspersimus*).

Less aggressive: the only named contemporaries in the surviving fragments—Volumnius, Vitulus, Atticus (Varro *Satires* 282, 411, 453)—seem to be minor characters; 'Atticus' was an impoverished senator, not Cicero's wealthy equestrian friend.

'Menippean' satires: Cicero *Academica* 1.8; Aulus Gellius 2.18.7, 13.31.1; Tertullian *Apologeticus* 14.8, Arnobius 6.23; ps.Probus on *Eclogues* 6.31 (p. 336 Hagen); Wiseman 2009b.137–43.

In his own name: Varro *Satires* 562 (*Varro*); 60, 175, 505 (*Marce*); cf. Lucilius 651W (*Lucilius*), 1075W (*Gai*).

Targeting corrupt senators: Varro *Satires* 64, 378, 452, 498–9, 512; Wiseman 2009b.148–50. Wide audience: Varro *Satires* 359, where someone complains to the narrator about 'what you publicize to the masses' (*quae ... in uulgum uulgas*).

Varro *Satires* 218 (Nonius 510L):

> *uosque in theatro, qui uoluptatem auribus*
> *huc aucupatum concucurristis domo,*
> *adeste et a me quae feram cognoscite,*
> *domum ut feratis ex theatro litteras.*

More substantial: for the increasingly elaborate decoration of temporary theatres, see Valerius Maximus 2.4.6, Pliny *Natural History* 21.6, 33.53, 35.23, 36.117 (Varro frr. 309–14 Funaioli).

Comic poets: Varro *Satires* 40, 356, 399, 522 (Plautus, Pacuvius, Ennius, Pompilius, Caecilius, Terence). *Double Marcus* programmatic: Varro *Satires* 58; Cèbe 1974.209–13.

Varro *Satires* 59 (Nonius 719L): *cum Quintipor Clodius tot comoedias sine ulla fecerit Musa, ego unum libellum non edolem, ut ait Ennius?* Quintipor Clodius is otherwise mentioned only in a quotation from Varro's correspondence (Nonius 168L, *epistula ad Fufium*).

Book to be read: Cicero *Academica* 1.4 and 8 (Varro on his readers); Varro *Satires* 304 ('You shouldn't touch my book, dear Petro, if this stage style irritates you').

Stage allusions: e.g. Varro *Satires* 51, 304, 353 (*scaena*); 218, 365, 513 (*theatrum*); 465, 570 (*cothurni*); 156, 353, 367 (comedy and tragedy); 531 (musician in *orchestra*), 355 (farewell to audience).

Soldier (Wiseman 2009b.113): Appian *Civil Wars* 4.47.202; cf. Varro *Res rusticae* 3.12.7 on his long absence in Spain, probably as legate to Pompey between 77 and 72 BC.

Vocatives: Varro *Satires* 8, 60, 66, 134, 175, 211, 304, 505, 562. Second-person singular: see Astbury 1985.134–5 for occurrences of *tu* and *tuus*.

Varro *Satires* 277 (Nonius 499L): *quid? qui uident et circumstant, non rident?—credo ridere: hiantis uideo, ridentes non audio*. Cf. *Satires* 531 (Nonius 69L) for another dialogue fragment.

Eumenides, first-person narrative: Varro *Satires* 142–7, 149–52, 154–5 (prose); 117 (*senarii*), 138 (trochaic *septenarius*), 141 (iambic *octonarius* followed by prose?); it evidently included reported dialogue (153, 157). Sung aria: 123–4. Hexameters: 125–7. Dialogue: 134–7. Great Mother and Galli: 150 (narrative setting); 119–21 (*senarii*), 140 (trochaic *septenarii*), 131–2 (Galliambics, horns and drums).

Aedile: Varro *Satires* 150, with Wiseman 1985.204–5, 269–72. Athens: 142 (Dionysia), 164 (Zeno), 165 (*porticus* and *dolium*). Possible final scene: 141 (*Attices philosophiae alumna*), 147 (*forenses*).

Expert on Plautus: Aulus Gellius 3.3.2–14 (Varro fr. 88 Funaioli). Jerome's partial list of Varro's works (Funaioli 1907.182) includes five books of *quaestiones Plautinae*, six books of *pseudotragoediae*, and three books each *de originibus scaenicis, de scaenicis actionibus* and *de actis scaenicis*.

Cicero *Pro Gallio* fr. 2 Crawford (Jerome *Epistles* 52.c.8):

> *his autem ludis—loquor enim quae sum ipse nuper expertus—unus quidam poeta dominatur, homo perlitteratus, cuius sunt illa conuiuia poetarum ac philosophorum, cum facit Euripiden et Menandrum inter se, et alio loco Socraten atque Epicurum disserentes, quorum aetates non annis sed saeculis scimus esse disiunctas. atque his quantos plausus et clamores mouet! multos enim condiscipulos habet in theatro, qui simul litteras non didicerunt.*

Cf. Varro *Satires* 302 (Menander); 6, 99, 490 (Socrates); 243, 315, 402 (Epicurus); 284 (Medea), 406 (Andromeda); the absence of Euripides' own name must be mere accident. Philosophers' banquet: Varro *Satires* 143–4.

6. A TURBULENT PEOPLE

Lucilius' great-nephew: Porphyrio and ps.Acro on Horace *Satires* 2.1.75; cf. ps.Acro on *Satires* 2.1.29 ('grandson'). Friend of Varro: Aulus Gellius 14.7.2; cf. Funaioli 1907.182 (Varro's *De Pompeio* in three volumes).

Charisma: Plutarch *Pompey* 1.2–2.5. Good looks: Pliny *Natural History* 7.53, 37.14. Legislation: Cicero *In Verrem* 1.45 (promise as consul designate), *De legibus* 3.22, 26; Velleius Paterculus 2.30.4, Plutarch *Pompey* 22.3.

Armies in being: Appian *Civil Wars* 1.121.561–2; cf. Plutarch *Pompey* 21.4. In recent years: the civil wars between Cn. Octavius and L. Cinna (consuls in 87) and M. Lepidus and Q. Catulus (consuls in 78).

6.1. The Political Stage

December 70 BC: Plutarch *Crassus* 12.3–4, *Pompey* 23.1–2; Appian *Civil Wars* 1.121.562–4. Presiding magistrate: Cicero *De republica* 2.55, Festus 154–5L; since Pompey was evidently elected first (from the order of names at Cicero *In Verrem* 2.3.123, Sallust *Catiline* 38.1 and ps.Asconius 189St), the *fasces* would be with Crassus in an even-numbered month.

Tablets taken to the treasury: inferred from Appian *Civil Wars* 1.121.564 (προγράψαι), with the formula *ad aerarium deferre* (Cicero *Philippics* 5.12, Livy 39.4.8, Suetonius *Diuus Augustus* 94.3, Tacitus *Annals* 3.51.2), εἰς τὸ ταμιεῖον ἀναφέρειν (Josephus *Antiquities* 14.221, Plutarch *Cato minor* 17.3).

Same stage for funerals: Polybius 6.52.1–3 (orator on Rostra); Diodorus Siculus 31.25.2, Suetonius *Diuus Vespasianus* 19.2 (actors); Appian *Civil Wars* 2.143–7.598–612 (Rostra as stage-set, orator, actors, audience as chorus); Wiseman 2009b.228–33. Same stage for *ludi*: implied by Livy 27.36.8 (Comitium used at *ludi Romani*); see in general Wiseman 2009b.153–70.

Pirates: Cicero *De imperio Cn. Pompei* 32–3, 53; Plutarch *Pompey* 24.6–8, Dio Cassius 36.21–2, Appian *Mithridatica* 93.

'Monarchy': Plutarch *Pompey* 25.2–3; cf. 30.3–4 (the same argument in 66 BC). Romulus: Dionysius of Halicarnassus *Roman Antiquities* 2.56.3–4; Plutarch *Romulus* 26.1–2, 27.1–7; Appian *Civil Wars* 2.114.476 (precedent for the Ides of March).

Senate discussion: Cicero *De imperio Cn. Pompei* 52 (Hortensius speech). Senate-house invaded: Dio Cassius 36.24.1–3. Crowded Forum: Cicero *De imperio Cn. Pompei* 44.

Piso on Romulus: Plutarch *Pompey* 25.4. Catulus: Cicero *De imperio Cn. Pompei* 59, Sallust *Histories* 5.24M, Velleius Paterculus 2.32.1–2, Valerius Maximus 8.15.9, Plutarch *Pompey* 25.5, Dio Cassius 36.36a. Man of integrity: Cicero *Pro Sestio* 101, *Philippics* 2.12; cf. *In Pisonem* 6 (*princeps senatus*); Dio Cassius 36.30.5.

The many: e.g. Cicero *Pro Cluentio* 110, *Pro Flacco* 96–7, *Ad Atticum* 2.3.4, Sallust *Histories* 3.48.6M (*multitudo*); Nonius 836L = Cicero *De republica* 6.1 (*multi*).

The few: e.g. Cicero *De lege agraria* 3.13, Sallust *Histories* 3.48.6M (*paucorum dominatio*); Caesar *De bello ciuili* 1.22.5, Hirtius *De bello Gallico* 8.50.2, Sallust *Jugurthine War* 27.2, cf. Augustus *Res gestae* 1.1 (*factio paucorum*); Sallust *Catiline* 20.7, 39.1, *Jugurthine War* 31.19, *Histories* 1.12M (*pauci potentes*).

Execution without trial: by Cicero in 63, punished by exile in 58. Political murder: of Clodius in 52, Caesar in 44. Civil war provoked: Pollio *FRHist* 56 F3 (Suetonius *Diuus Iulius* 30.4, Plutarch *Caesar* 46.1).

Cicero *De imperio Cn. Pompei* 1–2 (trans. Michael Grant, Penguin Classics, 1969):

> *quamquam mihi semper frequens conspectus uester multo iucundissimus, hic autem locus ad agendum amplissimus, ad dicendum ornatissimus est uisus, Quirites, tamen hoc aditu laudis, qui semper optimo cuique maxime patuit* ...

facile intellexi, Quirites, et quid de me iudicaretis et quid aliis praescriberetis. nunc cum et auctoritatis in me tantum sit quantum uos honoribus mandandis esse uoluistis, et ad agendum facultatis tantum quantum homini uigilanti ex forensi usu prope cotidiana dicendi exercitatio potuit adferre, certe et, si quid auctoritatis in me est, apud eos utar qui eam mihi dederunt, et si quid in dicendo consequi possum, iis ostendam potissimum qui ei quoque rei fructum suo iudicio tribuendum esse duxerunt.

For the scene, see Wiseman 2009b.155–7.

Audience for forensic speeches: Cicero *Brutus* 289–90; cf. *De oratore* 1.68 (tribunal), *Pro Caelio* 67 (*subsellia*); Catullus 53, Cicero *Brutus* 192 (*corona*). As Cicero observed to the judges in one trial, 'You see what a crowd there is in the Forum, so many types of people, so many different pursuits' (*Pro Caelio* 21).

Orators as actors: Cicero *De oratore* 2.338 (*oratoris scaena*), *Brutus* 290 (like Roscius), *De amicitia* 97 (*in contione, id est in scaena*); for political life in general as a *theatrum*, cf. *In Verrem* 2.5.35, *Ad Q. fratrem* 1.1.42, *Pro Rabirio Postumo* 42; for the orator's *actio*, i.e. delivery or performance, see *De oratore* 1.128 and 3.213–27.

6.2. Pompey and the Theatre

Pompey's achievement: Pliny *Natural History* 7.97–8 (quoting contemporary documents), Plutarch *Pompey* 45.23 (annual tribute raised from 50 million to 85 million *denarii*).

Theophanes (*FGrH* 188): Cicero *Pro Archia* 24 (already his *rerum scriptor* in 62 BC); Strabo 11.5.1 C503 (συστρατεύσας τῷ Πομπηίῳ); cf. Cicero *Ad Atticum* 2.5.1, 2.17.3, 5.11.3, 9.1.3, Caesar *De bello ciuili* 3.18.3 (political adviser). Alexander's historians: e.g. Arrian *Anabasis* pref.2 (Aristobulus and Ptolemy), 4.10.12 (Callisthenes); Pearson 1960.

Plutarch *Pompey* 42.4 (trans. Rex Warner, Penguin Classics 1958):

καὶ γὰρ εἰς Μιτυλήνην ἀφικόμενος τήν τε ἀγῶνα τὸν πάτριον ἐθεάσατο τῶν ποιητῶν, ὑπόθεσιν μίαν ἔχοντα τὰς ἐκείνου πράξεις. ἡσθεὶς δὲ τῷ θεάτρῳ περιεγράψατο τὸ εἶδος αὐτοῦ καὶ τὸν τύπον, ὡς ὅμοιον ἀπεργασόμενος τὸ ἐν Ῥώμῃ, μεῖζον δὲ καὶ σεμνότερον.

Unheard-of privilege: Velleius Paterculus 2.40.4 (a law of the tribunes T. Ampius and T. Labienus), Dio Cassius 37.21.4.

Cicero *Ad Atticum* 1.18.6:

sed interea πολιτικὸς ἀνὴρ οὐδ' ὄναρ *quisquam inueniri potest. qui poterat, familiaris noster (sic est enim, uolo te hoc scire) Pompeius, togulam illam pictam silentio tuetur suam.*

Cicero *Ad Atticum* 1.16.11:

...illa contionalis hirudo aerari, misera ac ieiuna plebecula, me ab hoc Magno unice diligi putat; et hercule multa et iucunda consuetudine coniuncti inter nos sumus, usque ut nostri isti comissatores coniurationis, barbatuli iuuenes, illum in sermonibus Cn. Ciceronem appellant. itaque et ludis et gladiatoribus mirandas ἐπισημασίας *sine ulla pastoricia fistula auferebamus.*

6.3. When Cicero Wasn't in Rome

Out of town April and May: Cicero *Ad Atticum* 2.417 (59 BC); *Ad Q. fratrem* 2.6.4, *Ad Atticum* 4.7 (56); *Ad Atticum* 4.6, 4.9 (55); *Ad familiares* 7.18.3, 16.10, 16.1315 (53); *Ad Atticum* 14.1–15.5 (44).

Departure date: *Ad Atticum* 14.1.1 (7 April); *Ad familiares* 7.18.3 (8 April); *Ad Q. fratrem* 2.6.4 (9 April). Return date: *Ad Q. fratrem* 2.6.4 (6 May, early because of a commitment); *Ad Atticum* 2.8.2, 14.14.6, *Ad Q. fratrem* 2.13.1 (1 June).

Social life: *Ad Atticum* 2.15.3 (Formiae), 5.2.2 (Cumae as *pusilla Roma*). Business postponed: *Ad Atticum* 14.5.2 (*res prolatae*, 11 April), *Ad familiares* 3.9.4 (*discessus senatus*, spring).

Out of town in November: *Ad Atticum* 4.8a (56 BC), 4.13.1 (55); *Ad Q. fratrem* 3.4.6 (54); *Ad familiares* 16.24.2, *Ad Atticum* 16.8–15 (44).

Avoiding the *ludi*: *Ad Atticum* 4.8a.1 (cf. 4.11.2 for Dionysius); *Ad Q. fratrem* 3.4.6 (leaving Rome the day the games begin); *De oratore* 1.24 (*ludorum Romanorum diebus*).

Cicero *De finibus* 3.7–8 (it is not clear which games are meant):

> nam in Tusculano cum essem uellemque e bibliotheca pueri Luculli quibusdam libris uti, ueni in eius uillam ut eos ipse ut solebam depromerem. quo cum uenissem, M. Catonem quem ibi esse nescieram uidi in bibliotheca sedentem multis circumfusis Stoicorum libris... 'quid tu' inquit 'huc? a uilla enim credo: et si ibi te esse scissem ad te ipse uenissem.' 'heri' inquam 'ludis commissis ex urbe profectus ueni ad uesperum.'

Ludi Apollinares: Cicero *Ad Atticum* 1.16.11, 2.19.3, 4.15.6 (Cicero present in 61, 59, and 54 BC); cf. 15.26–16.2 (absent in 44, because intending to go to Greece). *Ludi Romani*: *Ad Atticum* 4.1.4–5 (Cicero returns from exile on 4 September); but cf. *Ad Q. fratrem* 3.1.1 (absent in 54 BC *ludorum diebus*), 3.1.14 (back in Rome 18 September).

Young Cicero: *In Verrem* 2.5.36, *Pro Murena* 40 (aedile's games); *In Verrem* 2.5.180–2 ('new man' against the *nobiles*). Executions: Sallust *Catiline* 55, Plutarch *Cicero* 22.1–2. Hostile citizens: Cicero *Pro Sulla* 30–1 (crowd in Forum, 62 BC), Dio Cassius 37.38.

Enemy of the People: Cicero *Pro Sulla* 21–2, *Ad Atticum* 1.16.10 (*regnum*); Plutarch *Cicero* 23.2 (δυναστεία); cf. Wiseman 2009b.209–10 on Dio Cassius 46.20.1–2 and ps.Sallust *In Ciceronem* 5–6.

Cicero *In P. Clodium et Curionem* fr. 19 Crawford (cf. *Ad Atticum* 1.16.9–10 for the occasion):

> ...homo durus ac priscus inuectus est in eos qui mense Aprili apud Baias essent et aquis calidis uterentur. quid cum hoc homine nobis tam tristi ac seuero? non possunt hi mores ferre hunc tam austerum et tam uehementem magistrum, per quem hominibus maioribus natu ne in suis quidem praediis impune tum, cum Romae nihil agitur, liceat esse ualetudini seruire.

Clodius: see Tatum 1999.

Cicero and Clodius, 4–7 September 57: *Ad Atticum* 4.1.5–6 (the People approved of Cicero's alliance with Pompey).

Conspicuously visible: Cicero *De domo* 100 (*in conspectu totius urbis*), 116 (*pulcherrimo prospectu*); *De haruspicum responso* 33 (view of city). House dispute: Cicero *Ad Atticum* 4.2.2–6, *De domo*, passim.

85   The People's Liberty: *Ad Atticum* 4.2.3 (*suam Libertatem ut defenderent*); cf. Dio Cassius 39.11.1, 39.20.3. Rebuilding: *Ad Atticum* 4.2.7 (early October), 4.3.4 (3 November).

Cicero *Ad Atticum* 4.3.3 (written 23 November 57):

itaque a.d. III Id. Nov. cum Sacra uia descenderem, insecutus est me cum suis. clamor, lapides, fustes, gladii; et haec improuisa omnia. discessi in uestibulum Tetti Damionis. qui erant mecum facile operas aditu prohibuerunt. ipse occidi potui; sed ego diaeta curare incipio, chirurgiae taedet.

Armed escorts: cf. *Pro Milone* 10, *Ad Q. fratrem* 2.9.2 (but outside the city). Particularly shocking: *Ad Atticum* 4.3.2.

Ludi Ceriales of 56 BC: Cicero *Ad Atticum* 4.7.3 (*c.*13 April), *De haruspicum responso* 8; Dio Cassius 39.20.3. Games of 55: Cicero *Ad Atticum* 4.6.4 (from Cumae, mid-April), 4.10.2 (Cumae, 22 April), 4.9.2 (Naples, 27 April).

Cato at the *ludi Florales*: Valerius Maximus 2.10.8, Seneca *Epistles* 97.8; cf. Martial 1. pref.

6.4. Pompey's Games

Greek habit: Cicero *Pro Flacco* 15–17; Posidonius F 253.98 = Athenaeus 5.213d (popular assembly in theatre, Athens 87 BC). The People's place: Cicero *Pro Murena* 38–40 (a patronizing account of the *ludi* as popular entertainment).

86   Pompey and Crassus consuls again: Plutarch *Pompey* 51.4–52.2, *Crassus* 15, *Cato minor* 41–2; Cicero *Ad Q. fratrem* 2.8.3.

Date of games: Valerius Maximus 2.4.6 (hot weather); Coarelli 1997.568 notes that Pompey's birthday was 29 September (Pliny *Natural History* 37.13, the day chosen for his triumph in 61 BC), so they probably followed immediately after the *ludi Romani*.

Victoria: Tiro, cited in Aulus Gellius 10.1.7 (not a confusion, *pace* Coarelli 1997.569). The temple was evidently later re-dedicated to Venus Victrix: Pliny *Natural History* 8.20 (games), Tertullian *De spectaculis* 10.5 (temple and steps). Other temples: Suetonius *Diuus Claudius* 21.1 (access via *cauea*); Degrassi 1963.180–1 (*Fasti Allifani*), 190–1 (*Fasti Amiternini*) for annual sacrifices to Venus Victrix, Honos and Virtus, Victoria, and Felicitas *in theatro marmoreo*.

Height of temple: cf. Gros 1999.37–8, putting its pediment at about 45m above ground level (the same height as the Capitol); Gros 1987.322–6 for the impact of the whole complex.

Date of speech: Asconius 1C. Piso in 58: Cicero *In Pisonem* 12–14, 26, 52; cf. *Post reditum in senatu* 16–18, *De domo* 62, *Pro Sestio* 54.

Cicero *In Pisonem* 65:

> instant post hominum memoriam apparatissimi magnificentissimique ludi, quales non modo numquam fuerunt sed ne quo modo fieri quidem posthac possint possum ullo modo suspicari: da te populo, committe ludis. sibilum metuis? ubi sunt uestrae scholae? ne acclametur times? ne id quidem est curare philosophi. manus tibi ne adferantur? dolor enim est malum, ut tu disputas; existimatio, dedecus, infamia, turpitudo uerba atque ineptiae. sed de hoc non dubito: non audebit accedere ad ludos.

Pompey's theatre: Gros 1999, Coleman 2000.221–2, Sear 2006.57–61. Capacity: the Constantinian *Notitia* on *regio* X (Richter 1901.373) gives 17,580; cf. Pliny *Natural History* 36.115 ('40,000'). *Praecinctiones*: Vitruvius 2.8.11 (metaphorical), 5.3.4, 5.6.2, 5.7.2. Divided *cauea*: Suetonius *Diuus Augustus* 44.2; cf. Vitruvius 2.8.11, Seneca *De tranquillitate animi* 11.8.

Segregated areas and access: Sear 2006.2 ('carefully arranged so that the different classes had minimal contact with each other'), Packer *et al.* 2007.517–19; see Vitruvius 5.3.4 for the height of the *praecinctio* wall. Separate access stairs are detectable in the Theatre of Marcellus (Sear 2006 figs. 12–13), for which Pompey's theatre must have been the design pattern.

Cicero *Ad familiares* 7.1.1:

> ... modo ut tibi constiterit fructus oti tui; quo quidem tibi perfrui mirifice licuit cum esses in ista amoenitate paene solus relictus. neque tamen dubito quin tu in illo cubiculo tuo, ex quo tibi Stabianum perforando patefecisti sinum, per eos dies matutina tempora lectiunculis consumpseris, cum illi interea qui te istic reliquerunt spectarent communis mimos semisomni. reliquas uero partis diei tu consumebas iis delectationibus quas tibi ipse ad arbitrium tuum compararas; nobis autem erant ea perpetienda quae Sp. Maecius probauisset.

'Not to your taste': Cicero *Ad familiares* 7.1.2. *Clytemnestra*: Accius frr. 291–301 Dangel. *Trojan Horse*: Macrobius *Saturnalia* 6.1.38; cf. Nonius 762L (Livius).

Cicero *Ad familiares* 7.1.2–3:

> quae popularem admirationem habuerunt, delectationem tibi nullam attulissent. quod si tu per eos dies operam dedisti Protogeni tuo, dum modo is tibi quiduis potius quam orationes meas legerit, ne tu haud paulo plus quam quisquam nostrum delectationis habuisti.

Slave *lectores*: Cicero *Ad Atticum* 1.12.4 (Cicero's Sositheus), 16.2.6 (Atticus' Salvius); Nepos *Atticus* 13.3, 14.1.

Authoritative translations: Wilkinson 1949.58, Shackleton Bailey 1978.79. *Cubiculum* not bedroom: e.g. Cicero *Ad Q. fratrem* 1.1.25, *Pro Scauro* 26, *Philippics* 8.29; Pliny *Letters* 1.3.1, Tacitus *Dialogus* 3.1.

Sp. Maecius as critic: Horace *Satires* 1.10.38 (epic poetry context) and *Ars poetica* 387, with scholiasts on both passages.

6.5. Poets and Dancers

89 Cicero *Ad Q. fratrem* 2.9.1:

> non mehercule quisquam μουσοπάτακτος libentius sua recentia poemata legit quam ego te audio quacumque de re, publica priuata, rustica urbana.

Archias the poet: Cicero *Pro Archia* 6 (*audiebatur a M. Aemilio* [cos. 115 BC]); cf. Varro *Satires* 517 = Nonius 373–4L (*acroasi bellorum hominum*).

Cicero *De officiis* 1.147:

> ut enim pictores et ii qui signa fabricantur et uero etiam poetae suum quisque opus a uulgo considerari uult, ut si quid reprehensum sit a pluribus id corrigatur, iique et secum et <ex> aliis quid in eo peccatum sit exquirunt, sic aliorum iudicio permulta nobis et facienda et non facienda et mutanda et corrigenda sunt.

Stone theatre (Coarelli 1997.272–3): Vitruvius 3.3.2, *Année Épigraphique* 1987.67 (*theatrum lapideum*); cf. Degrassi 1963.190–1 (*Fasti Amiternini*), where Pompey's theatre is the *theatrum marmoreum*.

Wooden theatres still used: Vitruvius 5.5.7 (*multa theatra quotannis Romae facta*).

Poets reading *in medio foro*: Horace *Satires* 1.4.74–5 (*c*.35 BC).

Ground-plan of Pompey's theatre: Coarelli 1997.539–41, Beacham 1999.65–7, Gagliardo and Packer 2006.

Cicero on mime: *De oratore* 2.251 (clowning); *Orator* 88, *De oratore* 2.242 (obscenity); *Pro Caelio* 64 (improvisation); *Ad familiares* 7.11.2, 14.3.2 (comment); *Ad familiares* 12.18.2 (poets); Seneca *Controuersiae* 7.3.8–9 (Cicero and Laberius as rival wits).

90 Cicero on *mimae*: *Pro Plancio* 30 (a *mimula* raped by his client); *Pro Roscio comoedo* 23 (Dionysia, who earned 200,000 HS per performance); *In Verrem* 2.3.83 (Verres' mistress); *Ad Atticum* 10.16.5, *Philippics* 2.20, 58, 62, 69 (Antony's mistress). *Ludi Florales*: Ovid *Fasti* 5.331–68, Valerius Maximus 2.10.8, Seneca *Letters* 97.8; Wiseman 2008.175–86.

Mimae as dancers: *ILLRP* 803.11–13 (Eucharis), Aulus Gellius 1.5.3 (Dionysia). *Mimae* as singers: Philodemus 12.7–8 Sider, cf. Plutarch *Pompey* 22.2–4 (Flora); Servius on *Eclogues* 6.11 (Cytheris).

91 Lucretius 4.978–83:

> per multos itaque illa dies eadem obuersantur
> ante oculos, etiam uigilantes ut uideantur
> cernere saltantis et mollia membra mouentis
> et citharae liquidum carmen chordasque loquentis
> auribus accipere, et consessum cernere eundem
> scaenaique simul uarios splendere decores.

Actaeon: Varro *Satires* 513 (*saltatoribus in theatro*); cf. Ovid *Metamorphoses* 3.138–252 for the scenario. Nymphs by night: Apollonius Rhodius 1.1223–4 (Artemis), Horace *Odes* 1.4.5–8 (Venus); cf. Ovid *Fasti* 5.367–8, Dio Cassius 58.19.1–2 (Flora's games).

Diomedes in *Grammatici Latini* 1.491–2 Keil = Kaibel 1899.61 (Wiseman 2014.262–4):

> primis autem temporibus, sic uti adserit Tranquillus, omnia quae in scaena uersantur in comoedia agebantur. nam et pantomimus et pythaules et choraules in comoedia canebant. sed quia non poterant omnia simul apud omnes artifices pariter excellere, siqui erant inter actores comoediarum pro facultate et arte potiores, principatum <sui> sibi artificii uindicabant. sic factum est <ut>, nolentibus cedere mimis in artificio suo ceteris, separatio fieret reliquorum. nam dum potiores inferioribus qui in communi ergasterio erant seruire dedignantur, se ipsos a comoedia separauerunt, ac sic factum est ut exemplo semel sumpto usus quisque artis suae rem exequi coeperit neque in comoediam uenire.

Pantomimus (Hall and Wyles 2008): Jerome *Chronicle* Ol. 189.3 (Pylades, 22 BC), Athenaeus 1.20.d–e (Bathyllus of Alexandria), Seneca *Controuersiae* 3.pref.10 (Pylades tragic, Bathyllus comic); Lucian *Saltatio* 34, Dio Cassius 54.17.4, Macrobius *Saturnalia* 2.7.12–18 (new in Augustus' time); but cf. Hall and Wyles 2008.380 (Priene, *c*.80 BC).

Cicero *Pro Rabirio Postumo* 35:

> audiebamus Alexandream, nunc cognoscimus. illinc omnes praestigiae, illinc, inquam, omnes fallaciae, omnia denique ab eis mimorum argumenta nata sunt.

Serious poets: Giancotti 1967 (Publilius); Panayotakis 2010 (Laberius); Wiseman 1985.183–206 (Catullus). Not everyone wants to believe that Catullus the mimographer was Catullus the love poet (e.g. Coleman 2006.83 n. 2, Panayotakis 2010.41–2 n. 73), but the evidence for it is strong (Goldberg 2011.214): Cicero *Ad familiares* 7.11.1 (Valerius paired with Laberius); Martial 5.30.3 (Catullus as playwright); Juvenal 8.185–6 (Catullus' *Phasma* and *Laureolus*), 13.110–11 (*mimus* by Catullus); Tertullian *Aduersus Valentinianos* 14 (Catullus' *Laureolus*); Priscian 6.7 and 73 = *Grammatici Latini* 2.200 and 258 Keil (Valerius' *Phormio*); for Catullus the love-poet as 'Valerius' see Charisius in *Grammatici Latini* 1.97 Keil (124 Barwick).

Publilius as *mimicae scaenae conditor*: Pliny *Natural History* 35.199, cf. Suetonius *De grammaticis* 13 (on Staberius Eros) for the approximate date. Fifth century BC: Suda Σ 893 (4.411 Adler) and Diogenes Laertius 3.18 on Sophron.

Scholiast on Lucan 1.543–4 (35–6 Usener):

> hoc est eclipsin passus est, Mycenisque nox fuit. sed hoc fabulosum inueni in libro Catulli qui inscribitur περὶ μιμολογιῶν [Mueller 1869; MSS *permimologiarum*]. qui ait <Atreum> primum ciuibus suis solis cursus ueros et ante inauditos ostendisse ac persuasisse illum contrarium signis omnibus ascendere et quod ceterae uagae stellae facere dicuntur: et ob hanc scientiam inclitum summoto fratre regnum accepisse.

For the Greek title, cf. Josephus *Vita* 16 (actor/dancer as μιμολόγος); Macrobius *Saturnalia* 2.7.13–18 (Greek-speaking *pantomimi*).

Laberius' astrological titles: Panayotakis 2010.129 (*Aries*), 156 (*Cancer*), 266 (*Gemelli*), 380 (*Taurus*), 391–2 (*Virgo*).

6.6. Before the Disaster

Spoils of conquest: details in Badian 1968.76–92. Private luxury: Cicero *Pro Murena* 76. Tyrannicide: details in Wiseman 2009b.177–210.

Pompey's escort: Plutarch *Pompey* 23.3. Pompey and Caesar as assassination targets: Plutarch *Pompey* 25.4 (66 BC); Sallust *Catiline* 49.4, Suetonius *Diuus Iulius* 14.2, Plutarch *Caesar* 8.2 (63); Cicero *Ad Atticum* 2.24.2–3, *In Vatinium* 24 (59); Caesar *De bello Gallico* 1.44.12, Cicero *De domo* 129 etc (58); Cicero *Ad Q. fratrem* 2.3.3–4 (56); Crawford 1974.455–6 (Brutus' *libertas* coin issue, 54); Asconius 38C, 51C (52); Caelius in Cicero *Ad familiares* 8.14.2 (50).

Caesar in Germany and Britain: *De bello Gallico* 4.16–38; Catullus 11.9–12, 29.11–12. Julia: Plutarch *Pompey* 53.1–4, *Caesar* 23.4. Cicero: *Ad Atticum* 4.5.1–3 ('palinode'), *De prouinciis consularibus* 18–47. Aristocrats' reaction: *Ad familiares* 1.7.7–8, 1.9.4–20.

Cicero *Ad Atticum* 4.15.6:

> redii Romam Fontei causa a.d. VII Id. Quint. ueni spectatum, primum magno et aequabili plausu—sed hoc ne curaris, ego ineptus qui scripserim.

7. RETHINKING THE CLASSICS: 59–42 BC

Authorial intention: see Woodman and Powell 1992.207–11 for a sensible brief discussion.

Triumphant election: Plutarch *Caesar* 14.1 (λαμπρῶς), cf. Cicero *Ad Atticum* 2.1.6 ('he has the wind behind him'). Caesar as *popularis*: Cicero *In Catilinam* 4.9 (63 BC); Suetonius *Diuus Iulius* 11.1 (65), 16.2 (62); Cicero *Ad Atticum* 2.21.1 (*dominatio iucunda multitudini*), cf. Appian *Civil Wars* 2.10.36, 2.12.42–13.46, Dio Cassius 38.1.1–2, 38.4.1–3 (59 BC); Plutarch *Cato minor* 51.5 (τοῦ δήμου θέλοντος ἀεὶ τὸν Καίσαρα μέγιστον εἶναι).

Varro as *XXuir agris diuidendis*: Varro *Res rusticae* 1.2.10, Pliny *Natural History* 7.176.

'Tyranny': Cicero *Ad Atticum* 2.14.1, 2.17.1; cf. 2.8.1 (*reges*), 2.9.1 (*dynastae*), 2.12.1 and 13.2 (*regnum*), 2.21.1 (*dominatio*). Cicero's view: *Ad Atticum* 2.18.1 (*neque iam quominus seruiamus recusamus*), 2.19.5 (*certi sumus perisse omnia*), 2.21.1 (*res publica . . . tota periit*).

Caesar's son: Augustus *Res gestae* 1.1 (*rem publicam a dominatione factionis oppressam in libertatem uindicaui*), 2 (avenging the assassins' *facinus* / ἀσέβημα).

7.1. Lucretius and Philodemus

Suffering mortals: Lucretius 6.1 (*mortalibus aegris*); cf. Homer *Odyssey* 11.19 (δειλοῖσι βροτοῖσι).

Lucretius 1.146–54:

> hunc igitur terrorem animi tenebrasque necessest
> non radii solis neque lucida tela diei
> discutiant, sed naturae species ratioque.

> principium cuius hinc nobis exordia sumet,
> nullam rem a nilo gigni diuinitus umquam.
> quippe ita formido mortales continet omnis,
> quod multa in terris fieri caeloque tuentur
> quorum operum causas nulla ratione uidere
> possunt ac fieri diuino numine rentur.

Lucretius 3.1011–19:

> Cerberus et Furiae iam uero et lucis egestas,
> Tartarus horriferos eructans faucibus aestus,
> qui neque sunt usquam nec possunt esse profecto.
> sed metus in uita poenarum pro male factis
> est insignibus insignis, scelerisque luella
> carcer et horribilis de saxo iactu' deorsum,
> uerbera carnifices robur pix lammina taedae;
> quae tamen etsi absunt, at mens sibi conscia facti
> praemetuans adhibet stimulos torretque flagellis.

Memmius: Lucretius 1.42–3 (nec Memmi clara propago talibus in rebus communi desse saluti); cf. 1.26 (Memmiadae nostro), 1.411, 1.1052, 2.143, 2.182, 5.8 (inclute Memmi), 5.93, 5.164, 5.867, 5.1282.

Patronage and hard work: Lucretius 1.136–45 (sperata uoluptas suauis amicitiae, 140–1); cf. also 3.419 (conquisita diu dulcique reperta labore).

World of work (Wiseman 1974.15–25): Lucretius 1.411, 4.75–80, 4.528–32, 4.563–4 (man in the crowd); 1.936–47, 2.847–51, 4.223–5 (pharmacy); 2.196–200, 4.296–9, 4.513–19 (manual work). Life of luxury (Wiseman 1974.22–5): 2.24–8, 2.34–6, 2.51–2, 4.304–7, 4.400–3, 4.1029, 4.1123–32, 5.1428; cf. 4.991–1006, 5.1063–72 (hunting-dogs).

Classic statement: Lucretius 1.922–47 (cf. 4.1–22), esp. 943–6: haec ratio plerumque uidetur | tristior esse quibus non est tractata, retroque | uulgus abhorret ab hac.

Philodemus: Cicero In Pisonem 68–72, with Nisbet 1961.183–8, Janko 2000.3–10; for the poems see Sider 1997. Volcano and villa: Wallace-Hadrill 2011, esp. 25–36 (eruption), 48–56 (Bourbons), 114–18 (villa).

Philodemus on the sound of poetry (ἀκοή, εὐφωνία, ἦχος etc): e.g. De poematibus 1.37, 40, 83, 93–4, 100–1, 128–9, 151, 166 (Janko 2000.225, 229, 279, 285, 299–301, 307–9, 327–9, 361, 381); 5.21, 23–4, 26–7, 29, 32 (Mangoni 1993.148, 151–2, 153–4, 156, 158). Philodemus on the poet's audience (οἱ ἀκούοντες): e.g. De poematibus 1.49 (Janko 2000.239); 5.16, 36 (Mangoni 1993.143, 162).

Philodemus De poematibus 1.161 (Janko 2000.373): δεῖν τὸν μὲν σοφιστὴν ζητεῖν τὴ[ν] ἀλήθ[εια]ν, τὸν δὲ πο[ητὴν τὰ πα]ρὰ τοῖς πολ[λοῖς εὐδοκι]μοῦντα. διὸ [ταύτην τὴν λέξι]ν καλλίστην ἔ[λεγε, τὴν] τοὺς ὄχλους [ψυχαγωγο]ῦσαν, οὐ τὴν [κατ]ὰ τὸ [γ' ὀ]ρθό[τατ]όν [τισι δ]ὴ θαυμασθεῖ[σαν]. Cf. also De poematibus 1.162 (Janko 2000.375) on οἱ ψυχαγωγοῦντες τὸν ὄχλον. See Janko 2000.143–54 on Andromenides.

Cicero *Academica* 1.4 (*sin a Graecorum artibus et disciplinis abhorrerent*...), cf. Lucretius 1.944–5 = 4.19–20.

Cicero *Academica* 1.5:

uides autem... non posse nos Amafini aut Rabiri similes esse, qui nulla arte adhibita de rebus ante oculos positis uulgari sermone disputant.

Cicero *Tusculan Disputations* 4.6 (*cuius libris editis commota multitudo contulit se ad eam potissimum disciplinam*); 1.6 (*suos libros ipsi legunt cum suis*), 2.7 (*legendi... inter se qui idem sentient*); cf. 1.55 for Epicureans as 'plebeian philosophers'.

Philosophers losing their audience: Cicero *Pro Caelio* 41 (*prope soli iam in scholis sunt relicti*). Stoics: Horace *Satires* 2.3.32–297, presented as Stertinius' oral teaching (*pace* Rawson 1985.53, who calls him 'primarily a writer'—but the question is whether he wrote only for readers).

98   Lucretius and the Muses: 1.117–19 (Ch. 5.1 above, on Ennius), 1.929–30 = 4.4–5, 6.47 (chariot), 6.92–5 (Calliope). Calliope and epic: *Anthologia Palatina* 9.504.1 (ἡρωίδος ἀοιδῆς); e.g. Virgil *Aeneid* 9.525, Ovid *Metamorphoses* 5.337–40, Statius *Siluae* 2.7.34–106 (on Lucan).

Epicurean view of the gods: Lucretius 1.44–9 = 2.646–51 (*semota ab nostris rebus*, 46 = 648); 2.1093–4, 5.146–73, 5.1169–82. Pious reaction: Dionysius of Halicarnassus *Roman Antiquities* 2.68.1, 8.56.1. Prophets: Lucretius 1.102–9, cf. 5.110–21 (Giants); Wiseman 1994.50–3.

Prayer to Venus: Lucretius 1.29–43. Quoted lines (1.41–3): *nam neque nos agere hoc patriai tempore iniquo* | *possumus aequo animo nec Memmi clara propago* | *talibus in rebus communi desse saluti.*

Romans as *Aeneadae*: e.g. Virgil *Aeneid* 8.648, Ovid *Fasti* 4.161, *Metamorphoses* 15.682, Silius Italicus 1.2. Memmius' Trojan descent: Virgil *Aeneid* 5.116–17; Torelli 1999.175–7.

Consular candidature (54 BC): Cicero *Ad Atticum* 4.15.7, 4.17.2; *Ad Q. fratrem* 2.15.4, 3.1.16, 3.2.3, 3.6.3. Bloodshed (55): Plutarch *Cato minor* 41.4, 43.4, *Crassus* 15.4–5; Dio Cassius 39.31.1, 32.2, 35.5.

7.2. Demetrius, Historians, Caesar

Demetrius *On Style* 215:

καὶ ὅλως δὲ ὁ ποιητὴς οὗτος (ποιητὴν γὰρ αὐτὸν καλοίη τις ἂν εἰκότως) ἐναργείας δημιουργός ἐστιν ἐν τῇ γραφῇ συμπάσῃ.

99   Ctesias (*FGrH* 688) and μῦθοι: Strabo 1.2.35, 11.6.3 (C 43, 507–8); Plutarch *Artaxerxes* 1.2, 6.6; Lucian *True History* 1.3, 2.31, *Philopseudes* 2.

Heracleodorus in Philodemus *On Poems* 1.199 (Janko 2000.429):

[πο]ήματα φάσκων τὰ [Δ]ημοσθένους καὶ [τὰ Ξενο]φῶντος, μᾶλλον [δὲ καὶ] τὰ Ἡροδότου, καί[τοι κατὰ] τὴν συνθήκην [ἑκάστου συγ]γράφο[ν]τος.

'Hearing or reading' history: Cicero *De finibus* 5.52 (*res gestas audire et legere*), *De senectute* 20 (*legere aut audire*); Caelius in Cicero *Ad familiares* 8.15.1 (*aut audisti aut legisti*); Sallust *Catiline* 53.2 (*mihi multa legenti multa audienti*), *Jugurthine War* 85.13 (*audire aut legere*). Humble audience for history: Cicero *De finibus* 5.52 (*homines infima fortuna . . . delectantur historiae*).

Valerius Antias (Livy 39.43.1 on his *fabulae*): Forsythe 2002, Rich 2005. Numa story: Arnobius 5.1–2 (Antias FRHist 25 F8); cf. Ovid *Fasti* 3.259–392, Plutarch *Numa* 15.3–6; Wiseman 2008.155–66.

Antias and the games: Censorinus *De die natali* 17.8, 10, 11 (Antias frr. 19P, 22P, 55P on *ludi saeculares*), Asconius 69C (Antias fr. 37P on *ludi Romani*), Livy 36.36.4 (Antias fr. 40P on *ludi Megalenses*), Livy 39.22.8–9 (Antias fr. 46P on *ludi uotiui*).

Antias and the Valerii in early Rome: Münzer 1891, Wiseman 1998a.75–89. Noble Valerii (M. Valerius Messalla Niger and M. Valerius Messalla Rufus): Syme 1979.262–4, 1986.227–8; Wiseman 1979.131–4.

Cicero's *ambitio*: *Ad Q. fratrem* 3.1.12, 3.5.3; cf. 3.6.1 for the strategy planned with Quintus. Censorship: *Ad Atticum* 4.2.6 (already in October 57). Priesthood: *Ad Atticum* 2.5.2 (already in April 59); *Ad familiares* 8.3.1, 15.4.13, *Philippics* 2.4, Plutarch *Cicero* 36.1 (elected augur in 53 or early 52). Consulship for Quintus: see Wiseman 1966 for evidence (circumstantial) and argument.

Cicero *Ad familiares* 5.12.4–5:

> multam etiam casus nostri uarietatem tibi in scribendo suppeditabunt plenam cuiusdam uoluptatis, quae uehementer animos hominum in legendo te scriptore tenere posit. nihil est enim aptius ad delectationem lectoris quam temporum uarietates fortunaeque uicissitudines. quae etsi nobis optabiles in experiendo non fuerunt, in legendo tamen erunt iucundae . . . si uero exitu notabili concluduntur, expletur animus iucundissima lectionis uoluptate.

Posterity: *Ad familiares* 5.12.1 (*commemoratio posteritatis ac spes quaedam immortalitatis*), 5.12.7 (*ad memoriae dignitatem*), 5.12.9 (*ut ceteri . . . ex libris tuis nos cognoscant*).

One man's experience: *Ad familiares* 5.12.5 (*uiri excellentis ancipites uariique casus*). A play with acts: 5.12.6 (*quasi fabulam . . . habet enim uarios actus*).

Artistic advantage: Woodman 1988.89–90; the visual aspect is implied in *Ad familiares* 5.12.5 (*intuentibus*). Demetrius *On Style* 215.

Demetrius on letter-writing: *On Style* 224 (γράφεται καὶ ὧρον πέμπεται τρόπον τινά), 226 (less suited to a ὑποκριτής), 225 (ἐπιδεικνυμένῳ ἔοικεν, of a letter by Aristotle).

Cicero's correspondence: see White 2010, esp. 20–1, 92–3 (letters read to others); 95–6 (elaborate compositions). Cicero *Ad Atticum* 15.17.2 (*litterae sic et* φιλοστόργως *et* εὐπινῶς *scriptae ut eas uel in acroasi audeam legere*); cf. *Ad familiares* 7.18.4 (*uel in contione recte legi*).

Narrative letter, 61 BC: Cicero *Ad Atticum* 1.16.1 (ὕστερον πρότερον Ὁμηρικῶς); 1.16.4 (Xenocrates, cf. Diogenes Laertius 4.7), 5 (*Ariopagitae*), 12 (Philip of Macedon, cf. Plutarch *Moralia* 178a-b); 1.16.5 (Homer *Iliad* 16.112–13).

Atticus busy in Greece on Cicero's behalf: e.g. *Ad Atticum* 1.15.1 (*curaque et effice ut ab omnibus et laudemur et amemur*); 2.1.2 on Cicero's history of his consulship in Greek (*curabis ut et Athenis sit et in ceteris oppidis Graeciae*).

101 Addressed to Senate and magistrates: Cicero *Ad familiares* 15.1–2 (*M. Tullius M.f. Cicero procos. s.d. cos. pr. tr. pl. senatui*); 10.35.1–2, 12.15.3 and 6 (*patres conscripti*); 15.2.4 (*decretum a nostro ordine*), 15.2.7 (*uestro senatus consulto*); cf. also Livy 27.2.1, Suetonius *Diuus Iulius* 56.6 (*ad senatum*).

Read aloud to Senate: Livy 32.31.6, 33.24.4 (by the *praetor urbanus*); Plutarch *Cato minor* 51.2. Read aloud to the People: Livy 32.31.6, 33.24.4, 45.1.8 (*ex auctoritate patrum*).

Commands conferred directly by the People: *lex Gabinia* 67 BC (Pompey and the pirates), *lex Manilia* 66 (Pompey and Mithridates), *lex Vatinia* 59 (Caesar and Gaul), *lex Trebonia* 55 (Pompey and Spain, Crassus and Syria).

Pompey's letter to Senate: Appian *Civil Wars* 2.28.107 (ἑκὼν ἀποθήσομαι τοῖς ἀπολαβεῖν θέλουσιν).

Change of protocol: Cicero *Ad familiares* 10.8, 10.35, 12.15 (*s.d. cos. pr. tr. pl. senatui populo plebique Romano*, 43 BC).

Caesar's taunt: Suetonius *Diuus Iulius* 22.2 (*se . . . insultaturum omnium capitibus*).

Populus Romanus: Caesar *De bello Gallico* 1.8.3, 10.2, 11.3, 12.6, 13.3, 14.1, 14.7, 18.9, 19.2, 30.2, 31.7, 31.14, 31.16, 33.2, 34.4, 35.2 (twice), 35.4 (twice), 36.1, 36.2 (twice), 36.5, 40.1, 40.3, 42.3, 43.8, 43.9, 44.5 (twice), 44.7 (twice), 44.9, 44.12, 45.1 (twice), 45.2, 45.3.

Not to the Senate: *pace* Gelzer 1968.171, Meier 1995.253, Marincola 1997.197, Raaflaub 2009.180.

Internal evidence (Wiseman 1998b.2): Caesar *De bello Gallico* 2.28.1–2 (Nervii effectively wiped out), 5.49.1 (60,000 Nervii and allies besieging the winter camps).

First four winters: Caesar *De bello Gallico* 1.54.3 (*ipse in citeriorem Galliam ad conuentus agendos profectus est*), 2.35.3 (*in Italiam profectus est*), 5.1.1 (*discedens in Italiam*).

Oppius and Balbus: Cicero *Ad Atticum* 4.16.8; *Ad Q. fratrem* 2.11.4, 3.1.8–10, 3.1.12–13, 3.1.18; *Ad familiares* 7.5.2, 7.6.1, 7.7.1–2, 7.9.1, 7.16.3, 7.18.3.

102 Winters of 53/2 and 52/1 BC (Wiseman 1998b.5–6): Caesar *De bello Gallico* 6.44.3 (*in Italiam ad conuentus agendos profectus est*); 7.90.8 (*ipse Bibracte hiemare constituit*), 8.2.1 (leaves Bibracte on 29 December), 8.4.1–3 (back in Bibracte for 18 days in February).

Ethnographic excursuses: *De bello Gallico* 5.12–14 (Britain), 6.11–20 (Gaul), 6.21–8 (Germany). Speeches: *De bello Gallico* 5.29–30 (Sabinus), 5.44.3 (Pullo), 6.35.8–9 (Gallic captive), 7.20 (Vercingetorix), 7.38 (Litaviccus), 7.77 (Critognatus).

Great Mother as bringer of victory: Livy 29.10.5, 29.14.14; Cicero *De haruspicum responso* 28; Plutarch *Marius* 17.5, 31.1; Virgil *Aeneid* 10.252–5.

Mount Ida: *Homeric Hymn to Aphrodite* 53–5 (Anchises); Homer *Iliad* 2.819–21, Hesiod *Theogony* 1010 (birth of Aeneas); Virgil *Aeneid* 3.5–6, 9.80–9, Ovid *Fasti* 4.264, 273–4 (Aeneas' ships). Cf. Suetonius *Diuus Iulius* 6.1 for Caesar on his own ancestry.

7.3. Caesar and Catullus

Pompey's trophy (probably a globe): Dio Cassius 37.21.2 (τῆς οἰκουμένης); cf. Coarelli 1996b.376–9 for the heroic statue from the site, holding a globe and identified as that of Pompey himself. Venus inscription: Diodorus Siculus 40.4 (τὰ ὅρια τῆς ἡγεμονίας τοῖς ὅροις τῆς γῆς προβιβάσας); cf. Cicero *Pro Sestio* 67. *Pro Balbo* 16.

Caesar in Britain 'beyond the known world': Plutarch *Caesar* 23.2 (ἔξω τῆς οἰκουμένης); cf. Dio Cassius 60.19.2 (AD 39), *Anthologia Latina* 417.4 SB (AD 43). Conquest of Oceanus: Florus 1.45.19; cf. Horace *Odes* 4.14.47–8 (Augustus), Dio Cassius 59.25.2–3 (Gaius); Suetonius *Diuus Claudius* 17.3, Seneca *Apocolocyntosis* 12.3, [Seneca] *Octavia* 39–40 (Claudius).

World's boundary: Strabo 1.1.8–9 C5–6; cf. Cornelius Nepos fr. 7P (Pomponius Mela 3.5.44, Pliny *Natural History* 2.170) on the Caspian as an inlet of the surrounding Ocean.

Britain as source of gold and silver: Cicero *Ad familiares* 7.7.1, *Ad Atticum* 4.6.7 (expectations disappointed, July 54 BC); Strabo 4.5.2 C199. Come home rich: e.g. Cicero *Ad familiares* 7.13.1 (*inaurari*), 7.16.3, 7.17.3 on C. Trebatius.

Crassus' ambitions: Plutarch *Crassus* 16.2 (Bactria, India, the 'outer sea'), *Comparison of Nicias and Crassus* 2.5 (Caspian, Indian Ocean), 4.2 (India), 4.4 (Babylon, Bactria etc). Publius Crassus: Cicero *Brutus* 282 (*Cyri et Alexandri similis esse uoluit*); Rawson 1991.418–26.

Moral high ground: e.g. Cato's attack on Caesar's treatment of the Germans (Plutarch *Cato minor* 51.1–4, *Caesar* 22.2–3, Appian *Celtica* 18), and Ateius Capito's attempt to stop Crassus' command on religious grounds (Cicero *De diuinatione* 1.29, Velleius Paterculus 2.46.3, Plutarch *Crassus* 16.3–6, Dio Cassius 39.39.5–6); cf. Cicero *De finibus* 3.75 (*nulla belli causa*).

Ahenobarbus: Plutarch *Cato minor* 41.2–5, *Pompey* 52.1–2, *Crassus* 15.2, Dio Cassius 39.31.1, Appian *Civil Wars* 2.17.64 (frightened off in January 55 BC); Suetonius *Diuus Iulius* 24.1, *Nero* 2.2 (recall threat). Support: inferred from Cicero *Ad Atticum* 4.13.1 (*altercationes* in Senate, November 55) and the fact that Ahenobarbus was elected.

Date of Caesar's return: Caesar *De bello Gallico* 4.36.1 (before the equinox); the Roman calendar at this time was nearly a month ahead of the sun (Holzapfel 1885.331–5).

Mamurra: Cornelius Nepos fr. 24P (Pliny *Natural History* 36.48), cf. Cicero *Ad Atticum* 7.7.6 on his wealth; Catullus 29, 57, 114, 115. Date of arrival: cf. Cicero *Ad Q. fratrem* 3.1.17, 3.1.25, *Ad Atticum* 4.18.5 (Britain to Rome in 27–8 days).

Caesar's two worlds: Velleius Paterculus 2.46.1 (*alterum paene... quaerens orbem*), Florus 1.45.16 (*quasi hic Romanus orbis non sufficeret, alterum cogitauit*), Servius on Virgil *Eclogues* 1.66 (*a poetis alter orbis dicitur*); cf. Philo *Legatio ad Gaium* 10, *Anthologia Latina* 421.5 and 424.10 SB, Josephus *Jewish War* 2.363, [Seneca] *Octavia* 26–7.

Catullus' versatility: see the evidence collected in Wiseman 1985.246–62. Satirical playwright: Cicero *Ad familiares* 7.11.3 (*sodalem nostrum Valerium pertimesco*), Martial 12.83. Invective poet: Catullus 36.5, 40.1–6, 116.7–8; Quintilian 10.1.96, Tacitus *Annals* 4.34.5, Diomedes in *Grammatici Latini* 1.495 Keil, Porphyrio on Horace *Odes* 1.16.24.

Catullus' targets: e.g. Aurelius and Furius (Catullus 15, 16, 21, 23), Thallus (25), Piso and Memmius (28, 47), Vibennius father and son (33), Egnatius (37, 39), Ameana (41, 43), Otho and Libo (54), Rufa (59), Rufus (69, 71, 77), Gellius (74, 80, 88–91), Gallus (78), 'Lesbius' (79), Aemilius (97), Victius (98), Silo (103), Cominius (108), Aufillena (110–11), Naso (112), Maecilia (113).

Chanted in the Forum: cf. Catullus 40.5 (*ut peruenias in ora uulgi*); Cicero *Ad Q. fratrem* 2.3.2 (*uersus obscenissimi*); Seneca *Controuersiae* 7.4.7 (Calvus on Pompey), with Plutarch *Pompey* 48.7.

Four months to wait: Juvenal 6.69 (from the *ludi plebeii* to the *Megalenses*).

Catullus 29:

> *quis hoc potest uidere, quis potest pati,*
> *nisi impudicus et uorax et aleo,*
> *Mamurram habere quod comata Gallia*
> *habebat uncti et ultima Britannia?*
> *cinaede Romule, hoc uidebis et feres?* 5
> *et ille nunc superbus et superfluens*
> *perambulabit omnium cubilia*
> *ut albulus columbus aut Adoneus?*
> *cinaede Romule, hoc uidebis et feres?*
> *es impudicus et uorax et aleo.* 10
> *eone nomine, imperator unice,*
> *fuisti in ultima occidentis insula,*
> *ut ista uestra diffututa mentula*
> *ducenties comesset aut trecenties?*
> *quid est alid sinistra liberalitas?* 15
> *parum expatrauit an parum elluatus est?*
> *paterna prima lancinata sunt bona,*
> *secunda praeda Pontica, inde tertia*
> *Hibera, quam scit amnis aurifer Tagus,*
> *nunc Gallicae timetur et Britannicae.* 20
> *quid hunc, malum, fouetis? aut quid hic potest*
> *nisi uncta deuorare patrimonia?*
> *eone nomine, urbis †opulentissime†,*
> *socer generque perdidistis omnia?*

See Badian 1977 for the reading of line 20. Optimate final phrase: Cicero *Ad Atticum* 1.16.5, 2.21.1; Livy pref.12.

Attacks on Mamurra: Catullus 41, 43 (mistress Ameana); 94 (adulteries); 114, 115 (estates); 105 (Muses); 115.8 (*mentula magna minax*).

'Once again': Catullus 54.6–7 (*irascere iterum meis iambis | immerentibus, unice imperator*); cf. 93 ('I don't much care about wanting to please you, Caesar...'). Calvus on Caesar: Suetonius *Diuus Iulius* 49.1, 73.

Catullus 57:

> pulcre conuenit improbis cinaedis
> Mamurrae pathicoque Caesarique.
> nec mirum: maculae pares utrisque,
> urbana altera et illa Formiana,
> impressae resident nec eluentur.   5
> morbosi pariter, gemelli utrique,
> uno in lecticulo erudituli ambo,
> non hic quam ille magis uorax adulter,
> riuales socii puellularum.
> pulcre conuenit improbis cinaedis.   10

Suetonius *Diuus Iulius* 73:

> *Valerium Catullum, a quo sibi uersiculis de Mamurra perpetua stigmata imposita non dissimulauerat, satis facientem eadem die adhibuit cenae, hospitioque patris eius sicut consuerat uti perseuerauit.*

Catullus from Verona (Wiseman 2007): Jerome *Chronica* Ol. 173.2; Catullus 35.3, 67.34; Ovid *Amores* 3.15.7, Pliny *Natural History* 36.48, Martial 1.61.1, 14.195, Nonius 876L, Macrobius *Saturnalia* 2.1.8, Priscian in *Grammatici Latini* 2.16 Keil, Veronese scholiast on Virgil *Eclogues* 6.1. Sirmio: Catullus 31; Wiseman 1987.307–70.

Family ties: Catullus 61.204–23, 68.92–8, 68.119–24, 72.4, 79.2–3. *Caristia*: Ovid *Fasti* 2.617–38, Valerius Maximus 2.1.8; Degrassi 1963.414.

Illyricum: Caesar *De bello Gallico* 5.1.5; cf. Suetonius *Diuus Iulius* 22.1, Dio Cassius 38.8.5. January: Caesar *De bello Gallico* 5.1.1 (*L. Domitio Ap. Claudio consulibus*), 5.1.2–4 (ships), 5.1.5 (*conuentibus Galliae citerioris peractis*). Dictating: cf. Suetonius *Diuus Iulius* 56.5 for composition en route.

Flattering letters: Cicero *Ad Q. fratrem* 2.14.4 (received 3 June), cf. *Ad Atticum* 4.15.10, 4.16.7. Building programme: Cicero *Ad Atticum* 4.16.8 (*Caesaris amici*, including Cicero himself).

Calvus as orator: Catullus 53; Cicero *Brutus* 283–4, *Ad familiares* 15.21.4; Seneca *Controuersiae* 7.4.6–8, Quintilian 10.1.115, Tacitus *Dialogus* 18.1, 25.4.

7.4. Catullus 61–64

Died young: Ovid *Amores* 3.9.61–2. *Terminus post quem*: Cicero *Ad familiares* 7.11.2, dated to 53 BC by the reference to *interregna* at 7.11.1 (cf. Dio Cassius 40.45.3). *Terminus ante quem*: Nepos *Atticus* 12.2 (32 BC).

Biographical sketch: text and translation at Wiseman 1985.207; cf. also Gaisser 1993.25–6, who attributes it to Gerolamo Squarzafico. For the likely sources (Jerome and a lost text excerpted from Suetonius), see Baehrens 1885.22 n.; for the possible survival of Suetonius *De poetis*, see Wiseman 1985.189–90 on the evidence of Giovanni Pontano (1460).

Recent statement: Feeney 2012.43; cf. Wiseman 1987.273 ('it is impossible to imagine *him* reading his works to the Forum crowd'), a brash assertion, and patently false.

'Materiality of the book': Catullus 1.1–2, 14.17–19, 14b, 22, 36.18–20, 68.33–6, 68.46, 95.7–8.

One single copy: Tarrant 1983a, Butrica 2007.24–30. When, why, and by whom: Butrica 2007.14–24, Du Quesnay and Woodman 2012.265–8.

106 Writing-tablets: Catullus 42 (*pugillaria, codicilli*), 50.2 (*tabellae*).

Parties: Catullus 27; cf. 12.2, 50.6 (*in ioco atque uino*); *pace* Parker 2009.206 ('nowhere in Catullus... do we find a single suggestion that the poets ever "performed" at their own or anyone else's *conuiuia*'). Hymn: Catullus 34; Wiseman 1985.96–9.

Catullus 40:

> *quaenam te mala mens, miselle Rauide,*
> *agit praecipitem in meos iambos?*
> *quis deus tibi non bene aduocatus*
> *uecordem parat excitare rixam?*
> *an ut peruenias in ora uulgi?*
> *quid uis? qualubet esse notus optas?*
> *eris, quandoquidem meos amores*
> *cum longa uoluisti amare poena.*

Biographical sketch (Wiseman 1985.207): *in iocis apprime lepidus, in seriis uero grauissimus extitit. erotica scripsit et epithalamium in Manlium.*

Manlius: Catullus 61.16 and 205–13; probably L. Manlius Torquatus, praetor in 49 BC (Caesar *De bello Gallico* 1.24.3), who died after the defeat at Thapsus in 46 (*De bello Africo* 96); he was also a literary figure (Cicero *Brutus* 265, cf. Pliny *Letters* 5.3.5).

Sung and danced: implicit at Catullus 61.12–14, 38, 116.

Latin 'to marry': *Oxford Latin Dictionary* s.vv. *ducere* 5(a), *deducere* 10(b). Garlanded houses: Statius *Siluae* 1.2.230–1, Juvenal 6.79.

Torches: Catullus 61.15, 77–8, 94–5, 114; Varro *De uita populi Romani* 78 Riposati = Nonius 161L (lit from hearth), Statius *Siluae* 1.2.231 ('blazing at street-corners'). Wooden stands: Juvenal 6.78 ('along the narrow streets').

Pipe-player, street outside: Plautus *Casina* 798–9 (*age tibicen, dum illam educunt huc nouam nuptam foras, | suaui cantu concelebra omnem hanc plateam hymenaeo mi*); cf. Terence *Adelphoe* 905 (*tibicina et hymenaeum qui cantent*).

107 Twenty-four stanzas: Catullus 61.1–35 (solo hymn), 36–45 (invitation to girls' choir), 46–75 (girls' song), 76–113 (solo address to bride).

Twenty-three stanzas: Catullus 61.114–23 (invitation to boys' choir), 124–58 (boys' song), 159–73 (solo address to bride), 174–228 (*epithalamium*). For the *Fescennina iocatio* (61.120), see Festus (Paulus) 76L, Servius on *Aeneid* 7.695, Porphyrio on Horace *Epistles* 2.1.145; for the walnuts thrown as confetti as the bride went in (cf. 61.121–33), see Pliny *Natural History* 15.86, Festus 178–9L, Servius on *Eclogues* 8.30.

All the neighbourhood: Statius *Siluae* 1.2.232 (*et pars immensae gaudet celeberrima Romae*); cf. Phaedrus 1.6.1–2, where the crowd at a wedding is the storyteller's audience.

Scholarly consensus: Fordyce 1961.236; Lyne 1978.175 and 183 (= Gaisser 2007.121 and 134).

Catullus 62: lines 1 and 7 for Olympus and Oeta, line 3 for the banquet, lines 4 and 59–65 for the bride and her duty. 'Free sphere of poetry': Fraenkel 1955.8 (also 1955.7, 'the place of this epithalamium is neither in Greece nor in Rome but in a poetic sphere of its own').

Competing for prize: Catullus 62.9, 11, 16; cf. Cicero *Ad Atticum* 4.15.6 (*ludi Apollinares*, 54 BC), *Année épigraphique* 2003.251–2 (festival of Anna Perenna, AD 156); Plato *Laws* 2.659b, Plautus *Amphitruo* 69, *Poenulus* 37, *Trinummus* 706, Phaedrus 5.5.5–7, Plutarch *Cato minor* 46.2–3, Juvenal 6.320–3.

Greek myth and mime: Catullus περὶ μιμολογιῶν, in Scholia Bernensia on Lucan 1.544. Drama titles (Wiseman 1985.192–4): *Phasma* (Juvenal 8.186), *Priapus* (Nonius 195L), *Phormio* (Priscian 6.7 and 73); the fourth title is *Laureolus* (Juvenal 8.186–7, Tertullian *Aduersus Valentinianos* 14). Hexameters in drama were an innovation by Rhinthon (Lydus *De magistratibus* 1.41, cf. Ch. 3.2 above).

Chorus for dance performance: cf. Jerome *Chronica* Ol. 189.3 (Pylades), Phaedrus 5.7.5 and 25 (Bathyllus); Manilius 5.483–4, Lucian *Saltatio* 68.

Catullus 63 (Wiseman 1985.199–206, dismissed by Nauta 2004.609): lines 8–10 and 21–2 for the musical instruments; lines 26 (*tripudiis*), 28 (*thiasus*) and 30 (*chorus*) for the dance. Galliambics (Wiseman 1985.200): Varro *Satires* 131–2 Astbury; cf. Ch. 5.4 above for the context.

Jerome *Chronica* Ol. 189.3 (Suetonius p. 301 Roth):

> Pylades Cilix pantomimus, cum ueteres ipsi canerent atque saltarent, primus Romae chorum et fistulam sibi praecinere fecit.

Lucian *Saltatio* 30 (cf. 34 for the Augustan date of the innovation):

> πάλαι μὲν γὰρ αὐτοὶ καὶ ᾖδον καὶ ὠρχοῦντο· εἶτ' ἐπειδὴ κινουμένων τὸ ἆσθμα τὴν ᾠδὴν ἐπετάραττεν, ἄμεινον ἔδοξεν ἄλλους αὐτοῖς ὑπᾴδειν.

The ultimate source was probably Pylades' own book on dance (Athenaeus 1.20d), which was no doubt used by both Suetonius and Lucian.

Epyllion: Lyne 1978.169 (= Gaisser 2007.112–13), Baumbach and Bär 2012. Defining example: Trimble 2012, esp. 78 ('we want to know not only what this peculiar poem is *like*, but what kind of thing it *is*').

Highly wrought *epos*: Lyne 1978.172–3 (= Gaisser 2007.118). *Epos* as hexameter poetry: Parthenius *Sufferings in Love* pref. (Lightfoot 1999.309), on mythical subjects for Cornelius Gallus.

Dancers in the theatre: Varro *Satires* 513 Astbury, Lucretius 4.973–83 (Ch. 6.5 above). Glamorous showgirls: Cicero *Ad familiares* 9.26.2, *Ad Atticum* 10.10.5, *Philippics* 2.58 (the *mima* Volumnia Cytheris); Servius on *Eclogues* 6.11 (Cytheris as singer); *De uiris illustribus* 82.2 (Cytheris as mistress of Brutus, Antony, and Cornelius Gallus).

Nereids' breasts: 64.17–18. Ariadne's clothes: 64.60–7, cf. 129; no doubt she was off stage for costume-changes at 64.76–85 and 116–23.

110   Labyrinth dance: 64.112–15; cf. Callimachus *Hymns* 4.310–13, Plutarch *Theseus* 21.1, Pollux 4.101.

Not static: contrast 64.61 and 126–9. The gods' justice: 64.188–97. Thunder: 64.205–6; cf. Vitruvius 5.6.8 (*cum tonitribus repentinis*), Phaedrus 5.7.23 (*deuolutis tonitribus*). Sharing narrative: 64.246–50. Drums and horns: 64.261–4.

Chiron and the river-god: 64.278–93. Deliberately ominous: 64.299–302 (Apollo not present); cf. Homer *Iliad* 24.62–3, Pindar *Nemeans* 5.41–4, Plato *Republic* 2.383a–b. Achilles and Polyxenia: 64.338–70. On with the wedding: 64.372. Light of day: 64.408.

Long poems: the others are poem 66, a Callimachus translation sent from abroad (Woodman 2012.148) to a prominent politician, though what he did with it is anybody's guess (Du Quesnay 2012.153–62); poem 67, a satirical dialogue for a Veronese audience; poem 68a, a self-exculpatory letter in verse to Manlius, perhaps the bridegroom of 61; and poem 68b, a long and elaborate elegiac poem for Allius, with a mythic narrative of the adulterous liaison between the poet and his 'shining goddess' for which Allius had provided practical help.

7.5. The Greek Stage in Rome

Murder of Clodius: Asconius 31–2C, Dio Cassius 40.48.2. Honourable men: Cicero *Pro Milone* 72–91, Asconius 41C (Brutus), 53–4C (Cato); Wiseman 2009b.188–91. Senate-house: Asconius 32–3C, Dio Cassius 40.49.2–3.

111   Death of Julia: Cicero *Ad Q. fratrem* 3.1.17, Plutarch *Caesar* 23.4, *Pompey* 53.4, Dio Cassius 39.64. Crassus and son at Carrhae: Plutarch *Crassus* 17–31.

What he could expect: Caelius in Cicero *Ad familiares* 8.14.2 (Caesar knew in 50 BC that he couldn't be safe once he left his army); cf. Caesar *De bello Gallico* 1.44.12 (aristocrats wanted Caesar dead in 58).

Caesar's special permission: Caesar *De bello ciuili* 1.32.3; Cicero *Ad Atticum* 7.1.4, 7.3.4, 9.11a.2, *Ad familiares* 1.32.3. Pompey: Appian *Civil Wars* 2.31.121 (ὑπὲρ τῆς πατρίδος), Plutarch *Pompey* 59.1 (βοηθεῖν τῇ πατρίδι). Martial law: Caesar *De bello ciuili* 1.5.3–5; Cicero *Ad familiares* 16.11.3, Dio Cassius 41.3.2–3.

Caesar's motive, publicly declared in *De bello ciuili* 1.22.5: *ut tribunos plebis in ea re ex ciuitate expulsos in suam dignitatem restitueret, ut se et populum Romanum factione paucorum oppressum in libertatem uindicaret.*

Venus Genetrix: *Fasti Arvalium, Pinciani* and *Praenestini* on 26 September (Degrassi 1963.34–5, 48, 134–5). Octavius: Nicolaus of Damascus *FGrH* 90 F 127.9.19 (δυοῖν ὄντοιν θεάτροιν, τοῦ μὲν 'Ρωμαικοῦ ... θατέρου δὲ 'Ελληνικοῦ); cf. Suetonius *Diuus Iulius* 39.1 for actors 'in all languages' at Caesar's games.

Ludi Graeci: Plutarch *Marius* 2.1 (101 BC); Cicero *Ad familiares* 7.1.3 (55), *Ad Atticum* 16.5.1 (44); *CIL* 6.32323.156–7 (17).

Eucharis' epitaph (*CIL* 6.10096 = *ILS* 5213 = *ILLRP* 803):

> heus oculo errante quei aspicis leti domus,
> morare gressum et titulum nostrum perlege,
> amor parenteis quam dedit natae suae,
> ubei se reliquiae conlocarent corporis.
> heic uiridis aetas cum floreret artibus
> crescente et aeuo gloriam conscenderet,
> properauit hora tristis fatalis mea
> et denegauit ultra ueitae spiritum.
> docta erodita paene Musarum manu,
> quae modo nobilium ludos decoraui choro   10
> et Graeca in scaena prima populo apparui.
> en hoc in tumulo cinerem nostri corporis
> infestae Parcae deposierunt carmine.
> studium patronae cura amor laudes decus
> silent ambusto corpore et leto tacent.
> reliqui fletum nata genitori meo
> et antecessi genita post leti diem.
> bis hic septeni mecum natales dies
> tenebris tenentur Ditis aeterna domu.
> rogo ut discedens terram mihi dicas leuem.   20

See Wiseman 1985.30–5 (where, however, line 11 is mistranslated), Starks 2008.128–30.

Allusions to Epicharmus: Cicero *Ad Atticum* 1.19.8, *Ad Q. fratrem* 3.1.23, *Tusculan Disputations* 1.15; Q. Cicero *Commentariolum petitionis* 39.

Allusions to Rhinthon: Cicero *Ad Atticum* 1.20.3, cf. Varro *Res rusticae* 3.3.9 (text uncertain); Lydus *De magistratibus* 1.41 (from Varro?) for Rhinthon's influence on Lucilius and the Roman satirists.

Allusions to Sophron: Varro *De lingua Latina* 5.179; cf. Lydus (as above) for Sophron's later influence on Persius. For Sophron as a dramatist, see Demetrius *On Style* 156 (δράματα), Solinus 5.13 (*in scaena*); it is not clear to me why his latest editor believes the mimes were only 'intended for sympotic performance ... a long way from those later stage-plays which also go by the name μῖμος' (Hordern 2004.8–9, cf. 28 'literary in character').

Theocritus and Sophron: scholiast to Theocritus 2 and 15 (pp. 269–70, 272, 305 Wendel), Hordern 2004.46–9 (text and translation), 142–7 (commentary). Theocritus and Epicharmus: *Anthologia Palatina* 9.600.

Theocritus scholarship: e.g. Hunter 1996.1–13, Acosta-Hughes 2012; cf. Cairns 1992.13–16 for sensible discussion of the hymn to Dionysus (Theocritus 26).

Short epics: Theocritus 24–5. Adonis festival: Theocritus 15 (Hunter 1996.116–38); for the start of the hymn (15.100–1) cf. Catullus 36.11–14. Moonlight spells: Theocritus 2 (Dickie 2001.99–104).

Pliny *Natural History* 28.19:

> *defigi quidem diris deprecationibus nemo non metuit . . . hinc Theocriti apud Graecos, Catulli apud nos proximeque Vergilii incantamentorum amatoria imitatio.*

Only two words: Servius on *Aeneid* 7.378 (Catullus 'hoc turben' dicit), referring to the ἴυγξ (Theocritus 2.17–63), the wheel is more usually called *turbo* in Latin. Alphesiboeus: Virgil *Eclogues* 8.64–108; cf. 5.73 for his skill in mime.

Virgil's beginnings (*Eclogues* 6.1–2):

> *prima Syracosio dignata est ludere uersu*
> *nostra nec erubuit siluas habitare Thalea.*

Thalea and comedy: e.g. *Anthologia Palatina* 9.504.10; cf. Crawford 1974.438 (no. 410.9) for the comic mask as her attribute already in Virgil's time.

7.6. The Ides of March, and After

Inviolability: Livy *Epitome* 116, Nicolaus of Damascus *FGrH* 90 F 130.22.80, Appian *Civil Wars* 2.106.442, Dio Cassius 44.5.3. Oath: Suetonius *Diuus Iulius* 84.2, Appian *Civil Wars* 2.145.604, Dio Cassius 44.7.4.

Bodyguard: Nicolaus of Damascus *FGrH* 90 F 130.22.80, Suetonius *Diuus Iulius* 86.1, Appian *Civil Wars* 2.109.455.

Liberators (Wiseman 2009b.217–8): e.g. Cicero *Ad Atticum* 14.12.2, *Philippics* 1.6. Vengeance: e.g. Appian *Civil Wars* 2.130.544–7, 3.60.247.

Friend and collaborator: Cicero *Ad Atticum* 4.16.8 (54 BC). Delighted: Cicero *Ad Atticum* 14.9.2, 14.12.1, 14.13.2, 14.14.4, 14.22.2.

Speech to the People: Cicero *Philippics* 6.1 (tribune), 6.9 (*Brutum . . . uestraeque libertati natum*), 6.19 (slavery). For contrary views of the People's feelings, compare Cicero *Philippics* 7.22 with Appian *Civil Wars* 3.59.243, 3.60.247 (Piso's speech).

Augustus *Res gestae* 1.1:

> *annos undeuiginti natus exercitum priuato consilio et priuata impensa comparaui, per quem rem publicam a dominatione factionis oppressam in libertatem uindicaui.*

The Greek version of *factionis* is τῶν συνομοσαμένων, 'the conspirators'.

Aim of triumvirate: Appian *Civil Wars* 4.8–9.33–8.

Dates: Tacitus *Dialogus* 17.2 (death of Cicero), Dio Cassius 47.18.3–4 (consecration), Degrassi 1963.134–5 (second battle of Philippi).

Head and hands: Livy in Seneca *Suasoriae* 6.17, Plutarch *Cicero* 48.4–49.1, Dio Cassius 47.8.3.

8. RETHINKING THE CLASSICS: 42–28 BC

Never forgotten: Velleius Paterculus 2.56.2–5, Valerius Maximus 5.3.4, Seneca *Controuersiae* 7.2, *Suasoriae* 6.19.

Triumviral period: see above all Osgood 2006 and Powell 2008, two excellent analyses that 'put the hawk of history back among the doves of literature' (Powell 2008.5).

8.1. Virgil's *Eclogues*

Eclogues: 1, 3, 5, 7, and 9 fully dramatic; 2 and 8 dramatic with narrative frame. Sung on stage: Donatus *Vita Vergili* 26.90–1 (*bucolica eo successu edidit ut in scaena per cantores crebro pronuntiarentur*). Dance: *Eclogues* 5.73 (Alphesiboeus), 6.27–8 (*Fauni feraeque*).

Tityrus: Virgil *Eclogues* 6.4; cf. 1.1, 5.12, 8.55, 9.23–5; *Georgics* 4.566. Mime-actress: Servius on *Eclogues* 6.11 (*dicitur autem ingenti fauore a Vergilio esse recitata, adeo ut cum eam postea Cytheris cantasset in theatro*...), grafting on to the occasion a chronologically unlikely story about Cicero. Apollo: *Eclogues* 6.3–5, 11–12, 82–3.

Prophecy: *Eclogues* 4.9–10 (Apollo and the golden age), 11–12 (Pollio), 13 (*scelus*), 46–7 (Fates).

Conscious reversal: *Eclogues* 4.10 for the presence of Diana and Apollo, conspicuously absent at Catullus 64.299–302; the allusions to Catullus 64 are clearest at *Eclogues* 4.31–6 (Thetis, Argo, Achilles).

Clemency (Weinstock 1971.233–43, Braund 2009.34–6): e.g. Cicero *Ad Atticum* 9.16.1, *Pro Marcello* 1; Crawford 1974.491 (no. 480.21); Appian *Civil Wars* 4.8.32.

Rejection of Sullan precedents: Caesar in Cicero *Ad Atticum* 9.7c.1 (cruelty); Appian *Civil Wars* 2.94.395, cf. Suetonius *Diuus Iulius* 38.1 (land for veterans); Brutus' claim to the contrary (Appian *Civil Wars* 2.140.586) is clearly tendentious.

End of clemency: Appian *Civil Wars* 4.8.32–3 (triumvirs' inaugural edict). Proscription: details in Hinard 1985.227–326. Dispossession: details in Keppie 1983.38–43, 49–69, 101–4.

Pollution ($\mu\acute{\upsilon}\sigma o\varsigma$, $\ddot{\alpha}\gamma o\varsigma$): Appian *Civil Wars* 1.2.5, 1.17.71 (murder of Ti. Gracchus); 2.118.494, 2.124.520, 2.127.531, 5.48.203 (murder of Caesar); cf. Ovid *Fasti* 3.705–6, 5.573–4. Accursed: Appian *Civil Wars* 2.133.556 ($\dot{\varepsilon}\nu\alpha\gamma\varepsilon\hat{\iota}\varsigma$); 2.124.520, 2.130.544 ($\dot{\alpha}\rho\alpha\acute{\iota}$); cf. 2.124.518–20, 2.130.544–5, 2.131.549–51, 2.145.604 (oath-breakers).

Dispossessed in Rome: Appian *Civil Wars* 5.12.48–50. Veterans in Rome: Dio Cassius 48.12.1. Insolence and indiscipline: Appian *Civil Wars* 5.15.61–3 (theatre, cf. Suetonius *Diuus Augustus* 14), 5.18.73.

Eclogues context: Servius and ps.Probus (texts in Coleman 1977.14), the latter citing Asconius Pedianus, date the *Eclogues* to 42/1 BC, when Virgil was 28.

8.2. Sallust

Turning the clock back: Appian *Civil Wars* 5.30.118 (ἡ ἀρχή πάτριος), 5.39.159 (ἡ πάτριος πολιτεία), 5.43.179 (ἀριστοκρατία), all in speeches attributed to L. Antonius.

Aristocracy and L. Antonius: Appian *Civil Wars* 5.21.84, 5.40.167 (οἱ ἄριστοι); 5.29.114, 5.40.168 (οἱ ἐπιφανεῖς); cf. Dio Cassius 48.8.1 ('the senators and the landowning class').

Italy as a war zone: Dio Cassius 48.9.5 ('all the cities'), 48.13.2–6 (Sentinum sacked and burned, Nursia abandoned), 48.14.5–6 (Perusia destroyed); Appian *Civil Wars* 5.28.108, 5.74.314. City of Rome militarized: Dio Cassius 48.13.5, 48.16.1; Appian *Civil Wars* 5.31.119.

Aristocracy and Sex. Pompeius: Appian *Civil Wars* 5.72.306, 5.74.317, 5.78.330 (οἱ ἐπιφανεῖς). Famine: Dio Cassius 48.7.4, 48.18.1, 48.31.1; Appian *Civil Wars* 5.15.60, 5.18.72, 5.67.280.

Rioting: Dio Cassius 48.31.4–6 (*ludi* context), Appian *Civil Wars* 5.68.284–9.

Date of Sallust's historical works: the *terminus post quem* for his retirement from political life to writing history is his proconsulship of Africa in 45 BC (Dio Cassius 43.9.2–3, Sallust *Catiline* 4.1–2), the *terminus ante quem* his death in 36/5 BC (Jerome *Chronica* Ol. 186.1); in those ten years he wrote the *Catiline*, the *Jugurthine War*, and five books of *Histories*.

Conspiracy: Sallust *Catiline* 4.3 (*de Catilinae coniuratione*), 23.1, 23.4, 24.1, etc. Battlefield (Pistoriae, northern Etruria): *Catiline* 57–61. Sulla's veterans and the dispossessed: *Catiline* 11.5–7, 28.4, 37.6–9.

Sallust *Catiline* 3.1–2:

> pulchrum est bene facere rei publicae, etiam bene dicere haud absurdum est; uel pace uel bello clarum fieri licet; et qui fecere et qui facta aliorum scripsere multi laudantur. ac mihi quidem, tametsi haudquaquam par gloria sequitur scriptorem et auctorem rerum, tamen in primis arduom uidetur res gestas scribere, primum quod facta dictis exaequanda sunt . . .

Sallust *Catiline* 8.5:

> at populo Romano numquam ea copia fuit, quia prudentissumus quisque maxume negotiosus erat; ingenium nemo sine corpore exercebat; optumus quisque facere quam dicere, sua ab aliis bene facta laudari quam ipse aliorum narrare malebat.

Sallust *Catiline* 53.2:

> sed mihi multa legenti multa audienti quae populus Romanus domi militiaeque mari atque terra praeclara facinora fecit, forte lubuit adtendere quae res maxume tanta negotia sustinuisset.

Fame and reputation: *Catiline* 1.3–4, 2.2, 3.2 (*gloria*); 2.9, 3.5 (*fama*). Apologia: *Catiline* 3.3–4.1.

Sallust's career: Asconius 37C, 51C (tribune 52 BC); Dio Cassius 40.63.4 (expulsion), 42.52.2 (position regained), 43.9.2–3 (profiteering); cf. ps.Cicero *In Sallustium* 19–20 for his ill-gotten wealth, including the famous *horti Sallustiani* (Tacitus *Annals* 13.47.2).

Retirement from politics: Sallust *Catiline* 4.1 (*mihi relicuam aetatem a re publica procul habendam decreui*).

Sallust *Catiline* 4.1–2:

> *non fuit consilium socordia atque desidia bonum otium conterere, neque uero agrum colundo aut uenando seruilibus officiis intentum aetatem agere, sed a quo incepto studioque me ambitio mala detinuerat, eodem regressus statui res gestas populi Romani carptim, ut quaeque memoria digna uidebantur, perscribere, eo magis quod mihi a spe metu partibus rei publicae animus liber erat.*

Ordinary people: Cicero *De finibus* 5.52 (*homines infima fortuna*).

General maxim: Sallust *Catiline* 2.3–4.

Sallust *Catiline* 2.5:

> *uerum ubi pro labore desidia, pro continentia et aequitate lubido atque superbia inuasere, fortuna simul cum moribus inmutantur.*

Sallust *Catiline* 10.3–4:

> *igitur primo pecuniae deinde imperi cupido creuit: ea quasi materies omnium malorum fuere. namque auaritia fidem probitatem ceterasque artis bonas subuortit; pro his superbiam crudelitatem deos neglegere omnia uenalia habere edocuit.*

Powerful few (*pauci potentes*): Sallust *Catiline* 30.4, 39.1; cf. 20.7, 58.11 (Catiline speeches); so too *Jugurthine War* 3.4, 41.7, 80.5, *Histories* 1.12M. It was not just Sallust's idea: see for instance Cicero *Verrines* 1.36, 2.1.155, *De lege agraria* 2.7, *Pro Caelio* 22, *De republica* 1.51; Caesar *De bello ciuili* 1.22.5; Diodorus Siculus 31.26.2, 37.2.1–2.

Sallust *Jugurthine War* 5.1–2:

> *bellum scripturus sum quod populus Romanus cum Iugurtha rege Numidarum gessit, primum quia magnum et atrox uariaque uictoria fuit, dehinc quia tunc primum superbiae nobilitatis obuiam itum est; quae contentio diuina et humana cuncta permiscuit eoque uecordiae processit ut studiis ciuilibus bellum atque uastitas Italiae finem faceret.*

Arrogance of *nobilitas*: Sallust *Jugurthine War* 30.3, 64.1; cf. 31.2, 31.12 (Memmius' speech), 85.13, 85.19, 85.38, 85.45, 85.47 (Marius' speech); already in *Catiline* 10.4, 12.2, 23.6.

Their own wishes (*ex lubidine sua*): *Jugurthine War* 31.7 (speech of Memmius), 42.4; cf. Dio Cassius 46.22.7 (πρὸς τὴν ἑαυτοῦ βούλησιν), ps.Sallust *In Ciceronem* 5 (*cum omnia iudicia omnes leges in tua lubidine erant*), on Cicero.

Caesar's assassins: Matius in Cicero *Ad familiares* 11.28.3 (*o superbiam inauditam!*).

Popular champions: Sallust *Jugurthine War* 31 (Memmius), 85 (Marius), *Histories* 1.55M (Lepidus), 3.48M (Macer). Worthy of ancestors: *Jugurthine War* 31.6, 31.17; *Histories* 1.55.23M, 3.48.1M.

Date of Sallust's death: Jerome *Chronica* Ol.186.1.

Victorious return: Appian *Civil Wars* 5.130.538–42, Dio Cassius 49.15.1–3. Grant of *sacrosanctitas*: Augustus *Res gestae* 10.1, Dio Cassius 49.15.5–6; cf. Appian *Civil Wars* 5.132.548, Orosius 6.18.34 (misdating the full *tribunicia potestas* granted in 23 BC).

8.3. Horace's *Satires*

Playboy lifestyle: Dio Cassius 43.9.3; Varro in Aulus Gellius 17.18, Asconius in ps.Acro on Horace *Satires* 1.2.41, Servius on *Aeneid* 6.612, ps.Cicero *In Sallustium* 13–16.

Rome as *maledica ciuitas*: Cicero *Pro Flacco* 68, *Pro Caelio* 38. Satirical observers: Suetonius *De grammaticis* 15.2 (Pompeius Lenaeus' *acerbissima satura*), Horace *Satires* 1.2.47–54 (cf. 1.10.46–7 for satire as a popular genre).

Horace *Epistles* 2.2.46–52:

> dura sed emouere loco me tempora grato
> ciuilisque rudem belli tulit aestus in arma
> Caesaris Augusti non responsura lacertis.
> unde simul primum me dimisere Philippi,
> decisis humilem pennis inopemque paterni
> et laris et fundi, paupertas impulit audax
> ut uersus facerem.

Cf. Horace *Satires* 1.6.71–80 (education), 1.6.48 (military tribune); *Odes* 2.7.9–16, 3.4.26 (Philippi).

Freedman's son: *Satires* 1.6.46 (*quem rodunt omnes*), *Epistles* 1.20.20–1 (*in tenui re*). Maecenas: *Satires* 1.6.45–64, 1.9.43–59, 2.1.75–8, 2.6.29–58; *Epistles* 1.20.23.

Poets profiting from *ludi*: Ovid *Tristia* 2.507–10, where the praetor is the equivalent of a pre-22 BC aedile (Dio Cassius 54.2.3–4).

'Iambic' epodes: Mankin 1995.6–9 (the Greek iambic background), 14–22 (Horace's metres).

Dramatic form: Horace *Epodes* 5, 17; *Satires* 2.1, 2.3, 2.4, 2.5, 2.7, 2.8. *Vates*-poet: *Epodes* 16, esp. lines 36 (*eamus omnis ciuitas*) and 66 (*uate me*). Plural audience: *Satires* 2.2.2–7; cf. 2.3.77–81 for the audience of Stertinius' homily, reported by Damasippus.

Ears of listener: *Satires* 1.10.7–10, with Gowers 2012.313 ('the illusion that satire is an oral performance'); cf. 1.4.18 (*loqui*), 2.3.6 (*dicere*), 2.4.89 (*audire*).

Like conversation: *Satires* 1.4.41–2 (*sermoni propiora*), 2.6.17 (*Musa pedestris*), *Epistles* 2.1.250–1 (*sermones . . . repentis per humum*); referred to as *sermones* at *Epistles* 1.4.1, 2.1.4.

Aedileship as career move: e.g. Plutarch *Sulla* 5.1, *Caesar* 5.5–6.3.

Sicilian war: Horace *Odes* 3.4.28; for Maecenas, cf. *Elegiae in Maecenatem* 1.41–2, Appian *Civil wars* 5.99.414. Exile: Horace *Satires* 2.1.59.

Aedileship as too expensive: Appian *Civil Wars* 4.41.173; Dio Cassius 48.53.4–6 (37 BC), 49.16.2 (36), 53.2.2 (28), 54.11.1 (19).

Horace and Lucilius: *Satires* 1.4.1–6 (Athenian Old Comedy), 1.4.23–33 (the guilty fear satire).

Satires 1.4.34–8:

> *faenum habet in cornu, longe fuge: dummodo risum*
> *excutiat, sibi non, non cuiquam parcet amico;*
> *et quodcumque semel chartis illeuerit, omnis*
> *gestiet a furno redeuntis scire lacuque,*
> *et pueros et anus.*

Distancing himself: *Satires* 1.4.7–13, 22–4.

Satires 1.4.65–70:

> *Sulcius acer*
> *ambulat et Caprius, rauci male cumque libellis,*
> *magnus uter timor latronibus; at bene si quis*
> *et uiuat puris manibus contemnat utrumque.*
> *ut sis tu similis Caeli Birrique latronum,*
> *non ego sum Capri neque Sulci; cur metuas me?*

Sulcius and Caprius: 'informers or prosecutors' according to the ancient commentators' guess; first (and I think rightly) identified as satirists by Ullman 1917.117–19.

Satires 1.4.71–8:

> *nulla taberna meos habeat neque pila libellos,*
> *quis manus insudet uulgi Hermogenisque Tigelli,*
> *nec recito cuiquam nisi amicis, idque coactus,*
> *non ubiuis coramue quibuslibet. in medio qui*
> *scripta foro recitent sunt multi quique lauantes:*
> *suaue locus uoci resonat conclusus. inanis*
> *hoc iuuat, haud illud quaerentis, num sine sensu*
> *tempore num faciant alieno.*

Observation and moral lessons: *Satires* 1.4.103–39. Mouth shut: 1.4.38 (*compressis labris*). 'If I have time': 1.4.138–9 (*ubi quid datur oti, | illudo chartis*).

Satires 1.10.37–9:

> *haec ego ludo*
> *quae neque in aede sonent certantia iudice Tarpa*
> *nec redeant iterum atque iterum spectanda theatris.*

Tarpa the competition judge (cf. Horace *Ars poetica* 387) was evidently Sp. Maecius Tarpa, who had selected the programme for the inaugural games at Pompey's theatre in 55 BC (Cicero *Ad familiares* 7.1.1, Ch. 6.4 above). He may have been still doing the same job, using a temple to hear the applicants' work before deciding—perhaps that of Hercules Musarum (Horsfall 1976.83–6) or that of Venus Victrix, as it now was, in Pompey's theatre itself (Gowers 2012.325).

Advice: *Satires* 1.10.73–4 (*neque tu ut miretur turba labores,* | *contentus paucis lectoribus*).

121 Far from the crowd: *Satires* 1.6.18 (*nos... a uulgo longe longeque remotos*); for the estate, cf. *Elegiae in Maecenatem* 1.33-6. Dining-couch and colonnade: *Satires* 1.4.133–4 (*cum lectulus aut me* | *porticus excipiet*). Cf. Gowers 2012.152: 'He ends by removing [Roman satire] to the private sphere and reducing it to a harmless leisure activity, a silent thought-process.'

Refusing the Lucilian role: *Satires* 1.6.23–5 (*uulgo recitare timentis ob hanc rem,* | *quod sunt quos genus hoc minime iuuat, utpote pluris* | *culpari dignos*).

Satires 2.1.44–6, 57–60:

> *nec quisquam noceat cupido mihi pacis. at ille*
> *qui me commorit (melius non tangere, clamo)*
> *flebit et insignis tota cantabitur urbe...*
> *ne longum faciam: seu me tranquilla senectus*
> *exspectat seu mors atris circumuolat alis,*
> *diues inops, Romae seu fors ita iusserit exsul,*
> *quisquis erit uitae, scribam, color.*

Lucilius' example: *Satires* 2.1.62–76, cf. 29 (*Lucili ritu*).

Caesar approves: *Satires* 2.1.84 (*iudice... laudatus Caesare*); cf. 2.1.10–20 (praise of 'unconquered Caesar' as a profitable subject for poets), which dates the poem in or after 36 BC.

Imperator Caesar (Syme 1958 = 1979.361–77): the name is first attested in 38 BC (Crawford 1974.535, no. 534). 'End of civil wars': Appian *Civil Wars* 5.132.546. Benefits of peace: Appian *Civil Wars* 5.130.539–42. Veterans: Keppie 1983.69–73.

War in the Balkans: Appian *Illyrian Wars* 12–28 (with details from Augustus' own memoirs). Maecenas: Dio Cassius 49.16.2 (τὰ ἐν τῇ πόλει...διῴκησεν).

Dramatic form: Horace *Satires* 2.1, 3, 4, 5, 7, 8. Games: Horace *Satires* 2.8.79 (*nullos his mallem ludos spectasse*).

8.4. Virgil's *Georgics*

Trained and commanded: Livy *Epitome* 129, Velleius Paterculus 2.79, Dio Cassius 48.49.2–51.5 (as consul in 37 BC), 49.14.3–4 (Agrippa's 'naval crown'), Appian *Civil Wars* 5.118–21.

122 No new aqueduct: Frontinus *De aquis* 8 (Aqua Tepula, 125 BC). Illegally tapped: Frontinus *De aquis* 75.2–76.1, cf. Cicero *Ad familiares* 8.6.4 (complaint of an aedile in 50 BC); Dio Cassius 49.42.2 (Aqua Marcia, 34 BC).

Aqua Iulia: Frontinus *De aquis* 9, cf. Dio Cassius 48.32.3 (40 BC—misdated?). Aedile after his consulship: Frontinus *De aquis* 9.1, 98.1; Pliny *Natural History* 36.104.

Fabric of the city: Strabo 5.3.8 C235, Pliny *Natural History* 36.104, Dio Cassius 49.43.1 (Agrippa rebuilds sewers, streets, public buildings). Welfare of the citizens: Dio Cassius 49.43.2 (Agrippa distributes free oil and salt).

Pliny *Natural History* 36.121:

> *Agrippa uero in aedilitate adiecta Virgine aqua ceterisque conriuatis atque emendatis lacus DCC fecit, praeterea salientes D, castella CXXX, complura et cultu magnifica, operibus iis signa CCC aerea aut marmorea imposuit, columnas e marmore CCCC, eaque omnia annuo spatio. adicit ipse aedilitatis suae commemoratione et ludos diebus undesexaginta factos et gratuita praebita balinea CLXX.*

The Aqua Virgo was built by Agrippa in 19 BC (Frontinus *De aquis* 10.1).

Regular annual games: to the list in Chapter 3.5 above, add the *ludi Victoriae* from 26 October to 1 November, instituted in 81 BC (Velleius Paterculus 2.27.6, Cicero *In Verrem* 1.31); at first, under Sulla's dictatorship, they were entrusted to a praetor (Crawford 1974.445 no. 421), but that honorific status is not likely to have continued.

The *ludi Victoriae Caesaris*, instituted in 46 BC, were given by the consuls in 34 (Dio Cassius 49.42.1), but that may have been exceptional; perhaps they were normally the *praetor urbanus'* responsibility, like the *ludi Apollinares* immediately preceding.

The *ludi Florales* gained an extra day by Caesar's reform of the calendar in 46 BC (cf. Macrobius *Saturnalia* 1.14.9), and an extra day was added to the *ludi Romani* in honour of Caesar in 44 (Cicero *Philippics* 2.110).

Six aediles: Dio Cassius 43.51.3, Pomponius in *Digest* 1.2.2.32 (Caesar's reform, 44 BC). Victorious Caesar: Dio Cassius 49.43.8, Appian *Illyrian Wars* 28.

Tokens and barbers: Dio Cassius 49.43.3–4. Mourning: e.g. Suetonius *Diuus Iulius* 67.2, *Diuus Augustus* 23.2.

Avoiding publicity: Donatus *Vita Vergili* 11, cf. 13 (he preferred Naples and Sicily to Rome). Naples: Virgil *Georgics* 4.563–4, cf. *Catalepton* 5 and 8 (if not by Virgil, then by someone well informed); *Papyri Herculanenses* 1082.11, *Pap. Herc. Paris* 2; details in Sider 1997.12–24.

Siro: Cicero *De finibus* 2.119; *Papyri Herculanenses* 312.14; Servius on *Eclogues* 6.13 and *Aeneid* 6.264.

Virgil and Maecenas: *Georgics* 1.2, 2.39–46, 3.40–2, 4.2; Horace *Satires* 1.5.39–49 (38 or 37 BC), 1.6.45–64, 1.10.81–3. Suggestions: *Georgics* 3.41 (*haud mollia iussa*).

Public performer: Donatus *Vita Vergili* 28–9 (Julius Montanus on Virgil's *uocem et os et hypocrisin*); Quinn 1982.85–7. So far written: the *Georgics* took seven years, and were finished by 30 BC (Donatus *Vita* 25).

'The leisured men...': Powell 2008.228, 263. Seneca's remark: *Epistulae* 86.15. Address to farmers: *Georgics* 3.288 (*hic labor, hinc laudem fortes sperate coloni*).

Country people at the games: Ovid *Fasti* 3.783 (*rusticus ad ludos populus ueniebat in urbem*); cf. Cicero *In Verrem* 1.54 ('crowd from all Italy'), Phaedrus 5.5, Calpurnius Siculus 7.1–6. Education: Varro *De lingua Latina* 6.18 (play at the *ludi Apollinares* 'taught the People'); see Rawson 1991.570–81 on drama as ethical instruction.

Virgil *Georgics* 1.24–8, 40–2:

> tuque adeo, quem mox quae sint habitura deorum
> concilia incertum est, urbisne inuisere, Caesar, 25
> terrarumque uelis curam, et te maximus orbis
> auctorem frugum tempestatumque potentem
> accipiat cingens materna tempora myrto...
> da facilem cursum atque audacibus adnue coeptis, 40
> ignarosque uiae mecum miseratus agrestis
> ingredere et uotis iam nunc adsuesce uocari.

Virgil *Georgics* 1.463–8, 489–97:

> solem quis dicere falsum
> audeat? ille etiam caecos instare tumultus
> saepe monet fraudemque et operta tumescere bella; 465
> ille etiam exstincto miseratus Caesare Romam,
> cum caput obscura nitidum ferrugine texit
> impiaque aeternam timuerunt saecula noctem...
> ergo inter sese paribus concurrere telis
> Romanas acies iterum uidere Philippi; 490
> nec fuit indignum superis bis sanguine nostro
> Emathiam et latos Haemi pinguescere campos.
> scilicet et tempus ueniet, cum finibus illis
> agricola incuruo terram molitus aratro
> exesa inueniet scabra robigine pila, 495
> aut grauibus rastris galeas pulsabit inanis
> grandiaque effossis mirabitur ossa sepulcris.

Ides of March: Appian *Civil Wars* 2.119.501, 120.507, 125.523, 135.565, 139.580–141.591. Two battles: Augustus *Res gestae* 2 (*qui patrem meum interfecerunt... uici bis acie*), Petronius *Satyrica* 121.111 (*gemina morte*); cf. Livy *Epitome* 124 (next day), Plutarch *Antony* 22.2–4 (a few days later), Appian *Civil Wars* 4.110–14, 117–31; there is no reason to suppose, as many do, that Virgil was referring also to Pharsalus (48 BC).

Virgil *Georgics* 2.161–4:

> an memorem portus Lucrinosque addita claustra
> atque indignatum magnis stridoribus aequor,
> Iulia qua ponto longe sonat unda refuso
> Tyrrhenumque fretis immittitur aestus Auernis?

I take it that lines 170–2, presupposing the events of 31 or 30 BC, belong to the final drafting of the complete text.

Portus Iulius: Suetonius *Diuus Augustus* 16.1, Dio Cassius 48.49.2–51.5; Frederiksen 1984.333–4 and pl. XIV.

Brothers' strife: Virgil *Georgics* 2.496 (*infidos agitans discordia fratres*), 510 (*gaudent perfusi sanguine fratrum*); cf. Lucretius 3.70–2, Catullus 64.399.

Romulus and the death of Remus: Cicero *De officiis* 3.41 (an offence against *pietas* and *humanitas*); Horace *Epodes* 7.17–18 ('Bitter fate drives the Romans, and the crime of a brother's killing'); Livy 1.7.2 (the most widely believed version), cf. 1.6.4 (their rivalry 'an ancestral evil').

Virgil *Georgics* 2.532–5:

> *hanc olim ueteres uitam coluere Sabini,*
> *hanc Remus et frater; sic fortis Etruria creuit*
> *scilicet et rerum facta est pulcherrima Roma,*
> *septemque una sibi muro circumdedit arces.*

Sabines: Cicero *In Vatinium* 36, *Pro Ligario* 32; Livy 1.18.4; Horace *Epodes* 2.41, *Odes* 3.6.37–44; Strabo 5.3.1 C228, Columella 1.pref.19.

Twins found Rome together: Cassius Hemina FRHist 6 F14 = Diomedes in *Grammatici Latini* 1.384 Keil (stressing equality and consensus), Diodorus Siculus 37.11.1 (document attributed to 91 BC), Varro *Res rusticae* 2.pref.4, 2.1.9, Livy 10.23.12, Conon FGrH 26 F 1.48.7, Strabo 5.3.2 C229, Pliny *Natural History* 15.77, Justin 43.3.1, Servius on *Aeneid* 6.777, Orosius 2.4.1, Lydus *De mensibus* p. 115, *De magistratibus* 1.3.

Twins rule Rome together: Virgil *Aeneid* 1.292–3 (*Remo cum fratre Quirinus | iura dabunt*), Propertius 2.1.23 (*regnaque prima Remi*), *Anthologia Palatina* 9.213.3 (Rome as the city of Remus); cf. Catullus 58.5 (Romans as *Remi nepotes*), Propertius 4.6.80 (Remus' standards), Juvenal 10.73 (*turba Remi*). Shared rule may be implied by the hymns that honoured them together (Dionysius of Halicarnassus *Roman Antiquities* 1.79.10), and the otherwise unexplained ritual 'in memory of Remus and Romulus' on 8 November (Lydus *De mensibus* p. 115); according to one author Remus even outlived Romulus (Egnatius in *Origo gentis Romanae* 23.6).

Seneca *Letters* 94.46 (quoting Sallust *Jugurthine War* 10.6):

> M. Agrippa uir ingentis animi, qui solus ex iis quos ciuilia bella claros potentesque fecerunt felix in publicum fuit, dicere solebat multum se huic debere sententiae: nam concordia paruae res crescunt, discordia maximae dilabuntur. hac se aibat et fratrem et amicum optimum factum.

Romulus' war against Amulius: Cicero *De republica* 2.4, Conon FGrH 26 F 1.48.5; Dionysius of Halicarnassus *Roman Antiquities* 1.79.12 (age), 1.84.8 (vengeance); Ovid *Fasti* 3.59 (age), 4.809 (vengeance); Justin 43.2.10 (*in ultionem...in uindictam*).

Twelve vultures: Suetonius *Diuus Augustus* 95 (augury), Appian *Civil Wars* 3.94.388, Dio Cassius 46.46.2 (soldiers). Palatine house: Dio Cassius 53.16.5 (because of Romulus), Josephus *Jewish Antiquities* 19.75 and 90 (hut in front of the *basileion*); Wiseman 2013.251–4.

Agrippa as contemporary: he died early in 12 BC in his fifty-first year (Pliny *Natural History* 7.46). From the beginning: Nicolaus of Damascus FGrH 90 F 127.7.16, 130.31.133; Velleius Paterculus 2.59.5.

Caesar as Romulus: Dio Cassius 53.16.7; cf. Suetonius *Diuus Augustus* 7.2, Florus 2.34.66. Agrippa as Remus: Servius on *Aeneid* 1.292 (*Remum pro Agrippa positum*); Agrippa too lived on the Palatine (Dio Cassius 53.27.5), and the imperial residence was sometimes called 'the house of Remus' (Propertius 4.1.9, Persius 1.73, Martial 12.2.6, Statius *Siluae* 2.7.60).

8.5. Virgil's 'Epyllion'

Mythological narrative (*Georgics* 4.315–558): 'As is often noted, the lines are in the style of an epyllion, in movement (with frame and picture constituting the whole as, for instance, with Cat. 64) and in language, which is elevated throughout' (Thomas 1988.202).

Eulogy of Cornelius Gallus: Servius on *Eclogues* 10.1 and *Georgics* 4.1. Gallus' death: Jerome *Chronica* Ol. 188.2; Suetonius *Diuus Augustus* 66.1–2, Dio Cassius 53.23.5–7, Ammianus Marcellinus 17.4.5. Slow composer: Donatus *Vita Vergili* 22–5.

Servius' report is widely disbelieved on a priori grounds (e.g. Griffin 1985.180–2), but it is hard to see when and why it should have been invented. Besides, a passage on Gallus would fit well between the description of Aristaeus as 'the Arcadian master' at 4.283 and the closing reference back to the *Eclogues* at 4.565–6: the home of Aristaeus in the story we have is not Arcadia but Thessalian Tempe (4.317), whereas Gallus in the *Eclogues* is placed in a conspicuously Arcadian setting (*Eclogues* 10.15, 26, 31–3, 55, 57).

Modern scholars tend to assume a wide distribution of the original *Georgics* text, which would then have had to be recalled or suppressed, and 'Rome in the early twenties was not like Stalin's Russia, with an efficient and ubiquitous police which could have enforced such a decree throughout the private houses of readers of poetry' (Griffin 1985.181). I think that is anachronistic (Ch. 1.3 above), but in any case what mattered were the copies in the public libraries, and later those used in schools; they of course would not contain the praises of a *persona non grata*, and it is from them that our texts ultimately derive.

Aristaeus legend: Apollonius Rhodius 2.506–27, Diodorus Siculus 4.81–3, Columella 9.2.4, Nonnus *Dionysiaca* 13.253–308, Probus on *Georgics* 1.14 (Varro Atacinus fr. 6 Courtney).

Cyrene: *Georgics* 4.321–2 (*quae gurgitis huius* | *ima tenes*); contrast Pindar *Pythians* 9.5–70 (Libya 52–8), Apollonius Rhodius 2.500–10 (Libya 505), Diodorus Siculus 4.81.1, Nonnus *Dionysiaca* 13.300–3.

Virgil *Georgics* 4.358–73 (Day Lewis 1966.120–1):

> 'duc, age, duc ad nos; fas illi limina diuum
> tangere' ait. simul alta iubet discedere late
> flumina, qua iuuenis gressus inferret. at illum   360
> curuata in montis faciem circumstetit unda
> accepitque sinu uasto misitque sub amnem.
> iamque domum mirans genetricis et umida regna
> speluncisque lacus clausos lucosque sonantis

> ibat, et ingenti motu stupefactus aquarum 365
> omnia sub magna labentia flumina terra
> spectabat diuersa locis, Phasimque Lycumque,
> et caput unde altus primum se erumpit Enipeus,
> unde pater Tiberinus et unde Aniena fluenta
> saxosusque sonans Hypanis Mysusque Caicus 370
> et gemina auratus taurino cornua uultu
> Eridanus, quo non alius per pinguia culta
> in mare purpureum uiolentior effluit amnis.

Castellum of the Anio aqueduct: Rodriguez Almeida 1981.87–92 and tav. VII, esp. 91 n. 16 (cf. Najbjerg and Trimble 2006.83–5); Frontinus *De aquis* 21 (*intra portam Esquilinam*).

Martial 10.20.4–9:

> i perfer: breuis est labor peractae
> altum uincere tramitem Suburae.
> illic Orphea protinus uidebis
> udi uertice lubricum theatri
> mirantisque feras auemque regem
> raptum quae Phryga pertulit Tonanti.

Lacus Orphei (Coarelli 1996a): listed as the first item for *regio V* in the Constantinian Regionary catalogues (Richter 1901.372); cf. Wiseman 2013.249 for the catalogues as a partially updated Augustan text.

Sea-cave: Virgil *Georgics* 4.418–24. Herd of seals: *Georgics* 4.394–5.

Virgil *Georgics* 4.429–32 (Day Lewis 1966.123):

> cum Proteus consueta petens a fluctibus antra
> ibat; eum uasti circum gens umida ponti
> exsultans rorem late dispergit amarum.
> sternunt se somno diuersae in litore phocae.

Lucian *Saltatio* 19:

> ὅπερ δὴ καὶ τοῖς νῦν ὀρχουμένοις πρόσεστιν, ἴδοις τ' ἂν οὖν πρὸς τὸν καιρὸν ὠκέως
> διαλλαττομένους καὶ αὐτὸν μιμουμένους τὸν Πρωτέα.

Proteus as prophet (*uates*): Virgil *Georgics* 4.387, 392, 450. Prophets sing: e.g. Ennius *Annales* 207 Sk, Cicero *In Catilinam* 3.18, Catullus 64.383, Livy 1.45.5, 1.55.6, 5.15.4; see in general Wiseman 2008.44–7.

Commentators puzzled: Mynors 1990.295. Aristaeus' offence: Virgil *Georgics* 4.454–9; the snake (but not the pursuit) is mentioned at Apollodorus 1.3.2 and Ovid *Metamorphoses* 10.10. Chorus of Dryads: Virgil *Georgics* 4.460, 532–3; cf. Ovid *Metamorphoses* 10.8–10 (Naiads).

Roman audience: like Aristaeus, spectator of the waters (*Georgics* 4.367, *spectabat*).

8.6. Livy and Horace

129 Triumvirate: Augustus *Res gestae* 7.1 (ten continuous years), Appian *Illyrian Wars* 28 (second five-year grant confirmed by People), Livy *Epitome* 132 (*finito IIIuiratus tempore*, 32 BC). Hellenistic monarch: Plutarch *Antony* 54.3–6, Dio Cassius 49.40.3–41.3.

Antony's war: Livy *Epitome* 132, Velleius Paterculus 2.82.4, Florus 2.21.2, Plutarch *Antony* 58.1–2, Dio Cassius 50.3.2; cf. Suetonius *Diuus Augustus* 17.2 (Antony declared a public enemy); Horace *Odes* 1.37.6–12, Propertius 3.11.31–2, Dio Cassius 50.5.4 (Cleopatra's ambitions). Divorce: Livy *Epitome* 132, Plutarch *Antony* 57.2–3, Dio Cassius 50.3.2.

Popular mandate: Augustus *Res gestae* 25.2 (*iurauit in mea uerba tota Italia sponte sua et me belli quo uici ad Actium ducem poposcit*); Suetonius *Diuus Augustus* 17.2 (*coniuratio...pro partibus suis*); Osgood 2006.357–62.

Caesar's deputies: Dio Cassius 51.3.5. Riots and conspiracy: Velleius Paterculus 2.88; Dio Cassius 50.10.3–5, 51.3.5–6.

The first question: Livy pref. 1 (*facturusne operae pretium sim si a primordio urbis res populi Romani perscripserim*); for the likely date, see Woodman 1988.128–34.

Livy pref. 4–5:

> *legentium plerisque...festinantibus ad haec noua quibus iam pridem praeualentis populi uires se ipsae conficiunt: ego contra hoc quoque laboris praemium petam, ut me a conspectu malorum quae nostra tot per annos uidit aetas, tantisper certe dum prisca illa tota mente repeto, auertam.*

Moral parabola: Livy pref. 9 (*ad haec tempora quibus nec uitia nostra nec remedia pati possumus*); the same diagnosis in Sallust *Catiline* 10, Diodorus Siculus 31.26.2, 37.3.1–4, Dionysius of Halicarnassus *Roman Antiquities* 2.74.5, 10.17.6.

Public vices: Sallust *Histories* 1.12M, Horace *Epodes* 7.1–4, Dionysius of Halicarnassus *Roman Antiquities* 2.11.3. 'Body politic' metaphor: Cicero *Pro Cluentio* 146, *In Catilinam* 1.31, *Ad Atticum* 2.20.3, *Pro Sestio* 135, *Philippics* 8.15. Political remedy (Woodman 1988.132–4): e.g. Cicero *Pro Milone* 68 (by arms); Livy 3.20.8, 22.8.5, Appian *Civil Wars* 2.23.84 (dictatorship).

Expected outcome: implied by the young Caesar's emphatic refusal (Augustus *Res gestae* 5.1, Velleius Paterculus 2.89.5, Suetonius *Diuus Augustus* 52, Dio Cassius 54.1.3–5).

130 Dramatic episodes: e.g. Sextus Tarquinius and Lucretia (1.53.4–60.2), Appius Claudius and Verginia (3.44.1–58.11). History enthusiasts: Polybius 9.1.2–4, Cicero *De finibus* 5.52. Livy's eloquence: Quintilian 10.1.101. For the Roman People: Pliny *Natural History* pref. 16.

Ancestor Iulus: Livy 1.3.2 (*quis enim rem tam ueterem pro certo adfirmet?*). Foundation story: 1.6.4 (*auitum malum, regni cupido*), 1.7.2 (*uolgatior fama*). Romulus: 1.15.8 (*multitudini tamen gratior fuit quam patribus, longe ante alios acceptissimus militum animis*).

Livy 1.16.4:

fuisse credo tum quoque aliquos qui discerptum regem patrum manibus taciti argueret; manauit enim haec quoque sed perobscura fama; illam alteram admiratio uiri et pauor praesens nobilitauit.

The final word may be an allusion to 'the noble lie' (Plato *Republic* 3.414b–415d); Livy was interested in philosophy (Seneca *Epistulae* 100.9), and will certainly have known the passage.

Caesar: cf. Appian *Civil Wars* 2.114.476 for the assassins' decision to kill Caesar at the Senate meeting, 'as was said to have happened to Romulus when he became tyrannical'. Lucius Brutus: Livy 1.59.6–7, with Wiseman 2009a.

Divus Iulius temple: Dio Cassius 47.18.4 (begun 42 BC), 51.22.2 (dedicated 29 BC).

Curia Iulia: Dio 47.19.1 (begun 42 BC), 51.22.1 (dedicated 29 BC); cf. 40.50.2–3, 49.5.2 (name of Sulla).

Saepta Iulia: Cicero *Ad Atticum* 4.16.8 (projected 54 BC), Dio Cassius 53.23.1–2 (dedicated 26 BC).

Apollo temple: Velleius Paterculus 2.81.3, Dio Cassius 49.15.5 (begun 36 BC); Virgil *Aeneid* 8.714–22, Propertius 2.31.1–16, Dio Cassius 53.1.3 (dedicated 28 BC); cf. Wiseman 2013.255–6 on the archaeological evidence for the previous house on the site. Overlooking Caesar's forecourt: implied by Horace *Carmen saeculare* 61–5, Ovid *Tristia* 3.1.33–8, 59–60; full argument in Wiseman 2012. Modest house: Suetonius *Diuus Augustus* 72.1.

Apollo colonnades: Propertius 2.31.1–8, *CIL* 6.32323.31–2 (17 BC), Augustus *Res gestae* 19.1, Ovid *Tristia* 3.1.61–4, Crawford 1996.518, 519 (AD 19), Velleius Paterculus 2.81.3.

Burial mound (*tumulus*): Virgil *Aeneid* 6.874; Tacitus *Annals* 3.4.1, 3.9.2, 16.6.2; Crawford 1996.521 (AD 19). Also called *Mausolaeum*: Strabo 5.3.8 C236, *CIL* 6.8686 = *ILS* 1577, Suetonius *Diuus Augustus* 100.4 (*siluas et ambulationes in usum populi*), 101.4. Cleopatra's (and Antony's) tomb: Suetonius *Diuus Augustus* 17.4, Plutarch *Antony* 86.4, Dio Cassius 51.15.1.

Normal context of lyric poetry: Horace *Odes* 3.11.6 (*diuitum mensis et amica templis*). Banquets and parties: e.g. *Odes* 1.36, 2.11, 3.19, 3.28. Hymns: e.g. *Odes* 1.10, 1.35, 2.19, 3.26. Formal context: e.g. *Odes* 3.1.1–4 (the singer as priest).

Absence in the east: see Millar 2000.18–30 for the evidence of his movements.

Ruinous temples: e.g. Jupiter Feretrius on the Capitol (Nepos *Atticus* 20.3, before Atticus' death in March 32 BC).

Horace *Odes* 3.6.1–16 (West 2002.63):

> *delicta maiorum immeritus lues,*
> *Romane, donec templa refeceris*
> *aedesque labentis deorum et*
> *foeda nigro simulacra fumo.*

> dis te minorem quod geris, imperas: 5
> hinc omne principium, huc refer exitum:
> di multa neglecti dederunt
> Hesperiae mala luctuosae.
> iam bis Monaeses et Pacori manus
> non auspicatos contudit impetus 10
> nostros et adiecisse praedam
> torquibus exiguis renidet.
> paene occupatam seditionibus
> deleuit urbem Dacus et Aethiops,
> hic classe formidatus, ille 15
> missilibus melior sagittis.

132 Antony's Parthian war: Livy *Epitome* 130, Velleius Paterculus 2.82.1–3, Plutarch *Antony* 37–51, Dio Cassius 49.24–32.

Horace *Odes* 3.6.33–44 (West 2002.65):

> non his iuuentus orta parentibus
> infecit aequor sanguine Punico,
> Pyrrhumque et ingentem cecidit 35
> Antiochum Hannibalemque dirum,
> sed rusticorum mascula militum
> proles, Sabellis docta ligonibus
> uersare glebas et seuerae
> matris ad arbitrium recisos 40
> portare fustis, sol ubi montium
> mutaret umbras et iuga demerit
> bobus fatigatis, amicum
> tempus agens abeunte curru.

Veterans demobilized: Horace *Odes* 3.4.37–8, Augustus *Res gestae* 16.1, Suetonius *Diuus Augustus* 17.3, Dio Cassius 51.4.5–6; Keppie 1983.73–82.

Horace *Odes* 1.2.1–4, 13–20 (West 2002.9);

> iam satis terris niuis atque dirae
> grandinis misit Pater et rubente
> dextera sacras iaculatus arces
> terruit urbem, ...
> uidimus flauum Tiberim retortis
> litore Etrusco uiolenter undis
> ire deiectum monumenta Regis 15
> templaque Vestae,
> Iliae dum se nimium querenti
> iactat ultorem, uagus et sinistra
> labitur ripa Ioue non probante u-
> xorius amnis. 20

Ilia: Varro *De lingua Latina* 8.80 (*Ilia ab Ilio*); Fabius Pictor *FGrH* 809 F 4, Ennius *Annales* 56 Sk, Virgil *Aeneid* 1.274, 6.773, Dionysius of Halicarnassus *Roman Antiquities* 1.76.3–79.4.

River-god (Tiber or Anio?): Ennius in Porphyrio on *Odes* 1.2.17; Ovid *Amores* 3.6.45–82, *Fasti* 2.598; Statius *Siluae* 2.1.99–100.

Ides of March: Porphyrio on *Odes* 1.2.17 (*querenti autem Iliae caedem Caesaris intellegendum*).

Horace *Odes* 1.2.21–6 (West 2002.9):

> audiet ciuis acuisse ferrum
> quo graues Persae melius perirent,
> audiet pugnas uitio parentum
> > rara iuuentus.
> quem uocet diuum populus ruentis
> imperi rebus?

'Persians': i.e. Parthians, against whom Caesar was about to lead an army when he was assassinated.

Horace *Odes* 1.2.41–52 (West 1995.11):

> siue mutata iuuenem figura
> ales in terris imitaris almae
> filius Maiae patiens uocari
> > Caesaris ultor:
> serus in caelum redeas diuque
> laetus intersis populo Quirini,
> neue te nostris uitiis iniquum
> > ocior aura
> tollat; hic magnos potius triumphos,
> hic ames dici pater atque princeps,
> neu sinas Medos equitare inultos
> > te duce, Caesar.

Prefect of Egypt: Ulpian in *Digest* 1.17.1 (*lege sub Augusto*), with Millar 2000.25.

Egypt *in potestatem populi Romani redacta*: Degrassi 1963.134–5 (*Fasti Praenestini* on 1 August), Macrobius *Saturnalia* 1.12.35 (senatorial decree, 8 BC), *CIL* 6.701–2 = *ILS* 91 (bases of obelisks set up in the Circus Maximus and Campus Martius); cf. Augustus *Res gestae* 27.1 (added to the *imperium populi Romani*). No senator was allowed to set foot in Egypt without special permission (Tacitus *Annals* 2.59.3).

Georgics at Atella: Donatus *Vita Vergili* 27.

Virgil *Georgics* 4.559–66 (Day Lewis 1966.128):

> haec super aruorum cultu pecorumque canebam
> et super arboribus, Caesar dum magnus ad altum
> fulminat Euphraten bello uictorque uolentis
> per populos dat iura uiamque adfectat Olympo.

> illo Vergilium me tempore dulcis alebat
> Parthenope studiis florentem ignobilis oti,
> carmina qui lusi pastorum audaxque iuuenta, 565
> Tityre, te patulae cecini sub tegmine fagi.

8.7. The Republic Restored

Public holiday: Dio Cassius 51.19.2, 51.20.3–4. 18 July (*dies Alliensis*): Cicero *Ad Atticum* 9.5.2, Livy 6.1.11, Lucan 7.409, Tacitus *Histories* 2.91.1, Festus (Paulus) 6L, Festus 348L.

Games for *Venus genetrix*: Dio Cassius 43.22.2, 45.6.4, 49.4.2; Seneca *Quaestiones naturales* 7.17.2, Pliny *Natural History* 2.93, Appian *Civil Wars* 3.28.107, Obsequens 68. *Ludi Victoriae Caesaris*: Suetonius *Diuus Augustus* 10.1, *CIL* 6.37836 = *ILS* 9349, Degrassi 1963.78 and 188–9 (*Fasti Maffeiani* and *Amiternini*).

1 August: *feriae ex s(enatus) c(onsulto) q(uod) e(o) d(ie) imp(erator) Caesar Diui f(ilius) rem public(am) tristissimo periculo liberauit* (Degrassi 1963.30–1, 134–5, 190–1: *Fasti Arualium, Praenestini* and *Amiternini*); Horace *Odes* 4.14.34–6, Macrobius *Saturnalia* 1.12.35 (*senatus consultum* of 8 BC), Dio Cassius 51.19.6.

Arrival ceremony: Velleius Paterculus 2.89.1, Dio Cassius 51.21.1–2. 'After that': Dio Cassius 51.21.2–3.

Agrippa: Livy *Epitome* 129, Seneca *De beneficiis* 3.32.4, Pliny *Natural History* 16.7, Dio Cassius 49.14.3–4 (Naulochus); Dio Cassius 51.21.3 (Actium), cf. Suetonius *Diuus Augustus* 25.3 ('Sicily' error for Actium?).

Spoils of war: Augustus *Res gestae* 15.1 (*plebei Romanae . . . ex bellorum manibis*), 15.3 (*colonis militum meorum . . . ex manibis*). Treasury: Suetonius *Diuus Augustus* 41.1. No sacrilege: Dio Cassius 51.17.6–8. Comparison: Tacitus *Annals* 1.17.4 (10 *asses* per day).

Spectacle and celebration: Velleius Paterculus 2.89.1–2. Three triumphs: Livy *Epitome* 133, Virgil *Aeneid* 8.714, Macrobius *Saturnalia* 1.12.35 (*senatus consultum* of 8 BC); Degrassi 1947.344–5 (*Fasti Barberiniani*); Suetonius *Diuus Augustus* 22, 41.1, *Tiberius* 6.4; Dio Cassius 51.21.5.

Divus Iulius temple: Dio Cassius 51.22.2–6; Degrassi 1963.190–1, 208 (*Fasti Amiternini* and *Antiates*). Curia and Victory altar: Dio Cassius 51.22.1–2 ('decorated with spoil from Egypt'); Degrassi 1963. 79, 174–5 (*Fasti Maffeiani* and *Vaticani*); cf. Suetonius *Diuus Augustus* 100.2.

Ludi Romani: cf. Augustus *Res gestae* 21.2, Dio Cassius 51.22.3 (the temple of Capitoline Jupiter decorated with Egyptian booty).

Birthday: Dio Cassius 51.19.2; Degrassi 1963.34–5, 48, 279 (*Fasti Arualium* and *Pinciani, Feriale Cumanum*). The day was later celebrated with games: Dio Cassius 54.8.5, 54.26.2, 54.30.5, 55.6.6, 56.46.4, 57.14.4; Degrassi 1963.80 (*Fasti Maffeiani*).

Caesar's and Agrippa's census: Dio Cassius 52.42.1 (29 BC), Augustus *Res gestae* 8.2 (*lustrum* completed in 28 BC). Carried out *censoria potestate*: Degrassi 1947.254–5 (*Fasti Venusini*); cf. Suetonius *Diuus Augustus* 27.5 ('without holding the censorship').

End of civil wars: Macrobius *Saturnalia* 1.12.35, quoting a *senatus consultum* of 8 BC (*finis ... bellis ciuilibus impositus*); Augustus *Res gestae* 34.1 (*postquam bella ciuilia exstinxeram*); Velleius Paterculus 2.89.3 (*finita uicesimo anno bella ciuilia*).

Emergency powers not necessary: Augustus *Res gestae* 34.1 (28–27 BC); Tacitus *Annals* 3.28.2, Dio Cassius 53.2.5 (28 BC).

Lustrum: Varro *De lingua Latina* 6.87, Livy 1.44.2, Dionysius of Halicarnassus *Roman Antiquities* 4.22.1–2.

Previous census: Cicero *In Verrem* 1.54, Plutarch *Pompey* 22.5–6. Failed censuses: Dio Cassius 37.9.3, Plutarch *Crassus* 31.1 (65 BC); Dio Cassius 37.9.4 (64); Cicero *Ad Atticum* 1.18.8 (61), 4.9.1, 4.16.8 (55); Dio Cassius 40.63.2–5 (50); *Fasti Colotiani* Degrassi 1947.273 (42).

Revision of Senate: Dio Cassius 52.42.1–5, Suetonius *Diuus Augustus* 35.1. New patricians: Augustus *Res gestae* 8.1 (*iussu populi et senatus*), Dio Cassius 52.42.5, Tacitus *Annals* 11.25.2.

Pliny *Natural History* 35.26 (on M. Agrippa, *uir rusticitati propior quam deliciis*):

> exstat certe eius oratio magnifica et maximo ciuium digna de tabulis omnibus signisque publicandis, quod fieri satius fuisset quam in uillarum exilia pelli.

For works of art as part of the censor's business, see Cicero *Ad familiares* 8.14.4, *Ad Atticum* 6.9.5 (50 BC).

Agrippa in the Campus Martius: *CIL* 6.31545 (*pons Agrippae*); Aulus Gellius 14.5.1, Dio Cassius 55.8.3 (*campus Agrippae*); Tacitus *Annals* 15.37.2 (*stagnum Agrippae*), 15.39.2 (*monumenta Agrippae*); Dio Cassius 53.23.1 (Saepta), 53.27.1 (Basilica Neptuni), 54.28.5 (planned tomb); Horace *Epistles* 1.6.26, scholiast on Juvenal 6.154 (*porticus Agrippae*); Pliny *Natural History* 34.13, 36.38, Dio Cassius 53.27.2 (Pantheon); Pliny *Natural History* 34.62, 35.26, 36.189, Martial 3.20.15, 3.36.6, Dio Cassius 53.27.1, 54.29.4, 66.24.2 (*thermae Agrippae*); Frontinus *De aquis* 10, 22 (Aqua Virgo); Pliny *Natural History* 3.17, Martial 4.18.1–2, Plutarch *Galba* 25.5, Tacitus *Histories* 1.31.2, Dio Cassius 55.8.4 (Porticus Vipsania).

Pompey's *horti*: Plutarch *Pompey* 40.5, 44.3; Asconius 33C, 36C, 50C, 51–2C. Taken by Antony: Cicero *Philippics* 2.109, Velleius Paterculus 2.60.3, Appian *Civil Wars* 3.14.50. Then by Agrippa: *CIL* 6.29781, 39807, with Coarelli 1997.548–56; cf. Dio Cassius 53.27.5 on Agrippa (and Messalla) taking over Antony's Palatine house.

All possible publicity: Dio Cassius 53.1.1; Sutherland 1984.79, Aug. no. 476 (*cistophori* minted in Ephesus with the legend *Imp. Caesar Diui f cos. VI libertatis p.R. uindex*).

Augustus *Res gestae* 8.2:

> in consulatu sexto censum populi conlega M. Agrippa egi. lustrum post annum alterum et quadragensimum feci, quo lustro ciuium Romanorum censa sunt capita quadragiens centum millia et sexaginta tria millia.

Previous occasion: Phlegon *FGrH* 257 F 12.6; cf. Livy *Epitome* 98 (900,000).

Augustus *Res gestae* 20.4:

> duo et octoginta templa deum in urbe consul sextum ex auctoritate senatus refeci, nullo praetermisso quod eo tempore refici debebat.

Anxiety laid to rest: Horace *Odes* 3.6.1–8; cf. Livy 4.20.7 ('founder and restorer of all the temples'), Ovid *Fasti* 2.59–66, Dio Cassius 53.2.4–5.

Augustus *Res gestae* 34.1:

> in consulatu sexto et septimo, postquam bella ciuilia exstinxeram, per consensum uniuersorum potens rerum omnium, rem publicam ex mea potestate in senatus populique Romani arbitrium transtuli.

Cancellation of triumviral measures: Tacitus *Annals* 3.28.2, Dio Cassius 53.2.5.

Quadrennial games: Dio Cassius 51.19.2 (voted), 53.1.3–6 (28 BC); cf. 54.19.8 ('games in honour of his sovereignty').

136 Apollo temple (Miller 2009.185–252): Degrassi 1963.36–7, 194–5, 209 (*Fasti Arualium, Amiternini* and *Antiates*); Propertius 2.31.1–16, Ovid *Tristia* 3.1.59–64, Velleius Paterculus 2.81.3, Asconius 90C, Josephus *Jewish War* 2.81, *Jewish Antiquities* 17.301, Suetonius *Diuus Augustus* 29.3, Dio Cassius 49.15.5, 53.1.3. Strictly speaking, it was the temple of Apollo and Diana (Vitruvius 3.3.4, Virgil *Aeneid* 6.69).

Apollo at Actium (Miller 2009.54–94): Propertius 2.34.61–2, 3.11.69–70, 4.1.3, 4.6.27–68; Virgil *Aeneid* 8.704–6, *Elegia in Maecenatem* 1.51–6, Ovid *Metamorphoses* 13.715.

Virgil *Aeneid* 8.714–22:

> at Caesar, triplici inuectus Romana triumpho
> moenia, dis Italis uotum immortale sacrabat,   715
> maxima ter centum totam delubra per urbem.
> laetitia ludisque uiae plausuque fremebant;
> omnibus in templis matrum chorus, omnibus arae;
> ante aras terram caesi strauere iuuenci.
> ipse sedens niueo candentis limine Phoebi   720
> dona recognoscit populorum aptatque superbis
> postibus; incedunt uictae longo ordine gentes.

Pace Miller (2009.206–10, and elsewhere), this is not a description of a triumphal procession.

Area Palatina: Josephus *Jewish Antiquities* 19.223 (εὐρυχωρία τοῦ Παλατίου), with Wiseman 2012.378–9. Possibly identical with *Roma quadrata*: Solinus 1.17 (from Varro) and Tzetzes on Lycophron *Alexandra* 1232, with Wiseman 2012.379–83.

Stage and auditorium: as for the *ludi Palatini* established in AD 14 (Josephus *Jewish Antiquities* 19.75–6 and 90); see Wiseman 2012.383–6 for its position 'in front of the imperial residence', and its exploitation of the hut from which Romulus supposedly took the founding auspices of Rome.

Lucius Varius: Hollis 2007.253–81. His *Thyestes* (Leigh 1996): Quintilian 3.8.45, 10.1.98 (as good as any of the Greeks), Tacitus *Dialogus* 12.6; according to an anonymous author (Hollis 2007.257–8), *Lucius Varius cognomento Rufus Thyesten tragoediam magna cura absolutam post Actiacam uictoriam Augusti ludis eius in scaena edidit, pro qua fabula sestertium deciens accepit.*

Cleopatra ode: Horace *Odes* 1.37.

Livy 2.1.1:

> liberi iam hinc populi Romani res pace belloque gestas, annuos magistatus imperiaque legum potentiora quam hominum peragam.

9. RETHINKING THE CLASSICS: 28 BC–AD 8

Augustan age (Breed 2004): Suetonius *Diuus Augustus* 100.3 (AD 14); cf. Horace *Odes* 4.15.4 (*tua, Caesar, aetas*), Augustus *Res gestae* 16.1 (*ad memoriam aetatis meae*).

13–16 January 27 BC (Lacey 1996.77–99): Ovid *Fasti* 1.587–616, Censorinus *De die natali* 21.8; Degrassi 1963.112–15, 279 (*Fasti Praenestini, Feriale Cumanum*).

Augustus *Res gestae* 34.2:

> quo pro merito meo senatus consulto Augustus appellatus sum et laureis postes aedium mearum uestiti publice coronaque ciuica super ianuam meam fixa est, et clupeus aureus in curia Iulia positus, quem mihi senatum populumque Romanum dare uirtutis clementiaeque iustitiae et pietatis causa testatum est per eius clupei inscriptionem.

The Greek text renders *corona ciuica* as ὁ δρύινος στέφανος ὁ διδόμενος ἐπὶ σωτηρίᾳ τῶν πολειτῶν.

Ennius (*Annales* 155 Sk): Suetonius *Diuus Augustus* 7.2, cf. Varro *Res rusticae* 3.1.2.

Romulus' *auguratorium*: Dionysius of Halicarnassus *Roman Antiquities* 2.5.1–2 and 14.2.2, with Wiseman 2013.251–4.

Towering marble: Ovid *Tristia* 3.1.59–60 (*gradibus sublimia celsis... candida templa dei*), cf. Virgil *Aeneid* 6.69 (*solido de marmore*). *Augur Apollo*: Horace *Odes* 1.2.32, Virgil *Aeneid* 4.376, Horace *Carmen saeculare* 61–2, Valerius Flaccus 1.2.34, Statius *Thebaid* 1.495.

Three or four generations: Caligula was Augustus' great-grandson, Nero his great-great-grandson (Tacitus *Annals* 1.42.1, 14.53.2).

Working republic: for elections (Jones 1955), see for instance Horace *Odes* 3.1.10–14, *Epistles* 1.6.49–55, Velleius Paterculus 2.92.3–4, Dio Cassius 54.6.1–3; for legislation, see for instance Frontinus *De aquis* 129 (*lex Quinctia*, Crawford 1996.793–800), Macrobius *Saturnalia* 1.12.35 (tribune's *plebiscitum*, 8 BC).

9.1. The Citizens, the Audience

Tacitus *Dialogus* 13.2:

> testis ipse populus, qui auditis in theatro Vergili uersibus surrexit uniuersus et forte praesentem spectantemque Vergilium ueneratus est sic quasi Augustum.

Horace *Odes* 2.13.21–32 (West 1998.89):

> quam paene furuae regna Proserpinae
> et iudicantem uidimus Aeacum
>   sedesque descriptas piorum et
>   Aeolis fidibus querentem
> Sappho puellis de popularibus,   25
> et te sonantem plenius aureo,
>   Alcaee, plectro dura nauis,
>   dura fugae mala, dura belli!
> utrumque sacro digna silentio
> mirantur umbrae dicere; sed magis   30
>   pugnas et exactos tyrannos
>   densum umeris bibit aure uulgus.

For Horace as the Roman Alcaeus (and Sappho), cf. *Odes* 3.30.10–14, 4.9.1–12, *Epistles* 1.19.26–33, 2.2.99.

Livy: 1.59–60 (expulsion of Tarquins), 2.19–20 (battle of Lake Regillus). His fame: Seneca *Controuersiae* 10.pref.2; Pliny *Natural History* pref.16 (*celeberrimus*), Pliny *Letters* 2.3.8 (*nomen* and *gloria*), Suda K2098, 3.158 Adler (πολὺ καὶ κλεινὸν ὄνομα).

Pollio as orator: see for instance Quintilian 1.8.10, 10.1.113, Tacitus *Dialogus* 17.1. As poet (Hollis 2007.215–18): Virgil *Eclogues* 3.86, Pliny *Letters* 5.3.5; cf. Catullus 12.6–9. As tragedian: Virgil *Eclogues* 8.9–10; Horace *Satires* 1.10.42–3, *Odes* 2.1.9–12; Tacitus *Dialogus* 21.7.

Pollio as historian (Woodman 2003.199–213): Horace *Odes* 2.1, esp. lines 6–8 on the danger. Pollio and Sallust: Woodman 2003.207–12.

Library: Pliny *Natural History* 35.10 ('the first to make works of genius public property'); cf. Ovid *Tristia* 3.1.71–2, Suetonius *Diuus Augustus* 29.5 (*atrium Libertatis*). His own house: Seneca *Controuersiae* 4.pref.2 (evidently a general invitation rather than a private *recitatio*).

Pollio as citizen: Suetonius *De grammaticis* 10.6 (*ciuili...sermone*), Pliny *Natural History* 7.115 (*principe oratore et ciue*); he was a lover of liberty (Cicero *Ad familiares* 10.31.2–3), and deeply disapproved of the optimate Cicero (Seneca *Suasoriae* 6.14–15).

140   Britain and Parthia: Virgil *Georgics* 3.20–33; Horace *Epodes* 7.7–10, *Odes* 1.21.14–16, 1.35.29–32, 3.5.2–4. The tribute imposed on the Britons by Caesar in 54 BC (Caesar *De bello Gallico* 5.22.4, Strabo 4.5.3 C200) had clearly not been paid; and the Roman People's war of vengeance against the Parthians (Dio Cassius 43.51.1) had been aborted by Caesar's murder.

Intended invasion: Dio Cassius 53.22.5, 53.25.2. Conquest of Spain (Rich 2009): Livy 28.12.12, Velleius Paterculus 2.90.2–3.

Gate of War: Dio Cassius 53.26.5; Augustus *Res gestae* 13 (*cum per totum imperium populi Romani terra marique esset parta uictoriis pax*); the Greek text of *Res gestae* 13 renders *Ianum Quirinum* as πύλην Ἐννάλιον.

Latin text (Vulgate): *ego murus, et ubera mea sicut turris, ex quo facta sum coram eo quasi pacem reperiens*. Divinely ordained peace: e.g. Origen *Contra Celsum* 2.30, Orosius 6.20.8, 6.22.5.

Apponius *In Canticum canticorum* 12.53 (CCL 19.291–2):

> *in cuius apparitionis die, quod Epiphania appellatur, Caesar Augustus in spectaculis, sicut Liuius narrat, Romano populo nuntiat regressus a Britannia insula totum orbem terrarum tam bello quam amicitiis Romano imperio pacis abundantia subditum.*

The best discussion of the quotation is still Mommsen 1954.

'A rare and precious item': Cameron 2012.499 (referring to AD 401), cf. 511–15 on late antique use of Livy, mainly via epitomators.

'Abundance of peace': Psalms 72 (71): 7.

Dies atri (including the day after the Nones, such as 6 January): Varro *De lingua Latina* 6.29, Livy 6.1.12, Macrobius *Saturnalia* 1.16.21. Augustus and Epiphany: Orosius 6.20.2–4.

Prayer to Fortuna: Horace *Odes* 1.35.29–30 (*serues iturum Caesarem in ultimos* | *orbis Britannos*). Tributary to Rome: Horace *Odes* 4.14.47–8, with Brunt 1990.103–4 (cf. 104–6 for the Parthians) and Braund 1996.77–8 (see 76–89 on Augustus and Britain in general).

Livy as eyewitness: e.g. 1.19.3 on the first closing of the Gate of War, after the battle of Actium.

Timing of Augustus' return: he was certainly back in Rome by 13 June, when he was too ill to attend the *feriae Latinae* on the Alban Mount (Degrassi 1947.151, *Fasti feriarum Latinarum*).

Augustus' commentaries (Smith 2009): Suetonius *Diuus Augustus* 85.1 (13 books *Cantabrico tenus bello*), Plutarch *Comparison of Demosthenes and Cicero* 3.1 (dedicated to Agrippa and Maecenas). They are often described as an autobiography, but the terminal point clearly implies that their main subject was the campaigns the young Caesar conducted in person (Rich 2009.155–6, 159).

9.2. Horace's *Epistles*

Free elections, canvassing: Velleius Paterculus 2.91.3, 2.92.3–4; Suetonius *Diuus Augustus* 40.2; Dio Cassius 53.21.6–7, 54.16.1, 55.5.3.

Horace *Odes* 3.1.10–14:

> ... *hic generosior*
> *descendat in Campum petitor,*
>   *moribus hic meliorque fama*
>   *contendat, illi turba clientium*
>   *sit maior.*

Horace *Epistles* 1.6.49–54:

> *si fortunatum species et gratia praestat,*
> *mercemur seruum qui dictet nomina, laeuum*
> *qui fodicet latus et cogat trans pondera dextram*

> *porrigere: 'hic multum in Fabia ualet, ille Velina;*
> *cui libet hic fasces dabit eripietque curule*
> *cui uolet importunus ebur.'*

Fickle citizens: Horace *Odes* 1.1.7–8 (*mobilium turba Quiritium*), *Epistles* 1.16.33–4. Defeat: *Epistles* 1.1.43 (*turpemque repulsam*); cf. Valerius Maximus 7.5 (*de repulsis*).

Easy terms: four of the *Odes* (1.6, 1.7, 1.18, 2.1) are addressed to ex-consuls, and aristocratic names are dropped at *Odes* 3.19.10–11 (Murena), 3.21.7 (Corvinus), *Epistles* 1.5.3 (Torquatus), 1.9.1–4 (Claudius Nero).

The People's favour: Horace *Epistles* 2.2.103 (*scribo et supplex populi suffragia capto*). Modern literary scholars: e.g. Brink 1982.316; cf. 327 on 'the similarity with a political canvass which H. finds in publishing or reciting'.

Horace *Epistles* 2.2.95–6:

> *mox etiam, si forte uacas, sequere et procul audi*
> *quid ferat et qua re sibi nectat uterque coronam.*

'Each' (*uterque*) refers to Horace and his elegiac counterpart, probably Propertius.

'At a distance' (*procul*): 'not necessarily a long one', says Brink (1982.323), but only because he thinks Horace was referring to a private *recitatio* (1982.316, 'listeners seem to be admitted'); abandon that preconception, and the word can have its natural meaning.

Current orthodoxy: quotation from Cairns 2010.72; cf. Fantham 2013.101 on Horace's odes as 'poems, not public performances'.

In the People's gift: Cicero *De imperio Cn. Pompei* 1–2, cf. *Pro Cluentio* 153 (*iudicio populi Romani*).

Horace *Epistles* 1.19.35–8:

> *scire uelis mea cur ingratus opuscula lector*
> *laudet ametque domi, premat extra limen iniquus:*
> *non ego uentosae plebis suffragia uenor*
> *impensis cenarum et tritae munere uestis.*

Fickle *plebs* (literally 'breezy', *uentosa*): cf. Cicero *Philippics* 11.17 (a proposal that was *populare et uentosum*); for the 'breeze' (*aura*) of popular favour, see for instance Cicero *De haruspicum responso* 43, Livy 3.33.7, Horace *Odes* 3.2.20, Virgil *Aeneid* 6.816.

Dinner invitations and other inducements to voters: Cicero *Pro Murena* 72–4, *Pro Plancio* 46–7; cf. Tacitus *Annals* 1.15.1 (*largitiones*). Gifts of old clothes seem to be attested only here.

Publication of *Odes*: Nisbet and Hubbard 1970.xxxv–vi. Horace's pride: *Epistles* 1.19.21–33 (innovative), 34 (*ingenuis oculisque legi manibusque teneri*).

Horace *Epistles* 1.19.39–40:

> *non ego nobilium scriptorum auditor et ultor*
> *grammaticas ambire tribus et pulpita dignor.*

Ambire as canvassing: Cicero *Pro Plancio* 9, *Philippics* 11.19, *De republica* 1.47; cf. Livy 3.72.2, 8.37.9, Suetonius *Diuus Augustus* 56.1 (*tribus circuire*).

Electoral voting units (Taylor 1960): Cicero *Pro Plancio* 38–9, 43, 54, *Pro Sestio* 114; Varro *Res rusticae* 3.17.1, Livy 8.37.11, Suetonius *Diuus Augustus* 56.1. The normal formula was *tribus ad suffragium uocare* (Livy 4.5.2, 6.38.3–4, 10.9.1, 10.24.18, 25.3.15, 45.36.7, 45.39.20), or *tribus suffragium inire* (Livy 3.71.3, 6.35.7).

Ten years earlier: Horace *Satires* 1.10.38–9 (*iudice Tarpa . . . spectanda theatris*).

Other judges: Gallus in Hollis 2007.224 (*non ego, Visce . . . Kato, iudice te uereor*); for Viscus, see also *Satires* 1.9.22, 1.10.83, 2.8.20. Cf. ps.Acro on *Satires* 1.10.83, referring to Viscus and his brother: 'some say they were critics.'

Valerius Cato: Suetonius *De grammaticis* 11.1, probably from Furius Bibaculus (*Cato grammaticus . . . qui solus legit ac facit poetas*); for the translation of *legit*, cf. Kaster 1995.17, Hollis 2007.123 and 143, though neither refers to the *ludi scaenici*. 'Making poets' may be meant in the sense of the People 'making' magistrates by election (e.g. Cicero *Pro Plancio* 9, *Ad familiares* 15.12.1).

Cf. Quinn 1982.116: 'the task of finding an audience for literature seems to have fallen to the critics.' I think that was true in a sense rather different from what Kenneth Quinn had in mind. He assumed that 'the only audience worth writing for' was a cultural elite; 'as it was small and the members of it in constant contact, it could be reached by oral performance' (Quinn 1982.164). He was uncomfortable with Horace's evidence: 'there were attempts, we gather, to turn poetry into some kind of stage-spectacular, and make the performance an entertainment rather than an intellectual occasion.' In my view it was always both.

Cicero on canvassing: *Pro Plancio* 24 (*appellaui populum tributim, submisi me et supplicaui*); cf. Tacitus *Annals* 1.15.1 (*precibus sordidis*).

Noble authors: Horace *Satires* 1.10.85–6 (*te, Messalla, tuo cum fratre simulque | uos, Bibule et Serui*), named among those whose good opinion he valued; for Publicola (adopted by L. Gellius) see also *Satires* 1.10.28–9, with Badian 1988.8 n. 11.

Bibulus' historical work: Plutarch *Brutus* 13.3, 23.6. Servius' poems: Ovid *Tristia* 2.441, cf. Pliny *Letters* 5.3.5. Torquatus: Horace *Epistles* 1.5.9 (defence of Moschus), *Odes* 4.7.23 (eloquence). Iullus Antonius (born c.43 BC): *Odes* 4.2, with ps.Acro on 4.2.33.

Vedius Pollio (Syme 1961 = 1979.518–29): Dio Cassius 54.23.5, Pliny *Natural History* 9.167 (the villa); Seneca *De ira* 3.41.2, *De clementia* 1.18.2, Dio Cassius 54.23.1–6 (his luxury and cruelty). Theatre and *odeion*: Günther 1913.29–47; Sear 2006.46–7, 129–30.

Horace *Epistles* 1.19.41–9:

> *hinc illae lacrimae. 'spissis indigna theatris*
> *scripta pudet recitare et nugis addere pondus'*
> *si dixi, 'rides' ait 'et Iouis auribus ista*
> *seruas; fidis enim manare poetica mella*

> te solum, tibi pulcher'. ad haec ego naribus uti 45
> formido et luctantis acuto ne secer ungui,
> 'displicet iste locus' clamo et diludia posco.
> ludus enim genuit trepidum certamen et iram,
> ira truces inimicitias et funebre bellum.

Star dancers: Suetonius *Diuus Augustus* 45.4, Dio Cassius 54.17.4–5, Macrobius *Saturnalia* 2.7.12–19. Transfer of jurisdiction: Dio Cassius 54.2.3–4.

9.3. Tibullus and Propertius

Roman love elegy: see now Gold 2012, Thorsen 2013. Gallus: Hollis 2007.219–52, esp. 224.

Quintilian 10.1.93:

> *elegia quoque Graecos prouocamus, cuius mihi tersus atque elegans maxime uidetur auctor Tibullus. sunt qui Propertium malint. Ouidius utroque lasciuior, sicut durior Gallus.*

Grand public occasions: e.g. Tibullus 2.5 (installation of Messalla Messallinus as XVuir s.f.); Propertius 3.11 and 4.6 (*ludi quinquennales* commemorating Actium?), 3.18 (funeral of Marcellus), 4.11 (funeral of Cornelia). For less grand public occasions, cf. Tibullus 2.1 (a rustic festival, probably the *Ambarualia*), Propertius 3.17 (hymn to Bacchus).

Quirites addressed: Propertius 3.4.3, 3.5.47–8. *Roma* addressed: Propertius 3.1.15, 3.11.36 and 55, 3.14.34, 4.2.49, 4.10.10, 4.11.37.

Possible dramatic performance: e.g. Tibullus 1.4 (dialogue with Priapus), 1.8 (speech by Marathus); Propertius 1.17 (the poet shipwrecked), 1.18 (the poet in the wilderness), 2.26a (Cynthia shipwrecked), 3.3 (speeches by Apollo and Calliope), 4.1 (dialogue with Horus), 4.2 (Vertumnus monologue), 4.3 ('letter' as actress's monologue?), 4.4 (speech by Tarpeia), 4.5 (speech by Acanthis), 4.7 and 4.8 (speeches by Cynthia), 4.9 (speeches by Hercules and priestess).

Addressed to individuals: Tibullus 1.1, 1.3, 1.7 (Messalla); 2.3 (Cornutus); Propertius 1.1, 1.6, 1.14, 1.22, 3.22 (Tullus); 1.4 (Bassus); 1.5, 1.10, 1.13, 1.20 (Gallus); 1.7, 1.9 (Ponticus); 2.1, 3.9 (Maecenas); 2.22 ('Demophoon'), 2.34 ('Lynceus'); 3.12 (Postumus).

Addressed to 'friends': Propertius 1.1.25, 3.21.15 (*amici*); 3.21.11 (*socii*). Unspecified plural addressees: Tibullus 2.3.79 (*ducite*); Propertius 2.1.1, 3.13.1 (*quaeritis*).

Modern preconceptions are exemplified by the note on Propertius 2.1.1 in the standard textual commentary (Heyworth 2007.104): 'The poet's opening address to his readers... how his public is reacting to this second book.'

Not mutually exclusive: Tibullus 1.7 on Messalla's triumph (25 September 27 BC: Degrassi 1947.86–7) is mainly a private celebration of Messalla's birthday, while Propertius 2.1 and 3.9 to Maecenas deal with the public themes the poet is reluctant to address in epic narrative; cf. also Propertius 3.12 to Postumus (an oblique tribute to 'the brave standards of Augustus') and 3.22 to Tullus (a patriotic eulogy of Italy).

'Shows, and what follows shows': Cicero *De finibus* 2.23 (*adhibentes ludos et quae sequuntur*), with Wiseman 1985.45–8.

Cicero *In Pisonem* 22:

> *cum conlegae tui domus cantu et cymbalis personaret, cumque ipse nudus in conuiuio saltaret; in quo cum illum suum saltatorium uersaret orbem, ne tum quidem Fortunae rotam pertimescebat: hic autem non tum concinnus helluo nec tam musicus iacebat in suorum Graecorum foetore atque uino; quod quidem istius in illis rei publicae luctibus quasi aliquod Lapitharum aut Centaurorum conuiuium ferebatur.*

Dancing naked at banquets was attributed also to the friends of Catiline (Cicero *In Catilinam* 2.23); cf. Cicero *Pro Murena* 13 (with Wiseman 1985.263–5). Other prominent Romans noted for their dancing were Marcus Caelius (Macrobius *Saturnalia* 3.14.15) and Sempronia, wife of Decimus Brutus the consul of 77 BC (Sallust *Catiline* 25.2).

Centaurs and Lapiths: Diodorus Siculus 4.70.2–3, Ovid *Metamorphoses* 12.210–26, Hyginus *Fabulae* 33.3.

Young Caesar: Suetonius *Diuus Augustus* 70.1 (*cena secretior*). Plancus: Suetonius *Tiberius* 5 (consul), *Diuus Augustus* 7.2 (27 BC), Dio Cassius 54.2.1 (censor); Velleius Paterculus 2.83.2 (*cum caeruleatus et nudus caputque redimitus arundine et caudam trahens, genibus innixus Glaucum saltasset*); see Hollis 2007.149–54 for Cornificius and his *Glaucus*.

Propertius 1.20.7–12 (Heyworth 2007.87–8):

> *hunc tu siue leges Vmbrae sacra flumina siluae,*
> *siue Aniena tuos tinxerit unda pedes,*
> *siue Gigantei spatiabere litoris ora,*
> *siue ubicumque uago fluminis hospitio,*
> *nympharum semper cupida defende rapina*
> *(non minor Ausoniis est amor Adryasin).*

Estates on the banks of Clitumnus: Pliny *Letters* 8.8.6 (*uillae... secutae fluminis amoenitatem*), cf. 8.8.4 on boating for pleasure (*per iocum ludumque fluitantibus*); for the woods and cult site, see Virgil *Georgics* 2.146–7, Propertius 2.19.25–6, Suetonius *Gaius* 43.1, Pliny *Letters* 8.8.1–5.

Estates at Tibur: e.g. Cicero *Philippics* 5.19 (Metellus Scipio, then Antony), [Cicero] *In Sallustium* 19 (Caesar, then Sallust), Suetonius *Diuus Augustus* 72.2 (Augustus).

Estates at Cumae, Baiae, and Puteoli: e.g. Cicero *Ad Atticum* 13.52.1, 14.11.2 (L. Marcius Philippus), *Ad familiares* 4.2.1 (Ser. Sulpicius Rufus), *Academica* 1.1 (M. Varro); Seneca *Letters* 55.2 (P. Servilius Vatia); Pliny *Natural History* 31.6 (Cicero, then C. Antistius Vetus); Tacitus *Annals* 11.1.3 (Valerius Asiaticus), 13.21.6 (Domitia Lepida), 15.52.1 (C. Piso), 16.19.1 (Petronius).

For the notoriety of Baiae in particular, see Varro *Satires* 44 Astbury (Nonius 226L); Cicero *Ad Atticum* 1.16.10, *Pro Caelio* 35,38; Seneca *Letters* 51.1–3 and 11–12.

Battle of gods and Giants, at the *campi Phlegraei* between Cumae and Puteoli: Diodorus Siculus 4.21.5; Strabo 5.4.4 C243, 5.4.6 C245, 5.4.9 C248.

Cruising downstream ('the river', unnamed, must be the Tiber): e.g. Tacitus *Annals* 3.9.2 (Cn. Piso, AD 20). Riverside estates on the Tiber north of Rome: Cicero *Pro Milone* 64 (Milo's at Ocriculum); Sulpicia in [Tibullus] 3.14.4, with Degrassi 1969 for the text (Messalla's at Eretum, cf. Valerius Maximus 2.4.5).

148 Hylas story: Virgil *Georgics* 3.6 ('who has not told of the boy Hylas?'); e.g. Apollonius Rhodius 1.1207–72, Theocritus 13, Virgil *Eclogues* 6.43–4.

Propertius 1.20.25–30 (Cairns 2006.246):

> *hunc duo sectati fratres, Aquilonia proles,*
> *hunc super et Zetes, hunc super et Calais,*
> *oscula suspensis instabant carpere palmis,*
> *oscula et alterna ferre supina fuga.*
> *ille sub extrema pendens secluditur ala*
> *et uolucres ramo summouet insidias.*

Cf. Butrica 1980.75 for a different version, translating a heavily emended text.

They give up: Propertius 1.20.31 (*cessit genus Orithyiae*). 'No other extant account': Butrica 1980.69.

Pool of Pegae: Propertius 1.20.34 (*grata domus nymphis umida Thyniasin*), cf. Apollonius Rhodius 1.1221–2.

Propertius 1.20.45–7 (Heyworth 2007.93):

> *cuius ut accensae Dryades candore puellae*
> *miratae solitos destituere choros*
> *prolapsum et leuiter facili traxere liquore.*

Feature of private theatre: Günther 1913.34. Cult site of Anna Perenna and the *nymphae sacratae*: Piranomonte 2002, Wiseman 2006; *Année épigraphique* 2003.251–3 (inscriptions, second century AD); for Anna Perenna herself as a nymph, see Ovid *Fasti* 3.653–4 and 659–60, Silius Italicus 8.182–3.

149 'Delia', 'Nemesis', and 'Cynthia': Ovid *Amores* 3.9.31–2 and 53–8, *Ars amatoria* 3.536, *Remedia amoris* 764; Martial 8.73.5–7, 14.189 and 193; Juvenal 6.7, Apuleius *Apologia* 10, Sidonius Apollinaris *Epistulae* 2.10.6.

Party girls: e.g. Tibullus 1.6.15–20; Propertius 2.3.17, 2.9.21, 2.15.51–2, 2.30.13–16, 2.33.25–40, 2.34.57; 3.5.21–1, 3.8.3–4, 3.10.21–8.

'Cynthia' a dancer: Propertius 2.3.17–18, 2.28.59–60, 2.30.37–8; 3.10.23–4. It is interesting that Propertius often refers to poetry (his own and others') as 'dances': e.g. 2.10.1, 2.34.42; 3.1.44, 3.2.16, 3.5.19–20.

Equestrian rank: Suetonius *Vita Tibulli*, cf. Horace *Epistles* 1.4.7 on Tibullus' wealth; evidence for the Propertii of Asisium is collected in Cairns 2006.1–34. Socially inferior: as made clear in Propertius 2.23–4.

Propertius 2.13.9–14:

> *non ego sum formae tantum mirator honestae*
> *nec si qua illustres femina iactat auos;*

> me iuuat in gremio doctae legisse puellae
> auribus et puris scripta probasse mea.
> haec ubi contigerint, populi confusa ualeto
> fabula: nam dominae iudice tutus ero.

Posthumous reputation: Propertius 3.1.21–2 (*at mihi quod uiuo detraxerit inuida turba | post obitum duplici faenore reddet honos*).

Envy of privilege: cf. Propertius 2.1.73 on Maecenas as the 'envious hope' (*spes inuidiosa*) of the young and ambitious.

'Throughout the city': Propertius 2.5.1–2, 2.24.1–2 and 7, 2.26.21–2, 2.32.23–4.

Circulation of texts: Propertius 2.24.1–2, 2.25.1–4; 3.1.17–18, 3.2.15–18, 3.3.19–21, 3.25.17. The reference to 'Cynthia' being read all over the Forum (2.24.2, *toto Cynthia lecta foro*) is puzzling: people could hardly read papyrus scrolls while walking about a crowded piazza. It may mean that the book was on display at more than one of the shops in the Forum porticos: cf. Cicero *Philippics* 2.21, Asconius 33C (Forum *librarii*); Horace *Epistles* 1.20.1–2 (Vertumnus and Janus); Horace *Satires* 1.4.71, *Ars poetica* 373 (books on columns).

Theatre and games: Propertius 2.16.33–4, 2.19.9–10, 2.22.3–10. Fourth collection: dated by the consulship of P. Cornelius Scipio, brother of Cornelia (4.11.65–6). 'Cynthia's' ghost: Propertius 4.7.

Asisium theatre: *Supplementa Italica* 23 (2007) 369–71, nos. 24–5. Augustan theatres: Sear 2006.12–14; Sear's catalogue gives an Augustan date for more than forty Italian theatres and more than twenty in the provinces.

9.4. Ovid and Virgil

Ovid *Tristia* 4.10.1–2:

> ille ego qui fuerim, tenerorum lusor Amorum,
> quem legis, ut nouis, accipe posteritas.

Birthplace and rank: Ovid *Tristia* 4.10.3–8; cf. *Amores* 2.1.1, 2.16.1–10, 3.15.3–14, *Fasti* 4.79–82 and 685–6, *Tristia* 2.111–14, *Ex Ponto* 1.8.41–2, 4.8.17–19. Date: *Tristia* 4.10.5–6; cf. *Fasti* 4.627–8 and 673–6 for young Caesar.

Came out as verse: *Tristia* 4.10.25–6; cf. Seneca *Controuersiae* 2.2.8–12 for Ovid at the rhetorician's school.

Triumuir capitalis: *Tristia* 4.10.31–5, cf. Dio Cassius 54.26.5–6 on the 'vigintivirate' posts. For this period in Ovid's life see also *Fasti* 4.384 (*decemuir stlitibus iudicandis*), *Tristia* 2.93–6 (*iudex* for the centumviral court).

Ovid *Tristia* 4.10.41–60:

> temporis illius colui fouique poetas,
> quotque aderant uates rebar adesse deos.
> saepe suas uolucres legit mihi grandior aeuo
> quaeque nocet serpens, quae iuuat herba, Macer.
> saepe suos solitus recitare Propertius ignes
> iure sodalicii quo mihi iunctus erat.
> Ponticus heroo, Bassus quoque clarus iambis,

> *dulcia conuictus membra fuere mei.*
> *et tenuit nostras numerosus Horatius aures,*
>   *dum ferit Ausonia carmina culta lyra.*   50
> *Vergilium uidi tantum, nec auara Tibullo*
>   *tempus amicitiae fata dedere meae.*
> *successor fuit hic tibi, Galle, Propertius illi;*
>   *quartus ab his serie temporis ipse fui.*
> *utque ego maiores, sic me coluere minores,*   55
>   *notaque non tarde facta Thalia mea est.*
> *carmina cum primum populo iuuenalia legi,*
>   *barba resecta mihi bisue semelue fuit.*
> *mouerat ingenium totam cantata per urbem*
>   *nomine non uero dicta Corinna mihi.*   60

For Aemilius Macer (and a younger Macer, who wrote epic), see Hollis 2007.93–115, 424–5; for Ponticus and Bassus, see Hollis 2007.426, 421.

151 Fictive mistress: cf. *Amores* 2.17.29–30, on a woman who boasted she was Corinna ('What wouldn't she have given for it to be true?'). On everybody's lips: cf. *Amores* 3.1.17–18 and 21 (at dinner parties and on street corners all over town).

Thalea: e.g. *Anthologia Palatina* 9.504.10 (comedy and good morals), 9.505.7–8 (comedy, mime and bad morals); she is Ovid's Muse also at *Ars amatoria* 1.264. For the common ground of love-elegy and mime, see McKeown 1979.

Nequitia: Propertius 1.6.26, 2.24.6, Ovid *Amores* 2.1.2, 3.1.17 (poet); Propertius 1.15.38, 2.5.2, 3.10.24 (Cynthia); Propertius 3.19.10, Ovid *Amores* 3.4.10, 3.11.37, *Heroides* 4.17 (amorous women); Propertius 2.6.30, Ovid *Ars amatoria* 2.392, *Heroides* 17.29 (amorous men); Ovid *Fasti* 1.414 (lecherous Silenus).

Her territory (i.e. stage-games): Ovid *Tristia* 2.279–80 (*ludi quoque semina praebent | nequitiae*). Strict ladies warned off: *Amores* 2.1.4 (*non estis teneris apta theatra meis*).

Virgil and Tibullus: Domitius Marsus fr. 7 (Hollis 2007.304); cf. Ovid *Amores* 1.15.25–8, 3.9. Date of Virgil's death: Donatus *Vita Vergili* 35.

Master-copy: Donatus *Vita Vergili* 34 (*uolumina* in the care of Virgil's freedman copyist, Eros). Greater than the *Iliad*: Propertius 2.34.66.

Augustus' letter: Donatus *Vita Vergili* 31 (*ut sibi de Aeneide, ut ipsius uerba sunt, uel prima carminis ὑπογραφή uel quodlibet κῶλον mitteretur*).

Syria: Augustus *Res gestae* 11, Dio Cassius 54.6.1. Samos: Dio Cassius 54.7.4 (21–20 BC), 54.11.7 (20–19). Pythagoras as 'the Samian': e.g. Ovid *Fasti* 3.153, *Metamorphoses* 15.60, *Tristia* 3.3.62; Virgil's Pythagoreanism is implicit in *Aeneid* 6.724–51.

Wish to burn the text: Donatus *Vita Vergili* 37–41, Probus *Vita Vergili*.

Donatus *Vita Vergili* 38 (attributed to 'Sulpicius Carthaginiensis'):

> *iusserat haec rapidis aboleri carmina flammis*
>   *Vergilius Phrygium quae cecinere ducem.*
> *Tucca uetat Variusque simul; tu, maxime Caesar,*
>   *non sinis et Latiae consulis historiae.*

Probus attributes the same poem to 'Servius Varus'.

Origins of Rome: Virgil *Aeneid* 1.6–7 ('whence the Latin race, the Alban fathers and the walls of lofty Rome'), 1.33, 1.257–79, 6.777–90, 7.601–10, 8.626–38, 12.166, 12.821–7.

9.5. Augustus and the 'Secular Games'

Not robust: details in Suetonius *Diuus Augustus* 81–2; cf. 33.1 and 72.2 for casual references to his poor health. Recurring illness: especially just before his birthday, 23 September (Suetonius *Diuus Augustus* 5.1, 81.2). Specific bouts of illness are attested in 46 BC (Nicolaus of Damascus *FGrH* 90 F127.19–21); 42 BC (Velleius Paterculus 2.70.1, Valerius Maximus 1.7.1 etc); 29 BC (Dio Cassius 51.22.9, Suetonius *Diuus Augustua* 43.5); 28 BC (Dio Cassius 53.1.6); 27 BC (*Fasti feriarum Latinarum*, Degrassi 1947.150); 25 BC (Dio Cassius 53.25.7); 24 BC (*Fasti feriarum Latinarum*, Degrassi 1947.150).

Four years earlier (23 BC): Suetonius *Diuus Augustus* 28.1, 59.1, 81.1; Dio Cassius 53.30.1–2.

Two of them conspired (Fannius Caepio and Varro Murena, 22 BC): Strabo 14.4.5 C670, Velleius Paterculus 2.91.2; Suetonius *Diuus Augustus* 19.1, *Tiberius* 8; Tacitus *Annals* 1.10.4, Dio Cassius 54.3.3–4.

Trial: Suetonius *Tiberius* 8 (prosecution of Caepio *apud iudices*). Floods and plague: Dio Cassius 53.33.5, 54.1.1. Food shortage: Augustus *Res gestae* 5.2, Dio Cassius 54.1.2.

People's protector: Tacitus *Annals* 1.2.1 (*ad tuendam plebem*). Powers of the tribunes (Lacey 1996.100–16): Augustus *Res gestae* 10.1; Dio Cassius 51.19.6 (30 BC, limited to first milestone), 53.32.5 (23 BC). The removal of the geographical limit, nowhere explicitly attested, is implied by the empire-wide use of *trib(unicia) pot-(estate)* as part of Augustus' titulature on inscriptions and coins; for an early example, see the bronze coinage minted by Publius Carisius, Augustus' legate in Further Spain in 23–22 BC (Sutherland 1984.41–2, cf. Dio Cassius 54.5.1–2 for the date).

A mile beyond: Livy 3.20.7; cf. Dio Cassius 8.87.6, Appian *Civil Wars* 2.31.123 (simplified to 'the city walls').

Demand for dictatorship: Augustus *Res gestae* 5.1 and 3 (22 BC), Velleius Paterculus 2.89.5, Suetonius *Diuus Augustus* 52, Dio Cassius 54.1.4. Food supply (*curatio annonae*): Augustus *Res gestae* 5.2; Dio Cassius 54.1.3.

Augustus *Res gestae* 11–12.1:

> aram Fortunae Reducis ante aedes Honoris et Virtutis ad portam Capenam pro reditu meo senatus consecrauit, in qua pontifices et uirgines Vestales anniuersarium sacrificium facere iussit eo die quo consulibus Q. Lucretio et M. Vinicio in urbem ex Syria redieram, et diem Augustalia ex cognomine nostro appellauit. ex senatus auctoritate pars praetorum et tribunorum plebis cum consule Q. Lucretio et principibus uiris obuiam mihi missa est in Campaniam, qui honos ad hoc tempus nemini praeter me est decretus.

For Fortuna Redux see also Degrassi 1963.194–5 (*Fasti Amiternini*), 279 (*Feriale Cumanum*); Sutherland 1984.45, nos. 53–6; Dio Cassius 54.10.3.

Tomb of Virgil: Donatus *Vita Vergili* 36 (before the second milestone on the road to Puteoli); cf. Statius *Siluae* 4.4.51–5, Pliny *Letters* 3.7.8.

Standard modern account: Beard, North, and Price 1998.1.6.

153 Looking after the public interest: as stated by Augustus when challenged by a resentful aristocrat in 22 BC (Dio Cassius 54.3.3, where τὸ δημόσιον evidently translates *res publica*); cf. Horace *Odes* 4.15.17 (*custode rerum Caesare*), with Griffin 2002.326–7.

In 23 BC Augustus had been granted proconsular *imperium* for life, which explicitly outranked that of other proconsuls and would not lapse as theirs did when he entered the city (Dio Cassius 53.32.5); in 19 BC he was granted 'the power of the consuls for life, to the extent of using the twelve *fasces* always and everywhere and sitting on a magisterial chair between the consuls at any time' (Dio Cassius 54.10.5, trans. Crook 1996.92).

'State of the republic': Augustus, quoted in Suetonius *Diuus Augustus* 28.2 (*ut optimi status auctor dicar*) and Aulus Gellius 15.7 (*in statu rei publicae felicissimo*); *SC de Cn. Pisone patre* 13–14 (*tranquillitas praesentis status r.p.*); Velleius Paterculus 2.91.2 (*hunc felicissimum statum*); Suetonius *Diuus Augustus* 28.2 (*ne quem noui status paeniteret*); Tacitus *Annals* 1.4.1 (*uerso ciuitatis statu*), 4.33.2 (*conuerso statu*).

Ludi saeculares: excellent summaries in Beard, North, and Price 1998.1.201–6, Malloch 2013.176–8 and 181–2. The Sibyl's instructions are reported in Phlegon of Tralles *FGrH* 257 F 37.5.4 (reprinted in Thomas 2011.277–8); the preliminary decrees of the Senate and edicts of the *XVuiri* are in *CIL* 6.32323.1–89; the record of the actual proceedings is in *CIL* 6.32323.90–152 = *ILS* 5050 (reprinted in Thomas 2011.274–6, translation in Beard, North, and Price 1998.2.140–4); the hymn is Horace *Carmen saeculare*, the subject also of *Odes* 4.6.29–44.

Saeculum: Censorinus *De die natali* 17.5–14. Portentous events: Varro fr. 70 Funaioli (Censorinus *De die natali* 17.8).

Books in Apollo's temple: Tibullus 2.5.1–18 (before 19 BC), cf. Virgil *Aeneid* 6.71–4; Suetonius (*Diuus Augustus* 31.1) was evidently mistaken in dating the transfer of the books to Apollo after 12 BC.

Augustus presiding: Augustus *Res gestae* 22.2 (*pro conlegio XVuirorum magister conlegii*).

Phlegon *FGrH* 257 F 37.5.4, lines 1–7:

ἀλλ' ὁπότ' ἂν μήκιστος ἴῃ χρόνος ἀνθρώποισιν
ζωῆς, εἰς ἐτέων ἑκατὸν δέκα κύκλον ὁδεύσας,
μεμνῆσθαι, Ῥωμαῖε, καὶ εἰ μάλα λήσει ἑαυτόν,
μεμνῆσθαι τάδε πάντα, θεοῖσι μὲν ἀθανάτοισι
ῥέζειν ἐν πεδίῳ παρὰ Θύβριδος ἄπλετον ὕδωρ,
ὅππῃ στεινότατον, νὺξ ἡνίκα γαῖαν ἐπέλθῃ
ἠελίου κρύψαντος ἑὸν φάος·

Instructions: lines 7–9 (*Moirai*), 9–10 (*Eileithyiai*), 10–11 (*Gaia*), 12–16 (Zeus and Hera), 16–18 (Apollo, ὅστε καὶ Ἥλιος κικλήσκεται), 18–22 (boys' and girls' choirs), 23–5 (matrons), 25–6 purification, 27–33 (offerings to δαίμοσι μειλιχίοισιν).

Phlegon *FGrH* 257 F 37.5.4, lines 33–5:

> ἤμασι δ' ἔστω
> νυξί τ' ἐπασσυτέρῃσι θεοπρέπτους κατὰ θώκους
> παμπληθὴς ἄγυρις· σπουδῇ δὲ γέλωτι μεμίχθω.

31 May–3 June: *CIL* 6.32323.90–154, esp. 91 (*Achiuo ritu*), 100–1 (*in scaena quoi theatrum adiectum non fuit, nullis positis sedilibus*), 108 (*in theatro ligneo quod erat constitutum in Campo secundum Tiberim*), 149 (*carmen composuit Q. Horatius Flaccus*), 153–4 (*ubi sacrificium erat factum superioribus noctibus et theatrum positum et scaena*).

Edict (*CIL* 6.32323.156–8):

> ludos, quos honorarios dierum VII adiecimus ludis sollemnibus, committemus Nonis Iun. Latinos in theatro ligneo quod est ad Tiberim h. II, Graecos thymelicos in theatro Pompei h. III, Graecos asticos in theatro quod est in circo Flaminio h. IIII.

Altar of Dionysus: e.g. Pratinas (*c*.500 BC) in Athenaeus 14.617b–c (ἐπὶ Διονυσιάδα ... θυμέλην). *Orchēstra* as opposed to stage: e.g. Simias (probably third century BC) in *Anthologia Palatina* 7.21.3; Gow and Page 1965.2.514.

Vitruvius 5.7.2:

> ...ampliorem habent orchestram Graeci et scaenam recessiorem minoreque latitudine pulpitum, quod logeion appellant, ideo quod apud eos tragici et comici actores in scaena peragunt, reliqui autem artifices suas per orchestram praestant actiones; itaque ex eo scaenici et thymelici Graece separatim nominantur.

City Dionysia: e.g. Thucydides 5.20.1 (ἐκ Διονυσίων εὐθὺς τῶν ἀστικῶν). Tragedy and comedy: e.g. Aristotle *Poetics* 1449a2–b9; 'satyr-play' had been part of the tragic competition (details in Seaford 1984.16–26), as was well understood in Rome (Horace *Ars poetica* 220–33).

Theatre of Marcellus (Ciancio Rossetto 1999, Sear 2006.61–5): Dio Cassius 43.49.2–3, 53.30.5 (Caesar); Augustus *Res gestae* 21.1, Dio Cassius 53.30.5 (Marcellus); Pliny *Natural History* 8.65, Suetonius *Diuus Augustus* 43.5 (dedication and games, 4 May 11 BC, immediately after the *ludi Florales*); games were held there also in 13 BC, wrongly assumed by Dio Cassius (54.26.1) to be the dedication.

The theatre presumably replaced the *theatrum et proscaenium ad Apollinis* set up by the censors of 179 BC (Livy 40.51.3); it had nothing to do with the theatre Caesar planned to build up against the *mons Tarpeius* (Suetonius *Diuus Iulius* 44.1), which is often mentioned in this context by modern authors but was evidently a quite different project.

Pylades and Bathyllus: Seneca *Controuersiae* 3.pref.10 and 16, Suetonius *Diuus Augustus* 44.4, Plutarch *Moralia* 711f, Athenaeus 1.20d–e, Dio Cassius 54.17.4–5 (18 BC), Jerome *Chronica* Ol. 189.3 (22–21 BC), Macrobius *Saturnalia* 2.7.12–19.

Pantomimus: Lucian *Saltatio* 34 (Augustus' time); Lada-Richards 2007, Hall and Wyles 2008.

Pylades to Augustus: Dio Cassius 54.17.5 (συμφέρει σοι, Καῖσαρ, περὶ ἡμᾶς τὸν δῆμον ἀποδιατρίβεσθαι); cf. Macrobius *Saturnalia* 2.7.19 for a slightly different version.

Their art Greek: cf. *Inschriften von Priene* 113.65 (Hall and Wyles 2008.380–1) for the earliest attestation of παντόμιμος, c.80 BC. Greek mythology: Lucian *Saltatio* 37–61; Pylades' roles were tragic and heroic, Bathyllus' satyric and pastoral (Seneca *Controuersiae* 3.pref.10, Persius 5.123, Plutarch *Moralia* 711f, Athenaeus 1.20.d–e).

Hecklers: Macrobius *Saturnalia* 2.7.16 (μωροί, μαινόμενον ὀρχοῦμαι).

Extravagant spectacle: Phaedrus 5.7.4–9 (one of Bathyllus' musicians on the crane), Manilius 5.484 (*chorus*), Lucian *Saltatio* 68 (musicians, actor, singers).

Livy on *ludi scaenici*: 7.2.13 (*hanc uix opulentis regnis tolerabilem insaniam*); fr. 56, in Censorinus *De die natali* 17.9 (*ludos saeculares Caesar ingenti apparatu fecit*).

156 Strabo 1.2.8 C20:

αὕτη μὲν οὖν πρὸς ὀλίγους, ἡ δὲ ποιητικὴ δημωφελεστέρα καὶ θέατρα πληροῦν δυναμένη· ἡ δὲ δὴ τοῦ Ὁμήρου ὑπερβαλλόντως.

Now ready: Jerome *Chronica* Ol. 190.4, recording Varius' and Tucca's editing of the *Aeneid* under 17–16 BC.

The Sibyl and Elysium: Virgil *Aeneid* 5.733–6, 6.538–43, 6.666–78.

Virgil *Aeneid* 6.788–84:

> *huc geminas nunc flecte acies, hanc aspice gentem*
> *Romanosque tuos. hic Caesar et omnis Iuli*
> *progenies magnum caeli uentura sub axem.*
> *hic uir, hic est, tibi quem promitti saepius audis,*
> *Augustus Caesar, diui genus, aurea condet*
> *saecula qui rursus Latio regnata per arua*
> *Saturno quondam* . . .

9.6. Horace and Ovid

The People's choice: as demonstrated at the consular elections when he was no longer a candidate (Dio Cassius 54.6.1–3, 54.10.1–2). Learned to live with it: Syme 1986, esp. 50–63 on the consuls of 16–7 BC (with commentary at Wiseman 1998.139–46).

Aristocratic friendships: Horace *Odes* 4.1.9–20 (Paullus Fabius Maximus, consul 11 BC), 4.2 (Iullus Antonius, consul 10 BC), 4.7.23 (Manlius Torquatus), 4.8.2 (C. Marcius Censorinus, consul 8 BC), 4.9.30–44 (M. Lollius, consul 21 BC); *Ars poetica* 6, 235 (Calpurnii Pisones).

Horace *Odes* 4.3.13–16:

> *Romae principis urbium*
> *dignatur suboles inter amabiles*

> uatum ponere me choros,
> et iam dente minus mordeor inuido.

Themes that appealed: Horace *Odes* 4.4 and 4.15 (campaigns of Drusus and Tiberius, 15 BC), 4.5 (prayer for Augustus' return, *c*.14 BC), 4.6 (hymn to Apollo). Last of the *Odes*: Griffin 2002, Miller 2009.307–10.

Horace *Odes* 4.15.1–4:

> *Phoebus uolentem proelia me loqui*
> *uictas et urbes increpuit lyra,*
> > *ne parua Tyrrhenum per aequor*
> > *uela darem.*

Cf. Virgil *Aeneid* 1.67 for *Tyrrhenum aequor*.

Palatine piazza (Ch. 8.7 above): Josephus *Jewish Antiquities* 19.223, with Wiseman 2012.378–9, 2013.253–4.

Horace *Odes* 4.15.4–8:

> *tua, Caesar, aetas*
> *fruges et agris rettulit uberes*
> *et signa nostro resitituit Ioui*
> > *derepta Parthorum superbis*
> > *postibus...*

Cf. Virgil *Aeneid* 8.721–2 for *superbis | postibus*.

Apollo's laurel: Ovid *Metamorphoses* 1.562–3. Fame and majesty: *Odes* 4.15.14–15, cf. Virgil *Aeneid* 1.281 ('I have given them *imperium* without limit').

Horace *Odes* 4.15.17–20:

> *custode rerum Caesare non furor*
> *ciuilis aut uis exiget otium,*
> > *non ira, quae procudit enses*
> > *et miseras inimicat urbes.*

China (*Seres*): *Odes* 4.15.23; cf. Virgil *Georgics* 2.121. Julian edicts: *Odes* 4.15.22; for Augustus' *edicta* see Suetonius *Diuus Augustus* 25.1, 28.2, 31.5, 42.2, 53.1, 56.1, 89.2; Ovid *Tristia* 2.135 and 5.2.58, Frontinus *De aquis* 99.3, Pliny *Letters* 10.65.3 and 79.2, Censorinus *De die natali* 17.9, Paulus in *Digest* 48.18.8, Hyginus in Campbell 2000.86.25, Macrobius *Saturnalia* 1.10.23.

Horace *Odes* 4.15.25–32:

> *nosque et profestis lucibus et sacris*
> *inter iocosi munera Liberi*
> > *cum prole matronisque nostris*
> > *rite deos prius apprecati*
> *uirtute functos more patrum duces*
> *Lydis remixto carmine tibiis*
> > *Troiamque et Anchisen et almae*
> > *progeniem Veneris canemus.*

The reference to 'our wives and children' from Horace the well-known bachelor (*Odes* 3.8.1) is paradoxical only to readers who forget that this was a public performance. Propaganda and cliché: Thomas 2011.260.

Golden Rome: Ovid *Ars amatoria* 3.113 (*nunc aurea Roma est*).

Ovid *Ars amatoria* 3.121–2:

> *prisca iuuent alios, ego me nunc denique natum*
> *gratulor: haec aetas moribus apta meis.*

Augustus' *saeculum*: Porcius Latro in Seneca *Controuersiae* 2.7.7 (*o nos nimium felici et aureo, quod aiunt, saeculo natos!*), Ovid *Tristia* 1.2.103 (*hoc duce...felicia saecula*); Cestius Pius in Seneca *Controuersiae* 3.7 (*qui hoc saeculum amatoriis non artibus solum sed sententiis impleuit*).

Aristocratic friends: Ovid *Tristia* 4.4.27–32, *Ex Ponto* 1.7.27–30, 2.2.97, 2.3.73–8 (Messalla Corvinus); *Ex Ponto* 1.2.129–36 (Paullus Fabius Maximus).

Addressed to individuals (Syme 1978.72–5): *Amores* 1.9.2 (Atticus), 2.10.1 (Graecinus), 2.18.1 (Macer). 'The *Amores* enlist no persons of high rank as patrons or protectors' (Syme 1978.76).

Read to the People: *Tristia* 4.10.57. Games of Ceres: *Amores* 3.10.1 and 47–8; cf. *Medicamina faciei femineae* 3–4 (the reference to Ceres' gifts appropriate to the occasion?), *Amores* 3.2.45 (Circus games of Victoria, 27–30 July?).

Performance: *Amores* 1.8.23–108 (Dipsas speech), 3.1.15–60 (Tragedy and Elegy speeches), 3.5 (dialogue of poet and dream-interpreter), 3.6.53–66 (Anio speech). Nymphs: *Amores* 2.11.33–40, 3.6.61–4. Danced for the People: Ovid *Tristia* 2.519, cf. 5.7.25 (danced *pleno theatro*).

Internal references: Ovid *Heroides* 3.1–4, 4.3–6, 4.10–14, 4.175–6, 5.1–2, 7.183–4, 10.3, 10.140, 11.1–4, 14.131–2, 15.1–4, 15.97–8.

Ovid *Heroides* 7.1–4:

> *sic ubi fata uocant udis abiectus in herbis*
> *ad uada Maeandri concinit albus olor.*
> *nec quia te nostra sperem prece posse moueri*
> *alloquor (aduerso mouimus ista deo)...*

Resolved to leave: *Heroides* 7.7 (*certus es ire*), cf. Virgil *Aeneid* 4.554 (*certus eundi*). Aeneas' sword: Virgil *Aeneid* 4.495, 4.507, 4.646–7; Ovid *Amores* 2.18.25, *Ars amatoria* 3.39–40, *Fasti* 3.549.

Ovid *Heroides* 7.183–4:

> *aspicias utinam quae sit scribentis imago!*
> *scribimus, et gremio Troicus ensis adest.*

Elsewhere: *Amores* 2.18.25–6 (*quodque tenens strictum Dido miserabilis ensem | dicat*). Actress (perhaps with a danced accompaniment): see Cunningham 1949 for the *Heroides* as 'lyric-dramatic monologues to be presented on the stage with music and dancing' (cf. *Ars amatoria* 3.341–6).

Second-person plural: e.g. *Ars amatoria* 1.267, 2.739, 3.6 (*uiri*); 2.537, 2.667 (*iuuenes*); 1.459, 2.733 (*iuuentus*); 1.617, 2.745, 3.57, 3.417, 3.479, 3.547, 3.811 (*puellae*); unspecified second-person plural addressees at 1.640–5, 2.1, 2.173–4, 2.593–6, 2.641, and *passim* in book 3.

Collective address: *Ars amatoria* 2.536 (*uulgus*), 3.811 (*mea turba*). Both together: *Remedia amoris* 41 (*iuuenes*), 49 (*puellae*), 69 (*homines*, gender-neutral), 608 (*uir, puella*), 814 (*femina uirque*).

Ovid *Remedia amoris* 361–4, 389–90:

> *nuper enim nostros quidam carpsere libellos,*
>   *quorum censura Musa proterua mea est.*
> *dummodo sic placeam, dum toto canter in orbe,*
>   *qui uolet impugnent unus et alter opus.* . . .
> *rumpere, liuor edax: magnum mihi nomen habemus;*
>   *maius erit* . . .

Sung throughout the world: cf. *Amores* 1.3.25 (*per totum orbem*), 1.15.8 (*in toto orbe*); *Tristia* 2.118 (fame *toto ab orbe*).

Date: *Remedia amoris* 155–8, with Henderson 1979.xi–xii. Augustus' daughter (2 BC): Velleius Paterculus 2.100.3; Seneca *De beneficiis* 6.32.1, *De breuitate uitae* 4.6; Pliny *Natural History* 7.149, 21.9; Tacitus *Annals* 1.53.1, 3.24.2, 4.44.3, 6.51.2; Dio Cassius 55.10.12–16.

Horace, died 8 BC: [Suetonius] *Vita Horati*, Jerome *Chron.* Ol. 192.4. Maecenas, died 8 BC: Dio Cassius 55.7.1. Agrippa, died 12 BC: Dio Cassius 54.28.3. Popular demonstrations: Suetonius *Diuus Augustus* 65.3, Dio Cassius 55.13.1 (AD 3).

9.7. Ovid's *Fasti*

Theatres (Sear 2006.57–67, 133–7): Augustus *Res gestae* 20.1 (Pompey's), Dio Cassius 54.25.2 (Balbus'), Pliny *Natural History* 8.65 (Marcellus').

Regionary catalogues (*Notitia* and *Curiosum*): Richter 1901 373 for a composite text. Augustan data: Coarelli 2012.114–5. The modern consensus, assuming that the catalogues' figures represent linear feet of seating space, would reduce the capacities to 7,700, 11,000, and 13,000–14,000 respectively (Coleman 2000.221–4).

Triumphantly popular: Ovid *Metamorphoses* 15.877–8 ('wherever Roman power extends over conquered lands, I shall be read on the lips of the people'). World of stories: *Metamorphoses* 1.3–4 (*primaque ab origine mundi* | *ad mea perpetuum* . . . *tempora carmen*).

Recent scholarship: e.g. Galinsky 1996.265–6, Lada-Richards 2013 (*pantomimus*); Curley 2013.95–216 (tragedy). However, modern treatment of 'audience and performance' in *Metamorphoses* (e.g. Wheeler 1999) is primarily concerned with 'fictive', 'implied', or 'narratorial' audiences, and takes for granted a 'shift from oral culture to book culture in the Hellenistic age' (Wheeler 1999.58, but see Ch. 1.4 above). For a different approach, see Wiseman 2008.210–30, esp. 220 (on *Metamorphoses* 14.320–434) and 221–2 (on 11.221–65).

Nymphs and Nereids: e.g. *Metamorphoses* 1.576 (listening to Peneus), 1.690–1 (companions of Syrinx), 3.505–7 (weeping for Narcissus), 8.571–2 (serving in Achelous' palace), 10.8–9 (companions of Eurydice), 13.736–7 (companions of Scylla), 14.264 (serving in Circe's palace), 14.326–8 (yearning for Picus), 14.623–4 (companions of Pomona), 15.490–1 (companions of Egeria).

Cf. *Ex Ponto* 4.16.35, on Ovid's contemporary Fontanus, who 'sang of the loves of nymphs and satyrs'—perhaps as dance libretti?

Without clothes: e.g. *Metamorphoses* 2.459, 3.178–92 (Diana and her nymphs), 4.356–7 (Salmacis), 5.601–3 (Arethusa), 10.578 (Atalanta), 11.237 (Thetis), 13.901 (Scylla).

160 Reader: Ovid *Fasti* 1.10 (*legendus*), 1.20 (*legenda*), 3.791 (*pagina*). Second-person singular addressee: *Fasti* 1.315, 1.317, 2.151, 2.405, 2.419, 3.878, 4.677, 5.376, 5.389, 5.493–4, 6.539, 6.649. As pupil: 1.45, 1.49, 1.632, 2.47, 2.246, 2.284, 2.381, 2.453, 2.514, 2.542, 2.583–4, 3.135–6, 3.435–6, 3.765, 3.795, 4.63, 4.418, 5.449, 5.489, 6.104, 6.170, 6.212, 6.283, 6.291–2. As witness: 1.75, 1.591, 1.631, 2.79, 2.154, 2.202, 2.391, 2.472, 3.87, 3.116, 3.406, 3.450, 3.459, 3.519, 3.837, 3.851, 5.486, 5.599, 5.732, 6.261.

Second-person plural addressees: *Fasti* 3.370 (*credite dicenti*), 5.1 (*quaeritis*), 5.347 (*mihi credite*), 6.551 (*quaeritis*); the only other example is at 6.195. For an analogy, see Ovid's contemporary Grattius (mentioned at *Ex Ponto* 4.16.34), whose poem on hunting with dogs is consistently addressed to a single addressee; on two occasions, however (Grattius 56 *reponite*, 125 *relinquite*), the second-person plural presupposes an audience.

Occasions for instruction: e.g. Plato *Laws* 10.887d, Pausanias 1.3.3; Varro *De lingua Latina* 6.18 (*ludi Apollinares*); Dionysius of Halicarnassus *Roman Antiquities* 1.31.2, 1.79.10, 8.62.3 (hymns, cf. Wiseman 2008.237).

Ovid *Fasti* 4.187–90:

> *scaena sonat ludique uocant. spectate, Quirites,*
> *et fora Marte suo litigiosa uacent.*
> *quaerere multa libet, sed me sonus aeris acuti*
> *terret et horrendo lotos adunca sono.*

Ovid *Fasti* 5.183,190:

> *mater ades florum ludis celebranda iocosis . . .*
> *hoc quoque cum Circi munere carmen eat.*

Cult site: Tacitus *Annals* 2.49.1; cf. Cicero *In Verrem* 2.4.106 and 2.5.187 for Libera as Proserpina.

Prompted story: Ovid *Fasti* 4.417 (*exigit ipse locus raptus ut uirginis edam*); *pace* Fantham 1998.174, there is no need to suppose that 'the poet presents his theme in self-conscious metaliterary form, *like* a formal religious narrative' (my emphasis), or to take the phrase as meaning merely 'required by the occasion'.

Ovid's interlocutors: *Fasti* 4.195–372 (Erato), 5.193–376 (Flora), 5.9–108 (Polyhymnia, Urania, Calliope), 6.19–88 (Juno, Iuuentas); cf. Degrassi 1963.58 (*Fasti Venusini*) for the sacrifice to Juno. The same argument applies to the speeches of Carmentis on 11 January (*Fasti* 1.480–536), Mars on 1 March (3.172–252), the shepherd on 21 April (4.747–76), Remus on 9 May (5.459–74), and Mars and Jupiter on 9 June (6.353–84).

Relationship with stage: Ovid *Fasti* 4.326 (*scaena testificata loquar*); cf. Wiseman 1998.25–34 (on *Fasti* 6.569–636), 48–51 (on 6.483–550), 72–4 (on 3.657–96); 2008.162–5 (on 3.259–392), 222–30 (on 3.459–516, 5.183–378).

Sequel: *Fasti* 3.473 alludes to Catullus 64.132–5, and 3.475 is a verbatim quotation of 64.143.

Ovid *Fasti* 3.471–3:

> *en iterum, fluctus, similis audite querellas!*
> *en iterum lacrimas accipe, harena, meas!*
> *dicebam, memini, 'periure et perfide Theseu'* ...

Also 3.480: *quid me* ... *seruabas* for 'why did you save me?'

Other Ovidian quotations: e.g. Mars at *Fasti* 2.488 and *Metamorphoses* 14.815 (*dixisti*), quoting Jupiter in Ennius *Annales* 54–5 Sk.

Dwindling asset: cf. *Tristia* 5.7.25–8 (AD 12), where Ovid makes the clearly false excuse 'I've never done anything for theatres'.

Fortune: Suetonius *Diuus Augustus* 65.1 (*Fortuna destituit*); cf. Seneca *De breuitate uitae* 4.1–4, Pliny *Natural History* 7.149. Heirs: Velleius Paterculus 2.102.3, Tacitus *Annals* 1.3.2–3. Adoption: Velleius Paterculus 2.103.1–3; Suetonius *Diuus Augustus* 65.1, *Tiberius* 15.2 (cf. 23 on *atrox Fortuna*).

Disliked by the People: Tacitus *Annals* 6.51.1, Suetonius *Tiberius* 21.2, 72.2, 75.1; for his arrogance, see Tacitus *Annals* 1.4.3 and 1.10.7, Suetonius *Tiberius* 68.3.

Popular pleasures: Tacitus *Annals* 1.54.2, 1.76.4, 4.62.2. Outrageous behaviour: Velleius Paterculus 2.126.2 (*theatralis seditio*); Tacitus *Annals* 1.77, 4.14.3, Suetonius *Tiberius* 37.2; Dio Cassius 56.47.2, 57.21.3.

Toxic question: the best account is still Levick 1976.47–67. Military crisis (Pannonian revolt, AD 6): Velleius Paterculus 2.110–14, Dio Cassius 55.29–32 and 34.7. Flood, fire, and famine (AD 5–8): Dio Cassius 55.22.3, 55.26.1–27.1, 55.31.3–4, 55.33.4.

Something stupid: Ovid refers to his *stultitia* at *Tristia* 1.2.100, 3.6.35; *Ex Ponto* 1.6.20, 1.7.44. The best discussions of Ovid's exile are Syme 1978.215–29 and Green 1982.44–59.

Prominent people: implied at *Tristia* 3.4.4. Too sensitive: *Tristia* 1.5.51–2, 2.207–8, 3.6.27–32, 4.10.99–100; *Ex Ponto* 1.6.21–4. Angry (*Caesaris ira*): *Tristia* 1.2.3, 1.2.61, 1.3.85, 2.124, 3.8.39, 3.11.17–18, 3.11.72, 3.13.11, 5.1.41; *Ex Ponto* 1.4.29, 1.9.28, 1.10.20, 2.2.19, 2.5.11, 2.7.55, 3.3.83, 3.6.7, 3.7.39, 3.9.27.

Added to the charge: *Tristia* 2.207 (*duo crimina*). No jury or Senate: *Tristia* 2.131–2. Edict: *Tristia* 2.133–8, 5.2.55–8.

No restrictions: *Ex Ponto* 3.6.11–12.

Ovid *Ex Ponto* 4.2.31–8:

162
> siue quod hinc fructus adeo non cepimus ullos
>   principium nostri res sit ut ista mihi,
> siue quod in tenebris numerosos ponere gestus
>   quodque legas nulli scribere carmen idem est.
> excitat auditor studium, laudataque uirtus
>   crescit, et immensum gloria calcar habet.
> hic mea cui recitem nisi flauis scripta Corallis
>   quasque alias gentes barbarus Ister habet?

For the Coralli (Syme 1978.165–6), see *Ex Ponto* 4.8.83, Strabo 7.5.12 (C318), Valerius Flaccus 6.88–94, Appian *Mithridatica* 69.293.

What Augustus wanted: cf. Finley 1983.55 on 'one implication of an oral culture: remove a man physically from the state and he has no lines of communication with the citizenry' (his example was Athenian 'ostracism').

10. UNDER THE EMPERORS

163 'Three theatres': Ovid *Ars amatoria* 3.394 (*terna theatra*), Strabo 5.3.8 C236 (θέατρα τρία), Suetonius *Diuus Augustus* 45.4 (*trina theatra*); *Fasti Ostienses* AD 112 (Degrassi 1947.201: *theatris tribus*). Praetorian Guard: Tacitus *Annals* 1.77.1 (AD 15), 13.24.1, 13.25.4; cf. Valerius Maximus 2.4.1 for the theatres as *urbana castra*.

Ovid and the People: *Tristia* 1.1.17–24, 2.87–8.

Transfer of authority: Tacitus *Annals* 1.4–13.

10.1. First-Century Poets

164 Astronomical poet: for the dates, see Manilius 1.898–903 (defeat of Varus *terminus post quem*), 2.509 (Augustus still alive). Sequence of poets: Manilius 2.1–48 (Homer, Hesiod, Aratus, Theocritus etc). All subjects dealt with: 2.49–52. Crowd: 2.52 (*turbamque ad nota ruentem*).

Manilius 2.136–8 (trans. Volk 2002.203–4):

> haec ego diuino cupiam cum ad sidera flatu
> ferre, nec in turba nec turbae carmina condam,
> sed solus, uacuo ueluti uectatus in orbe.

Great predecessor: Lucretius 1.926–30 = 4.1–5; cf. Manilius 2.49–56.

Smallest crowd: Manilius 2.144 (*minima est quae turba per orbem*). Majority: 2.145–8; for *dulcemque per aures | adfectum* (2.147–8), cf. Ovid *Metamorphoses* 5.308–9, where the Muses are accused of deceiving the crowd with mere entertainment (*indoctum uana dulcedine uulgus | fallere*).

Untrodden paths: *Aetna* 8 (*per insolitum... itur*), 24 (*ignotas molimur... curas*); the poem is dated before AD 79 by the absence of any reference to Vesuvius. Deception, base, impious: *Aetna* 29 (*fallacia uatum*), 40 (*turpe... carmen*), 42 (*impia... fabula*).

Aetna 74–9, 91–2:

> haec est mendosae uulgata licentia famae.
> uatibus ingenium est: hinc audit nobile carmen.
> plurima pars scaenae rerum est fallacia. uates
> sub terris nigros uiderunt carmine manes
> atque inter cineres Ditis pallentia regna;
> mentiti uates Stygias undasque canesque...
> debita carminibus libertas ista, sed omnis
> in uero mihi cura.

Cf. Goodyear 1965.118, who damned line 76 as spurious on the grounds that 'so abrupt and direct a reference to the stage is inappropriate, since it is clear that the author is not thinking primarily of dramatic poetry'—a remarkable example of the power of preconception.

Tacitus *Annals* 11.13.1 (trans. Woodman 2004.201–2):

> at Claudius... munia censoria usurpans theatralem populi lasciuiam seueris edictis increpuit, quod in Publium Pomponium consularem (is carmina scaenae dabat) inque feminas inlustris probra iecerat.

Pomponius: Pliny *Natural History* 7.80, 14.56; Quintilian 10.1.98; Tacitus *Annals* 5.8.2, 12.27.2–28.2; Pliny *Letters* 3.5.3, 7.17.11; Manuwald 2001.243–8 for his play *Aeneas*.

Persius 1.13–17, 40–2, 63:

> scribimus inclusi, numeros ille, hic pede liber,
> grande aliquid quod pulmo animae praelargus anhelat.
> scilicet haec populo pexusque togaque recenti
> et natalicia tandem cum sardonyche albus
> sede leges celsa...
>   'rides' ait 'et nimis uncis
> naribus indulges. an erit qui uelle recuset
> os populi meruisse?'...
> 'quis populi sermo est?'

Juvenal 7.43–7:

> scit dare libertos extrema in parte sedentis
> ordinis et magnas comitum disponere uoces;
> nemo dabit regum quanti subsellia constant
> et quae conducto pendent anabathra tigillo
> quaeque reportandis posita est orchestra cathedris.

Rant: Juvenal 1.1 (*semper ego auditor tantum?*), 12–13 (*Frontonis platani conuolsaque marmora clamant | semper et adsiduo ruptae lectore columnae*); Ti. Catius Caesius Fronto was consul in AD 96 (Pliny *Letters* 2.11.3 and 8, 4.9.15, 6.13.2).

Statius: Hardie 1983.58–65 for his career.

Juvenal 7.82–7:

> *curritur ad uocem iucundam et carmen amicae*
> *Thebaidos, laetam cum fecit Statius urbem*
> *promisitque diem: tanta dulcedine captos*
> *adficit ille animos tantaque libidine uulgi*
> *auditur. sed cum fregit subsellia uersis,*
> *esurit intactam Paridi nisi uendit Agauen.*

Paris (executed AD 83): Martial 11.13, Juvenal 6.87, Suetonius *Domitian* 3 and 10.1, Dio Cassius 67.3.1.

Emperor's favour: e.g. *Siluae* 3.1.62, 4.2.5–17, 4.2.63–7.

Statius *Siluae* 5.2.160–3:

> *ei mihi! sed coetus solitos si forte ciebo*
> *et mea Romulei uenient ad carmina patres,*
> *tu deris, Crispine, mihi, cuneosque per omnis*
> *te meus absentem circumspectabit Achilles.*

Coetus in line 160 is Gronovius' emendation for *questus* in the MSS.

Pretentious amateurs: Juvenal 3.9 for 'poets reciting in the month of August' (not at the *ludi scaenici*, therefore) as one of the horrors of urban life.

10.2. First-Century Playwrights

Pomponius (Cichorius 1922.423–32): Pliny *Epistles* 7.17.11, Quintilian 8.3.31. Seneca (Griffin 1976): Ulpian *Digest* 36.1.1.1 for his consulship.

'Recitation drama': Goldberg 2000.225 (cf. 226, 'the recitations of Senecan tragedy ... became an exercise by and for the definition of an educated elite'); the idea originated with Zwierlein 1966, is frequently accepted without argument (e.g. Curley 2013.36–7 and *passim*), but is rightly contested by Boyle 2008.xl–xlii.

Cultured elite: e.g. Ferri 2003.2–3 on the 'gentrification' of literature, 55 on 'a snobbish reluctance, on the part of the elite, to produce elaborate dramas ... and expose them to the whimsical reaction of the uneducated'. No evidence is offered for either notion.

Neutralizing evidence: Fitch 2000.7, who according to Ferri (2003.55 n. 137) 'somewhat overstates the case for performance'. Burden of proof: Wiseman 2008.201–2.

Curiatius Maternus (Manuwald 2001.78–86): Tacitus *Dialogus* 11.4 (senator), 17.3 (date).

Usual procedure: e.g. Horace *Ars poetica* 386–9 and 419–52, Pliny *Epistles* 7.17.11. Caused offence: Tacitus *Dialogus* 2.1 (*cum offendisse potentium animos diceretur*).

Tacitus *Dialogus* 3.2–4 (trans. Russell and Winterbottom 1972.433):

> tum Secundus 'nihilne te,' inquit, 'Materne, fabulae malignorum terrent quo minus offensas Catonis sui ames? an ideo librum istum apprehendisti ut diligentius retractares et, sublatis si qua prauae interpretationi materiam dederunt, emittere Catonem non quidem meliorem, sed tamen securiorem?'
>
> tum ille: 'leges tu quid Maternus sibi debuerit, et agnosces quae audisti. quod si qua omisit Cato, sequenti recitatione Thyestes dicet: hanc enim tragoediam disposui iam et intra me ipse formaui. atque ideo maturare libri huius editionem festino ut dimissa priore cura nouae cogitationi toto pectore incumbam.'
>
> 'adeo te tragoediae istae non satiant' inquit Aper 'quo minus omissis orationum et causarum studiis omne tempus modo circa Medeam, ecce nunc circa Thyesten consumas, cum te tot amicorum causae, tot coloniarum et municipiorum clientelae in forum uocent, quibus uix suffeceris, etiam si non nouum tibi ipse negotium importasses, ut Domitium et Catonem, id est nostras quoque historias et Romana nomina, Graeculorum fabulis aggregares.'

Politically sensitive: see also Tacitus *Dialogus* 11.2, possibly referring to a play on Nero (Kragelund 2002.38–40, 95–8).

Public performance: Tacitus *Dialogus* 10.5 (*te ab auditoriis et theatris in forum et ad causas et ad uera proelia uoco*).

Phantom genre: Wiseman 2008.200–9. To be performed: Pliny *Letters* 7.17.3 (*tragoediam, quae non auditorium sed scaenam et actores* [*poscit*]).

Premature rejoicing in AD 41: Josephus *Jewish Antiquities* 19.167–84 (speech of the other consul), 187–8, 230; Suetonius *Gaius* 60 (temples). Amnesty: Suetonius *Diuus Claudius* 11.1.

Josephus *Jewish Antiquities* 19.227–8:

> οἱ μὲν ἀξιώματος τε τοῦ προτέρου ὀρεγόμενοι καὶ δουλείαν ἔπακτον αὐτοῖς ὕβρει τῶν τυράννων γενομένην φιλοτιμούμενοι διαδιδράσκειν χρόνῳ παρασχόν, ὁ δὲ δῆμος φθόνῳ τε πρὸς ἐκείνην καθιστάμενος καὶ τῶν πλεονεξιῶν αὐτῆς ἐπιστόμισμα τοὺς αὐτοκράτορας εἰδὼς καὶ αὐτοῦ καταφυγὴν ἔχαιρεν Κλαυδίου τῇ ἁρπαγῇ στάσιν τε ἔμφυλον, ὁποία καὶ ἐπὶ Πομπηίου γένοιτο, ἀπαλλάξειν αὐτῶν ὑπελάμβανον τοῦτον αὐτοκράτορα καθιστάμενον.

The historians Josephus probably used were the elder Pliny and/or Cluvius Rufus and/or Fabius Rusticus (*FRHist* 80, 84, 87).

Cato as symbol: Sallust *Catiline* 53.2–54.6; Horace *Odes* 1.12.35–6, 2.1.24; Virgil *Aeneid* 8.670, Manilius 4.87; Valerius Maximus 2.10.7, 5.1.10; Lucan 1.128, 9.18 etc; for Cato in Seneca, see Griffin 1976.190–4.

Audience loyal to the Caesars: e.g. Phaedrus 5.7.25–8, Pliny *Panegyricus* 54.1–2, Suetonius *Diuus Augustus* 89.3.

Octavia: Boyle 2008; cf. Tarrant 1983c. 379–81 for the manuscript tradition, Barnes 1982 and Kragelund 1982.38–52 for the date of production, Wiseman 2004.265–72 for a conjectural reconstruction of its staging. An early production date is suggested by the emphasis on the post-fire famine (*Octavia* 833, Suetonius *Nero*

45.1), which turned out to be less severe than had been feared (Tacitus *Annals* 15.39.2). 'Haughty harlot': *Octavia* 125 (*superba paelex*).

Citizens' chorus: *Octavia* 288–308 (Tarquins), 676–82, 877–90 (Gracchi); Lucan 6.795–9, with Wiseman 2004.263.

Nero's urban estate: Martial *De spectaculis* 2, Suetonius *Nero* 31.1–2, 38; Champlin 2003.178–209. Sibyl: quoted by Dio Cassius 67.18.4.

10.3. Prose Fiction and History

Ancient novels: Whitmarsh 2008, Cueva and Byrne 2014 for recent coverage; Reardon 1989 for translated texts of the Greek novels. Petronius' *Satyrica*: Schmeling 2011.xii–xvii (date and authorship), xxii (recitations for 'coterie').

Macrobius *In Somnium Scipionis* 1.2.7–8:

> *fabulae, quarum nomen indicat falsi professionem, aut tantum conciliandae auribus uoluptatis aut ad hortationis quoque in bonam frugem gratia repertae sunt. auditum mulcent uel comoediae, quales Menander eiusue imitatores agendas dederunt, uel argumenta fictis casibus amatorum reperta, quibus uel multum se Arbiter exercuit uel Apuleium non numquam lusisse miramur. hoc totum fabularum genus, quod solas aurium delicias profitetur, e sacrario suo in nutricum cunas sapientiae tractatus eliminat.*

For 'plots' (*argumenta*) as 'made-up events which nevertheless could have happened', see *Rhetorica ad Herennium* 1.13, with Morgan 1993.189–90. For Petronius as 'Arbiter', see Tacitus *Annals* 16.18.2 (*elegantiae arbiter*).

Apuleius as *Platonicus*: e.g. Charisius 314 Barwick (*Grammatici Latini* 1.240 Keil), Augustine *City of God* 8.12.3, 8.14.2; cf. Apuleius *Florida* 15.26 (*noster Plato*).

Sophist: Harrison 2000. Any genre: Apuleius *Florida* 20.5–6 (songs, dialogues, hymns, histories, satires, 'your Apuleius does all those, and cultivates all nine Muses equally'); details of his works in Harrison 2000.10–36.

Theatres: e.g. Apuleius *Florida* 5.1 (*in theatro conuenistis*), 9.4 (*consessum in auditorio*), 18.10 (*pro amplitudine auditorii*).

Compare Philo *De congressu* 64–6 (Alexandria, first century AD): 'Practically every day the auditoria and the theatres are full, and the philosophers are in full flow, stringing together their lectures on virtue without even taking breath. But what's the use of what they say? Instead of concentrating, people turn their attention elsewhere ... deaf to the subject of the lecture, present only in body and absent in thought, no different from images or statues. Any who do pay attention sit there just listening, and leave remembering nothing of what was said; they came for the pleasure of listening, not to benefit from it.'

Apuleius *Florida* 18.1–5:

> *tanta multitudo ad audiendum conuenistis ut potius gratulari Carthagini debeam, quod tam multos eruditionis amicos habet, quam excusare, quod philosophus non recusauerim dissertare. nam et pro amplitudine ciuitatis frequentia collecta et pro magnitudine frequentiae locus delectus est. praeterea in auditorio hoc genus spectari debet non pauimenti marmoratio nec proscaenii contabulatio nec scaenae columnatio, sed nec culminum eminentia nec lacunarium refulgentia*

nec sedilium circumferentia, nec quod hic alias mimus halucinatur, comoedus sermocinatur, tragoedus uociferatur, funirepus periclitatur, praestigiator furatur, histrio gesticulatur ceterique omnes ludiones ostentant populo quod cuiusque artis est, sed istis omnibus supersessis nihil amplius spectari debet quam conuenientium ratio et dicentis oratio.

Display speech (Harrison 2000.122–5): *Florida* 18.37–8 (hymn), 39–43 (dialogue).

Notable feature: full discussion in Panayotakis 1995 (Petronius), May 2006 (Apuleius). Greek 'romances': Perry 1967.

One of the earliest: Reardon 1989.17–21. Syracuse theatre: Chariton 8.7.1, 8.7.3, 8.8.13–15; cf. Homer *Odyssey* 9.1–11 (the bard in the hall) for an analogous self-referential device.

Greek novels as δράματα: Photius *Bibliotheca* 94 (73b27–9); cf. 73 (50a7) and 87 (66a27) on Heliodorus, 87 (66a16) on Achilles Tatius, 94 (73b24) on Iamblichus, 166 (107a7, 111a34) on Antonius Diogenes. Poet of comedy: Photius *Bibliotheca* 166 (111a35) on Antonius Diogenes as ποιητὴς κωμῳδίας.

Orator's job: Cicero *De legibus* 1.5 (*opus... oratorium maxime*), *Orator* 65–6 (style of *sophistae*); cf. *De oratore* 2.51, 2.62–4, *Orator* 37–9. For Cicero and historiography in general, see Brunt 1993.181–209 (first published 1979), Woodman 1988.70–116.

Contentious and political: e.g. Horace *Odes* 2.1.1–8 (Pollio), Seneca *Controuersiae* 10. pref.8 (T. Labienus), Tacitus *Annals* 4.34–6 (Cremutius Cordus), Suetonius *Diuus Claudius* 41.2 (young Claudius); Labienus and Cremutius were forced to commit suicide.

Polite gathering: e.g. Seneca *Letters* 95.2, Suetonius *Diuus Claudius* 41.1; Pliny *Letters* 1.13.3, 7.17.3–4, 9.27.

Inconspicuous evidence: ps.Acro on Horace *Satires* 1.3.86 (*in spectaculo*), Suda K2098 (παμπλείστους ἀκούειν) = FRHist 48 T1, 54 T1; Dionysius of Halicarnassus *Roman Antiquities* 11.1.1–2 (history as instruction 'for practically everyone', including οἱ πολλοί).

Aristides and Lucian: Bowersock 1969.36–40, Jones 1986.6–23 for the essentials. Between poets and orators: Aelius Aristides 28.68 (τοὺς μεταξὺ τῶν ποιητῶν τε καὶ ῥητόρων); at 28.72 he calls Thucydides a ποιητής.

Competitive, festivals: e.g. Aelius Aristides 27.46, 33.22–8, 51.31–4. Audience: Aelius Aristides 28.153, 29.16, 48.30 (theatre); 34.42 (καὶ τῶν δεξιῶν καὶ τῶν οὕς τοὺς πολλοὺς ὀνομάζομεν), 34.55 (liberal education, dancers and mimes). Aristides on οἱ πολλοί: e.g. 28.98–119, 29.4, 34.1, 34.38–45.

Two things: Lucian *Historia* 7–9 = Loeb vol. 6 pp. 10–14.

Lucian *Historia* 10:

οὐδὲ τερπνὸν ἐν αὐτῇ τὸ κομιδῇ μυθῶδες καὶ τὸ τῶν ἐπαίνων μάλιστα πρόσαντες παρ' ἑκάτερον τοῖς ἀκούουσιν, ἢν μὴ τὸν συρφετὸν καὶ τὸν πολὺν δῆμον ἐπινοῇς, ἀλλὰ τοὺς δικαστικῶς καὶ νὴ Δία συκοφαντικῶς προσέτι γε ἀκροασαμένους.

Objective, honouring truth: Lucian *Historia* 38–9 = Loeb vol. 6 pp. 52–4.

Lucian *Historia* 39 = Loeb vol. 6 p. 54:

ὅλως πῆχυς εἷς καὶ μέτρον ἀκριβές, ἀποβλέπειν μὴ εἰς τοὺς νῦν ἀκούοντας ἀλλ' εἰς τοὺς μετὰ ταῦτα συνεσομένους τοῖς συγγράμμασιν.

172 Writing for posterity: e.g. Dionysius of Halicarnassus *Roman Antiquities* 1.1.2 (on 'those who have chosen to leave monuments of their own mind to posterity'), Pliny *Natural History* pref.6 (first for the *uulgus* and *turba*, then for 'those who have leisure for *studia*'), Aulus Gellius 17.12.2 ('leaving it written in books').

Present-day audience: Lucian *Historia* 44 (ὡς μὲν τοὺς πολλοὺς συνεῖναι, τοὺς δὲ πεπαιδευμένους ἐπαινέσαι).

Lucian *Historia* 58 = Loeb vol. 6 p.70:

ἢν δέ ποτε καὶ λόγους ἐροῦντά τινα δεήσῃ εἰσάγειν... ἐφεῖταί σοι τότε καὶ ῥητορεῦσαι καὶ ἐπιδεῖξαι τὴν τῶν λόγων δεινότητα.

Brought on stage: cf. Arnobius 5.1, on Valerius Antias *FRHist* 25 F8 (*inducitur Iuppiter*); Ovid *Fasti* 3.305, on the same story (*prodit Numa*); both verbs, like Lucian's εἰσάγειν, are regularly used to express 'Enter X' in the stage sense.

Lucian *Somnium* 12 = Loeb vol. 3 p. 224:

...εἰς σὲ πάντες ἀποβλέψονται· κἂν πού τι λέγων τύχῃς κεχηνότες οἱ πολλοὶ ἀκούσονται, θαυμάζοντες καὶ εὐδαιμονίζοντές σε τῆς δυνάμεως τῶν λόγων.

Rhetor: Lucian *Prometheus es* 2 = Loeb vol. 6 p. 420 (ἐς τὰ πλήθη παριόντες καὶ τὰς τοιαύτας τῶν ἀκροάσεων ἐπαγγέλλοντες); *Apologia* 15 = Loeb vol. 6 p. 210 (ἐπὶ ῥητορικῇ δημοσίᾳ μεγίστας μισθοφορὰς ἐνεγκάμενον).

Lucian *Apologia* 3 = Loeb vol. 6 p. 194:

πάλαι μέν, ὦ φιλότης, ὡς εἰκός, εὐδοκίμηταί σοι τουτὶ τὸ σύγγραμμα καὶ ἐν πολλῷ πλήθει δειχθέν, ὡς οἱ ἀκροασάμενοι διηγοῦντο, καὶ ἰδίᾳ παρὰ τοῖς πεπαιδευμένοις ὁπόσοι ὁμιλεῖν αὐτῷ καὶ διὰ χειρὸς ἔχειν ἠξίωσαν.

Audience as οἱ πολλοί: e.g. Lucian *Bis accusatus* 33, *Rhetorum praeceptor* 20, *Harmonides* 3 = Loeb vol. 3 p. 146, vol. 4 p. 160, vol. 6 p. 220. Audience as ὁ πολὺς λεώς: e.g. *Piscator* 25, *Rhetorum praeceptor* 17, *Fugitiui* 3 = Loeb vol. 3 p. 40, vol. 4 p. 156, vol. 5 p. 58. Audience as τὸ πλῆθος or τὰ πλήθη: e.g. *Bis accusatus* 34, *Rhetorum praeceptor* 26, *Nauigium* 1 = Loeb vol. 3 p. 148, vol. 4 p. 170, vol. 6 p. 430. Lucian's work as δημόσιόν τι: *Harmonides* 3 = Loeb vol. 6 p. 220.

10.4. Lucian in the Theatre

173 Lucian in the theatre: e.g. *Zeuxis* 12, *Harmonides* 3 = Loeb vol. 6 pp. 168, 222; also implied by his use of θεαταί, e.g. *Piscator* 25, *Navigium* 1 = Loeb vol. 3 p. 40, vol. 6 p. 430. Acted: e.g. *Bis accusatus* 33 = Loeb vol. 3 p. 146 (ὑποκρινόμενος). Drama: e.g. *Pro imaginibus* 29, *Pseudologista* 10 = Loeb vol. 4 p. 334, vol. 5 p. 384 (τὸ δρᾶμα).

Commonly accepted view: Jones 1986.14, citing Bellinger 1928. Cf. Hopkinson 2008.2: 'In the dialogues the declaimer's rhetorical training will have equipped him to give the various speakers distinctive voices.'

First paragraph: Bellinger 1928.3. Presuppositions recur: quotations from Bellinger 1928.8, 24, 24–5, 27. Final paragraph: Bellinger 1928.40. His constant use of 'stage' and 'scene', presumably metaphorical, presupposes a virtual performance which I think is better understood as a real one.

Several dialogues (*Dialogi meretricum* 12 and 13, *Bis accusatus*, *Fugitiui*, *Timon*): Bellinger 1928.16–17 ('it must be confessed that Lucian's handling of them is inferior'), 36–7 ('Lucian's extremes of carelessness').

Characters shouting: *Piscator* 1–2 = Loeb vol. 3 pp. 2–4 (the speakers are named haphazardly as Plato, Chrysippus, Epicurus, Aristippus, Empedocles, Aristotle, Pythagoras, and Diogenes); Bellinger 1928.35.

Gods on Olympus: *Iuppiter tragoedus* 33–53, *Timon* 1–19 = Loeb vol. 2 pp. 140–68, 326–40. Up from the underworld: *Charon* 1 = Loeb vol. 2 p. 396; cf. Pollux 4.132 on αἱ χαρώνιαι κλίμακες, with Cicero *Pro Sestio* 126, [Seneca] *Octavia* 593 for its use on the Roman stage. Mountains: *Charon* 3 (ἐπικυλινδοῦντες), 5 (ἐπικυλινδείσθω, μηχανή, twin peaks) = Loeb vol. 2 pp. 402–6.

Lucian *Dearum iudicium* 5 = Loeb vol. 3 pp. 390–2:

— ἐπειδὴ δὲ πλησίον ἤδη ἐσμέν, ἐπὶ τῆς γῆς, εἰ δοκεῖ, καταστάντες βαδίζωμεν, ἵνα μὴ διαταράξωμεν αὐτὸν ἄνωθεν ἐξ ἀφανοῦς καθιπτάμενοι.

— εὖ λέγεις, καὶ οὕτω ποιῶμεν. ἐπεὶ δὲ καταβεβήκαμεν, ὥρα σοι, ὦ Ἀφροδίτη, προιέναι καὶ ἡγεῖσθαι ἡμῖν τῆς ὁδοῦ· σὺ γὰρ ὡς τὸ εἰκὸς ἔμπειρος εἶ τοῦ χωρίου πολλάκις, ὡς λόγος, κατελθοῦσα πρὸς Ἀγχίσην.

Goddesses undressing: *Dearum iudicium* 9–10 = Loeb vol. 3 pp. 396–8.

'Twice accused' dialogue (Loeb vol. 3 pp. 84–150): *Bis accusatus* 1–7 (conversation 'in heaven'), 8–9 (descent to Attica), 10–11 (Pan), 12–13 (Athenian court), 14 (the Syrian ῥήτωρ), 33 (Dialogue's complaint). Pan as Athenian resident: Euripides *Ion* 936–8, Aristophanes *Lysistrata* 911, Pausanias 1.28.4.

Lucian *Bis accusatus* 33 = Loeb vol. 3 p. 146:

πῶς οὖν οὐ δεινὰ ὕβρισμαι μηκέτ' ἐπὶ τοῦ οἰκείου διακείμενος, ἀλλὰ κωμῳδῶν καὶ γελωτοποιῶν καὶ ὑποθέσεις ἀλλοκότους ὑποκρινόμενος αὐτῷ;

Menippus and Varro (Wiseman 2009b.131–51): Aulius Gellius 1.17.4, 2.18.7, 3.18.5, 13.11.1, 13.23.4, 13.31.1; Macrobius *Saturnalia* 1.7.12, 2.8.2, 3.12.6, 5.20.13; [Probus] on Virgil *Eclogues* 6.31 (p. 336 Hagen).

Menippus and Lucian: *Piscator* 26 (accomplice in his 'comedy'), *Bis accusatus* 33 (dug up to terrorise Dialogue) = Loeb vol. 3 pp. 42, 146; cf. *Icaromenippus* (Loeb vol. 2 pp. 268–322), *Menippus* (Loeb vol. 4 pp. 72–130).

Suda s.v. *Phaios* (Φ 180 Adler):

εἰς τοσοῦτον τερατείας ἤλασεν ὥστε Ἐρινύος ἀναλαβὼν σχῆμα περιῄει, λέγων ἐπίσκοπος ἀφῖχθαι ἐξ ᾅδου τῶν ἁμαρτανομένων, ὅπως πάλιν κατιὼν ταῦτα ἀπαγγέλλοι τοῖς ἐκεῖ δαίμοσιν. ἦν δὲ αὐτῷ ἡ ἐσθὴς αὕτη· χιτὼν φαιὸς ποδήρης, περὶ

αὐτῷ ζώνη φοινικῆ, πῖλος Ἀρκαδικὸς ἐπὶ τῆς κεφαλῆς ἔχων ἐνυφασμένα τὰ δώδεκα
στοιχεῖα, ἐμβάται τραγικοί, πώγων ὑπερμεγέθης, ῥάβδος ἐν τῇ χειρὶ μειλίνη.

Cf. Diogenes Laertius 6.9.102, where the passage is used of Menedemus.

Help from his friends: e.g. *Nigrinus* (Loeb vol. 1 pp. 98–138), where the introductory letter makes it clear that the second speaker is Lucian himself.

10.5. Integrating Evidence

Authors in the theatre: see also Petronius *Satyrica* 90.5.

Aulus Gellius 18.5.2–4:

> ibi tunc Iuliano nuntiatur ἀναγνώστην quendam, non indoctum hominem, uoce admodum scita et canora Ennii annales legere ad populum in theatro. 'eamus' inquit 'auditum nescio quem istum Ennianistam'; hoc enim se ille nomine appellari uolebat. quem cum iam inter ingentes clamores legentem inuenissemus—legebat autem librum ex annalibus Ennii septimum—hos eum primum uersus perperam pronuntiantem audiuimus... [the mispronounced lines were Ennius *Annales* 236–7 Sk] neque multis postea uersibus additis, celebrantibus eum laudantibusque omnibus, discessit.

Corinth theatre scene: Apuleius *Metamorphoses* 10.30–4 (text and translation in Hall and Wyles 2008.386–90); May 2008 for discussion and bibliography.

Unlike 'all-mime': rightly pointed out by May 2008.339, who however goes on to say 'the interpretation of the action has to be inferred entirely from the silent *pantomime* dance itself' (my italics); the concept of 'meta-pantomime' (May 2008.357–8) seems to me an unnecessary complication.

Homer: Apuleius *Metamorphoses* 10.30.1; for the authorship of *Cypria* (West 2013.32–4), cf. Aelian *Varia historia* 9.15, Proclus in Photius 319a (5.157 Henry), Tzetzes *Chiliades* 13.633–4; Homer was often assumed to be the author of all the 'Trojan cycle' epics (West 2013.28–30). Original narrative: Proclus in Davies 1988.31; West 2013.75–9.

Lucian: *Dearum iudicium* 9–11 (Loeb vol. 3 pp. 396–400); *Dialogi marini* (Loeb vol. 7 pp. 178–236). Andromeda: *Dialogi marini* 14.3 = Loeb vol. 7 pp. 228–30 ('half-naked from the breasts down').

Spectacle: Lucian *Dialogi marini* 15.1 (ἡδίστου θεάματος), 15.3 (ἡδὺ θέαμα) = Loeb vol. 7 pp. 232–4.

Lucian *Dialogi marini* 15.3 = Loeb vol. 7 pp. 234–6:

> ἡμεῖς δὲ πάντες ἡσυχίαν ἄγοντες οὐδὲν ἄλλο ἢ θεαταὶ μόνον τῶν γιγνομένων παρηκολουθοῦμεν, Ἔρωτες δὲ παραπετόμενοι μικρὸν ὑπὲρ τὴν θάλασσαν, ὡς ἐνίοτε ἄκροις τοῖς ποσὶν ἐπιψαύειν τοῦ ὕδατος, ἡμμένας τὰς δᾷδας φέροντες ᾖδον ἅμα τὸν ὑμέναιον, αἱ Νηρεΐδες δὲ ἀναδῦσαι παρίππευον ἐπὶ τῶν δελφίνων ἐπικροτοῦσαι ἡμίγυμνοι τὰ πολλά, τό τε τῶν Τριτώνων γένος καὶ εἴ τι ἄλλο μὴ φοβερὸν ἰδεῖν τῶν θαλασσίων ἅπαντα περιεχόρευε τὴν παῖδα· ὁ μὲν γὰρ Ποσειδῶν ἐπιβεβηκὼς ἅρματος, παροχουμένην τὴν Ἀμφιτρίτην ἔχων, προῆγε γεγηθὼς ὁδοποιῶν νηχομένῳ τῷ ἀδελφῷ· ἐπὶ πᾶσι δὲ τὴν Ἀφροδίτην δύο Τρίτωνες ἔφερον ἐπὶ κόγχης κατακειμένην, ἄνθη παντοῖα ἐπιπάττουσαν τῇ νύμφῃ.

Tombs like dwellings or temples: Borg 2013.9–40, cf. Zanker and Ewald 2012.27–8;   177
the best-known examples of 'streets of tombs' are those at Isola Sacra, north of
Ostia, and beneath the basilica of St Peter's in Rome.

Sarcophagi reliefs and mythology: brilliantly discussed in Zanker and Ewald 2012
(24–6 on viewing in tombs).

Louvre sarcophagus (fig. 22): Herdejürgen 1996.93–5 no. 26, Tafeln 28–31; Zanker
and Ewald 2012.295–7. Closed-mouth masks: Lucian *Saltatio* 29 = Loeb vol. 5
p. 240. Masks in lunettes: Herdejürgen 1996.51–3.

Diana's nymphs: Ovid *Metamorphoses* 3.165–81, Nonnus *Dionysiaca* 5.307–11.
Actaeon: Hyginus *Fabulae* 180 (deliberate voyeurism), Nonnus *Dionysiaca*
5.303–7 and 475–8 (tree); Varro *Satires* 513 (*saltatores in theatro*), Pollux 4.141   178
(antlered mask). Priapus on stage: Augustine *City of God* 6.7.2.

Basel sarcophagus (fig. 23): Schmidt 1968; Zanker and Ewald 2012.357–9.

Grief-stricken spectators: quotation from Zanker and Ewald 2012.357.   179

For the bearded figure as a 'messenger speech', see Green 1994.57–8 (on Tarentine
vases of the fourth century BC): 'Very often he stands slightly to the side of the
action as depicted, and he has his fingers raised in the gesture of speech or
clutches his head in agony and disbelief. It is noticeable too that he is regularly
present at scenes of action and violence of a kind that by convention
and practicality were not represented on the Greek stage. That is, he gives
messenger speeches, reporting on the unseen action of a story, an action that
is then envisaged by the vase-painter and depicted on the vase.' Euripides:
Medea 1121–230.

Indecency: Tertullian *De spectaculis* 10.4 (*lasciuia*), 10.5 (*turpitudo*); 17.1, 17.5–6, 20.5,
29.5 (*impudicitia*). For a running commentary on *De spectaculis*, with up-to-date
bibliography, see Lugaresi 2008.377–427.

Tertullian *De spectaculis* 17.6:

> si et doctrinam saecularis litteraturae ut stultitiae apud deum deputatam aspernamur, satis
> praescribitur nobis et de illis speciebus spectaculorum quae saeculari litteratura lusoriam uel
> agonisticam scaenam dispungunt.

The standard English and French translations (Roberts and Donaldson 1869.25,
Glover and Rendall 1931.277, Turcan 1986.247) seem to me quite wide of the
mark, and Lugaresi (2008.409) passes over the sentence in silence; perhaps he too
is unsure what it means.

Dispungere: For the various meanings, see *Thesaurus linguae Latinae* 4.1437.7–37.
Agones: Tertullian *De spectaculis* 3.2, 10.13, 11.1, 29.5.

Literature as 'stage teachings': *De spectaculis* 29.4 (*si scaenicae doctrinae delectant*),   180
urging good Christians to prefer biblical works.

10.6. Christians

Games of Flora (Wiseman 2008.175–86): Valerius Maximus 2.10.8 (*priscus mos
iocorum*), Seneca *Letters* 97.8, Martial 1.pref. Third and fourth centuries: Historia

Augusta *Elagabalus* 6.5 (the orgiast emperor's self-justification), Ausonius 14.16.25–6 (the games watched by those who say they didn't).

Brought up as evidence: Tertullian *De spectaculis* 17.3–4, [Cyprian] *De spectaculis* 5–6, Minucius Felix *Octauius* 25.8, Arnobius 7.33, Lactantius *Diuina institutio* 1.20.6–10, Augustine *City of God* 2.27.1.

What sort of deities: Tertullian *Apologeticus* 15.1–3, Arnobius 4.35; Augustine *City of God* 2.8.1–3, 2.25.6, 2.26–7, 4.27.3–5, etc.

From the pagans themselves: Varro *Antiquitates diuinae* frr. 7 and 10 Cardauns (Wiseman 1998.18–19), Dionysius of Halicarnassus *Roman Antiquities* 2.18.3 (Wiseman 2009b.92–3); Tertullian *Ad nationes* 2.1.9–11, Augustine *City of God* 6.5–7 (verbatim quotations from Varro at 6.5.2 and 7). Citadel: Tertullian *De spectaculis* 10.5 (*arcem omnium turpitudinum*), cf. 10.6 (*daemonia*).

Not a convincing argument: Augustine *City of God* 6.9.8–9, 8.1.1.

181 Arnobius 4.35:

> *sedent in spectaculis publicis sacerdotum omnium magistratuumque collegia, pontifices maximi et maximi curiones, sedent quindecimuiri laureati et diales cum apicibus flamines, sedent interpretes augures diuinae mentis et uoluntatis, nec non et castae uirgines perpetui nutrices et conservatrices ignis, sedet cunctus populus et senatus, consulatibus functi patres, diis proximi atque augustissimi reges; et quod nefarium esset auditu, gentis illa genetrix Martiae, regnatoris et populi procreatrix amans saltatur Venus et per adfectus omnes meretriciae uilitatis impudica exprimitur imitatione bacchari. saltatur et Magna sacris compta cum infulis Mater et contra decus aetatis illa Pessinunta Dindymene in bubulci unius amplexu flagitiosa fingitur adpetitione gestire, nec non et illa proles Iouis Sophoclis in Trachiniis Hercules pestiferi tegminis circumretitus indagine miserabiles edere inducitur heiulatus, uiolentia doloris frangi atque in ultimam tabem diffluentium iecerum maceratione consumi.*

The same three dance plots are cited by Arnobius at 7.33, along with Europa, Leda, Ganymede, and Danae.

Eyes and ears: e.g. Tertullian *De spectaculis* 1.3, 17.5; Lactantius *Diuina institutio* 6.21.1 and 8, Paulinus of Nola *Epistulae* 16.7, Augustine *City of God* 2.27.4.

Song of the Sirens (Kahlos 2006.57–9): e.g. Clement of Alexandria *Stromateis* 6.11.89, *Protrepticus* 12.118.2; Origen *Contra Celsum* 2.76, Jerome *Epistulae* 22.18.2; Paulinus of Nola *Epistulae* 16.7, 23.30; Ambrose *De fide ad Gratianum* 3.1.4, Basil *De legendis gentilium libris* 4.

Received through the ears: e.g. Lucian *Menippus* 3 = Loeb vol. 4 p. 78 (hearing Homer and Hesiod); Arnobius 4.30 (hearing *fabulae* about the gods), 4.32 (*fabulae* 'placed in the ears' by poets' inventions); Jerome *Epistulae* 21.13 (poets' song 'capturing the ears' as food for demons).

Literature as an integral part: Tertullian *De spectaculis* 17.6 (*saecularis litteratura*), *Apologeticus* 14.2 (*litterae uestrae*), followed by 14.2–6 on poets, 15.1–3 on mimes; Arnobius 4.33 (*luxuriantes litterae*), 4.36 (burn your *litterae!*), with 4.35 for the transition from poets to actors; Augustine *City of God* 2.25.6, 6.5.5, 6.6.5, 6.7.5 on poets and actors as parallel categories.

Augustine *Sermones* 241.5 (*Patrologia Latina* 38.1135–6):

> *Virgilio non placet doctrina de animarum reditu in corpora. animas in ea opinione beatas esse non posse. exhorruit quidam auctor ipsorum, cui demonstrabatur, uel qui inducebat apud inferos demonstrantem patrem filio suo. nostis enim hoc prope omnes; atque utinam pauci nossetis. sed pauci nostis in libris, multi in theatris, quia Aeneas descendit ad inferos, et ostendit illi pater suus animas Romanorum magnorum uenturas in corpora. expauit ipse Aeneas, et ait*
> >   'o pater, anne aliquas ad caelum hinc ire putandum est
> >   sublimes animas, iterumque ad tarda reuerti
> >   corpora?'
> *credendumne est, inquit, quod eant in caelum et iterum redeant?*
> >   'quae lucis miseris tam dira cupido?'
> *melius filius intelligebat quam pater exponebat.*

Four classic authors (Marrou 1965.405–6): implied by Arusianus Messius *Exempla elocutionum ex Vergilio Sallustio Terentio Cicerone digesta* (AD 395), *Grammatici Latini* 7.449 Keil; cf Ausonius 8.56–65 (adding Horace). Branded on the memory: Orosius 1.18.1 (*ludi litterarii disciplina nostrae quoque memoriae inustum est*).

A fact that he deplored: see Lugaresi 2008.535–694 for a full analysis of Augustine's hostility to the theatre. Before his conversion, he had himself been an enthusiast (*Enarrationes in Psalmos* 147.7: *nos quoque ibi sedimus et insaniuimus*).

Preserve of the elite: Kenney 1982.10.

Bibliography

Acosta-Hughes 2012: Benjamin Acosta-Hughes, '"Nor when a man goes to Dionysus' holy contests" (Theocritus 17.112): Outlines of Theatrical Performance in Theocritus', in Kathryn Bosher (ed.), *Theatre Outside Athens: Drama in Greek Sicily and South Italy* (Cambridge University Press): 391–408.

Ammerman 1990: A. Ammerman, 'On the Origins of the Roman Forum', *American Journal of Archaeology*, 94: 627–46.

Andrén 1940: Arvid Andrén, *Architectural Terracottas from Etrusco-Italic Temples*. Acta Instituti Romani Regni Sueciae 6. Lund: C. W. K. Gleerup.

Andreussi 1996: M. Andreussi, '"Murus Servii Tullii": mura repubblicane', in Eva Margareta Steinby (ed.), *Lexicon Topographicum Urbis Romae*, vol. 3. Rome: Quasar: 319–24.

Arata 1990: F(rancesco) P(aolo) A(rata), '5.1. Terracotte architettoniche', in Cristofani 1990: 119–29.

Astbury 1985: Raymond Astbury (ed.), *M. Terentii Varronis saturarum Menippearum fragmenta*. Leipzig: B. G. Teubner.

Astin 1978: A. E. Astin, *Cato the Censor*. Oxford: Clarendon Press.

Bacilieri 2001: Cinzia Bacilieri, *La Rappresentazione dell'Edificio Teatrale nella Ceramica Italiota*. BAR International Series 997. Oxford: Archaeopress.

Badian 1968: E. Badian, *Roman Imperialism in the Late Republic*. Oxford: Blackwell.

Badian 1977: E. Badian, 'Mamurra's Fourth Fortune', *Classical Philology*, 72: 320–2.

Badian 1988: E. Badian, 'The Clever and the Wise: Two Roman *Cognomina* in Context', *Bulletin of the Institute of Classical Studies Supplement*, 51: 6–12.

Baehrens 1885: Aemilius Baehrens (ed.), *Catulli Veronensis liber*, vol. 2. Leipzig: Teubner.

Baehrens 1886: Aemilius Baehrens (ed.), *Fragmenta poetarum Romanorum*. Leipzig: Teubner.

Barnes 1982: Timothy D. Barnes, 'The Date of the *Octavia*', *Museum Helveticum*, 39: 215–17.

Battaglia and Emiliozzi 1979: Gabriella Bordenache Battaglia and Adriana Emiliozzi, *Le ciste prenestine*, I Corpus: 1.1. Rome: Consiglio nazionale delle ricerche.

Battaglia and Emiliozzi 1990: Gabriella Bordenache Battaglia and Adriana Emiliozzi, *Le ciste prenestine*, I Corpus: 1.2. Rome: Consiglio nazionale delle ricerche.

Baumbach and Bär 2012: Manuel Baumbach and Silvio Bär, 'A Short Introduction to the Ancient Epyllion', in Manuel Baumbach and Silvio Bär (eds.), *Brill's Companion to Greek and Latin Epyllion and its Reception*. Leiden: Brill: ix–xvi.

Beacham 1999: Richard C. Beacham, *Spectacle Entertainments of Early Imperial Rome*. New Haven: Yale University Press.

Beard et al. 1991: Mary Beard, Alan K. Bowman, Mireille Corbier, Tim Cornell, James L. Franklin, Jr., Ann Hanson, Keith Hopkins, and Nicholas Horsfall, *Literacy in the Roman World*. JRA Supplement 3. Ann Arbor, Mich.: Journal of Roman Archaeology.

Beard, North, and Price 1998: Mary Beard, John North, and Simon Price, *Religions of Rome*, 2 vols.: 1. *A History*; 2. *A Sourcebook*. Cambridge: Cambridge University Press.

Beazley 1963: J. D. Beazley, *Attic Red-Figured Vase-Painters*, ed. 2. Oxford: Clarendon Press.

Bellelli 2011: Vincenzo Bellelli, 'Un'iscrizione greca dipinta e i culti della Vigna Parrocchiale a Caere', *Studi Etruschi*, 74: 91–124.

Bellinger 1928: Alfred R. Bellinger, 'Lucian's Dramatic Technique', *Yale Classical Studies*, 1: 1–40.

Betti Sestieri and De Santis 2000: Anna Maria Bietti Sestieri and Anna De Santis, *Protostoria dei popoli latini: Museo Nazionale Romano Terme di Diocleziano*. Milan: Electa.

Bing 1988: Peter Bing, *The Well-Read Muse: Present and Past in Callimachus and the Hellenistic Poets*. Göttingen: Vandenhoeck & Ruprecht.

Borg 2013: Barbara E. Borg, *Crisis and Ambition: Tombs and Burial Customs in Third-century CE Rome*. Oxford: Oxford University Press.

Bowersock 1969: G. W. Bowersock, *Greek Sophists in the Roman Empire*. Oxford: Clarendon Press.

Boyle 2008: A. J. Boyle (ed.), *Octavia attributed to Seneca*. Oxford: Oxford University Press.

Braund 1996: David Braund, *Ruling Roman Britain: Kings, Queens, Governors and Emperors from Julius Caesar to Agricola*. London: Routledge.

Braund 2009: Susanna Braund (ed.), *Seneca, De Clementia*. Oxford: Oxford University Press.

Breed 2004: Brian W. Breed, '*Tua, Caesar, aetas*: Horace Ode 4.15 and the Augustan Age', *American Journal of Philology*, 125: 245–53.

Brink 1982: C. O. Brink, *Horace on Poetry: Epistles Book II: The Letters to Augustus and Florus*. Cambridge: Cambridge University Press.

Brunt 1990: P. A. Brunt, *Roman Imperial Themes*. Oxford: Clarendon Press.
Brunt 1993: P. A. Brunt, *Studies in Greek History and Thought*. Oxford: Clarendon Press.
Burkert 1987: Walter Burkert, *Ancient Mystery Cults*. Cambridge, Mass.: Harvard University Press.
Butrica 1980: James L. Butrica, 'Hylas and the Boreads: Propertius 1.20.25–30', *Phoenix*, 34: 69–75.
Butrica 2007: J. L. Butrica, 'History and Transmission of the Text', in Marilyn B. Skinner (ed.), *A Companion to Catullus*. Malden, Mass.: Blackwell: 13–34.
Cairns 1992: Francis Cairns, 'Theocritus, *Idyll* 26', *Proceedings of the Cambridge Philological Society*, 38: 1–38.
Cairns 2006: Francis Cairns, *Sextus Propertius: The Augustan Elegist*. Cambridge: Cambridge University Press.
Cairns 2010: Francis Cairns, 'The Mistress's Midnight Summons: Propertius 3.16', *Hermes*, 138: 70–91.
Cameron 1995: Alan Cameron, *Callimachus and his Critics*. Princeton: Princeton University Press.
Cameron 2012: Alan Cameron, *The Last Pagans of Rome*. New York: Oxford University Press.
Campbell 2000: Brian Campbell, *The Writings of the Roman Land Surveyors* (JRS Monographs 9). London: Society for the Promotion of Roman Studies.
Canali De Rossi 2005: Filippo Canali De Rossi, *Le relazioni diplomatiche di Roma* vol. I. Rome: Herder.
Carafa 1998: Paolo Carafa, *Il Comizio di Roma dale origini all'età di Augusto*, BCAR Supplement 5. Rome: 'L'Erma' di Bretschneider.
Carandini 2007: Andrea Carandini, *Roma: il primo giorno*. Bari: Laterza.
Carlucci 2006: Claudia Carlucci, 'Osservazioni sulle associazioni e sulla distribuzione delle antefisse di II fase appartenenti ai sistemi decorativi etrusco-laziali', in I. Edlund-Berry, G. Greco, and J. Kenfield (eds.), *Deliciae Fictiles III*. Oxford: Oxbow: 2–21.
Cèbe 1974. Jean-Pierre Cèbe (ed.), *Varron, Satires ménippées*, Collection de l'École française de Rome 9, vol. 2. Rome: École française.
Champlin 2003: Edward Champlin, *Nero*. Cambridge, Mass.: Harvard University Press.
Chassignet 1986: Martine Chassignet (ed.), *Caton, Les Origines (fragments)*. Collection Budé. Paris: Les Belles Lettres.
Ciancio Rossetto 1999: P. Ciancio Rossetto, 'Theatrum Marcelli', in Eva Margareta Steinby (ed.), *Lexicon Topographicum Urbis Romae* vol. 5. Rome: Quasar: 31–5.
Cichorius 1922: Conrad Cichorius, *Römische Studien: Historisches, Epigraphisches, Literaturgeschichtliches aus vier Jahrhunderten Roms*. Leipzig: Teubner.

Clarke 2008: Katherine Clarke, *Making Time for the Past: Local History and the Polis*. Oxford University Press.

Coarelli 1993: F. Coarelli, 'Comitium', in Eva Margareta Steinby (ed.), *Lexicon Topographicum Urbis Romae* vol. 1. Rome: Quasar: 309–14.

Coarelli 1996a: Filippo Coarelli, 'Lacus Orphei', in Eva Margareta Steinby (ed.), *Lexicon Topographicum Urbis Romae* vol. 3. Rome: Quasar: 171.

Coarelli 1996b: Filippo Coarelli, *Revixit ars: arte e ideologia a Roma dai modelli ellenistici alla tradizione repubblicana*. Rome: Quasar.

Coarelli 1997: Filippo Coarelli, *Il Campo Marzio dalle origini alla fine della repubblica*. Rome: Quasar.

Coarelli 2009: Filippo Coarelli, 'La romanizzazione della Sabina', in *Reate e l'Ager Reatinus: Vespasiano e la Sabina dalle origini all'impero*. Rome: Quasar: 11–16.

Coarelli 2012: Filippo Coarelli, *Palatium: Il Palatino dalle origini all'impero*. Rome: Quasar.

Coarelli 2013: Filippo Coarelli, *Argentum signatum: le origini della moneta d'argento a Roma*. Studi e materiali 15. Rome: Istituto italiano di numismatica.

Coffey 1976: Michael Coffey, *Roman Satire*. London: Methuen.

Coleman 1977: Robert Coleman (ed.), *Vergil: Eclogues*. Cambridge Greek and Latin Classics. Cambridge University Press.

Coleman 2000: Kathleen Coleman, 'Entertaining Rome', in Jon Coulston and Hazel Dodge (eds.), *Ancient Rome: The Archaeology of the Eternal City*. Oxford: Oxford University School of Archaeology: 210–58.

Coleman 2006: Kathleen M. Coleman (ed.), *Martial: Liber Spectaculorum*. Oxford: Oxford University Press.

Cornell 1995: T. J. Cornell, *The Beginnings of Rome: Italy and Rome from the Bronze Age to the Punic Wars (c.1000–264 BC)*. London: Routledge.

Courtney 1993: Edward Courtney (ed.), *The Fragmentary Latin Poets*. Oxford: Clarendon Press.

Crawford 1974: Michael H. Crawford, *Roman Republican Coinage*. Cambridge: Cambridge University Press.

Crawford 1985: Michael H. Crawford, *Coinage and Money under the Roman Republic: Italy and the Mediterranean Economy*. London: Methuen.

Crawford 1996: M. H. Crawford (ed.), *Roman Statutes*. BICS Supplement 64, 2 vols. London: Institute of Classical Studies.

Crawford 2011: M. H. Crawford et al. (eds.), *Imagines Italicae: A Corpus of Italic Inscriptions*. BICS Supplement 110, 3 vols. London: Institute of Classical Studies.

Cristofani 1980: Mauro Cristofani, 'Reflets de l'art classique', in *Prima Italia: Arts italiques du premier millénaire avant J.C.* Exhibition catalogue, Musées Royaux d'Art et d'Histoire, Brussels: 173–5.

Cristofani 1990: Mauro Cristofani (ed.), *La grande Roma dei Tarquinii: catalogo della mostra*. Rome: 'L'Erma' di Bretschneider.
Crook 1996: J. A. Crook, 'Political History, 30 B.C. to A.D. 14', in Alan K. Bowman, Edward Champlin, and Andrew Lintott (eds.), *The Cambridge Ancient History*, ed. 2, vol. 10: *The Augustan Empire, 43 B.C.–A.D. 69*. Cambridge: Cambridge University Press: 70–112.
Csapo 2010: Eric Csapo, *Actors and Icons of the Ancient Theater*. Malden, Mass.: Wiley–Blackwell.
Csapo and Miller 2007: Eric Csapo and Margaret C. Miller (eds.), *The Origins of Theater in Ancient Greece and Beyond*. New York: Cambridge University Press.
Csapo and Slater 1994: Eric Csapo and William J. Slater, *The Context of Ancient Drama*. Ann Arbor, Mich.: University of Michigan Press.
Cueva and Byrne 2014: Edmund P. Cueva and Shannon N. Byrne (eds.), *A Companion to the Ancient Novel*. Malden, Mass.: Wiley–Blackwell.
Cunningham 1949: Maurice P. Cunningham, 'The Novelty of Ovid's *Heroides*', *Classical Philology*, 44: 100–6.
Curley 2013: Dan Curley, *Tragedy in Ovid: Theater, Metatheater, and the Transformation of a Genre*. Cambridge: Cambridge University Press.
Curtis 2011: Paul Curtis (ed.), *Stesichoros's Geryoneis*. Mnemosyne Supplement 333. Leiden: Brill.
Davies 1988: Malcolm Davies (ed.), *Epicorum Graecorum fragmenta*. Göttingen: Vandenhoeck & Ruprecht.
Davies 1991: Malcolm Davies (ed.), *Poetarum Melicorum Graecorum Fragmenta*, vol. 1. Oxford: Clarendon Press.
Day Lewis 1966: C. Day Lewis, *The Eclogues, Georgics and Aeneid of Virgil*. London: Oxford University Press.
De Santis 2009: Andrea De Santis, 'La valle reatina: la strutturazione del territorio dal III sec.a.C. al I sec.d.C.', in *Reate e l'Ager Reatinus: Vespasiano e la Sabina dalle origini all'impero*. Rome: Quasar: 31–8.
Dearden 2004: Chris Dearden, 'Sicily and Rome: The Greek Context for Roman Drama', *Mediterranean Archaeology*, 17: 121–30.
Degrassi 1947: Atilius Degrassi (ed.), *Inscriptiones Italiae*, XIII *Fasti et elogia*, fasc. 1 *Fasti consulares et triumphales*. Rome: Libreria dello stato.
Degrassi 1963: Atilius Degrassi (ed.), *Inscriptiones Italiae*, XIII *Fasti et elogia*, fasc. 2 *Fasti anni Numani et Iuliani*. Rome: Istituto poligrafico dello stato.
Degrassi 1969: Attilio Degrassi, '*Aeretinae matronae*', in Jacqueline Bibauw (ed.), *Hommages à Marcel Renard* II. Collection Latomus 102. Brussels: Latomus: 173–7.
Derrida 1976: Jacques Derrida, *Of Grammatology*. Baltimore: Johns Hopkins University Press.

Dickie 2001: Matthew W. Dickie, *Magic and Magicians in the Greco-Roman World*. London: Routledge.
Dover 1993: Kenneth Dover (ed.), *Aristophanes Frogs*. Oxford: Clarendon Press.
Du Quesnay 2012: Ian Du Quesnay, 'Three Problems in Poem 66', in Du Quesnay and Woodman (2012): 153–83.
Du Quesnay and Woodman 2012: Ian Du Quesnay and Tony Woodman (eds.), *Catullus: Poems, Books, Readers*. Cambridge: Cambridge University Press.
Duckworth 1952: George E. Duckworth, *The Nature of Roman Comedy: A Study in Popular Entertainment*. Princeton: Princeton University Press.
Fantham 1998: Elaine Fantham (ed.), *Ovid Fasti Book IV*. Cambridge Greek and Latin Classics. Cambridge: Cambridge University Press.
Fantham 2013: Elaine Fantham, *Roman Literary Culture: From Plautus to Macrobius*. Baltimore: Johns Hopkins University Press.
Feeney 2005: Denis Feeney, 'The Beginnings of a Literature in Latin', *Journal of Roman Studies*, 95: 226–40.
Feeney 2007: Denis Feeney, *Caesar's Calendar: Ancient Time and the Beginnings of History*. Sather Classical Lectures 65. Berkeley and Los Angeles: University of California Press.
Feeney 2012: Denis Feeney, 'Representation and the Materiality of the Book in the Polymetrics', in Du Quesnay and Woodman 2012: 29–47.
Ferri 2003: Rolando Ferri (ed.), *Octavia: A Play Attributed to Seneca*, edited with introduction and commentary by Rolando Ferri. Cambridge Classical Texts and Commentaries 41. Cambridge: Cambridge University Press.
Filippi 2004: Dunia Filippi, 'La *domus regia*', *Workshop di archeologia classica* 1: 101–21.
Finley 1983: M. I. Finley, *Politics in the Ancient World*. Cambridge: Cambridge University Press.
Fitch 2000: John G. Fitch, 'Playing Seneca?', in George W. M. Harrison (ed.), *Seneca in Performance*. London: Duckworth: 1–12.
Fordyce 1961: C. J. Fordyce, *Catullus: A Commentary*. Oxford: Clarendon Press.
Forsythe 2002: Gary Forsythe, 'Dating and Arranging the Roman History of Valerius Antias', in Vanessa R. Gordon and Eric W. Robinson (eds.), *Oikistes: Studies in Constitutions, Colonies, and Military Power in the Ancient World, Offered in Honor of A. J. Graham*. Leiden: Brill: 99–112.
Fortunati 1993: F. R. Fortunati, 'Il tempio delle Stimmate di Velletri: il rivestimento arcaico e considerazioni sul sistema decorativo', in Eva Rystedt, Charlotte Wikander, and Örjan Wikander (eds.), *Deliciae Fictiles: Proceedings of the First International Conference on Central Italic Architectural Terracottas*. Acta Instituti Romani Regni Sueciae 4° 50, Stockholm: Paul Astrom: 256–65.

Fraenkel 1955: Eduard Fraenkel, 'Vesper adest' (Catullus LXII)', *Journal of Roman Studies*, 45: 1–8.
Fraser 1972: P. M. Fraser, *Ptolemaic Alexandria*. Oxford: Clarendon Press.
Frederiksen 1984: Martin Frederiksen, *Campania*. London: British School at Rome.
Funaioli 1907: Hyginus Funaioli (ed.), *Grammaticae Romanae fragmenta*. Leipzig: Teubner.
Gabba 2000: Emilio Gabba, *Roma arcaica: storia e storiografia*. Storia e letteratura 205. Rome: Edizioni di storia e letteratura.
Gagliardo and Packer 2006: Maria C. Gagliardo and James E. Packer, 'A New Look at Pompey's Theatre: History, Documentation, and Recent Research', *American Journal of Archaeology*, 110: 93–122.
Gaisser 1993: Julia Haig Gaisser, *Catullus and his Renaissance Readers*. Oxford: Clarendon Press.
Gaisser 2007: Julia Haig Gaisser, *Oxford Readings in Classical Studies: Catullus*. Oxford: Oxford University Press.
Galinsky 1996: Karl Galinsky, *Augustan Culture: An Interpretive Introduction*. Princeton: Princeton University Press.
Gallia 2007: Andrew B. Gallia, 'Reassessing the "Cumaean Chronicle": Greek Chronology and Roman History in Dionysius of Halicarnassus', *Journal of Roman Studies*, 97: 50–67.
Gelzer 1968: Matthias Gelzer, *Caesar: Politician and Statesman*. Oxford: Blackwell.
Gelzer 1993: Thomas Gelzer, 'Transformations', in Andrew Stewart *et al.* (eds.), *Images and Ideologies: Self-Definition in the Hellenistic World*. Hellenistic Culture and Society 12. Berkeley: University of California Press: 130–51.
Gerhard *et al.* 1897: E. Gerhard *et al.*, *Etruskische Spiegel* 5. Berlin: Georg Reimer.
Giacchero 1974: Marta Giacchero (ed.), *Edictum Diocletiani et collegarum de pretiis rerum venalium*. Pubblicazioni dell'Istituto di storia antica e scienze ausiliarie dell'Università di Genova 8. Genoa: Istituto di storia antica.
Giancotti 1967: Francesco Giancotti, *Mimo e gnome: studio su Decimo Laberio e Publilio Siro*. Biblioteca di cultura contemporanea 98. Messina: G. D'Anna.
Gill and Wiseman 1993: Christopher Gill and T. P. Wiseman (eds.), *Lies and Fiction in the Ancient World*. Exeter: University of Exeter Press.
Glover and Rendall 1931: T. R. Glover and Gerald H. Rendall (trans.), *Tertullian: Apology, De Spectaculis; Minucius Felix*. Loeb Classical Library 250. London: Heinemann.
Gold 2012: Barbara K. Gold (ed.), *A Companion to Roman Love Elegy*. Chichester: Wiley–Blackwell.
Goldberg 1995: Sander M. Goldberg, *Epic in Republican Rome*. New York: Oxford University Press.

Goldberg 1998: Sander M. Goldberg, 'Plautus on the Palatine', *Journal of Roman Studies*, 88: 1–20.
Goldberg 2000: Sander M. Goldberg, 'Going for Baroque: Seneca and the English', in George W. M. Harrison (ed.), *Seneca in Performance*. London: Duckworth: 209–31.
Goldberg 2005: Sander M. Goldberg, *Constructing Literature in the Roman Republic: Poetry and its Reception*. New York: Cambridge University Press.
Goldberg 2011: Sander M. Goldberg, 'Roman Comedy Gets Back to Basics', *Journal of Roman Studies*, 101: 206–21.
Goodyear 1965: F. R. D. Goodyear (ed.), *Aetna*. Cambridge Classical Texts and Commentaries 2. Cambridge: Cambridge University Press.
Gow and Page 1965: A. S. F. Gow and D. L. Page (eds.), *The Greek Anthology: Hellenistic Epigrams*. Cambridge: Cambridge University Press.
Gowers 2012: Emily Gowers (ed.), *Horace Satires Book I*. Cambridge Greek and Latin Classics. Cambridge: Cambridge University Press.
Gratwick 1982: A. S. Gratwick, 'The Satires of Ennius and Lucilius', in E. J. Kenney (ed.), *The Cambridge History of Classical Literature* II.1: *The Early Republic*. Cambridge: Cambridge University Press: 156–71.
Green 1982: Peter Green, *Ovid: The Erotic Poems*. Penguin Classics. Harmondsworth: Penguin Books.
Green 1994: J. R. Green, *Theatre in Ancient Greek Society*. London: Routledge.
Green 1995: J. R. Green, 'Theatrical Motifs in Non-Theatrical Contexts on Vases of the Later Fifth and Fourth Centuries', in Alan Griffiths (ed.), *Stage Directions: Essays in Ancient Drama in Honour of E. W. Handley*. BICS Supplement 66. London: Institute of Classical Studies: 93–121.
Green 1996: J.R. Green, 'Messengers from the Tragic Stage: The A. D. Trendall Memorial Lecture', *Bulletin of the Institute of Classical Studies*, 41: 17–30.
Griffin 1976: Miriam T. Griffin, *Seneca: A Philosopher in Politics*. Oxford: Clarendon Press.
Griffin 1985: Jasper Griffin, *Latin Poets and Roman Life*. London: Duckworth.
Griffin 2002: Jasper Griffin, '"Look your last on lyric": Horace, *Odes* 4.15', in T. P. Wiseman (ed.), *Classics in Progress: Essays on Ancient Greece and Rome*. Oxford: Oxford University Press: 311–32.
Griffith 2007: Mark Griffith, '"Telling the Tale": A Performing Tradition from Homer to Pantomime', in Marianne McDonald and J. Michael Walton (eds.), *The Cambridge Companion to Greek and Roman Theatre*. Cambridge: Cambridge University Press: 13–35.
Gros 1987: Pierre Gros, 'La Function symbolique des edifices théâtraux dans le paysage urbain de la Rome augusteénne', in *L'Urbs: espace urbain et histoire*. Collection de l'École française de Rome 98. Rome: École française: 319–46.

Gros 1999: P. Gros, 'Theatrum Pompei', in Eva Margareta Steinby (ed.), *Lexicon Topographicum Urbis Romae* vol. 5. Rome: Quasar: 35–8.

Günther 1913: R. T. Günther, *Pausilypon: The Imperial Villa near Naples*. Oxford: Oxford University Press.

Habinek 1998: Thomas N. Habinek, *The Politics of Latin Literature: Writing, Identity, and Empire in Ancient Rome*. Princeton: Princeton University Press.

Hall 2014: Jonathan M. Hall, *Artifact and Artifice: Classical Archaeology and the Ancient Historian*. Chicago: University of Chicago Press.

Hall and Wyles 2008: Edith Hall and Rosie Wyles (eds.), *New Directions in Ancient Pantomime*. Oxford: Oxford University Press.

Halliwell, Russell, and Innes 1995: Stephen Halliwell (ed.), *Aristotle Poetics*; Donald Russell (ed.), *Longinus On the Sublime*; Doreen C. Innes (ed.), *Demetrius On Style*. Loeb Classical Library 199. Cambridge, Mass.: Harvard University Press.

Hanson 1959: John A. Hanson, *Roman Theater-Temples*. Princeton Monographs in Art and Archaeology 33. Princeton: Princeton University Press.

Hardie 1983: Alex Hardie, *Statius and the Silvae: Poets, Patrons and Epideixis in the Graeco-Roman World*. Arca 9. Liverpool: Francis Cairns.

Harris 1989: William V. Harris, *Ancient Literacy*. Cambridge, Mass.: Harvard University Press.

Harrison 2000: S. J. Harrison, *Apuleius: A Latin Sophist*. Oxford: Oxford University Press.

Havelock 1966: Eric A. Havelock, 'Pre-Literacy and the Pre-Socratics', *Bulletin of the Institute of Classical Studies*, 13: 44–67.

Havelock 1982: Eric A. Havelock, *The Literate Revolution in Greece and its Cultural Consequences*. Princeton: Princeton University Press.

Henderson 1979: A. A. R. Henderson (ed.), *P. Ovidi Nasonis Remedia Amoris*. Edinburgh: Scottish Academic Press.

Hendriks, Parsons, and Worp 1981: I. H. M. Hendriks, P. J. Parsons, and K. A. Worp, 'Papyri from the Groningen Collection 1: Encomium Alexandreae', *Zeitschrift für Papyrologie und Epigraphik*, 41: 71–83.

Herdejürgen 1996: Helga Herdejürgen, *Stadtrömische und italische Girlandensarkophage, erster Faszikel*. Die antiken Sarkophagreliefs VI.2.1. Berlin: Deutsches archäologisches Institut.

Heyworth 2007: S. J. Heyworth, *Cynthia: A Companion to the Text of Propertius*. Oxford: Oxford University Press.

Hinard 1985: François Hinard, *Les Proscriptions de la Rome républicaine*. Collection de l'École française de Rome 83. Rome: École française.

Hollis 2007: Adrian S. Hollis, *Fragments of Roman Poetry c.60 BC–AD 20*. Oxford: Oxford University Press.

Holloway 1994: R. Ross Holloway, *The Archaeology of Early Rome and Latium*. London: Routledge.

Holzapfel 1885: Ludwig Holzapfel, *Römische Chronologie*. Leipzig: Teubner.

Hopkinson 2008: Neil Hopkinson (ed.), *Lucian: A Selection*. Cambridge Greek and Latin Classics. Cambridge: Cambridge University Press.

Hordern 2004: J. H. Hordern, *Sophron's Mimes: Text, Translation, and Commentary*. Oxford: Oxford University Press.

Horsfall 1976: Nicholas Horsfall, 'The Collegium Poetarum', *Bulletin of the Institute of Classical Studies*, 23: 79–95.

Horsfall 1985: Nicholas Horsfall, 'CIL VI 37965 = CLE 1988 (Epitaph of Allia Potestas): A Commentary', *Zeitschrift für Papyrologie und Epigraphik*, 61: 251–72.

Horsfall 1995: Nicholas Horsfall, 'Rome Without Spectacles', *Greece and Rome*, 42: 49–56.

Horsfall 2003: Nicholas Horsfall, *The Culture of the Roman Plebs*. London: Duckworth.

Hughes 2006: Alan Hughes, 'The "Perseus Dance" Vase Revisited', *Oxford Journal of Archaeology*, 25: 413–33.

Humm 1999: Michel Humm, 'Le Comitium du forum romain et la réforme des tribus d'Appius Claudius Caecus, *Mélanges de l'École française de Rome (Antiquité)*, 111: 625–94.

Hunter 1996: Richard Hunter, *Theocritus and the Archaeology of Greek Poetry*. Cambridge: Cambridge University Press.

Hutchinson 2008: G. O. Hutchinson, *Talking Books: Readings in Hellenistic and Roman Books of Poetry*. Oxford: Oxford University Press.

Janko 2000: Richard Janko (ed.), *Philodemus. On Poems Book I*. Oxford: Oxford University Press.

Jocelyn 1980: H. D. Jocelyn, 'The Fate of Varius' Thyestes', *Classical Quarterly*, 30: 387–400.

Jones 1955: A. H. M. Jones, 'The Elections under Augustus', *Journal of Roman Studies*, 45: 9–21.

Jones 1986: C. P. Jones, *Culture and Society in Lucian*. Cambridge, Mass.: Harvard University Press.

Kahlos 2006. Maijastina Kahlos, '*Perniciosa ista inanium dulcedo litterarum*: The Perils of Charming Literature in Paulinus of Nola, Ep. 16', *Maia*, 43: 53–67.

Kahn 1979: Charles H. Kahn, *The Art and Thought of Heraclitus: An Edition of the Fragments with Translation and Commentary*. Cambridge: Cambridge University Press.

Kaibel 1899: Georgius Kaibel (ed.), *Comicorum Graecorum fragmenta*, I fasc. 1. Berlin: Weidmann.

Kannicht 2004: Richard Kannicht (ed.), *Tragicorum Graecorum fragmenta (TGrF)*, vol. 1: *Euripides*. Göttingen: Vandenhoeck & Ruprecht.

Kassel and Austin 2001: R. Kassel and C. Austin (eds.), *Poetae comici Graeci (PCG)*, vol. 1: *Comoedia Dorica mimi phlyaces*. Berlin and New York: De Gruyter.

Kaster 1995: Robert A. Kaster (ed.), *C. Suetonius Tranquillus: De Grammaticis et Rhetoribus*. Oxford: Clarendon Press.

Kenney 1982: E. J. Kenney, 'Books and Readers in the Roman World', in E. J. Kenney and W. V. Clausen (eds.), *The Cambridge History of Classical Literature II: Latin Literature*. Cambridge: Cambridge University Press: 3–32.

Kenyon 1951: Frederic G. Kenyon, *Books and Readers in Ancient Greece and Rome*. Oxford: Clarendon Press.

Keppie 1983: Lawrence Keppie, *Colonisation and Veteran Settlement in Italy 47–14 B.C.* London: British School at Rome.

Kierdorf 1979: Wilhelm Kierdorf, *Laudatio funebris: Interpretationen und Untersuchungen zur Entwicklung der römischen Leichenrede*. Beiträge zur klassischen Philologie 106. Meisenheim am Glan: Anton Hain.

Kondratieff 2010: Eric Kondratieff, 'The Urban Praetor's Tribunal in the Roman Republic', in Francesco de Angelis (ed.), *Spaces of Justice in the Roman World*. Columbia Studies in the Classical Tradition 35. Leiden: Brill: 89–126.

Kragelund 1982: Patrick Kragelund, *Prophecy, Populism, and Propaganda in the 'Octavia'*. Opuscula Graecolatina 25. Copenhagen: Museum Tusculanum.

Kragelund 2002: Patrick Kragelund, 'Historical Drama in Ancient Rome: Republican Flourishing and Imperial Decline?', *Symbolae Osloenses*, 77: 5–105.

Kübler 1927: B. Kübler, 'Lictor', *Paulys Realencyclopädie*, 13: 507–18.

Lacey 1996: W. K. Lacey, *Augustus and the Principate: The Evolution of the System*. Arca 35. Leeds: Francis Cairns.

Lada-Richards 2007: Ismene Lada-Richards, *Silent Eloquence: Lucian and Pantomime Dancing*. London: Duckworth.

Lada-Richards 2013. Ismene Lada-Richards, '*Mutata corpora*: Ovid's Changing Forms and the Metamorphic Bodies of Pantomime Dancing', *Transactions of the American Philological Association*, 143: 105–52.

Lane 1979: Eugene N. Lane, 'Sabazius and the Jews in Valerius Maximus', *Journal of Roman Studies*, 69: 35–8.

Leigh 1996: Matthew Leigh, 'Varius Rufus, Thyestes and the Appetites of Antony', *Proceedings of the Cambridge Philological Society*, 42: 171–97.

Levick 1976: Barbara Levick, *Tiberius the Politician*. London: Thames & Hudson.

Lewis 1974: Naphtali Lewis, *Papyrus in Classical Antiquity*. Oxford: Clarendon Press.

Lightfoot 1999: J. L. Lightfoot, *Parthenius of Nicaea: The Poetical Fragments and the Ἐρωτικὰ Παθήματα*. Oxford: Clarendon Press.

Lloyd 1975: Alan B. Lloyd, *Herodotus Book II: Introduction*. Études préliminaires aux religions orientales dans l'empire romain 43. Leiden: Brill.

Lowrie 2009: Michèle Lowrie, *Writing, Performance, and Authority in Augustan Rome*. Oxford: Oxford University Press.

Lugaresi 2008: Leonardo Lugaresi, *Il teatro di Dio: Il problema degli spettacoli nel cristianesimo antico (II–IV secolo)*. Supplementi Adamantius 1. Brescia: Morcelliana.

Lyne 1978: R. O. A. M. Lyne, 'The Neoteric Poets', *Classical Quarterly*, 28: 167–87.

Malloch 2013: S. J. V. Malloch (ed.), *The Annals of Tacitus Book 11*. Cambridge Classical Texts and Commentaries 51. Cambridge: Cambridge University Press.

Mangoni 1993: Cecilia Mangoni (ed.), *Filodemo: Il quinto libro della Poetica (PHerc. 1425 e 1538)*. Naples: Bibliopolis.

Mankin 1995: David Mankin (ed.), *Horace Epodes*. Cambridge Greek and Latin Classics. Cambridge: Cambridge University Press.

Manuwald 2001: Gesine Manuwald, *Fabulae praetextae: Spuren einer literarischen Gattung der Römer*. Zetemata 108. Munich: C. H. Beck.

Marincola 1997: John Marincola, *Authority and Tradition in Ancient Historiography*. Cambridge: Cambridge University Press.

Marrou 1965: Henri-Irénée Marrou, *Histoire de l'éducation dans l'antiquité*. Paris: Éditions du Seuil.

Marshall 2006: C. W. Marshall, *The Stagecraft and Performance of Roman Comedy*. Cambridge: Cambridge University Press.

May 2006: Regine May, *Apuleius and Drama: The Ass on Stage*. Oxford: Oxford University Press.

May 2008: Regine May, 'The Metamorphosis of Pantomime: Apuleius' *Judgement of Paris* (*Met.* 10.30–34)', in Hall and Wyles 2008: 338–62.

McKeown 1979: J. C. McKeown, 'Augustan Elegy and Mime', *Proceedings of the Cambridge Philological Society*, 25: 71–84.

Meier 1995: Christian Meier, *Caesar: A Biography*. London: HarperCollins.

Meyer 1980: Jørgen Chr. Meyer, 'Roman History in Light of the Import of Attic Vases to Rome and Etruria in the Sixth and Fifth Centuries BC', *Analecta Romana Instituti Danici*, 9: 47–68.

Meyer 2004: Elizabeth A. Meyer, *Legitimacy and Law in the Roman World: Tabulae in Roman Belief and Practice*. Cambridge: Cambridge University Press.

Michels 1967: Agnes Kirsopp Michels, *The Calendar of the Roman Republic*. Princeton: Princeton University Press.

Millar 2000: Fergus Millar, 'The First Revolution: Imperator Caesar, 36–28 BC', in *La Révolution romaine après Ronald Syme: bilans et perspectives*. Entretiens sur l'antiquité classique 46. Geneva: Fondation Hardt: 1–30.

Miller 2009: John F. Miller, *Apollo, Augustus, and the Poets*. Cambridge: Cambridge University Press.
Mommsen 1886: Theodor Mommsen, 'Die Tatius-legende', *Hermes*, 21: 570–87.
Mommsen 1906: Theodor Mommsen, *Gesammelte Schriften*, vol. 4. Berlin: Weidmann.
Mommsen 1954: Theodor E. Mommsen, 'Augustus and Britain: A Fragment from Livy?', *American Journal of Philology*, 75: 175–83.
Moretti 1968: L. Moretti (ed.), *Inscriptiones Graecae urbis Romae*, fasc. 1. Rome: Istituto Italiano per la storia antica.
Morgan 1993: J. R. Morgan, 'Make-believe and Make Believe: The Fictionality of the Greek Novels', in Christopher Gill and T. P. Wiseman (eds.), *Lies and Fiction in the Ancient World*. Exeter: University of Exeter Press: 175–229.
Muecke 1993: Frances Muecke (ed.), *Horace Satires II*. Warminster: Aris & Phillips.
Muecke 2005: Frances Muecke, 'Rome's First "Satirists": Themes and Genre in Ennius and Lucilius', in Kirk Freudenburg (ed.), *The Cambridge Companion to Roman Satire*. Cambridge: Cambridge University Press: 33–47.
Mueller 1869: L. Mueller, 'Der Mimograph Catullus', *Rheinisches Museum*, 24: 621–2.
Münzer 1891: Fridericus Münzer, *De gente Valeria: dissertatio inauguralis historica*. Oppolae: Erdmann Raabe.
Mura Sommella 2011: Anna Mura Sommella, 'La dea col tutulo dal tempio arcaico del Foro Boario', in Patricia Lulof and Carlo Rescigno (eds.), *Deliciae Fictiles IV: Architectural Terracottas in Ancient Italy*. Oxford: Oxbow: 177–87.
Mynors 1990: R. A. B. Mynors (ed.) *Virgil: Georgics*. Oxford: Clarendon Press.
Najbjerg and Trimble 2006: Tina Najbjerg and Jennifer Trimble, 'The Severan Marble Plan since 1960', in Roberto Meneghini and Riccardo Santangeli Valenzani (eds.), *Formae urbis Romae: nuovi frammenti di piante marmoree dallo scavo dei Fori imperiali*. BCAR Supplement 15. Rome: 'L'Erma' di Bretschneider: 75–101.
Nauta 2004: Ruurd R. Nauta, 'Catullus 63 in a Roman Context', *Mnemosyne*, 57: 596–628.
Nisbet 1961: R. G. M. Nisbet (ed.), *Cicero In L. Calpurnium Pisonem oratio*. Oxford: Clarendon Press.
Nisbet and Hubbard 1970: R. G. M. Nisbet and Margaret Hubbard (eds.), *A Commentary on Horace: Odes Book I*. Oxford: Clarendon Press.
North 1989: J. A. North, 'Religion in Republican Rome', in F.W. Walbank *et al.* (eds.), *The Cambridge Ancient History*, VII part 2, ed. 2. *The Rise of Rome to 220 BC*. Cambridge: Cambridge University Press: 573–624.
North 1992: J. A. North, 'Deconstructing Stone Theatres', in *Apodosis: Essays presented to Dr. W. W. Cruickshank to Mark his Eightieth Birthday*. London: St Paul's School: 75–83.

Nünlist 2009: René Nünlist, *The Ancient Critic at Work: Terms and Concepts of Literary Criticism in Greek Scholia*. Cambridge: Cambridge University Press.

Oakley 1998: S. P. Oakley, *A Commentary on Livy Books VI–X*, vol. 2. Oxford: Clarendon Press.

Olson and Sens 2000: S. Douglas Olson and Alexander Sens (eds.), *Archestratos of Gela: Greek Culture and Cuisine in the Fourth Century B.C.* Oxford: Oxford University Press.

Osgood 2006: Josiah Osgood, *Caesar's Legacy: Civil War and the Emergence of the Roman Empire*. Cambridge: Cambridge University Press.

Packer 2007: James E. Packer, 'Drawing Pompey: Three Centuries of Documenting Pompey's Theatre (1833–2006)', in Anna Leone, Domenico Palombi, and Susan Walker (eds.), *Res bene gestae: ricerche di storia urbana su Roma antica in onore di Eva Margareta Steinby*. LTUR Supplement 4. Rome: Quasar: 257–78.

Packer *et al.* 2007: James E. Packer, John Burge, and Maria C. Gagliardo, 'Looking Again at Pompey's Theater: The 2005 Excavation Season', *American Journal of Archaeology*, 111: 505–22.

Page 1981: D. L. Page (ed.), *Further Greek Epigrams*. Cambridge: Cambridge University Press.

Panayotakis 1995: Costas Panayotakis, *Theatrum Arbitri: Theatrical Elements in the Satyrica of Petronius*. Mnemosyne Supplement 146. Leiden: Brill.

Panayotakis 2010: Costas Panayotakis (ed.), *Decimus Laberius: The Fragments*. Cambridge Classical Texts and Commentaries 46. Cambridge: Cambridge University Press.

Parker 2009: Holt N. Parker, 'Books and Reading Latin Poetry', in William A. Johnson and Holt N. Parker (eds.), *Ancient Literacies: The Culture of Reading in Greece and Rome*. New York: Oxford University Press: 186–229.

Patai and Corral 2005: Daphne Patai and Will H. Corral (eds.), *Theory's Empire: An Anthology of Dissent*. New York: Columbia University Press.

Pearson 1960: Lionel Pearson, *The Lost Historians of Alexander the Great*. APA Monographs 20. Philadelphia: American Philological Association.

Pearson 1987: Lionel Pearson, *The Greek Historians of the West: Timaeus and his Predecessors*. APA Monographs 35. Atlanta, Ga.: American Philological Association.

Pensabene 1988: Patrizio Pensabene, 'Scavi nell'area del tempio della Vittoria e del santuario della Magna mater sul Palatino', *Archeologia laziale*, 9: 54–67.

Perry 1967: Ben Edwin Perry, *The Ancient Romances: A Literary-Historical Account of Their Origins*. Sather Classical Lectures 37. Berkeley and Los Angeles: University of California Press.

Peruzzi 1998: Emilio Peruzzi, *Civiltà greca nel Lazio preromano*. Studi dell'Accademia Toscana 'La Columbaria' 165. Florence: Leo S. Olschki.

Pfeiffer 1949: Rudolfus Pfeiffer, *Callimachus*, vol. 1. Oxford: Clarendon Press.
Pfeiffer 1968: Rudolf Pfeiffer, *History of Classical Scholarship: From the Beginnings to the End of the Hellenistic Age*. Oxford: Clarendon Press.
Piranomonte 2002: Marina Piranomonte (ed.), *Il santuario della musica e il bosco sacro di Anna Perenna*. Milan: Electa.
Powell 2008: Anton Powell, *Virgil the Partisan: A Study in the Re-integration of Classics*. Swansea: Classical Press of Wales.
Purcell 2003: Nicholas Purcell, 'Becoming Historical: The Roman Case', in David Braund and Christopher Gill (eds.), *Myth, History and Culture in Republican Rome*. Exeter: University of Exeter Press: 12–40.
Quinn 1982: Kenneth Quinn, 'Poet and Audience in the Augustan Age', in Hildegard Temporini and Wolfgang Haase (eds.), *Aufstieg und Niedergang der römischen Welt* II.30. Berlin: De Gruyter: 75–180.
Raaflaub 2009: Kurt Raaflaub, '*Bellum Civile*', in Miriam Griffin (ed.), *A Companion to Julius Caesar*. Malden, Mass.: Wiley Blackwell: 175–91.
Rawson 1981: Elizabeth Rawson, 'Chariot-Racing in the Roman Republic', *Papers of the British School at Rome*, 49: 1–16.
Rawson 1985: Elizabeth Rawson, *Intellectual Life in the Late Roman Republic*. London: Duckworth.
Rawson 1991: Elizabeth Rawson, *Roman Culture and Society: Collected Papers*. Oxford: Clarendon Press.
Reardon 1989: B. P. Reardon (ed.), *Collected Ancient Greek Novels*. Berkeley and Los Angeles: University of California Press.
Rehm 2007: Rush Rehm, 'Festivals and Audiences in Athens and Rome', in Marianne McDonald and J. Michael Walton (eds.), *The Cambridge Companion to Greek and Roman Theatre*. Cambridge: Cambridge University Press: 184–201.
Rhodes 1981: P. J. Rhodes, *A Commentary on the Aristotelian Athenaion Politeia*. Oxford: Clarendon Press.
Rich 2005: John Rich, 'Valerius Antias and the Construction of the Roman Past', *Bulletin of the Institute of Classical Studies*, 48: 137–61.
Rich 2009: John Rich, 'Cantabrian Closure: Augustus' Spanish War and the Ending of his Memoirs', in Christopher Smith and Anton Powell (eds.), *The Lost Memoirs of Augustus and the Development of Roman Autobiography*. Swansea: Classical Press of Wales: 145–72.
Richter 1901: Otto Richter, *Topographie der Stadt Rom*. Handbuch der klassischen Altertums-Wissenschaft 3.3.2. Munich: C. H. Beck.
Ridgway 1992: David Ridgway, *The First Western Greeks*. Cambridge: Cambridge University Press.
Ridgway 1996: David Ridgway, 'Greek Letters at Osteria dell'Osa', *Opuscula Romana*, 20: 87–97.

Robert 1959: Jeanne Robert and Louis Robert, 'Bulletin épigraphique', *Revue des Études Grecques*, 72: 149–283.

Robert 1979: Jeanne Robert and Louis Robert, 'Bulletin épigraphique', *Revue des Études Grecques*, 92: 413–541.

Roberts and Donaldson 1869: Alexander Roberts and James Donaldson (eds.), *The Writings of Tertullian*, vol. 1. Ante-Nicene Christian Library, vol. XI. Edinburgh: T. & T. Clark.

Robinson 2004: E. G. D. Robinson, 'Reception of Comic Theatre amongst the Indigenous South Italians', *Mediterranean Archaeology*, 17: 193–212.

Rodriguez Almeida 1981: Emilio Rodriguez Almeida, *Forma urbis marmorea: Aggiornamento generale 1980*. Rome: Quasar.

Russell and Winterbottom 1972: D. A. Russell and M. Winterbottom (eds.), *Ancient Literary Criticism: The Principal Texts in New Translations*. Oxford: Clarendon Press.

Säflund 1932: Gösta Säflund, *Le mura di Roma repubblicana: Saggio di archeologia romana*. Acta Instituti Romani Regni Sueciae 1. Lund: Gleerup.

Schenkeveld 1992: Dirk M. Schenkeveld, 'Prose Usages of ἀκούειν "To Read"', *Classical Quarterly*, 42: 129–41.

Schmeling 2011: Gareth Schmeling, *A Commentary on the Satyrica of Petronius*. Oxford: Oxford University Press.

Schmidt 1968: Margot Schmidt, *Der Basler Medeasarkophag: ein Meisterwerk spätantoninischer Kunst*. Monumenta artis antiquae 3. Tübingen: Ernst Wasmuth.

Schweitzer 1955: B. Schweitzer, 'Zum Krater des Aristonothos', *Römische Mitteilungen*, 62: 78–106.

Seaford 1984: Richard Seaford, *Euripides. Cyclops, with Introduction and Commentary*. Oxford: Clarendon Press.

Sear 2006: Frank Sear, *Roman Theatres: An Architectural Study*. Oxford: Oxford University Press.

Sewell 2010: Jamie Sewell, *The Foundation of Roman Urbanism 338–200 BC: Between Contemporary Foreign Influence and Roman Tradition*, JRA Supplement 79. Portsmouth, RI: Journal of Roman Archaeology.

Shackleton Bailey 1978: D. R. Shackleton Bailey (trans.), *Cicero's Letters to his Friends*, vol. 1. Harmondsworth: Penguin.

Sider 1997: David Sider (ed.), *The Epigrams of Philodemos: Introduction, Text, and Commentary*. New York: Oxford University Press.

Skutsch 1985: Otto Skutsch (ed.), *The Annals of Quintus Ennius*. Oxford: Clarendon Press.

Smith 2009: Christopher Smith (ed.), 'The Memoirs of Augustus: Testimonia and Fragments', in Christopher Smith and Anton Powell (eds.), *The Lost Memoirs of Augustus and the Development of Roman Autobiography*. Swansea: Classical Press of Wales: 1–13.

Solin 1981: Heiki Solin, 'Sulle dediche greche di Gravisca,' *Parola del passato*, 36: 185–7.
Snell 1971: Bruno Snell (ed.), *Tragicorum Graecorum fragmenta (TGrF)*, vol. 1. Göttingen: Vandenhoeck & Ruprecht.
Sommella Mura 1990: Anna Sommella Mura, 'Il tempio arcaico e la sua decorazione', in Cristofani 1990: 115–18.
Starkie 1938: Walter Starkie, *The Waveless Plain: An Italian Autobiography*. London: John Murray.
Starks 2008: John H. Starks, jr, 'Pantomime Actresses in Latin Inscriptions', in Hall and Wyles 2008: 110–45.
Starr 1991: Raymond J. Starr, 'Reading Aloud: *Lectores* and Roman Reading', *Classical Journal*, 86: 337–43.
Strecker 1884: C. Strecker, *De Lycophrone, Euphronio, Eratosthene comicorum interpretibus*. Greifswald.
Sutherland 1984: C. H. V. Sutherland, *The Roman Imperial Coinage*, rev. edn., vol. 1. London: Spink.
Syme 1958: Ronald Syme, 'Imperator Caesar: A Study in Nomenclature', *Historia*, 7.172–88.
Syme 1961: Ronald Syme, 'Who was Vedius Pollio?', *Journal of Roman Studies*, 51: 23–30.
Syme 1978: Ronald Syme, *History in Ovid*. Oxford: Clarendon Press.
Syme 1979: Ronald Syme, *Roman Papers*, vols. 1–2. Oxford: Clarendon Press.
Syme 1986: Ronald Syme, *The Augustan Aristocracy*. Oxford: Clarendon Press.
Tagliamonte 1996: G. Tagliamonte, 'Iuppiter Optimus Maximus Capitolinus, aedes, templum, fino all' a. 83 a.C.', in Eva Margareta Steinby (ed.), *Lexicon Topographicum Urbis Romae* vol. 3. Rome: Quasar: 144–8.
Taplin 1993: Oliver Taplin, *Comic Angels and Other Approaches to Greek Drama through Vase-Paintings*. Oxford: Clarendon Press.
Taplin 2004: Oliver Taplin, 'A Disguised Pentheus Hiding in the British Museum?', *Mediterranean Archaeology*, 17: 237–41.
Taplin 2007: Oliver Taplin, *Pots and Plays: Interactions between Tragedy and Greek Vase-painting of the Fourth Century BC*. Los Angeles: J. Paul Getty Museum.
Taplin 2012: Oliver Taplin, 'How was Athenian Tragedy Played in the Greek West?', in Kathryn Bosher (ed.) *Theatre Outside Athens: Drama in Greek Sicily and South Italy*. Cambridge: Cambridge University Press: 226–50.
Taplin and Wyles 2010: Oliver Taplin and Rosie Wyles (eds.), *The Pronomos Vase and its Context*. Oxford: Oxford University Press.
Tarrant 1983a: R. J. T[arrant], 'Catullus', in L. D. Reynolds (ed.), *Texts and Transmission: A Survey of the Latin Classics*. Oxford: Clarendon Press: 43–5.
Tarrant 1983b: R. J. T[arrant], 'Plautus', in L. D. Reynolds (ed.), *Texts and Transmission: A Survey of the Latin Classics*. Oxford: Clarendon Press: 302–7.

Tarrant 1983c: R. J. T[arrant], 'The Younger Seneca: Tragedies', in L. D. Reynolds (ed.), *Texts and Transmission: A Survey of the Latin Classics*. Oxford: Clarendon Press: 378–81.

Tatum 1999: W. Jeffrey Tatum, *The Patrician Tribune: Publius Clodius Pulcher*. Chapel Hill, NC: University of North Carolina Press.

Taylor 1960: Lily Ross Taylor, *The Voting Districts of the Roman Republic*. Papers and Monographs of the American Academy in Rome 20. Rome: American Academy.

Thomas 1988: Richard F. Thomas (ed.), *Virgil Georgics*: vol. 2. Books III–IV. Cambridge Greek and Latin Classics. Cambridge: Cambridge University Press.

Thomas 2011: Richard F. Thomas (ed.), *Horace Odes Book IV and Carmen Saeculare*. Cambridge Greek and Latin Classics. Cambridge: Cambridge University Press.

Thorsen 2013: Thea S. Thorsen (ed.), *The Cambridge Companion to Latin Love Elegy*. Cambridge: Cambridge University Press.

Todisco 2002: Luigi Todisco, *Teatro e spettacolo in Magna Grecia e Sicilia: Testi immagini e architettura*. Biblioteca di Archeologia 32. Milan: Longanesi.

Torelli 1992: Mario Torelli, *L'arte degli Etruschi*. Rome and Bari: Laterza.

Torelli 1999: Mario Torelli, *Tota Italia: Essays on the Cultural Formation of Roman Italy*. Oxford: Clarendon Press.

Torelli 2011: Mario Torelli, '*Fictilia tecta*: Riflessioni storiche sull'arcaismo etrusco e romano', in Patricia Lulof and Carlo Rescigno (eds.), *Deliciae Fictiles IV: Architectural Terracottas in Ancient Italy*. Oxford: Oxbow: 3–15.

Trendall 1987: A. D. Trendall, *The Red-Figured Vases of Paestum*. London: British School at Rome.

Trendall 1989: A. D. Trendall, *Red-Figure Vases of South Italy and Sicily: A Handbook*. London: Thames & Hudson.

Trimble 2012: Gail Trimble, 'Catullus 64: The Perfect Epyllion?', in Manuel Baumbach and Silvio Bär (eds.). *Brill's Companion to Greek and Latin Epyllion and its Reception*. Leiden: Brill: 55–79.

Turcan 1986: Marie Turcan (ed.), *Tertullien: Les Spectacles (De spectaculis)*. Sources Chrétiennes 332. Paris: Éditions du Cerf.

Ullman 1917: B. L. Ullman, 'Horace on the Nature of Satire', *Transactions of the American Philological Association*, 48: 111–32.

Vermaseren 1977: Maarten J. Vermaseren, *Cybele and Attis: The Myth and the Cult*. London: Thames & Hudson.

Volk 2002: Katharina Volk, *The Poetics of Latin Didactic: Lucretius, Vergil, Ovid, Manilius*. Oxford: Oxford University Press.

Walbank *et al.* 1989: F. W. Walbank, A. E. Astin, M. W. Frederiksen, and R. M. Ogilvie (eds.), *The Cambridge Ancient History*, ed. 2, vol. 9, part 2: *The Rise of Rome to 220 BC*. Cambridge: Cambridge University Press.

Wallace-Hadrill 2011: Andrew Wallace-Hadrill, *Herculaneum Past and Future*. London: Frances Lincoln.
Warmington 1935: E. H. Warmington (ed.), *Remains of Old Latin 1: Ennius and Caecilius*. Loeb Classical Library. Cambridge, Mass: Harvard University Press.
Weinstock 1971: Stefan Weinstock, *Divus Julius*. Oxford: Clarendon Press.
Welsh 2011: Jarrett T. Welsh, 'Accius, Porcius Licinus, and the Beginning of Latin Literature', *Journal of Roman Studies*, 101: 31–50.
Werner 1963: Robert Werner, *Der Beginn der römischen Republik: historisch-chronologische Untersuchungen über die Anfangszeit der libera res publica*. Munich: R. Oldenbourg.
Werner 2009: Shirley Werner, 'Literary Studies in Classics: The Last Twenty Years', in William A. Johnson and Holt N. Parker (eds.), *Ancient Literacies: The Culture of Reading in Greece and Rome*. New York: Oxford University Press: 333–82.
West 1995: David West, *Horace Odes I: Carpe Diem*. Oxford: Clarendon Press.
West 1998: David West, *Horace Odes II: Vatis Amici*. Oxford: Clarendon Press.
West 2002: David West, *Horace Odes III: Dulce Periculum*. Oxford University Press.
West 2013: M. L. West, *The Epic Cycle: A Commentary on the Lost Troy Epics*. Oxford: Oxford University Press.
Wheeler 1999: Stephen M. Wheeler, *A Discourse of Wonders: Audience and Performance in Ovid's Metamorphoses*. Philadelphia: University of Pennsylvania Press.
White 2009: Peter White, 'Bookshops in the Literary Culture of Rome', in William A. Johnson and Holt N. Parker (eds.), *Ancient Literacies: The Culture of Reading in Greece and Rome*. New York: Oxford University Press: 268–87.
White 2010: Peter White, *Cicero in Letters: Epistolary Relations of the Late Republic*. New York: Oxford University Press.
Whitmarsh 2008: Tim Whitmarsh (ed.), *The Cambridge Companion to the Greek and Roman Novel*. Cambridge: Cambridge University Press.
Wilkinson 1949: L. P. Wilkinson (trans.), *Letters of Cicero*. London: Geoffrey Bles.
Wilson 2008: Peter Wilson, 'Costing the Dionysia', in Martin Revermann and Peter Wilson (eds.), *Performance, Iconography, Reception: Studies in Honour of Oliver Taplin*. Oxford: Oxford University Press: 88–127.
Winsbury 2009: Rex Winsbury, *The Roman Book: Books, Publishing and Performance in Classical Rome*. London: Duckworth.
Winter 2009: Nancy A. Winter, *Symbols of Wealth and Power: Architectural Terracotta Decoration in Etruria and Central Italy, 640–510 BC*. MAAR Supplement 9. Ann Arbor, Mich.: University of Michigan Press.
Wiseman 1966: T. P. Wiseman, 'The Ambitions of Quintus Cicero', *Journal of Roman Studies*, 56: 108–15.

Wiseman 1974: T. P. Wiseman, *Cinna the Poet and Other Roman Essays*. Leicester: Leicester University Press.

Wiseman 1979: T. P. Wiseman, *Clio's Cosmetics: Three Studies in Greco-Roman Literature*. Leicester: Leicester University Press.

Wiseman 1985: T. P. Wiseman, *Catullus and His World: A Reappraisal*. Cambridge: Cambridge University Press.

Wiseman 1987: T. P. Wiseman, *Roman Studies, Literary and Historical*. Liverpool: Francis Cairns.

Wiseman 1994: T. P. Wiseman, *Historiography and Imagination: Eight Essays on Roman Culture*. Exeter: University of Exeter Press.

Wiseman 1995: T. P. Wiseman, *Remus: A Roman Myth*. Cambridge: Cambridge University Press.

Wiseman 1998: T. P. Wiseman, *Roman Drama and Roman History*. Exeter: University of Exeter Press.

Wiseman 2004: T. P. Wiseman, *The Myths of Rome*. Exeter: University of Exeter Press.

Wiseman 2006: T. P. Wiseman, 'The Cult Site of Anna Perenna: Documentation, Visualization, Imagination', in Lothar Haselberger and John Humphrey (eds.), *Imaging Ancient Rome: Documentation—Visualization—Imagination*. JRA Supplement 61. Portsmouth, RI: 51–61.

Wiseman 2007: T. P. Wiseman, 'The Valerii Catulli of Verona', in Marilyn B. Skinner (ed.), *A Companion to Catullus*. Malden, Mass.: Blackwell: 57–71.

Wiseman 2008: T. P. Wiseman, *Unwritten Rome*. Exeter: University of Exeter Press.

Wiseman 2009a: T. P. Wiseman, 'A Puzzle in Livy', *Greece and Rome*, 56: 203–10.

Wiseman 2009b: T. P. Wiseman, *Remembering the Roman People*. Oxford: Oxford University Press.

Wiseman 2010a: T. P. Wiseman, 'The City that Never Was: Alba Longa and the Historical Tradition', *Journal of Roman Archaeology*, 23: 433–9.

Wiseman 2010b: T. P. Wiseman, 'Velleius Mythistoricus', in Christina S. Kraus, John Marincola, and Christopher Pelling (eds.), *Ancient Historiography and its Contexts: Studies in Honour of A. J. Woodman*. Oxford: Oxford University Press: 73–83.

Wiseman 2012: T. P. Wiseman, '*Roma Quadrata*, Archaic Huts, the House of Augustus, and the Orientation of Palatine Apollo', *Journal of Roman Archaeology*, 25: 371–87.

Wiseman 2013: T. P. Wiseman, 'The Palatine, from Evander to Elagabalus', *Journal of Roman Studies*, 103: 234–68.

Wiseman 2014: T. P. Wiseman, 'Suetonius and the Origin of Pantomime', in T. J. Power and R. K. Gibson (eds.), *Suetonius the Biographer*. Oxford: Oxford University Press: 256–72.

Woodman 1988: A. J. Woodman, *Rhetoric in Classical Historiography*. London: Croom Helm.
Woodman 2003: A. J. Woodman, 'Poems to Historians: Catullus 1 and Horace, *Odes* 2.1', in David Braund and Christopher Gill (eds.), *Myth, History and Culture in Republican Rome: Studies in Honour of T. P. Wiseman*. Exeter: University of Exeter Press: 191–216.
Woodman 2004: A. J. Woodman, *Tacitus: The Annals*. Indianapolis: Hackett.
Woodman 2012: Tony Woodman, 'A Covering Letter: Poem 65', in Ian Du Quesnay and Tony Woodman (eds.), *Catullus: Poems, Books, Readers*. Cambridge: Cambridge University Press: 130–52.
Woodman and Powell 1992: Tony Woodman and Jonathan Powell (eds.), *Author and Audience in Latin Literature*. Cambridge: Cambridge University Press.
Zanker and Ewald 2012: Paul Zanker and Björn C. Ewald, *Living with Myths: The Imagery of Roman Sarcophagi*. Oxford: Oxford University Press.
Zevi 1995: Fausto Zevi, 'Demarato e i re "corinzi" di Roma', in A. Storchi Marino (ed.), *L'incidenza dell'antico: studi in memoria di Ettore Lepore*, I. Naples: Luciano editore: 291–314.
Ziolkowski 1992: Adam Ziolkowski, *The Temples of Mid-Republican Rome and their Historical and Topographical Context*. Saggi di storia antica 4. Rome: 'L'Erma' di Bretschneider.
Zwierlein 1966: Otto Zwierlein, *Die Rezitationsdramen Senecas*. Beiträge zur klassischen Philologie 20. Meisenheim am Glan: Hain.

Index of Passages

Aetna
  74–9 and 91–2: 164
Apponius
  In Canticum Canticorum 12.53: 140
Apuleius
  Apologia 39.2: 69
  Florida 18.1–5: 170
Arnobius
  Aduersus nationes 4.35: 181
Athenaeus
  Deipnosophistae 14.615a-e: 57–8
Augustine
  Sermones 241.5: 181–2
Augustus
  Res gestae 1.1: 113
  8.2: 135
  11-12.1: 152
  20.4: 135
  34.1: 135
  34.2: 138

Cassiodorus
  Variae 37.3 and 5: 4
Catullus
  29: 103–4
  40: 106
  57: 104
  63: 108
  64: 109–10
  On Mime-Performances: 92
Cicero
  Academica 1.5: 97
  Ad Atticum 1.16.11: 82
  1.18.6: 82
  4.3.3: 85
  4.15.6: 93
  Ad familiares 5.12.4-5: 99–100
  7.1.1-3: 87–8
  Ad Q. fratrem 2.9.1: 89
  De finibus 3.7–8: 83
  De imperio Cn. Pompei 1-2: 81
  De officiis 1.147: 89
  In P. Clodium et Curionem fr. 19 Crawford: 84
  In Pisonem 22: 147
  65: 86
  Pro Gallio fr. 2 Crawford: 78
  Pro Rabirio Postumo 35: 92

Tusculan Disputations 1.34: 70
Corpus inscriptionum Latinarum
  6.10096: 111
  6.32323.156-8: 154

Demetrius
  On Style 215: 98
Diomedes
  Grammatici Latini 1.491-2 Keil: 91
Dionysius of Halicarnassus
  Roman Antiquities 7.72.1–73.4: 43–4
Donatus
  Vita Vergili 38: 151

Ennius
  Annales 12-13 Skutsch: 66–7
  fr. 28.4-8 Courtney: 69
  fr. 39 Courtney: 68
  fr. 45 Courtney: 70
Epicharmus
  PCG F 287: 68
Euhemerus
  FGrH 63 F 20: 68

Fabius Pictor
  FGrH 809 F 13(b) = FRHist 1 F 15: 43–4

Gellius, Aulus
  Noctes Atticae 5.18.9: 73
  10.6.2: 41
  18.5.2-4: 175–6

Heraclitus
  fr. 104 Diels = 59 Kahn: 22
Herodotus
  1.23–24.1: 17
  5.67.1 and 5: 17
Homer
  Iliad 18.502-6: 11
  18.603-6: 11
  Odyssey 8.258-64: 11
Homeric Hymns
  Apollo 166-73: 67
  Hermes 53-9: 23
Horace
  Epistles 1.6.49-54: 142
  1.19.35-40: 142

Horace (cont.)
  1.19.41–9: 146
  2.2.46–52: 119
  2.2.95–6: 142
  Odes 1.2.1–4 and 13-26: 132–3
  1.2.41–52: 133
  2.13.21–32: 139
  3.1.10–14: 141
  3.6.1–16: 131
  3.6.33–44: 132
  4.3.13–16: 156
  4.15.1–8: 157
  4.15.17–32: 157
  Satires 1.4.34-8: 120
  1.4.65–78: 120
  1.10.37–9: 120
  2.1.44–6 and 57–60: 121
  2.1.69–74: 76

Jerome
  Chronica Ol. 189.3: 109
  Epistles 52.c.8: 78
Josephus
  Jewish Antiquities 19.227–8: 168
Juvenal
  7.43–7: 165
  7.82–7: 165

Lactantius
  Institutio diuina 1.11.35: 68
  1.18.10: 70
  5.9.20: 75
Livy
  pref. 4–5: 129
  1.16.4: 130
  2.1.1: 137
  7.2.3–8: 25
  27.37.7 and 13: 48
  34.54.4–8: 54
  fr. 55: 140
Lucian
  Apologia 3: 172
  Bis accusatus 33: 175
  Dearum iudicium 5: 174
  Dialogi marini 15.3: 176
  Historia 10: 171
  39: 171
  58: 172
  Saltatio 19: 128
  30: 109
  Somnium 12: 172
Lucilius (ed. Warmington)
  791–2: 75
  897: 75
  1145–51: 75
Lucretius
  1.117–19: 66
  1.146–54: 95
  1.922–47: 96

  3.1011–19: 95
  4.978–83: 91

Macrobius
  In Somnium Scipionis 1.2.7–8: 170
Manilius
  2.136–8: 164
Martial
  10.20.4–9: 126

Nonius Marcellinus (ed. Lindsay)
  31: 24
  54: 75
  481: 75
  499: 77
  510: 76
  719: 77
Nossis
  Anthologia Palatina 7.414: 41

Ovid
  Ars amatoria 3.121-2: 157
  Ex Ponto 4.2.31-8: 161–2
  Fasti 3.471–3: 161
  4.187–90: 160
  5.183 and 190: 160
  Heroides 7.1–4 and 183–4: 158
  Remedia amoris 361–4 and 389–90: 159
  Tristia 4.10.1–2: 150
  4.10.41–60: 150

Persius
  1.13–17: 165
  1.40–2: 165
Philodemus
  On Poems 1.199: 99
Phlegon of Tralles
  FGrH 257 F 37.5.4: 153
Plato
  Ion 535b-e: 64
  Laws 7.815c: 36–7
Plautus
  Amphitruo 64–8: 52
  Aulularia 717–20: 53
  Captiui 1–3 and 10–14: 52
  Curculio 465–86: 57
  Menaechmi 72–6: 60
  Miles Gloriosus 79–82: 52
  Poenulus 1–45: 53–4
  Pseudolus 401–5: 63
  1081–3: 51
  Truculentus 9–12: 60
Pliny (elder)
  Natural History 13.68 and 70: 4
  21.7: 24
  28.19: 112
  35.26: 135
  36.121: 122

Index of Passages

Pliny (younger)
  Letters 4.7.2: 9
Plutarch
  Life of Pompey 42.4: 82
Polybius
  3.31.12–13: 72
  6.53.1–3: 71
  9.1.2: 72
  30.22.1–12: 57–8
'Probus'
  Grammatici Latini 4.231
    Keil: 66
Propertius
  1.20.7–12: 147
  1.20.25–30: 148
  1.20.45–7: 148
  2.13.9–14: 149

Quintilian
  Institutio oratoria 10.1.93: 146

Sallust
  Catiline 2.5: 117
  3.1–2: 116
  4.1–2: 117
  8.5: 116
  10.3–4: 117
  53.2: 116
  Jugurthine War 5.1–2: 117–18
Scholiast on Cicero
  88 Stangl: 84
Scholiast on Lucan
  35–6 Usener: 92
Sempronius Asellio
  FRHist 20 F 2: 73
Seneca
  Letters 94.46: 125
Servius
  on *Georgics* 3.24: 61
Statius
  Siluae 5.2.160–3: 166

Strabo
  1.2.8 (C20): 156
Suda
  s.v. *Phaios* (Φ180 Adler): 175
Suetonius
  De grammaticis 2.2: 48
  Diuus Iulius 73: 104
  fr. 191 Reifferscheid: 91

Tacitus
  Annals 11.13.1: 165
  14.20.2: 61
  Dialogus 3.2–4: 167
  13.2: 139
Terence
  Hecyra 1–5: 59
  28-45: 60
Tertullian
  De spectaculis 17.6: 179
Thucydides
  1.22.4: 71

Varro
  De lingua Latina 5.65: 68
  6.69: 75
  De uita populi Romani fr. 23 Riposati: 24
  Menippean Satires 59: 77
  218: 76
  277: 77
Virgil
  Aeneid 6.788-84: 156
  8.714–22: 136
  Georgics 1.24–8 and 40–2: 123
  1.463–8 and 489-97: 123–4
  2.161–4: 124
  2.532–5: 124
  4.358–73: 126
  4.429–32: 128
  4.559–66: 133
Vitruvius
  De architectura 5.7.2: 154

General Index

Accius, L., playwright 87
Achilles, legendary hero 33, 53, 110, 166
  shield of 10–11
Actaeon, legendary hunter 177–8
  danced in theatre 91, 128, 178
Actium, battle of 129, 132, 134, 136
actor-managers 52–3, 63
Adonis, Alexandrian festival of 112
Adrastus, cult of at Sicyon 17
aediles, curule 43, 47, 49, 54
aediles, plebeian 41, 42, 49, 84
aedileship, expense of 119, 121
Aegeus, in Catullus 110
Aemilius Paullus, L., conqueror of
  Macedon 50, 59, 101
Aemilius Scaurus, M., consul 115 BC 89
Aeneas, Trojan hero 45, 48, 123, 130,
  132–3, 169
  in Virgil 151, 156, 158, 182
  Romans as *Aeneadae* 98
Aeschylus, Athenian playwright 23, 46
Aesculapius (Asklepios), healing god 44, 170
Aesop, fabulist 68
Agamemnon, in *cista* scene 33
Agonalia (9 Jan., 21 May, 11 Dec.) 28
agora, creation of at Rome 10, 14, 21
Agrippa, M. Vipsanius, consul 37 BC 121–2,
  124–5, 129, 134, 152, 159
  as aedile 122, 127, 128–9
  as censor 134–5
  at *ludi saeculares* 154
  on concord 125
Alcaeus, in Horace 139
Alcinous, Homeric king 11–14, 58
Alexander 'the Great', king of Macedon 40, 50,
  81, 103
Alexandria 92, 95, 129, 134
  library at 3, 45, 48, 49
'all-mime' (*pantomimus*) 91–2, 109, 128, 155,
  159, 161, 166, 176, 177
Alphesiboeus, Virgilian mime 112
Amafinius, Epicurean preacher 97
Ambivius, L., actor-manager 59–60
Ambracia, siege of 70
Amphitrite, consort of Poseidon 176
Anchises, father of Aeneas 68, 156, 157, 174
Ancus Marcius, legendary Roman king 14

Andromeda, in Varro and Lucian 78, 176
Andromenides, literary theorist 97
Anicius Gallus, L., consul 160 BC 57–8, 60
Anio, river and aqueduct 126, 147
Anna Perenna, cult site of 148
Antonius, Iullus, consul 10 BC 143
Antonius, L., consul 41 BC 115–6
Antonius, M. ('Antony'), consul 44 BC 113, 114,
  116, 129, 121, 132, 135
Antonius Julianus, rhetorician 175–6
Antiochus III, Seleucid king 5, 45, 132
Aper, M., in Tacitus 167, 168
Aphrodite (see also Venus) 174, 176
Apollo (see also Phoebus) 63, 115–16, 147
  as Helios 153
  games of, see *ludi Apollinares*
  Palatine temple of 130–1, 136, 138,
    153–4, 157
  Roman cult of 23, 55
Apponius, biblical commentator 140–1
Apuleius, sophist and fiction writer 170, 171
  describes dance performance 176
Apulia, red-figure vases in 31, 34
aqueducts 40, 120–1, 126–7
Ara Maxima, altar of Hercules 15
Archelaus, king of Macedon 23
Archestratus of Gela, poet of fish 69
Archias of Antioch, poet 89
area Palatina 136
Arethusa, Virgilian nymph 126
Argiletum, street in Rome 126
Argonauts 109, 148
Argos, Greek city 17
Ariadne, consort of Dionysus 30
  in Catullus and Ovid 109–10, 160
Arion of Lesbos, poet and musician 17, 46
Aristaeus, Virgilian beekeeper 125–6, 128
Aristarchus, Greek playwright 53
Aristides, Aelius, sophist 171
aristocrats, behaviour of 5, 74–5, 93, 94–5, 113,
  115, 117–18, 152
Aristodemus, ruler of Cumae 19
Aristophanes, Athenian playwright 23, 46, 52, 120
Aristoteles ('Aristotle'), philosopher 17, 19, 46
  on *mimesis* 33–5
  on poets as makers 63, 99
  on Rome 26

General Index

Arnobius, Christian polemicist 180–1
Artemis (see also Diana) 33
Ascanius, son of Aeneas 45
Asinius Pollio, C., consul 40 BC 5, 115
  as historian 139–40
Asisium, theatre at 149
astici, meaning of 154–5
astrology, and mime 92
Ateius Capito, Roman jurist 41
Athenaeus of Naucratis, learned author 57
Athenian drama 20, 23, 30–1, 33, 46, 75, 119–20, 179
Athenian pottery, in Italy 19, 31–2
athletic competitions 11, 43, 45, 179–80
Atreus, legendary king 92
Attalus III, king of Pergamum 61
Atticus, T. Pomponius, friend of Cicero 82–3, 85, 93, 94, 97
  as learned author 47
  as political agent 100
Attis, in Catullus 108
Augustalia, calendar innovation 152–3
Augustinus, Aurelius (St Augustine) 180, 181–2
Augustus, see Caesar
aulaea, meaning of 61
Aurelius, C., public-spirited farmer 79–80
'authorial intention' 94

Bacchic ritual 31, 33, 35–6, 41, 177
  suppressed at Rome 42, 50, 69
Baebius, Cn., curule aedile 200 BC 49
Baehrens, Emil 67
Baiae, site of country houses 84
Balbus, L. Cornelius, agent of Caesar 101, 102
Balbus, theatre of 159
Ballio, Plautine pimp 51
Bathyllus of Alexandria, 'all-mime' dancer 155, 159, 176
Bellinger, Alfred R. 173–4
Bing, Peter 6
Birrius, Horatian mugger 120
Blaisos of Capri, playwright 41–2
books, ancient 4–6, 103
bookshops, ancient 6, 120, 269
boxers, at *ludi* 58, 60
Britain, attempted conquest of 93, 102, 140–1
Brundisium, as fish market 69
Brutus, D. Iunius, assassin 113
Brutus, L., legendary liberator 130
Brutus, M. Iunius, assassin 110, 119, 130, 152

Caelius, Horatian mugger 120
Caere, Etruscan city 10, 20, 59
Caesar. C. Julius, statesman and author 80, 94, 99, 117, 126, 129, 168
  as *popularis* 5, 93, 111, 113, 115, 118, 163
  building projects of 105, 273
  Commentaries of 101–2, 141

  murder of 113, 124, 130, 132–3
  triumph of 111, 112
Caesar Augustus (see also Octavius) 94, 119, 155, 163
  achieves peace by conquest 140
  at *ludi saeculares* 153–6
  and Virgil 151, 156
  as protector of the People 152–3, 157, 163
  Commentaries of 141
  house of 138, 157
  late years of 159, 161–2, 163
  military campaigns of 140, 151
  Res gestae of 135, 138
Cairns, Francis 148
Calchas, Homeric prophet 63
calendar, Roman 26–8, 152, 160
Caligula, see Gaius
Callimachus, poet and scholar 45–6
Calliope, Muse of epic 98
Calpurnius Bibulus, historian 143
Calvus, C. Licinius, poet and orator 104, 105
Camenae, goddesses of inspiration 65, 67
Cameron, Alan 7
Campania, red-figure pottery in 32, 34
Campus Martius, building projects in 85–6, 130–1, 135
Capitol, in Rome 19, 40, 43
  as site for *ludi scaenici* 55, 89
Caprius, fierce satirist 120
Carbo, Papirius, corrupt senator 75
carmen, carmina 27, 64, 164–5
Carmentalia (11 and 15 Jan.) 27
Carmentis, mother of Evander 15, 27
Carthage, wars with Rome 40, 45, 49
Cassiodorus, on papyrus 4
Cassius, C., corrupt senator 75
Cassius Longinus, C., assassin 119, 152
Cassius Hemina, historian 73
Castor and Pollux, Roman cult of 22–3, 44
Cato, M. Porcius, consul 195 BC 70–1, 72
Cato, M. Porcius, senator and Stoic 83, 85, 110, 168, 180
  subject of play 167–8
Catullus, C. Valerius, poet and playwright 80, 94, 103–10, 125
  dance librettos? 108–10, 160–1
  on Caesar and Mamurra 103–5
  on magic 112
  on mime 92, 108
  on weddings 106–7
Catulus, C. Lutatius, consul 242 BC 45
Catulus, Q. Lutatius, consul 78 BC 80
cauea, meaning of 52, 60–1, 86, 163
Centaurs, drunkenness of 147
Ceres (see also Demeter) 123, 160
Cerialia (19 April) 27
  games of, see *ludi Ceriales*
  Roman cult of 20, 22, 27, 42, 55, 59

Charinos, theatrical impresario 30
Chariton, writer of fiction 170–1
Charon's ladder, stage device 174
Chiron, in Catullus 110
Christians 179–82
choros, choroi 11, 15, 17, 43–4, 57–8, 108, 154
Cicero, M. Tullius, consul 63 BC 55, 70, 80, 91, 110, 112, 113–14, 182
  dialogues of 83, 169
  letters of 82–3, 85, 87–9, 99–100, 114
  political position 84–5, 93, 99
  speeches to the Roman People 81
  when absent from Rome 83–5, 168
  on canvassing for office 143
  on Epicureans 97
  on historical style 99–100, 171
  on learning from the stage 9
  on Roman malice 118
  on 'mime' 90, 92
  on poets and the public 89
  on popular enthusiasm for history 9, 73, 99, 130
  on prophets 64
  on the origin of Rome 10
  on Varro? 78
Cicero, Q. Tullius, anxious brother 88, 99
Cincius Alimentus, L., historian 10
Circe, witch-goddess 18, 26
Circeii, Roman colony at 26
Circus Flaminius, as site for *ludi scaenici* 55, 89, 154–5
circus games, see *ludi circenses*
Circus Maximus 24, 43, 47, 51
  as site for *ludi scaenici* 55, 56, 57–9, 89, 160
cistae, engraved scenes on 33, 38–9, 41, 45
Clastidium, victory as subject of play 70
Claudia, aggrieved patrician lady 41, 49
Claudius, emperor 165, 168, 169
Claudius, Ap., consul 307 BC 41
Claudius Cento, C., consul 240 BC 47
Claudius Pulcher, P., consul 249 BC 41
Claudius Quadrigarius, historian 73
Cleanthes, philosopher 5
Cleisthenes, Athenian statesman 17
Cleisthenes, ruler of Sicyon 17
Cleopatra, queen of Egypt 129, 131, 134, 137
Clitumnus, river 147
Clodius Pulcher, P., tribune 58 BC 84–5, 86
codex, codicillus 3
coinage, origin of at Rome 40
comitium, in Roman Forum 26
competition, in drama and poetry 23, 30, 82, 108, 120, 143, 146, 148, 155
Consualia (21 Aug., 15 Dec.) 27
Consus, Roman cult of 24–5, 27
copyists, expense of 5
'Corinna', in Ovid 150–1
Corinth, Greek city 17, 19, 176

Cornelius Nepos, biographer 114
Cornificius, Q., senator and poet 147
Cotta, L. Aurelius, corrupt senator 75
Crassus, L. Licinius, consul 95 BC 83
Crassus, M. Licinius, consul 70 BC 79–80, 86, 102–3, 111
Crassus, P. Licinius, ambitious commander 102–3, 111
Cratinus, Athenian playwright 23, 120
Creusa, legendary murder victim 178–9
Crispinus, absent friend 166
Cronos (see also Saturn) 22, 23
Croton, Greek city in Italy 23
Ctesias of Cnidos, historian 98–9, 100, 170
Cumae, Greek city in Italy 19, 26, 69
Curia Iulia 130, 134, 138
Curiatius Maternus, playwright 167–8
curtains, at theatres 61
'Cynthia', in Propertius 149
Cypria, pseudo-Homeric epic 176, 196
Cyrene, Virgilian nymph 125–6, 128

Dacians, in Horace 131–2
dancers, in theatres 91, 108–9, 127–8, 158, 171, 176, 181
dancing-girls (see also *mimae*) 31–3, 127
dancing-place, see *choros*
'Delia', in Tibullus 149
Delphi, Roman dedication at 23
Demeter (see also Ceres) 20, 27, 59
Demetrios, playwright 30
Demetrius, literary critic 7, 98–9, 100, 171
Demodocus, Homeric bard 11–14
Demosthenes, Athenian master-orator 70, 98, 99
Derrida, Jacques vii
dialogue, as performance 112, 114–5, 172–4
Dialogue, personified 174–5
Diana (see also Artemis) 33, 91, 106, 154, 177–8
didaskaloi, didaskaliai 46, 58
Dido, queen of Carthage 158
Diodorus Siculus, historian 114
Diogenes, Cynic philosopher 78
Diomedes, grammarian 91
Dionysia, Athenian festival 20, 28, 46, 78, 155
Dionysiac drama (see also satyr-plays) 20, 31, 33–5, 41, 45, 48
Dionysius, freedman of Atticus 83
Dionysius of Halicarnassus, historian 10
  on *ludi Romani* 43–4
Dionysus (see also Bacchic ritual, Liber) 17, 41, 177
  Athenian cult of 20, 154–5
  on 'Pronomos vase' 30–1
Dioscuri (see also Castor and Pollux), in Italy 22–3
dissignator, in theatre 53
dithyramb, choral hymn to Dionysus 17, 35

General Index

Divus Augustus, temple of 168
Divus Julius, temple of 115, 130, 134, 168
Domitius Ahenobarbus, L., consul 54 BC
  103, 104
Dryads (see also nymphs) 128, 147, 148

Egypt 3, 47, 139
  property of Roman People 133, 134
elections, under Augustus 141–2
Eleithyia, goddess of childbirth 44, 153–4
Eleuthereus, cult title of Dionysus 20
'elite culture' vii, 8, 65, 68, 89, 142, 163, 166,
  182, 265
Elpenor, comrade of Odysseus 26
enargeia 98–9
Ennius, Q., poet and playwright 65–70, 75
  Annales read in theatre 175–6
  as reincarnation of Homer 67
  on august augury 138
Ephesus, Ionian city 22
epic poetry, audience of 64, 65–7
Epicharmus, Syracusan playwright 20, 68, 112
Epicurus, Athenian philosopher 78, 95, 97
'epyllion', phantom genre 109, 125
Erato, helpful Muse 160
Eratosthenes of Cyrene, polymath 45, 46
Esquiline gate, in Rome 126, 127
Etna, poem on 164
Etruria, red-figure pottery in 32, 34
Euclio, Plautine character 52
Euhemerus, Sicilian author 68
Eumaeus, Homeric swineherd 22
Eumenes, king of Pergamum 5
Eumenides, Varronian satire 77–8
Eupolis, Athenian playwright 23, 120
Euripides, Athenian playwright 23, 45, 78, 179
  Bacchae illustrated 31–2
  Iphigeneia at Aulis illustrated 33, 38–9
  plots used as *phlyakes* 41
Eurydice, Virgilian heroine 128
Evander, Arcadian exile 15
exostra, stage device 167

Fabius Pictor, Q., historian 10
  on *ludi Romani* 43–5, 47, 58
Falerii, pottery from 33, 36
Fates (*Moirai, Parcae*) 110, 111, 115, 153–4, 158
Faunus and Picus, local deities 99
Feeney, Denis 105
female performers, see dancing-girls, *mimae*
Feralia (21 Feb.) 28
'Fescennine' verses 25, 107
flamines, Roman priests 27, 181, 202
Flora, Roman cult of 42, 43, 47–8, 55
  games of, see *ludi Florales*
Fonteius, giver of games 93
Fontinalia (13 Oct.) 27
Fordyce, C.J. 107

Fortuna, goddess 141
Forum Bovarium, in Rome 15–17
Forum Romanum 26–7, 79
  activities in 57, 76, 78, 84, 103, 120
  as site for *ludi scaenici* 56–7, 89
  origin of 2, 14, 163
Fraenkel, Eduard 107
Fronto, recitation host 165
Fulvius Nobilior, M., consul 189 BC 70
funerals, in Roman Forum 27, 71
Furies 77, 95
Furrina, *flamen* of 27
Furrinalia (25 July) 27

Gabinius, A., consul 58 BC 80, 147
Gaius ('Caligula'), emperor 168
Galli, priests of Great Mother 77, 108
Galliambic, frenetic dance measure 77, 108
Gallus, C. Cornelius, poet 114, 146, 147, 150
  disgrace and suicide 125
games, see *ludi*
Gaul, conquest of 93, 101–2, 103–4
Gauls, capture of Rome by 23, 25
Gellius, Aulus, learned author 41, 175
Geryoneus, cattle of 15
Giants, battle with gods 98, 147
Glaucus, subject of poetry and dance 147
Gorgon, head of 30, 33, 39
Gracchus, Ti. Sempronius, tribune 133 BC 74,
  115, 169
gradus, in theatres 61–2
Graviscа, Etruscan port 22
Great Mother (Magna Mater) 55, 77, 108, 181
  games of, see *ludi Megalenses*
  temple of 55–6, 77
Greek culture in Rome 8, 25–6, 46, 50, 72–3
'Greek games' at Rome 111–12, 154–5

Hadrian, emperor 19, 48, 177
hairy-suited performer (Papposilenus)
  30, 33, 43
Hannibal, Carthaginian commander 49, 132
Havelock, Eric 22
Helios, sun-god 153
Hellenistic culture 6–7, 44–5, 95
Hephaestus (see also Volcanus) 10, 27
Hera (see also Juno) 174
Heracleodorus, literary theorist 99
Heraclitus, Ionian philosopher 22, 68
Herculaneum, library at 96
Hercules (Herakles), legendary hero 15–16, 18,
  44, 148, 181
Hermes (see also Mercury) 18, 23, 174, 176
Hermippus, pipe-player 57
Hermodorus, Ionian lawgiver 22
Herodotus of Halicarnassus, historian 71, 99
  on Cleisthenes of Sicyon 17

Hesiod, poet taught by Muses 63–4, 122, 123
Hiero, ruler of Syracuse 23
Himera, Greek city in Sicily 15
Himeros, on 'Pronomos vase' 30–1
Hippias son of Pisistratus, ruler of Athens 19
historians, audiences for 71–3, 99–100, 101–2, 116, 130, 171–2
historical drama 70, 167–9
histrio, Etruscan for 'actor' 25
Homer 17, 22, 33, 63, 65, 98, 100, 155, 164
  as evidence for the seventh century BC 10–14, 21, 28
  as public performer 6, 7, 67
  Cypria danced 176
  texts of 2, 3
Horatius Flaccus, Q. ('Horace'), poet and satirist 80, 94, 114, 118–21, 131–3, 141–6, 150, 156–7, 159
  addresses Roman People 119, 131–2, 135, 156
  at *ludi saeculares* 154
  friend of the rich and powerful 121, 142–3, 146, 149, 156
  on audiences for lyric 131
  on Augustus and Britain 141
  on Cleopatra 137
  on elections 140–1
  on Greek culture in Rome 8
  on Lucilius 75–6, 120–1
  on 'publication' 5, 120
  on Remus 124
Hylas, as love object 147–8

Ida, mountain in Phrygia 102, 108, 174
Ilberg, Hugo 66
Ilia, mother of Romulus and Remus 132
Illyricum, wars in 104–5, 122, 132, 134
Ion, rhapsode 64
Ionians, in Italy 22
Iphigeneia, in *cista* scene 33, 38
Isthmian Games 19
'Italian comedy' 41
Iulus, son of Aeneas 130, 156
Iuuenalis, D. Iunius ('Juvenal'), satirist 165
Iuuentas, daughter of Juno 160

Jason, legendary hero 178
judgement of poets 88, 142–3, 146, 149
Jugurtha, king of Numidia 117
Julia, daughter of Augustus 159, 161
Julia, daughter of Caesar 93, 111
Julius Persius, friend of Apuleius 170, 175
Juno (see also Hera) 48, 154, 160
Jupiter (see also Zeus) 68, 79, 98, 99, 110, 132, 181
  and Ganymede 126–7
  Capitoline temple of 19–20, 40, 43, 55, 154
  flamen of 27, 181
  games of, see *ludi plebeii*, *ludi Romani*
  guarantor of Roman power 157
  Ides sacred to 27
Juvenal, see Iuuenalis

Kenney, E.J. vii

Laberius, D., playwright 92
Lactantius, L., Christian polemicist 180
Laelius, C., consul 140 BC 76
Lapiths, Thessalian people 126, 147
Larentalia (23 Dec.) 27
Lares, mother of 27
Latin colonies 40, 42, 74
Latins, absorbed into Roman state 40
Latinus, son of Odysseus and Circe 18
Latium, derivation of name 22, 42
law-code, Roman 22, 24
Lemuria (9, 11, 13 May) 27
Lentulus Lupus, L., consul 156 BC 75
Lepidus, M. Aemilius, consul 78 BC 118
Lepidus. M. Aemilius, triumvir 113, 129
letters, as literary form 100–1
Liber (see also Dionysus) 123, 157, 161
  Roman cult of 20, 22, 27, 42, 59
Libera, cult partner of Liber and Ceres 20, 22, 27, 42, 59, 160
Liberalia (17 March) 20, 27, 28, 41, 51, 203
Liberty, goddess of 84, 85
libraries 5, 83, 131, 139
librarii 6
Licinia Eucharis, dancer 111, 112
Licinius Macer, C., tribune 73 BC 118
lictors, at *ludi* 53, 58
listeners vii, 7, 64–5, 72–3, 116, 119, 164, 171, 181, 284
literacy, extent of 8–9
Livius, T. ('Livy') 15, 51, 94, 129–31, 139
  on Augustus in 24 BC 140–1
  on Livius Andronicus 48
  on freedom and law 137
  on privileged seats at *ludi* 54
  on the origin of Roman drama 25, 155
  on the origin of Rome 10
Livius Andronicus, L., poet and playwright 46–7, 48, 65, 69
Locri, Greek city in Italy 23
'Longinus', literary critic 7
Lowrie, Michèle 7–8
Lucanus, Annaeus, M. ('Lucan'), poet 169
  commentary on 92
Lucceius, L., senator and historian 99–100
Lucian of Samosata, sophist 171–5, 176
  on 'all-mime' 109, 128
  on historians 171–2
Lucilius, C., satirist 74–6, 77, 79, 118
  as model (or not) for Horace 120–1

General Index

Lucretius, T., philosophical poet 80, 95–6, 98, 164
  on dancers 91
  on Ennius 66, 98
Lucrine lake, in Virgil 124
ludi circenses 24, 45, 82, 180
ludi saeculares 153–6, 159
ludi scaenici 20, 45, 50, 73, 80, 90–1, 92, 99, 110, 143, 154, 159, 163, 180, 181
  ludi Apollinares 49, 55, 82, 83, 89, 93, 115
  ludi Ceriales 42, 49, 51, 84, 85, 89, 122, 158, 160
  ludi Florales 41, 47–8, 49, 84, 85, 89, 90, 122, 160, 180
  ludi Megalenses 49, 58, 59, 84, 89, 102, 108, 122, 141, 160
  ludi plebeii 43, 49, 55, 84, 85, 89, 103, 116, 122
  ludi Romani 43–4, 47, 48, 49, 54, 55, 58, 83–4, 89, 122, 134
  ludi Victoriae 86, 122, 203
Lupercalia (15 Feb.) 28
Lutatius Catulus, C., consul 242 BC 45
Lycidas, Virgilian herdsman 115
Lyne, Oliver 107
Lysimachus, pipe-player 57

Macedon, Roman conquest of 50, 57
Macer, ornithological poet 150
Macrobius, on fiction 169–70
Maecenas, C., friend of Caesar Augustus 121, 129, 133, 147, 159
  Esquiline estate of 121
  patron of poets 119, 121, 122, 131, 136, 142, 146, 149
Maecius Tarpa, Sp., judge of poetry 87, 88, 120, 143
Maenius, C., consul 338 BC 26, 28, 29, 36
Magna Mater, see Great Mother
Maia, mother of Hermes 23, 133
Mamurra, Caesarian officer 103–4
Manilius, C., tribune 66 BC 81
Manilius, M., astronomical poet 164
Manlius Torquatus, patrician bridegroom 106–7
Manlius Torquatus, orator 143
Marcellus, M. Claudius, consul 222 BC 70
Marcellus, M. Claudius, aedile 23 BC 155
  theatre of 155, 159
Marcipor, pipe-player 49
Marius, C., consul 107 BC 101, 118
Marius, M., friend of Cicero 86–8, 100
Mars, father of Romulus 40, 181
  flamen of 27
Martialis, M. Valerius, poet ('Martial') 5, 126–7
masks, theatrical 174–5, 177–9
Matralia (11 June) 27
Matuta, Roman cult of 27
Medea, legendary murderess 78, 167, 178

Medusa, in *cista* scene 33, 39
Meliboeus, Virgilian herdsman 115
Memmius, C., patron of Lucretius 95–6, 98
Memmius, C., tribune 111 BC 118
Memory, see Mnemosyne
Menander, Athenian playwright 49, 78, 170
Menippus of Gadara, Cynic philosopher 76, 175
Mercury (see also Hermes) 18, 52, 133
  Roman cult of 22, 23
Messalla, see Valerius
Metellus Macedonicus, Q., consul 143 BC 75
mimae (see also dancing-girls) 90–1, 109
'mime' (see also 'all-mime') 87, 89–92, 151, 171, 178
Minerva, escorts Hercules to Olympus 15–16
Mithridates, king of Pontus 81, 86, 93
Mitylene, theatre at 81–2
Mnemosyne (Memory), mother of the Muses 63, 65
Moeris, Virgilian herdsman 115
Moirai, see Fates
Moneta, identified as Mnemosyne 65
Mucius Scaevola, Q., consul 117 BC 75
Muses (see also Calliope, Erato, Thalea) 63, 65, 89, 96, 98, 100, 103, 110, 111, 160, 164
musicians, at *ludi scaenici* 49, 57–8, 91, 109–10, 119, 155, 176
  in *ludi Romani* procession 43, 45
  on pottery and *cistae* 30–1, 33

Naevius, Cn., poet and playwright 42, 48, 65, 70, 87
Naples (Neapolis), Greek city in Italy 26, 122, 133
Naulochus, battle of 121, 134
Nausicaa, Phaeacian princess 11
Neapolis, see Naples
'Nemesis', in Tibullus 149
Neptunalia (23 July) 27
Neptune (see also Poseidon) 27
Nereids (see also nymphs) 109, 159, 176–7
Nero, emperor 169
Nestor, Homeric king 69
'Nestor's cup', at Ischia 10
Nossis, on Rhinthon 41
Notus, wind-god 176
novels, ancient 169–71
Numa, legendary king 99, 132
Nünlist, René 7
nymphs (see also Dryads, Nereids) 147–9, 159
  Bacchic imitation of 35–6
  on stage 91, 109, 127–8, 148, 158

Oceanus, circumambient river 11, 102
Octavia, wife of Antony 129
Octavia, wife of Nero 169

Octavius, C. (see also Caesar Augustus) 95, 111, 112, 113
  as 'young Caesar' 116, 118, 119, 121, 125, 129, 131, 147, 150
  house of 125, 131, 136, 138
  in Virgil and Horace 123, 133
  victorious return to Rome 134–7
Octavius Lampadio, C., literary scholar 48
odeion, recital hall 143–5
Olympian Zeus, Athenian temple of 19
Opalia (19 Dec.) 27
Oppius, C., agent of Caesar 101, 102
orators, as actors 81
orchestra, meanings of 58–9, 154, 165
Orpheus, legendary singer 127, 128
  pool of, in Rome 126–7, 128
Ostia, Roman colony at 25, 80
Ovidius Naso, P. ('Ovid') 15, 94, 146, 150–1, 157–62
  as public performer 151, 158
  exile of 150, 161–2
  Fasti, plural addressees 160
  Heroides, as performance 158

Paestum, vase-painters at 32–3, 35
Palaestrio, Plautine slave 52
Palatine hill (see also *area Palatina*) 125, 130, 136, 138
  as site of *ludi scaenici* 55, 89, 157, 160
  etymology of 15
Pales, shepherds' goddess 27
Palilia, see *Parilia*
Pallantion, town in Arcadia 15
Pallas Athene, see Minerva
Pan, goat-god 36, 44, 45, 174
pantomimus, see 'all-mime'
Papposilenus, see hairy-suited performer
papyrus 3–6, 47, 48, 123, 163
Parcae, see Fates
Parilia (21 April) 27
Paris, 'all-mime' dancer 165–6
Paris, judge of goddesses 174, 176
Parthenius of Nicaea, mythographer 114
Parthians 132, 140, 141, 151
Pausanias, on choruses and tragedies 9
Pausilypon (Posilippo), villa at 143–5
Pegae, home of nymphs 148, 149
Pegasus, born from Medusa's neck 33, 39
Peleus, in Catullus 109–10
Peneus, river, in Virgil 125
Pentheus, tragic victim 31
Periander, ruler of Corinth 17
Persephone, daughter of Demeter 20, 59
Perseus, killer of Medusa 29–30, 33
Persius Flaccus, A., satirist 165, 169, 171
Petronius Arbiter, fiction writer 169–70
Phaeacia, games at 11–14, 15, 58
Phemius, Homeric bard 14

Philippi, battle of 113, 119, 124
Philodemus of Gadara, poet and literary theorist 96–7, 99, 122
phlyakes, 'fooleries' 41
Phoebus (see also Apollo) 136, 157
Photius, on novels 171
Pisistratids, Athenian ruling family 19
Piso, C. Calpurnius, consul 67 BC 80
Piso, L. Calpurnius, consul 58 BC 86, 96, 147
Plancus, L. Munatius, consul 42 BC 147
Plato, philosopher 98, 169, 170, 174
  on Bacchic ritual 35–6
  on 'noble lie' 255
  on poetic performance 22
  on rhapsodes 64
  on stories heard at sacrifices 8–9
  on theatre competitions in Italy 23
Plautus, T. Maccius, comic playwright 1, 6, 49, 50–5, 62, 63, 76, 78
  Amphitruo 52
  Asinaria 53
  Aulularia 52
  Captiui 52
  Curculio 57
  Menaechmi 60
  Miles gloriosus 52, 54
  Poenulus 53–4, 63
  Pseudolus 51
  Truculentus 60
Plebeian games, see *ludi plebeii*
Plinius Caecilius Secundus, C. ('younger Pliny') 5, 9, 168
Plinius Secundus, C. ('elder Pliny') 4, 24, 112, 135
Pollux, see Castor
Polybius of Megalopolis, historian 71–4, 99, 130
  on Anicius' *ludi scaenici* 57–8
  on the Roman political system 73–4
Polyphemus, at Caere 10
Pompeii, view from 87–8
Pompeius Magnus, Cn. ('Pompey the Great') 79–80, 81, 84, 99, 101, 103, 111, 135, 168
  theatre of 61, 81–2, 85–7, 89–90, 92, 102, 109, 114, 119, 154–5, 159
Pompeius Magnus, Sex., commander in Sicily 116, 118, 119, 121, 124
Pomponius Secundus, P., consul AD 44 165, 166–7, 168
Pomponius Secundus, Q., consul AD 41 168
Poppaea Sabina, empress 169
populus Romanus, see Roman People
Portunalia (17 August) 27
Portus Iulius, in Virgil 124
Poseidon, sea-god (see also Neptune) 11, 44, 176
  honoured at Rome 19, 27

General Index

Poseidonia, Greek city in Italy 32
Posillipo, see Pausilypon
Postumius Albinus, Sp., consul 186 BC 50
Powell, Anton 123
Praeneste, city of Latium 33, 37, 38
Praetorian Guard 163, 168
praetors, in charge of *ludi* 49, 51, 146, 159
preconception, power of 7, 281
Priapus, phallic god 178
Pronomos, pipe-player 30
Propertius, Sex., poet 94, 146, 147–9, 150, 151
prophets (see also Sibyl, *uates*) 27, 63–4, 67, 79, 128, 131–2
proscaenium, meaning of 51, 174
Proteus, legendary shape-shifter 128
Protogenes, slave *lector* 88
Ptolemy II Philadelphus, king of Egypt 3, 5, 45, 69, 112
'publication' 5–6, 9, 94, 123, 163, 167, 172, 182
Publilius Pellio, T., actor 49
Publilius Syrus, playwright 92
Puteoli, theatre at 175
Pylades of Cilicia, 'all-mime' dancer 109, 155, 159, 176
Pylos, as fish market 69
Pyrrhus, king of Epirus 37, 45, 132
Pythagoras of Samos, philosopher 20, 151

quindecimuiri s.f., priestly college 153, 154, 181
Quinn, Kenneth 265
Quintilianus, M. Fabius ('Quintilian'), on elegy 146
Quintipor Clodius, bad playwright 77
Quirinalia (17 Feb.) 27
Quirinus, as deified Romulus 40, 132
   flamen of 27
Quirites, significance of name 40

Rabirius, Epicurean preacher 97
Ravidus, attacked by Catullus 106
Reate, home of Varro 76
'recitation drama', phantom genre 166–7, 168
Regillus, lake, battle of 23, 139
Regulus, M. Aquillius, wealthy senator 9, 163
Remus, twin of Romulus 124–5, 130
Rhinthon, Sicilian playwright 40–1, 43, 45, 112, 178
Robigalia (25 April) 27
Roma, significance of name 10, 15
Roman People, as audience at *ludi* 53, 102, 110, 142–3, 149, 153–4, 165, 166, 181
   inspired by funerals 71, 80
   loyal to Caesars 163, 168
   political role of 79–80, 101, 111, 113
   subject of Roman history 71, 116–17, 129
Romans, descended from Achaeans 26
Rome, S. Omobono site 15, 17

Romulus, founder of Rome 19, 25, 40, 45, 48, 68, 70, 133
   fratricide? 124–5, 130
   hut on Palatine 125, 260
   'tyranny' of 80
rostra, in Roman Forum 26, 27, 79
Rubustini, Apulian people 31
Rudiae, home of Ennius 69
Ruvo di Puglia, vases from 31

Sabidius Severus, friend of Apuleius 170, 175
Sabines 40, 124
   Sabine women, capture of 25, 70
saeculum, as new age 153, 156, 157
Saepta Iulia 130
Sagra, river, battle of 23
Sallustius Crispus, C. ('Sallust'), historian 80, 94, 114, 116–18, 125, 182
   on listening to history 99, 116
   on *populares* 118
Samos, Augustus at 151
Sappho, in Horace 139
sarcophagi, iconography of 177–9, 181
satire, as dramatic form 25, 76–7
satura, meaning of 69, 78, 91
Saturn (see also Cronos) 22, 23, 27, 80
   gives name to Latium 22, 42, 156
Saturnalia (17 Dec.) 27
satyr-plays (see also Dionysiac drama) 20, 30–1, 36, 45
satyrs and *silēnoi* 20–1, 36, 43, 69, 110, 177
scaena, meaning of 51, 60, 78, 167, 180
Schenkeveld, Dirk 7
scholia, ancient literary commentaries 7, 46
Scipio Aemilianus, P., consul 147 BC 76
Scipio 'Africanus', P., conqueror of Hannibal 49, 54, 70, 101
Secundus, Julius, in Tacitus 167
Seethiasos, marine revelry 176–7
Sempronius Asellio, historian 73
Sempronius Tuditanus, M., consul 240 BC 47
Seneca, L. Annaeus, consul AD56 123, 125
   plays of 1, 166–7
Servius, Virgilian commentator 61–2, 125
Shackleton Bailey, D.R. 88
Sibyl, prophetess 153, 155, 156, 169
Sicyon, Greek city 17
sikinnis, Greek satyric dance 43
Silenus, song of 114
Simaetha, Theocritean sorceress 112
Sirmio, home of Catullus 104
Siro, Epicurean philosopher 122
Skiras of Tarentum, playwright 41–2
Skutsch, Otto 67
slaves, in theatre 54
Socrates, Athenian philosopher 64, 78
Sopatros of Paphos, playwright 41

sophists 97, 170–2
Sophocles, Athenian playwright 23, 46, 181
Sophron of Syracuse, playwright 112
Sotades of Maronea, poet of low life 69
stage games, see *ludi scaenici*
Starkie, Walter 64
Statius, P. Papinius, poet 165–6
Stesichorus of Himera, early poet 15, 46, 58
Strabo of Amaseia, geographer 156
Subura, district in Rome 126
Suda, on playwrights 46
Suessa Aurunca, home of Lucilius 74
Suetonius Tranquillus, C., learned
    author 48, 62
  on Catullus? 105
  on comedy and 'all-mime' 91–2, 108–9
Sulcius, fierce satirist 120
Sulla, L. Cornelius, consul 88 BC 74, 76, 80, 115,
    116, 130
Sulmo, home of Ovid 150
Sulpicius Rufus, Ser., poet 143
Surrentum, as fish market 69
sword-fighters, at *ludi* 60
Syracuse, Greek city in Sicily 23, 171
  drama at 20, 112

tabulae, see writing-tablets
Tacitus, Cornelius, historian 61, 163
  on playwrights 165, 167–8
  on Virgil in the theatre 139, 140
Tarentum (Taras), Greek city in Italy 31, 33,
    37, 69
  playwrights from 41, 47
Tarpa, see Maecius
Tarquinius Superbus, L. ('Tarquin'), Roman
    king 19, 20, 22, 23, 130, 139, 169
Tarracina, Roman colony at 25
temple dedications, dating of 22, 40
Terentius, C., curule aedile 200 BC 49
Terentius Afer, P. ('Terence'), comic
    playwright 1, 6, 49, 50, 51, 59–61, 62, 182
  Hecyra 59–60
Terminalia (23 Feb.) 27
Tertullianus, Q. Septimius
    ('Tertullian') 179–80, 181
Thalea, Muse of comic drama 112, 150–1
theatre games, see *ludi scaenici*
theatres, permanent 1, 2, 51, 60–1, 85, 89, 149,
    159, 163, 166, 170
theatres, temporary 50–62, 84, 89, 127, 136, 154
theatrum, meaning of 51, 174
Theocritus of Syracuse, poet and
    playwright 112, 114
Theodorus of Boeotia, pipe-player 57
Theophanes of Mitylene, historian 81–2
Theopompus, pipe-player 57
Theseus, in Catullus and Ovid 110, 160–1
Thetis, in Catullus 109–10

Thucydides, Athenian historian 71–2
thumelici, meaning of 154–5
Thyestes, legendary king 92, 136, 167
Tiber, river 126, 147, 153–4
Tiberius, stepson of Augustus 161
Tibullus, Albius, poet 146, 149, 150, 151
Tibur (Tivoli), site of country houses 147
Tigellius Hermogenes, bookshop
    frequenter 120
tightrope-walkers, at *ludi* 59, 60, 170
Tityrus, Virgilian herdsman 114, 115, 133
Tomis, site of Ovid's exile 161
Transpadane Italy 101, 104–5, 112, 124
'tribe' (*tribus*), voting district 142–3
Tritons, in Lucian 176–7
triumphs, as public holidays 40, 57, 58, 70
trumpeter, at games 53
Tubulus, L. Hostilius, corrupt senator 75
Tucca, Plotius, saves *Aeneid* 151, 156
Tullus Hostilius, legendary Roman king 14
Tusculum, site of country houses 83
Twelve Tables, see law-code

uates, meaning of 63–4, 164

Valerius Antias, historian 99
Valerius Cato, judge of poetry 143, 146
Valerius Messalla, M., consul 61 BC 99
Valerius Messalla, M., consul 53 BC 99
Valerius Messalla Corvinus, M., consul
    31 BC 143, 146, 147
Valerius Publicola, orator 143
Varius, L., poet and playwright 136, 151, 156
Varro, M. Terentius, learned author 8, 24, 79,
    94, 112, 114
  as satirist 74, 76–8, 89, 91, 118, 175
  on 'mythic theology' 180
  on the origin of Roman drama 25, 47,
    62, 78
Vedius Pollio, private theatre of 143, 146, 148
Veii, Etruscan city 17–18, 23, 25
Velitrae (Velletri), town in Latium 18
Vennonius, historian 73
Venus (see also Aphrodite) 91, 181
  ancestress of Iulii 111, 123, 134, 157
  ancestress of Romans in general 98, 181
  great-grandmother of Romulus 68
  'Victrix', in Pompey's theatre 226
Vercingetorix, Gallic leader 102
Vergilius Maro, P. ('Virgil') 6, 15, 75, 80,
    114–15, 122–8, 139, 150, 181
  Aeneid of 151, 182
  as public performer 122–3
  heard in theatre 139, 182
  Eclogues, sung and danced 114, 146
  replaces eulogy of Gallus 125
  on magic 112
  on post-Actium games 136, 157

Verona, home of Catullus 104
Vesta, Roman cult of 27, 132
　　Vestal Virgins, at theatre 181
Vestalia (9 June) 27
Vesuvius, eruption of 97
Vibius Viscus, judge of poetry 143, 146
Victory, goddess of 86, 134
violence, in Roman politics 74
Virgil, see Vergilius
Vitruvius, on theatres 154
vividness, see *enargeia*
Volcanalia (23 August) 27
Volcanus ('Vulcan'), god of fire 27, 164
Volturnalia (27 August) 27

Volturnus, *flamen* of 27
Vulcan, see Volcanus

wedding ceremony 106–7
Wilkinson, L.P. 88
women and children, in theatre 54
writing-tablets (*tabulae, pugillaria*) 3, 80, 106

Xenophon, Athenian author 98, 99

Zeno, Stoic philosopher 78
Zephyrus, wind-god 176
Zetes and Calais, sons of the North Wind 148
Zeus (see also Jupiter) 44, 176